THE OXFORD HANDBO

C000231544

THEOLOGICAL
ETHICS

THE OXFORD HANDBOOK OF

THEOLOGICAL ETHICS

Edited by

GILBERT MEILAENDER

AND

WILLIAM WERPEHOWSKI

OXFORD

UNIVERSITY PRESS

OXFORD
UNIVERSITY PRESS

Great Clarendon Street, Oxford OX2 6DP

Oxford University Press is a department of the University of Oxford.
It furthers the University's objective of excellence in research, scholarship,
and education by publishing worldwide in

Oxford New York

Auckland Cape Town Dar es Salaam Hong Kong Karachi
Kuala Lumpur Madrid Melbourne Mexico City Nairobi
New Delhi Shanghai Taipei Toronto

With offices in

Argentina Austria Brazil Chile Czech Republic France Greece
Guatemala Hungary Italy Japan Poland Portugal Singapore
South Korea Switzerland Thailand Turkey Ukraine Vietnam

Oxford is a registered trade mark of Oxford University Press
in the UK and in certain other countries

Published in the United States
by Oxford University Press Inc., New York

© Oxford University Press 2005

The moral rights of the authors have been asserted
Database right Oxford University Press (maker)

First published 2005
First published in paperback 2007

British Library Cataloguing in Publication Data

Data available

Library of Congress Cataloguing in Publication Data

Data to follow

Typeset by SPI Publisher Services, Pondicherry, India
Printed in Great Britain by
Biddles Ltd., King's Lynn, Norfolk

ISBN 978–0–19–926211–3 (Hbk.)   978–0–19–922722–8 (Pbk.)

1 3 5 7 9 10 8 6 4 2

CONTENTS

LIST OF CONTRIBUTORS

Harlan Beckley is Director of the Shepherd Program for the Interdisciplinary Study of Poverty and Human Capability and Fletcher Otey Thomas Professor of Religion at Washington and Lee University in Lexington, Virginia.

Robert Benne is Director of the Roanoke College Center for Religion and Society in Salem, Virginia.

Jana Bennett is Assistant Professor of Theology at Hampden-Sydney College in Hampden-Sydney, Virginia.

Lisa Sowle Cahill is the J. Donald Monan, S.J., Professor of Theology at Boston College.

Paul J. Griffiths holds the Schmitt Chair in Catholic Studies at the University of Illinois in Chicago.

Vigen Guroian is Professor of Theology at Loyola College in Maryland.

Amy Laura Hall is Assistant Professor of Theological Ethics at Duke University Divinity School in Durham, North Carolina.

Stanley Hauerwas is Gilbert T. Rowe Professor of Theological Ethics at Duke University in Durham, North Carolina.

James F. Keenan, SJ, is Professor of Theological Ethics at Boston College, in Chestnut Hill, Massachusetts.

Robin W. Lovin is Professor of Ethics at Southern Methodist University in Dallas, Texas.

Gerald P. McKenny is Associate Professor of Christian Ethics and Director of the John J. Reilly Center for Science, Technology, and Values at the University of Notre Dame.

Lois Malcolm is Associate Professor of Systematic Theology at Luther Seminary, in St Paul, Minnesota.

Gilbert Meilaender is the Phyllis and Richard Duesenberg Professor in Christian Ethics at Valparaiso University.

Richard B. Miller is Director of the Poynter Center for the Study of Ethics and American Institutions, and Professor in the Department of Religious Studies, Indiana University.

Douglas F. Ottati is the M. E. Pemberton Professor of Theology at Union Theological Seminary in Virginia and the Presbyterian School of Christian Education.

Gene Outka is Dwight Professor of Philosophy and Christian Ethics at Yale University in New Haven, Connecticut.

Stephen J. Pope is Associate Professor of Social Ethics in the Department of Theology, Boston College.

Jean Porter is the John A. O'Brien Professor of Moral Theology at the University of Notre Dame.

R. R. Reno is Associate Professor of Theology at Creighton University, in Omaha, Nebraska.

William Schweiker is Professor of Theological Ethics at the University of Chicago in Chicago, Illinois.

David H. Smith is Nelson Poynter Senior Scholar at Indiana University in Bloomington, Indiana.

William C. Spohn is the Augustin Cardinal Bea SJ Distinguished Professor of Theology at Santa Clara University.

Max Stackhouse is the Rimmer and Ruth de Vries Professor of Reformed Theology and Public Life at Princeton Seminary.

Kathryn Tanner is Professor of Theology at the University of Chicago Divinity School.

Philip Turner is Dean, the Berkeley Divinity School at Yale (retired).

Bernd Wannenwetsch is University Lecturer in Ethics, Oxford University.

Darlene Fozard Weaver is Assistant Professor of Theology at Villanova University in Villanova, Pennsylvania.

John Webster is Professor of Systematic Theology at the University of Aberdeen.

William Werpehowski is Professor of Christian Ethics and Director of the Center for Peace and Justice Education at Villanova University in Villanova, Pennsylvania.

Sondra Wheeler is the Martha Ashby Carr Professor of Christian Ethics at Wesley Theological Seminary in Washington, DC.

D. M. Yeager is Associate Professor at Georgetown University in Washington, DC.

INTRODUCTION

GILBERT MEILAENDER AND WILLIAM WERPEHOWSKI

An introduction to a book such as this one serves prospective readers best if it tells them what they should know in order to determine whether it is the sort of book they want to read. Providing that information is our aim here.

The various Handbooks published by Oxford University Press are not aimed at beginners; nor are they aimed only at scholars who work in a particular field. Their target falls somewhere between those two groups—those who know a good bit, who would be in a position to do advanced work in a field, and who might be helped and stimulated by a survey of the field. We think and hope that this volume will do that for readers interested in the field of theological ethics. So this is a Handbook not in ethics generally but in a certain kind of ethics, and it attempts to survey that field.

Nevertheless, the task of surveying a field can be accomplished in many different ways, and we have chosen a particular approach. Readers should understand that it is the collection of essays, taken as a whole, that surveys the field of theological ethics. We have assigned specific topics to our contributors, but we have not asked them to provide a survey of the topic on which they write. On the contrary, we have permitted, and even encouraged, them to do more than catalogue what has been said on the topic. Ethics is, after all, a normative discipline, and it has seemed appropriate to us that contributors should, as they see fit, develop their own constructive arguments. Thus, a reader of these essays will do more than learn 'about' a variety of topics in theological ethics; he or she will also enter into the ongoing conversation that constitutes theological ethics.

At the same time, as we noted above, this Handbook treats not some generic area known as ethics, but the discipline of theological ethics in particular. That is, it contemplates the moral life as it is lived, imagined, and spoken of within the more encompassing field of Christian theology, for which thought and action can never be neatly separated. This is, of course, not the only angle from which one might think about the moral life, but it is one that has deeply influenced our civilization and that continues to shape the lives of large numbers of people.

There is, to be sure, no single vision of how ethics ought to fit into the larger enterprise of Christian theology, and, just as we have invited our contributors to shape their essays in accord with their own normative commitments, we have done the same in developing the structure of this Handbook. (We have not, however, limited the contributors to those who share our vision.) At the very outset of his *Institutes*, John Calvin articulates two related premises: that 'without knowledge of self there is no knowledge of God', and that 'without knowledge of God there is no knowledge of self'. However these may be 'mutually connected' in a person's life (and the connection may work differently in the lives of different people), Calvin suggests that 'the order of right teaching requires that we discuss the former [knowledge of God] first, then proceed afterward to treat the latter [knowledge of ourselves]'.

The structure of this Handbook should suggest to a discerning reader that we have, at least in a general way, followed Calvin's lead. That is, we begin with a set of essays on 'dogmatics and ethics', intimating thereby that, whatever may be true of other kinds of ethics, Christian theological ethics must treat the shape of the moral life and the meaning of our humanity within the context of who God is and what God does. (One need not think of this as peculiarly indebted to Calvin, however; after all, the *Summa Theologiae* begins in the *Pars Prima* with God and only thereafter turns to man.) It is, of course, possible, to adopt the opposite strategy, as much of modern theology has done, and begin with the human subject, moving from that starting-point to talk of God. (And, indeed, some of our contributors do so.) But the structure of this Handbook, even if not each of its essays, suggests that theological ethics is, finally, a branch of dogmatics. Those with any Barthian inclinations at all might wish to go even further and argue that—since in Jesus Christ our human life has been taken into God's own life—the character and structure of our life cannot be a free-standing topic but *must* be part and parcel of theology. That, at any rate, is how things look from within the circle of faith.

The opening section of essays under the rubric of 'dogmatics and ethics' is followed by four sections whose essays deal, respectively, with the *sources* of Christian moral knowledge, the *structure* of Christian life, the *spirit* of Christian life, and the *spheres* of Christian life.

Almost any kind of systematic ethical reflection will need to consider the sort of people we ought to be, the goals we ought to seek, and the actions we ought to do or decline to do. For a Christian ethic, however, developed within the contours sketched by dogmatic theology, this generic sort of ethical reflection will be shaped in important ways by Christian faith. Ethical reflection must necessarily draw on a range of *sources*. Almost everyone is likely to make use of personal (or communal) experience and, to a greater or lesser degree, human powers of reason. In addition to these, Christians rely on authoritative texts, even though it is no easy matter to explain how scriptural texts function in moral reflection. In addition, Christians do not—or, at least, should not—think of themselves as free-floating philosophers of the moral life. Their thinking takes place within—and is instructed and disciplined by—the community of believers, both living (as a present community of discourse) and dead (as a tradition of discourse). How one makes use of these diverse sources of moral insight has often been a matter of controversy among Christians, and it remains an ongoing project within theological ethics.

Among the standard topics of theological ethics are some that deal with the *structure* or shape of the Christian life and some that deal with what we may call the *spirit* of the Christian life. Perhaps the two most general ways of giving Christian structure to the moral life—ways that, still today, correspond in very rough form to Roman Catholic and Protestant approaches—have been in terms of virtue and vocation. But there are other terms—such as 'responsibility'—that have risen to special prominence in more recent times; there are perennial topics—such as the place of 'rules' in Christian life—that affect our understanding of life's shape; and there are limits—most especially death—which give their own structure to life. To treat only such topics, however, is to fall considerably short of all that theology has wanted to say about the meaning of life in Christ, and—in order to capture not only the structure but also the spirit of this life—we have included essays on what have traditionally been regarded as the three chief theological virtues: faith, hope, and love.

Instructed by the variety of sources from which they gain moral knowledge about both the structure and the spirit of their life, Christians live within a variety of *spheres* that give a distinctively social or institutional cast to life. These spheres—such as government, family, economy, and culture—have sometimes been spoken of in terms such as 'orders of creation' or 'mandates'. We have preferred the simple term 'spheres', especially because we have included here as a sphere of Christian life a community not generally included when one thinks in terms of orders of creation: namely, the church. It would be, to say the very least, inadequate to depict the social setting of Christian life in terms only of those communities—such as government and economy—which are shared by those within and without the church. For, in fact, some of the deepest problems Christians encounter when thinking about how they ought to live—and some of the issues that have most troubled recent reflection in theological ethics—have to do precisely with how one manages the intricate simultaneities required to live within the church and the other spheres of life.

Finally, in the last section of this Handbook, we gather together essays that treat the structure not of the Christian life itself but of the discipline of theological ethics. We do this by offering essays that revisit and re-examine a few works (most of them single volumes by scholars in theological ethics or moral theology) that have given a kind of shape or structure to ethics, especially as it has become a distinct and specialized branch of theological study. These are not necessarily the best books ever written in theological ethics (though at least several of them might lay justified claim to such a title); rather, they are books that have given students of Christian ethics a vision of the whole, a sense of how the disparate materials of the discipline can be gathered together in coherent and constructive ways. To revisit and rethink books of this sort is perhaps as instructive a way into the field of theological ethics as one can imagine.

Of course, any of the essays in this volume may be read by itself for insight into a particular topic, and we hope many of them will be read in this way. Better still, however, is to take the handbook whole, to read it as a mode of entry into the focused (yet also quite diverse) conversation that is the continuing tradition of discourse we call 'theological ethics'.

PART I

DOGMATICS
AND ETHICS

CHAPTER 1

CREATION AND ETHICS

LISA SOWLE CAHILL

THE doctrine of creation expresses a basic dimension of religious experience, by dislocating the centrality of human concerns within the universe. Even while promising human salvation, Christianity begins in awareness that humans are not ultimate, and that in a higher source of existence lies hope for the brokenness of our condition. Religion directs attention away from human projects to a transcendent power on which we are dependent, and it addresses human suffering by proposing an alternative path in greater conformity to that power.

'Creation', a doctrine whose biblical foundation is the first three chapters of Genesis, expresses for Christians the knowledge that God, not humans beings, is at the centre of the universe. The destiny proper to humans is to recognize and conform to the presence and will of God. The theology of creation sets the human condition against the magnificent horizon of God's sovereignty, goodness, and justice; it places humans within a universe of other beings whose existence is prior to humanity and who have, in God's eyes, a value in themselves; it judges human life in so far as it departs from and defaces the world as God made it to be.

The biblical creation narratives (Genesis 1 and 2) form a unity with the story of 'the Fall' (Genesis 3). When the first three chapters are read as part of the entire book of Genesis, and linked to the Pentateuch, then creation becomes an integral component of the story of salvation focused on Abraham, to be carried forward, according to Christian faith, in Jesus Christ. 'Creation', from the standpoint of faith traditions, is not some prehistoric event that constitutes a temporal prelude to the human history of sin and redemption. Instead, creation captures one dimension of humanity's entire existence before God. It is one symbolic strand in a multi-layered narrative of human suffering, guilt, and hope, a narrative to which creation, redemption, church, and eschatology afford interdependent points of entry. The claim that Genesis offers 'scientific' evidence of the origins of the universe, and the claim that scientific evidence disproves divine creation, are equally misguided. (On the Enlightenment origins of this debate, as well as on its fruitlessness, see Clifford 1991: 219–40, and Gilkey 1959, 1995.)

Historically, the doctrine of creation takes one of its earliest forms in the credal formulation, 'I believe in God, the Father almighty, maker of heaven and earth'. As developed theologically by the Church Fathers, especially Augustine, a focus of the doctrine is *creatio ex nihilo*, 'creation out of nothing', which recognizes the infinite difference between God and the world, the utter dependence of everything that exists on the divine, and the world's beginning in time along with its inevitable end (see Gilkey 1959; Gunton 1997).

This essay will focus not on any one authoritative doctrinal formulation of creation, but on aspects of the theology of creation that are important for Christian ethics today. I will first argue that the idea of creation has been used in five key ways in the Christian tradition, then make five critical points about how this doctrine has functioned in the past and ought to function in the future. In relation to ethics, the doctrine of creation has often been used to defend a foundation or minimum of human morality that survives the fact of sin and that can provide a natural basis for just social life. I will argue that this approach needs to be nuanced and amplified, so that Christian theology can more adequately meet the challenge of working for justice in a global and interreligious context. Confronting problems like economic oppression, gender discrimination, racism, ethnic violence, and environmental degradation, different traditions must, can, and do co-operate to solve common problems while still maintaining and valuing distinct faith identities. To invoke creation is not to bracket religious identity while pursuing common human moral values. Rather, creation is a symbolic point of unity among religious traditions. It can underwrite religious commitment to uphold continuities and commonalities in human moral experience and obligation across traditions.

USES OF THE DOCTRINE OF CREATION IN CHRISTIAN TRADITION

The idea of creation has been used in an essentially optimistic way in Christian tradition to affirm that all beings are good, and that evil and suffering are not part of the original meaning of existence. Creation is a premiss that allows believers to define part of existence as we know it as due to 'sin', and to define other aspects as revelatory of the divine will. It looks forward to redemption in God, as the origin and *telos* of all. Ethically, the doctrine of creation has sometimes led to a positive, interventionist ethic, in which humans are even seen as 'co-creators' with God *vis-à-vis* human history and nature (Hefner 1989). An alternative outcome is a positive ethic of social justice, in which justice for the earth is connected to justice within and among human communities, but which requires setting significant restraints on human projects for the sake of the common good (McFague 2001: 71–126, 205–10).

This general perspective can be sorted into at least five components.

1. *Creation puts existence under God's ordering power and providence.* The two creation accounts in the first and second chapters of Genesis both show God creating everything that exists through an orderly progression from inanimate to animate creatures, and finally to humanity. In the historically later and more concise Priestly version in Genesis 1, God's speech ('Let us make...', 'Let there be...') represents the engagement of divine intentionality in the creative process. After creating the universe, God approves it. 'God saw everything that he had made and indeed, it was very good' (Gen. 1: 31; NRSV throughout). The historically earlier version in Genesis 2 displays the human condition through a more extended folkloric story of the creation of the first man and woman. It characterizes the non-human scene on which humans arrive in terms of interdependent beauty. 'Out of the ground the Lord God made to grow every tree that is pleasant to the sight and good for food...' (Gen. 2: 9). While the unexplained intrusion of the serpent on Eve's innocence connotes the absurdity of evil, the course of events in the garden and after the Fall still takes place essentially within the purview of God's authority. God has both the power to discover and punish the offenders (3: 8–19, 23–4), and to look down the road to future events and possible salvation (3: 15, 19). In the poetry of the Psalms and the Wisdom of Solomon, God is praised as Creator, present in and guiding the works of his hand. 'The heavens are telling the glory of God; and the firmament proclaims his handwork' (Ps. 19: 1).

> For you love all things that exist
> and detest none of the things that you have made;
> for you would not have made anything if you had hated it.
> How would anything have endured if you had not willed it?
> or how would anything not called forth by you have been preserved?
>
> (Wisd. 11: 4–5)

In books five and seven of his *Confessions*, Augustine celebrated the goodness of all creation, rejecting the Manichaean belief that the material world is the product of a god of darkness, and his interpretation of Genesis held that, through God's continuing providence, creation has potential for growth toward greater beauty and order (Williams 1999). Thomas Aquinas spoke of God's providence as ordering the world to its divinely ordained end (1948: I. 22. 1), and he believed that the multiplicity and ordering of the natural world is an indicator of the existence and goodness of God (Aquinas 1948: I. 2. 3; see Jenkins 2003). John Calvin, among the most eloquent of theological proclaimers of divine purpose in creation, calls God's works a 'beautiful theatre' of God's glory, and admires 'the very order of events' in creation as evidence of 'the paternal goodness of God' (Calvin 1981: I. 14. 20; I. 14. 2). In a contemporary restatement of trust in the goodness and divine guidance of creation, Sallie McFague expresses a sense of God that arises in gratitude toward the power that created us and in assurance of its blessing. 'It is the awareness that life, my life and all other life, is included within God's life, and God's life or reality is defined by love. Life, then, is a gift of love, and therefore, whatever happens in life will be "well"' (McFague 2001: 133).

Although the evil and suffering present in the world have always constituted a challenge to religious affirmations of God's creative and sustaining goodness, mainstream Christian tradition has sought none the less to maintain trust in God's providence. A counterpart to the doctrine of creation as good and manifesting God's design is the view that evil must be attributed to human sinfulness, that sin affects not only human behaviour but even the working of the natural world. The evil caused by sin is believed to be overcome ultimately by God's ordering of history toward divinely ordained purposes (for a general discussion of evil and theodicy, see Tilley 1987). The Creator's providence may permit evil as a concomitant of human freedom, but it neither causes evil nor is overcome by it.

2. *The doctrine of creation permits identification of some aspects of concrete existence as sin.* Human religious experience and theological reflection begin from an existential situation of suffering and the search for solutions to the questions and trials of life. The idea of creation functions as a premiss from which part of the human situation can be defined as contrary to God's will, as non-normative, and as non-necessary. When God discovers the guilty parties hiding from him in Eden, he tells them in no uncertain terms that their predicted suffering is 'because' of their wrongdoing (Gen. 3: 14, 17), not because of the nature of things. The theology of creation, then, is part of a religious world-view that resists resignation to evil. It is an important element in a religious reading of the world that gives rise to hope by first permitting judgement on what is but ought not to be. If humans have caused evil in the world, it follows that they are responsible to reverse this evil, and that some evils at least can be defeated by resistance.

Interpreting active resistance to suffering as a mandate of the biblical stories of creation and fall is today a vigorous theological emphasis. Traditionally, the evil of a defaced created order was more often seen to be an inevitable punishment for sin, one that could not be remedied within history. The solution, then, was to find solace and transformation within the Church and in hope of eternal life. For example, Luther has 'no doubt that before sin the air was purer and the water more prolific; yes even the sun's light was more beautiful and clearer'. After the Fall, however, the earth, which 'is innocent and would gladly produce the best products', is 'prevented by the curse which was placed upon man because of sin' (Luther 1955: 205, 204). Calvin grants that the image of God 'imprinted on the fair form of the universe' is now 'inefficient' in bringing us to God because of human sinfulness; this is why we have the consolation and support of the revealed Word (Calvin 1981: I. vi. 66). Neither Augustine, Aquinas, nor the Reformers held out much hope of transforming the world as we know it. Yet Aquinas, with his theory of the natural law (discussed below), had more confidence than the others that the historical order still retains inherent structures of justice.

Despite these and other historical precedents, simple resignation in the face of difficulty and injustice is not demanded by a biblically grounded doctrine of creation as affected by the fall of humans. The so-called curses of God—pain in childbirth and male rule for the woman, hard agricultural labour and low yield for the man—are clearly set against God's original intention. They are not in fact presented biblically as God's will for the human future, even given the reality of sin. The 'curses' should be read as declarative rather than prescriptive statements; in them, God announces the consequences of human action. God certainly does not demand that future human action refrain from attempting to rectify the broken situation caused by sin. In fact, the opposite seems to be required if we take seriously creation's original goodness and the divine distress at its despoilment suggested by God's persistent questioning of the offending pair (Gen. 3: 9–18). 'Sin interrupts God's creative work and wounds the heart of God' (Sponheim 1999: 99). The doctrine of a good creation in contemporary theology implies that humans have an obligation to undo the evil effects of their sin on the human body, human relationships, and the created environment. While sin cannot be conquered by human effort alone, and while final victory over evil is eschatological, humans still have an ethical obligation to reduce evil in the world.

3. *A theology of creation allows us to recognize and promote aspects of human experience that respect and restore human well-being and that of the rest of creation.* Sin disturbs and distorts the creation, but does not entirely destroy its goodness. Human beings can still glimpse God's glory and discern the outlines of God's will in themselves, in human relationships and societies, and in the world around them. The most central vocabulary and body of Christian thought capturing the accessibility to human knowledge of created goodness, and its normative claim on human behaviour, is the tradition of 'natural law'. Most famously developed by Thomas Aquinas, the natural law tradition has precedents in non-Christian philosophers, especially the Stoics and Aristotle, and parallels in virtually every major Christian theologian, from St Paul (Rom. 1: 14–15, 18–20) onward. The major

difference among these voices is not so much whether they hold that human morality should conform to a created 'natural' order, but whether they believe that reason's ability to know this order is more or less intact, the will's ability to choose it more or less free, and the connection of the natural order to salvation more or less positive. (For a general discussion of natural law, see Pope 2001, and his essay in this volume, Chapter 9 below.)

The most positive and optimistic contemporary proponents of natural law ethics have been those working in the Catholic social tradition, rooted in the thought of Aquinas. From the end of the nineteenth century onward, papal social encyclicals have addressed issues of the day in terms of justice and the common good (Coleman 1991). Recent studies have called attention to the religious and theological contexts and premises of the development of theories of natural law in this tradition (Porter 1999). It is true, none the less, that Catholic natural law has in the past served, and continues to serve, as a sturdy basis on which to begin cross-cultural and inter-religious discourse about human moral behaviour and social relationships.

In addition to its role in theories of natural law, the theology of creation is part of an important and long-standing line of Christian thought that sees the fact that all persons are creatures of God, and made in the image of God (Gen. 1: 27), as offering a viable basis on which to affirm common moral insights. There are human moral experiences, values, and obligations to one another and to society that are recognizably similar across cultures. For example, Aquinas observed that all human cultures accord respect to the need to protect and preserve life; to form sexual and reproductive unions, and to nurture and educate the young; to live co-operatively with others in society; and to seek knowledge about God (1948: I. II. 94). Although it is a long way from such general inferences about the nature of the good life to specific cultural norms and practices, the basic idea that all humans value and seek certain key components of well-being and happiness is an invaluable source of mutual respect and compassion. The idea that all humans share a created nature supports this idea.

Many Protestant authors, in both the Reformed and the Lutheran traditions, as well as Orthodox theologians, affirm something like the natural law as a basis for morality. Thus, for instance, Michael Northcott (relying on O'Donovan 1984), writes:

The original ordering of creation towards God, and internally towards itself, and towards the human as the most godlike aspect of creation, has deep moral and theological significance. The Christian moral project therefore requires affirmation of the original *telos* (purpose or end) and shape of created and material life, and of the marks of creation's original relatedness to God which we may still find in ourselves and in the rest of the natural order. (2001: 216)

Pre-modern authors accepted that hierarchies in the patterns of access to material and social goods were 'natural', and that humans had the right and even the duty to 'dominate' or 'subdue' the rest of the created world (as is suggested by the language of Gen. 2: 28). Since the Enlightenment, however, the rising ideal of human equality has helped theologians challenge received hierarchies. A salient example is patriarchy, supposedly licensed by the fact that the woman was taken from the man's rib (Gen. 2: 22), implying that she is inferior and subordinate. Newer readings note that both man and woman were formed by a personal creative act of God, from some pre-existing matter (indeed, a higher-order working material in the woman's case than in the man's (Gen. 2: 7)!). The fact that they are called into a 'one flesh' unity can be seen as a paradigm for co-operative, non-hierarchical human community in general (for a feminist reading of Genesis, see Trible 1978).

Similarly, the rights of humanity over the natural environment have been moderated in recent decades by theologies of reciprocity, if not equality, between humanity and non-human creation. The creation of the first human from 'the slime of the earth' denotes a natural bond between humanity and the rest of creation. Just as human nature, with its bodily, psychological, spiritual, and social requirements, forms a basis for ethical insight and for practical consensus about the pursuit of human flourishing, so does the natural world, endangered as it is by human patterns of exploitation (Hessel and Ruether 2000; Christiansen and Grazer 1996). The natural environment provides a shared horizon against which all cultures and societies must gauge the effects of human projects.

4. *Creation looks forward to the redemption of all creatures in Christ.* Christian praise of God as 'Creator' presumes that the transcendent power of God's creative goodness has been experienced even within the historical situation of human suffering. To affirm the doctrine of creation is to glimpse the possibility of rescue from the shadow side of the human condition. The doctrine of creation takes the eschatological reality of salvation that begins already within history, and connects it with the origins of the universe and the ground of its being. The grace of redemption meets and restores human identity and relationships as they were created to be, and also perfects nature.

Early Christians interpreted the significance of Jesus in light of traditions about creation and God's presence in it, sometimes imaged by the figure of Wisdom or Sophia (Prov. 8) (see Clifford 1991: 199–208; 1996: 34–6). New Testament texts linking creation to redemption in Christ include the Prologue of John's Gospel (John 1: 1–14), its parallel in the Christological hymn of Paul's letter to the Colossians (1: 15–20), 2 Corinthians (the 'new creation' in Christ, 5: 17), and Romans 8. In the latter, a link is drawn between the suffering of the whole created world and human bodily suffering (exemplified by women's suffering in child-birth). 'All creation is groaning in labour pains even until now.' Just as the faithful have the Spirit and await 'the redemption of our bodies', so the whole natural universe is blessed by the intercession of Christ's Spirit, through the Spirit's 'inexpressible groanings' that mediate divine compassion (Rom. 8: 22–3, 26). The idea of creation, integrally related to redemption, underlines the restoration and reconciliation of all things in Christ. It diminishes the exaggerated anthropomorphism that has often been the engine of human triumphalism over the rest of creation.

According to Karl Barth, humanity was created to be called into covenant with God; redemption in Christ fulfils not only humanity, but also the creation. In Barth's view, humans are privileged in relation to God, but can never be dissociated from the cosmos of which they are a small part. In Jesus Christ, God reveals the created universe as the sphere of God's dealings with humanity, and summons humans to a restored relationship with the divine. This restoration is the restoration of creation; the theology of creation constitutes a recognition of this intrinsic relationship. 'The knowledge communicated by the Word of God is the knowledge of creation in its indissoluble connexion with the covenant and therefore the knowledge of heaven and earth as the cosmos of man in covenant with God' (Barth 1960: 11). In the Roman Catholic tradition especially, the concept of 'sacramentality' connects the presence of God in and through creation to God's incarnation in Christ (Himes and Himes 1990).

In his Christological reading of creation, Jürgen Moltmann uses the phrase 'creation for glory' to indicate that creation will be consummated as 'the home and dwelling place of God's glory'. This future is already anticipated by the historical indwelling of the Holy Spirit in all things. 'The bond of love, participation, communication and the whole complex warp and weft of interrelationships determines the life of the one, single creation, united in the cosmic Spirit' (Moltmann 1985: 5). In Christ's resurrection, humanity is resurrected; in or with humanity, the whole creation is restored by Christ (O'Donovan 1984: 31; Northcott 2001: 213–16).

The dynamic relationship between human evil and suffering, the recognition of creation as establishing a partially lost but still recognizable ideal, the hope of salvation inherent in ascribing the normative claim of the ideal to a transcendent authority, the confirmation of this hope in Christ, and the ethical implications of that hope, are well captured in two simple assertions with which Paul Sponheim opens *The Pulse of Creation*. 'Transformation is needed. We could be other than we are.' 'God wills and works to change things for the better... and the lives of Christians are to contribute to that change' (1999: p. ix).

5. *Creation can sponsor an ethics of responsibility qualified by an ethics of restraint, linking ecology and social justice.* I have already proposed that the Christian doctrines of sin and fall are part and parcel of the very ability to distinguish the facets of the human reality that are aberrations, and should be changed, from those that reveal the possibility of life in conformity with God's purposes. As James Gustafson stated it almost thirty years ago, 'One ought to be moral because the

ultimate power, God...intends that human action conform to his purposes and activity for the well-being of the whole creation' (Gustafson 1975: 25–6). This way of putting the matter calls forth human responsibility while placing human interests in a larger perspective. God creates new possibilities for human and natural welfare that human action should seek to realize. At the same time, human beings ought to proceed with a sense of self-criticism and humility, deriving from acknowledgement of human finitude and fallibility (Gustafson 1975: 67).

Some authors, accentuating the dynamic and even evolutionary process through which life has emerged and changed on earth, call on humans to be 'co-creators' with God in realizing new possibilities that can benefit humanity (Hefner 1976, 1989). Yet the global ecological crisis that has become ever more apparently acute over the past five decades, seen in light of the doctrine of creation, prompts a different analysis. Here human hubris is responsible not only for degradation of the natural environment, but for pervasive social injustices in human use and abuse of natural resources (see Northcott 1996 for a general analysis). Both the commodification of nature and the spread of exploitative human relations have been exacerbated in the global economy by the dominance of a world market system under the control of elites in the 'first world' (Northcott 1996: 48). Although theologies using the metaphor of co-creation do not endorse exploitation, the metaphor none the less diminishes a critical approach to human projects. Rather than raising humans to partnership with the divine, a view of humans as sinful and in need of repentance may be called for.

Elizabeth Johnson notes that interest in the natural world as a theological topic declined among both Catholics and Protestants after the sixteenth century, giving way to a preoccupation with God and the human self. She claims that, in the third millennium, emerging knowledge about the age of the earth and the complexity of its ecosystems, and about the vastness of the universe, have called our attention back to the wonder of our environment (Johnson 2000: 8, 3). Theologically, creation is being rediscovered. Challenges to moral and social practice follow from this. They concern both the earth and the human lives dependent on it and upon each other. 'Solidarity with victims', a theme of liberation theology, should be extended to non-human life systems and species; moreover, 'economic poverty coincides with ecological poverty, for...the poor suffer disproportionately from environmental destruction' (Johnson 2000: 15). Though this is not an entirely new point, the amount of attention it has received in recent theological treatments of environmental ethics marks it as one whose importance is being newly recognized (see Hessel and Ruether 2000; Christiansen and Grazer 1996).

To correct human abuses of creation and the injustice toward other humans that follows, an ethic of sacrifice and restraint will be necessary on the part of the privileged. Sallie McFague's plea for a theology that can liberate North American Christians from their patterns of consumption, and hence liberate the natural world and other peoples from oppression, coheres well with the rediscovery of the theological value of creation furthered by Johnson. 'Theology by relatively comfortable North American Christians ought not to focus on personal salvation, in this world or the next, but on lifestyle limitations, on developing a philosophy of "enoughness," and realizing that the cruciform way of Christ means making sacrifices so that others might live' (McFague 2001: 33). Perhaps another way to put this point is to say that personal salvation can occur only in a communal context, in relationships with God and others that reflect and restore the goodness of creation. The Genesis creation stories reinforce the Christian belief that salvation happens corporately in a new 'reign of God', 'body of Christ', or 'family' of believers. The way of salvation includes sacrifice that rights the communal imbalances that result from human sin.

CRITIQUE AND DEVELOPMENT OF THE DOCTRINE OF CREATION

Although Christian theologians, not surprisingly, tend to turn to Christology to link creation with redemption and with social, ecological ethics, biblical scholars have shown the importance of viewing the Pentateuchal history of creation in its own right. Thus, one important development is to regard creation as part of God's salvific action in the Hebrew Bible (Christian Old Testament), especially the first five books (Pentateuch or Tanak). Second, a very serious critical question that must be posed to any 'redemptive' solution to the conflict and suffering besetting creation is whether these realities are really at odds with God's 'design', attributable to human sin, and remediable by divine grace or human action.

Third, if the theology of creation is integrally related to redemption, then Christology and Trinitarian theology may also require renovation. These doctrines must correspond to a theology of creation as a dynamic process, revelatory of God's will, and the scene of redemption of humans and the cosmos. A fourth development—in which a theology of creation may provide a meeting point for many religious traditions—is demanded by interreligious co-operation on global social issues, especially in relation to the ecological crisis. Finally, a contemporary theology of creation should envision the continuing, creative, and dynamic empowerment of all creatures in the world through the presence and power of God. This applies to the natural environment as well as to human victims of oppression.

These five points will be addressed in turn. Overall, their impact is to qualify or expand the five aspects of contemporary creation theologies already discussed. The most challenging is the second question, about how humans are to judge and evaluate the purposes of God. In the end, this question may have to be answered experientially and communally, as systematic theological proposals and doctrinal propositions are tested in the life of the Church. At the same time, the Church itself is never free from sinful bias and must humbly submit its favoured interpretations of God's Word to the tests of experience, science, philosophy, and alternative theological construals of Scripture and tradition.

1. *Creation and redemption are already counterparts in the Hebrew Bible.* Thirty years ago, Claus Westermann asserted that 'the activity of the God who saves' is just as central to the Old Testament as to the New, and that the construction of the Pentateuch relates creation and salvation. The centre-piece of the first five biblical books is God's saving action in leading his people out of Egypt. This key action is developed by means of the history of the patriarchs, which shows the character of the people in relation to God before the Exodus event. God's graciousness to humans is taken back to the origins of the world, so that the history of his people can be based on what has gone before. Thus 'creation' is not a past event, but a process that dynamically continues (Westermann 1974: 121–2). The people of God live out of creation, in covenant, and toward the fulfilment of the redemptive presence of God that has always accompanied Israel in her faithfulness, waywardness, suffering, and restoration.

A special focus of the creation–redemption trajectory is established by the creation of humanity in God's image (Gen. 1: 27–8). Despite the fact that the Genesis creation stories are a composite of diverse strands of tradition, Thomas Mann (1991) identifies two literary devices that link these stories together and establish a creation–redemption trajectory. These devices are the 'generations' formula, which occurs eleven times in Genesis, and the divine 'promises' of blessing (children, land, nationhood, and above all relation to God). The promises begin immediately after the creation of male and female in God's image (Gen. 1: 28), and are eventually extended to 'all the families of the earth' through Abraham (Gen. 12: 3) (Mann 1991: 342–3). Generational connection and faithful divine promise link the creation of humanity with a family history and a community under God that is redemptive. Sinful humanity is redeemed in the entire history of salvation, a history in which humanity's created destiny to serve as an image or representative of God on earth is restored.

The image of God in humans does not consist in certain human attributes, or in 'human nature' understood in a static way, but in collective relationships that represent the relation of God to creation (Westermann 1974: 55–60, 73; Hall 1986). Human relationships and human communities that reflect divine love and justice, and a human relation to the earth that 'tills' and 'keeps' it (Gen. 2: 15), restore God's image in humanity. The bestowal of blessing on Noah and his sons in Genesis 9, with its companion outlawing of murder, confirms that human life in the image of God especially excludes the killing of other human beings (9: 6).

It is necessary to clarify the process of redemption revealed in the Hebrew Bible in order to modify triumphalist or exclusionary Christian theologies that limit God's saving action to the churches founded in Christ's name. If we appreciate that the Book of Genesis already communicates redemption without specific reference to Christ, we may be more ready to see God's saving work in other religious traditions. As a Christian doctrine, creation has inherent ecumenical potential.

2. *The God of creation is awesome and mysterious.* Both the Israelite and the Christian stories of creation–redemption assume a God who is beneficent, provident, and reconciling—a God who has placed humanity at the pinnacle of creation and who ultimately wills human well-being. This consoling view helps believers to overcome, if not exactly to resolve, the problem of evil in the world, and the ambivalence of human nature and the natural world in relation to moral purposes. A challenging counter-proposal has been made by the Reformed theologian, James Gustafson (1981, 1984, 1994, 2003). Gustafson insists that naïve and superficial assurances of divine favour do not meet the tests of human experience, of historical and scientific knowledge about the natural world, or—most crucially—of true piety before divine sovereignty. He presses his point in a recent work: 'Does any historical and other human evidence count against our teaching and preaching about a providential Deity who provides redemption and hope to those in despair, to the people of nations devastated by decades of strife in Asia, Africa, or Central America? If God is gracious, is God also impotent to actualize those gracious purposes in natural and human-generated catastrophes?' (Gustafson 2003: 100–1). Gustafson answers his own rhetorical questions by Calvinistic resort to a mysterious and mighty God whose entirety Jesus Christ does not reveal to believers. 'The Almighty has his own purposes' (Gustafson 2003: 109).

Important in forming Gustafson's challenge is his conviction (following John Calvin and Jonathan Edwards) that nature is a conduit of God's glory. Reading nature's signs honestly, however, requires us to contend with empirical and scientific information about the conflicts inherent in the 'balance' of the ecosphere. The conditions that sustain life and its 'evolution' are the same conditions that permit and even require the destruction of some beings for the survival of others. An 'anthropocentric' Christianity that makes the most of biblical symbols to absolutize human well-being is, for Gustafson, idolatrous. He advocates a 'theocentric' alternative in which God's will is accepted as revealed in the book of nature and history, in which the 'radical dependence' of humanity on the divine is acknowledged, and in which human redemption consists in a faithful attempt to relate to all things as they relate to God, in so far as we can understand that (1994: 48).

Nature inspires respect, wonder, and awe, but its lesson is that the human species is a part of natural processes, not the zenith on which all creation is naturally focused. 'God is the source of human good but does not guarantee it' (1994: 48). Gustafson warns: 'We might idealize a world in which the values in particular relations work harmoniously for the good of the whole; we might eschatologize this, looking toward some coming or eternal kingdom in which this harmony will be realized. But, I believe, it is not ours to know such things' (1994: 106). In contrast to traditional theologies of creation, Gustafson does not attribute 'providence' to God, if by that is meant divine intentions leading all that exists to a harmony in which the importance of every individual is confirmed. Nor does Gustafson attribute human suffering and the natural conflict of life with life to an original human sin that marred an otherwise harmonious origin. The asymmetry of natural flourishing is for Gustafson an indicator of divine mystery, properly evoking a sense of awe and worship, not a desperate attempt to rewrite the divine purposes to suit human ends.

The collision of Gustafson's realism with the confidence of most creation theology in the certainty of divine beneficence is striking. Equally immersed in the wonder of creation, Sallie McFague draws an opposite inference about the nature of the divine and of the divine dispositions toward humanity. God is love, and we are created to love God intimately, she proclaims, appealing to her own experience of nature, read in the light of a Christian faith that is more traditional in so far as its trust and optimism are concerned. For McFague, nature is the route to sure knowledge of 'the existence of everything within divine love' (McFague 2001: 136). This clash of interpretations throws into relief the role of personal and communal experience in shaping the convictions with which theologians approach the idea of creation. A key aspect of experience is human suffering, whether understood optimistically as a proper object of resistance and change, or pessim- istically as an inevitable fact of created being.

Gustafson's demand that suffering be accepted as not contrary to the divine will has not met with wide agreement. Nevertheless, his challenge must be taken seriously. Paul Sponheim meets it more successfully than many, understanding that God is met in the midst of the negative. In suffering, 'we meet the one who as creator is truly Other, who interrupts our sense of the very limits of reality' (1999: 62). Grasping the truth and the possibility of a different reality requires imagin- ation. 'The Christian turn to creation is really a spiraling down to that which grounds and animates the distinctive Christian reading of things and at the same time links the Christian with all the others' (1999: 130).

The imaginative act of faith is and should be interdependent with biblical symbols, theological traditions, church authorities, human experience, knowledge of history and the natural world, and philosophical explanations of the human condition. The circular nature of these criteria does not permit the indisputable verification of any one interpretation of even central biblical themes like creation. These criteria do, however, commend the constant revisitation of one's own point of departure in light of correctives, and the continual re-examination of how a given theological focus point like creation is appropriated and practised. Gustaf- son's hard questions do not defeat Christian trust in God's promises and hope for redemption of the human condition. They do, however, caution against 'cheap grace', and urge the renewal of faith communities so that they may more authentically and persuasively embody the presence and care of God that they in theory proclaim.

3. *Creation theology today demands the reintegration of doctrines.* The great Trinitarian and Christological doctrines of the Christian tradition take the problem of human salvation as their point of departure. Doctrinal controversy and development over the centuries represent the struggle of believers to understand and articulate how God is redemptively present in Jesus Christ. In the twentieth century God's redemptive presence throughout human history received an emphasis absent in the past, as did the correlation of human redemption with the redemption or salvific restoration of the cosmos. While the event of God's self-disclosure in Christ has of course continued to be definitive for Christian belief, God's immanence in the entire creation and in all cultures has become increasingly important theologically. This shift in emphasis has led to new efforts to understand the relationships among the creator, the redeemer, and the 'sustainer', i.e., God's or Christ's 'Spirit' present in history and the world. The symbolism of God as Spirit can strengthen awareness of the creation–redemption trajectory in Christianity; this symbolism also has promising ecumenical resonance.

These explorations obviously involve far more than can be addressed in one essay on creation. This volume's contributions on redemption, church, and eschatology will further understanding of recent work in these areas. For present purposes it will be useful (if not entirely adequate) to stress that theologies of the Spirit have been among the most fruitful outcomes or counterparts of recent interest in creation. Past Christian development of God as Spirit construed the Spirit primarily as the Spirit of Christ present in the faith community. Yet there are also analogues in the Hebrew Bible to New Testament Spirit symbolism for God. Feminist theologians like Elisabeth Schussler Fiorenza (1983) and Elizabeth Johnson (1994) have developed the importance of the figure of Wisdom (in Wisdom, Proverbs, and Sirach) as a feminine personification of the divine, and as a background resource for New Testament characterizations of Jesus endowing him with qualities of this female figure (in 1 Corinthians, Matthew, and John). Lady Wisdom personifies the presence of God in the creation and the created world, and her activities are often described in imagery borrowed from the natural universe (Proverbs 8). Wisdom is 'the fashioner of all things' (Wisd. 7: 22); 'she is a breath of the power of God and a pure emanation of the Almighty' (Wisd. 7: 25); 'she reaches mightily from one end of the earth to the other and she orders all things well' (Wisd. 8: 1).

The Prologue to John's Gospel, drawing on the Wisdom tradition, envisions creation through the Logos, or Word, of God, and with this imagery understands the significance of Jesus not only as a revelation of God, but as also participating in creation (John 1: 1–4, 14). Spirit imagery is used to communicate both God's presence in Christ to the world (at his baptism and at Pentecost) and God's presence in creation through Wisdom (Wisd. 7: 22). The extensive collection published as *Christianity and Ecology* includes a major section entitled 'Creator, Christ and Spirit in Ecological Perspective' (Hessel and Ruether 2000: 3–124). The effect and importance of recent work on Trinitarian symbolism, with regard to theologies of creation, lies in the fact that the traditionally almost exclusive emphasis on the incarnation of God in Jesus Christ, as a unique and absolute revelation of God, is being moderated. Though Christ is incontrovertibly the centre of Christian identity, the divine presence in the cosmos—creating, sustaining, and redeeming—is being reappropriated through symbols with a looser connection to the historical figure of Jesus. This development leads to the next critical point.

4. *Interreligious co-operation to protect global common goods, especially the natural environment, draws inspiration from the symbol of creation and its attendant theologies. In turn, the theology of creation is seen in new perspective.* Many religious traditions have appealed to some idea that the cosmos reveals a sacred order to underwrite the value and purpose of earthly existence, and to establish ideals and norms for transformative action in the world.

Pythagoreans, for example, found in the depths of nature a mystical realm of musical and numerical enchantment. Ancient Israelites read the universe as an expression of divine Wisdom. Egyptians delved beneath the surface of nature to the realm of Maat, Indians to the domain of Dharma, and Taoists to the Tao. Stoics read the cosmos as the outward manifestation of an inner rationality that they called Logos. And the Gospel of John pierced beneath all things to an eternal Word that was in the beginning with God, and that was God.... Traditionally, almost all religions and philosophies read the universe as a revelation of order or purpose. (Haught 2004: 12)

Sallie McFague uses the phrase 'common creation story' to refer to the universal and increasingly recognized fact that the universe is characterized by unity, differentiation, and interdependence, as well as to the common origin of all that exists in a universe that has evolved this way (McFague 1993: 43–5).

Religious traditions around the world unite in protest against rising levels of threat to the delicate webs of life in which theologies of creation recognize intrinsic value and which they summon humanity to protect. Paul Knitter believes that 'the more the religions of the world can ground themselves in this earth and the more deeply they can connect with the nature and needs of this planet, the more they will find themselves interconnected. The more deeply religious persons become ecologically attuned, the more effectively they will become ecumenically connected' (Knitter 2001: 366). Although there may be resistance in 'the academy' to grand schemes of meaning or 'metanarratives', there are certainly 'metaproblems' that the human race must confront. Saving the earth from imminent ecological disaster is one of them. We confront an ethical and ecological challenge to devise a shared way of acting in the world. Shared practices of sustainability and justice could be nourished by an earth mysticism, developing for an age more conscious of an entire imperilled planet the 'nature mysticism' attested by Christian figures such as Bernard of Clairvaux, Francis of Assisi, Hildegard of Bingen, and Jonathan Edwards (see Soelle 2001: 97–112). Such practices might lead to a shared religious story of 'common creation'. A common creation story or shared practices need not be inimical to the rootedness of all religious participants in particular and rich traditions, for it would emerge from and bring together the mutual concerns of many faiths (Knitter 2001: 368–9; see also Adams 1993).

5. *The earth as well as human beings must be liberated and empowered.* Social ethics grounded in creation theology tends to stress the unity of the human species. Its reformist agenda is oriented toward greater equality and participation for all those human beings and communities that have been excluded from the bounty of creation in the past and present, and are virtually certain to be so in the future. Divine creation establishes a normative pattern of existence that is dynamic, but structured by spiritual and moral values. A 'preferential option for' and 'empower-ment of' the poor is the dominant theme of liberation theologies that seek justice for the poor of the earth. A liberating theology of creation makes a preferential option for the poor earth itself, as well as for oppressed peoples. It judges human sinfulness in light of divine transcendence, inspires interreligious transformative action, and works toward the restoration of all beings, including the earth, to the abundance and unity that reflect their deepest nature.

What a Christian theology of creation must not do, however, is assume that the symbol of creation is its property alone, or that redemption can be isolated from the continuing dynamic of creation. Moreover, a natural fact, and a theological enigma, is disharmony and violence within the natural world, even granting credence to evolutionary theories that depict progressive emergence of higher life forms, and the necessity of death for new life to emerge (see Polkinghorne 2001). Narratives of human temptation and fall are a reminder not only that the socially and ecologically unjust *status quo* reflects human guilt and cannot be accepted, but that the appearance of evil in the world cannot be completely grasped by human understanding. Nevertheless, it is to be repented and resisted. The healing of humanity and the earth demands practical political, religious, and theological co-operation among the world's faiths and cultures.

Among Christian doctrines, creation is salient in its capacity to affirm the natural moral sense of humanity, the calling of all persons and communities to restored relationships with God, and the presence of the divine in all cultures and through the created world. The doctrine of creation responds to a primal human experience of fault lines in the universe as we know it and to a pervasive human longing to align ourselves with the ultimate source and truth of our being.

References and Suggested Reading

Adams, C. J. (1993). 'Introduction', in C. J. Adams (ed.), *Ecofeminism and the Sacred*, New York: Continuum, 1–9.

Aquinas, Thomas (1948). *Summa Theologiae*. New York: Benziger.

Barth, K. (1960). *Church Dogmatics*, III: *The Doctrine of Creation*, Part II. Edinburgh: T. & T. Clark.

Calvin, John (1981). *Institutes of the Christian Religion*, 2 vols. Grand Rapids, Mich.: Eerdmans.

Christiansen, D. and Grazer, W. (ed.) (1996). *'And God Saw That It Was Good': Catholic Theology and the Environment*. Washington: United States Catholic Conference.

Clifford, A. (1991). 'Creation', in F. Schussler Fiorenza and J. Galvin (eds.), *Systematic Theology: Roman Catholic Perspectives*, Minneapolis: Fortress Press, 193–248.

—— (1996). 'Foundations for a Catholic Ecological Theology of God', in Christiansen and Grazer (1996), 23–46.

Coleman, J. A. (ed.) (1991). *One Hundred Years of Catholic Social Thought: Celebration and Challenge*. Maryknoll, NY: Orbis.

Gilkey, L. (1959). *Maker of Heaven and Earth*. New York: Doubleday.

—— (1995). 'Evolution, Culture, and Sin: Responding to Philip Hefner's Proposal', *Zygon*, 293–308.

Gunton, C. E. (ed.) (1997). *The Doctrine of Creation: Essays in Dogmatics, History, and Philosophy*. Edinburgh: T. & T. Clark.

Gustafson, J. M. (1975). *The Contributions of Theology to Medical Ethics*. Milwaukee: Marquette University Theology Department.

—— (1981). *Ethics from a Theocentric Perspective*, I: *Theology and Ethics*. Chicago: University of Chicago Press.

—— (1984). *Ethics from a Theocentric Perspective*, II: *Ethics and Theology*. Chicago: University of Chicago Press.

—— (1994). *A Sense of the Divine: The Natural Environment from a Theocentric Perspective*. Cleveland: Pilgrim Press.

—— (2003). *An Examined Faith: The Grace of Self-Doubt*. Minneapolis: Fortress Press.

Hall, D. J. (1986). *Imaging God: Dominion as Stewardship*. Grand Rapids, Mich.: Eerdmans; New York: Friendship.

Haught, J. F. (2004). 'The Unfinished Universe: Does Creation Tell a Story?', *Commonweal*, 130/5, 12–14.

Hefner, P. (1976). 'The Foundations of Belonging in a Christian Worldview', in P. Hefner and W. W. Schroeder (eds.), *Belonging and Alienation: Religious Foundations for the Human Future*, Chicago: Center for the Scientific Study of Religion, 161–80.

—— (1989). 'The Evolution of the Created Co-Creator', in T. Peters (ed.), *Cosmos as Creation*, Nashville: Abingdon, 211–33.

Hessel, D. T. and Ruether, R. R. (eds.) (2000). *Christianity and Ecology: Seeking the Well-Being of Earth and Humans*. Cambridge, Mass.: Harvard University Center for the Study of World Religions Publications.

Himes, M. J. and Himes, K. R. (1990). 'The Sacrament of Creation: Toward an Environmental Theology', *Commonweal*, 117/2, 42–9.

Jenkins, W. (2003). 'Biodiversity and Salvation: Thomistic Roots for Environmental Ethics', *Journal of Religion*, 83, 401–20.

JOHNSON, E. A. (1994). *She Who Is: The Mystery of God in Feminist Theological Discourse.* New York: Crossroad.

—— (2000). 'Losing and Finding Creation in the Christian Tradition', in Hessel and Ruether (2000), 3–22.

KNITTER, P. F. (2001). 'Deep Ecumenicity versus Incommensurability: Finding Common Ground on a Common Earth', in Hessel and Ruether (2001), 365–81.

LUTHER, MARTIN (1955). 'Lectures on Genesis, Chapters 1–5', in Jaroslav Pelikan (ed.), *Luther's Works*, I, St Louis: Concordia, 3–359.

McFAGUE, S. (1993). *The Body of God: An Ecological Theology.* Minneapolis: Augsburg Fortress.

—— (2001). *Life Abundant: Rethinking Theology and Economy for a Planet in Peril.* Minneapolis: Fortress Press.

MANN, T. W. (1991). ' "All the Families of the Earth": The Theological Unity of Genesis', *Interpretation*, 45, 341–53.

MOLTMANN, J. (1985). *God in Creation: A New Theology of Creation and the Spirit of God.* San Francisco: Harper & Row.

NORTHCOTT, M. S. (1996). *The Environment and Christian Ethics.* Cambridge: Cambridge University Press.

—— (2001). 'Ecology and Christian Ethics', in R. Gill (ed.), *The Cambridge Companion to Christian Ethics*, Cambridge and New York: Cambridge University Press, 209–27.

O'DONOVAN, O. (1984). *Resurrection and Moral Order: An Outline for Evangelical Ethics.* Leicester: Intervarsity Press.

POLKINGHORNE, J. (ed.) (2001). *The Work of Love: Creation as Kenosis.* Grand Rapids, Mich., and Cambridge: Eerdmans.

POPE, S. J. (2001). 'Natural Law and Christian Ethics', in R. Gill (ed.), *The Cambridge Companion to Christian Ethics*, New York and Cambridge: Cambridge University Press, 77–95.

PORTER, J. (1999). *Natural and Divine Law: Reclaiming the Tradition for Christian Ethics.* Ottawa: Novalis.

SANTMIRE, H. P. (1985). *The Travail of Nature: The Ambiguous Ecological Promise of Christian Theology.* Philadelphia: Fortress Press.

SCHUSSLER FIORENZA, ELISABETH (1983). *In Memory of Her: A Feminist Theological Reconstruction of Christian Origins.* New York: Continuum.

SCHWEIKER, W. (2004). *Theological Ethics and Global Dynamics: In the Time of Many Worlds.* Oxford: Blackwell.

SMULDERS, P. (1975). 'Creation, I. Theology', in K. Rahner (ed.), *The Encyclopedia of Theology: The Concise Sacramentum Mundi*, New York: Seabury, 313–18.

SOELLE, D. (2001). *The Silent Cry: Mysticism and Resistance.* Minneapolis: Fortress Press.

SPONHEIM, P. R. (1999). *The Pulse of Creation: God and the Transformation of the World.* Minneapolis: Fortress Press.

TILLEY, T. W. (1987). 'Evil, Problem of', in J. A. Komonchak, M. Collins, and D. A. Lane (eds.), *The New Dictionary of Theology*, Wilmington, Del.: Michael Glazier, Inc., 360–3.

TRIBLE, P. (1978). *God and the Rhetoric of Sexuality.* Philadelphia: Fortress Press.

WESTERMANN, C. (1974). *Creation.* Minneapolis: Fortress Press.

WILLIAMS, R. (1999). 'Creation', in A. Fitzgerald (ed.), *Augustine through the Ages: An Encyclopedia*, Grand Rapids, Mich., and Cambridge, 251–4.

WRIGHT, J. H. (1987). 'Providence', in J. A. Komonchak, M. Collins, and D. A. Lane (eds.), *The New Dictionary of Theology*, Wilmington, Del.: Michael Glazier, Inc., 815–18.

CHAPTER 2

REDEMPTION AND ETHICS

R. R. RENO

MORAL reflection involves an odd combination of seemingly opposite concerns. On the one hand, the very substance of ethics is prohibition and exhortation. For St Thomas Aquinas, the first principle of the natural law is that 'good is to be sought and done, evil to be avoided' (1966: q. 94, a. 2). The presumed dynamism is patent. Our lives are in play, with moral commandments guiding and directing. The 'shalts' and 'shalt nots' are to human freedom as a shove or a push to our bodies. They seek to make a difference, to create a gap between who we presently are and what we are to become. In this way, morality shapes, presses, and moulds as an engine of change. In the true sense of the word, we *suffer* morality. On the other hand, moral theory and reflection are also preoccupied with continuity. According to St Thomas, God governs all things and directs them toward their final ends. For rational creatures, this governance is not extrinsic. We are not morally pushed and pressed by an external force. Instead, we share in the divine governance of all things by virtue of the natural law, a structuring force operative within our aptitudes and activities (1966: q. 91, a. 2). Being good does not entail being something other than a human being. Our becoming righteous is a real difference, and yet that becoming takes place within a genuinely human framework.

Taken together, change and continuity provide the agenda for meta-ethical reflection. The most fundamental criterion for any ethical vision is the question of whether it affirms difference without discontinuity. Difference is necessary. The force of the 'shalt' and 'shalt not' must be real and transformative; otherwise, normative language is otiose. At the same time, discontinuity is not permitted. Transformation cannot be so severe as to entail destruction. The pressure of morality must not trail off into violation and oppression. It is this combination of pushing, pulling, and shaping demand with reassurance that the human person can endure change that provides moral theory with its deepest puzzles.

The oddly nesting phenomena of moral relativism and intense pressures to change moral prejudices, the authoritarianism of therapeutic language, the increasingly widespread and conformist consensus that 'authenticity' is the highest good: these and other counter-intuitive and dysfunctional dimensions of contemporary culture reflect anxieties about difference and discontinuity. Where premodern moralists argued over just which moral principles were apt and why, we argue over whether moral principles exist, or whether they are 'healthy' ways to structure our lives. We think that we need not—we ought not—suffer morality, not because of a commitment to immorality, but because we find moral prohibitions inhumane and moral ideals unrealistic. For all the grand ambitions of the Enlightenment, all the soaring rhetoric of Romanticism, all the social change encouraged and endorsed by modernity, we seem to have settled upon the conclusion that moral difference entails an unacceptable discontinuity. Obligation oppresses, and commandment crushes: such are the commonly accepted alliterations of our day.

I do not have the space or inclination to analyse systematically the atmosphere of the age, as I have attempted to do elsewhere (Reno 2001). My goal is to show how Christianity approaches the puzzle of difference without discontinuity, a puzzle all the more difficult and pressing because the Christian vision of redemption endorses a radical difference for each and every human person. 'Flesh and blood does not inherit the kingdom,' writes St Paul. 'We will all be changed, in a moment, in the twinkling of an eye, at the last trumpet' (1 Cor. 15: 50, 52). At the same time, Christian hope insists that no inhumane or unrealistic discontinuity marks the movement of change. On the contrary, echoing the prophet Hosea, St Paul assures his reader, 'Death has been swallowed up in victory' (1 Cor. 15: 54). Paul reiterates this theme of change and continuity in countless ways. Romans 6 speaks of the transition from death to sin undergirded by the crucified and risen Jesus. 2 Corinthians 4 tells of the travails of discipleship, again, sustained by the continuity of Jesus' identity: 'We are afflicted in every way, but not crushed; perplexed, but not driven to despair; persecuted, but not forsaken; struck down, but not destroyed; always carrying in the body the death of Jesus, so that the life of Jesus may also be visible in our bodies' (2 Cor. 4: 8–10). This, then, is the promise of the Christian ethics of redemption for which Paul is the great meta-ethicist. We can seek something beyond ourselves—fellowship with God!—and we can accept the disciplinary structures of a Christian ethic directed toward that end, without destroying our bodies or renouncing our individualities.

In order to explain this promise, I think it useful to divide the problem of change and continuity into two distinct issues. The first has to do with a leading Pauline and postmodern preoccupation—'the body'. Put succinctly, the Christian view of redemption endorses rather than cancels the intrinsic goodness of creation. Continuity is affirmed. At the same time, redemption entails a transformation rather than a simple affirmation of the created order. The body is not destroyed or denied, but it is altered and changed. There is a real difference. As a contemporary *provocateur* might put the matter, redemption 'circumcises' creation. The second issue concerns freedom, another great Pauline concern. The term 'freedom', however, is notoriously ambiguous and contentious, and I propose to set it aside. The central issue at stake in St Paul's use of freedom is the question of personal participation in new life in Christ. One can give oneself entirely to God without abandoning selfhood. The logic of atonement best expresses the reasons why Christianity views the redemption of the individual as consistent with affirming rather than abandoning one's identity. I propose, then, to consider these two separate aspects of the Christian vision of redemptive change under separate heads: first, the fate of the body, and second, the role of individuality.

THE CIRCUMCISION OF CREATION

Imagine a contemporary American college professor who takes up St Paul's Letter to the Romans for the first time. Reading the first chapter, she is outraged by the regressive and puritanical attitude toward sexual desire. St Paul's rhetorical evocation of the descent of the human race into sin culminates in a condemnation of homosexual acts. According to St Paul's genealogy of morals, the primal spiritual perversion of idolatry is manifest in the perversion of the most primal desires of our bodies. To violate the first commandment of the Decalogue so distorts the human condition, so disorders moral judgement, that it leads to a violation of all the laws of the Torah, even the commandment that precedes sin itself: be fruitful and multiply.

As our imaginary professor grasps the logic of St Paul's argument, the wide sweep of Christian morality floods into her thoughts. She thinks, not just of Roman Catholic sexual morality, which she regards as ridiculously outmoded, but of the whole structure of Western moral thought. 'My God,' she whispers under her breath, 'it is all here: the relentless assault upon our desires, the tireless repression of what is natural, the towering burden of guilt. Nietzsche is surely right. Christianity is the source of our self-hatred. Thankfully, we live in more enlightened times, and people are allowed to live according to much healthier and more natural principles.'

With these sobering thoughts about St Paul's aggressive demands, reinforced by a glance at his apparent fear of homosexuality and, indeed, human sexuality in general ('It is well for a man not to touch a woman'—1 Cor. 7: 1), as well as reflection on what surely seems to be his self-hatred ('I do not do what I want, but I do the very thing I hate'—Rom. 7: 15), our college professor turns to diagnosis. 'Christianity', she speculates, 'is bewitched by the Metaphysics of Presence. It desires to escape from the quotidian and everyday in order to dwell with the unchangeable and eternal. It wishes to burst the bounds of finitude and grasp the univocal and impassible. Yes, again, Nietzsche is right. Christianity is Platonism for the masses.' The moment of insight suddenly puts everything she dislikes about Christianity into a clear light. 'Now I see why Christianity is dogmatic and Puritanical. It hates the irreducible plurality of the particular. It cannot endure the weight of the body. It seeks radical transcendence, and it will slash and burn its way through ordinary life in order to maintain its goal. Look at the way in which missionaries lay waste to indigenous cultures. See how the life of the mind is crushed under the weight of dogma. The faithful are only too eager to gather up the *realia* of life—ethnic identity, a child's innocent questions, sexuality—and pile it up on to a glorious *auto de fé* fueled by Church-mandated discipline.'

Our college professor may be over agitated, but she is not merely beholden to febrile postmodern theory. A sober voice from the twentieth century anticipated her analysis. Joseph Soloveitchik's mid-twentieth century classic, *Halakhic Man*, is primarily concerned to expound a religious phenomenology of Judaism. Solo-veitchik juxtaposes the spiritual gestalt of halakhic man to what he calls *homo religiosus*. For Soloveitchik, *homo religiosus* reflects the natural religious impulse of most men and women to seek radical transcendence as an escape from worldliness, either in ecstatic transport or through severe ascetic self-denial. In both cases, 'the body' is a problem to be overcome. '*Homo religiosus* is dissatisfied, unhappy with this world,' writes Soloveitchik. 'He searches for an existence that is above empirical reality. This world is a pale image of another world' (1983: 13). Redemptive aspiration, for *homo religiosus*, is discontinuous with creation, even antithetical.

Soloveitchik is circumspect about the relationship between the Christian view of redemption and the aspirations of *homo religiosus*. His goal is to describe Judaism, and, by and large, he leaves the question of Christianity to Christian theologians. None the less, writing in the early 1940s, Soloveitchik is drawn into a diagnosis of the failures of Christianity. I quote a long section in full, for Soloveitchik is articulating one of the most fundamental criticisms of the Christian vision of redemption, a criticism that gives moral seriousness to reactions of our postmod-ern literary scholar, whose thoughts are too often trivialized by postmodern rhetorical gestures and moral prejudices.

The strange, disturbing dualism that blossoms forth in other religions is grounded in the fragmentation of life into many different sectors. The universal *homo religiosus* not infre-quently sets up markers and draws sweeping demarcation lines—till here is the divine-heavenly-transcendental realm and from this point on the realm of earthly, bodily life.

Homo religiosus, praying in his house of worship, prostrated on the cold stone floor, repeating over and over the old litany *non mea voluntas sed tua fiat*—not my will be done, only Thine—is not at that moment a this-worldly man, possessor of riches and chattels, estates and factories, who drives his impoverished workers ruthlessly, and whose hands are often stained with the blood of the outcast and the ill-gotten gain wrung from the hands of the unfortunate. For him the world of prayer and the world of reality have nothing to do with each other.... The heavenly kingdom does not come into the slightest contact with the earthly kingdom.... The man in the sanctuary and the man in the marketplace are two separate and distinct personalities who have absolutely nothing in common with one another. How many noblemen have bowed down before the cross in the spirit of abject submission and self-denial, confessed their sins with scalding tears and bitter cries and in the very same breath, as soon as they left the dim precincts of the cathedral, ordered that innocent people be cruelly slain. (1983: 92–3)

What are we to make of this analysis? At root, whether in the voice of a postmodern literary professor or a modern orthodox rabbi, the criticisms amount to an indictment of the Christian view of redemption. Christianity is all for change and difference, but it is disloyal to the world because it sees redemption as a form of escape from finitude. The particulars of the indictment are diverse. In this passage, Soloveitchik evokes the brutalities of Christendom, brutalities that culminated in the orgy of violence and genocide that was sweeping through Christian Europe as he was writing. Others might focus on ways in which Christian dogmatism brutalizes the intellect. Still others might emphasize the ways in which guilt-ridden Christians do violence to their souls. In contemporary American politics, not a few commentators bemoan the ways in which devout Christians seem increasingly aggressive in the public arena. These particulars coalesce around what is, at root, a theological intuition: Christianity endorses radical transcendence, a view of redemption that is indifferent toward creation and does not respect the limits of finitude.

What, then, is the response of the defendant? The temptation is to register protest. The Creeds speak against the indictment. 'How can such a charge be made? Does not Christian doctrine affirm that God created the world and called it good, and on this ground did not the early church attack Gnostic teachings at every turn? What about the Incarnation? Is not the whole point of Christianity that God comes into human flesh?' Scriptural citations can be massed and arrayed in battalions. 'Does not St Paul insist that we are raised in our bodies? Does not Job say that he will see God in his body?' The great cloud of witnesses is all well and good, but counter-citation is not the same as counter-argument. How can one link an affirmation of the intrinsic goodness of creation with the real difference of redemption?

The basic argumentative strategy of the Christian tradition has been to think through the relationship between Jesus and the one Lord and God who creates the world. In the early centuries of Christianity, following John 1: 1, theologians argued that the Logos who was incarnate in Jesus of Nazareth is the Logos by which the Father creates the heavens and the earth. The upshot of this dogmatic conclusion is a mandate both to presuppose in general and to discern in detail continuity across the changes wrought by redemption in Christ. The logos or logic of new life in Christ, so this dogmatic conclusion implies, is co-ordinated with the logos or logic of finite existence. Creation is completed and fulfilled in redemption; it is not cancelled or ignored.

St Irenaeus of Lyon offers a clear illustration of this dogmatic move. His treatise, *Against the Heresies*, was written against Gnostic rivals, who were willing to give up on continuity in order to heighten the difference of redemption. The specific criticism that Irenaeus advances against them is that they are 'wicked interpreters' of Scripture (1989: book I, preface, 1). They abuse the literal sense of Scripture because they presuppose a redemptive scheme of escape from finitude. This scheme is supported, argues Irenaeus, by a theological distinction between a lower divine power (or powers) that structures creation and the higher divine power that redeems. Irenaeus can be numbingly complex in his descriptions of this Gnostic distinction and the various interpretations of the Bible that result, but here I simply note that the underlying charge that Irenaeus advances against the Gnostics is similar to the charge Soloveitchik mounts against Christianity: an assumed discontinuity between creation and redemption leads to an abuse of the former as a mere means to achieve the latter. That is, he charges that his Gnostic adversaries promote a view of redemption that is 'anti-body'. Clearly, then, Irenaeus does not endorse the project of *homo religiosus*; he refutes it.

Irenaeus's arguments rely on countless reformulations of basic Trinitarian teaching. 'There is but one God, who made all things by His Word,' writes Irenaeus in a characteristic passage, 'and not, as they allege, that the Creator was one, but the Father of the Lord another' (1989: book III, 11, 1). The unity of divine identity ensures a continuity between the act of creation and the initiative of redemption. For this reason, Irenaeus reads the language of immanence and presence in the Gospel of John metaphysically. To say that, in Christ, the Logos 'came to what was His own' (John 1: 11) reinforces the Trinitarian teaching that the Logos by which God creates the world is the Logos by which the world is redeemed. The 'body' of creation is not alien to the 'spirit' of redemption.

By adopting a Trinitarian hypothesis about God's identity, Irenaeus is able to unite the original agency of God in creation with the unique agency of God in redemption. This allows him to affirm the difference that redemption makes, while blocking all disjunctive accounts of the 'newness' of Christian faith and life. The underlying goal of the vast array of complex arguments that make up the last three books of *Against the Heresies* is to demonstrate the continuity of divine purpose. For the most part, Irenaeus works toward this goal by emphasizing the fulfilment of the prophecies, teachings, commandments, and histories of the Old Testament. However, we should beware of thinking that this is merely a literary or textual exercise. For Irenaeus, the Scriptures are the privileged window on to the structured reality of divine agency, manifest in all things. Irenaeus calls this structured reality the divine 'economy', or dispensation. His countless detailed exegetical arguments, therefore, are pieces of a larger argument designed to show how human history and created reality have an anticipatory shape that leans toward fulfilment in Christ. The Son who comes to redeem is with the Father as the Logos of creation.

Because the divine economy has an anticipatory structure, the decisive and transformative coming of the Logos in the flesh of the man Jesus of Nazareth is not a shock or a blow to the body of creation. It is, to use one of Irenaeus's technical terms, a recapitulation, a 'summing up' of all things, a fulfilment and completion, rather than a cancellation and new beginning (1989: book III, 26, 6). In such a view, the 'space' of redemption is not the disembodied realm of spirit; it is the consummated and completed body of creation. The 'time' of redemption is not the timeless eternal, but the 'fullness of time', the filling up of history with that toward which it has been leaning from the outset (1989: book III, 26, 7).

We should beware, however, of the temptation to think that the force of Irenaeus's argument rests in concepts such as recapitulation. For Irenaeus, and for the Christian tradition broadly, the decisive claim is about God: God, who is united with himself, is the source of creation and redemption. He creates toward the end of drawing all things to himself. How one describes the ontological conditions for this process of fulfilment, how one describes the process itself, the role of Jesus of Nazareth in that process, the anomaly of evil within the created order, and so forth—these are the questions that provoke theological debates. The crucial point is that the continuity between creation and redemption is a presupposition of those debates, if they are to be undertaken as debates within Christian theology. Because the Son is *homoousios* with the Father (as the Nicene Creed would subsequently formulate Irenaeus's position), continuity is analytic to the Christian account of the sovereign and undivided lordship of God.

If we return to our imagined college professor, the upshot is not a reassurance that Christianity teaches what she would like it to teach. Rather, the point is that Christian morality seeks to shape the soul, and such shaping is a rightfully human act and ambition. Christian moral demands involve a formation of and not assault upon our finite, embodied realities, a humanizing project of self-correction and even self-perfection, not an inhumane endeavour that leads to self-mutilation. Christianity does not want to renounce or transcend that body. Rather, as the evident aggressiveness of traditional Christian norms so amply demonstrates, a theological ethic wishes to shape the body. Chastity, for example, whether in a married or in a celibate state, is not a neglect or assault upon the body. It is an ambitious project of ordering bodily desire. The same holds for disciplines of the tongue, such as prohibitions against lying, slander, and gossip, as well as the whole range of Christian teaching on wealth, violence, and social order.

In these and many other specific instances, there is a drive toward holiness in the disciplines of the Christian life. The Sermon on the Mount is challenging, even frightening, because it raises the level of moral demand to heights that seem unendurable. There is an 'unnatural' quality to self-sacrificial love, and no theory of natural law and no moral epistemology can demonstrate or prove continuity. For this reason, we should say that a Christian ethic of redemption 'circumcises' the body. Only a faith in the unity of the Father with the Son in whom all things are created and through whom all things are redeemed can sustain the conclusion that the knife of circumcision that cuts into the heart of the faithful divinizes rather than deforms. The confidence that one can strive for righteousness without renouncing one's humanity rests on the identity of God, not on a metaphysical principle. The continuity across change is theological, not natural (see Reno 1996: 108–33).

ATONEMENT AND PERSONAL IDENTITY

When I conjure in my mind the objections friends and acquaintances make to Christian ethics, the focus is not only on the fate of our bodies. I find that many people worry about personal identity. Christian ethics, like all traditional ethical systems, has an authoritarian tone: 'Do this, and don't do that.' I can easily hear a voice of objection: 'What about my own judgements? What about the unique circumstances of my life?' Here, the concern is not with reason considered abstractly or with human nature in general. Instead, the worry is much more particular. What is the fate of our identities as unique and individual persons?

Great modern figures such as Rousseau and Emerson based their criticisms of traditional morality around this worry about individuality. Rousseau's *First* and *Second Discourses* emphasize the ways in which prevailing social mores alienate human beings and corrupt the intrinsic dignity of each person. People bend and distort themselves so that they can fit into prevailing social categories and succeed according to dominant social norms. We become calculating social animals rather than spontaneous, free human beings.

Emerson does not follow Rousseau's specific theories of the origins of social alienation, but he joins in Rousseau's broad condemnation of the dehumanizing effects of social conformity. The crucial similarity between the two is a common judgement that the disciplinary structures of social life force changes upon the individual that create a discontinuity between our true selves and our social selves. When Emerson says that 'imitation is suicide', he is drawing attention to the spiritual death that stems from self-alienation. When we stretch ourselves to meet the standards and goals set by others, we risk waking up one morning drowning in the responsibilities of marriage, children, job, and mortgage, feeling as though we have lost touch with all the passions and desires that once animated and moved us, finding ourselves frightened by self-recognition as we read T. S. Eliot, 'We are the hollow men / We are the stuffed men.'

Ironically, Rousseau's and Emerson's diagnosis of self-loss in social conformity has become conventional wisdom in our time. 'Question Authority' is a bumper-sticker philosophy that flows directly from the worry that collective demand will corrupt individual integrity. Moreover, the therapeutic atmosphere of contemporary culture is saturated with variations on the fundamental Rousseauian and Emersonian strategy of resistance to self-alienation: Be yourself! For most proponents of traditional morality, the modern and postmodern quest for authenticity seems but a cover for self-indulgence and a justification for immoralities. This reaction misdiagnoses the deep structure of Rousseauian and Emersonian protests against the shaping demands of morality. For at root, the worry concerns atonement. Both Rousseau and Emerson are profoundly pessimistic about any form of personal change that is not internally motivated. They despair of the possibility of linking who we presently are to the persons whom traditional morality would discipline us to become. They cannot see how a man or woman subjected to the disciplines of commandments can be 'at-one' with him or her self. Both see morally mandated personal development as a form of self-destruction, a spiritual act of immolating one's desires and impulses for the sake of something extrinsic to the self. Thus, in order to affirm a loyalty to individuality, both Rousseau and Emerson reject all forms of moral discipline that are not tailored by our consciences for our own unique circumstances, for our distinctive needs as individuals, for our intensely personal sensibilities and feelings. Only in this way can we be both morally ambitious and 'at-one' with ourselves.

The concern about self-loyalty is present in classical Christian literature as well. St Augustine's story of his conversion to Christianity turns on the same problem of atonement and personal identity that worries Rousseau and Emerson. As a young man, he read Cicero's *Hortensius*. 'The book', he says, 'changed my feelings.' 'It gave me different values and priorities,' Augustine reports. 'Suddenly every vain hope became empty to me, and I longed for the immortality of wisdom' (1998: III. 4). With this newfound zeal, Augustine embarked on a search for the truth, a search that took him down the blind alley of Manichaeanism, a search that foundered on the problem of evil and the difficulty of conceptualizing God as pure spirit—all problems closely related to the question of the relationship of body to spirit and the issues we have considered above.

For Augustine, the search was difficult and involved setbacks, but in the end, he came to see the truth of Christianity. Yet, this was not enough. For all his intellectual gains, nothing had changed for him as an individual. 'I myself was exceedingly astonished', he reports, 'as I anxiously reflected how long a time had elapsed since the nineteenth year of my life, when I began to burn with a zeal for wisdom, planning that when I had found it I would abandon all the empty hopes and lying follies of hollow ambitions. And here I was already thirty, and still mucking about in the same mire in a state of indecision' (1998: VI. 11).

The problem Augustine faced is one of personal identity, not human nature. Augustine was convinced that chastity is virtuous, and that virtue is a fulfilment and not a diminishment of his nature as a rational creature. He had no difficulty imagining a transformed human nature. Yet, he could not change. 'Fettered by the flesh's morbid impulse and lethal sweetness, I dragged my chain, but was afraid to be free of it' (1998: VI. 12). Augustine sought change, but he could not change, for he wished to be loyal to himself. 'Now I had discovered the good pearl. To buy it I had to sell all that I had; and I hesitated' (1998: VIII. 1). Augustine loved his habits, and he could not conceive of living without them, not because he thought them good, but simply because the habits were *his*.

Augustine's story of his spiritual journey dramatizes the true nature of a major resistance to the Christian view of redemption, a resistance expressed in such influential modern form by Rousseau and Emerson: the disjunctive demand of Christian ethics seems to require a death of the self, a renunciation of personal identity. In his modest divine comedy, *The Great Divorce*, C. S. Lewis fills in the details of this resistance. The spectral souls who are met by the Solid People at the entrance to heaven can only journey toward God if they will give up their doubts, vices, and shame. In Lewis's account, few do, and the reason is simple. They cannot imagine being *themselves* without the very qualities of the soul that alienate them from God. As the hissing lizard of lust warns the frightened man in a scene that echoes Augustine's hesitations, '[Without me] how could you live?' (1946: 101).

For all its affirmation of the continuity of creation and redemption, Christian theology has no interest in allaying the existential anxiety that naturally arises when we wonder whether our individual desires, commitments, habits, and projects can really endure an other-worldly ethic. For the other-worldly character of Christian ethics stems from the fact that 'the world' is not the created order. Rather, the worldly life of human beings is structured by the disorder of sin. Sin is a fundamentally unnatural and purely personal reality that shapes our identities. Sin cannot corrupt our human nature. Even the most pessimistic Augustinians in the Christian tradition have denied that sin is essential to the human condition. None the less, sin structures our personalities and gives shape to our habits. Sin is not a peripheral defect, an unfortunate but subsidiary feature of our lives. Sin determines our identities, and if we are to be loyal to ourselves in our current condition, then we must affirm our sinfulness, for it defines our life projects and self-images. By contrast, as Augustine was well aware, not to have this propensity toward evil, while it may not entail being superhuman, does entail becoming a different person.

Because human beings are personally invested in a life of sin, the personal disjunction of redemption is very real. Again, St Paul does not back away from the starkest possible language: 'We know that our old self was crucified with [Christ] so that the body of sin might be destroyed.... Whoever has died is freed from sin' (Rom. 6: 6–7). For the martyrs of the early church, the question of loyalty to Christ did entail physical life and death, but this is only the most visible and evident witness to the disjunctive structure of a Christian ethics of redemption. The Pauline language of death does not denote a physical cessation of life. At issue is who we are, as individuals: our loyalties, our commitments, our hopes and aspirations. The gospels report Jesus saying, 'Those who find their life will lose it, and those who lose their life for my sake will find it' (Matt. 10: 39 and parallels). St Augustine felt the horror of loss. It was not as though Augustine was unable to imagine a human being living a celibate life, any more than it was impossible for the Rich Young Man in the gospels who was disappointed by Jesus' commandment to sell all his possessions to imagine a life of poverty. The world has plenty of examples to show that it is possible to be human and celibate or poor. Rather, the problem for Augustine and the Rich Young Man was personal: How can *I* be celibate or poor without dying to my current projects, loyalties, and commitments? And if I do so die, then will I even be myself anymore? This is a problem of atonement.

The solution to this aspect of the problem of continuity of personal identity parallels the solution to the problem of the continuity of the body. It rests in the identity of Jesus Christ as the Son of God. In this case, however, it not just his identity as the incarnate Logos that secures continuity. He is *pro nobis*, 'for us', as the incorporative power of redemption. In some classical accounts of atonement, this incorporative power is discussed in terms of an exchange or substitution. Others describe a representative or pedagogical role that Jesus fills. In these different approaches, the metrics of analysis can focus on debt, penalty, sacrifice, or moral influence. Each account has its advantages and disadvantages, but what unifies atonement theory is a common concern to show that the changes both effected and demanded by the Christian view of redeemed life can be met. A link can be established between old and new, between death to sin and life, and that link is to be found in Christ.

Dietrich Bonhoeffer provides an analysis that highlights this aspect of atonement theory. Describing the logic of redemption, Bonhoeffer observes: 'God does not "overlook" sin; that would mean not taking human beings seriously as personal beings in their very culpability' (1998: 155) Whatever God does for human beings in Christ, it must be a 'doing' that accounts for the reality of our lives as we actually live them. Bonhoeffer continues with the central affirmation of all atonement theory: 'God does take human beings seriously in their culpability, and therefore only punishment and the overcoming of sin can remedy the matter' (1998: 155). This Christ endures in our place. Readers must not founder over Bonhoeffer's use of punishment as the metric to describe the conditions for divine seriousness about the particularity of human life. He might have used satisfaction or sacrifice or pedagogy or some other as yet undiscovered concept to describe the bridging function that links the person who has died to his old self with the one who lives as a new person in Christ. The crucial point is that Jesus Christ does what is necessary to establish the link; he effects atonement, and we participate in that atonement.

One of the greatest problems with atonement theory is that the terms are so often abstract. Debts must be paid, satisfaction must be offered, sacrifice must be made. This seems remote from Rousseau's and Emerson's concerns about authenticity. In the letters of St Paul, from which a great deal of Western Christian atonement theory draws its inspiration, the link is more evident, because Paul sees the incorporative power of Jesus Christ as enacted in the lives of believers as well as before the judgement seat of God. 'Do you not know', Paul asks the Christians in Rome, 'that all of us who have been baptized into Christ Jesus were baptized into his death? Therefore we have been buried with him by baptism into death, so that, just as Christ was raised from the dead by the glory of the Father, so we too might walk in newness of life' (Rom. 6: 3–4). At issue is not an abstract reconciliation of cosmic accounts. God is not up in heaven calculating debts and payments. Rather, for Paul, God is doing something here and now, and that 'doing' is addressed to concrete individuals. The incorporative power of Jesus Christ, given objective form in the sacrament of baptism and subjective form in faith, carries the believer across the difference between a life dominated by sin and a life that stretches toward righteousness. For this reason, Paul can use the greatest possible image of disjunction—death—while still affirming a continuity of personal identity. Jesus Christ is the enduring power across this disjunction. He has died and has been raised. The promise of the Gospel is that we can participate in that bridging reality. The upshot is atonement: however great the moral demands, we can stretch toward them, even stretch to the point of dying to ourselves, without simply severing our lives. To put the matter in scriptural terms more familiar to students of classical theories of atonement: in Christ, we can draw near to the holiness of God without being consumed by the purifying fires of judgement.

One of the clearest expressions of this confidence that radical moral demand is consistent with self-loyalty may be found in John Paul II's encyclical on fundamental questions in moral theology, *Veritatis Splendor*. The dominant theme of the encyclical is the sovereignty of moral truth, not only as universal and unchanging, but as commanding the loyalty of the whole person. The ideal of moral perfection flows from this sovereignty, and John Paul II's specific reflections on technical questions in Roman Catholic moral theology are detailed defences of the scope and depth of moral truth against various efforts to narrow and soften ethical obligations. One of the most important discussions concerns the relationship between divine law and human freedom. There, John Paul II engages contemporary forms of Rousseau's and Emerson's worry about self-alienation with a dogmatic claim: 'Patterned on God's freedom, man's freedom is not negated by his obedience to the divine law; indeed, only through this obedience does it abide in truth and conform to human dignity' (1993: § 42). The demands of Christian ethics, even the counsels of perfection that press the follower of Christ toward supernatural ends, are a fulfilment rather than a diminishment of our individuality.

In order to make good on this claim, John Paul II must provide some account of atonement. He does not adopt or articulate any theory of atonement. He does, however, reiterate the basic dynamics of Romans 6. For John Paul II, the sovereignty of moral truth 'is confirmed in a particularly eloquent way by Christian martyrdom' (1993: § 90). Spiritual death to the dominion of worldly powers may well be accompanied by physical death. The earthly kingdom may hang her traitors. Yet, the eloquence of the martyrs rests in more than the extremity of their obedience. For John Paul II, as for the early church, the eloquence of martyrdom is evangelical, not Stoic, for the path of suffering and death recapitulates the way of Jesus Christ. In the same way, the less visible suffering of any who feel the painful death of worldly loyalties—hating mother and father, plucking out the eyes of lust, selling possessions dearly loved—this very real personal grief and travail under the disciplines of moral perfection recapitulate the way of the Man of Sorrows.

For John Paul II, the basic logic of classical atonement theory functions, in a figural rather than an analytic fashion. We can endure being stretched across the demands of discipleship because Christ has gone before us to establish the way. As is the case in a formal theory of atonement, Christ supports the transition as the power of redemption. At this point the concerns of Rousseau and Emerson return. John Paul II's immoderate affirmation of the goal of moral perfection and his embrace of the ideal of martyrdom would seem to vindicate the judgement that Christian faith does violence to the human person. Christianity may promise redemption, but it seems to nurture a death wish, a ruthless self-denial that relishes suffering. One need not be an ideologue or a knave to worry that the sovereignty of a moral truth that is most visible in martyrdom leaves no room for individuality, no space for personal uniqueness, no scope for the projects and loyalties that fill our lives and shape our identities. Far from being 'at-one' with ourselves in Christ, the perfection of Christian moral demands seems to drive a wedge into our lives and split us in two: a thin sliver of righteousness and obedience over and against the vast reality of our lives.

Were the Israelites at the base of Mount Sinai right to exclaim in fear, 'Do not let God speak to us, or we will die'? (Exod. 20: 19). Just as faith in Christ as the Son of God who is *homoousios* with the Father is the crucial premise for a theological argument demonstrating the continuity of the body across redemptive change, so also is a faith in Christ as the one who died for us and was raised the crucial premise for showing the personal continuity of atonement. Because Jesus Christ is who he is, Christian ethics can endorse the sovereignty and severity of moral truth and, at the same time, affirm that devotion to righteousness is a life project that is marked by personal continuity. Obedience to the commandments of God will put to death the body of our sin, but it will not destroy our individuality.

No anthropological scheme or theory of freedom can demonstrate the truth of the Christian affirmation that we endure a death to our old selves in Christ. Like the fate of our bodies, the destiny of our personalities rests in the identity of God. None the less, a return to St Augustine allows us to see that the Christian vision of redemptive change can drive a wedge into life and consume profoundly intimate loyalties and habits in fires of self-discipline, while still affirming personal continuity. On this point, the crucial aspect of his *Confessions* is not any particular theological argument that Augustine makes. Instead, what stands out is the successful literary combination of disjunction with continuity. Augustine both pushes away his past in repudiation and draws it near in memory.

The key to the success of Augustine's ability in creating a rhetoric of both disjunction and continuity is the underlying structure of repentance. To both renounce and own the main features of one's life, as does Augustine in the voice of repentance, creates a literary effect that we might rightly call atonement. It is possible because, at every turn, Augustine's penitent voice places the reality of his life into the hands of God. He concludes his extended address to God that opens the *Confessions* with these words: 'Dust and ashes though I am, let me appeal to your pity, since it is to you in mercy that I speak, not to a man, who would simply laugh at me. Perhaps you too may laugh at me, but you will relent and have pity on me' (1998: 1. 6). God's identity as the one who comes as the power of redemption, not Augustine's as the one who seeks, is the key to the possibility of owning his past as, indeed, his own, while, at the very same time, disowning it as governed by sin. God atones for those whose lives are broken, as was Augustine's, across the difference between love of self and desire for the divine.

Donald MacKinnon was one of the more idiosyncratic theologians of the twentieth century, and his capacity to think against the grain of conventional theological fashions led him to recognize that we often puzzle out our deepest questions in disguised or muddled forms. Writing in the 1960s, when the key questions of morality and religion were framed in epistemological terms, he offered a cautionary word of dissent: 'The philosopher of religion easily tends to think that the greatest obstacles today in the way of religious belief are to be found in the unintelligibility and inadmissibility of such fundamental concepts as that of a creator God, an immaterial soul, etc. But it may be that as a matter of empirical fact, the most deep-seated unwillingness to take seriously the claims of the Christian religion has its roots in a sharp criticism of Christian ethics, of the Christian image of the good life' (1968: 51).

I have little doubt that MacKinnon was correct. However much Rudolf Bultmann's 'modern man' was incapable of believing in the 'mythological world-view' of pre-modern culture, I am certain that postmodern men and women are capable of believing almost anything. Ours is a sceptical age, and the fruit of scepticism is most often credulity. We know that we cannot know, so we cast our lot with what is convenient or alluring or exciting or familiar. When truth is a matter of taste, then we should not be surprised that some people lap up astrology as eagerly as others do ice cream. For this reason, the revulsion that postmodern men and women feel toward Christian ethics eclipses older worries about reason and revelation. That revulsion is, of course, diverse, both in object and in intensity. None the less, as I have outlined, in large part the revulsion stems from the way in which redemptive hope endorses a disjunctive, other-worldly ethic, one that seeks a transformed body and a new identity in Christ.

I have attempted to show the theological cogency of this ethical demand, a cogency that rests on the clarity of the Christian identification of Jesus Christ as the Son of God, who for us and for our salvation, became incarnate, was crucified, and was raised by the Father. But cogency rarely convinces. When your friend is white with fear before take-off, you can set out to explain the principles of aerodynamics, hydraulics, pilot training, and so forth. Yet, if he tosses off all your explanations by saying, 'But how can I know that modern science and technology and training really work?', then you have little recourse. The same holds for Christian ethics and the redemptive moral demands it endorses. I can show how the machinery of Trinitarian and Christological doctrine ensures that the flights of Christian moral ambition are consistent with safe landings, both in body and in personal identity; but if the modern world falls back upon its doubts and says, 'But how can you prove that Jesus really is the incarnate Son of God who died for us and for our salvation?', then I have little recourse other than to reiterate Karl Barth's assertion that the grace of God *is* the answer to the ethical question. When all the explaining is done, only the power of the facts of air travel can overcome a man's doubts about the possibilities of flight. When all the theological analysis has been unwound, only the power of the great divine fact, the God who is who he is, can overcome our fears of moral change.

REFERENCES AND SUGGESTED READING

AQUINAS, THOMAS (1966). *Summa Theologiae*, vol. 28. Oxford: Blackfrairs.
AUGUSTINE (1998). *Confessions*. Oxford: Oxford University Press.
BARTH, KARL (1957). *The Church Dogmatics*, vol. II/2. Edinburgh: T. & T. Clark.
BONHOEFFER, DIETRICH (1998). *Sanctorum Communio: Dietrich Bonhoeffer's Works*, vol. 1. Minneapolis: Fortress Press.
BOYARIN, DANIEL (1994). *A Radical Jew: Paul and the Politics of Identity*. Berkeley: University of California Press.
DAWSON, JOHN DAVID (1995). *Literary Theory*. Minneapolis: Fortress Press.
—— (2002). *Christian Figural Reading and the Fashioning of Identity*. Berkeley: University of California Press.

DENNEY, JAMES (1903). *Atonement and the Modern Mind.* New York: A. C. Armstrong.

EMERSON, RALPH WALDO (1929). *Essays: First and Second Series.* New York: Houghton Mifflin.

HARE, JOHN (1996). *The Moral Gap: Kantian Ethics, Human Limits, and God's Assistance.* Oxford: Clarendon Press.

IRENAEUS (1989). *The Ante-Nicene Fathers*, vol. 1. Grand Rapids, Mich.: Eerdmans Publishing.

JOHN PAUL II (1993). *Veritatis Splendor.* Rome: Libreria Editrice Vaticana.

LEWIS, C. S. (1946). *The Great Divorce.* New York: Macmillan.

LUBAC, HENRI DE (1983). *A Brief Catechesis Concerning the Relationship of Nature and Grace.* San Francisco: Ignatius Press.

MACKINNON, DONALD (1968). *Borderlands of Theology.* New York: Lippincott.

MENKE, KARL-HEINZ (1991). *Stellvertretung: Schuesselbegriff christlichen Lebens und theologische Grundkategorie.* Einsiedeln: Johannes Verlag.

MOBERLY, R. C. (1901). *Atonement and Personality.* London: John Murray.

PARFIT, DEREK (1984). *Reasons and Persons.* Oxford: Clarendon Press.

RENO, R. R. (1996). *The Ordinary Transformed: Karl Rahner and the Christian Vision of Transcendence.* Grand Rapids, Mich.: Eerdmans Publishing.

—— (2001). 'American Satyricon', *First Things*, 116, 35–41.

—— (2002). *Redemptive Change: Atonement and the Christian Cure of the Soul.* Harrisburg, Pa.: Trinity Press.

ROUSSEAU, JEAN-JACQUES (1964). *The First and Second Discourses.* New York: St. Martin's Press.

SOLOVEITCHIK, JOSEPH (1983). *Halakhic Man.* New York: Jewish Publication Society. Originally published in Hebrew in 1944.

WOLF, SUSAN (1982). 'Moral Saints', *Journal of Philosophy*, 79, 419–39.

CHAPTER 3

....

ESCHATOLOGY
AND ETHICS

....

KATHRYN TANNER

ESCHATOLOGY, or the theology of last things, is a Christian doctrine with a rather direct bearing on ethical questions via its influence on psychological dispositions to act. (For an account of the way Christian beliefs affect dispositions to act that is more complex than anything I can offer here—an account that includes, for example, the importance of situation and of the additional beliefs one holds—see Tanner 1992: 1–34.) Perhaps for this reason, eschatology is a major topic in much of contemporary Christian thought concerned, as this author is, to promote social and political activism. What one believes about the end of things affects how one feels about the world in which one lives and one's attitude towards efforts to make the world a better place. Disgust and appreciation for the life one leads, contentment and discontentment with one's lot, resignation and resistance to the social order, hope and despair of change, eagerness and reluctance to take action, optimism and pessimism about bettering human life, triumphalism and humility about what has been achieved so far, are all associated at one time or another with the theology of last things. The direction of the doctrine's influence—whether it helps to motivate or discourage action for the world's improvement—depends on a number of variables that are associated with historical tensions in the way the doctrine has developed in the Christian tradition.

VARIABLES IN THE DEVELOPMENT
OF DOCTRINE

The degree to which all dimensions of life are represented at the eschaton is one such factor. Some eschatologies are cosmic in scope, telling us, for example, to expect a new heaven and earth in which peace reigns among all living creatures; while others limit attention to human life—in hopes, for instance, of human replacements for the fallen angels in heaven. Among the latter, human-centred sort, sometimes the corporate dimensions of human existence are played up—in talk, for instance, about the kingdom or city of God. Sometimes individuals are the major concern—for example, when eschatology has the existential meaning of being open to the future or where the primary question is reward or punishment after death. Not every account of the eschaton, furthermore, includes all the various sides of human life: physical and spiritual, intellectual and sensible. Quite often, indeed, the ultimate good of human life at its end—say, the beatific vision of God—highlights the excellent exercise of intellectual or spiritual, rather than physical, capabilities, and defines that excellence in terms of avoidance of bodily based passions or dependence on sense faculties. The dimensions of existence not included in the eschaton are evidently not perfectible in a way that would allow them to count as ultimate goods and are likely to be, therefore, of at most penultimate concern in a moral life. The widest possible eschaton—where the natural world appears in all its glory, human community is transformed along with individual lives, and fulfilment includes both the material and the spiritual sides of life—would, to the contrary, encourage moral responsibility with a similarly universal range, commitment to furthering the good of the whole planet and its peoples in every respect possible.

The extent to which the eschaton mirrors life as we know it is another major factor. Because it represents the consummate good of creation, the eschaton gives us no reason to question the moral adequacy of those features of the contemporary world that turn up again there; slave-holders therefore waxed eloquent about masters and slaves in heaven and their segregated lots. Our moral imaginations find no expansion beyond the given in those respects; the eschaton does not prompt us to improve those aspects of the world, because the eschaton gives us no reason to think that there is anything better. At the other extreme, a merely fantastic eschaton makes us despair of ever getting there from here; we would seemingly have to start from scratch to make any headway. Our attention focused by eschatology on goods impossible in this world, we become distracted from and sour on the achievable ones. The middle point of such descriptions of the eschaton—the one that would foster maximum dissatisfaction with the *status quo* while underpinning a strong call for action—seems an eschaton that contrasts as much as possible with this world yet one that is recognizably this world transformed.

The location of the eschaton also proves to be an influence. Will the eschaton occur in this world or the next? On earth or in heaven? As the final moment of human history or beyond it? In this life or after death? In the latter set of cases, the eschaton tends to take on a compensatory function. We expect little from this life and are resigned to that fact by hopes of what is to come once we leave all this behind; we can put up with what little we have if we expect everything to be changed in a world beyond this one. The eschaton exerts no pull on us, it does not prompt us to act, because we do not expect the eschaton ever to enter our world.

Another consideration is the mechanism of the eschaton's realization. Especially when the disjunction in content and location between the world as we know it and the eschaton is great, the final state of things tends to be brought about by God's action alone; God must be called in to set things right, and our responsibilities cease. Where God acts alone to bring in the eschaton, change from this world to the next is also often pictured as immediate and without process. This world simply ends, and a new world begins by divine power, since nothing within this world has the capacity to bring the eschaton closer to realization through gradual, progressive action. Our struggle for the good—painful, effort-filled action that takes time—is therefore devalued relative to God's own immediate achievement of the world that is to come; and expectations of the good to be achieved by way of our struggles often drop away. If action to better the world is to be motivated by eschatology, human action should then have some place in bringing about the eschaton. We should not, however, ever be left to our own devices. To the extent that work to bring about the eschaton becomes our sole responsibility, to that same extent there is no remedy for despair should our efforts prove fruitless, and nothing to stop our finalizing the good of the best that we can do. Where eschatology suggests that human action is necessary but always and in every respect empowered and corrected by God's own action to bring about the eschaton, a call for human action can be combined with a chastened recognition of the difficulties to be faced and a realistic sense of what can be achieved by human action.

A TEMPORALIZED OR DE-TEMPORALIZED ESCHATON?

A final factor—one that the rest of this essay addresses in some detail—concerns whether or not, and (if so) the manner in which, the eschaton is temporalized. This seems to me a more fundamental set of tensions in Christian eschatology (for reasons that will become apparent below) than the more familiar tension between an already realized eschaton and one yet to come. The 'last' in the 'last things' that eschatology discusses is ambiguous. It may mean ultimate—the highest good that consummates creation—in which case nothing much is indicated directly about the time of the eschaton's occurrence. It might have occurred at the beginning, when the world was first created, and been lost; it might be breaking in, even realized, now. Or 'last' may have an essentially temporal sense: what comes at the end of time, either as the last moment of the temporal sequence or 'after' it, so to speak, when the temporal unrolling of the world (or, more personally speaking, one's lifetime) has finished. Temporalized in either fashion, the eschaton is associated with the future—with the immediate future in case time is up, but more commonly with a distant future, the eschaton as not yet here, the eschaton one awaits.

Future-oriented eschatologies have generally been dominant for the last 200 years in the West, undoubtedly encouraged by the rise of historical consciousness in modernity. Things have not always been this way, and are unlikely to remain unchanged; the future cannot be bound to the past or the present. Human beings are, moreover, responsible for these changing circumstances of their social worlds. Improvement by social means is possible, the errors of past and present thereby corrected. Human beings exist in a constant state of dissatisfaction with the achievements of past and present, and act according to the imperative of permanent revolution, in order to usher in the new.

Modern eschatologies typically incorporate these modern hopes for a better future through progressive historical movement, and repudiate both resignation in the face of what is and despair about a better life to come. What these eschatologies often temper is modern enthusiasm over the ability of human beings to bring heaven on earth. Checked is the unwarranted optimism of modernity, optimism that must overlook the sufferings and injustices that remain, or, when beset by unexpected difficulties, optimism that promotes inconsolable despair. Every good that human beings achieve can be surpassed by the final good that God promises; and some genuine evils—such as transience and death—are simply beyond the powers of human beings to remedy, and so must be left to God. Modern eschatologies also insist—on pain of irrelevance—that the final good is not the product of a wholly naturalistic historical process. God must be at work in and for the world if it is to come to its end.

In probably the best and most influential example of this sort of modern eschatology—Jürgen Moltmann's *Theology of Hope* (1975)—both these modifications to a modern sensibility amount to a deepening of the future orientation of action in modern movements for social change. Constantly looking towards the future keeps progressive social action from ever stopping with what has been achieved in the past and the present, and from ever saying that the end has finally come. So as to make clear that naturalistic processes are insufficient to bring about the final good of the world, God's future, unlike any ordinary future, takes on a kind of causal primacy *vis-à-vis* past and present. God's future is not the simple unrolling of past and present processes. Instead, God's future comes to this world—it takes the form of an *adventus*—so as to set history in movement, so as to draw past and present towards itself. The future—not the past and the present—becomes in this way the real motor of history.

If eschatology is not temporalized in this way, it is argued (again most forcefully and influentially by Moltmann), social action for the world's improvement finds no encouragement. An eschaton realized in the present or past absolutizes the good of some already achieved state, and so short-circuits the critical impulse essential to social reform; there is nothing new, nothing better, to come. An eschaton not indexed to time—an eternal eschaton—affords no principle for distinguishing one time from another in terms of the progressive achievement of the good in history. Every time is like every other, differences devalued, with reference to an eternal eschaton, equally near or far from every historical period. An eschatology consisting, in sum, of 'the epiphany of the eternal in the present' is simply a recipe, then, for social stasis.

I would like to dispute this association of de-temporalized eschatologies with inaction and complacency by developing in the rest of this essay a de-temporalized eschatology with the opposite effects. But I would also like to suggest that future-oriented eschatologies do not have as much going for them now as they once did. Progressive social action now is less a matter of rejecting the fixities of the past and setting matters in motion, and more a matter of finding new organizations for the flow of people and things. In our postmodern world nothing is fixed any more, everything is already in motion, fluidity the rule. The problem is not stability and inelasticity, but the unjust way that things are presently set in motion—for example, on the economic front, the way in which capital flows in and out of nation-states to bankrupt them, or the way in which corporations outsource to take advantage of low-paid workers in foreign countries, the way in which populations move, or are hampered from moving, by immigration restrictions. Social action to improve the world is no longer defined by the decision to be open to the future, to throw oneself open to the new, but by decisions about how persons, products, and processes are to circulate and be arranged in space. Once political and economic questions fundamentally concern such matters as the transnational migrations of workers, shifting sites of production and consumption in a world dominated by multinational corporations, the connection or disconnection of regions to global financial and media networks, and the ways in which bodies are corralled, measured, and manipulated, 'prophecy involves a geographical rather than historical projection' (Berger 1974: 44). Incorporating and correcting these postmodern movements for social change in the way in which modern eschatologies have done would suggest, therefore, a more spatialized than temporalized eschatology.

The optimism of modernity has also fallen by the wayside. Neo-liberalism seems the only game in town with the breakup of the Soviet Union and the turn of China to the forces of the free market. Even if we had other model states to go on, the speed of contemporary life gives us no time to consider them. The complex, decentralized networks of monetary and communication media make it very difficult, moreover, to analyse the problems of contemporary life in ways that would identify agents and mechanisms for change. In short, we have difficulty imagining where to go from here and how to get there.

Eschatology would presumably counter these trends—for example, by helping to expand our imagination for the possible configurations of life—but some of the forces for pessimism in contemporary life are more intransigent. They seem not so much problems as indisputable facts. Modernity has simply shown its dark side in the terrors of the last century. The ills that come with every social advance are more apparent than ever before: ecological disaster from attempts at ecological inter- vention; hate group and terrorist organizing from the same internet that links us, etc. Indeed, the risks only seem to increase with every improvement. Naturalism is now associated more with fatalism than with confidence in the powers of human achievement: death, transience, and failure seem simply the irremediable stuff of life. Things will ultimately come to a bad end of cosmic proportions if the physicists are right: dissipation or conflagration is our universe's sorry future.

One has the option of course as a theologian of trying to dispute all this. Things are not so bad; a successful resolution of things is possible in any case with God's help. The cosmic crunch, for example, may be averted by divine power, or the universe recreated from cosmic death by some renewed divine act of *creatio ex nihilo*. But is there a way for eschatology to incorporate a less optimistic world-view directly and as it stands? Or is eschatology really only amenable to a fairly sanguine estimation of human history's and the globe's future prospects? Eschatology might be able to incorporate a less optimistic world-view, I suggest again, were eschat- ology to be de-temporalized.

This would mean uncoupling the eschaton from hopes for the world's future. We have our hope in God whether or not things are likely to turn out well in the end, whether or not things are likely to turn out badly in the end. Social action for the world's improvement, to which we are called by such an eschatology, would be uncoupled too from expectations of success; we are called to act, irrespective of the likelihood of success or failure. De-temporalized eschatology would become, then, a socially progressive creed, unaltered, for all times, whether confident or jaded.

But can a de-temporalized eschatology encourage social action for the world's betterment? If Christian eschatology does not offer specifically future hopes, what might motivate action to bring in a better future for humans and the planet? Without expectations of a better world to come, what disturbs complacency concerning the world as it seems to work now? Without hopes for the future of this world, what can Christian eschatology do to alleviate despair in the face of present injustice and suffering? What is to prevent the sense that all our efforts to better the world are simply futile?

To put the same set of worries another way, has too much of contemporary pessimism been conceded by a de-temporalized eschatology? What is to prevent such an eschatology from simply being co-opted by a nihilistic cultural moment? Christian eschatology in that case would simply confirm the untoward contemporary understandings of world, self, and community that scientific predictions of the world's end, for example, already play into and foment: (1) a desperate foreboding about the ultimate futility of efforts to improve the human situation and conditions of the planet—what is the difference if everything is to end in some cosmic crunch?—and (2) an irresponsible, simply self-interested focus on goods that can be had in the moment without much expenditure of effort. As the Bible gives shocked expression to such a view of the moral space of human life: 'They said to themselves in their deluded way: "Our life is short and full of trouble, and when man comes to the end there is no remedy; no man has ever been known to return from the grave... come then, let us enjoy the good things while we can, and make full use of the creation, with all the eagerness of youth... Down with the poor and honest man! Let us tread him under foot... For us let might be right!"' (Wisd. 2: 1, 6, 10, NEB).

I need to explain, then, how an eschatology for a world without a future manages to avoid hopelessness in the face of present trouble, complacent inactivity regarding suffering and injustice, and irresponsible self-concern. I need to explain how my eschatology does not bring with it the loss of eschatology as political theology, the loss of active, socially committed challenge to structures of oppression, injustice, and ecological devastation that is so much a part—and rightly so—of many modern, future-oriented eschatologies. The explanations won't make much sense, however, without first developing in greater detail the character of this de-temporalized eschatology.

ESCHATOLOGY FOR A WORLD WITHOUT A FUTURE

Just as creation in its essential meaning does not refer to what happens in the beginning (in contradistinction to what happens after), so the central claim of eschatology does not refer to what happens at the end (in contradistinction to what happens before). Creation refers to a relationship of dependence upon God which holds whether or not the world has a beginning, and whatever the worldly mechanism by which it may have come to be. Understood in a similar way, the eschaton—consummation in the good—has to do primarily with a new level of relationship with God, the final one surpassing what we are simply as creatures, beyond which there is no other. Eschatology's fundamental interest is in the character of this relationship to God and not in what the world is like or what happens to it considered independently of that relationship—say, at its end. One retains a religious interest in the future of things *as they exist in this new relationship with God*—that is, one wants to know the consequences for the world that this consummate relationship with God brings with it. But the world has this future whether or not the world *considered in itself* ends and whatever the process by which it does; the world will have this future, irrespective of such events, because it has this future in virtue of the character of its relationship with God. Worries about the final, future state of things are undercut, since the world can enjoy this new level of relationship with God however badly things turn out.

This new level of relationship with God can be called eternal life in God. While continuing and consummating God's faithful commitment to the creature's good as that is manifest in creation, eternal life is a greater gift, and brings in its train greater gifts, than the relationship with God that creatures enjoy simply as creatures. The unconditionality of eternal life marks one such difference from the relationship with God that creatures enjoy simply as such. With eternal life it becomes clear how relationship with God as the source of all benefit cannot be broken by sin, suffering, or death; relations with a life-giving God are maintained unconditionally from God's side. Whatever might happen, God remains faithful to a life-giving relationship with us and empowers us, through Christ, for faithfulness to that same life-giving mission, too. The relationship is also unconditional, then, in that what we should be in it—the image of God's own relationship with us—is maintained or shored up from God's side (in virtue of the free favour and mercy of God in Christ) despite our own failings, sufferings, and sin. In the relationship of eternal life, God sets us in and upholds our position in relation to God, whatever we do, whatever happens to us. Despite the fact of human failing, faithlessness, and death, we *are* alive in God.

Eternal life is, secondly, not the same sort of relationship as the rather external one that exists between God and creatures: our very identity as creatures is redefined so as to be essentially constituted by relationship with God. Separation from God is now impossible in a way it was not for us simply as creatures. The meaning of this new identity is that our dependence upon God for our existence is now complete: in Christ we essentially *are* that relationship to God in a way that simply being creatures of God does not entail.

The model for this aspect of life in God is the Incarnation. (For a fuller description of the Christology employed here and throughout, see Tanner 2001.) Jesus is the one who lives in God, the one who is all that he is as a human being without existing independently of God, the human being whose very existence is God's own; this is the meaning of 'hypostatic union'. Otherwise expressed, in Jesus God becomes the bearer of our very human acts and attributes. By grace—by virtue, that is, of a life-giving relationship with Jesus that is ours in the power of the Spirit—we enjoy something like the sort of life in God that Jesus lives. We (and the whole world) are to live in God as Jesus does, through Him.

Eternal life is, in the third place, a greater gift than the relationship enjoyed simply by creatures because of the gifts it brings with it. Those gifts are not just the consummate expression of the sort of finite goods appropriate to creatures, but divine gifts. As a consequence of the Incarnation, the very powers and character of God shine through Jesus' human acts and attributes—giving Jesus' acts and attributes a salvific force (e.g., so as to overcome and heal the consequences of sin) and eventuating in the manifest glorification of Jesus' own human being in the Resurrection. So for us, life in Christ brings not just created goods but divine attributes such as imperishability and immortality, which are ours only through the grace of Christ in the resurrection of our bodies.

Understood in the way I have been describing, eternal life promotes a more spatialized than temporalized eschatology. The future-oriented eschatology of a future-oriented society here gives way to an eschatology in keeping with the present epoch, which, as Michel Foucault describes it, is 'the epoch of space. We are in the epoch of simultaneity; we are in the epoch of juxtaposition... of the side by side, of the dispersed... [O]ur experience of the world is less that of a long life developing through time than that of a network that connects points and intersects with its own skein' (Foucault 1986: 22). Eternal life is not the endless extension of present existence into an endless future, but a matter of a new quality of life in God, at the ready, even now infiltrating, seeping into the whole. Eternal life is less a matter of duration than a matter of the mode of one's existence in relation to God, as that calibre of relation shows itself in a new pattern for the whole of life.

At the most fundamental level, eternal life is ours now in union with Christ, as in the future. It is therefore not directly associated with the world's future and not convertible to the idea that the world will always have a future or further time. Here the eschaton cannot be understood primarily as what comes *from* the future to draw the time of this world ever onward. It is not associated especially with any particular moment of time (past, present, or future), and therefore such an understanding of the eschaton has no stake in any reworked, theological account of temporal relations in which a coming future is given primacy over present and past times.

Besides the fact that it is not temporally indexed in any of these ways, eternal life is also spatialized in that it suggests a living *in* God, a kind of placement within the life of God. Since there may come a time when the world no longer exists, this placement in God cannot be equated with God's presence or placement within the world. A kind of indwelling of God in us is, however, a consequence of life in God, just as the Incarnation has as its consequence a human life lived by the power of God. In imitation of Christ, we live in God, and therefore the life we lead has a kind of composite character to match our new composite personhood: God's attributes become in some sense our own; they are to shine through our lives in acts that exceed human powers, and in that way become established as part of a reborn sense of self. The consequences of that indwelling work themselves out in lives with a temporal flow, but they are being worked out now as much as at any time in the future. Now, as after our deaths, there is, moreover, no end to the flow, as a terminal point for religious preoccupation, because the inexhaustible fullness of God's gifts makes itself felt in creatures in the form of an ever-expanding reception of gifts.

Eternal life is also understood in spatial terms so as to become a realm or sphere. Eternal life is a kingdom of God, comparable to an Old Testament sense of righteousness as a new pattern of relationships to which the righteous commit themselves. Eternal life is a new 'power-charged area, into which [humans] are incorporated and thereby empowered to do special deeds' (Von Rad 1962: 376). This realm of eternal life is not other-worldly, either in the sense of becoming a part of the picture after death—i.e., in the sense that one enters into it only after death—or in the sense of marking a spiritualized, merely personal attitude to events of this world. Instead, eternal life exists now in competition with another potentially all-embracing structure or pattern of existence marked by futility and hopelessness—the realm of death, in the broadest biblical sense of that. One exists in this realm of eternal life now, and it extends as far as that other realm of death does, under which, as Paul says, the whole created universe groans (Rom. 8: 22). Eternal life infiltrates, then, the present world of suffering and oppression, to bring life, understood as a new pattern or structure of relationships marked by life-giving vitality and renewed purpose.

Eternal life as a given for all time to come is a present reality. We possess now, in an unconditional fashion, life in God as a source of all good; and therefore we need not wait for death to pass from the realm of death to that of life. 'He who hears my words and believes... has eternal life; he does not come into judgment, but has [already] passed from death to life' (John 5: 24). 'So if anyone is in Christ, there is a new creation; everything old has passed away; see everything has become new!' (2 Cor. 5: 17). As Bernhard Anderson discusses the point:

[A]lready in the old age people may taste the power of the age to come; already in the old age the leaven of God's kingdom is at work; already in the time of the old creation a new creation is beginning. Thus, the relation between the two ages... is neither a straight-line continuity nor a disjunctive discontinuity. Rather it is continuity and discontinuity. People are called to live in the zone where the circles overlap—where there is discontinuity with the old age even while the old age continues. (1994: 238)

Eternal life's ever present reality does not mean that the full consequences of our entrance into eternal life are immediately evident. A world of blessings—now, as after death—are the expected effects of life in God, and therefore life in God permits no simple spiritualization of God's gifts. Eternal life is to bring about life in all the extended biblical senses of that term—abundance, longevity, fruitfulness, individual well-being, and communal flourishing in justice and peace—in this world and after its death. At the world's death, when we no longer exist as independent beings apart from God, when we no longer have even an apparent existence outside of God, such goods must have some greater and different manifestation in the life we continue to live in God—i.e., in the form of a new, sanctified, and imperishable life that carries us beyond the loss of our own powers of living in death. But the realization of these goods of life obviously takes time, in that their recipients progressively unroll over the course of the world's history, and in that the process of receiving them is very often a temporally extended one for most things in the world. We and the world are to exhibit all the good consequences of life in God as the signs or manifestations of our entrance into it. 'We . . . have crossed over from death to life; we know this, because we love our brothers. The man who does not love is still in the realm of death' (1 John 3: 14–16, NEB). But given a world of hatred and injustice, eternal life is evidently not ours in a way that precludes more to come in manifestation of it. The familiar tension between already and not yet, understood as a temporal dynamic, returns for all these reasons, but within the fundamental de-temporalized eschatological frame of eternal life. Not yet manifest in a world still progressively unfolding, and in a world of suffering and tribulation, are the full consequences that follow from the decisive fact of eternal life, already, forever, and fully ours. This 'more to come' is the world's living out or adequate reflection of what is already completely the case: this 'more', for example, is a life with others that properly reflects what follows from life in God, a life in God that has already been granted to us completely and irrevocably from God's side and that remains an ever empowering source for all the goods of life. The tension between present achievement and future promise holds, as a temporal matter, for the consequences of eternal life, then. Eternal life itself, as the consummate form of relationship with God, remains in its unsurpassable achievement unchanged, with no more to come, becoming neither more nor less with time.

This relationship between eternal life and the benefits it brings finds its model in the way in which the Incarnation enables the saving effects of Jesus' life and death. The Incarnation, understood as the Word's assuming the humanity of Jesus as its own, is an unchanging, and in that sense temporally unindexed, fact of Jesus' existence from beginning to end. As the constitutive feature of Jesus' reality, it is responsible for the remarkable character of Jesus' entire life for the sake of life. All that Jesus does and 'enjoys' to further the good throughout the course of his life and death in a world of sin (healing, delivering, blessing, dying for our sakes) is a consequence of his life in God as the incarnate Son of God. What Jesus does and what he suffers are the unfolding of the meaning of life in God (i.e., the meaning of incarnation) as that power for life enters into fully historical human existence and struggles to overcome a world of suffering, exclusion, and despair. The more to come in our lives and the world's—e.g., the end of the host of death-dealing consequences of sin—is, similarly, the now effort-filled unrolling during the time of the world (and after it) of what life in God should bring with it—life in the entirety of its connotations.

ACTION FOR THE WORLD'S BETTERMENT

How does the eschatology I am developing stimulate action for the better in this life? It might not seem to do so, for a number of reasons. Because eternal life is an unconditional, already realized possession, nothing we do is necessary to bring it about or to sustain it; this might suggest (erroneously, as I shall argue) that action is not obligated in any way *by* life in God. The present possession of eternal life might also seem to compensate for all other disappointments in a way that would simply reconcile us with them; even when matters could be improved by human action, we would not see any need to do so because we already have all that we need simply in virtue of life in God. Finally, hope that sustains action in the face of obstacles and disappointment seems shattered by the world's eventual end, and thereby hope for the future of the world itself seems gone as the primary spur to present action.

While on the viewpoint I am developing one need not deny that the future will be different from the present, criticism of the present is not fuelled primarily by the difference between present realities and what one expects the future to bring. Instead, criticism of the present is prompted, and complacency about it prevented, by a recognition of the disparity between the realm of life and the realm of death as those two realms or powers wrestle for supremacy in the here and now. One is led to see the way in which the world currently runs as an insufferable, unacceptable affront, not by the disparity between the present and God's coming future, but by the utter disjunction between patterns of injustice, exclusion, and impoverishment, which make up the realm of death, and the new paradigm of existence empowered by life in God as a force working in the present. In short, complacency is ruled out not by a transcendent future but by a transcendent present—by present life in God as the source of goods that the world one lives in fails to match.

The shape of Jesus' life is this new paradigm of existence struggling in the here and now over the shape of life in the world. That pattern of action is one that ministers divine beneficence to others, in correspondence to Jesus' own ministering of the Father's beneficence to humanity—healing, nourishing, attending to the needs of the world—what Jesus did in his own life, a prior ministry that empowers our own. We are disgruntled with the world as it is in light of Jesus as our world's future, but rather than coming to us from the future simply, Jesus is the new paradigm of the world's existence already realized (in the past of his own life) and as a present force at work at all times for the good in our lives as Christians. Not simply a future yet to be for us, and not simply the past achieved by Christ, our future is present in us as Christ, ours by the Spirit, works even now, and ever after, to shape us according to the pattern of his own life.

Action is the proper response to a world that is not the way it should be, because, although human action does not bring about life in God (that is God's unconditional gift to us), human action of a certain sort is what life in God requires of us. This is so, first of all, simply because life in God is not inactive, a resting in God in the form of contemplation or adoration. Life in God does not break forth in the form of a static epiphany but in and through the way in which our lives are set in motion. Life in God fundamentally just means sharing in God's own dynamic Trinitarian life of indivisible threefold movement as that dynamism is extended outward to us, to include us, in this triune God's relations with us in Christ. Eternal life means a community of life with God in Christ, a community of action in which we are taken up into Christ's own action for the world. As Jesus does the life-giving work of the Father through the power of the Holy Spirit, we, in virtue of our union with Christ, are to do the same.

Eternal life turns attention, then, not just to the benefits we are to receive through Christ—our being healed, purified, and elevated by Christ in the power of the Spirit—but to our active participation in Christ's own mission. That participation, you might say, just *is* the primary benefit—performing the work of the Father as Jesus did. It is the final benefit, in that it is what all the others enable. Once healed, purified, and elevated, we are perfected so as to participate in Christ's mission to the world, no longer simply responding to what God does for and to us, but acting for others in conformity with Christ's own service in the kingdom of righteousness.

In this way, the blessings of eternal life forbid complacency about our own good fortune, forbid the self-satisfaction that so often comes with the living of a blessed life. The chief blessing is a relationship with God manifest in active obedience to God's own mission to the world. That mission is one that turns one away from gifts received towards the needs of others still to be met in a world of poverty, greed, and oppression. The mission is one of strife and struggle against the *status quo* of a sinful world.

In this life, life in God sets a task for us, secondly, as a proper sign or witness to our fellowship with God in Christ: we are to be a holy people, and in that way demonstrate through the character of our deeds what it means to be God's own. Eternal life calls for a certain way of living to signal one's willing entrance into the realm of God's life-giving being. Only a particular way of living in this world—living so as to counter suffering, oppression, and division—corresponds to life in God, achieved in Christ.

Third, although everything has already been given to us, in a certain sense everything still remains to be done in conformity with that fact. We have everything we need in Christ to live different lives of righteousness; we have a sure promise and firm foundation for another kind of life in Christ. What remains outstanding is growth in openness to this gift and growth in living a life that shows throughout its course the pattern of that gift. Just as the fact of incarnation needed to be worked out in Jesus' life, through the entrance of divine powers into human life and their transformation of it, so our union with Christ needs to be worked out in ours, in an even more difficult struggle against active sin in our own lives and outside them. The more to come, the consummation of our lives in Christ, is the parallel in our lives to the theanthropic operations of Christ's life and their effects—a transformed pattern of human action for the world's good. Assumed by the Word from the very first to be its own, the humanity of Christ was worked over, during the course of Jesus' life, so as to show forth perfectly the power of God for life. Made one with Christ through the Spirit, and empowered by the gift of Christ's Spirit, we struggle, in ways never completed in this life, to eradicate sin and match the life intended for us by Christ's taking of us—sinful and suffering—to be his own.

Eternal life amounts, furthermore, to an unconditional imperative to action, in that this life in God remains an empowering source of our action for the good, whatever the obstacles and failings of Christians. Assumed into Christ's life, our lives are continuously fed by the workings of Christ in us through the power of the Spirit, however sorry their state. The imperative to act is also unconditional, in that it is not affected by considerations of success. Irrespective of any likelihood that one's actions to better the world will succeed, and even if one knows that all one's achievements will come to nothing with the world's end, one is obligated to act, simply because this is the only way of living that makes sense in light of one's life in God. This is the only possibility for us given our reality as God's own. Without primary concern for the consequences of one's actions, one acts out of gratitude for the life in God that one has been given, one acts out of joyful recognition that a certain course of action is part of those good gifts that stem from a special relationship with God. In this way, non-moral forms of appreciation and response inform a Christian sense of obligation.

In another sense, action is also a conditional imperative; one is also acting in an attempt to bring about a world that more closely matches the one that life in God should bring. Although eternal life is not conditional on our action, since it is in a primary sense already, fully, and irrevocably achieved through God's action in Christ, the blessings in the world that should naturally follow from it are yet in some significant sense conditional in the world as we know it. Blessings flow from life in God, but their egress from that source can be blocked by sin, understood as the effort to turn away from relations with the triune God (and one's fellows), the One from whom all goods flow. In this life, action that accords with the life-giving forces of God runs into the obstructions posed by our world as a realm of death—forces promoting impoverishment, suffering, exclusion, and injustice. One is called to act to counter such forces in the effort to bring in another kind of life.

This action cannot, moreover, be delayed in hopes of more propitious circumstances to come. Action is present oriented, and therefore realistic. One must work with what one has, and that means figuring out the present workings of the world, with, for example, the help of the physical and social sciences, in order to intervene as best one can. Action has an urgency, moreover; every moment counts. As scientists describe it, the world does not have an indefinite extension into the future; nor will a second chance for action come again by way of a future reinstatement of the world now suffering loss. In religious terms, 'the source for every gaze towards the future is life today, in fellowship with God'. Future hopes do not lure us away from a concern with the present; 'the religious depth of the present is in fact the only thing that can offer grounds for [those future hopes]' (Schillebeeckx 1981: 800).

Failure to succeed is not, however, a reason for despair. Certainly, if our action is not motivated primarily *by* hopes for success, the failure of those hopes is no cause to give up the fight. But to the extent that our hopes *are* for the furthering of God's blessings through our own action, those hopes can be sustained even in the most dire and hopeless of circumstances. One can continue to hope in God, and specifically in God's gift of eternal life, since that is not conditioned by those circumstances or by our own failure because of them. The motor of blessings and of our own action to promote them—eternal life—is something already and forever achieved without us, not something our action brings about or sustains, and therefore our hopes in it are not subject to disappointment when our actions fail to have the effects we desire. A hope, then, to counter despair in the present comes not from the idea that God is the coming future, but from the fact that, despite appearances to the contrary in a world of sin, God has already in fact assumed our lives. What draws our action and the world ever onward is not a future running ahead of us but a steadfast and unshakeable rock (Christ) as the source of that movement, the fund and fountain of what should be an ever expanding feast. On the basis of the fact that in Christ we already have all we need to do so, on the basis of the fact that even now we live in God as Christ does through Christ's mercy, we can hope to have done our part before the end of time. Indeed, we can continue to hope in the world's (and our) further benefit after that end comes, but this is no hope in the world in itself, for that world ends (and has already ended *as* something in and of itself); it is a hope in the world whose new identity essentially means nothing other than life in God.

Indeed, in the interim before the world ends, for our part we should expect defeat as much as success. One with Christ who in his mission of benefit suffered humiliation and defeat to all appearances at the hands of the powers, we must prefer defeat to success everywhere that such success means being favoured by death-dealing forces at work in human life. Better to go to the cross in faithfulness to the mission of a gift-giving God than to reap the riches of a kingdom of death:

[T]o be sacrificed is . . . as long as the world remains the world, a far greater achievement than to conquer; for the world is not so perfect that to be victorious *in the world* by adaptation to the world does not involve a dubious mixture of the world's paltriness. To be victorious in the world is like becoming something great in the world; ordinarily to become something great in the world is a dubious matter, because the world is not so excellent that its judgment of greatness unequivocally has great significance—except as unconscious sarcasm. (Kierkegaard 1962: 288)

References and Suggested Reading

ANDERSON, BERNHARD (1994). *From Creation to New Creation*. Minneapolis: Fortress Press.

BERGER, JOHN (1974). *The Look of Things*. New York: Viking Press.

FOUCAULT, MICHEL (1986). 'Of Other Spaces', *Diacritics*, 16, 22–7.

IRENAEUS (1989). 'Against Heresies', in *Ante-Nicene Fathers*, vol. 1. Grand Rapids, Mich.: Eerdmans.

KIERKEGAARD, SØREN (1962). *Works of Love*. New York: Harper & Row.

MOLTMANN, JÜRGEN (1975). *Theology of Hope*. New York: Harper & Row.

——(1996). *The Coming of God*. Minneapolis: Fortress Press.

NIEBUHR, H. RICHARD (1969). *The Kingdom of God in America*. Philadelphia: Westminster Press.

ORIGEN (1973). *On First Principles*. Gloucester, Mass.: Peter Smith.

PANNENBERG, WOLFHART (1969). *Theology and the Kingdom of God*. Philadelphia: Westminster Press.

RUETHER, ROSEMARY RADFORD (1970). *Radical Kingdom*. New York: Harper & Row.

SCHILLEBEECKX, EDWARD (1981). *Christ: The Experience of the Lord*. New York: Crossroad Publishers.

TANNER, KATHRYN (1992). *The Politics of God*. Minneapolis: Fortress Press.

——(2001). *Jesus, Humanity, and the Trinity*. Minneapolis: Fortress Press.

VON RAD, GERHARD (1962). *Old Testament Theology*, I. New York: Harper & Row.

CHAPTER 4

ECCLESIOLOGY AND ETHICS

BERND WANNENWETSCH

THEOLOGY is less like a building where each brick touches only the few others next to it and more like a web where everything is sensitively connected to everything else. If only for this reason there would be justification for assuming an ecclesiological dimension in ethics as well as an ethical dimension in ecclesiology. This claim should seem all the more evident because it finds strong backing in Scripture. The so-called ethical code in the Old Testament is not made up of a general oriental morality with particular religious overtones, but precisely circumscribes the particular ethos of a *covenant people*. This is why, for example, the commandments in the Decalogue are framed in covenantal language (as in the preamble: I am the Lord, your God) and covenantal narrative (Exod. 19 f.: Deut. 6 ff.). In similar fashion, the moral exhortations in the New Testament are typically framed in the *pluralis ecclesiasticus*. Paul, for example, customarily addresses his congregations as whole bodies, as indicated by the repeated opening line 'brothers' that sets the stage for moral exhortations. When he challenges the believers to discern, judge, and live according to the gospel, he is actually presupposing and envisioning a *community* of discernment, a *body* of judgement, and a *communal* witness to the gospel (Rom. 12: 2).

Given strong evidence of the mutual indwelling of ecclesiology and ethics in Scripture and in the formative first period of the Christian tradition, where the institution of public penitence in particular characterized the Church as a moral community, it must seem all the more striking that in the modern era this knot has been widely ignored if not cut altogether. Ecclesiological debates in this era have typically revolved around the relation that the Church has with other entities such as the State, or that one church has with another, or they have concerned internal principles of ordering such as the structure of ministries. These debates are, of course, not without (at times strong) ethical significance, but they are rarely debated as matters of *common* morality.

Ethics, on the other hand, has tended to be understood in modernity as having to do primarily with general rules and individual excellence. Even for those who did not want to base their attitude towards the Church predominantly on the experience of the religious wars that had shattered the European continent and seemingly altogether discredited religion in its institutional form as a proper basis for a morality of peaceful coexistence, it appeared that while the Church could assist in the promoting and discussing of moral principles, it could not effectively incubate them.

When Enlightenment and post-Enlightenment thinkers such as Kant proposed to set out moral rules in universal fashion, subject to reason alone, they did not (in the majority of cases) intend to sever the linkage of ethics and Christianity; on the contrary, they wished to uphold and strengthen Christianity's moral principles by providing them with a less particularistic foundation than church doctrines. These philosophers intended precisely to cut the knot that had tied ethics to the *Church*. A Church-based morality was regarded as a paradigmatic instance of the old 'heteronomy' that for too long had prevented the coming of age of mankind. What Kant's principle of the 'will that is alone good' substituted for was precisely the Church, since the authority of the maxims of the will drawn from reason replaced the authority by which the maxims of the Church were seen to be drawn from God's own reason or revelation.

By and large, modern theologians found it not too difficult to embrace the new universal foundation of morality, as the gain seemed considerable and the sacrifice small. After all, the material principles of the new ethics, such as reciprocity, seemed not incompatible with the Christian tradition. And the Church had not lost its social role either, since, as Kant conceded, there was still the need to *motivate* people actually to put into practice the moral commands that they perceived as reason's summoning (Kant 1934). Since the task of moral motivation would keep the Church busy enough, it would hardly find time to lament having been pushed out of the business of finding and formulating the rules themselves.

There were, of course, those not content with limiting the scope of Christian ethics to the motivation and application of rules that had been established without any accounting of the Christian doctrinal tradition. Yet, even when Christian ethicists looked for doctrinal anchoring points for their business, they tended to look not at ecclesiology but at other doctrinal *topoi* that were perceived to be more fertile grounds in which to plant an ethics—such as creation (natural law, moral incarnationalism), Christology (discipleship), or eschatology (pilgrimage). Some exceptions to this rule in former generations, such as Dietrich Bonhoeffer, will be of particular interest to us, and it is only fair to note that the situation has improved in the course of the last two decades or so. The persistent modern neglect of the knot has given way to a new interest in ecclesiology, and this precisely as a function of new trends in ethics, particularly in the USA.

With the renaissance of Aristotelian moral philosophy, rivalling the reign of Kantian individualism, moral communities have become a genuine matter of new interest, in particular as a breeding ground for civic virtues and a sorely needed counterweight to the (allegedly) morally neutral state and its patent inadequacy in the gestation of such virtues. Within the framework of communitarian thought, it would appear only natural that religious bodies provide the strongest exemplars of such moral communities in embodying particularly thick descriptions of communal morality (MacIntyre 1990).

While, therefore, a good deal of the new interest in church and ecclesiology for moral reasons appears to be a result or a particular outworking of the logic that drives the communitarian cause, there has emerged another strand of thought that should not be confused with communitarianism despite certain similarities. Theologians such as John Howard Yoder (1992, 1994, 1997) and Stanley Hauerwas (1995) have found a significant following when they claim that the Church as a body and a people has an *inherent* ethical and even political character. In Hauerwas's often quoted phrase: 'The church does not have a social ethic; the church is a social ethic' (1983: 99). Whoever wishes to get to know the social ethics of the Church is better advised to look at the way in which the Church actually lives its communal life as a body than to examine a list of moral precepts that the Church administers. The nature of the gospel is to be embodied, and the nature of the Church is to embody the gospel, including its moral grammar. In a nutshell, these theologians reminded us of the elementary theological truth according to which ecclesiology *is* ethics, and ethics *is* ecclesiology.

I will defend this insight and its critical value over against individualized, dehistoricized, and disembodied accounts of morality and Christian ethics in particular, while at the same time attempting to add depth by exploring the dialectic which elucidates why the Church that 'is' a social ethic still needs to 'have' a social ethic. Working from within my own Lutheran theological commitments, I will advance my argument with particular reference to Bonhoeffer, Luther, and Augustine.

In section (1) below I examine Dietrich Bonhoeffer as a still under-acknowledged forefather of the new ecclesio-ethical emphasis. His treatment of the Church as a 'distinct sociological type' (1998: 252) underlies the all-important claim that the Church is *not* and should not be made the fundament of Christian ethics. Rather than having or needing a *foundation*, Christian ethics is given an ever new *beginning* in worship (Wannenwetsch 1996, 2003). Section (2) argues that the Church both 'is' and 'has' a social ethic. That is, the Church cannot content itself with lively and controversial debates about moral matters, but must at the same time venture unambiguous moral proclamation. In section (3) I examine Luther's notion of the hiddenness of the Church as a liberating alternative to the scheme of visibility or invisibility. The position developed in these sections will, finally, be tested in section (4) by considering the controversial issue of an 'ethical *status confessionis*': that is, are there moral issues (in addition to doctrinal issues) in which the very identity of the Church is at stake?

BEGINNING ETHICS FROM THE CHURCH AS A SOCIOLOGICAL TYPE *SUI GENERIS*

It is striking that, despite the prevalence of Christological emphasis in his theology, Bonhoeffer avoided immediately deriving his ethics from Christology as he encountered it, for example, in accounts of an 'incarnational ethics' within Anglo-Saxon theological idealism. Instead, he found the ethical locus of Christ-ology in ecclesiology. 'The point of departure for Christian ethics is the body of Christ, the form of Christ in the form of the Church, and the formation of the church in conformity with the form of Christ' (1955: 64). This move must seem remarkable, given that Bonhoeffer was the sharpest critic of the (Protestant) Church of his day, which he found in lamentable shape. His starting with ecclesi-ology was obviously motivated by his persistent claim that ethics is to be 'entirely concrete' (1955: 66). This concreteness is not geared to an arsenal of 'ought' claims but to the insurmountable 'is', to the reality that exists in Christ and is recognized through Christ. Yet, this is not a cloudy 'all encompassing reality' that can be grasped anywhere or in the depths of one's own inwardness, but it finds its ascribed location, according to God's promise, in the Church. The Church lives as the Body of Christ, and it is the concrete and material way in which the 'gestalt' of Christ is experienced within space and time.

In this light, the other leading metaphor of Bonhoeffer's ethics—'conformation (*Gleichgestaltung*) to Christ'—receives its particular shape as a primarily *social* process. The 'new man' in the *gestalt* of Christ is not the individual subject on her path of 'imitating Christ' but the new human race (Eph. 2: 15) that God has called into being as the Church of Jews and Gentiles. Since the moral process of conformation to Christ is happening within the real presence of Christ's Body (1955: 63), Bonhoeffer maintained that Christian ethics cannot be construed in idealistic fashion, setting up ideas which become aims in a process of moral realization. 'God hates this wishful dreaming', as found in projects of Church 'development' (1996: 36) or in 'Christian programs' of 'Practical Christianity' (1955: 60) which are born from human desire that denies the God-given reality of the Body.

If this was as far as it went, one could misread Bonhoeffer's move as ending up in a blunting Church positivism that would engender an ecclesiastical ethics which outdoes even caricatures of papal moral unilateralism. It is therefore essential to understand Bonhoeffer's turn to the Church against the backdrop of his firm standing within the Lutheran tradition and its core ecclesiological conviction that the Church is but the creature of the word. The Church does not exist in and of itself, but precisely 'in' those genuine practices that constitute its own being in the first place: the proclamation of the word in preaching and the administering of sacraments (1998: 270). Christian liturgy makes one thing clear in a paradigmatic way: the Body of Christ experiences its own activity as receiving itself from and participating in God's activity; it acts in, with, and under God's acting. The Church is God's 'work' (*poiema*), 'created for good works that he has prepared beforehand that we may walk in them' (Eph. 2: 10).

It is precisely this peculiar non-foundational understanding of the Church as depending on the ever new arrival of Christ's presence in the 'lovely means' (Luther) of word and sacraments that compelled Bonhoeffer to speak of the Church as a 'distinct sociological type'. In his first doctoral thesis, *Sanctorum Communio*, he demonstrated how existing sociological categories such as 'association' or 'community' fall short of encapsulating the nature of the Church, since they are incapable of rendering an intelligible account of 'evangelical-ecclesial forms' such as baptism, confirmation, or assembly (1998: 256 f.). If, for example, someone decides to separate from the Church, she is not simply 'ending her membership', any more than one can 'join' the Church as any other association. The significance of these peculiar forms requires an understanding of the Church precisely as Church and under no other category. 'Church is a form of community *sui generis*, namely community of Spirit as community of love. In it the basic sociological types of society (*Gesellschaft*), community (*Gemeinschaft*), and association of authentic rule (*Herrschaftsverband*) are combined and transcended' (1998: 266).

Bonhoeffer's characterization of the Church from within its own 'gestalt' was deliberately directed against Ernst Troeltsch's influential distinction of types of 'self-realisation of the Christian social idea'. Troeltsch had described the 'church type' under the general rationale of a 'mass organization', which has to pay for its influential role in the shaping of public life by adjusting its own moral standards to that public life, thereby inevitably resulting in an 'ethic of compromise'. He contrasted the 'church type' with the 'sect type' in which the radical realization of a Christian 'love-ethic' is necessarily bound up with a deliberate renouncing of any effect it might have in the shaping of society (Troeltsch 1992; Bonhoeffer 1998: 268 *passim*).

By demonstrating that the liturgical existence of the Church does not prevent but actually ensures a peculiar worldliness, Bonhoeffer's ecclesiology has the potential to overcome this unfortunate alternative. Precisely because the enhypostatic existence of the Church does not 'own' its constitutive features—word and sacrament—Bonhoeffer could describe the proper ecclesial self-understanding as 'church for others' (1971: 382). Another critical and topical gain of Bonhoeffer's anti-foundational ecclesiology is that it prevents a Christian ethics that wishes to account for the central role of the Church from being absorbed into the communitarian logic, thereby baptizing *any* sort of *conventional* ethos and ethics a moral community might engender. Christian ethics should be concerned with what the Church has to say, but more so with the word that the Church has to hear. To the relationship of these two aspects we now turn.

THE SOCIAL ETHICS THAT THE CHURCH HAS: THE NEED FOR MORAL PROCLAMATION

Why was it that Paul took the reality of the church as brotherhood for granted and still felt the need actively to remind the church of this, its own reality, exhorting believers to behave as brothers and sisters? It must be acknowledged that the Church does have, and actually has to have, a social ethics, in that it is entrusted with the task of proclaiming the gospel that cannot be separated from its social and moral dimension. Though there have always been aspects of the gospel's moral dimension that are difficult to understand and controversial, there has also always existed a *consensus ecclesiae* that covers a far wider range of issues and convictions which are uncontroversial and make up the material for the Church's moral proclamation.

At least from the perspective of a Western European Protestant, it seems worth stating that the task of unambiguous moral proclamation belongs to the Church Catholic and should not be left to the Roman Catholic Church alone, as the strange reluctance in many Protestant churches in this respect seems to assume, leading all too often to contentment with the facilitation of ethical debates and/or with criticizing Catholic moral proclamations. Ethical debates, of which there is no shortage in Protestant churches, are not quite moral proclamation, though they are certainly a necessary feature on the way towards unambiguous moral proclamation, in so far as they help to formulate afresh the *consensus ecclesiae* as it emerges from a communal listening to the gospel. While reclaiming the ethic that the

Church *has* in terms of its task of moral proclamation seems unambiguous and straightforward in itself, it needs to be seen how this claim relates to Hauerwas's famous statement (that the Church *is*, rather than *has*, an ethic). A theological mind will sense that the two claims can hardly be as mutually exclusive as they sound, but must rather enjoy a dialectical relationship. Yet, it will be instructive to analyse in some detail how the assumed dialectic actually works.

It might be just a matter of the right order in emphasis. Thus, it would seem that priority must be given to Hauerwas's dictum. It needs to be established first that the Church *is* a social ethics by sheer virtue of the gift of its existence as Christ's Body, before it can be analysed in terms of its relation to the task of moral proclamation to the surrounding society. Were it the other way round, the Church would be caught in the 'credibility' trap, by having to embark on the vain and desperate business of trying to validate the proclamation through its own moral integrity. Yet the validity of the ethic that the Church *has* can never simply be a function of the ethic that the Church *is*. The Church must preach the word according to its moral dimension, irrespective of its own shortcomings in living out this word in its midst. Any endeavour by the Church to 'back' the credibility of its proclamation or even to safeguard its efficiency through its own excellence would leave it with a very poor alternative. It would lead it either to the adoption of a moralizing regime, aiming at a *societas perfecta*, or—more likely under contemporary circumstances—to the lowering of standards of the proclamation itself.

While it is often said that liberal moral attitudes are the result of a cultural accommodation of Christian values to the spirit of the time in permissive societies, we must be aware of the grounding of these attitudes in a moralized ecclesiology. The idea that we cannot ask more of the people in terms of the Church's moral proclamation to society than we are capable of accomplishing ourselves completely misrepresents the problem. It is true that we should not ask more of others than we ask of ourselves, but the standard of this asking cannot be determined by what we have accomplished or are willing to try, but must be set according to what the gospel asks from us.

Notwithstanding the validity of what I said above about the order in which the 'having' of the Church's social ethic (as proclamation) must be preceded by the 'is' of its faithful existence as a body, there is also a sense in which the 'have' actually precedes the 'is'. By this I mean the word that the Church *has* to hear; for it is itself the first addressee of its own proclamation. The Church can never assume that it 'knows' the commandments, for example, or the exhortations of the Sermon of the Mount, in the sense that they have been fully absorbed into the Church's life and so are completely embodied. The fact that Christians keep listening to these words over and over again in worship and catechesis suggests a genuinely non-proprietary understanding of 'having' an ethic. The Church does not 'own' its ethic as one owns property. As Luther's characterizing of the word as *verbum externum* insisted, there is no exclusive right of usage and interpretation of the word that entitles the

Church to flaunt it before the rest of the world without the need for the Church itself to listen further. Though not a property, the word can be said to be the 'possession' of the Church, as the proclamation of the word (and the sacraments) is precisely *what* the faithful share in as a body (O'Donovan 2002: 20 ff.).

Of course, the emphasis that Yoder and Hauerwas place on the 'is' was directed against precisely the attitude that claimed to 'have' an ethic presentable to the outside world just like any other bundle of 'ideas', 'concepts', etc. In this respect, the Church cannot 'deal' with its ethics as with a commodity, but is called to communicate the ethics that it 'has', which is nothing but the word to which it must first listen. In this vein, it would be quite right to say that the Church's main business is preaching to itself, though audibly enough for the world to overhear. Lest we build up false alternatives here, it is important to understand the ethics that the Church 'has' as encompassing the whole complex of preaching the word to itself, listening, debating, accommodating, and re-accommodating its inner life to the gospel—including the recognition of its own failure and sin.

To take an example, should the recent crisis in North American Catholic dioceses about sexually abusive priests silence the Church on issues of sexual morality? Would silence be a proper way for the Church to acknowledge the credibility problem into which it has manoeuvred itself? This conclusion would seem evident only on the basis of a simplistic account of credibility in which the 'is' of the Church's social ethics provides the warrant for the 'have' of its proclamation; it would further mean to limit the notion of the 'Church's proclamation' to the communication by which it turns to the outside world. If, however, we understand 'proclamation' as including the full extent to which the Church is *addressed* by the gospel, responding to it in its inner life and work, confessing its failures and readjusting its practice, then it will be clear that the 'overflow' of this proclamation towards the wider society need not present a credibility problem. In fact, as unpleasant as the experience must have been for the Catholic Church in the USA, if it is serious about being itself the first addressee of its moral proclamation, the current predicament may in the longer run strengthen rather than weaken the witness of this Church.

BEYOND VISIBILITY AND INVISIBILITY: THE HIDDEN CHURCH

If we are to unwrap further the 'credibility' problem that the Church's proclamation faces, we must come to terms with the issue of the Church's visibility or invisibility and the moral accounts that these respective emphases engender. As a rough mapping, we could expect the stressing of the Church's invisibility to go hand in hand with an individualistic account of ethics or even engender a spiritualist indifference towards all moral conduct. It seems likely, for example, that the 'moral' libertarians against whom Paul is reacting in his letters to the Corinthians are of the same mind-set as those who are charged with 'showing contempt for the church' in their reckless behaviour of excluding poorer participants at the Eucharist. Just as the former assume that bodily relations cannot affect their respective spiritual standing and that they are therefore free to engage in rambling sexual encounters, the latter spiritualize and individualize the Eucharist when they 'go ahead each with his own supper' (1 Cor. 11: 22 *passim*; NRSV).

Ecclesiological accounts that focus on the visible Church, on the other hand, will tend to favour either perfectionist ethics ('sectarian' in Troeltsch's terminology) or (again in terms of Troeltsch's classification) an 'ethic of compromise'. The question is, of course, whether the basic distinction between visible and invisible Church is really inevitable or even suitable. We shall see in the following paragraphs that Martin Luther's approach to the issue points to a better alternative.

Early in his conflict with the papal Church, the reformer typically stressed what we might call the trans-visibility of the Church. We must note that Luther never speaks of the 'invisibility' of the Church as a noun or in an attributive way even when stressing that 'nobody can see it'. What he means by this does not echo a Platonic demeaning of matter, according to which the invisible and purely spiritual Church would count as the true and beautiful while the visible would appear as a defective copy—spoiled by matter, tainted by necessity and hopelessly caught in the web of worldly presumptions, strife, and boredom.

By contrast, Luther's stressing of the trans-visibility of the Church results from his reading of the third article of the Creed where the Church is confessed as a matter of *belief*, not sight. 'If this article is true it follows that nobody can see or feel the holy Christian church, and no one should say: Look, it is here or there.... The holy Christian church speaks therefore: I believe one holy Christian church. But the presumptuous church of the pope says: I see a holy Christian church.... The former says: The Church does not depend on a human being, the latter says: The Church is built upon the pope' (WA 7: 685 f., my translation). Luther is reacting against a blunt empirical account of the Church which identifies the *una sancta* with one existing church body, thereby bestowing a quasi-divine quality on canon law and its rulings even when they are found to contradict Scripture.

The reformer's emphasis on the Church as the object of belief corresponds to his defining it as 'an assembly of hearts in one faith' (*Works* 39: 65). 'Regardless of whether a thousand miles separates them physically, they are still called one assembly in spirit, as long as each one preaches, believes, hopes, loves, and lives like the other' (*Works* 39: 65). Luther likens the two dimensions of the Church— spiritual and bodily—to that of a human being, and though he admits that there should be no separation between the two (*Works* 39: 70), it is the former, the assembly of faith, that counts as the true Church (*Works* 39: 68 f.). We find Luther's deliberate move to interpret the *communio sanctorum* of the third article in the personal sense (*genitivus subiectivus*) of a *congregatio* echoed in the formulation of the Augsburg Confession's article VII (*de ecclesia*): 'The church is the assembly of saints in which the gospel is taught purely and the sacraments are administered rightly' (*Book of Concord*, 32).

What is striking in this definition is that the Church is defined not just as a body but as an event. It is not exhaustively described in personal terms, not even as the assembly of true believers or saints, but through a particular practice: word and sacrament. In the wake of his controversy with the spiritualist wing of the Reformation, Luther became increasingly interested in the pastoral question of how one can ever know where the true Church is encountered. His answer was given in terms of two essential identification marks, the *notae ecclesiae*: word and sacrament. In maintaining that both must be present for the Church to be the true Church, another blow was struck against any ecclesiological positivism. 'Wherever you see that the gospel is absent, there you should not doubt the church to be absent, too, in spite of their baptising and eating from the table' (WA 7: 721). It is ultimately because 'the whole life of the church depends upon the word of God' (*tota vita et substantia ecclesia est in verbo dei*, WA 7: 722) and is therefore qualified as a matter of belief, that Luther characterizes the church as hidden: 'Therefore the church is called in Ps. 9 (v. 1) almuth, abscondita' (WA 7: 723, my translations).

The gain in Luther's concept of the 'hidden' church over against the scheme of visibility/invisibility is considerable. Hidden means neither invisible nor visible. What is hidden is visible only to the eyes of faith; yet, it is a reality that can be experienced in the flesh. The true Church does not exist behind or beyond the visible Church but is hidden *within* it, in which *multi hypocrati et mali admixti sunt* as article VIII of the Augsburg Confession states. The *communio sanctorum* that the Creed confesses can be understood in two ways: in the personal sense (of a *genitivus subiectivus*) as the *congregatio vere credendum*, and in the non-personal sense (of a *genitivus obiectivus*) as communication in word and sacrament. According to the first sense, the Church is fully invisible as the community of faith that spans the world and the ages. According to the second sense, the Church is fully visible as the concrete visual happening in the font and around the altar. Luther's notion of hiddeness is the key that prevents a blunt equation of both senses, which would eventually lead to an absorbing of the invisible church into the visible. His emphasis on the pure proclamation of the gospel that is to qualify the visual sacraments and which is always susceptible to the discerning of the spirits places another barrier before empiricist accounts of the Church. It does so by accounting for God's freedom and the crucial role that the Spirit assumes in the constitution and reconstitution of God's people. Though God promises to be present in the proclamation of the gospel and the administration of the sacraments, it is still up to God himself to fulfil this promise at his chosen time, and his presence cannot be operationalized in terms of a self-realization of the Church through its sacramental life.

As Luther puts it in the Large Catechism's treatment of the third article: 'To this article...I cannot give a better title than "sanctification"' (*Book of Concord*, 415). The Spirit makes us holy, Luther says, 'through the Christian Church, the forgiveness of sins, the resurrection of the body and the life everlasting' (*Book of Concord*, 416). This emphasis has crucial implications for the relationship between the Church and ethics. On the one hand, Luther encourages an understanding of the Creed's article on the Church in terms of its moral scope—as an article about sanctification. On the other hand and within this stated purpose, the Church—together with the practice of reconciliation and the suffering of resurrection—is assigned the precise role of a *means* by which the Spirit accomplishes sanctification; a *mere* means, as it were, since the authorship belongs to the Spirit and not the Church. If we say that sanctification is not engendered *by* the Church but only *through* it, we are still speaking of a *necessary* means which works towards sanctification in a multitude of ways: through mutual encouragement and exhortation, the exemplars of the saints, through preaching and nourishing at the Lord's table.

What is the gain of all this for our overall question? The decisive *moral* point in Luther's account of the Church as a hidden reality is, I take it, precisely *to prevent it from hiding*—to prevent the Church from hiding itself behind its invisibility or visibility. The first type of hiding is easier to spot: in terms of our previous discussion of the social ethics that the Church 'is' or 'has', such hiding would essentially mean to deny the relevance of the 'is' by ignoring the fact that the life of the body of believers is 'a letter of Christ, read by all men' (2 Cor. 3: 3). In the case of serious moral transgressions happening in its midst, it would mean for the Church to deny its corporate responsibility and escape into the rhetoric of the 'weakness of individuals', indicating that these cannot be taken to represent the Church at all.

It is within the framework of self-hiding versus God-given hiddenness that the classical debates about the Church as sinner (*ecclesia peccatrix*) are best situated, and prime material would be provided through the fragile tradition of ecclesiastical 'declarations of guilt' such as the Stuttgart declaration of the Protestant churches in Germany after the downfall of the 'Third Reich' or John Paul II's recent plea for forgiveness for the past failings of his Church. With all their shortcomings and sometimes overly cautious tone, these declarations nevertheless show how the Church can step out of its hiding by publicly accounting for its responsibility as a visible body. By taking on the guilt of individual members as its own and relinquishing its own (self-)righteousness, the Church is faithfully witnessing to God's future, in which will occur the eschatological separation of sheep from goats that must not be anticipated before the day appointed.

There are also ways—perhaps more subtle—by which the Church is tempted to hide behind its visibility. Where everything is assumed to be out in the open, without any eschatological surplus and without the ever new need of divine authorization, the Church easily falls prey to the reigning ideology of self-promotion and marketing of its own cause. In short, the Church will eventually behave like what Bonhoeffer called an 'organization'. Whereas hiding behind invisibility will tend to encourage antinomian accounts of morality, hiding behind visibility will typically mean to approach moral matters in a bureaucratic vein, handling delicate issues in formalized fashion and replacing the genuine Christian grammar of *parenesis* (Wannenwetsch 2002) with the language of decrees. As an example, we might think of the Roman Catholic practice of annulling, on the basis of some formal failure at the outset, marriages of couples who have actually lived a marital life together. Another example would be provided by various attempts in the history of the Church to safeguard the efficacy of its ministry through human means: sometimes by usurping worldly power as when, for example, the Church used the power of magistrates to bring parishioners out of the pub and into church on Sunday morning, and at other times presenting itself in moral purity as a community of the unspoiled through simple expulsion of failing members.

THE PROBLEM OF AN ETHICAL
STATUS CONFESSIONIS

The second tendency—to hide behind visibility—has also been embodied in numerous sectarian movements that have accompanied and challenged the pilgrim Church throughout the ages. These movements have raised a fundamental question: Are there moral questions within the Church which impinge on not only the functionality (*bene esse*) of the body but challenge its very identity as Church (its *esse*)? This question has been discussed within the ecumenical movement of the twentieth century under the heading of 'ethical *status confessionis*' (Lorenz 1983). The essence of the question is, of course, as old as the Church itself, and it seems that contemporary Christianity could learn a great deal from the Church of the patristic age and its dealings with serious moral transgressions and heretical movements that threatened church unity on moral grounds. The Church responded to these problems through its institution of public penitence, on the one hand, and through the development of a theology of unity and schism which was worked out by theologians such as Augustine of Hippo. What were the principles underlying both responses, and what is their significance for the topic of 'ethics and ecclesiology' today?

In the light of the distinctions developed above, it can be said that the institution of public penitence in the patristic age fits well the notion of the hidden Church that we analysed in Luther. That is, it represents a phenomenon that is completely unintelligible under the scheme of 'visibility' or 'invisibility'. The institution of public penance does not hide behind invisibility; for it assumes that the sin of individual members must inevitably affect the whole body, and that the body must act to expel the sin from its midst. At the same time, however, public penitence does not hide behind visibility, since it does not simply expel the sinner but keeps the bond of unity with him or her throughout the process that unfolds from excommunication to reconciliation. The sin of individual members is, in other words, borne by the whole body, which is summoned to continue to pray and care for the penitents while interrogating itself as to what part the congregation might have in their failing.

It goes without saying that the existence and functioning of public penitence presupposed the steady practice of unambiguous moral proclamation. The aim of reconciling and reintegrating the excommunicated was as essential in defining the body's unity as it was inherent in the institution of public penitence. While maintaining that some practices, by their very nature, distance a sinner from the body, because they are incompatible with the body's faith and life, the institution of public penitence enabled the Church to resist the temptation to construe its unity on the basis of ostracism and expulsion. Instead, it deliberately based its unity and moral integrity on reconciliation. The mode of regulating conflicts in its midst was to be no other than the mode of its very existence as a community of the reconciled (Eph. 2: 16).

This marked the central difference between the Catholic Church and heretical movements such as the Donatists, who denied the possibility of a second penitence and based the validity of the sacraments on the uncompromised moral integrity of the administering persons. It is noteworthy that Augustine developed his case against the Donatists not by diminishing the importance of moral life for the identity of the Church, but by seeing its true, and higher, significance. Together with the Donatists, he holds that the Church can be the Church only if a kind of ethical *status confessionis* exists. Ironically, for Augustine, the Donatists themselves provide the prime example of this truth. Although, as Augustine concedes, they can hardly be blamed for a lax morality or a lack of Christological seriousness, they nevertheless count as exemplars of those 'who deny with deeds'. 'You confess it in words, you deny it by your deeds. You can deny things, you see, by your deeds.' Augustine goes on to explain this surprising move further: 'What is denying by your deeds? Being proud and making schisms; making your boast not in God, but in man. That's how Christ is denied by deeds; Christ, of course, loves unity' (Sermon 185, in *Works: Sermons*, III/5: 340).

With this Augustine turns the tables. In spite of the Donatists' claim to a higher and purer morality, it is precisely here—in the moral realm—that they are failing.

This is because the Church's unity, though established by Christ himself and bestowed as his gift, still entails a moral claim. It must be maintained as the 'unity of the spirit in the bond of peace' (Eph. 4: 3). For Augustine this is especially evident in the Eucharist: 'Therefore receive and eat the body of Christ, yes, you that have become members of Christ in the body of Christ; receive and drink the blood of Christ. In order not to be scattered and separated, eat what binds you together' (Sermon 228B, in *Works: Sermons*, III/6: 262). The 'higher morality' of the heretics, which causes them to call into question the validity of the Church's sacraments when administered by former apostate priests, undermines exactly the core practice of 'eating the bond of unity', and therefore threatens the very identity of the Church as the communion of reconciliation. Because the heretics are keen to divide Christ's garment, Augustine argues that they love not unity but their own excellence. Pride is the 'mother' of all heresy, and the Donatists act as the 'children of pride' (Sermon 346B, in *Works: Sermons*, III/10: 82). This line of thought is not unlike Paul's argument in his letters to the Corinthians, where the moral issue about eating meat offered to idols was not to be settled by determining who was right (the 'strong'), but by summoning the strong to be concerned not with the integrity of their own consciences but with the consciences of those who are 'weak' (1 Cor. 10: 28 f.).

It may seem easy to dismiss Augustine's argument as circular. The Church calls for living within the bond of love, and living with love requires obedience to the Church. Yet Augustine would surely have agreed with the Donatists that the Church must have agreement about the central practices of its way of life and must separate itself from those who do not agree. His emphasis upon unity does not make it the single or highest moral concern, to which all other moral truths must be sacrificed. He means simply to note that the Church's moral discussions must be undertaken in the love of unity rather than the love of pride. Any handling of moral transgression or division that does not reflect Christ's love of unity will inevitably lead to moral corruption—a corruption that is all the more serious in kind if it comes (self-)deceptively wrapped in moral clothes.

Augustine's attempt to hold together the Church's faith and life points to a perennial necessity. Although any depiction of the works (i.e., the deeds of individual members within the Church or corporate action by Church bodies) is secondary to the chief task of proclaiming the gospel (which always calls for a way of life that goes beyond any current state of its embodiment in the life of the Church), there is a positive relationship between works and proclamation—a relationship which Bonhoeffer characterized as 'preparing the way' (1955: 321, 324). This task is not one of validating or verifying the proclamation (as the metaphor is actually negatively geared to clear ground rather than establish ground itself), but it is, nevertheless, a necessary feature of the Church's witness. Since the Church cannot be distinguished from its task of witnessing as though this was only one of its functions and not its mode of existence, moral questions can at times be determinative of the Church's identity and witness. To deny this possibility would mean to deny the corporeality of the Church, as any body consists of 'works'. Negative experiences with schismatic movements that were quick to declare a *status confessionis* where, in fact, their own hubris was at stake, should not license recent principled denials of the possibility of an ethical *status confessionis*, whether they are made in the name of a misunderstood doctrine of justification by faith alone or in the name of a liberal ideology that regards ethical matters as private or as a matter of socio-economic evolution and therefore always in flux. Contrary to the assumption that underlies these denials, only as we acknowledge that a core of moral convictions—no less than soteriological doctrines—constitutes the Christian faith can we give due weight to ecclesial conflicts about moral matters. Though the *status confessionis* points to the existence of a painful moment in which debate must give way to cathartic action, this moment does not end debate, but induces and fuels it. In fact, as an acknowledged ground for such debates, the theologoumenon *status confessionis* aims to prevent itself from really happening as an event.

More important than agreement on every issue is that the Church agree about *which* questions and practices belong to its moral *esse* rather than to its *bene esse*. For example, differences in judgement about licit sexual practices within marriage belong at a level different from questions about sexual activity outside marriage, which, in turn, belong to a level different from questions about sexual activity that is not limited by the differention of male and female. It is a vital part of the Church's moral task to clarify where there may be legitimate disagreement and where not, and to distinguish conduct that hampers or suspends the community from conduct that actually puts an end to it.

In the light of this task, it seems wise to distinguish a few general types. It makes a difference if we are talking about moral flaws within a church's life, about its practical toleration of such behaviour, or, by contrast, a church's actual licensing of it through explicit or implicit approval. The first type cannot constitute a *status confessionis* and will be dealt with sufficiently through moral exhortation (or excommunication) within the affected church body. For this first and, of course, for the second type also, one should follow Calvin's conviction that it is committing the sin of pride to separate from a church for reason of moral flaws alone—that is, as long as the preaching of the gospel and the administration of sacraments are basically intact (*Institutes*, IV/1, 12 ff.).

While it is deplorable to see a church turning a blind eye to certain behaviour that contradicts its moral *esse*, it is still 'only', as it were, compromising itself, not yet corrupting moral doctrine. Only where the latter happens can the *status confessionis* be declared without the sort of pride that Augustine depicted as destructive of the church's life. Just as with doctrinal heresy, ethical heresy must be a matter of *public proclamation*, not of individual behaviour or lax church policies. This need not confine the *status confessionis* to *explicit* public declarations which contradict the *moralis consensus ecclesiae*; public relevance may also be achieved through a symbolic act whose significance has been made unequivocal through the preceding course of action or debate.

The recent installation of the first openly homosexual bishop in the Anglican diocese of New Hampshire has been widely recognized an act of this quality. Other contemporary examples of an ethical *status confessionis* would be the South African Dutch Reformed Church's proclaiming of apartheid as being in accord with biblical principles, or the German Protestant churches' adoption of the Aryan paragraph during the regime of the Nazis.

Once a case of ethical *status confessionis* is commonly perceived, further questions arise. Will separation, expulsion (of a group), or schism be the only available alternatives, or are there other viable options? This is the question that the Anglican communion of churches, in the aftermath of the New Hampshire case, decided to explore in a patient consultative process. In this faithful endeavour, they face a difficulty that they share with many other churches today.

Though the debates about an ethical *status confessionis* are aimed at answering a different question from the question that led to the practice of public penitence, there is an interdependence of both moments. The replacement of the penitence rite with private or general confession in the vast majority of churches has produced a situation in which it has become increasingly difficult to address the problem of the Church's moral *esse* or *bene esse* in any depth. The resulting privatized notions of morality have inevitably undermined our sense of the importance of the moral integrity of the body as a whole. As long as the Church's ability to discern when its moral identity is at stake is underdeveloped, and as long as it is unable to distinguish between such cases and others in which its own weakness has hampered its common life and diminished its witness to its own moral teaching, it is likely that any construal of 'ethics and ecclesiology' will find it hard effectively to transcend the idea of the Church as (merely) 'another moral resource'.

References and Suggested Reading

Augustine (1991–). *The Works of Saint Augustine: A Translation for the 21st Century.* Brooklyn, NY: New City Press.

Barth, K. (1954). 'The Christian Community and the Civil Community', in R. G. Smith (ed.), *Against the Stream: Shorter Post-War Writings 1946–1952*, London: SCM Press.

Bonhoeffer, D. (1955). *Ethics.* London: SCM Press.

—— (1971). *Letters and Papers from Prison.* London and New York: SCM Press.

—— (1996). *Life Together and Prayerbook of the Bible. Dietrich Bonhoeffer Works*, vol. 5. Minneapolis: Augsburg Fortress Press.

—— (1998). *Sanctorum Communio: A Theological Study of the Sociology of the Church. Dietrich Bonhoeffer Works*, vol. 1. Minneapolis: Augsburg Fortress Press.

Calvin, J. (1960). *Institutes of the Christian Religion.* Philadelphia: Westminster Press.

EVERETT, W. J. (1988). *God's Federal Republic: Reconstructing our Governing Symbol*. New York: Paulist Press.

GUROIAN, V. (1994). *Ethics after Christendom: Toward an Ecclesial Christian Ethic*. Grand Rapids, Mich.: Eerdmans.

HAUERWAS, S. (1981). *A Community of Character: Toward a Constructive Christian Social Ethic*. Notre Dame, Ind., and London: University of Notre Dame Press.

—— (1983). *The Peaceable Kingdom: A Primer in Christian Ethics*. Notre Dame, Ind., and London: University of Notre Dame Press.

—— (1995). *In Good Company: The Church as Polis*. Notre Dame, Ind., and London: University of Notre Dame Press.

HEBERT, A. G. (1935). *Liturgy and Society: The Function of the Church in the Modern World*. London: Faber & Faber.

KANT, I. (1934). *Religion within the Limits of Reason Alone*. New York: Harper & Row.

LORENZ, E. (1983). *The Debate on Status Confessionis: Studies in Christian Political Theology*. Geneva: Lutheran World Federation.

Lumen Gentium: Dogmatic Constitution on the Church (1966). In W. Abbott (ed.), *The Documents of Vatican II*, New York: Guild Press, 14–101.

LUTHER, M. (1883–). *Werke: Kritische Gesamtausgabe*. Weimar (WA).

—— (1955–). *Works*, ed. J. Pelikan and H. T. Lehman, 54 vols. Philadelphia and St Louis: Fortress Press.

MacINTYRE, A. (1990). *Whose Justice? Which Rationality?* Notre Dame, Ind.: University of Notre Dame Press.

O'DONOVAN, O. (2002). *Common Objects of Love: Moral Reflection and the Shaping of Community*. Grand Rapids, Mich., and Cambridge: Eerdmans.

The Book of Concord: The Confessions of the Evangelical Lutheran Church, ed. T. G. Tappert, and J. Pelikan. Philadelphia: Fortress Press, 1959.

TROELTSCH, E. (1992). *The Social Teaching of the Christian Churches*. Louisville, Ky.: Westminster Press.

WANNENWETSCH, B. (1996). 'The Political Worship of the Church. A Critical and Empowering Practice', *Modern Theology*, 12, 269–99.

—— (2002). 'Members of One Another: Charis, Ministry and Representation. A Politico-Ecclesial Reading of Romans 12', in G. Bartholomew *et al.* (eds.), *A Royal Priesthood?: The Use of the Bible Ethically and Politically*, Carlisle and Grand Rapids, Mich.: Paternoster and Zondervan, 196–220.

—— (2003). 'Liturgy', in W. Cavanaugh and P. Scott (eds.), *Blackwell Companion to Political Theology*, Oxford: Blackwell, 76–90.

—— (2004). *Political Worship: Ethics for Christian Citizens*. Oxford: Oxford University Press.

WEBBER, R. E. and CLAPP, R. (1988). *People of the Truth: The Power of the Worshipping Community in the Modern World*. San Francisco: Harper & Row.

YODER, J. H. (1992). *Body Politics: Five Practices of the Christian Community before the Watching World*. Nashville: Discipleship Resources.

—— (1994). *The Priestly Kingdom: Social Ethics as Gospel*. Notre Dame, Ind.: University of Notre Dame Press.

—— (1997). *For the Nations: Essays Public and Evangelical*. Grand Rapids, Mich., and Cambridge: Eerdmans.

ZIZIOULAS, J. D. (1993). *Being as Communion: Studies in Personhood and the Church*. Crestwood, Mo.: St Vladimir's Press.

CHAPTER 5

DIVINE GRACE AND ETHICS

GILBERT MEILAENDER

THAT in Jesus Christ God has freely and graciously become friend of sinners and justifier of the ungodly is the heart of the Christian gospel and the centre of Christian life. It would be hard to imagine Christian hymnody without its praise for this divine grace to sinners.

> How vast your mercy to accept
> The burden of our sin,
> And bow your head in cruel death
> To make us clean within,

says a hymn dating (in its Latin version) from the eighth century. The wonder of grace is, as we might expect, a staple of hymns inspired by Reformation teaching. 'Salvation unto us has come / By God's free grace and favor.' In the bleeding Saviour on the tree Isaac Watts discerned 'Amazing pity, grace unknown, / And love beyond degree'. 'There's a wideness in God's mercy', written by Frederick Faber, a nineteenth-century convert from Anglicanism to Roman Catholicism, affirms even that 'There is grace enough for thousands / Of new worlds as great as this', and the reformed slave-trader, John Newton, believed he had experienced an 'Amazing Grace' capable even of saving 'a wretch like me'.

The language of worship must, of course, sometimes be given greater precision in the language of dogmatic theology, and this is surely true for ethics as a branch of dogmatics. Questions about how God's grace works in human beings to produce a transformation that involves, as St Paul writes in Romans 12, the renewal of their minds and a discernment of God's will are among the most complicated and controverted of issues in Christian theology.

From among the many topics one might take up in an essay on the place of grace in the Christian life, I will focus here on three: (1) the necessity of God's prevenient grace if the power of sin is to be overcome and we are really to *love* God, (2) the relationship of grace and *faith* in bringing about the justification and renewal of sinners, and (3) the contours of a life that is energized by confidence in divine grace already bestowed in Jesus, but, at the same time, lived in *hope*. Although this will leave much unsaid, it nevertheless draws into the orbit of grace many important themes of Christian moral reflection. It gives us one angle on the three chief theological virtues, it takes up themes deeply embedded in the Scriptures, and it directs our attention to topics that have been stumbling-blocks for ecumenical understanding and agreement.

'APART FROM ME YOU CAN DO NOTHING'

Jesus' words in John 15: 5, which became so important to Augustine as he wrestled with Pelagianism, direct us to grace as the starting-point of the Christian life. Taken in the abstract, of course, the claim that apart from God human beings can do nothing raises far-reaching questions about the genuineness of human freedom. And, in fact, it has always been difficult for Christian thinkers to be simultaneously anti-Manichaean and anti-Pelagian. In the face of a quite natural, recurring (Manichaean) tendency to make sense of human moral experience by describing our human nature as a battleground between good and evil principles, Christian thinkers will want to assert human power of choice. In the face of an equally natural (Pelagian) desire to take seriously this created power of choice as the moving force in the moral life, Christian thinkers will want to assert that, apart from God's grace, our power of choice is always governed by the direction of our will, which is now enslaved to sin. So many loves—some clearly good, others suspect—come quite naturally to us, and we may be uncertain how to love with a whole heart or whether we are capable of such love.

The division within sinful human beings is memorably depicted by St Paul in Romans 7: 18–19: 'I can will what is right, but I cannot do it. For the good that I would I do not; but the evil which I would not, that I do' (RSV throughout). Although interpreters will probably always disagree about who the 'I' of Romans 7 is, I think it best to read Paul as depicting here the divided will (not of those who are in Christ, but) of children of Adam; for Romans 6 makes clear that Christians are no longer to be described as enslaved to sin, and Romans 8: 2 asserts that the indwelling Spirit of Jesus 'has set me free from the law of sin and death'.

Perhaps the most memorable description of the divided will comes in Augustine's *Confessions*, when he depicts his struggle to give himself whole-heartedly to God and his inability to accomplish this simply by willing to do it. Having heard the story of Victorinus—himself a scholar and rhetorician like Augustine, who, upon becoming a Christian, had made public profession of his faith—Augustine writes,

> I was on fire to be like him ... but I was held back, and I was held back not by fetters put on me by someone else, but by the iron bondage of my own will. ... And the new will which I was beginning to have and which urged me to worship you in freedom and to enjoy you, God, the only certain joy, was not yet strong enough to overpower the old will. ... So my two wills, one old, one new, one carnal, one spiritual, were in conflict, and they wasted my soul by their discord. (1963: VIII. 5)

He could not order his loves rightly simply by willing to do so, because, as he notes, 'I, no doubt, was on both sides' (1963: VIII. 5). The division cut so deeply into his soul that he could not, by his own power, simply place himself on one side or the other. Only later, after the climactic scene in the garden, would it be the case that when 'I willed, I should will it thoroughly' (1963: VIII. 8).

The grace of God alone can overcome this division within the self, and—though it is true that such a strong theology of grace gives rise to a number of difficulties, a few of which I consider below—we should not be so concerned about the difficulties that we miss the importance of divine grace for Christian ethics. Robert Merrihew Adams has called attention to a 'gaping hole' in most modern ethical theories. 'They have nothing to say to us in a situation of helplessness' (1999: 224). Adams is concerned chiefly to commend the moral significance of actions which, though seemingly pointless, carry symbolic value, but his observation can be extended to the whole of the moral life. Learning to love the good, to bring into right order our fragmented and dispersed loves, and to overcome our idolatrous loves, is a task that may well evoke in us a sense of helplessness. We may be forced to say, with Augustine, 'I, no doubt ... [am] on both sides'. An ethical theory that cannot speak to such helplessness 'abandons us in what is literally the hour of our greatest need' (Adams 1999: 224).

It is also true, however, that a theology of grace raises problems for Christian ethics. Most obviously, perhaps, it may lead us to wonder whether human beings ever act freely and whether, in avoiding Pelagianism, we may flirt with a Manichaean depiction of our nature as entirely lacking the power of choice. Although Luther's *Bondage of the Will* admits of varying interpretations, and may not be internally consistent, there are moments in the argument when such flirtation seems present. For example, his well-known image of the human will as a 'beast of burden' might be thought to leave no room for the power of choice. 'If God rides it, it wills and goes where God wills....If Satan rides it, it wills and goes where Satan wills; nor can it choose to run to either of the two riders or to seek him out, but the riders themselves contend for the possession and control of it' (Luther 1972: 65–6).

It should perhaps not surprise us that at other moments Luther draws back and looks for ways to do justice to a distinctively human power of choice through which God's grace can work. 'For heaven, as the saying goes, was not made for geese' (Luther 1972: 67). We should, I think, join Luther in those moments when he draws back and say something not unlike what Augustine says in book v of *City of God*, where two issues concern him. One is whether we can sensibly speak of human freedom if God knows the future. Augustine's answer—a good one—is that among the causes which God foreknows are our choices. 'It does not follow, then, that there is nothing in our will because God foreknew what was going to be in our will; for if he foreknew this, it was not nothing that he foreknew' (Augustine 1984: v. 10).

The more difficult question, however, is whether God causes to be what comes to be through our choices (which he foreknows). We may freely choose, Augustine says, but only God gives the power of achievement (1984: v. 10). Here, I suspect, we confront mysteries that are more than problems to be solved. It may help if we think of human life as a drama, whose author is God, and in which we play the parts given us. Having created characters of the sort we are, the author cannot simply manipulate them—at least, not if he wishes to write well. But perhaps a sufficiently inventive author may still be able to incorporate all his characters' choices into the plot of a story that ends in accord with his design.

Dorothy Sayers, herself the author of both stories and plays, explores such an analogy with great ingenuity in *The Mind of the Maker*. An author has both characters and plot with which to work, but bringing them together in a coherent and satisfying story is no easy task. Sayers grants that authors have far more control over their characters than parents have over their children. But even of characters in a story it is true, she writes, that 'unless the author permits them to develop in conformity with their proper nature, they will cease to be true and living creatures' (Sayers 1979: 67). Indeed, 'the free will of a genuinely created character has a certain reality, which the writer will defy at his peril' (Sayers 1979: 67). Suppose the plot of the story seems to require from characters behaviour that is simply not 'in character'. What then? An author may 'behave like an autocratic deity and compel the characters to do his will whether or not', but this, of course, is unlikely to make for a good story. Alternatively, '[t]he humanistic and sensitive author may prefer to take the course of sticking to his characters and altering the plot to suit their development. This will result in a less violent shock to the reader's sense of reality, but also in an alarming incoherence of structure' (Sayers 1979: 69–70). The right way out of such difficulties—requiring authorial skill of the highest order—permits characters to act in accord with their natures, while yet bringing the plot to the ending the author had envisioned. 'In language to which we are accustomed in other connections', Sayers concludes, 'neither predestination nor free will is everything, but, if the will acts freely in accordance with its true nature, it achieves by grace and not by judgment the eternal will of its maker, though possibly by a process unlike, and longer than, that which might have been imposed upon it by force' (1979: 75).

The genuineness of human volition is not the only issue, however. A strong theology of grace, because it seems to obliterate all penultimate distinctions in the light of the ultimate either/or of God's verdict, may also seem sometimes to paralyse our powers of moral judgement and render us unable or unwilling to acknowledge moral goodness when we see it. It may, in Reinhold Niebuhr's terms, make us 'indifferent to relative moral discriminations' (1964: 190). Even the best of human achievements is tainted by our sin and falls short of the perfect love God wants from us; therefore, a strong theology of grace is 'always in danger of heightening religious tension to the point where it breaks the moral tension, from which all decent action flows' (Niebuhr 1964: 196).

This issue, though in different terms, came to the centre of theological attention in the Protestant Reformation with the question whether sin remains in the Christian. Roman Catholics answered that sin, in its most precise sense, does not remain. Although an inclination to sin (concupiscence) does remain even in Christians, the Holy Spirit dwells within them and, hence, there can be nothing in them that God condemns. The Council of Trent's Decree concerning original sin states the position clearly.

If anyone denies that by the grace of our Lord Jesus Christ which is conferred in baptism, the guilt of original sin is remitted, or says that the whole of that which belongs to the essence of sin is not taken away, but says that it is only canceled or not imputed, let him be anathema. For in those who are born again God hates nothing. . . . But this holy council perceives and confesses that in the one baptized there remains concupiscence or an inclination to sin, which, since it is left for us to wrestle with, cannot injure those who do not acquiesce but resist manfully by the grace of Jesus Christ. (Schroeder 1941: 23)

In the *Joint Declaration on the Doctrine of Justification*, confirmed in 1999, Lutherans and Roman Catholics sought a way past this anathema. Thus, when Lutherans say that those who are justified are still sinners and that their sin constitutes opposition to God, 'they do not deny that, despite this sin, they are not separated from God and that this sin is a "ruled" sin [that is, the believer is no longer enslaved by it]' (Lutheran World Federation and the Roman Catholic Church 2000: 4. 4, 29). Roman Catholics, on the other hand, do not deny that remaining concupiscence (which they decline to call sin) 'is objectively in contradiction to God and remains one's enemy in lifelong struggle' (2000: 4. 4, 30). The issue is 'whether man's historical existence is such that he can ever, by any discipline of reason or by any merit of grace, confront a divine judgment upon his life with an easy conscience' (Niebuhr 1964: 141).

Perhaps we cannot do so—and should not. Without the Lutheran emphasis, therefore, Christian ethics is always in danger of appearing too self-contained, too ready to assume divine grace—and then move on. But, as Anthony Lane notes, we also need the finely grained moral distinctions between better and worse if there is to be any Christian ethical reflection at all:

On the one hand it is true that we are all sinners, all in need of God's mercy. But if that is all we can say we end up with a moral relativism.... It would have been wrong, for example, for white South Africans under apartheid to deflect criticism with the, doubtless true, statement that deep down all people are racists. (2002: 176)

Christian ethics can scarcely deny that divine grace—the indwelling power of the Holy Spirit—makes a difference, a moral difference, in our lives and loves.

Even apart from the gracious bestowal of the Holy Spirit which leads ultimately to salvation, we may well—with the Calvinist strand of Christian thought—speak also of 'common' grace: a 'non-salvific attitude of divine favor toward all human beings' (Mouw 2001: 9). This common grace has generally been thought to include the many natural blessings which God bestows on his creatures, as well as the ability even of unbelievers to do acts that serve the common good. One might, of course, speak of these as the work of providence rather than grace; yet it does not seem wrong to think of them as unmerited blessings of the Creator. Calvin, in fact, speaking in particular of the gift of reason and understanding, writes that we ought to see in it 'the peculiar grace of God' (1960: II. 14).

More significant for Christian ethics, however, would be a category of common grace that includes the moral worth of our actions. Probing just this possibility, Richard Mouw invites us to consider a case such as the following: suppose a marriage between non-Christians has been broken by wrongdoing but is now repaired and reconciled through patient love and forgiveness. Christian theology would not say that this husband and wife are saved (or justified) when they rebuild their marriage; nevertheless, Christians who see the hand of God at work in human life may be inclined to discern here the presence of a healing grace. We want to say, Mouw suggests, that 'God judges the inner states of the unbelieving couple who have experienced marital reconciliation to be better than the inner states associated with their former alienation' (2001: 43). Hence, from one angle—an important angle—we want and need to say that these spouses, whether reconciled or unreconciled in their marriage, are not in right relation with God apart from the gracious gift of the Holy Spirit. But we need another angle of vision as well—enabling us to acknowledge that even God is not indifferent to the relative moral discriminations we must make in judging human action.

'God's love has been poured into our hearts through the Holy Spirit which has been given us'

These words of St Paul in Romans 5: 5 point toward what has been perhaps the deepest (and most ecumenically divisive) problem in Christian reflection on the meaning of divine grace and the role of faith. In his influential tracing of the interactions of *agapē* and *eros* in Christian thought, Anders Nygren rightly notes that Augustine 'delights' to quote Romans 5: 5 in order to describe how, through the work of the Holy Spirit, God infuses the grace of renewal, thereby giving to believers what he has commanded and making possible ascent to fellowship with God on the basis of holiness (1953: 455). For Nygren this understanding of grace is a distortion of the true *agapē* motif, but, interestingly, he can use the same passage from Romans to describe—favourably in his view—how St Paul regards *agapē* as a kind of divine '"pneumatic fluid"' which is infused into believers and, through them, passed on to others (1953: 129). Even their own agapeic works, it seems, are really God's work—which is one way to be certain that human 'works' do not displace grace in theological ethics.

We need only contrast Nygren's way of organizing our understanding of the Christian life with Kenneth Kirk's equally wide-ranging and learned depiction of life as a journey toward *The Vision of God* to begin to appreciate just how deep this issue goes. Is grace fundamentally a *gift* bestowed by God, and the Christian's grace-given faith, then, formed by love? Or is grace fundamentally God's *favour* toward sinners, and the Christian's response one of faith that trusts this promised favour? The first approach risks constantly turning our attention inward—to how we are doing or what moral progress we are making—and such an inward turn is, of course, precisely a turn away from the power of grace that comes from outside us. The second approach risks depicting the Christian life as resting content in our sinful condition as if it were acceptable to a gracious God.

We may, of course, want to say 'yes' to both of these ways of structuring the Christian life, while doing our best to avoid their dangers, and that may be wise. History shows, though, that this is by no means easy. That the Bible often speaks of God's grace as favour toward sinners, and that therefore the Reformation emphasis must be affirmed, is beyond dispute. It is also true, however, that the Bible—and even St Paul—can think of grace as a gift bestowed on and infused into believers. Thus, in his greeting at the outset of 1 Corinthians, St Paul writes: 'I give thanks to God always for you because of the grace (*charis*) of God which was given you in Christ Jesus…so that you are not lacking in any spiritual gift (*charism*).' The favour of God, enacted and displayed in Jesus, takes form and shape in the character of believers.

In this, as so often, Augustine has already displayed the rough contours of our problem. Thus, for example, in his important treatise 'On the Spirit and the Letter' he notes that the righteousness of God of which St Paul speaks is not that by which God himself is righteous—a standard that we must attain—but 'that with which He endows man when He justifies the ungodly' (1948: 471). Hence, God's right-eousness is not a requirement but a free gift. Nevertheless, in Augustine's formu-lation cited above, this gift is not simply the *favor Dei* which we are invited to rely upon and trust. It is something more like a substantive endowment, a healing of the interior person (Augustine 1948: 494). The gift of grace is placed, therefore, in service of healing and renewal. 'The law was therefore given, in order that grace might be sought; grace was given, in order that the law might be fulfilled' (Augus-tine 1948: 487).

The Scholastic distinction between uncreated and created grace deals in different language with similar concerns. 'Uncreated grace' refers to the favour of God, which, through the indwelling of the Holy Spirit, effects a created habit of grace within the soul. It is this habit of soul that fits one for God's presence and is the basis of justification. But one need only read Karl Rahner's intricate essay 'Some Implications of the Scholastic Concept of Uncreated Grace' to begin to appreciate how difficult it is to describe in a satisfactory way the relationship between uncreated and created grace. Shall we say—as, Rahner notes, St Paul seems to suggest—that what comes first is the indwelling of the Holy Spirit (uncreated grace), and that the Spirit, in turn, creates in believers an inner quality of right-eousness or a habit of grace? Shall we say, in other words, that every created grace is a 'consequence and a manifestation of the possession of this uncreated grace'? (Rahner 1965: 322). Or shall we say, as Rahner characterizes Scholastic teaching, that the Holy Spirit can dwell in believers only in so far as their very person has been renewed—in short, that apart from created grace no indwelling of the Spirit could be possible? (Rahner 1965: 322).

In the *Summa Theologiae* Aquinas resolves the issue in the following manner: even though grace is indeed God's own gracious favour, which can hardly be possessed or disposed of by human beings, it is also what Thomas O'Meara has called 'a form of life', and not just a transitory divine favour provided again and again (O'Meara 1997: 262). In q. 110, a. 1, of the *Prima Secundae* of the *Summa* Aquinas asks whether grace 'set[s] up something' in the human soul—in particu-lar, whether divine grace can become a 'quality' of the human soul. Distinguishing various uses of the term 'grace', Aquinas notes first how it may refer to the love or favourable attitude that one person has toward another, 'as we might say that this soldier has the king's grace and favour' (Aquinas 1972: q. 110, a. 1). It may also, however, mean a gift that is given freely, 'as we might say, "I confer on you this grace"'. And the crucial question, then, is whether the first of these meanings implies or requires the second, whether grace does indeed 'set up' something in the soul. Aquinas holds that it does, even though the first objection he considers in q. 110, a. 1, states (as clearly as Luther could have) why one might think otherwise:

It seems that grace does not set up something in the soul. For as a man is said to have the grace and favour of God, so too he is said to have the grace and favour of man.... Now when a man is said to have the grace and favour of a man, nothing is set up in the one who has the other's grace; but in the one whose grace he has there is set up a certain approval. Therefore when a man is said to have God's grace, nothing is set up in his soul; all that is signified is a divine approval.

To this objection Aquinas replies by distinguishing between the way in which one has the favour of another human being and the way in which one has God's favour.

Even when someone is said to have man's grace and favour, it is implied that there is something in him pleasing to man, just as when someone is said to have God's grace and favour; but there is a difference. For what is pleasing to us in someone else is presupposed to our love for him; but what is pleasing to God is caused by the divine love.

That is, even the 'form of life', the 'quality' that is 'set up' in the soul and becomes one's possession, permitting us to say that one 'has God's grace' (*gratiam Dei habere*), even this quality is a supernatural gift that has first been given by God (*a Deo proveniens*) (Aquinas 1972: q. 110, a. 1). It is this quality of the soul that, fully developed, fits one for God's presence. It is not simply God's favourable attitude toward us; it is a 'form of life', a gift that takes up residence within the person's character. But to speak of this gift simply as our possession would hardly be adequate. Better to say, as Theo Kobusch does in explicating Aquinas: 'The absolutely nonmanipulable is present only in the mode of gift (*donum*)' (2002: 212).

Likewise, Luther's view, though surely emphasizing grace as divine favour toward sinners, is much more complex than has sometimes been appreciated. Thus, for example, in 'Against Latomus', an important early treatise, he distinguishes (and relates) what he calls 'grace' and 'gift'.

A righteous and faithful man doubtless has both grace and the gift. Grace makes him wholly pleasing so that his person is wholly accepted ... but the gift heals from sin and from all his corruption of body and soul.... Everything is forgiven through grace, but as yet not everything is healed through the gift. The gift has been infused, the leaven has been added to the mixture. It works so as to purge away the sin for which a person has already been forgiven.... A person neither pleases, nor has grace, except on account of the gift which labors in this way to cleanse from sin. (Luther 1958: 229)

If the language is not that of the Scholastics, perhaps the patterns of thought are not as far removed from each other as we have sometimes supposed.

Hence, we would paint far too neat a picture if we were simply to play off against each other grace as divine favour (external to us) and grace as (interior) divine gift—and think of these as Reformation versus Roman Catholic emphases. For, while the languages are very different—returning 'again and again' to the promised grace, or growing 'more and more' in the grace that has been given—the structural problems are related (Hunsinger 2000: 299–300). It is not easy to understand, in Luther's language, why one who is the object of God's favour, who is pleasing to God, need purge away sin or do anything more than, simply, trust that good news. It is not easy to understand, in Aquinas's language, why one in whom a new, supernatural form of life has taken root need return time and again with renewed faith to the promise that, despite his sin, God looks on him with favour. If we emphasize our need to return again and again to the promise of God's favour, we seem to undermine the love of God that has been poured into our hearts through the Holy Spirit. If we emphasize the sense in which this new life of love becomes more and more our possession, becomes habitual, we seem to undermine the sense in which it is, finally, God's continuing gift and work in us. Neither emphasis is entirely safe without the other.

Reinhold Niebuhr helpfully distinguishes 'two aspects of the life of grace', which he calls 'grace as power' and 'grace as pardon' (1964: 124, 107). Noting that it is always difficult to express both aspects of the experience of grace without seeming to do an injustice to one or the other, Niebuhr writes:

The theologies which have sought to do justice to the fact that saints nevertheless remain sinners have frequently, perhaps usually, obscured the indeterminate possibilities of realizations of good in both individual and collective life. The theologies which have sought to do justice to the positive aspects of regeneration have usually obscured the realities of sin which appear on every new level of virtue. (1964: 125)

One way to understand much of Karl Barth's doctrine of reconciliation in volume IV of his *Church Dogmatics* is to read him as trying to give full expression to both aspects of grace. He 'elevated reconciliation to preeminence so that justification became a subordinate concept which described reconciliation as a whole—as also did sanctification, justification's simultaneous counterpart' (Hunsinger 2000: 304).

This is, I suspect, the best that Christian ethics can manage or should try to manage. The one gracious work of God in Christ, reconciling the world to himself, will—this side of the eschaton—always have to be described in the languages of both pardon and power. These are different but necessary ways of describing how God's Spirit draws human lives into the story of Jesus. The language of pardon speaks to Christians' continuing experience of sin in their lives; the language of power reflects the truth that the Spirit of Christ does, indeed, dwell in believers. Both languages will, therefore, be necessary to say everything that needs to be said about the place of grace in Christian life.

In adopting this position, I am returning to something like the 'double justification' formula on which (some) Catholics and (some) Protestants reached agreement at the Regensburg Colloquy in 1541 (Yarnold 1988). That colloquy, the last serious attempt to avoid a permanently divided church before the decisions of the

Council of Trent made such a hope futile, affirmed that 'living faith is that which both appropriates mercy in Christ, believing that the righteousness which is in Christ is freely imputed to it, and at the same time receives the promise of the Holy Spirit and love' (Lane 2002: 234). More than 450 years later, in the *Joint Declaration on the Doctrine of Justification*, Lutherans and Catholics adopted a formula not unlike that of Regensburg:

We confess together that God forgives sin by grace and at the same time frees human beings from sin's enslaving power and imparts the gift of new life in Christ. When persons come by faith to share in Christ, God no longer imputes to them their sin and through the Holy Spirit effects in them an active love. These two aspects of God's gracious action are not to be separated. (2000: 4. 2, 22)

We are not likely to do much better than this in our own attempts to distinguish without separating the *charis* and the *charism* bestowed on those who are in Christ. But when both aspects of grace are seen and emphasized properly, Christian ethics will help to form people whose lives give evidence of 'a combination of increasing humility [in the face of grace as pardon] and increasing achievement [made possible by grace as power]' (Ramsey 1950: 200).

'THROUGH JESUS WE HAVE OBTAINED ACCESS TO THIS GRACE IN WHICH WE STAND, AND WE REJOICE IN OUR HOPE OF SHARING THE GLORY OF GOD'

These words of St Paul in Romans 5: 2 invite us to consider the relationship between the grace bestowed on believers and the future glory for which they hope. Although salvation is a gift that has, in some sense, already been bestowed on believers, it is also a future state not yet attained, toward which one must 'press on', as Philippians 3: 12 puts it. The object is not, of course, simply one's personal salvation. It is the reign of God inaugurated in Jesus' death and resurrection but still to be revealed for every eye to see. Yet, however certain is the fact that God's rule will one day be manifested, confidence that any one of us in particular will be saved and share in that reign might seem to be premature or presumptuous. For within human history Christians are always 'on the way', and we need to discern how this truth determines the contours of a life pleasing to God.

Grace having been bestowed in Jesus Christ, we ought to live with confidence that God will make good on the promise of which the Spirit of Jesus serves as down payment. The reign of God not yet having been manifested, however, we must 'press on' toward something that is present now chiefly as the object of our hope. To 'press on' or to 'hope' must mean more than just to 'await' or 'anticipate'. It suggests difficulty while on the way, and it might seem even to suggest uncertainty of outcome. Were there no uncertainty, after all, why would one need the virtue of hope? Then expectation would suffice. Yet, it is 'hope of sharing the glory of God' that St Paul commends even to those who have already through Jesus 'obtained access to this grace in which we stand'.

Precisely what to say about the character of Christian hope has not been easy to work out. Thus, for example, a decree from the sixth session of the Council of Trent, while readily granting that 'no pious person ought to doubt the mercy of God, the merit of Christ and the virtue and efficacy of the sacraments', none the less asserts of believers that 'each one, when he considers himself and his own weakness and indisposition, may have fear and apprehension concerning his own grace, since no one can know with the certainty of faith, which cannot be subject to error, that he has obtained the grace of God' (Schroeder 1941: 35). The cadence seems quite different in John Wesley's famous description of his Aldersgate experience: 'I felt my heart strangely warmed. I felt I did trust in Christ, Christ alone for my salvation; and an assurance was given me that he had taken away *my* sins, even *mine*, and saved *me* from the law of sin and death' (Whaling 1981: 107). That same assurance is nicely articulated in a stanza from one of Charles Wesley's hymns:

> By faith we know thee strong to save
> (Save us, a present Savior thou!)
> Whate'er we hope, by faith we have,
> Future and past subsisting now.
>
> (Whaling 1981: 188)

Take Trent seriously, and we may be uncertain how to say, with St Paul, that we now stand in grace and can rejoice (rather than be anxious) in our hope. Take the Wesleys seriously, and our sense of being still 'on the way' may seem threatened, and anticipation rather than hope may be sufficient to shape the way we live.

We should note how deeply embedded in different understandings of grace are these differing assessments of the meaning of hope, and they take us back to issues discussed in the previous section. When grace is understood chiefly as the pardoning promise of God, which makes Christ's righteousness the sinner's own, the significance—before God—of what we do, of individual actions, almost inevitably recedes. In turn, then, our assurance for the future does not depend on what the character of our deeds may be, but, rather, on the promised mercy of God. When grace is understood chiefly as a power that moves us to become—through our deeds and through our traits of character—holy in God's eyes, assurance of future salvation might seem premature before the completion of this process of perfection.

At least for those of us who are not Thomists, it may seem that even the angelic doctor is pulled in several different directions. In IaIIae, q. 112, a. 5, of the *Summa* ('can a man know that he has grace?') Aquinas distinguishes three different ways in which one might know something: (1) through a special revelation, (2) through one's own cognitive capacities, and (3) by signs in one's life. To take them in reverse order, we may see signs in our life suggesting the working of God's grace, but that knowledge can never be perfect or complete. There are many things we may know through our own capacities, and even some things that we may know with certainty, but we cannot know with certainty things that are only in God's power. 'In this sense no one can know that he has grace.' (Here Aquinas refers to 1 Cor. 4: 4: 'I am not aware of anything against myself, but I am not thereby acquitted. It is the Lord who judges me.') Finally, it is indeed possible that 'by a special privilege God sometimes reveals this to people, so that the joy of complete security may begin in them even in this life, and so that they may carry out remarkable tasks more confidently and courageously and endure the evils of this present life; so it was said to Paul, *My grace is sufficient for you.*'

In St Thomas's specific discussion of the virtue of hope, in IIaIIae, qq. 17–22 of the *Summa*, his angle seems slightly different. In q. 18, a. 4, he says that hope involves the expectation of future salvation, and—replying to a possible objection to the effect that since hope of salvation 'comes by way of grace and merits', we cannot be assured in this life that we have grace—he says: 'Hope does not put its trust primarily in grace already received but in the divine omnipotence and mercy.... To anyone having faith, this omnipotence and mercy of God are certainties.' We would, I think, be faithful to Aquinas's complexities if we said: Although grace has been bestowed by the Spirit, salvation remains future, and the way toward it must be traversed. Our question about certitude, then, asks whether Christians can be assured that they will, indeed, arrive at the promised destination. Faith (understood as cognitive, as knowledge) does not enable us to know with certainty that we will be among the saved. But putting the matter that way is thinking of one's life in the third person, as an observer might—and no one can *live* that way. We can, on the other hand, say that the 'omnipotence and mercy of God are certainties' when grasped in the first person by faith (understood not as knowledge but as trust). This is not to look at one's life from the outside; it is to turn to God and cling to his promises in confidence.

A useful comparison might be with the way the marriage vow must be taken. It cannot be simply a prediction about what may happen in the future, for any honest prediction must reckon with the fact that some marriages end in divorce. One cannot take the vow from that perspective of a third-person observer. I cannot say, 'Yes, I will be faithful to you—unless, of course, I am one of those who turns out to

fail in this commitment.' Or, at any rate, if I say this, she is not likely to think I have
taken the vow she wants from me. But I can meaningfully, even in the midst of
living out that vow, hope that I will be faithful to it. That is, I can recognize that the
way of faithfulness is arduous and strewn with temptations. Indeed, just as my
spouse wants something more from me than a prediction of the future, even so she
also wants to see in me this hope that sets its course with a clear recognition of the
difficulties.

On this topic, as on those taken up in the two previous sections, the *Joint
Declaration on the Doctrine of Justification* articulates substantial consensus. This
comes out most clearly in a Roman Catholic affirmation whose cadence is not
precisely that of Trent:

With the Second Vatican Council, Catholics state: to have faith is to entrust oneself totally
to God, who liberates us from the darkness of sin and death and awakens us to eternal life.
In this sense, one cannot believe in God and at the same time consider the divine promise
untrustworthy. No one may doubt God's mercy and Christ's merit. Every person, however,
may be concerned about his salvation when he looks upon his own weaknesses and
shortcomings. Recognizing his own failures, however, the believer may yet be certain that
God intends his salvation. (2000: 4. 6, 36)

If this is the kind of assurance with which Christians, shaped by grace, live toward
the future God has promised, we might ask, finally and all too briefly, what
difference it makes for the contours of our life.

One of the most influential streams of modern moral philosophy, and of much
everyday moral reflection, has been what moral theorists call 'consequentialism'.
This view holds that it is our responsibility to determine and seek to achieve the
best overall state of affairs in all that we do. It suggests, however, a kind of
presumption about our control of the future that sits uneasily in a life shaped by
hope, whose assurance rests not in our mastery but in God's promises.

In the first section above, I explored briefly the analogy of the story, focusing on
the author's role in working out the plot even in the face of 'recalcitrant' characters
(of his own creation). Now we can focus for a moment on the characters and on
what it would mean for them to think of themselves as characters in a drama
written by the divine author. They know the part given them, and each must play
his part in his own way, with his own particular flair and interpretation. But none
of the characters is the dramatist or the director, and none of them knows how the
plot is satisfactorily to be worked out. That is essentially our situation. C. S. Lewis
put the metaphor this way:

We do not know the play. We do not even know whether we are in Act I or Act V. We do not
know who are the major and who the minor characters. The Author knows.... That it has a
meaning we may be sure, but we cannot see it. When it is over, we may be told. We are led to
expect that the Author will have something to say to each of us on the part that each of us
has played. The playing it well is what matters infinitely. (Lewis 1960: 105–6)

This is a quite different picture of the moral life from imagining ourselves responsible for achieving the best possible state of affairs. Christians are under authority, called to act faithfully within the limits of history, even when it is not apparent that such faithfulness leads in the direction of the greatest good overall.

There is no way to live such a life except in hope that the God revealed in Jesus will complete what remains incomplete in our own achievements, and such hope—a hope that goes well beyond any empirical evidence—must be the gift of God's grace. Indeed, we may well say with Barth that what 'derives and proceeds' from our own capacities alone, however noble it may sometimes be, 'can never be Christian faith, nor Christian love, nor Christian hope' (1962: 939). On the contrary, if the division within our being is to be overcome and our loves rightly ordered, if faith in God's favour toward us is to renew and energize our lives in habits of virtue, and if genuine hope is to free us for both love and faithfulness—if all this is to happen in human lives, we must credit the mystery of divine grace so powerfully gestured at in a hymn by Bianco da Siena:

> And so the yearning strong,
> With which the soul will long,
> Shall far outpass the pow'r of human telling;
> No soul shall guess his grace
> Till it become the place
> Wherein the Holy Spirit makes his dwelling.

References and Suggested Reading

ADAMS, ROBERT MERRIHEW (1999). *Finite and Infinite.* Oxford: Oxford University Press.

AQUINAS, THOMAS (1966). *Summa Theologiae*, vol. 33. Oxford: Blackfriars.

—— (1972). *Summa Theologiae*, vol. 30. Oxford: Blackfriars.

AUGUSTINE (1948). 'On the Spirit and the Letter', in Whitney J. Oates (ed.), *The Basic Writings of Saint Augustine*, New York: Random House, 461–518.

—— (1963). *Confessions.* New York: Mentor Books.

—— (1984). *City of God.* New York: Penguin Books.

BARTH, KARL (1962). *Church Dogmatics, IV/3.2.* Edinburgh: T. & T. Clark.

BRONDOS, DAVID A. (2004). 'Sola Fide and Luther's "Analytic" Understanding of Justification', *Pro Ecclesia*, 13, 39–57.

CALVIN, JOHN (1960). *Institutes of the Christian Religion.* Philadelphia: Westminster Press.

HUNSINGER, GEORGE (2000). *Disruptive Grace: Studies in the Theology of Karl Barth.* Grand Rapids, Mich.: William B. Eerdmans.

KIRK, KENNETH E. (1932). *The Vision of God.* London: Longmans, Green and Co.

KOBUSCH, THEO (2002). 'Grace (Ia IIae, qq. 109–114)', in Stephen J. Pope (ed.), *The Ethics of Aquinas*, Washington: Georgetown University Press, 207–18.

LANE, ANTHONY N. S. (2002). *Justification by Faith in Catholic–Protestant Dialogue.* London and New York: T. & T. Clark.

LEWIS, C. S. (1960). *The World's Last Night and Other Essays*. New York: Harcourt Brace Jovanovich.

THE LUTHERAN WORLD FEDERATION AND THE ROMAN CATHOLIC CHURCH (2000). *Joint Declaration on the Doctrine of Justification*. Grand Rapids, Mich.: William B. Eerdmans.

LUTHER, MARTIN (1958). *Luther's Works*, vol. 32. Philadelphia: Fortress Press.

—— (1972). *Luther's Works*, vol. 33. Philadelphia: Fortress Press.

MOUW, RICHARD J. (2001). *He Shines in All That's Fair: Culture and Common Grace*. Grand Rapids, Mich.: William B. Eerdmans.

NIEBUHR, REINHOLD (1964). *The Nature and Destiny of Man*, II. New York: Charles Scribner's Sons.

NYGREN, ANDERS (1953). *Agape and Eros*. London: SPCK.

O'MEARA, THOMAS F., OP (1997). 'Virtues in the Theology of Thomas Aquinas', *Theological Studies*, 58, 254–85.

PFÜRTNER, STEPHAN, OP (1964). *Luther and Aquinas on Salvation*. New York: Sheed and Ward.

PIEPER, JOSEF (1997). *Faith, Hope, Love*. San Francisco: Ignatius Press.

RAHNER, KARL (1965). *Theological Investigations*, I. Baltimore: Helicon Press.

RAMSEY, PAUL (1950). *Basic Christian Ethics*. New York: Charles Scribner's Sons.

SAYERS, DOROTHY L. (1979). *The Mind of the Maker*. San Francisco: Harper & Row.

SCHROEDER, H. J., OP (trans.) (1941). *Canons and Decrees of the Council of Trent*. St Louis, Mo.: B. Herder.

WAWRYKOW, JOSEPH P. (1995). *God's Grace and Human Action: 'Merit' in the Theology of Thomas Aquinas*. Notre Dame, Ind., and London: University of Notre Dame Press.

WHALING, FRANK, (ed.) (1981). *John and Charles Wesley: Selected Prayers, Hymns, Journal Notes, Sermons, Letters and Treatises*. New York: Paulist Press.

YARNOLD, EDWARD (1988). '*Duplex iustitia*: The Sixteenth Century and the Twentieth', in G. R. Evans (ed.), *Christian Authority: Essays in Honour of Henry Chadwick*, Oxford: Clarendon Press, 204–23.

PART II

SOURCES OF MORAL KNOWLEDGE

CHAPTER 6

....

SCRIPTURE

....

WILLIAM C. SPOHN

INTRODUCTION

....

WHEN Christians reflect seriously about how to live, they inevitably appeal to Scripture. Although this appeal is inevitable for Christians, there is no consensus on how it should be made. For the past forty years, scholars have debated how Scripture should be part of discussions about this way of life. The historical-critical method and then more recent social-scientific scholarship have made possible a more nuanced appeal to Scripture through deeper understanding of biblical texts and contexts. More recent studies of rhetoric and response have focused on listeners' interaction with the texts. If previous generations saw biblical scholarship and ethics proceeding on separate tracks, that is no longer the predominant view. Exegesis has an ethical direction that needs to be acknowledged, since every biblical scholar brings moral perspectives and interests to the text (McDonald 1993). At the same time, ethicists have realized that every literary genre, not just rules and principles, can guide the moral agent and community. The great historical narratives, the paradigms of Exodus and the Cross and the Resurrection, personal exemplars, prophetic vision, and the rich language of praise and lament shape the moral perception, dispositions, and character of believers (Bartlett 1983; Ricoeur 1995; Pleins 2001).

Resistance to this closer integration comes from two different groups, who object to any normative use of Scripture for either doctrine or ethics. Some exegetes view their work as strictly descriptive, providing no path from what a text meant to what it might mean for believers today. They are concerned that drawing inferences from a biblical text for life today usually wrenches the text from its unique historical context and ignores contradictory voices within Scripture (Deidun 1998). In addition, some postmodern critics reject normative thinking in any form, because it restricts the range of diverse meanings that the text might inspire. In the most radical version of this view, no text stands over against the reader; the text is whatever the reader chooses to make of it (Patte 1995). All interpretations are valid except for those that would violate 'the other'. If, however, these critics were to spell out the vague ethics of justice they take for granted, they would have to acknowledge the normative dimension of their own critique.

While postmodernism rightly points out that normative thinking has been used oppressively, a scripture that offers no normative guidance has ceased to be 'Scripture'. As David Kelsey has shown, there is a triadic relation among a scripture, a tradition, and a community (1975: 89–119). A given community of faith finds its identity and calling in the text that stands at the origin of its tradition, which is constituted to a significant degree by the continuing interaction of the community with that text. Even though those relations get spelled out in various ways by different theological and denominational traditions, the triadic relation still holds. The question then becomes *how* Scripture is authoritative in communities of faith, rather than *whether* it should be authoritative in some general sense.

Although the churches need to attend to the fruits of biblical scholarship, the academy is probably not the best place to determine what the appropriate role of Scripture is in the Christian way of life. The Hebrew Scriptures and the New Testament do not and should not function as 'Scripture' for the pluralist secular academy. The academic setting of most scholarship dictates that biblical works get treated as historical, political, and literary documents rather than the authoritative revelation of God.

The Lens of Character and Virtue

The most adequate ethical approach to Scripture is that of character and virtue ethics. While the ethics of principles and the ethics of consequences are also represented in the texts, they are subordinate to the ethics of character. The Christian way of life is not a set of ideals, though it strives for the redeemed creation where God will reign fully. It is not a set of principles, though it centres on the twofold Love Command, and its scope is delimited by the moral boundaries of the Decalogue. Neither ideals nor principles capture the relationships to Christ, God, and neighbour that constitute this way of life. Because it reshapes the fundamental identity and dynamics of the person, however, the most appropriate ethical approach is the ethics of virtue and character.

Every book of the New Testament envisions a transformation of 'heart', a conversion of the core intellectual and emotional reality of the Christian. More than a change of behaviour or direction, what is required is a change of heart: unless the roots are sound, the fruit will be bad (Luke 6: 43–5). Character ethics looks to being as the basis of doing, because our actions flow from the sorts of persons we are. The virtues and integrity we bring to any situation determine how we will perceive what is going on and how we are disposed to act humanely. At the same time, character is defined by choices that become habits: we become what we do. In this framework, moral discernment, the capacity to discover what is right and good, takes precedence over justification, the ability to explain logically the moral reasons for action. Discernment should not be divorced from justification, since principles often help us notice what is morally salient, and reference to them keeps discernment honest.

Ethical reflection is more adequate the more comprehensively it considers moral experience. Considering character and virtue offers a broader purchase on moral experience than simply analysing moral discourse. Courage and compassion, for instance, depend more on perceiving moral challenges and framing them accurately than on the ability to make a logical argument. In similar fashion, reflecting theologically on Scripture in Christian ethics ought to attend to the ways in which the whole range of biblical literature, from prophecy to psalms of lament to parables, shapes the moral vision and emotions of individuals and communities (Gustafson 1974; Saliers 1979, 1980). It will have to attend to practices like baptism and eucharistic liturgy, forgiveness and hospitality to the poor, that communities employ to form the hearts and minds of the individuals in a way of life that is faithful to the gospel. In order to do justice to questions about conduct, Christian ethics must consider the sources of conduct in the hearts of disciples and in the communities that form them.

Sources and Tasks

Since Christian ethics is ecclesial, it will have different sources from philosophical ethics. Whereas philosophical ethics depends upon the interaction between moral theory and empirical data, Christian ethics adds two additional sources: Scripture and tradition (the historical process in which the gospel has been understood and applied). Most Christian ethicists accept that an adequate argument in their discipline must draw upon all four sources (Spohn 1995a). Even though there is no formula to determine the relative weight given to the respective sources and theologians dispute what to do when the sources fail to agree, they realize that ignoring any of the sources will lead to a deficient argument.

Before making my constructive proposal, it will be important to distinguish the various aspects of listening to Scripture in ethical reflection. Moving immediately from biblical texts to moral conclusions while ignoring our presuppositions and theological vision usually leads to an uncritical and self-serving 'application' of Scripture.

Methodist biblical scholar Richard B. Hays carefully distinguishes four tasks (1996: 3–7). The first is exegetical, since accurate descriptive knowledge of the text in its historical, social, and literary context is indispensable. The original meaning does not exhaust the text's potential, but it does exercise control over the range of readings it can sustain. The second task is hermeneutical. Since no text is self-interpreting, one must critically acknowledge the frameworks of meaning within which the texts are considered. For example, the 'household code' texts of the pastoral epistles will be read by feminist critics quite differently from how they will be read by those coming from an evangelical or liberation theology perspective. The third task is synthetic, in which the great diversity of Scripture is organized around certain central theological symbols or concepts. The choice of those symbols over alternative construals must be justified theologically. Should a theology of redemption based on the cross of Jesus be central, or should the organizing framework be the Incarnation, where creation is based in the grace of Christ? Finally, the pragmatic task brings the fruit of the previous processes to bear on particular moral questions described with the best empirical information. This final task is a complex discernment made in the light of biblical themes and paradigms in relation to the empirical information relevant to the issue at hand.

The synthetic task is the one most likely to be skipped over, even by professional scholars in hermeneutics. Theological commitments, especially when taken for granted, greatly influence which parts of the Bible are selected, how they are read, and which method of ethics is employed (Spohn 1995b). For example, Martin Luther's commitment to the dialectic of sin and grace conforms to his focus on Romans and Galatians and also makes an ethics of disposition preferable to an ethics of obligation (Luther 1959). Liberation theologians focus on the Synoptic Gospels because they graphically portray Jesus' option for the poor and oppressed, which extends God's liberating work epitomized in the Exodus. This stance calls for an ethics of solidarity with, and justice for, the poor based on analysis of contemporary social structures that oppress them (Sobrino 1993). In what follows, I will stake out my own approach, which (a) gives primacy to the Synoptic Gospels' portrayal of discipleship, (b) as configured by the Cross and Resurrection of Jesus, in order, (c) to shape the character of Christians and their communities.

DISCIPLESHIP SHAPED BY THE CROSS
AND RESURRECTION

The New Testament presents a way of life through the story of the life of Jesus of Nazareth. That way takes Jesus' entire life as its fundamental norm and inspiration. Loyalty and obedience to Jesus reshaped the lives of the disciples, and the same process goes on for contemporary believers in relation to the risen Christ. Discipleship expresses both radical personal commitment to God in Christ and the process of becoming his followers in the company of others whom he calls. The Synoptic Gospel narratives portray how Jesus called and formed the first disciples. They are the paradigms for how the risen Lord continues to call people to become his disciples and devote their lives to the reign of God in the world.

The New Testament pattern of discipleship displayed in the gospel narratives is shaped by the Cross and Resurrection of Jesus in which the narratives culminate. The destiny of Jesus internally structures the accounts of discipleship, because the gospels were written backwards, from the vantage of the Cross and Resurrection of Jesus. The journey that begins with the summons to 'come and follow me' ends with the scandal of the cross and the triumph of the resurrection. That culminating experience transforms the disciples to preach and live the gospel in the power of the Spirit. Jesus' disciples were more apprentices than students, since they learned his message as it was embodied in his person, words, and deeds. Notwithstanding the Gospel of John's lengthy self-expositions, Jesus did not preach about himself but about God's reign over the world that was breaking out in his ministry. The characteristics of the reign of God are shown in his parables, healings, table fellowship, and teaching. That is why the whole life of Jesus sets the path for discipleship. 'Discipleship' stresses that this way of life is entered by travelling in his company and friendship, not simply by studying it.

Although discipleship is not a central symbol in the Pauline literature, the end of Jesus' life defines the beginning of Christian life in baptism. Christian life begins by being plunged into the watery grave of death to emerge to a new life and destiny 'in Christ'. This act foreshadows the new path for the baptized, which is to share the destiny of Christ in dying to death and living to God (Bonhoeffer 2003). Breaking radically with one's former life is a dying to the old way of life and a rising to a new existence in Christ (Rom. 6: 1–12; Col. 3: 1–11). 'Therefore we have been buried with him by baptism into death, so that, just as Christ was raised from the dead by the glory of the Father, so we too might walk in newness of life' (Rom. 6: 4; NRSV). Paul urges the Romans to use their imaginations to recognize the analogy between the dying and rising of Christ and their dying to old ways and living the new moral existence which is now possible because the same divine power that raised Jesus from the dead is animating them. For Christians, moral life flows out of, and ratifies, the resurrected life that has been given them. The old ways of sin must constantly be put to death, and the promise of new life must be lived out by dedication and committed action: 'so too we might walk in the newness of life'.

Character of the Disciple
and the Community

There are two angles of vision on character: one focuses on the individual, the other on the community (Cahill 2002). The first looks to the change which this new relation to God in Christ works in the individual. It probes that gradual trans-formation of the person through moral psychology—that is, the dynamics of perception, dispositions, intentions, and identity as shaped by the virtuous habits that are at once the fruits of the Spirit and the chosen dispositions of the individual. My preference for beginning with moral psychology may stem from my Catholic background, but also from the fact that each disciple is called by name and must decide in free obedience to follow Christ. While character owes much to a good community, the community cannot make the fundamental life decisions that give each character its unique shape.

The second angle on character is more common to contemporary Protestant ethicists, who attend to the character of the community that is called into existence as the Body of Christ in the world (Hauerwas 1981, 1985; Fowl and Jones 1991). Disciples are called to affiliate with an actual group of people which has a distinctive moral stance; in other words, this way of life is not a solitary journey, but occurs in and with the graced people of God. The practices inculcated by the community, from eucharist to hospitality to non-violence, shape the virtuous habits of individual members. Protestants may have greater reluctance to spell out the changes worked by the Spirit in the individual lest the primacy of grace be obscured. Methodist theologian Stanley Hauerwas, who pioneered this approach, analyses Christian virtues in conversation with the work of Aristotle and Alasdair MacIntyre (Hauerwas and Pinches 1997). In general, however, those who look to character through the lens of community place greater emphasis on religious practices than on moral psychology.

The Character of the Disciple

Christians become conformed to the 'mind of Christ' (1 Cor. 2: 15) by using their imaginations under the grace of the Spirit. The imagination grasps the fundamental pattern of Jesus' life as the pattern for their lives to follow. Paul's moral exhortations frequently follow the lines of this basic analogy: as Jesus did in regards to X, so too you should do. This analogical reasoning is most succinctly expressed in Paul's plea to the Corinthians to be generous in contributing to the hard-pressed churches in Palestine: 'For you know the generous act of our Lord Jesus Christ, that though he was rich, yet for your sakes he became poor, so that by his poverty you might become rich' (2 Cor. 8: 9). Note that Paul does not appeal to an ethical principle or issue a command; instead, he asks them to use their imaginations: as Jesus was graciously generous to you, even to the point of giving everything to you, so too you should be generous to your fellow Christians. The suffering and rising of Jesus provide the normative pattern for their action. Gratitude for his gift to them provides the inspiration, the moral energy, for them to show a comparable generosity. Because the call is rooted in the gift received, it leads to an action that corresponds to that gracious gift. Their giving generously in love even to the point of loss will be met by God's bountiful response and gratitude from the Jewish Christians. Paul's allusion to the seed sown in the ground that yields a good harvest alludes to the symbolic subtext of his appeal, the Cross and Resurrection of Jesus.

Jesus' self-giving for the sake of others sets the pattern which is more fully elaborated in the kenotic hymn of Phil. 2: 5–11. This costly Christian love does not focus on the sacrifices made by the self but on the neighbours in need (Outka 1972). The new life given in baptism is the dynamic Spirit of Jesus which expresses itself in a 'christomorphic life'—that is, a life that manifests the distinctive qualities of Jesus' life (Hays 1996: 46, 27–32; Sittler 1998: 24–48). Paul urges his congregations to imitate Christ, because they have already begun to participate in the life of Christ through the Spirit given to them. Not only are Christians on the way, the way is in them because the life of Christ is in them.

The life of Jesus that is symbolically compressed in Paul is narratively displayed in the gospels. The radical self-giving of God in Christ is refracted through the prism of narrative into a set of qualities that is normative for the disciples. Jesus' characteristic virtues are ingredients in the gospel stories that define them: love, compassion, obedience, radical trust in God, solidarity with the broken, gratitude, and fidelity. If the character of the Christian is formed from the inside out in Paul's writings, it is formed from the outside in when it comes to the gospels. The disciples hear what Jesus teaches and watch what he does, and so do those who would be his disciples in subsequent generations. Today's Christians draw the analogy between how Jesus treated people then and how they should act today.

In terms of moral psychology, analogical reflection is one of the most important ways in which the gospel influences action faithful to it. Analogical reflection moves from a familiar pattern to new experience, looking for similarities and dissimilarities. The new situation is both like and unlike the original paradigm case. Because there are always dissimilarities, analogical thinking does not seek to copy the original pattern. If the dissimilarities are too pronounced, then it becomes clear that this is the wrong paradigm case for this particular problem case. The paradigm functions not as a model to be copied but a prototype that encourages adaptation that is both creative and faithful. As we shall see below, spiritual practices fund Christians' imaginations with biblical images and stories that guide their moral reflection and also develop the virtuous habits that help them see how to act.

Most analogies have four terms: A is to B as C is to D. We move from the paradigm case to the problem case, inferring from A and B what D, the missing term in the problem case, should be. However, the scriptural pattern of analogical reflection is not a simple four-term ratio. If it were, it would take this form: 'Do unto others as Jesus did to people like them.' The immediate response to such advice might well be, 'Why should I? Why should the example of Jesus be an authoritative paradigm for me?' Between the paradigm case and the problem case there needs to be a set of terms that expresses the present recognition of grace, a personal perception of what Christ has done for me. Without some parallel in my own experience, the gospels' stories are only historical accounts. I might notice interesting parallels in them to present problems, but I would not hear the imperative of faith. I might notice a pattern, but it is unlikely that I would be motivated or compelled to follow it.

In the full analogy of biblical moral reflection there are three sets of terms: the paradigm case, the personal recognition case, and the problem case. Those three sets contain six terms, but four elements. To put it schematically: $\frac{A}{B} :: \frac{A}{C} :: \frac{C}{D}$ Spelling it out verbally: As Christ did to his first disciples, so he has done to you, and so you should do likewise to these neighbours. The formal authority that Scripture has in the community of faith becomes existential when the Word gets personal confirmation, when the believer recognizes that the One spoken of in Scripture has been acting in his or her own life in a way that ought to lead to acting in similar ways toward others.

To spell out the three sets of terms, consider how the story of Jesus and Zacchaeus the tax collector (Luke 19: 1–10) has moral import. The story helps Christians recognize and remember how Jesus has acted when they were alienated. The memory of that welcoming mercy sets the pattern and evokes the desire to act in a corresponding way to the outcasts and alienated in their own context. The analogical reflection goes like this: As Jesus welcomed Zacchaeus (as A is to B), so Jesus has welcomed you (so A is to C); therefore, you ought to welcome others who are outcasts in a corresponding manner (so too C is to D). That middle set of terms establishes the link between the story and the appropriate action because it makes Christians aware that they have also been forgiven and restored by Christ. Then the story of Zacchaeus stands not as a distant moral example to be admired, but as a reminder that the gift they have received contains a call. 'As you have freely received, so freely give' (Matt. 10: 8; Gustafson 1975: 101–3, 114–16). Gratitude moves the memory of grace into a response that takes 'the shape of the engendering deed' (Sittler 1998: 24). Gratitude does not seek to pay God back for grace, but to 'go and do likewise' (Luke 10: 37) to those in need. When the stories and characters of Scripture give believers the right lenses to see what has happened to them, they become motivated to transfer that gift into creative and faithful action toward the neighbour.

It certainly takes critical skills to spot the similarities and dissimilarities between the prototype and the problematic situation. However, unless the person perceives some resonance between the stories of Scripture and personal experience, it is unlikely that the stories will speak with authority. Biblical stories lead to moral insight just as theological concepts do:

> If theological concepts yield no such insight they are of no value, they have no authority for a person. The religious person who uses these concepts often has a more complex pattern of authorization. Symbols and concepts have authority not only because they enable the theologian to perceive aspects and dimensions of circumstances but also because they are confirmed in the religious dimensions of his experience. (Gustafson 1975: 123)

As narrative theology insists, the story of liberation from captivity, of being lost and then found by God, of being welcomed to the Lord's table, has to be *my* story as well. It will not be enough to identify with it as the story of the tradition in which I stand. That story becomes authoritative when it reveals what has been occurring in my own history, and that the One who acted then is acting in characteristic fashion in my life (Niebuhr 1960: 54–66, 84–90).

Regular spiritual practices of meditation and preaching open the space where life and story mutually illumine each other. As I hold my life up to it, the story illumines my experience; in turn, my memories of undeserved forgiveness and reconciliation bring the story alive for me. The analogical imagination appreciates *what* Jesus did for Zacchaeus, but also catches *how* he acted, the attitude and stance he took toward the tax collector. Because virtues are skills, they need stories and images to display how they operate. Analogical discernment seeks to act in a way that harmonizes with the story, to be creatively hospitable in a different era with different kinds of outcasts. Discernment does not seek a command, an imperative that will be the same for every Christian. It channels the urgency of grace into appropriate expression in unique contexts as understood by an agent with unique gifts and limitations. For some, hospitality will push the boundaries of race and class in personal relations and hiring practices; for others, it may inspire a welcoming stance toward a difficult family member or work in a soup kitchen or dedication to develop affordable housing.

Over time, stories like Zacchaeus and the Prodigal Son will enter into the dispositional pattern of compassion. It becomes a 'story-shaped' disposition as it gets scripted by these remembrances and energized by gratitude. These stories also display the shadow of the virtue, the tension of grace in the face of sin. The grumbling good citizens of Jericho and the angry older brother sulking outside the party show that compassion is a choice made in the face of anger and resentment. They do not fade from our emotional repertoire, but in the company of Jesus, resentment and anger do not belong (Lauritzen 1988).

Action inspired by the gospel stories leads to habitual dispositions in the heart, and so defines character. As grace conspires with human development, so the believer becomes disposed, has a readiness, to see situations as calling for virtuous ways of acting. The hospitable person spots the opportunities to welcome strangers and friends and finds delight in doing so. Hospitality becomes more than duty, although sometimes it can be quite challenging. As this fruit of the Spirit matures, it can become a metaphor for the person's fundamental stance toward the world (Ogletree 1983; Sedgwick 1999).

Analogies and moral principles   I believe that every type of biblical literature invites analogical reflection (Spohn 1999). Hays distinguishes four common modes of ethical discourse in Scripture: rules, more general principles, paradigms, and the symbolic world as the framework for moral discernment (Hays 1996: 209). Biblical paradigms and frameworks have the greatest potential for ethical reflection because of the overall narrative form of the New Testament and the necessity of reasoning analogically from it. Scripture does not contain timeless truths that can be extracted from the ore of 'culturally conditioned' rules and stories. Rather, communities bring their own situations up to the paradigms and symbolic world of the New Testament to seek how to respond faithfully and creatively: 'We will seek, under the inspiration and guidance of the Holy Spirit, to reread our own lives within the narrative framework of the New Testament, discerning analogies— perhaps startling ones—between the canonical stories and our community's situation' (Hays 1996: 303). To emphasize the tension between the two situations, Hays calls this a process of 'metaphor making' (1996: 299). Although the moral work of imagination is often described today as metaphorical, when the terms are spelled out, it becomes clear that analogy captures the process better than metaphor.

What role do moral norms play in a Christian ethics of character and virtue? Moral principles articulated in the Decalogue and the twofold Love Command play an important role in reflection (Outka 1992). Although there is a tendency among biblical interpreters to downplay rules and principles, James Childress argues that concrete moral norms 'can establish presumptions and burdens of proof for the moral life' that are crucial in moral justification (Childress 1984). Principles shape character by being the standards we attempt to live up to and by clearly ruling out actions that would make us vicious. Commands focus the challenge that the gospel makes to our customary ways of behaving (Fowl and Jones 1991). Commands like the 'hard sayings' of Jesus can and often should disrupt practices and dispositions that have compromised the gospel in our lives (Barth 1957).

Biblical rules and principles have an analogical aspect that is often overlooked. They cannot be detached from the narratives. Biblical stories and images are not merely illustrations of underlying principles, they enter into them constitutively. Any appeal to biblical principles is inherently analogical because of the paradigms built into them. Biblical principles are not exceptional in this regard: the Aristotelian tradition concurs that practical reasoning is rooted in the particular, and invariably refers to paradigmatic cases (Jonsen and Toulmin 1988). Contemporary Aristotelian moral philosopher Alasdair MacIntyre argues that moral principles cannot be understood without familiarity with their typical cases, and vice versa: 'principles are empty without examples' (Cosgrove 2002: 62; MacIntyre 1984*b*).

The unsystematic and *ad hoc* nature of biblical prescriptions reflects how the mind actually works. 'If moral reasoning involves...grasping moral norms through concrete examples, then the Bible's characteristic way of moving from the particular to the general (and often concentrating on the particular without moving very far toward the general) is a virtue and not a liability' (Cosgrove 2002: 67). Seeking analogies between paradigms and problem cases, therefore, is not a refuge for the logically feeble, but is 'a natural reflex of any use of principles to decide a specific moral question' (2002: 61).

Central New Testament principles are unions of paradigm and norm. The parable of the Good Samaritan enters into what it means to love as a neighbour. That pericope concludes with an imperative that invites analogous thinking: 'Go and do likewise' (Luke 10: 37). Washing the disciples' feet becomes the paradigm for the new commandment that Jesus gives the disciples at the Last Supper. It stands as a cameo for the full standard: namely, the whole life of Jesus as the norm and motivation for that love: 'Just as I have loved you, so you are to love one another' (John 13: 34). Since that 'you' includes the believer in the middle term of personal recognition, the command has continuing relevance and authority. When specific rules are expressions of an underlying moral rationale, they too can be used analogically. Specific action guides are markers or signs of their underlying rationales, which are the loci of moral authority.

Analogical reflection arises both from the narrative shape of Scripture and the fundamental imperative of discipleship which seeks to follow the way of life inaugurated in Jesus Christ. The diverse images, stories, and teachings of the gospels cohere around his life, which is the basic norm of Christian existence. The climax of the life of Jesus, his cross and resurrection, epitomizes that life and integrates the disparate sayings and happenings related in the gospels. For example, because the Beatitudes and the admonition to 'turn the other cheek' (Matt. 5: 3–12, 39) correspond to Jesus' attitudes at the climax of his life, they should be ranked ahead of the cleansing of the Temple (Matt. 20: 12–13) as paradigms for discipleship. Analogies can of course be misused, and communities need openness to the other sources, particularly to an accurate reading of the tradition and human moral wisdom, to use analogies wisely (Gustafson 1974).

The Character of the Community

Having examined how Scripture shapes individual character, we now turn to the way in which Christian communities form disciples to correspond to the ways of Jesus Christ. Moral reflection is a communal enterprise in the New Testament, a feature that is difficult for us to imagine in a more individualist culture. The New Testament's preferred location of moral reflection is the community of faith, not the isolated conscience; the subject of moral development is not the individual but the faithful community (Johnson 1983). Even though apostles like Peter and Paul exercised moral leadership, the full church was the locus of moral discernment, since it alone had the resources to hear and respond to God's word. The life of discipleship is not geared to develop virtuous individuals but to usher in the reign of God. In Pauline terms, the new life given in baptism aims to build up the Body of Christ.

One cannot adequately examine a scripture without reference to the communities and traditions in which it functions. The focus, therefore, should not be upon how individual scholars use biblical texts in moral discourse. Asking how ethicists should 'use' Scripture ignores the prior question of how Scripture shapes Christians and the communities to which they belong. It is communities that convey the central stories, symbols, and moral convictions that shape the character of their members. Even though believers belong to several communities, the community of faith ought to be the one that makes primary claim upon them (Hauerwas 1981, 1985; Hauerwas and Pinches 1997). The New Testament writings witness to the perennial struggle to bring other loyalties and commitments into line with the values of the one God manifest in Christ and present in the Spirit.

If communities play so central a role in shaping believers, ethicists need to assume a new form of research. They should examine the practices of communities of faith as they strive to interpret the word of God as communities of moral discourse. This examination will necessarily involve broader sociological and political realities. Most of the values that orient character are inculcated through relationships in communities that are central to the person's identity (O'Connell 1998). As the philosopher Josiah Royce argued (1969), every community has a cause to which it is accountable, and the members of that community hold themselves accountable to each other in terms of their common cause.

This new research will necessarily involve empirical study of the practices of actual communities, because the Christian Church does not exist generically but only in particular locations with particular traditions, spiritualities, and limitations. Denominational disagreements on neuralgic issues such as homosexuality and military intervention in the 'war on terrorism' stem not only from their methods of reading Scripture but even more from the varying polities, histories, and social locations within which biblical texts are considered. The aim of this study of diverse communities will not be to produce a single model for community discernment but to assess relatively adequate practices within the diversity and fragmentation of the Body of Christ.

Community practices   In order to draw some theological conclusions from these descriptions of how Scripture functions in congregations, it will be necessary to appeal to some common New Testament criteria. It would not be honest to endorse those ways of discerning which produce judgements that the theologian already favours. Theology reflects on the life of faith to make it more integral and consistent, just as ethics tries to do for the moral life. In order to do Christian ethics theologically, one has to reflect on the self-understanding of a community of belief, from within the circle of a lived tradition. At the same time, the theologian will have to realize that tradition's limits in living the gospel and the resources for its reform that are offered by other communions and by aspects of culture beyond the churches.

I propose New Testament practices as the normative basis for evaluating community moral discernment of Scripture for several reasons: (a) they are constitutive of authentic Christian community; (b) they are the means whereby believers come to recognize in their own lives God's presence and action that is paradigmatically expressed in Scripture; and (c) practices bring out the social dimension of virtue ethics.

First we need to define 'practices'. Every community and culture inculcates its characteristic virtues by the exemplars it holds up for emulation and the practices that form these central virtues. In MacIntyre's philosophical account, practices are socially constituted human behaviours that are worth doing in themselves, contain their own standards of excellence, and expand the human capacities of the practitioner (1984a: 187–8). He cites friendship and playing a musical instrument as examples of practices that meet this definition. These activities are not evaluated instrumentally as techniques for getting something beyond the activity. They are evaluated internally by reference to their own standards of excellence. The agent's intention is crucial in distinguishing practice from technique. If one played the saxophone primarily to pay the rent, it would be evaluated as a means to an end. Although a practice might in one order have instrumental significance (as friendships make for a more enjoyable life), that value is subordinated to the inherent value of the practice (the good of the friend and the friendship).

This notion of practices has been employed and expanded by theologians. They are beginning to analyse certain activities that Christian communities use to inculcate the Christian way of life as practices (Dykstra 1997; Volf and Bass 2002). MacIntyre's notion of practices gets relocated in the relationship to God in Christ: friendship with God subsumes and orders all the inherent and instrumental goods involved in virtuous practices. The theological criteria for practices are not only internal but are also measured as responses to God's action in Christ. These practices also have a teleological dimension beyond what MacIntyre described, since, as Paul insists, all the gifts and practices in the community are meant to build up the Body of Christ to the glory of God. Religious activities that were intended exclusively for the sanctification of the individual or gaining heavenly reward would remain at the level of techniques.

(a) The New Testament mandates a distinctive set of practices as constitutive ingredients in this way of life. For instance, baptism, eucharist, hospitality, prayer, forgiveness, sexual fidelity, service, and solidarity with the poor are not optional but necessary features of Christian communities. There is no complete list of practices in the New Testament, since they are embedded in the gospel accounts or mentioned in *ad hoc* fashion in the letters to various churches. It would be difficult to imagine a professedly Christian community that did not engage in regular forms of prayer, preaching the Word, reconciling with enemies, and serving those in need. These practices shape disciples, just as from the beginning when the first disciples entered their apprenticeship in the ways of the Kingdom of God. They were sent out to do the same works as Jesus, even if they barely comprehended what they were about (Matt. 10: 1–11: 9). Their persistent ambition, scrambling for honour, and self-importance showed how mixed their motives were. They needed the scandal of the cross and resurrection to convert their hearts to serve God's purposes in Jesus' ways.

  If the practices are ways to learn from the outside in, they are equally the human activities that help disciples learn from the inside out, because they co-operate with the divine self-giving that is the Spirit of Jesus conferred at baptism. As Luther wrote, practices are also the marks by which the Body of Christ is known to the world (1966; Braaten and Jenson 1999). Christian communities continue to shape the dispositions of their members through these regular, committed New Testament practices. To the extent that core practices are missing or inauthentic, their formation is compromised, just as it was at Corinth with its fractious eucharistic assemblies.

(b) Practices are the ordinary ways that communities educate their members to recognize God's continuing action in their lives and appreciate that grace as a continuing re-enactment of the ways the Lord acted in the history of Israel and Jesus acted towards the people of his day. They bring peoples' lives into harmony with the way of life displayed in the gospels. Rooted in the life of a believing community, these practices are the 'schools of the affections', the places where the individual's dispositions are trained to resemble the dispositions of Jesus. Through these communally based practices, they come to see the world through new eyes and become ready to respond with the mercy, obedience, justice, courage, trust, and fidelity that God has shown them in Christ and they have witnessed in the community. Reformed theology calls these the ordinary 'means of grace', because they are the usual vehicles through which grace reshapes hearts and minds.

The communal practices of authentic spirituality, largely neglected in Christian ethics, provide the link between the gospels and the moral life of Christians.

Congregational studies are needed, since different Christian traditions give priority to different New Testament practices and emphasize their corresponding virtues. Evangelicals stress baptismal commitment, the preaching of the word, and the obedience of faith. Luther strove for a balance of internal practices such as word and sacrament with external practices of witness and service (Hutter 1994; Stortz 1998). Radical Reformation churches like the Mennonites stress the non-violent cross, fraternal correction, and lives of service. Roman Catholics emphasize the Eucharist and solidarity with the poor, as well as contemplative practices that bear some resemblance to the transcendent worship that is central to Eastern Christianity. Rather than seeing these as competing versions of the one, true ecclesiology, they should be considered as different facets of the universal Body of Christ taking shape in quite distinctive cultural contexts but equally accountable as regards living a life 'worthy of the gospel of Christ' (Phil. 1: 27). The different emphases also stand as a salutary witness to the narrowness of any tradition in its customary practices.

(c) The radically social New Testament vision of the moral life might not seem to fit into the 'old wineskins' of virtue and character ethics, which tend to emphasize individual interiority and personal growth. The charges of perfectionism and individualism made against virtue ethics can be addressed by considering the virtues from the perspective of the practices that shape them. Practices do expand human capacities, but not by directly aiming at doing so. Virtuous practices engage us in values that transcend the self. While it is true that fidelity in marriage, for example, enhances the quality of life of each of the partners, the discipline of married life should draw them beyond self-interest so that the good of the marriage and family and serving the broader community become paramount. Christian fidelity in marriage, like the other virtuous practices, is not geared to create moral virtuosi but to serve the Lord in a way that corresponds to the love of Christ and God's covenant fidelity (Eph. 5: 21–33). Perfectionism is the pitfall of those who are blind to the goods of practices that transcend self-interest.

CHRISTIAN ETHICS AS A SPIRITUAL PRACTICE

Christian Reformed theologian Allen Verhey proposes that Christian ethics is best understood as a spiritual practice. His account describes his own communion and presents a normative recommendation for others. Christian ethics arises out of the spiritual practice of reading Scripture prayerfully in community and articulates the moral dynamics of this core practice of faith. It connects present experience with God's characteristic ways of acting. Reading the story of Jesus faithfully, Christians 'learn to remember, and such remembering is to own a past as one's own and to own it as constitutive of identity and community and as determinative of discern-ment' (2002: 165). Christian ethics is therefore not primarily a scholarly enterprise, but a communal practice done 'by way of reminder' of 'the story Christians love to tell and long to live' (2002: 74). The story of Jesus as recounted in the gospels and remembered by the early communities normatively shapes the community's sense of who it is and is called to become.

This 'remembering' is the inherent good at which the practice of reading Scripture aims. Verhey specifies three pairs of virtues internal to the practice that determine whether it hits the mark: holiness and sanctification, fidelity and creativity, discipline and discernment (2002: 66–71). This means that the primary test of any Christian ethics is internal to the practice itself. This does not mean that there is not also accountability to the best of human wisdom. Arguments should be logically consistent and coherent with experience. Christians should be willing and able to give a rational account of their actions to persons of good will who share their humanity and polity but not their faith. However, conceiving Christian ethics as a practice means rather that the criteria it must measure up to are moral rather than formal; they focus on the moral aspects of how the practice is done rather than on discourse alone.

As a spiritual practice, ethics moves out from a prayerful and critical reading of the story of Jesus to the issues that challenge the community of faith. Verhey invites the reader to contemplate the text of the Good Samaritan, for example, alongside investigation of the problem of access to health care. Raising the central disposition highlighted in the story as a normative stance to the problem, he writes that 'compassion leads to costly care' (2002: 481) and a commitment to access for the poor that goes beyond the logic of the marketplace. Others may see different policy approaches giving expression to compassion, but the direction should be set by the paradigmatic Samaritan. This ethics of discernment lets the story of Jesus challenge the other stories that First World Christians too often accept as normative, like the marketplace individualism of Adam Smith or the calculating fairness of John Rawls's liberal justice.

Although remembering the story of Jesus and living faithfully are worthwhile in themselves, they ought to have consequences. While the Church has to be itself, its 'self' is always oriented towards God and God's purposes in the world. Jesus proclaimed God's in-breaking reign and called disciples to set captives free, heal the sick, and reconcile the estranged in the world. For this to occur, congregations need to attend to the challenges from secular society and different parts of the globe, not merely to the familiar voices from their own race and class.

For communal discernment to succeed, the core practices must be functioning well and all the gifts of the Spirit operating in the community. Only through their combined exercise will it 'grow up in every way into him who is the head, into Christ, from whom the whole body... as each part is working properly, promotes the body's growth in building itself up in love' (Eph. 4: 15, 16). When some functions or charisms exercise disproportionate influence and others are suppressed, the discernment of the community is adversely affected. When viewed through the lens of character, therefore, Christian ethics is just as much a moral and spiritual enterprise as it is an intellectual discipline. It requires faithful communities as well as faithful scholars.

References and Suggested Reading

Barth, K. (1957). *Church Dogmatics*, II/2: *The Doctrine of God*. Edinburgh: T. & T. Clark.
Bartlett, D. (1983). *The Shape of Scriptural Authority*. Philadelphia: Fortress Press.
Bonhoeffer, D. (2003). *Discipleship*. Minneapolis: Fortress Press.
Braaten, C. E. and Jenson, R. W. (eds.) (1999). *Marks of the Body of Christ*. Grand Rapids, Mich.: Eerdmans.
Cahill, L. S. (2002). 'Christian Character, Biblical Community, and Human Values', in W. P. Brown (ed.), *Character & Scripture: Moral Formation, Community, and Biblical Interpretation*, Grand Rapids, Mich.: Eerdmans, 3–17.
Childress, J. (1984). 'Scripture and Christian Ethics', in C. Curran and R. McCormick (eds.), *Readings in Moral Theology IV: The Use of Scripture in Moral Theology*, New York: Paulist Press, 178–212.
Cosgrove, C. H. (2002). *Appealing to Scripture in Moral Debate*. Grand Rapids, Mich.: Eerdmans.
Deidun, T. (1998). 'The Bible and Christian Ethics', in B. Hoose (ed.), *Christian Ethics: An Introduction*, Collegeville, Minn.: Liturgical Press, 3–46.
Dykstra, C. (1997). 'Reconceiving Practice in Theological Inquiry and Education', in N. Murphy, B. J. Kallenberg, and M. T. Nation (eds.), *Virtues and Practices in the Christian Tradition: Christian Ethics after MacIntyre*, Harrisburg, Pa.: Trinity Press International.
Fowl, S. E. and Jones, L. G. (1991). *Reading in Communion: Scripture and Ethics in Christian Life*. Grand Rapids, Mich.: Eerdmans.
Gustafson, J. M. (1974). *Theology and Christian Ethics*. Philadelphia: Pilgrim Press.
—— (1975). *Can Ethics be Christian?* Chicago: University of Chicago Press.
Hütter, R. (1994). 'The Church as Public: Dogma, Practice, and the Holy Spirit', *Pro Ecclesia*, 3, 252–7.
Hauerwas, S. (1981). *A Community of Character: Toward a Constructive Christian Social Ethic*. Notre Dame, Ind.: University of Notre Dame Press.
—— (1985). *Character and the Christian Life: A Study in Theological Ethics*. 2nd edn. San Antonio, Tex.: Trinity University Press.
—— (1993). *Unleashing the Scripture: Freeing the Bible Captivity to America*. Nashville: Abingdon Press.

HAUERWAS, S. and PINCHES, C. (1997). *Christians Among the Virtues: Theological Conversations with Ancient and Modern Ethics*. Notre Dame Ind.: University of Notre Dame Press.

HAYS, R. B. (1996). *The Moral Vision of the New Testament: A Contemporary Introduction to Christian Ethics*. San Francisco: HarperCollins.

JOHNSON, L. T. (1983). *Decision Making in the Church: A Biblical Model*. Philadelphia: Fortress Press.

JONSEN, A. R. and TOULMIN, S. (1988). *The Abuse of Casuistry: A History of Moral Reasoning*. Berkeley: University of California Press.

KELSEY, D. (1975). *The Uses of Scripture in Recent Theology*. Philadelphia: Fortress Press.

LAURITZEN, P. (1988). 'Emotions and Religious Ethics', *Journal of Religious Ethics*, 16, 307–24.

LUTHER, M. (1959). 'The Large Catechism', in T. G. Tappert and J. Pelikan (eds.), *The Book of Concord: The Confessions of the Evangelical Lutheran Church*, Philadelphia: Fortress Press, 357–461.

—— (1966). 'On the Councils and the Church', in E. W. Gritsch (ed.), *Luther's Works*, xl, St Louis, Mo.: Concordia, 3–178.

MCDONALD, J. I. H. (1993). *Biblical Interpretation and Christian Ethics*. New York: Cambridge University Press.

MACINTYRE, A. (1984a). *After Virtue: A Study in Moral Theory*, 2nd edn. Notre Dame, Ind.: University of Notre Dame Press.

—— (1984b). 'Does Practical Reasoning Rest on a Mistake?', *The Monist*, 67, 498–513.

NIEBUHR, H. R. (1960). *The Meaning of Revelation*. New York: Macmillan.

O'CONNELL, T. E. (1998). *Making Disciples: A Handbook of Christian Moral Formation*. New York: Crossroads.

OGLETREE, T. W. (1983). *The Use of the Bible in Christian Ethics*. Philadelphia: Fortress Press.

OUTKA, G. (1972). *Agape: An Ethical Analysis*. New Haven: Yale University Press.

—— (1992). 'Universal Love and Impartiality', in E. N. Santurri and W. Werpehowski (eds.), *The Love Commandments: Essays in Christian Ethics and Moral Philosophy*, Washington: Georgetown University Press, 1–103.

PATTE, D. (1995). *Ethics of Biblical Interpretation: A Reevaluation*. Louisville, Ky.: Westminster John Knox Press.

PLEINS, J. D. (2001). *The Social Visions of the Hebrew Bible: A Theological Introduction*. Louisville, Ky.: Westminster John Knox Press.

RICOEUR, P. (1995). *Figuring the Sacred: Religion, Narrative, and Imagination*. Philadelphia: Fortress Press.

ROYCE, J. (1969). 'The Philosophy of Loyalty', in J. J. McDermott (ed.), *Josiah Royce: Basic Writings*, II, Chicago: University of Chicago Press, 915–1013.

SALIERS, D. E. (1979). 'Liturgy and Ethics: Some New Beginnings', *Journal of Religious Ethics*, 7, 173–89.

—— (1980). *The Soul in Paraphrase: Prayer and the Religious Affections*. New York: Seabury Press.

SEDGWICK, T. F. (1999). *The Christian Moral Life: Practices of Piety*. Grand Rapids, Mich.: Eerdmans.

SITTLER, J. (1998). *The Structure of Christian Ethics*. Louisville, Ky.: Westminster John Knox Press.

SOBRINO, J. (1993). *Jesus the Liberator: A Historical Theological View.* Maryknoll, NY: Orbis Books.

SPOHN, W. C. (1995*a*). 'Morality on the Way of Discipleship: The Use of Scripture in *Veritatis Splendor*', in M. Alsop and J. O'Keefe (eds.), Veritatis Splendor: *American Responses*, Kansas City, Mo.: Sheed and Ward, 83–105.

——(1995*b*). *What Are They Saying about Scripture and Ethics?*, 2nd edn. New York: Ramsey; Toronto: Paulist Press.

——(1999) *Go and Do Likewise: Jesus and Ethics.* New York: Continuum.

STORTZ, M. E. (1998). 'Practicing Christians: Prayer as Formation', in K. L. Bloomquist and J. R. Stumme (eds.), *The Promise of Lutheran Ethics*, Minneapolis: Fortress Press, 55–73.

VERHEY, ALLEN (2002). *Remembering Jesus: Christian Community, Scripture, and the Moral Life.* Grand Rapids, Mich.: Eerdmans.

VOLF, M. and BASS, D. C. (2002). *Practicing Theology: Beliefs and Practices in Christian Life.* Grand Rapids, Mich.: Eerdmans.

CHAPTER 7

....

DIVINE COMMANDS

....

LOIS MALCOLM

A DIVINE command ethics holds that morality is contingent on God's will. An act, state of affairs, or character trait—or some combination of these—is moral (right or wrong, good or evil) if God wills it. Some divine command ethics hold the extreme position that only what God commands or prohibits is moral. Others prefer the label 'theological voluntarism' because it focuses on what God wills in general, rather than simply on what God commands or prohibits (Murphy 2002*b*). Divine command ethics or theological voluntarism can either be normative (what one should do) or meta-ethical (why one should be moral in the first place).

The classic critique of divine command ethics is found in the *Euthyphro* dialogue (1948: 11). Paraphrased for monotheists, the question is: Does God command something because (a) it is good, or is it good because (b) God commands it? If (a) is true, then it appears that morality is independent of God's will.

Conversely, if (b) is true, then it appears that there is no independent standard for accepting or rejecting God's commands. This would seem to make acceptance of God's commands arbitrary and capricious. How does one judge whether a command is consistent with what is morally right? This question is especially acute for believers who take seriously the normative content of biblical injunctions, since they often differ on how to interpret and apply those injunctions to everyday life. For example, Protestants and Roman Catholics place greater weight on different kinds of normative sources; Protestants traditionally have stressed Scripture, whereas Roman Catholics stress, in addition to Scripture, the magisterium and personal revelation in prayer (Idziak 1979).

Moreover, if (b) is true, then it appears that there is no basis for identifying God's moral qualities apart from simply saying that God wills them. If a divine command ethics relies solely on God's will and not on claims about what is right or good, then what is the basis for praising God's moral qualities when there is no independent moral standard independent of divine will? Are we simply equating God's goodness with God's will? If there is no independent standard of goodness for evaluating God's will, do we not simply have a moral tautology? And if this is, indeed, a moral tautology—that God's goodness is simply the same thing as God's will or power—then does this not simply valorize omnipotence? This is perhaps the most poignant criticism of a divine command ethics. It asks whether such an ethic does not, in fact, define the good in terms of the glorification of ultimate power, and whether—in an age of heightened technological power and worldwide ethnic conflict—this is, indeed, the best way to chart the connection between divine power and finite goodness (Schweiker 1998: 247).

Most recent defenders of divine commands (following their nominalist predecessors in the late medieval period) have accepted the terms of the dilemma Socrates posed in the *Euthyphro* and seek to offer a cognitive defence of the plausibility of divine command ethics or theological voluntarism on philosophical grounds (see, e.g., Adams 1987c, 1999; Murphy 2002b; and Quinn 1990, 1991a). In contrast, the major biblical and theological traditions that deal with divine commands offer a different construal of the relationship between divine commands and conceptions of the good from that in Socrates' dilemma. By way of a genealogy of these traditions, I aim to bring to the fore the range of conceptual resources they offer for reasoning publicly about divine commands and to demonstrate that they reconstrue the terms of Euthyphro's dilemma with a performative—and, indeed, one might say, counterfactual—resolution to the age-old problem of the conflict between power and goodness.

I begin with the chief biblical traditions that inform Christian theological reflection on divine commands: Moses (and the Ten Commandments), Jesus (and the double-love commands), and Paul (and his understanding of the law's functions within human existence). Next, I trace the development of the nominalist focus on divine commands within the context of earlier theological contributions (by Irenaeus, Augustine, and Thomas Aquinas). I then examine how the Reformers (Martin Luther and John Calvin) appropriate—and nuance—this nominalist understanding of divine commands, and briefly discuss their influence on strains of modern and contemporary forms of voluntarist thought. My own constructive contribution, offered by way of a critical appropriation of Karl Barth's theology of divine commands, seeks to depict a 'theonomous' account of divine commands (a term that will be defined in the course of the argument)—one that presupposes a Trinitarian understanding of God and the Reformers' distinctions among the 'uses of the law'.

BIBLICAL TRADITIONS

Within Judaism and Christianity the core experience at the heart of any divine command theory is the experience of the people of Israel on Mount Sinai (Levenson 1985). The experience is described with a range of vivid metaphors (Exod. 19: 16–25)—from thunder, lightning, a mysterious cloud on the mountain, and a blast of a trumpet (which could be a hurricane) to a description of a mountain wrapped in smoke (which could be a volcano). There is quaking and the people tremble. Indeed, they are warned not to 'break through' to YHWH or 'look' at what is going on, so that he does not 'break out' against them (vv. 21, 22; Levenson 1985: 15).

There are two contrasting movements in this experience. The first is an 'intersection' between God and Israel; they meet at Mount Sinai, where Moses, Israel's representative to God, ascends to meet God. The second is a 'barrier' between God and Israel, which, if transgressed, will turn this moment of 'destiny' into one of 'disaster' (Levenson 1985: 15, 16). Rudolf Otto, the theologian and historian of religion, describes the twofold quality of this experience as one of 'mysterium tremendum et fascinans', a Latin expression which can be rendered as 'a fearsome and fascinating mystery' (Otto 1923). The 'indivisible charm and threat' of this experience makes it 'eminently exotic, lying outside the boundaries of what is familiar' (Levenson 1985: 16).

Nonetheless, this theophany cannot be divorced from the larger context of God's relation to Israel as covenant partner. The covenant between YHWH and the Israelites hews to the pattern of an ancient Near Eastern vassal treaty. The overlord offers sustenance and protection; the vassals offer exclusive devotion (worship of one God) and acts of fealty (observance of the commandments). This means, on the one hand, that God's right to rule needs to be established. Thus, the Decalogue (the Ten Commandments) is introduced with YHWH's claim to have brought the Israelites out of slavery in Egypt (Exod. 20: 2). On the other hand, the commandments (*mitsvot*) are given to a people who are capable of responding as *real partners* in this covenant. As such, they are addressed as a community that already shares patterns of linguistic, social, and political organization that extend over time and space (Novak 2001). God's command is not merely experienced within the transient immediacy of a dyadic encounter (Novak 2001: 472).

Even more deeply, within the canon of the Old Testament (or Hebrew Bible) traditions about 'command' (e.g., in Exod. 20) already presuppose traditions about 'creation' (e.g., Gen. 1–3). As Paul Althaus has pointed out, within biblical thinking, God's command (*Gebot*; cf. 'commandments' as *mitsvot*) is a 'summons' or 'call' to live out of the fundamental 'offer' (*Angebot*) or 'gift' of truth, life, and freedom that lies at the heart of creaturely existence (1966: 8–11). The command itself is a means for respecting human freedom, the human capacity to respond—or not respond—to this offer or gift.

Further, this summons does not come in a vacuum but presupposes that all creatures derive intrinsic worth from the fecundity of God's life. This is what lies at the heart of all Jewish and Christian criticisms of forms of Gnosticism—that revelation does not take one *out* of the world but comes *to* and *for* us *in* the world (Novak 2001: 475). It lies at the heart of Jewish and Christian conceptions of 'natural law', which in their classic forms (e.g., in Aquinas or Maimonides) are not understood to contradict divine commands (Fox 1990). What gives the commands their moral and ethical force is not simply that God issues them, but that they resonate with our deepest creaturely sense of what is good, true, alive, and freeing (Althaus 1966). God is not only present in our world in intensified moments of command; rather, God permeates all of our creaturely experience. In the Scripture itself, we find God named as YHWH ('Lord') and *elohim* ('God', or 'divinity'), the latter expressing a more mediated, less personal, sense of the divine presence within creation (Novak 2001: 475; see Gen. 20: 11; Exod. 1: 17, 3: 13–14, 5: 2).

God's covenant relationship with human beings, with its call for obedience, leads not to sheer 'heteronomy'—the strictly external meeting of a demand. Rather, as the Hebrew Bible scholar Jon Levenson has suggested (1994: 142 ff.), it can be characterized as a 'dialectic of covenantal theonomy'—drawing on Paul Tillich's concept of 'theonomy' as a means for moving beyond either a false 'heteronomy' or a false 'autonomy' (1951: 85 ff.). If 'heteronomy' means a law coming from an external authority (*hetero* (other) + *nomos* (law)) and 'autonomy' a law coming from one's self (*auto* (self) + *nomos* (law)), then 'theonomy' means a law coming from God (*theos* (God) + *nomos* (law)). What one finds in the story of redemption from Egypt and the Sinaitic covenant—and the Abrahamic covenant that precedes them—is a dynamic whereby 'those who stand under covenantal obligation by nature and necessity are continually called upon to adopt that relationship by free decision' (Levenson 1994: 148). Thus, Levenson asserts, God's omnipotence in the Hebrew Bible is best understood not as a 'static attribute' but as a 'dramatic enactment' whereby God's absolute power realizes itself in 'achievement' and 'relationship' (1994: p. xiv).

This 'dialectic of covenantal theonomy' raises the same questions that the *Euthyphro* raises, but it does so not from the standpoint of an external observer but from the standpoint of a God and a people who are *deeply engaged* in relationship with each other. In this relationship, there is real movement back and forth between both parties. On the one hand, in Genesis 22, Abraham is told to 'bind' Isaac—a prime example of human *heteronomy* before God's inscrutable command. On the other hand, in Genesis 18, Abraham pleads with God not to destroy Sodom—a prime example of human *autonomy* over divine decrees. God saves Sodom because Abraham appeals: 'Shall not the judge of all the earth do what is just?' (Gen. 18: 25). In the larger theology of the Hebrew Bible, or Old Testament, human judgement neither 'replaces the inscrutable God who commands' nor merely 'becomes superfluous within the life lived in faithfulness to him' (Levenson

1994: 153). Rather, both *obeying* and *arguing* are depicted as important aspects of humanity's relationship to God (Levenson 1994: 153–6).

In the Gospels of the New Testament, Jesus of Nazareth also treats divine decrees—and their articulation in law—as something to be *obeyed* and *argued* about. Jesus is an observant Jew who came not to 'destroy' but to 'fulfil' the law (Matt. 5: 17). None the less, in the tradition of the prophets who condemned 'empty' worship and the teaching of 'human precepts as doctrines' (Mark 7: 7; cf. Isa. 1: 10–20, 58: 1–4; Amos 5: 21–4), he frequently challenges those who 'neglect the weightier demands of the law: justice and mercy and faith' (Matt. 23: 23). Moreover, in the tradition of the lament psalms, he expresses his hesitations about God's will for his own life, as the Passion narratives depict so vividly—from the scene in the Garden of Gethsemane (Mark 14: 36) to the scene on the cross at Golgotha (Mark 15: 34).

Jesus' teaching on the law summarizes the two great 'love commands' found in the Hebrew Scripture, or Old Testament (Mark 12: 28–34; cf. Matt. 22: 34–40; Luke 10: 25–8). Reiterating the covenantal focus on the intrinsic connection between God's rule, on the one hand, and just and merciful relationships among people, on the other, these commands lie at the heart of any Christian response to Euthyphro's dilemma. They affirm that the first commandment—'love the Lord your God' with all your heart, soul, mind, and strength (cf. Deut. 6: 4–5)—cannot be divorced from the second—'love your neighbour as yourself' (cf. Lev. 19: 18; see also Rom. 13: 9; Gal. 5: 14; Jas. 2: 8). The second command echoes the ethical standard of the 'golden rule' given elsewhere in both the Jewish and the Christian Scriptures—'Do to others as you would have them to do you' (Luke 6: 31, NRSV; cf. Matt. 7: 12; see also Lev. 19: 18; Tobit 4: 15). To recognize that there are no greater commandments than these is, according to Jesus, to be 'not far from the kingdom of God' (Mark 12: 34). In addition to reaffirming God's covenant at Sinai, this summary reiterates prophetic injunctions that argued for an intrinsic connection between 'love and justice' and 'waiting continually for your God' (Hos. 12: 6; cf. Mic. 6: 8). They are, in turn, reiterated throughout the New Testament—especially in Paul's appeals regarding the relationship between 'freedom' and 'love' (e.g., in Gal. 5: 13–15) and the Johannine focus on the link between 'God's love' and 'a brother or sister in need' (1 John 3: 11–17; John 13: 31–5).

Although Jesus' teaching reaffirms Old Testament covenantal themes, his interpretation of God's commands is rigorist and eschatological. There is an apocalyptic urgency in his call to participate in the reign of God that is 'breaking out' among the people. Disciples are to forgo normal kinship ties and be ready to give their wealth to the poor (Mark 10: 17–31; cf. Matt. 19: 16–30; Luke 18: 18–30). One's 'neighbour' includes not only friends but also enemies (Luke 6: 27–36); it is the 'Samaritan'—an outsider regarded with hostility—who exemplifies what it means to be a neighbour (Luke 10: 25–37). Finally, Jesus radicalizes specific injunctions— one is to avoid not simply murder but also anger, not simply adultery but also lust, and so on (Matt. 5: 21–48). Jesus' call is to be 'perfect ... as your heavenly Father is perfect' (Matt. 5: 48).

The other major New Testament thinker on the commandments is Paul, whose analysis of how the law functions within human existence—from three distinct vantage points—was to have a profound influence on the Reformers many centuries later. First, in line with Jewish and Stoic influences, he presupposes that God's 'eternal power and divine nature' has been understood and seen by all people through creation, and not simply through divine revelation or command (Rom. 1: 20; cf. Wisd. 13: 1–9; see also Acts 17).

Second, he argues that even if all people—Jews and Gentiles—have had access to the law, all none the less are under the power of sin (Rom. 3: 1–20; cf. Ps. 14: 2–3). At the root of their sin is the refusal to 'honour' (or 'glorify') God as God; this is the source of all other sins or vices (see, e.g., Rom. 1: 29 for one list; cf. Gal. 5: 19–23 among many other lists of vices in the New Testament). As a result, they are conflicted within themselves; the law is impotent to help them out of this conflict (Rom. 7: 12, 14; Gal. 2: 21). Only justification by Christ's grace as a gift can save them (Rom. 3: 24).

Finally, Paul contends that, in spite of its impotence, the law is not to be overthrown (Rom. 3: 31). Indeed, a major portion of Paul's letters consists of appeals to live according to the 'law of the Spirit of life' (the sphere in which the Spirit is dominant) and not according to the 'flesh' (the sphere in which sin is dominant) (see, e.g., Rom. 8 and 12: 1, 2). It is only by being 'transformed' by the 'renewing' of one's mind—and thus enabled to see things from the vantage point of the new age (or world) ushered in by Christ's Spirit—that one can 'discern' God's 'will', which Paul equates with what is 'good and acceptable and perfect' (Rom. 12: 2).

HISTORY OF CHRISTIAN THEOLOGY

Several early contributions to our overall thinking about divine commands are important to note. Irenaeus's major insight, which he articulated in his critique of Marcion and the Gnostics, was that a Jewish understanding of creation still holds for Christians. God's creation is good, and a natural law is accessible to all people through their observation of creation. Further, he argued for the normative authority for Christians of the Old Testament (the Hebrew Bible) and thus, by implication, of the revelation of the Ten Commandments (see *Against the Heresies*).

Augustine made two important contributions (see, e.g., *The City of God*). First, he interprets Jesus' double-love commands by way of a distinction between *caritas* (love) and *cupiditas* (concupiscence). With *caritas*, one loves others (and even one's self) for God's sake—and therefore as ends to be enjoyed in themselves simply because they have been endowed by God with intrinsic worth. With *cupiditas*, one loves others (and, again, even one's self) simply as a means for one's own purposes—and therefore without regard for their inherent value.

A second contribution evolved in his conflicts over grace with Pelagius. Earlier in his life, Augustine affirmed that we are able, as creatures, to perceive and enact the law—a position quite close to that later held by Pelagius. Later in his own life, Augustine increasingly stressed our dependence on divine election with regard to matters of grace and salvation, and with regard to our capacity to perceive and enact the good.

Augustine's understanding of grace was to have a profound influence on Western Christianity, although those who claimed him as a predecessor found themselves arguing for either the 'mind' or the 'will' as the central locus within human existence for encountering God. In his *Summa Theologiae*, Aquinas argued for the former, contending that human beings are rational beings who participate in natural law by way of reason—a natural law that reflects what inheres in God's mind. Revealed 'divine law' does not contradict this natural law; it only offers a clearer picture of it. Even his explanations of cases in the Bible where God appears to command what is irrational or against natural law are based on the assumption that God would not will what is contrary to God's nature. When seen from the standpoint of God's own 'mind', such commands do not violate God's nature (see, e.g., *Summa Theologiae* 1.2, q. 94, a. 5, ad. 2).

By contrast, Franciscans like Bonaventure, a contemporary of Aquinas, stressed the centrality of love in talking about humanity's encounter with God—although he still presupposed universal patterns in creation that could, at least initially, lead one to God (see *The Soul's Journey into God*). Franciscans in the late medieval period, however, tended toward nominalism, the view that individuals are the primary reality, and universal concepts mere mental descriptions of features shared by individuals. Theological expressions of nominalism drew on the biblical idea of covenant in order to stress the fact that God is wholly free in relationship to the world and could (and theoretically still can) create other physical and moral laws than those now operative. In spite of their stress on radical divine freedom, however, most late medieval nominalists also held that God has bound God's 'absolute power' (*potentia absoluta*) through creation and revelation to act in certain ways. On the basis of this binding of God's freedom—God's 'ordained power' (*potentia ordinata*)—God can be trusted as reliable.

The ethics of divine commands became a primary focus for theologians and philosophers in this late medieval period—the most prominent being William of Occam, Gabriel Biel, Jean Gerson, and John Duns Scotus (see Idziak 1979: 1–38). We note what the Cambridge Platonist Ralph Cudworth—who opposed divine command ethics—wrote about them several centuries later: They 'zealously contend…that there is nothing absolutely, intrinsically, and naturally good and evil, just and unjust, antecedently to any positive command or prohibition of God; but that the arbitrary will and pleasure of God... by its commands and prohibitions is the first and the only rule and measure thereof' (*Treatise Concerning Eternal and Immutable Morality*, quoted in Idziak 1979: 3). Arguments for a divine command ethics rested on theological beliefs about God's omnipotence and ultimate freedom, on the one hand, and humanity's dependence on God as creator, on the other. Much more historical work needs to be done analysing what these later medieval thinkers actually taught about divine commands, for their statements are often embedded in discussions of other theological and ethical questions. Further, they did not all teach the same thing; for example, some have questioned whether Scotus is appropriately termed a divine command ethicist, since he also seems to have had a place for natural law.

Nonetheless, a new idea of God emerged with the rise of nominalist philosophy and its critique of Aristotelian metaphysics—along with, we should add, the devastation of the Black Death and the papal schism that brought the medieval world and the coherence of its world-view to an end. This God overturns all eternal standards of truth and justice, and puts the will in place of reason, and freedom in place of necessity and order (Gillespie 1996: 24, 25). Indeed, it can be argued that Luther's crisis of faith came about precisely because of his uncertainty about God's goodness, on the one hand, and about his own capacity to will the right response to God's will, on the other. In response to this uncertainty, Luther stressed a radical disjunction between law and gospel in his early theology: the law 'kills, curses, accuses, judges, and demands'; by contrast, the gospel of Jesus Christ brings forgiveness of sins, life, and salvation. By highlighting the law's accusatory character, this understanding of the law further developed Pauline insights into the character of sin as a failure to 'glorify' (Paul) or 'trust' (Luther) God. The reason why the law can only accuse, according to Luther, is that human beings will misuse even the 'best' (the law and wisdom) in the 'worst' manner—to justify themselves rather than trust in God (see the *Heidelberg Disputation (1518)*; Forde 1997).

By the mid-1520s, in reaction to the rise of the more radical wing of the Reformation—which held to a more antinomian view of the law than Luther—he expanded, but did not replace, his earlier dualistic understanding of law and gospel with a more dialectical conception of God's twofold rule (as law and gospel) in two kingdoms (spiritual and temporal) (Lazareth 2001). This expansion reached its climax with the 'double use of the law' (*duplex usus legis*). The first is the civic use (*usus civilis*): God ordains civic laws in order to restrain transgressions within human communities. We should note that Luther's understanding of this use is not quite as positive as Aquinas's understanding of natural law, since its primary function is to restrain destructive behaviour—although he does in some contexts (e.g., in the *Large Catechism*) have a more positive understanding of how God works through patterns within creation. The second is the 'theological use' (*usus theologicus*), which he captured very vividly in his earlier work. Its function is simply to reveal to human beings their sin and the well-deserved wrath of God, and to drive them to God's Word, which justifies sinners in Christ. It is only on the basis of the freedom which this justification gives that Christians can—living out of the fruits and gifts of the Spirit—attend to their 'neighbour's' need (since they no longer need to use the neighbour as a means for their own justification) (cf. Meilaender 2003).

By contrast, Philip Melanchthon introduced a 'threefold function of the law' (*triplex usus legis*) in his *Christian Doctrine* (*Loci Communes* (1535)). In addition to Luther's two uses, Melanchthon argued for a third, 'didactic use' (*usus didacticus*) to instruct the regenerate morally. John Calvin followed Melanchthon, arguing, in his *Institutes of the Christian Religion* (1536), that 'the gospel did not so entirely supplant the entire law as to bring forward a different way of salvation'. Rather, the gospel 'confirms' and 'satisfies' what the law had promised (book 2, ch. 9, sect. 4, and ch. 10, sect. 2). Thus, the gospel differs from the law only in its clarity of manifestation. Calvin presupposes Luther's civil and theological uses of the law (though he reverses their order), but then argues that the law's principle use is its third use—its 'didactic' use. In the hearts of the faithful among whom the Spirit of God already lives and reigns, this use of the law both (1) instructs Christians so that their understanding is in better conformity with God's will and (2) exhorts them so that their obedience in Christ is confirmed, and disobedience restrained. In addition to a stress on the third use of the law, Calvin also placed a greater stress than did Luther on the human capacity to know God and God's laws through creation (through the *sensus divinitatis*, sense of divinity, in all people, and what he called 'common grace'—as opposed to 'special grace') and on the possibility of establishing a just Christian society (or commonwealth) in this world.

MODERN AND CONTEMPORARY PROPOSALS

This Reformation legacy has influenced at least two strains of voluntarism (forms of thought focused on the primacy of the will) in modern moral thought: theological and philosophical. These strains are brought to our attention by two types of critics of divine command ethics: modern liberals (versus the theological strain) and traditional Roman Catholics (versus the philosophical strain).

First, modern liberals criticize the Reformation's influence on Puritan morality because of its heteronomous character; it relies on divine will rather than human autonomy. Among others, Kai Nielsen represents a generation of secular ethicists who argued that each person must make his own ethical choices, with his own finite and fallible awareness, and to do this, one needed to presuppose that morality was logically independent of religion. The viability of religious belief depends on our sense of good and bad, and not vice versa (Nielsen 1961). These ethicists sought to liberate themselves from the kind of Puritan theology that sought to assert, and as far as possible prove, that 'the arbitrary will of God must also be good' (Miller 1954: ch. 1).

Second, traditional Roman Catholics criticize the Reformation's influence on the voluntarism of much contemporary ethical thought because its focus on the will—human and divine—appears to undermine any kind of rational reflection on the *telos*, or end, of morality toward which human natural desires also aim (see Pinckaers 1995: chs. 10, 12, 13; see Mouw 1991: chs. 3, 4). Jacques Maritain, for example, combined a critique of the voluntarism and individualism in modern ethical thought with a critique of Luther's celebration of the 'individual will... stand[ing] solitary and naked before God and Christ' (1955: 18). In his footsteps, Alasdair MacIntyre (1981) criticized the 'Occamism' of Reformation thinking, with its punctiliar focus on the will's choices rather than rational reflection on the true end, or *telos*, of human desires. In addition to these critics, many have noted how Immanuel Kant's deontological ethics, with its stress on freedom's recognition of the categorical imperative abstracted from all prudential ends, epitomizes a secularized appropriation of a Reformation divine command ethics (cf. Kant 1996). Yet others have drawn parallels between Thomas Hobbes's conception of the state as the Leviathan and Calvin's conception of God as an ideal monarch of a theocracy (see Mouw 1991: ch. 6).

If Kant echoes the Reformers' understanding of the law's positive functions (as, e.g., civic or didactic), then a number of post-Kantian thinkers can be seen as echoing the law's accusatory function. Paul Tillich uses the term 'transmoral' to describe Luther's depiction of the conscience's experience of *Anfechtungen* (tempting attacks) and *Angst* (dread) in the face of God's wrath, on the one hand, and of joy in the face of its justification, on the other (1963: 77–81). Judgement stands 'beneath' the conscience; justification stands 'above' it. He goes on to describe Friedrich Nietzsche's 'will to power' as yet another example of such a 'transmoral conscience', since its creative and destructive power lies above morality. Likewise, he describes Martin Heidegger's 'call of conscience' as defined in relation to our 'being toward death' as yet another 'transmoral' appeal (Tillich 1963: 77–81). Finally, Søren Kierkegaard's interpretation of God's command to Abraham to sacrifice Isaac as a 'teleological suspension of the ethical' can also be classed as 'transmoral'—even though it results not from God's wrath against sin but simply from a command that confounds human ethical reflection (Kierkegaard 1983).

Most contemporary defenders of divine command ethics have tended to be philosophers who seek to defend the *theological* strain of voluntarist thought (in response to critics like Nielsen (1961)). Their defence, however, is philosophical—seeking to demonstrate how theological voluntarism accounts for *formal* features of morality that are not accountable on other grounds (Murphy 2002*b*). One argument, for example, contends that it offers an account of the non-naturalistic character of morality—the sense in which it appears to come not merely from natural properties (i.e., descriptions of natural states of affairs) but from non-natural ones (Adams 1973; cf. Moore 1903: sect. 13). Related to this is the argument that theological voluntarism accounts for the 'overridingness' of morality—the fact that it demands absolute allegiance over all other claims (Murphy 2002b). Divine command ethics or theological voluntarism provides an account of why moral norms have more binding power than other values (e.g., prudential values) when they conflict (cf. Sidgwick [1907]: 1981: 497–509). A third argument contends that theological voluntarism offers an account of the 'impartiality' of morality—the sense in which it takes not merely a personal perspective, but an impartial one, the point of view, in Henry Sidgwick's words, of 'the universe' ([1907]: 1981: 382). Since the 'universe' *per se* does not have a perspective, theological voluntarism accounts for morality's impartiality by claiming that it arises from the demands of someone who is not only impartial or objective but who also has a supreme love for all creatures, the proper objects of morality (Murphy 2002b).

These defences have focused on how theological voluntarism accounts for theories of obligation, and not on how it accounts for other normative properties (e.g., theories of value). Indeed, they have gone so far as to 'modify' their accounts of divine commands by allowing for other grounds of normative reasoning even in their evaluation of divine commands. Robert M. Adams, for example, has contended that if God were to command something cruel, this would imply that God did not have the character of being loving, implying that it would not be wrong to disobey the command. In his more formal terms, 'when I say "it is wrong to do X," (at least part of) of what I *mean* is that it is contrary to God's command to do X. "It is wrong to do X" *implies* "it is contrary to God's command to do X." But "it is contrary to God's command to do X" implies "it is wrong to do X" only if it is assumed that God has the character I believe him to have, of loving his human creatures' (1987c: 100; cf. his later work, Adams 1999).

This, implies, however, that a divine command ethics is partly dependent on a person's independent evaluation of what God has commanded. Adams concedes this point, but maintains that it does not entail abandoning a divine command ethics. One can still argue that the non-naturalistic character of obligation is best accounted for by a divine command ethics, even if one does not maintain that *all* value concepts must be understood in terms of God's commands (1987c). None the less, as William Schweiker has pointed out, such a modified divine command ethics does not provide a *theological* account of God's goodness. Although it 'properly shifts the discussion of the character of God from power to goodness'—by allowing for *values* to be considered in the evaluation of God's commands—it does not provide a means for integrating theologically 'judgments about moral rightness and wrongness' with 'inquiry into nonmoral values' (Schweiker 1998: 256). In fact, '[i]t leaves open the question of how we are to think about the relation between

God's goodness [God's being] and judgments about actions [what God commands]' (Schweiker 1998: 256).

By contrast, Barth, the foremost divine command theologian in the twentieth century, offers a robust *theological* account of the relation between *God's being* (God's goodness or love) and *God's act* (God's freedom and power). Drawing on both Calvinist and Lutheran strains of Reformation thought, Barth retrieves the Reformers' stress on the Word of God (as 'law and gospel', or 'command' and 'election') by way of Kant's and Kierkegaard's conceptual categories. In line with this complex of influences, his divine command ethics is defined over against modern liberal and Roman Catholic theories of value, which, in his view, do not do justice to the sheer autonomy and otherness of God's command (1957: 520–32).

His position clearly falls on the nominalist side of the Euthyphro debate.

'When God confronts man with his command,' he argues, 'what he wills is purely *ad hoc* actions and attitudes which can only be thought of as historically *contingent* even in their necessity, acts of obedience to be performed on the spot in a specific way, *pure decisions* the meaning of which is not open to discussion, because they do not point to a higher law, but is rather contained in the fact that God has *decided* in this way and spoken accordingly, so that human decisions can only *obey* or *disobey* the divine decision.' (1957: 674, my italics)

Nonetheless, Barth gives content to this command (1957: 552–606). Power as power has no divine claim on us. The divine claim that addresses us has content—Jesus Christ. Jesus Christ gives God's command its 'teleological power'. God's command (the Law) is merely the form in which we hear and respond to the human good, the Word of God (the Gospel). The inner meaning and ground of the command of God (the act of God being God) is Jesus Christ, the Word of God (God's being-in-act). God's very *being* is defined by an *act of grace* founded in divine election and not by the exercise of power. God's 'essence' and God's 'act' are one and the same thing. 'God gives Himself to man entirely in his revelation. But not in such a way as to give Himself a prisoner to man. He remains free, in operating, in giving Himself' (1957: 674). Yet this freedom is not merely the 'meaningless idea of a divine *potentia inordinata*'; rather, it is 'the *potentia ordinata* that is the real freedom and omnipotence of God' (1957: 606).

Yet, as Schweiker has observed, although Barth offers a theological understanding of the relationship between goodness and power, he none the less defines both (i.e., God's election—'goodness'—and God's command—'power') in relation to Jesus Christ (1998: 259). In doing this, does Barth not collapse all of ethics into Christology? Is the moral value of creaturely existence—its goodness in and of itself—defined solely in terms of humanity's election in Jesus Christ? On the one hand, Barth contends that 'power as power' has no claim upon us. Yet, if the goodness that defines this power is defined solely in relation to God's election in Jesus Christ, does Barth not, once again, collapse all human goodness into divine will? Are we not, once again, left with the tautology that divine goodness is to be equated with divine will? If this is true, does he not return us to yet another version of Euthyphro's dilemma: that the good is only good because God's wills (elects) it to be so in Jesus Christ?

At the heart of these questions is the question of whether Barth does justice to the status of creaturely goodness in and of itself (as creation) or whether he has collapsed all of creation—and therefore also ethics, which is about the human good—into Christology. This is a central difficulty in Barth's ethics—a criticism raised across the theological spectrum, by Roman Catholics (e.g., Werpehowski (1981)), Lutherans (e.g., Wingren (1961)), Reformed (e.g., R. Niebuhr (1941)), and, most recently, Jews (e.g., Novak (2001)). In Thomistic categories, Barth appears to collapse natural law and grace. In the Reformers' categories, he not only collapses law and gospel, but also fails to distinguish among the uses of the law. He collapses the 'civil' and 'didactic' uses of the law (having only a 'Christian' ethic) and fails to distinguish the law's accusatory function from these other uses.

Richard Mouw has helpfully attempted to broaden the focus that Barth narrows Christologically. Mouw does this with a thought-provoking sketch of a Trinitarian understanding of divine commands (1991: 150–75). Drawing on a classic essay by H. R. Niebuhr, which had criticized the 'christomonism' of Barth's ethics and argued for a full-bodied Trinitarian account of the ethical task (1946), Mouw argues for a Calvinist divine command ethics that attends to all three Persons of the Trinity, and not only to Christ (the Second Person). With regard to the Father (the First Person), Mouw discusses, in addition to Roman Catholic appeals to natural law, Abraham Kuyper's Calvinist appeals to 'world-order' and creational 'laws' established by the First Person Creator. With regard to the Spirit (the Third Person), he discusses the contributions of Pentecostals and charismatics, on the one hand, and liberationists, on the other—both of which groups address God's immanent presence in ethical agency.

DIVINE COMMANDS AND A THEONOMOUS DIALECTIC

To summarize the argument so far, Barth's theology of divine commands helps us rethink the terms of Euthyphro's dilemma. He contends that God's command is to be obeyed above all else. Yet he also contends that the inner meaning—the 'teleological power'—of this command is God's election in Jesus Christ. Thus, he presupposes a standard of goodness beyond sheer power. Most importantly, he thinks God's *act* in relation to God's *being*, thus offering an *inner theological* ground for relating ultimate (or divine) power and ultimate (or divine) goodness. Nevertheless, as Schweiker and others have pointed out, his dogmatics defines all ethics as a moment within Christology. Thus, following Mouw, a more explicitly *Trinitarian* account of God's commands provides a means for thinking about the relation of divine commands to doctrines of creation and the Spirit.

In accord with our reading of classic biblical texts on divine commands and the Reformers' conception of the 'uses of the law', this Trinitarian corrective enables us to outline an understanding of divine commands that entails both 'heteronomous' and 'autonomous' moments within a larger 'theonomous' dialectic. On the one hand (with regard to its 'autonomous' moments), God's command cannot be divorced from the biblical themes of covenant and creation. Not only is an 'other' addressed by the command (as implied by 'covenant'), but the command (*Gebot*) is a summons to live out of the offer (*Angebot*) that lies at the heart of one's creaturely existence (as implied by 'creation') (Althaus 1966). First, God's command respects humanity's freedom; we have a will that can respond or not respond, and thus are real partners in the enactment of the command. Second, God's command comes not only from outside us, but resonates with our deepest yearnings for truth, life, and goodness. As Augustine understood so brilliantly in his interpretation of the double-love command, loving God with all our hearts is really the only true way to love creatures (ourselves and others), since the very act of loving God so transforms our will that we actually are able (i.e., have the *power*) to perceive and enact for ourselves and one another the *goodness*—the truth, the life, and freedom—that is already ours as creatures (without needing to manipulate that goodness for some other purpose than simply enjoying its intrinsic worth) (Schweiker 2000; Vacek 1996).

On the other hand (with regard to its 'heteronomous moments'), this command does *not* always appear to us as gift. We also experience it as 'law' (*Gesetz*)—as demand, as something alien to us (Althaus 1966: 12–21; cf. Meilaender 2005). Power and goodness do not always cohere in our own actions and character or in the world around us. Paul captures the former in his depiction of two internal competing wills (Rom. 7: 21–3). The prophets (e.g., Amos, Hosea, Jeremiah) capture the latter in their cries for justice and defence of the powerless; Paul echoes their corporate judgement when he describes God's destructive power to use 'things that are not, to reduce to nothing things that are' (1 Cor. 3: 28; cf. Jer. 9: 24).

Moreover, by melding his—and Christ's—experience of God's wrath against sin (cf. Paul) with the protest of the righteous sufferer (cf. the lament psalms), Luther grasps a complex intuition about this 'heteronomous moment'—that it can entail not only guilt but also a sense of despair and protest against God. Yet another dimension of this 'moment' is expressed in the story of Abraham's near sacrifice of Isaac with its (in Kierkegaard's words) 'teleological suspension of the ethical'. Here the issue is neither guilt nor protest but the sense of a divine claim that seems to transcend even the most obvious of ethical injunctions.

Of course, the story of Abraham itself may suggest that this sense of a divine claim 'beyond' the ethical is not without ambiguity. Indeed, it can be used to sanction religious images of a demonic god (not bound by truth or justice) or, in secular terms, a nihilism not unlike Heidegger's 'being towards death' or Nietzsche's 'will to power'. Thus, as Levenson has suggested, Abraham's story (in Gen. 22) must be set alongside other texts (like Gen. 18 and, we might add, the lament psalms), which indicate that God is a trustworthy—if at times unpredictable—partner, who not only calls us to moral accountability but also is responsive to our moral arguments.

These autonomous and heteronomous moments point to the 'performative' character of the commands. Obedience to them is a counterfactual challenge to the conflict between power and goodness (within us and the world around us). Response to their summons is a bold enactment of God's claim that creation is, indeed, good; that the reign of God will, indeed, prevail; and that ultimately nothing can separate us from God's love in Christ Jesus—not even the ills (personal or corporate) we suffer and protest against (Rom. 8: 38, 39; note that Paul quotes Ps. 44: 22, the epitome of a lament psalm, right before this). In other words, for Christians, the double-love commandment is a 'theonomous' summons to participate in God's own enactment—through Jesus Christ and the Spirit's power—of the fact that (1) ultimate goodness is powerful enough to overcome evil, because (2) ultimate power is good enough to bind itself to creating, redeeming, and sustaining finite life—in all its inherent integrity and otherness (cf. Schweiker (1998)).

This participation entails allowing God's Spirit to so transform and renew our minds that we can, in fact, perceive and enact God's reign in our midst—precisely in the face of what appears to contradict it (Rom. 12: 2). Luther's focus on spontaneity and being 'above scrutiny' (cf. 1 Cor. 2: 15) captures the sense of power and autonomy which the Spirit gives in this discernment. Calvin's focus on exhortation—which resonates with a Jewish understanding of *halakhah* as the law that instructs and guides—captures how the Spirit gives wisdom in this discernment, a wisdom that has external and internal resonances (with, e.g., Scripture and tradition, on the one hand, and one's internal law, on the other). Indeed, this discernment—and the reflection and judgement it entails—is not merely a private task. It does not pertain to some Gnostic flight out of the worlds in which we live—and the forces (political, psychological, biological, and so on) actually at play within them. The one whose will is being discerned (the God of the Bible) is a God passionately and intimately concerned with actual history and the actual creaturely goods—personal and corporate—that constitute the integrity of our lives within it.

These concerns are not merely academic. In contrast to G. E. M. Anscombe's influential assertion some decades ago that a 'divine law conception of ethics' no longer survives (1958), the fact remains—as sociologists (e.g., Berger (1999)) and students of religion (e.g., Jenkins (2002)) continue to remind us—that a large percentage of Jews, Christians, and Muslims throughout the world still presuppose, at least in word if not always in deed, that morality is in some way governed by divine will. Indeed, one could argue that a central task for public reasoning about this will—and the commands identified with it—is not the cognitive defence of its plausibility but the task of discerning what that will actually is and what it might mean to live in accordance with it in the very complexity of our lives (where power and goodness do not always cohere). For Jews and Christians, what lies at the heart of that task is, in some sense, quite clear. The 'ancient, protean, and strangely resilient' story of God's commands calls us to defend publicly the moral and spiritual dignity (and the concrete goods that dignity entails) not only of those who are like us (or agree with us or are useful for our purposes) but of all people, whether they stand within or outside our communities (Levenson 1993: 232).

REFERENCES AND SUGGESTED READING

ADAMS, R. M. (1973). 'A Modified Divine Command Theory of Ethical Wrongness', in G. Outka and J. P. Reeder, jun. (eds.), *Religion and Morality*, Garden City, NY: Anchor, 318–47; repr. in Adams 1987*c*: 97–122.

——(1979). 'Divine Command Metaethics Modified Again', *Journal of Religious Ethics*, 7, 66–79; repr. in Adams 1987*c*: 144–63.

——(1987*a*). 'Autonomy and Theological Ethics', *Religious Studies*, 15, 191–4.

——(1987*b*). 'Divine Commands and the Social Nature of Obligations', *Faith and Philosophy*, 4, 262–75.

——(1987*c*). *The Virtue of Faith and Other Essays in Philosophical Theology*. Oxford: Oxford University Press.

——(1999). *Finite and Infinite Goods: A Framework for Ethics*. Oxford: Oxford University Press.

ALTHAUS, P. (1966). *The Divine Command*. Philadelphia: Fortress Press.

ANSCOMBE, G. E. M. (1958). 'Modern Moral Philosophy', *Philosophy*, 33, 1–19.

AQUINAS (1964–). *Summa Theologiae*. New York: McGraw-Hill.

AUGUSTINE (1998). *The City of God Against the Pagans*. Cambridge: Cambridge University Press.

BARTH, K. (1957). *Church Dogmatics*, vol. II/2. Edinburgh: T. & T. Clark.

BERGER, P. (1999). *The Desecularization of the World: Resurgent Religion and World Politics*. Grand Rapids, Mich.: Eerdmans.

BONAVENTURE (1998). *The Soul's Journey into God*. New York: Paulist Press.

BRUNNER, E. (1947). *The Divine Imperative*. Philadelphia: Westminster Press.

CALVIN, J. (1960). *Institutes of the Christian Religion*, 2 vols. Philadelphia: Westminster Press.

FORDE, G. (1997). *On Being a Theologian of the Cross: Reflections on Luther's Heidelberg Disputation (1518)*. Grand Rapids, Mich.: Eerdmans.

FOX, M. (1990). 'Maimonides and Aquinas on Natural Law', in *Interpreting Maimonides*, Chicago: University of Chicago Press, 124–51.

GILLESPIE, M. (1996). *Nihilism before Nietzsche*. Chicago: University of Chicago Press.

HARE, J. (2001). *God's Call: Moral Realism, God's Commands, and Human Autonomy.* Grand Rapids, Mich.: Eerdmans.

HARRIS, M. (2003). *Divine Command Ethics: Jewish and Christian Perspectives.* London: Routledge.

HELM, P. (1991). *Divine Commands and Morality.* Oxford: Oxford University Press.

HENRY, C. (1957). *Christian Personal Ethics.* Grand Rapids, Mich.: Eerdmans.

IDZIAK, J. M. (1979). *Divine Command Morality: Historical and Contemporary Readings.* New York: Edwin Mellen.

—— (1997). 'Divine Command Ethics', in P. L. Quinn and C. Taliaffero (eds.), *A Companion to Philosophy of Religion*, Oxford: Blackwell, 453–9; repr. in *The Virtue of Faith*, Oxford: Oxford University Press, 2000, 123–7.

IRENAEUS (1992). *Against the Heresies.* New York: Paulist Press.

JENKINS, P. (2002). *The Next Christendom: The Coming of Global Christianity.* Oxford: Oxford University Press.

KANT, I. (1996). *The Critique of Practical Reason.* New York: Prometheus.

KIERKEGAARD, S. (1983). *Fear and Trembling.* Princeton: Princeton University Press.

LAZARETH, W. (2001). *Christians in Society: Luther, the Bible, and Social Ethics.* Minneapolis: Fortress Press.

LEVENSON, J. (1985). *Sinai and Zion: An Entry into the Jewish Bible.* Minneapolis: Winston Press.

—— (1993). *The Death and Resurrection of the Beloved Son: The Transformation of Child Sacrifice in Judaism and Christianity.* New Haven: Yale University Press.

—— (1994). *Creation and the Persistence of Evil: The Jewish Drama of Divine Omnipotence.* San Francisco: Harper & Row.

LUTHER, M. (1963). 'Lectures on Galatians (1535)', in *Luther's Works*, xxvi–xxvii, St Louis, Mo.: Concordia Publishing House.

MACINTYRE, A. (1981). *After Virtue.* Notre Dame, Ind.: University of Notre Dame Press.

MARITAIN, J. (1955). *Three Reformers: Luther—Descartes—Rousseau.* New York: Charles Scribner's Sons.

MEILAENDER, G. (2005). 'Hearts set to Obey', in C. E. Braaten and C. R. Seitz (eds.), *I Am the Lord Your God: Christian Reflections on the Ten Commandments*, Grand Rapids, Mich.: Cerdmans, 253–75.

MILLER, P. (1954). *The New England Mind: The Seventeenth Century.* Cambridge, Mass.: Harvard University Press.

MOORE, G. E. (1903). *Principia Ethica.* Cambridge: Cambridge University Press.

MOUW, R. J. (1991). *The God who Commands: A Study in Divine Command Ethics.* Notre Dame, Ind.: University of Notre Dame Press.

MURPHY, M. C. (1998). 'Divine Command, Divine Will, and Moral Obligation', *Faith and Philosophy*, 15, 3–27.

—— (2002a). *An Essay on Divine Authority.* Ithaca, NY: Cornell University Press.

—— (2002b). 'Theological Voluntarism', in E. N. Zalta (ed.), *The Stanford Encyclopedia of Philosophy*, URL = <http://plato.stanford.edu/archives/fall2002/entries/voluntarism-theological/>.

NIEBUHR, H. R. (1946). 'The Doctrine of the Trinity and the Unity of the Church', *Theology Today*, 3, 371–84.

NIEBUHR, R. (1941). *Nature and Destiny of Man*, I. New York: Scribner's.

NIELSEN, K. (1961). 'Some Remarks on the Independence of Morality from Religion', *Mind*, 70, 175–86.

NOVAK, D. (2001). 'Karl Barth on Divine Command: A Jewish Response', *Scottish Journal of Theology*, 54/4, 463–83.

OTTO, R. (1923). *The Idea of the Holy*. New York: Oxford University Press.

PINCKAERS, S. (1995). *The Sources of Christian Ethics*. Washington: The Catholic University of America Press.

PLATO (1948). *Euthyphro, Apology, Crito*. Indianapolis: Bobbs-Merill Company.

QUINN, P. L. (1990). 'The Recent Revival of Divine Command Ethics', *Philosophy and Phenomenological Research*, 50 (suppl.), 345–65.

—— (1991*a*). *Divine Commands and Moral Requirements*. Oxford: Clarendon Press.

—— (1991*b*). 'The Primacy of God's Will in Christian Ethics', *Philosophical Perspectives*, 6, 493–513.

SCHWEIKER, W. (1998). 'Divine Command Ethics and the Otherness of God', in O. Summerell (ed.), *The Otherness of God*, Charlottesville, Va.: University Press of Virginia, 246–65.

—— (2000). 'And a Second is Like It: Christian Faith and the Claim of the Other', *Quarterly Review*, 20/3, 233–47.

SIDGWICK, H. ([1907] 1981). *The Methods of Ethics*. London: Macmillan.

TILLICH, P. (1951). *Systematic Theology*, I. Chicago: University of Chicago Press.

—— (1963). *Morality and Beyond*. New York: HarperCollins.

VACEK, E. C. (1996). 'Divine-Command, Natural-Law, and Mutual-Love Ethics', *Theological Studies*, 57, 633–53.

WERPEHOWSKI, W. (1981). 'Command and History in the Ethics of Karl Barth', *Journal of Religious Ethics*, 9, 298–320.

WINGREN, G. (1961). *Creation and Law*. Philadelphia: Muhlenberg Press.

CHAPTER 8

TRADITION IN THE CHURCH

PHILIP TURNER

THREE SENSES OF TRADITION

TRADITION, when used in connection with Christian thought and practice, is a word with at least three different but nonetheless related meanings. Each of these has a distinctive set of issues connected with it. Both the meanings and the connected issues will be discussed in the remarks that follow. Throughout this discussion, varied though it will be, one overarching issue presents itself, though in various guises. In Christian thought and practice, tradition serves to link the present life and witness of the Church to the original witness of the Apostles. It is something like a bridge thrown across the chasm of time. The question is whether or not the connection forged in fact connects the present life and teaching of the Church to the original witness to Jesus in a way that is faithful. To put the matter in another way, in Christian thought the question addressed by the notion of tradition is how the Church is to remain faithful to the original witness of the Apostles and at the same time address in a cogent way the changes and chances of history.

The bridge-like quality of tradition is captured well by the first two of its three meanings. In Greek and Latin the nouns translated in English as 'tradition' (*paradosis* and *traditio*) are both related to verbs meaning to hand or give over. Thus, in its original meaning, 'tradition' connotes not only what is passed on but also the processes by means of which tradition's content is adequately transmitted. This double meaning is present in both the New Testament and the writings of the Church Fathers. There is, however, a third meaning, distinctively more contemporary, that has attached itself to the term. Tradition is then said to refer not only to what is handed over and to the process by means of which the transmission occurs; it refers also to an entire form of life, a matrix of language and practice, that generates both the process of transmission and its content (MacIntyre 1981, 1988, 1990).

Thus, to cite the example of the Christian tradition of marriage (an example that will be used in illustrative ways throughout the course of this essay), one can say that, in the Christian tradition, marriage is understood as an institution that carries the moral requirement of fidelity and permanence between the parties involved. These two requirements form a central aspect of the *content* of the Christian tradition about marriage. This moral content, however, is passed on by means of a certain process that includes teaching, the marriage rite, literary and other artistic works, exemplary lives, and a host of social practices that order the domestic relations of marital partners. However, both the tradition of fidelity and permanence and the process by means of which these requirements are passed on are themselves engendered and given force by a larger complex of belief and practice in which fidelity and permanence (being primary characteristics of God's relationship with his people) have even wider religious and moral significance. This wider context is frequently termed 'tradition', and it provides the matrix within which the particular traditions that Christians espouse about marriage both arise and are passed on.

The Content of Tradition

Tradition in the New Testament   The notion of tradition as teaching and practice with a particular content appears with frequency (but not apart from conflict) within the pages of the New Testament (Hanson 1962: 10–11). The word *paradosis* is used thirteen times. Nine of these references are negative—referring as they do to the *paradosis* of the Jewish elders that Jesus contrasts unfavourably with the 'word' or 'commandment of God' (Matt. 15: 2, 3, 6; Mark 7: 3, 5, 8, 9, 13; Gal. 1: 14). In the Gospels of Matthew and Mark, Jesus condemns the teaching, or the tradition, of the Pharisees and the Scribes because their traditions represent 'the precepts of men', rather than the 'commandment of God' (Matt. 15: 2–9; Mark 7: 3–13). The Apostle Paul, by implication, makes a similar contrast when he links his devotion to 'the traditions of my fathers' to his persecution of the Church; and then goes on to compare his devotion to the traditions of his fathers to his present devotion to God's Son (Gal. 1: 13–17).

All the references to *paradosis* cited above refer to *halakha*; that is, to Jewish interpretations of the Law (rather than to the Law itself) that Jesus and the early Church held to be misinterpretations of divine truth and faithful practice. There are, however, positive references to a specifically Christian *paradosis* to be found. 1 Cor. 11: 2 and 2 Thess. 2: 15, 3: 6, use the word to refer to practices and teaching that have been handed over by Paul; and, consequently, because of their apostolic origin, they are to be honoured and kept. There are other references in which the word *paradosis* does not appear but which clearly refer to Christian teaching and practice that have authority precisely because they have been passed on as the tradition of the Apostles. Luke 1: 2; Rom. 6: 17; 1 Cor. 11: 23 ff., 15: 1 ff.; 2 Pet. 2: 21; Jude 3 refer variously to 'a narrative of the things delivered to us', a 'standard of teaching', receiving 'from the Lord what I also delivered to you', 'the gospel, which you received', 'the holy commandment delivered to them', and 'the faith once delivered to the saints'.

Taken together, these references to delivering or handing over have a particular content and concern most fundamentally the words and works of Jesus. They also refer to short formulas like the actions at the Last Supper. Some are of a more theological character, in that they contain Christological statements or accounts of Christ's resurrection. If one surveys all the references to 'passing on', one can say by way of summary that the contents of tradition, as understood and positively regarded by the writers of the New Testament, include summaries of Jesus' life and teaching and Christian belief, along with accounts of the moral and religious practices and virtues that characterize the common life of the Church. In short, the content of tradition includes both belief and practice. Noting this fact, Yves Congar warned against separating 'too sharply the "tradition" of paschal faith from the "tradition" of apostolic rules of conduct'. Both, he insisted, are to be granted authority because both build up the Church. Together, 'they integrate the true religious relationship which the faithful must have with God in Christ' (Congar 1967: 10).

With respect to the authority of the content passed on, Paul's reference to receiving 'from the Lord' (1 Cor. 11: 23) what he has passed on is of particular importance. A good case has been made for holding that, whenever Paul refers to passing on what he has received, he understands the transmission to be 'from the Lord', but through the Church (Hanson 1962: 11). Noting this usage, Oscar Cullmann has argued that, at least for Paul, Christ himself takes the place of Jewish *Halakha* (Cullmann 1956: 66). Jesus now delivers through the Church a tradition that is faithful to God. The risen and ascended Christ hands over the truth about God, and he does so as both its content and its author. Christ thus stands as the one who hands tradition over to the Apostles, who in turn pass the tradition on to those who come to faith through their witness. The Apostles are of crucial importance for this transmission, because they are the direct witnesses of Jesus' life, death, resurrection, and ascension. Therefore, the tradition that comes from them is considered true rather than false.

The canon of Scripture and the rule of faith This all too brief discussion of tradition in the New Testament indicates clearly that from the beginning *paradosis*, though utterly necessary to gain a purchase on the truth about God, was regarded as both reliable and unreliable. As time passed and the distance between the Apostles and the present increased, the issue of tradition's veracity took on new complexities. Adequacy of content became a burning issue. Its truth or falsehood was an issue not only between Jews and Christians but also within the Church itself. It is tradition that serves to link past and present, but time and distance, along with human limitation and perversity, produce diverse traditions. The question naturally arises as to which version or versions are genuine.

In the early centuries of the history of the Church, two criteria emerged for deciding disputes concerning the veracity of the content of tradition—the *canon of Scripture* and the *rule of faith*. The criterion of greatest authority was the *canon of Scripture*. For Christ, the Apostles, and the authors of the books of the New Testament, 'Holy Scripture' is a term that refers to that collection of writings that came to be known as the Old Testament and, more recently, 'the Hebrew Scriptures'. It was not until the fifth century that the canon assumed the form now found in the New Testament. Nevertheless, by the end of the second century the Church as a whole accepted (in addition to the books of the Old Testament) the four gospels, the book of Acts, the Pauline letters (including the Pastorals), and at least two of the Catholic Epistles (1 John and 1 Peter) as Holy Scripture. These writings were accorded authority because they were associated with the original witness of the Apostles and because of greater age. For these reasons (apostolic origin and age), their witness was deemed true. Consequently, from an early date, Holy Scripture became the standard point of reference in the process of distinguishing between the faithful and the unfaithful content of tradition.

Another test employed for assaying the content of tradition was the *rule of faith*. The *rule of faith* is not to be confused with a creed, in that it was not considered a universally accepted token of orthodoxy. Its authority was more local than that of a creed. It was, according to R. P. C. Hanson, 'simply an account, divided into subjects, of the content of the preaching and teaching of the Church contemporary with the writer who mentions or quotes the rule of faith' (Hanson 1962: 93). Among others, Irenaeus, Tertullian, Hippolytus, and Origen give accounts of the *rule of faith* as they received it. The *rule*, as rendered by each, is variously named and given slightly different content. Despite this variety, the accounts given of the *rule* each has received are remarkably similar. All refer to a similar standard of teaching by which the content of *paradosis* is to be judged (Hanson 1962: 86–91).

The content of the *rule* as rendered by these authors was clearly designed to help distinguish false from true teaching. In making these determinations, the *rule of faith* is only rarely (and ambiguously) referenced as a form of tradition the content of which has authority independent of that of Holy Scripture. Indeed, serious doubts have been cast by both Protestant and Roman Catholic scholars upon the once common claims that there are authoritative traditions with contents not found in Holy Scripture (Congar 1964: 41–5; Hanson 1962: 102–8). The *rule of faith*, rather, was regarded by the Church Fathers as a summary of the correct way of reading Holy Scripture. It was considered to be a form of tradition that does not add truth absent from Holy Scripture; rather, it provides an *epitome* of what the Holy Scriptures are about.

The development of doctrine?   Apostolic origin, in the minds of the Church Fathers, gives authority to both the *canon of Scripture* and the *rule of faith*. The Fathers were not, however, critical in the modern sense. In their minds, faithful tradition does not change, but minimal historical knowledge makes it clear that tradition, both in respect to faith and morals, has changed and does change. To cite once more, and at some length, the example of Christian tradition of teaching and practice with respect to marriage, there have been significant changes and differences through the ages; and these changes and differences have, in various ways and at various times, become points of contention. In the West, no fewer than five accounts (four Christian and one more secular) of the marital relationship have come to form aspects of a complex and sometimes conflicted view of the nature and moral requirements of that estate. John Witte has characterized them as (1) the Catholic sacramental model, (2) the Lutheran social model, (3) the Calvinist covenantal model, (4) the Anglican commonwealth model, and (5) the Enlightenment contractarian model (Witte 1997: 2–12). Comparison of these variations in tradition reveals both reconcilable differences in emphasis and potentially irreconcilable points of conflict.

In respect of the specifically Christian traditions, the Catholic sacramental model, as articulated in the mid-twelfth century, viewed marriage (though less optimal than celibacy) as a natural association created by God for the care and nurture of children in the service and love of God. Because of sin, marriage serves also to restrain lust and to direct natural passion to constructive social purpose. These marital 'goods' require a lifelong relationship of fidelity and love. When marriage is entered into with these intentions and is consummated, it assumes the dignity of a sacrament that supplies sanctifying grace that, in turn, allows for the fulfilment of the goods of marriage and the signification of the relationship between Christ and the Church.

At the time of the Reformation, Protestants rejected both the subordination of marriage to celibacy and the notion that marriage is a sacrament. Lutherans developed a social model of marriage rooted in their doctrine of the two kingdoms. Marriage was seen as a social estate rather than a sacred one. Marriage is ordained by God but directed to human ends. Its goods lie within the earthly rather than the heavenly kingdom. Within the earthly kingdom, it is best viewed as a voluntary relationship that serves, in the providence of God, for procreation and protection, for the revelation of sin and the need for grace, for the restriction of promiscuity, and for the promotion of love, restraint, and other virtues.

Calvinist accounts of marriage mirror in many ways those of Lutherans, but the goods and requirements of marriage are placed in a different context—that of a covenant involving God, the couple, and the entire community of the faithful. The couple make their commitments before God and each other, parents give their consent to the union, two witnesses serve as God's priests, the minister blesses the couple and reminds them of their duties, and the magistrate registers the couple and protects their persons and property. Because God is the major party to the covenant, Calvinist thought, unlike Lutheran thought, added a more distinctively spiritual dimension to marriage (though not a sacramental one). Marriage under God became for them a school of charity that leads to sanctification.

In the Anglican tradition, yet another model of marriage became ascendant. Marriage was conceived as 'a little commonwealth'. As Witte notes, 'This model embraced the sacramental, social, and covenantal models but went beyond them' (Witte 1997: 8). The central calling of family life was at one and the same time to serve the common good of the couple, the children, the Church, and the state. Each household contained a variety of offices in sub- and super-ordinate relationship one with another. Each, therefore, was to be a model commonwealth that, on a small scale, through its stability and good order, mirrored and strengthened the larger commonwealth of the nation.

Even this brief summary of the tradition of marriage in the Western Church suggests both variety and conflict. Things have been made even more complicated by the growth of another tradition of thought and practice that has itself been generated by a larger (secular) tradition matching the third sense of the word mentioned at the outset. In the eighteenth century another tradition, many of whose advocates defined themselves in direct opposition to their Christian inheritance, met the complex Christian tradition outlined above (Gay 1966: 256–419; Beiser 1996: 3–19; Byrne 1996: 1–52). In response both to new learning and to the religious strife of the period, the liberalism of the Enlightenment appeared on the scene. This tradition (fuelled by influences from classical philosophy, a critical approach to tradition, and the advances of science) places maximum moral value on human autonomy rather than divine order. Consequently, it tends to see marriage not as an estate ordered in a pre-set way by God, but as a purely voluntary relationship the terms of which may be chosen by the parties involved. This liberal tradition of marriage advocates the abolition rather than the reform of many aspects of the Christian one. The elevation of the moral importance of autonomy is accompanied by a principle of equality that calls into question traditional hierarchies. Marriages, with increasing frequency, are preceded by pre-nuptial agreements that spell out the terms of a particular marriage contract. Further, notions of pre-set duties that attach to the roles of husband, wife, and child are replaced by the notion of the natural rights that each member of a household holds in opposition to the others. More recently, the principle of autonomy has been used to challenge the traditional link between marriage and heterosexual relations. In short, the content of the liberal tradition concerning marriage is in many ways less a development of Christian thought and practice and more the result of the emergence in the West of a very different tradition in the third, broader sense of the term mentioned at the outset of this discussion.

How are these changes and divisions in Christian tradition (along with others of even greater significance) to be viewed? How is one to judge the results of the meeting of the liberal tradition with that of the Western Christian tradition? How is one to judge the results of the meeting of Christian tradition with other world religions and other cultures rooted in alternative world-views? To repeat the initial question about the significance of tradition, how in the midst of these changes and conflicts is the faith and practice of the Church to remain faithful to the witness of the Apostles and at the same time address the contingencies presented by history?

Tradition, Transmission, and Adjudication

Questions such as these necessarily bring discussions of the content of tradition into relationship with discussions of the second sense of the word identified above: namely, the processes by means of which tradition is to be passed on. In passing tradition on, both standards for judging adequacy and processes for transmission come into relationship with each other. Perusal of Christian history suggests that there have been at least six very different answers given to the way in which standards of judgement can be joined successfully to a process of transmission. For the sake of convenience these answers can be labelled as Roman Catholic developmental, Eastern Orthodox conciliar, Protestant confessional, Anglican con-sensual, Evangelical biblical, and Sectarian communal. Each of these seeks to link standards of judgement with processes of transmission. Each comprises a strategy for distinguishing true from false tradition. Each provides a way of linking apos-tolic witness with present circumstance; and each has proved to be in itself a major cause of Christian division.

The Roman Catholic developmental strategy, as given classical expression by John Henry Newman in *An Essay on the Development of Doctrine*, posits an organic development in the tradition of the Church that roots itself in a central core, or 'deposit', handed over to the Apostles by Christ that then grows exponentially through the ages. Newman most frequently likens this organic process to the development of a mind from youth to maturity. He proposes seven tests that can be used to distinguish true from false developments (Newman 1974: 116–48). However, these seven tests need confirmation from an office in the Church empowered by God to adjudicate in difficult cases. In a final sense, the power of adjudication resides in the Bishop of Rome (Newman 1974: 165–78; *Catholic Encyclopedia* 2003). Through the teaching authority of the Church that resides collectively in the bishops with the Pope at their head, the faith and practice of the Church is both passed on and protected from error.

Eastern Orthodox Christians have eschewed central adjudicative authority and have been reluctant to provide a clearly defined and permanent criterion for the adequacy of tradition other than God himself (Meyendorff 1978: 20). In this respect they like to distinguish themselves from Western Christians, who have turned to quite identifiable standards and mechanisms for making these determinations. To be sure, among Orthodox Christians doctrinal and ethical disputes are normally settled by reference to the decisions of ecumenical councils, but not on all occasions. Sometimes authoritative decisions are given by local councils, or even by general consensus. The Eastern Orthodox conciliar strategy holds that doctrine develops only in the sense that concrete issues must be addressed. As the Church addresses issues, tradition does not grow in an expansive manner. Rather, it gives a fresh statement of eternal truth, which does not change. For the Eastern Orthodox it is less the case that tradition develops and more the case that eternal truth must be expressed in new ways, depending upon circumstances (Meyendorff 1978: 19). The adequacy of this expression can be gleaned from councils and consensus, but final judgements lie in the hands of God rather than in precisely identifiable human formulations, agents, or mechanisms.

The Protestant strategy has centred on 'confessions', 'articles', and 'catechisms' that define how the Bible's witness to God is rightly to be understood and applied in life's various circumstances. Typically, these statements address matters of both faith and morals (Bicknell 1956; Tappert 1959). They are used to interpret the import of Holy Scripture, to instruct the faithful, and to judge the adequacy of the content of tradition as it is passed on. From the sixteenth through the early twentieth centuries, among Protestants, interpretive authority with respect to these statements was located in very large measure among theologians, most of whom held posts in universities. However, the secularization of universities has left vague the locus of authority to interpret and apply the confessions.

Anglicanism most certainly springs from the Reformation, and during the course of its history it has used a confession in the form of the Thirty-Nine Articles of Religion to ensure that its clergy pass on a faithful account of apostolic faith and practice. The Articles touch on both doctrinal matters such as the Trinity and the person of Christ, and upon moral matters such as works of supererogation and the swearing of oaths. However, as time has passed, use of the Articles of Religion as a means of preserving tradition through a disciplined clergy has declined, and another method of ensuring the adequacy of tradition's transmission has emerged (Sykes 1995; P. W. Turner 2003). That method allows open and reasonably free discussion of issues, both theological and moral, but preserves tradition through constancy of practice. At present, among Anglicans, theological and moral tradition is embedded in liturgical practices more than in doctrinal or moral statements; and they have been slow to change practice (and with it teaching) until a fairly wide consensus is present. However, in recent years, increasing politicization of ecclesial governance and wider cultural and theological diversity among Anglicans have led to a greater willingness to change practice before wide consensus has been reached. As a result, within the Anglican Communion, tradition is increasingly seen as a matter more of debate and conflict than of unifying heritage.

Evangelical and Sectarian Christians have evolved a distinctive method of remaining faithful to the apostolic witness. In different ways, both Evangelicals and more 'sectarian' Christians are leery of tradition. They often, though not always, view it as an example of faithlessness rather than fidelity (Yoder 1984: 63–79). When confronted with an issue, Evangelicals tend to go not to tradition but directly to Holy Scripture (Bloesch 1982: 51–78). In their view, the Holy Scriptures are perspicuous. They can speak for themselves if the Holy Spirit is present. The believer is thus called upon to allow the Bible to speak to current circumstances in an immediate way, either through the voice of a trusted preacher or through the internal testimony of the Holy Spirit. Neither creeds, nor confessions, nor ecclesiastical authorities are to impose themselves between the Bible and the individual believer's mind and heart.

Christians of a more sectarian bent share the Evangelicals' suspicion of the mediating authority of tradition. They share also a belief in the ability of the Holy Spirit to speak to the present through the witness of Holy Scripture. However, correct understanding of the Bible's meaning for the present is to be determined within a community whose common life and worship provide, as it were, the sacred space in which God's Spirit may be assumed to be present (Yoder 1984: 24–44). In this space, the Bible is read and discussed until the community has reached a common mind in respect to questions of both belief and practice.

TRADITION EMBEDDED IN PRACTICE

Alasdaire MacIntyre points out that tradition develops in part by means of arguments internal to itself, and the processes mentioned above are intended to ensure that reliable means are available for ensuring the adequacy of tradition's content (MacIntyre 1981: 6–21). However, Jaroslav Pelikan has reminded his readers that tradition is more often than not passed on in continuity rather than in conflict with what has gone before. Pelikan notes that for centuries Christians have been breaking bread and drinking wine, and he goes on to say, 'If that is a self-evident truth, it is also a massive instance of continuity amid change, and a prime instance of the reality of tradition' (Pelikan 1984: 48).

Continuity is maintained in the midst of conflict because tradition, as it is actually passed on, is, more often than not, embedded in daily practices rather than ecclesial mechanisms or argumentative treatises. The two most common forms of embedding are liturgical and biographical. It is through both liturgy and the lives of exemplary Christians that tradition is most conservatively, most effectively, and most frequently passed on. On the whole, contemporary discussions of tradition have failed to give adequate attention to the processes whereby tradition is actually transmitted. That is, discussion of tradition has focused largely on conflicts in respect to the content of tradition or upon tradition as a matrix of thought and action that generates a host of more particular beliefs and practices. If, however, the focus of attention falls upon *liturgical practices* and *exemplary lives*, tradition as the activity of passing on begins to gain more and more significance.

Better than half a century of work in the field by social anthropologists has more than demonstrated the importance of liturgy for passing on tradition. A prime example is the research of Victor Turner, who, in a series of ground-breaking studies, has shown *liturgy* to be a form of activity in which belief and practice are embedded in things said, shown, and done (V. Turner 1961, 1968, 1969). The religious and moral meaning of liturgical action is contained more in symbolic than in discursive expression (P. W. Turner 1976: 113–23). The symbols deployed in what is said, shown, and done within liturgical contexts have their origins in basic narratives and in bodily and organic elements that both form the foundations of human life and provide social identity to liturgy's participants. The narrative flow of liturgy and the symbolic actions it contains, in Victor Turner's phrase, at one and the same time prove to be both 'storehouses' (of meaning and information) and 'powerhouses' (of emotive force).

Liturgy links both meaning and power in forms of action that change only slowly, if at all. As such, they serve as affective and effective means of passing on the beliefs and practices that define a tradition. Furthermore, they do so in a way that temporarily shuts out tradition's more intellectualist and conflict-related aspects. Thus, for example, in Christian liturgies for the blessing of marriage, the story of God's purposes for marriage is told, promises are made to seek jointly the fulfilment of those purposes, hands are joined, rings are given and received, and kisses exchanged. Among Eastern Orthodox Christians, the couple is 'crowned' as a sign that, within the compass of their marriage, they participate in Christ's victory over death (Meyendorff 1984: 21–43). In Eastern Orthodox, Roman Catholic, and some

Protestant ceremonies the story and the symbolic actions that carry the tradition of marriage are linked in an even more direct way to Christ's death and resurrection. That is, the entire marriage liturgy is placed within the Holy Eucharist, which, through its own symbolic actions, tells the entire story of God's plan for salvation. In these and many other ways marriage liturgies illustrate the point that tradition embedded in practice at one and the same time screens out disputed issues and imprints what has been received upon those who will become tradition's living carriers into the future.

The lives of the saints provide a second example of the transmitting force of tradition embedded in practice. It may well be that a life lived is an even more powerful vehicle for the passing on of tradition than liturgical practice. One need think no further than the life of St Francis of Assisi to find a convincing example. The stories of St Francis's life, both historical and legendary, display fundamental Christian beliefs and practices in ways that have impressed generation after generation (de Voragine 1993: 220–9; Spoto 2003). The iconography in the basilica in Assisi, particularly as found in the frescos of Giotto, depicts the life of Francis as that of an ideal disciple. Giotto's frescos are clearly intended to pass on the tradition of imitating Christ so firmly embedded in the saint's life (Goulet, McInally, and Wood 1994: 29–46). The five window bays in the upper nave of the basilica show events from the life of the saint that are intended to induce an imitation of his life by those who view the story. So Giotto shows the saint breaking out of the prison of worldly possessions, taking off an old life and putting on a new one, shunning the quest for glory and honour, obeying the call to rebuild God's church, giving up everything to obey God's call, embracing the poor, interceding for all humankind, and preaching the Gospel to the entire creation, including the animals. What Giotto presents is Christian belief and practice embedded in a life, and he does so with the direct intent of passing on this tradition.

The example of the Giotto frescos reminds one that tradition is passed on in other forms of practice, most notably artistic. The growing crisis in the ability of churches to pass on communal traditions suggests a need to focus more attention on this and other forms of tradition's transmission than now is common. In this respect, what might be called 'domestic liturgy', practices of piety within the home, are of particular importance. To grasp the extraordinary effectiveness of this way of passing on tradition, one need read no further than Liz Harris's remarkable account of 'domestic liturgy' among Hasidic Jews (1985). Reading Harris's account of functioning 'domestic liturgy' makes one aware immediately of the erosion among Christians of domestic practices that involve people within their domestic space in the regular practice of prayer, Bible reading, and contemplation of the lives of the saints. Once this decline is noted, it is difficult to escape the conviction that the erosion of these domestic practices (along with other means for passing on tradition) indicates a crisis in the wider sense of Christian tradition—that wider matrix of belief and practice that generates particular traditions and the means of passing them on.

TRADITION AS GENERATIVE MATRIX

It is likely that this wider crisis is responsible in part for bringing discussion of tradition in its third sense to the fore, and for generating what Gene Outka has aptly named the 'particularist turn' in Christian ethics (Outka 1996). In recent years, Hans Frei, George Lindbeck, John Howard Yoder, and Stanley Hauerwas, among many others, have turned their attention to the erosion of the Christian tradition (in the broader sense of the term) within Western society; and they have suggested that the challenge before the churches is the reconstitution of this tradition as a cultural matrix that generates beliefs and practices that are in fact distinctively Christian. Frei referred in a negative manner to what he called 'the eclipse of the biblical narrative'. By this phrase he suggested that, in the nineteenth and twentieth centuries, interpretive theories which assume that the meaning of the Bible must be found at some level below or beyond the Bible's story-line have served to shut out the formative power of the story itself (Frei 1974). As a result, Christian identity has been compromised. Lindbeck argued that theology, and so also tradition, are best understood not as informative propositions about objective realities or as symbols expressive of inner feelings but as 'communally authoritative rules of discourse, attitude, and action' (Lindbeck 1984: 16–18). Lindbeck implies in all his work that the Christian tradition is in crisis because Christians have, as it were, forgotten how to speak the Christian language and in fact are speaking a sort of pidgin. Yoder speaks of the corruption of distinctively Christian belief and practice by the alliance made between Christianity and its surrounding culture when Constantine made Christianity the religion of the Empire (Yoder 1984: 135–7, 1994: 55–8). Hauerwas, in a host of articles, returns again and again to the way in which Christian tradition has been obscured and corrupted by the power of the liberal cultural assumptions spawned by the Enlightenment (Hauerwas 1981: 72–86). Each of these authors, in the face of one or another form of cultural erosion, pleads for the reconstitution of Christian tradition in the broad sense; and they propose this reconstitution as the primary theological task of their generation.

The 'particularist turn' has served in an appropriate manner to focus attention upon the central importance of tradition as a source of religious knowledge, practice, and identity. It is important to note, however, that discussions of the nature and importance of tradition among theologians are part of a larger discussion about the nature and authority of tradition that is taking place within Western culture as a whole. It is further important to note that the renewed importance attached to tradition has brought with it a number of highly contested issues. There are at least three of these that are of signal importance for theological ethics.

Universal forms of moral knowledge? The first has to do with the existence (or non-existence) of moral knowledge that, as it were, transcends the limits of particular traditions, and so makes possible moral converse between persons who have been formed by very diverse ones. This issue has assumed particular importance in contemporary debate because of the intense (and often dangerous) moral conflicts that arise both within pluralistic civil societies and between peoples from markedly different cultures and civilizations. Even a brief survey of ethical writing reveals a variety of attempts to find a basis for common morality that is not rooted in a particular tradition (Outka and Reeder 1993). They range from various theories of natural law to a search for comprehensive knowledge that would allow some final settlement of contested issues.

It lies beyond the compass of an essay of this sort to adjudicate debates of this magnitude. What can be done is to indicate briefly the sorts of things that people who insist upon the necessity of standing in a particular tradition have to say in response to the issue as posed. Negatively, they point out both that a survey of human societies does not yield broad moral agreement and that the sort of comprehensive knowledge that might settle moral disputes seems always elusive. In a more positive vein, they insist that it is simply impossible to stand outside tradition and adopt, as it were, 'a view from nowhere'. Most insist, however, that dependence on tradition does not entail moral relativism of the sort that makes it impossible to make universal moral claims. Alasdaire MacIntyre has made the point forcefully in this way: 'There is nothing paradoxical at all in asserting that from within particular traditions assertions of universal import may be and are made, assertions formulated within the limits set by the conceptual, linguistic and argumentative possibilities of that tradition, but assertions which involved the explicit rejection of any incompatible claim' (cited in Outka 1996: 102).

Dependence on tradition also does not make it impossible to argue constructively in ways that engage people from other moral traditions. Even extreme forms of dependence on tradition need not deny the possibility of finding, if only on an *ad hoc* basis, points of moral agreement with people from other traditions (Yoder 1984: 40–4). Indeed, less extreme forms will in fact assume, because there are certain necessary elements of human social life, that mutually intelligible forms of moral appeal can and will be found in any moral debate (Boyle 1992: 3–28). What they deny is that these mutually intelligible forms of appeal exist as graspable truth outside and beyond particular moral traditions.

Learning from emergent conditions and other traditions?   Another issue posed by the particularist turn is the extent to which tradition, both as specific content and as generative matrix, may be legitimately influenced by contact with other traditions or emergent cultural factors. Either or both of these eventualities may well confront a tradition not only with difference but also with new issues not heretofore addressed. When such circumstances arise, as they have in the past with (among other things) usury, marriage and divorce, slavery, and religious freedom, it seems difficult to deny that changes have occurred in a regnant tradition that in fact alter both its generalities and specifics in very radical ways (Noonan 1993: 662–8).

To return once more to the example of marriage, John Witte has shown that the meeting of Christian traditions of marriage and the more individualistic tradition of human autonomy spawned by the Enlightenment has produced alterations not only in the understanding and practice of marriage but also in the larger world-view that generates this practice. His summary of these changes is captured by the title of his book, *From Sacrament to Contract*. With respect to tradition understood as generative matrix, the liberalism of the Enlightenment did not eliminate, but it did at one and the same time reduce, the significance of a pre-established moral order and elevate the moral importance of human autonomy. This change has led to alterations in the specific moral content of the marital relationship. Its value is measured more by personal satisfaction than social benefit. Its terms and condi-tions are less entered into than freely chosen. The character of the relationship is determined less by status and more by rights. Its termination has increasingly been legitimized by free choice rather than pre-set and rather limited conditions.

The question is how these changes are to be viewed by one who stands within Christian tradition both in its broad (generative matrix) and in its narrow sense (specific content). Staunch defenders of the 'particularist turn' will be hard pressed not to conclude that these changes in certain specific ways represent some form of corruption. On the other hand, those whom Noonan has referred to as 'Modern-ists', tend to see tradition as a projection of human need, and so subject to legitimate change in response to such need (Noonan 1993: 671). 'Modernists' will thus be inclined to take a more positive view of change. In this case, it will be seen as a progressive alteration brought on by social change, new experience, and new understanding. Once more, it is impossible here to adjudicate a debate of this scope, but it does seem that the historical changes cited above make problematic a number of views—namely, those asserting that moral practices ought to remain forever fixed, or that the insights of other traditions should be rejected out of hand, or that new conditions and experience are in and of themselves justification for changing or jettisoning a tradition (Hollenbach 1996: 70).

The continuing identity of tradition?   If one admits that cultural contingency can have effects on tradition in legitimate ways, the question of the continuity and staying power of tradition arises. Here again, the Christian tradition faces severe challenges. Ernst Troeltsch noted well over a century ago the historical character of Christianity. It is a movement necessarily in relationship with the changing aspects of culture and society; and, as a result, it faces the possibility that at some point it will have changed so much that it becomes discontinuous with its origins. Indeed, one of the charges that more conservative Christians now level at liberal Christians is that they have in fact brought about such a metamorphosis. The counter-charge is, of course, that traditionalists now hold to beliefs and practices rendered untenable by new learning, social change, and experience.

How, then, is one to assess and seek to establish the staying power of Christian tradition? Here one arrives at what is perhaps the heart of the current debate over the place of tradition in Christian theology and ethics. The examples of changes in tradition adduced thus far (usury, marriage, slavery, and religious freedom) suggest the inadequacy of a form of 'confessional obedience' that is so wary of alternative traditions that it returns again and again to the text of the Bible as a *single* authoritative source that governs both its internal relations and its relations with a host society. These examples also suggest that positions such as those of Richard Rorty and Mark Taylor, who, like Nietzsche, hold that social change has simply rendered Christian tradition irretrievably lost, go too far (Outka 1996: 106). The weight of evidence favours the view that Christian tradition—even with the developments, disputes, and discontinuities pointed out by historians of Christian ethics such as Noonan and Witte—none the less manifests sufficient continuity to retain both integrity and recognizability. The examples cited suggest also that continuity and change can be satisfactorily linked only by holding in tension the following items: (1) adherence to canonical texts; (2) the governing seriousness of received tradition; (3) a thoughtful engagement with the intellectual and social trends of the various societies in which believers live; and (4) willingness on the basis of compatibility with received tradition both to incorporate aspects of these trends and to judge some of them unacceptable.

The challenge of continuity and change is well illustrated once more by the meeting of traditions now occurring in debates over the nature and goods of marriage. The received Christian tradition views men and women as creatures made in the image of God and subject to divine will. Marriage is a form of relationship the terms of which have been established by God in creation. Men and women may choose to enter into this relationship or not, but they may not choose its terms. Once having entered it, they are to be parted only by death. Short of death, the only allowable reasons for ending the relationship are if a marriage has not been properly entered, if it has been destroyed by some grievous offence like adultery, or if, because of sin, it has suffered a death analogous to physical death.

The alternative tradition views men and women first as *persons*, *selves*, and *individuals* who possess freedom and reason. As reasonable and free beings they have a right to pursue self-chosen goals as long as the pursuit of these goals does no harm to others. Marriage is one way to pursue the goals an agent may set for him- or herself. As such, it is a form of relationship the terms of which may, within certain legally defined limits, be set by the parties involved. It may also, within certain legally defined limits, be ended by the choice of one or both of the parties.

The issue presented by the meeting of these two traditions is whether and how the Christian tradition (in all three of the senses identified above) can, at one and the same time, maintain its central tenet that marriage is an institution 'ordained by God' for certain predetermined ends, yet accommodate the focus on individual choice and individual flourishing that lies at the heart of the Enlightenment tradition. It would appear on the surface at least that each might be enriched by the other, but the way in which a focus on personal choice and individual flourishing is to be incorporated into the notion of an order that is not the creature of human will, without compromising both options, is far from obvious.

The answer in part depends upon keeping in dynamic tension the four factors mentioned above. Within Christianity, the staying power of tradition depends upon maintaining a dynamic tension between loyalty to authoritative texts, deference to received tradition, thoughtful engagement with intellectual and social trends, and willingness to accept or reject novelty on the basis of compatibility with received tradition. However, successful negotiation of these shoals by all accounts of Christian tradition depends to some extent on the character of common life within the Church. Right discernment depends upon the presence within the Church and within the lives of individuals of those virtues and graces (faith, hope, love, patience, kindness, sympathy, forgiveness, truthfulness, courage, wisdom, justice, temperance) that make possible a grasp of tradition's import, the peaceful resolution of conflict, and finally unity of both belief and practice. In the end, tradition's staying power is linked to and rests upon the presence of virtue within the life of the community that it both defines and sustains.

REFERENCES AND SUGGESTED READING

BEISER, JAMES M. (1996). *The Sovereignty of Reason: The Defense of Rationality in the Early English Enlightenment*. Princeton: Princeton University Press.

BICKNELL, E. J. (1956). *A Theological Introduction to the Thirty-nine Articles of the Church of England*. London: Longmans, Green and Co.

BLOESCH, DONALD G. (1982). *Essentials of Evangelical Theology*, I: *God, Authority & Salvation*. San Francisco: Harper & Row Publishers.

BOYLE, JOSEPH (1992). 'Natural Law and the Ethics of Traditions' in Robert P. George (ed.), *Natural Law Theory: Contemporary Essays*, Oxford: Oxford University Press, 3–30.

BYRNE, JAMES M. (1996). *Religion and the Enlightenment from Descartes to Kant*. Louisville, Ky.: Westminster John Knox Press.

Catholic Encyclopedia, xv (2003). 'Tradition and Living Magisterium.' Online edition.

CONGAR, YVES (1964). *Tradition and the Life of the Church*. London: Burns & Oates.

—— (1967). *Tradition and Traditions: An Historical and a Theological Essay*. New York: Macmillan.

CULLMANN, OSCAR (1956). *The Early Church*. London: SCM Press.

DE VORAGINE, JACOBUS (1993). *The Golden Legend: Readings on the Saints*, trans. William Granger Ryan. Princeton: Princeton University Press.

FREI, HANS (1974). *The Eclipse of the Biblical Narrative: A Study in Eighteenth and Nineteenth Century Hermeneutics*. New Haven: Yale University Press.

GAY, PETER (1966). *The Enlightenment: The Rise of Modern Paganism*. New York: W. W. Norton & Company.

GOULET, XAVIER, MCINALLY, CIRAN, and WOOD, JOSEPH (1994). *The Basilica of Saint Francis: A Spiritual Pilgrimage*. Assisi: Casa Editrice Franciscana.

HANSON, R. P. C. (1962). *Tradition in the Early Church*. London: SCM Press.

HARRIS, LIZ (1985). *Holy Days: The World of a Hasidic Family*. New York: Collier Books.

HAUERWAS, STANLEY (1981). *A Community of Character: Toward a Constructive Christian Social Ethic*. Notre Dame, Ind.: University of Notre Dame Press.

HOLLENBACH DAVID, S J, (1996). 'Tradition, Historicity, and Truth in Theological Ethics', in Lisa Sowle Cahill and James F. Childress (eds.), *Christian Ethics: Problems and Prospects*, Cleveland: Pilgrim Press, 60–75.

LINDBECK, GEORGE (1984). *The Nature of Doctrine: Religion and Theology in a Postliberal Age*. Philadelphia: Westminster Press.

MACINTYRE, ALASDAIR (1981). *After Virtue: A Study in Moral Theory*. Notre Dame, Ind.: University of Notre Dame Press.

—— (1988). *Whose Justice? Which Rationality?* Notre Dame, Ind.: University of Notre Dame Press.

—— (1990). *Three Rival Versions of Moral Enquiry: Encyclopaedia, Genealogy, and Tradition*. Notre Dame, Ind.: University of Notre Dame Press.

MEYENDORFF, JOHN (1978). *Living Tradition: Orthodox Witness in the Contemporary World*. Chestwood, NY: St Vladimir's Seminary Press.

—— (1984). *Marriage: An Orthodox Perspective*. Crestwood, NY: St Vladimir's Seminary Press.

NEWMAN, JOHN HENRY (1974). *An Essay on the Development of Christian Doctrine*. Harmondsworth: Pelican Books.

NOONAN, JOHN T. jun. (1993). 'Development in Moral Doctrine', *Theological Studies*, 54, 662–77.

OUTKA, GENE (1996). 'The Particularist Turn in Theological and Philosophical Ethics', in Lisa Sowle Cahill and James F. Childress (eds.), *Christian Ethics: Problems and Prospects*, Cleveland: Pilgrim Press, 93–118.

—— and REEDER, JOHN P., jun. (eds.) (1993). *Prospects for a Common Morality*. Princeton: Princeton University Press.

PELIKAN, JAROSLAV (1984). *The Vindication of Tradition*. New Haven: Yale University Press.

SPOTO, DONALD (2003). *Reluctant Saint: The Life of Francis of Assisi.* London: Penguin Compass Books.

SYKES, STEPHEN (1995). *Unashamed Anglicanism.* Nashville: Abingdon Press.

TAPPERT, THEODORE G. (ed.) (1959). *The Book of Concord: The Confession of the Evangelical Lutheran Church.* Philadelphia: Fortress Press.

TURNER, PHILIP W. (1976). 'Come, Let us Eat and Drink', in *Theology and Culture: Essays in Honor of Albert T. Mollegen and Clifford Stanley,* Supplementary Series, 7 *Anglican Theological Review.*

—— (2003). 'Tolerable Diversity and Ecclesial Integrity: Communion or Federation?', *Journal of Anglican Studies,* 1/2 (Dec.), 24–46.

TURNER, VICTOR (1960). *Ndembu Divination: Its Symbolism and Technique,* Rhodes Livingstone Papers, no. 31. Manchester: Manchester University Press.

—— (1961). *Chihamba, the White Spirit,* Rhodes Livingstone Papers, no. 33. Manchester: Manchester University Press.

—— (1967). *The Forest of Symbols.* Ithaca, NY: Cornell University Press.

—— (1968). *The Drums of Affliction.* Oxford: Oxford University Press.

—— (1969). *The Ritual Process: Structure and Anti-Structure.* Chicago: Aldine Press.

WITTE, JOHN jun. (1997). *From Sacrament to Contract: Marriage, Religion and Law in the Western Tradition.* Louisville, Ky.: Westminster John Knox Press.

YODER, JOHN HOWARD (1984). *The Priestly Kingdom: Social Ethics as Gospel.* Notre Dame, Ind.: University of Notre Dame Press.

—— (1994). *The Royal Priesthood: Essays Ecclesiological and Ecumenical.* Scottsdale, Pa.: Herald Press.

CHAPTER 9

REASON AND NATURAL LAW

STEPHEN POPE

THE centre of theological ethics is God—the 'ineffable one', 'the nameless one', and 'holy mystery', who remains always incomprehensible to human reason (see Rahner 1985: 46–7, 65–6). The conclusions reached through exercising the powers of human intelligence will therefore have a secondary significance to the kind of knowledge communicated in revelation and experienced in faith. The God of Christian theological ethics, the concern of this essay, is revealed as Creator and Redeemer. Faith in this God leads one to affirm that an ordering wisdom lies behind both the inherent *logos* of the natural world and the explicit revelation communicated in Scripture and the Christian tradition.

Scripture, the written record of God's self-communication to humanity, is the single most important source for theological ethics. Yet, since theology is generated by faith seeking understanding, theological ethics employs the various cognitive capacities that we group together under the term 'reason'. Scholars of course differ, sometimes vehemently, over what 'reason' means, how it functions, and what role it ought to play within theological ethics (see Gustafson 1978).

The doctrine of 'natural law' constitutes a particular subset of the larger question of the place of reason and philosophy in theological ethics. Its adherents tend to be Roman Catholic, but not always so. Its meaning is anything but unproblematic and obvious. In spite of having been subject to wave after wave of criticism in the history of philosophy and theology, natural law continues to appeal to those who believe that ethics must be grounded in being and the moral life based on what is good for human beings. Periodic disclosures of human wickedness and horrors—lynchings, secret police abductions, or death squad assassinations—reawaken our sense of the importance of objective moral standards to which evil-doers can be held accountable. Reminders of human goodness inspire gratitude for positive moral capacities bestowed on us by the Creator and elicited by grace.

Theological ethics is drawn to natural law for two fundamental reasons. First, it advances a form of moral realism which affirms that moral standards are based in reality, and in this sense 'objective', rather than manufactured by human decisions. Second, some ethicists are attracted to natural law for its universal scope and its claim to apply to all human beings—rich as well as poor, conqueror as well as conquered, men as well as women.

Yet the ancient and medieval contexts from which natural law doctrine emerged are now long gone. It is thus helpful to keep in mind that concepts taken out of context can generate misunderstanding and confusion unless explicated with care and interpreted in ways that make sense to new audiences. Consider the meaning of 'natural'. When the ancients understood the good life to be 'according to nature', they meant according to what is best, most noble, or most excellent in human nature. Moderns, on the other hand, understand 'nature' according to the methodology of the natural sciences as what occurs with some frequency under natural conditions. Classical philosophy and modern science refer to 'nature' in entirely different senses, but references to both continue to shape contemporary moral discourse. Even to understand what is meant by 'natural law' presents a significant challenge for us.

This essay begins with a brief discussion of the historical origins of the notion of natural law and its medieval development, then proceeds to examine its modern transformations, more recent theoretical developments, and contemporary challenges. Since not every aspect of such a complex topic can be examined adequately in an essay-length treatment, this essay will focus on how 'nature' functions normatively within natural law ethics.

ORIGINS

The ancient precursors to natural law appealed to nature (*physis*) as morally prior to social convention and positive law (*nomos*). Plato's *Gorgias* argued against Callicles' understanding of natural justice as the 'law of nature' by which the strong rule the weak (Plato 1961a: 483E). The *Republic* examined the 'natural justice' that exists in the properly ordered soul and city-state (Plato 1961b). Aristotle distinguished actions that are 'legally just' from those that are 'naturally just' (Aristotle

1941a: 1134^{b}18). Cicero's *De Re Publica* (1929: 3. 22) first advanced the explicit claim that the 'natural law' provides universal moral principles obliging not only Roman citizens but all human beings. He opposed the claim of what later came to be called 'moral positivism', according to which binding moral claims are not discovered in human nature but rather are 'posited' by the will of some authority. Outside such a will, positivism holds, there is no binding moral standard.

Though the early Church and the Patristic age reflected on the virtues, the moral law, and natural justice, the first high tide of natural law reflection came with Thomas Aquinas. He understood natural law in the context of a more encompassing theological framework that assimilated Aristotelian and Neoplatonic metaphysics to Christian doctrine. Thomas appropriated Aristotle's definition of 'nature' as an intrinsic principle of movement and rest (see Aristotle 1941b: 192^{b}14 ff.; Aquinas 1948: I, 29, 1 ad 4; all subsequent references to the work of Thomas are also to the *Summa Theologiae*; citations specify volume, question, and article). In this philosophy, a being's 'nature' is what it is when fully developed. A being's *telos*, or end, then, reveals its nature, both how it characteristically acts and how it is characteristically acted upon. In Thomistic cosmology, the Creator governs the world by arranging the parts in proper relation to the whole cosmos and by providing individual beings with natures proper to their own actions. Just as grace perfects, and does not destroy, nature, so the cardinal virtues are perfected by the theological virtues. The virtues lead to 'beatitude', or complete flourishing.

As 'rational animals', human beings must freely choose and intelligently pursue their end. Morality provides a path to true and perfect happiness, experienced partially in this life and completely in the next. 'Flourishing' functions as the justification for virtues and moral standards rather than as the intentional and direct goal of every act. The agent asks herself, 'What is the right thing to do?' or 'What would a good person do in this situation?' rather than 'Which of these actions will most contribute to my flourishing?' (let alone, 'Which of these options will make me happier?').

Of all animals, human beings alone possess intellect. Thomas followed Aristotle in distinguishing between the speculative intellect, which considers truth for its own sake, and the practical intellect, which seeks to understand in order to act appropriately. Both forms of intellectual activity move from premises to conclusions. Practical reasoning begins from fundamental premises known by the intellect to be true and grasped by the natural disposition that Thomas called 'synderesis'. The properly functioning human mind recognizes without effort that every agent acts for an end, and that 'the good is what all things seek after' (Aquinas 1948: I-II, 94, 2). From this principle flows the first precept: do good and avoid evil. Every specific moral decision ought to accord with this first principle of practical reason.

Practical reasoning directs human action in two ways: general and particular. Reason applies general knowledge of moral principles to particular cases in light of specific knowledge of their details. The virtue of prudence, or practical wisdom, habitually leads the moral agent who possesses it to act in a 'fitting' manner (Aquinas 1948: I-II, 57, 2, 5). Moral reasoning can go astray either through ignorance of the particulars of a case or by ignorance of the general moral principle (or principles) relevant to it (Aquinas 1948: I-II, 76, 1).

The process of moral reasoning results in an act of conscience, a particular judgement to act or refrain from acting. Good judgements are based on proper understanding and lead to reasonable decisions. Reason is competent to control, and proper control is exercised in light of reason shaped by the right purposes (Aquinas 1948: I-II, 18, 9). Being directed to an appropriate end, of course, is not simply a matter of reasoning about it. Appetites must be well disposed to their proper end through the 'habits' of the moral virtues—not only prudence, but also justice, temperance, and fortitude. If they are not disposed to their proper end—if 'right reason' is not complemented by 'right desire'—then moral reasoning itself will be derailed (Aquinas 1948: II-II, 47, 4). Natural law is thus 'rational' but not 'rationalist'.

Thomas's understanding of 'nature' and 'reason' converged in his account of law. Thomas understood 'law' as an ordinance of reason, ordered to the common good, made by one who has care for a community, and communicated publicly (Aquinas 1948: I-II, 90, 4). 'Law' governs in analogous ways the created world ('eternal law'), human behaviour ('natural law'), particular human political communities ('temporal law' or 'positive law'), and the Christian life ('divine law'). The human person is made in the 'image of God' and endowed with free choice. Since each person has the capacity to choose to accept (or to reject) the moral principles of the eternal law, Thomas defined natural law as 'the rational creature's participation in the eternal law' (Aquinas 1948: I-II, 91, 2). ('Natural' for Thomas did not mean 'automatic' or 'mechanistic'.) This participation is both reasonable and natural: each person must use his or her reason to discover what accords with 'right reason' in any particular situation, and 'right reason' always conforms to the order inscribed by the Creator in nature.

Practical reason proceeds from indemonstrable or self-evident principles. The most fundamental obligation, as we have seen, is to 'do good and avoid evil'. The principles of the natural law take as their 'matter' natural inclinations: the inclination for existence common to all beings, the generic inclinations to reproduction and sexual relations shared by all animals, and the specifically human inclinations to political life, truth seeking, and spirituality held in common by all human beings. Practical reason thus applies the principles of the natural law to the expression of natural human inclinations expressed in different domains of existence—sex, marriage and family, life, communication, property, and so forth.

Two additional features of practical reason must be kept in mind. First, practical reasoning, unlike speculative reasoning, deals with individual and contingent matters, and therefore its judgements are not characterized by absolute necessity (see Aquinas 1948: I-II, 3, 6 ad 2). They are true 'for the most part', but do not always hold. Moral principles therefore need to be interpreted with sensitivity to the particular nuances of concrete cases, not applied rigidly and mechanistically (see Aquinas 1948: I-II, 96, 1, 6).

Second, this process of derivation acknowledges a gradation in the authority made by different kinds of moral claims. What is taken by one community to be an application of the natural law can be dispensed with in another community when it is determined to be detrimental to the common good, justice, and virtue (see Aquinas 1948: I-II, 100, 8; see also I-II, 97, 6; 97, 4 ad 3). A change in circumstances can mean that the secondary precepts of the natural law do not apply in these cases; it does not imply, however, that the secondary precepts are invalidated (see Kossel in Pope 2002: 169–93).

Since human nature includes body and soul, the human good is material as well as spiritual, intellectual, and moral. Human nature and the good proportionate to it, like both the political community and the universe as a whole, is structured hierarchically. Human nature is oriented to lower goods (of the body), to relatively higher goods (of the soul), and to an ultimate good (God). Practical reason is equipped to grasp the essentials of this order, though it also benefits from the detail, clarity, and assurance of revelation. Most importantly, divine law orients the person to an otherwise unknown destiny—the Beatific Vision—but rather than obliterating the naturally human in favour of an exclusively other-worldly good, this end calls forth its deepest potentialities.

The moral life orders the lower powers to serve the higher, and both to contribute to love of God and love for neighbour. Acts of virtue are rewarding in and of themselves; vicious acts constitute their own punishment. The wicked do not always recognize their own misery, but this kind of ignorance is in itself an added dimension of self-inflicted punishment. The thief, liar, and murderer work contrary to their own happiness not only in the afterlife but also in this one. The saint, on the other hand, achieves true beatitude even when suffering.

Natural Law Challenged

The Thomistic interpretation of the natural law has been subjected to a wide variety of significant criticisms throughout the history of philosophy and theology. Rather than examine each particular criticism in detail, a task that would require volumes, I will confine myself to a broad overview of a few important features of this challenge. After this brief overview, I will consider various ways in which natural lawyers have responded to these challenges and then make an assessment of the current state of the question.

A series of massive shifts in the way we understand nature began in the seventeenth century and had a seismic effect on how we think about natural law (see Taylor 1989; Pinckaers 1995; MacIntyre 1981). One of the most important of these shifts for our topic was triggered in 1859 by the publication of Charles Darwin's *The Origin of Species*. 'Darwin's dangerous idea', as philosopher Daniel Dennett (1995) calls it, called into question many of the presuppositions taken for granted by natural law ethicists. Investigations into animal intelligence deflate exaggerated claims about the uniqueness of human reason; the field of genetics has been taken to lower our estimate of the moral power, or freedom, at the disposal of human agents; neurophysiology and cognitive science raise questions about the influence of the brain on the mind (and even the existence of the soul); and studies of animal sociality suggest that morality is only an extension of primate strategies for affiliation, coalition building, and the management of aggression. Evolutionary theory regards human behaviour in an increasingly mechanistic way, and as the discoveries of genetics multiply, the prestige of mechanistic anthropology expands.

Scientific views of the natural world and our place in it are not particularly comforting. Evolutionists typically depict nature as a heartless, cruel, cold place where all species are eventually eliminated by the relentless, wasteful, and bloody process of natural selection (see Huxley 1894; Williams 1988; Hausfater and Hrdy 1984). Nature is morally purposeless, so whatever purposes it is given must come from human choices. Since human action is itself the product of the same causal forces that control the rest of nature, the argument runs, we cannot be expected to break from those forces in a very dramatic way.

Reason on this view works most powerfully in a scientifically reductive manner, breaking down problems into their most elementary parts and then subjecting them to empirical investigation. Evolutionists studying the behaviour of particular organisms can make testable predictions in light of certain constraints. Reason also functions in other ways, of course, but once reason moves away from the scientific (and mathematical) enterprise, it declines in reliability. Reason, *contra* Kant, is not the primary guide for human life—'Genes are the primary policy makers; brains are the executives' (Dawkins 1976: 60). This is especially the case when reason moves into morality. Instrumental reason is competent to indicate the means for implementing moral values, but it has no way of examining the legitimacy of these values themselves (see Weber 1958 [1919]).

The destructive implications of this view for the 'moral law' are clear. Nature is purposeless and amoral. Morality is the product of cultural evolution, which facilitates co-operation, group bonds, and social control. Nature contains neither an objective moral law nor an inherent moral order within which human beings function. Nature belies the claim made by the South African human rights activist Archbishop Desmond Tutu, for example, and accepted by all natural law ethicists, that 'this universe has been constructed in such a way that unless we live in accordance with its moral laws we will pay the price for it' (Tutu 1997: 196).

Evolutionists do not infer, however, that we are fated to be immoralists. In fact, the opposite is the case: they argue that our only hope lies not in the rescue operation of a transcendent deity but in the willingness of courageous human beings to assume responsibility for building more fair, just, and tolerant communities. Instead of legitimizing selfishness, clannishness, and chauvinism, most evolutionary moralists strive to endorse mainstream liberal values such as liberty, individual rights, and tolerance. Because there is no natural law, in other words, moral order has to be *created* by human agents. Morality allows us to override, at least to some extent, the complete indifference of nature to human affairs (see Nitecki and Nitecki 1993; Rose 1998; O'Hear 1997).

CONTEMPORARY APPROACHES
TO THE NATURAL LAW

All ethical theories operate on the basis of a description, implicit or explicit, of the morally relevant traits of human nature; relatively more sound ethical positions are based on relatively more adequate accounts of human nature. Conversely, defective presuppositions about human nature can cripple an ethical theory.

Contemporary advocates of natural law ethics work within the context of a cultural world that lacks any consensus about an objective basis for moral claims. Natural law is challenged by historicism as well as by naturalism. Naturalism, we have just seen, denies that there is either a transcendent purpose to life or a metaphysical basis for affirming that any moral claims are true and binding on all human beings. Historicism claims that reality is composed only of individual entities, and that it is therefore impossible to make claims that apply to all people. Because human beings exist only as particular individuals living at particular times and in particular cultures, there can be no universal moral claims. Both naturalism and historicism work with the underlying premiss that the world is valueless and purposeless, except when values and purposes are created by human choices. There is no shared humanity, only a vast collection of individuals from the same species locked in various modes of competition against one another.

Natural law ethicists respond to this challenge in a variety of ways. One strategy suggests a return to the golden age of natural law. Those who defend what can be called, for lack of a better term, 'revived Thomism' continue to produce translations and commentaries on Thomistic texts and their modern commentators (see, e.g., McInerny 1982, 1992).

A second approach to natural law focuses on the exercise of practical reason within the context of specific problematic cases. The 'public philosophy' developed by John Courtney Murray, SJ, pursues natural law as the basis of moral discourse in pluralistic societies governed by representative democracy (see Murray 1960). Murray and other admirers of Pope John XXIII's *Pacem in Terris* critically appropriate modern insights into the nature of human rights and combine them with the older Thomistic focus on duties and the common good (see Hollenbach 2003).

A third, revisionist position interprets natural law in light of the 'historical consciousness' promoted by the Second Vatican Council (see, e.g., McCormick 1989). Revisionist natural law holds that the rightness or wrongness of acts depends on whether they are beneficial or harmful to the person, rather than on their conformity to nature. Identifying an act as 'contrary to nature' indicates its 'relative disvalue', but not necessarily its moral impermissibility. An act is only morally wrong when, other things being equal, there is no proportionate reason justifying it (McCormick 1989: 134).

Two other innovative approaches to natural law are particularly important today: the new natural law theory and the personalist natural law theory.

THE NEW NATURAL LAW THEORY

A new approach to natural law has been developed partly in opposition to both revisionist natural law and revived Thomism. Germain Grisez, John Finnis, and their colleagues constructed a 'new natural law theory' (see Finnis 1980; Grisez 1983), because they did not believe that the received theory was any longer philosophically viable. Their theory holds that the 'first principles of practical reason' give rationality to the process of moral decision making. Its first principles are known 'in themselves' (*per se nota*), comprehended immediately when their meaning and reference are understood, and indemonstrable. Advocates of this theory know that it stands or falls with legitimate metaphysics, e.g., regarding human freedom, but they attempt to eschew the kind of explicit metaphysical foundations for the theory developed by the neo-Scholastics and revived Thomists.

The distinctiveness of this approach lies in its attempt to address the 'naturalistic fallacy' objection by arguing that practical reason, not speculative reason, derives a set of moral implications from a principle that is already normative rather than purely descriptive (Grisez 1965). Rather than draw moral norms from some set of facts about human nature, the new theory derives particular moral norms from more general moral norms. The first principle of practical reason is itself both normative and 'underivable'. All other principles are derived from it by reason alone (for this among other reasons it is often associated with the ethics of Kant).

Practical reason identifies several basic goods: life, knowledge, aesthetic appreciation, play, friendship, practical reasonableness, and religion (see, *inter alia,* Finnis 1980: 86–90). Particular items have from time to time been added to or subtracted from this catalogue, so, for example, it later came to include 'the marital good' (George 1996: 5). Basic goods are intrinsically valuable and universally recognized as such. The key moral principle holds that it is *always* wrong to intend to destroy an instantiation of a basic good (see Finnis 1980: 118–23). So, for example, since life is a basic good, murder is always wrong.

The 'new natural law' presents a formidable ethical theory in terms that are intelligible to contemporary philosophers. Though this position does not rely on faith in any explicit way, and in fact claims to be purely rational, it has been used by many Catholics to provide a contemporary theoretical defence of the moral teachings of the magisterium. It is no coincidence that the content of the 'new natural law' happens to agree with almost every item of moral teaching found in the *Catechism of the Catholic Church.*

The 'new natural law theory' has been subject to significant philosophical criticisms. First, lists of basic goods are notoriously ambiguous—e.g., are all religions, including cults, instantiations of a basic value? Second, it holds that basic goods are incommensurable and cannot be subjected to 'weighting', but it is not clear that one cannot reasonably weight, say, religion as a more important good than play. The claim that basic goods cannot be 'attacked' seems to deny the experience of deep moral conflict between competing goods.

Finally, this position is criticized for isolating its philosophical interpretation of human nature from other descriptive accounts of the same and for operating without empirical evidence. It proposes natural law without nature. Finnis opines, for example, without offering any evidence, that same sex relations of every kind fail to offer intelligible goods of their own, but only 'bodily and emotional satisfaction, pleasurable experience, unhinged from basic human reasons for action and posing as its own rationale' (Finnis 1998: 153, 151). This theory reasons a priori from principles to what must in fact be the empirical case, but not in the reverse direction.

Personalist Natural Law

A fifth reading of the natural law comes from Pope John Paul II, the tradition's most representative figure in living memory. A staunch opponent of the widespread moral relativism of the modern world, the pope denounced the departure of historic Christian cultures from the gospel and their gradual slide away from the objective moral law.

Unlike the previous approaches to moral knowledge, John Paul II spoke first and foremost from an explicitly scriptural perspective. This pleased Protestants, who have been critical of natural law on the grounds that it assigned reason more authority than revelation (see Barth 1961: 3–31; Niebuhr 1979 [1935]: ch. 5, but modified in 1941: I; but also Hütter and Dieter 1998). The pope's account of natural law drew from Scripture, but also built on Thomistic precedents, and incorporated modern notions of human dignity and human rights. This account of natural law was developed on the distinctively personalist and Christocentric anthropology presented by the Second Vatican Council's 'Pastoral Constitution on the Church in the Modern World': 'only in the mystery of the incarnate Word does the mystery of man take on light' (Flannery 1988: 922).

Yet the pope did anything but break away from the natural law—on the contrary, he assumed its relevance even when he engaged in scriptural exegesis on moral matters. The encyclical *Veritatis Splendor* enunciated familiar themes from the natural law tradition. Natural law is 'inscribed' in the heart of every person, grounded in the human good, and prohibits 'intrinsically evil acts' (John Paul II 1993: par. 81). Reason is a gift of God, but takes its proper orientation from faith— especially today, when knowledge of the natural law has been blurred in the 'modern conscience'. Unlike the emphasis of 'public philosophy' and the 'new natural law theory', the pope's ethic repeatedly insisted that an adequate grasp of the natural law depends on revelation, faith, and adherence to the teachings of the magisterium. As an 'expert in humanity', the Church has the most profound grasp of the principles of the natural law, and also the best vantage point from which to understand its secondary principles and their application.

This is not to say that the pope gave up on reason or regarded natural law as less intrinsically intelligible than did other natural lawyers. He, like the others, would have agreed with the revisionist denial that there are any 'mysterious ethical norms which are simply impervious to human insight' (McCormick 1989: 204). John Paul II continued to reaffirm the ancient view of moral standards as inherently intelligible. The increasing appeal of human rights around the world (by ordinary people, if not always by their governments) confirms the accessibility of the moral law. Natural law *qua* human rights provides the basis for the infusion of ethical principles into the political arena of pluralistic democracies. It also provides criteria for holding accountable criminal states or transnational actors that violate human dignity by engaging, for example, in 'genocide, abortion... deportation, slavery, prostitution... [and] degrading conditions of work which treat laborers as mere instruments of profit' (John Paul II 1993: par. 80, citing *Gaudium et Spes*, par. 27). Natural law holds out the best resource for countering both amoral relativism and the tyrannical misuse of power (see John Paul II 1995: par. 70).

The pope's personalist natural law theory gave an important place to fixed, knowable, and clear moral rules that apply to communities as well as to individuals. Its treatment of reproductive issues is illustrative. States as well as couples, no matter what difficulties and hardships they face, 'must abide by the divine plan for responsible procreation' (John Paul II 1995: par. 97). Sounding a theme from Pope Pius XI and Pope Paul VI, John Paul II warned his listeners that 'The moral law obliges them in every case to control the impulse of instinct and passion, and to respect the biological laws inscribed in their person' (1995: par. 97).

Natural law thus proscribes not only artificial contraception, abortion, infanticide, and euthanasia, but also newer biomedical procedures regarding experimentation with human embryos and human cloning. Natural law also provides moral criteria for assessing economic and political systems. Though there is no one correct model of an economic or political system, natural law does require that any given economic or political order affirm human dignity, promote human rights, foster the unity of the human family, and support meaningful human activity in every sphere of social life (see John Paul 1987: par. 41, in O'Brien and Shannon 1992: 424–5; John Paul II 1991: par. 43, in O'Brien and Shannon 1992: 471–2).

John Paul II's personalist interpretation of natural law has been criticized on several grounds. First, it stressed law at the expense of reason and nature. As the Dominican Thomist Herbert McCabe observed of *Veritatis Splendor*, 'despite its frequent references to St. Thomas, it is still trapped in a post-Renaissance morality, in terms of law and conscience and free will' (McCabe 1994: 67; see also Spohn 1995). Second, the pope was criticized for an inconsistent eclecticism that did not coherently relate biblical, natural law, and rights-oriented language in a synthetic vision. He switched from one kind of argument to another without indicating how the different parts are integrated into a coherent whole. Third, he was charged with a highly selective and ahistorical understanding of natural law. Thus, what he described as 'unchanging' precepts prohibiting intrinsically evil acts have at times been changed. As John Noonan put it, in the long history of Catholic ethics, one finds that 'what was forbidden became lawful (the cases of usury and marriage); what was permissible became unlawful (the case of slavery); and what was required became forbidden (the persecution of heretics)' (Noonan 1995: 194). Fourth, critics argued that John Paul II had an underdeveloped sense of 'historical consciousness', and therefore consistently slighted the contingency, variability, and ambiguities of historical particularity (see Curran 2002: 61–6). This can lead to an absolutist and legalistic reading of the natural law that obscures the need for the virtue of prudence. Fifth, this approach to natural law also led feminists to accuse the pope of failing to attend sufficiently to the oppression of women in the history of Christianity and to downplay the need for change in the structures of the Church (see Cahill 1998; Traina 1999).

To his credit, the pope was more concerned with the fundamental basis of the natural law than are proponents of most of the other positions examined here. His approach was theological and ontological: nature is creation, the human creature must be understood in personal terms, and the person must always act in accordance with the plan of the Creator. This theological understanding of creation, however, is never informed, co-ordinated with, or even placed in contact with scientific ways of viewing nature. This is not because the pope denied the proper autonomy of science. On the contrary, his treatment of the Galileo case, the status of evolutionary science, and his endorsement of the dialogue between science and theology all indicate the contrary (see John Paul II 1986: 22, 1996). His categorization of evolutionary science as pertaining to the body but not to the soul, however, implies that the core of the person lies outside the province of science. His approach to natural law proceeded on the basis of phenomenological, metaphysical, and theological reflection on the human person, while ignoring scientific data and theories about human behaviour. The insulation of this theological perspective is understandable in the writings of a figure whose concern is primarily pastoral, but the same is not true for others of like mind in the academy who have the time and talent to address this important but neglected issue.

PROSPECTS FOR NATURAL LAW

These natural law theories fail to relate their teleological views of human behaviour—its orientation to the good—to contemporary accounts of humanity or the natural world. This lacuna is due in part to disciplinary specialization, but it will need to be addressed if the natural law tradition is to continue to develop. The natural law tradition generally disagrees with those modern ethical theories that deny the necessity of considering broad metaphysical and anthropological issues. Natural law doctrine roots moral standards—both 'precepts' and 'virtues'—in the human good. Its interpretation of the human good depends in turn on an account of human nature—its powers, potentialities, and inclinations. The question, 'What is right and wrong?' can only be addressed in light of the broader question, 'What is the human good?', and helpful reflection on this question in turn depends on how one answers the question, 'What is human nature?'

The most fundamental philosophical issue here concerns 'teleology', or the presence of 'purpose' or 'goals' in nature. The early modern opponents of natural law first denied the existence of purpose in the natural world as a whole, and then extended this denial to human nature itself, where purposes came to be identified with human choices, conventions, or cultures. Natural law ethics evaporates if nature is purposeless.

The intellectual journey of philosopher Alasdair MacIntyre illustrates the importance of re-establishing a sense of the purposeful character of nature. His seminal work *After Virtue* attempted to retrieve Aristotle's virtue ethics without also drawing on what MacIntyre called his 'metaphysical biology' (McIntyre 1980: 152, 183). At that time MacIntyre believed it possible to base virtue ethics on a social teleology provided by the goods internal to communal 'practices' (MacIntyre

1981: 175 f.). A person is a 'story telling animal' whose identity and purposes come not through nature but through the narratives of living traditions. His next major work, *Whose Justice? Which Rationality?* moved beyond Aristotle to an appropriation of Thomas Aquinas's virtue ethics, thus inclining him towards a greater appreciation of the moral significance of the natural law and human nature (MacIntyre 1988: 181, 194 f.). MacIntyre's more recent writing, *Dependent Rational Animals* (1999), employs naturalistic observations about natural functions of animals (notably dolphins) as a means for thinking about natural purposes. 'I now judge that I was in error in supposing an ethics independent of biology to be possible,' writes MacIntyre (1999: p. x). But here MacIntyre draws from biology to underscore the reality of human vulnerability and disability in relation to which the 'virtues of acknowledged dependence' (1999: ch. 10) must be developed and exercised. Unfortunately, MacIntyre's interest in animality is usually restricted to various forms of weakness or disability. He does not reflect on how the behavioural traits of animals are related to larger questions of natural purposes. He thus begins, but does not complete, the development of a new teleological view of human nature upon which a revitalized natural law could be built.

The continued development of natural law ethics depends on re-establishing a sense of the purposefulness of the natural world in general and of human nature in particular. Given the magnitude of this task, an essay of this sort can provide only rudimentary outlines of how such reflection might proceed.

First, we need to reflect more carefully on the way in which the cosmos is structured to sustain moral purpose—i.e., 'teleologically'. The term 'teleology' is used in so many ways that it is nearly impossible to avoid misunderstanding (see Ayala 1970 and 1989); yet natural law ethics has no alternative but to use it or something like it. Natural law ethicists need to be clear that they are not suggesting that every event in the universe exists to produce a predetermined goal: e.g., that the occurrence of mutations in DNA is directed by some sort of biological planning agent. The purpose of the universe exists in and through the interaction of chance and necessity that constitute its overall design.

The universe has been 'fine-tuned' to give rise to at least one planet with physical conditions that allow for the emergence and maintenance of life. The Earth provided conditions that were hospitable first to beings marked by some elemental forms of information processing, then to beings capable of consciousness, and finally to beings capable of self-consciousness. The earliest forms of life gave rise to organisms with increased capacities for movement, sensitivity, awareness, and responsiveness. Organisms moved only by chemical reaction gave rise to organisms moved by apprehensions, drives, and emotions. Spontaneity was complemented by restraints imposed by the social ordering of animals living in groups. Increased environmental demands called forth expanding behavioural repertoires, increasingly complex emotional responses, and more and more sophisticated mechanisms of information processing.

This broad evolutionary context gave rise to a particularly intelligent primate, *Homo sapiens*, whose social life, even in its earliest phases, was made possible by complex forms of symbolic communication, especially language. Human intelligence, like that of other primates, was originally suited to simple problem solving—e.g., how to move across complex terrain to get food or how to fend off threats from aggressors—but our ancestors gradually gained capacities of heart and mind that allowed them to be captivated by wonder and to reflect on questions for their own sake. Music, art, poetry, and religion came to express 'contemplative' as well as 'practical', or socially functional, purposes.

A closely related development occurred morally: the necessity of making choices for instrumental purposes gave rise to the capacity to care about goods and persons for their own sakes. The development of the human sense of compassion and awareness of justice came to extend moral concern beyond one's own circle of 'reciprocators' to any human being in need or any person suffering from injustice. Some aspects of the basic human sense of fairness expand upon a proto-moral sense of equity shared with other social primates (see de Waal 1996; Brosnan and de Waal 2003). The universal appeal of the golden rule testifies to this moral development in the species and to the natural roots of justice. The emergence of human cognitive and moral abilities was also accompanied by the emergence of a capacity for religious self-transcendence. The culmination of the evolutionary process consists in the ability of the cosmos, through human beings, to understand its existence as gift, to respond to its Creator with awe, gratitude, and fidelity, and to undertake responsibility for the well-being of those spheres of creation within which it is possible to do so.

The word 'teleology' is used here in two senses. First, the 'cosmic evolution' of the universe as a whole is teleological in that it has given rise to increasingly complex structures and forms of life from which a species capable of intelligent and loving behaviour has emerged. Second, human nature is also teleological in that it is naturally oriented both to specific goods and, more importantly, to the good as such. Moral systems around the world bear witness to this natural orientation.

Human nature is inclined to a variety of goods. The human good includes, as Thomas would put it, 'external goods' and 'goods of the body', and therefore ethics must take into account the considerable pre-rational, biological roots of human nature (see Porter 1999: ch. 1). Biology considers a range of goods that comprise part of what Thomas called 'temporal happiness', but this end is, at its best, radically incomplete, since the biological does not encompass even psychological, social, or cultural goods, let alone moral and religious ones, in their own right. Evolutionary theory, then, will always fail to satisfy those who seek in it a complete account of the natural law. Indeed, evolutionists need to be subjected to critical scrutiny when they present a kind of quasi-natural law argument suggesting that the values of our own particular culture are best suited to address our natural needs as human beings (see Beckstrom 1993 and Buss 1994).

The human good also includes not only 'external goods' and 'goods of the body' but 'goods of the soul' that are not reducible to other goods. Since what is 'natural' for the human person is not simply what is 'biological' or 'organic' or 'genetic', the attempt comprehensively to explain or justify natural law in terms of evolutionary theory is bound to fail. The 'natural' includes the full range of inclinations identified by Thomas, including those desires common to rational beings: for knowledge, for life in political community, and for union with God. These distinctively human orientations point to the highest good which we are capable of desiring: the knowledge and love of God. They also imply, in contrast to the 'new natural law theory', a kind of general hierarchy among the goods to which human beings are naturally oriented.

Clearly, human nature is ordered not only to the good. History attests to our susceptibility to corruption, bias, and excessive self-concern. The juxtaposition of various kinds of adaptations and motivations leaves the modern human psyche fraught with moral complexity, ambiguity, and tension. At the same time, though, widespread resentment over such evils and their passionate uncovering and denunciation themselves testify to the more fundamental human inclination to the good.

The teleological interpretation of humanity makes it absolutely critical to distinguish two senses of the word 'natural': the statistical and the normative. The statistical sense of nature is merely what occurs with some frequency under natural conditions. In this sense of the word it is entirely 'natural' for some male animals to practice infanticide, to kill conspecifics from other groups, and to engage in forced copulation with fertile females (see Daly and Wilson 1988). Acts like these were probably also placed by natural selection on our own evolved menu of behavioural options in the course of our evolutionary past because in the distant past they were 'fitness enhancing' under certain conditions (see Midgley 1978; Barkow, Cosmides, and Tooby 1992; Pinker 1997).

The normative sense of the 'natural' relates this repertoire of behavioural 'givens' residing in our human nature to the morally more fundamental inclination to the good. The latter provides a comprehensive position from which to interpret the former. Biologically based emotional proclivities and motivations are objects of deliberate moral choices and behaviourally developed habits. The 'phenotypic plasticity' of 'open programs' (Mayr 1988: 68) allows for, and even requires, choices that accumulate to shape our more or less persisting habits. Natural law ethics, then, is not an alternative to an account of ethics in terms of 'virtues', but closely dependent on it. We distinguish pre-moral natural *proclivities* like sexual attraction and in-group loyalty from moral *virtues* like marital love and ordered patriotism and *vices* like sexual promiscuity and xenophobia. The proclivities are pre-personal and pre-rational inclinations; the virtues are a reasonable and morally ordered set of dispositions. Higher-level intellectual and affective capacities enable us to act in ways that run counter to our 'fitness interests', so the moral challenge put to us—as both responsible agents and as moral communities—is to shape the expression of the array of our evolved proclivities in ways that accord with 'right reason'. The moral life is a matter of gradually shaping these emotional responses into forms that promote the human good.

This view of reason and nature provides a way of interpreting the moral law. A right way of acting is not ethically obligatory or legitimate simply because it is 'natural', in the scientific sense, as 'evolved' or 'genetically based', but it is obligatory because it accords with what is good for human beings, considered comprehensively. The obligatory character of morality—the 'law'—binds the person to moral standards that promote the well-being, or flourishing, of the person and his or her community. It is wrong to murder, to be sexually unfaithful, to steal, to lie, and to cheat, because doing so undermines the good of both self and others. General norms are not matters of arbitrary taste or idiosyncratic preferences, but reflect judgements about structures of living that promote human flourishing. Our basic orientation to the good is not extinguished by wrongdoing: even liars resent being lied to, and those who steal get morally outraged when stolen from. Virtues and law, like reason and nature, are generally complementary to one another.

In natural law ethics, true moral objectivity is achieved in concrete acts through the exercise of the virtue of prudence. What is objectively binding in a particular situation, in other words, is what is most in keeping with the first principle of practical reason: do good and avoid evil. General moral knowledge includes various beliefs about which aspects of our inherited behavioural repertoire ought to be approved of, acted upon, and promoted—and which ought to be inhibited, sublimated, or closely monitored. It also includes general knowledge of which kinds of acts tend to undermine the human good and which kinds of acts promote it, but moral decision making only succeeds when attention is focused on concrete goods and evils at stake in particular situations. The virtue of prudence is lacking when moralists insist on adhering to rules that, in concrete situations, damage human lives. Rather than prescribing a universal and exhaustive moral code proper for all times and all people, our understanding of natural law must be dynamic, flexible, and open to new developments as a result of changing human circumstances.

The virtue of prudence functions most effectively when it enables the agent to perceive the morally salient factors at stake in concrete human experiences. It is in and through concrete experience that people discover, appropriate, and deepen their understanding of what constitutes true human flourishing. Interpretations of these experiences are influenced by membership in particular communities shaped by particular stories. Discovery of the natural law, Pamela Hall notes, 'takes place within a life, within the narrative context of experiences that engage a person's intellect and will in the making of concrete choices' (Hall 1994: 37).

Our grasp of the natural law and our ability to exercise the virtue of prudence are tutored in community. A properly social understanding of human nature under-scores the dependence of virtue generally on community. People are formed and trained in virtue by the stories and exemplars handed down through traditions. Life in community shapes the affections, imagination, and practical rationality through which moral standards are interpreted (see Spohn 1999). This returns us to the importance of Scripture, tradition, and the Church, all of which play critically important roles in shaping identity and one's sense of the full range of what is meant by human flourishing. Advocates of natural law ethics, then, draw not only from science and moral philosophy, but also from Scripture and tradition in their effort to develop a more appropriate, precise, and comprehensive account of genuine human flourishing. Only in this way will contemporary natural law reasoning contribute to the development of an ongoing moral tradition, rather than simply perpetuate time-worn platitudes and abstract, universal rules.

REFERENCES AND SUGGESTED READING

ALLSOPP, MICHAEL E. and O'KEEFE, JOHN J. (ed.) (1995). *Veritatis Splendor: American Responses*. Kansas City, Mo.: Sheed and Ward.

AQUINAS, THOMAS (1948). *Summa Theologiae*. Rome: Marietti.

ARISTOTLE (1941*a*). *Ethica Nicomachea*, trans. W. D. Ross, in McKeon (1941), 935–1126.

—— (1941*b*). *Physica*, trans. R. P. Hardie and R. K. Gaye, in McKeon (1941), 21–397.

—— (1941*c*). *Politica*, trans. Benjamin Jowett, in McKeon (1941), 1127–324.

AYALA, FRANCISCO J. (1970). 'Teleological Explanations in Evolutionary Biology', *Philosophy of Science*, 37, 1–15.

—— (1989). 'Can "Progress" be Defined as a Biological Concept?', in Matthew H. Nitecki (ed.), *Evolutionary Progress*, Chicago and London: University of Chicago Press, 75–96.

BARKOW, JEROME H., COSMIDES, LISA, and TOOBY, JOHN (eds.) (1992). *The Adapted Mind: Evolutionary Psychology and the Generation of Culture*. New York: Oxford University Press.

BARTH, KARL (1961). *Church Dogmatics*, III/4. Edinburgh: T. & T. Clark.

BECKSTROM, JOHN H. (1993). *Darwinism Applied: Evolutionary Paths to Social Goals*. Westport, Conn.: Praeger.

BROSNAN, SARAH F. and DE WAAL, FRANS B. M. (2003). 'Monkeys Reject Unequal Pay', *Nature*, 425 (Sept.), 297–9.

BUSS, DAVID M. (1994). *The Evolution of Desire: Strategies of Human Mating*. New York: Basic Books.

CAHILL, LISA SOWLE (1998). 'Accent on the Masculine', in Curran and McCormick (eds.), (1998), 53–60.

CICERO, MARCUS TULLIUS (1929). *De Re Publica: On the Commonwealth*, trans. George Holland Smith and Stanley Barney Smith. Indianapolis: Bobbs-Merrill.

CURRAN, CHARLES E. (2002). *Catholic Social Teaching 1891–Present: A Historical, Theological and Ethical Analysis*. Washington: Georgetown University Press.

—— and McCORMICK, RICHARD, SJ (eds.) (1998). *John Paul II and Moral Theology: Readings in Moral Theology*, no. 10. New York/Mahwah, NJ: Paulist Press.

DALY, MARTIN and WILSON, MARGO (1988). *Homicide*. New York: Aldine de Gruyter.

DAMASIO, ANTONIO (1994). *Descartes' Error: Emotion, Reason, and the Human Brain*. New York: Avon Books.

DAWKINS, RICHARD (1976). *The Selfish Gene.* New York: Oxford University Press.

——(1986). *The Blind Watchmaker.* New York: W. W. Norton.

DENNETT, DANIEL C. (1995). *Darwin's Dangerous Idea: Evolution and the Meanings of Life.* New York: Simon and Schuster.

DE WAAL, FRANS B. M. (1996). *Good Natured: The Origins of Right and Wrong in Humans and Other Animals.* Cambridge, Mass.: Harvard University Press.

FINNIS, JOHN (1980). *Natural Law and Natural Rights.* New York: Oxford University Press.

——(1983). *Fundamentals of Ethics.* Washington: Georgetown University Press.

——(1998). *Aquinas: Moral, Political, and Legal Theory.* Oxford: Oxford University Press.

FLANNERY, AUSTIN (ed.) (1988). *Vatican Council II: The Conciliar and Post Conciliar Documents*, rev. edn. Northport, NY: Costello Publishing Co.

GEORGE, ROBERT P. (ed.) (1996). *Natural Law, Liberalism, and Morality.* New York: Oxford University Press.

——(1999). *In Defence of Natural Law.* Oxford: Clarendon Press.

GRISEZ, GERMAIN (1965). 'The First Principle of Practical Reason: A Commentary on *Summa Theologica* IaIIae, q. 94, a. 2', *Natural Law Forum*, 10, 162–201.

——(1970). 'Toward a Consistent Natural Law Ethics of Killing', *American Journal of Jurisprudence*, 15, 64–96.

——(1983). *The Way of the Lord Jesus*, II: *Living a Christian Life.* Chicago: Franciscan Herald Press.

GUSTAFSON, JAMES M. (1978). *Protestant and Roman Catholic Ethics: Prospects for Rapprochement.* Chicago: University of Chicago Press.

HALL, PAMELA (1994). *Narrative and the Natural Law.* Notre Dame, Ind.: University of Notre Dame Press.

HAMILTON, EDITH, and CAIRNS, HUNTINGTON (ed.) (1961). *Plato: Collected Dialogues.* Princeton: Princeton University Press.

HAUSFATER, GLENN and HRDY, SARAH BLAFFER, (1984). *Infanticide: Comparative and Evolutionary Perspectives.* Chicago: Aldine.

HOLLENBACH, DAVID, SJ (2003). *The Global Face of Public Faith: Politics, Human Rights, and Christian Ethics.* Washington: Georgetown University Press.

HÜTTER, REINHARD and DIETER, THEODOR (eds.) (1998). *Ecumenical Ventures in Ethics: Protestants Engage Pope John Paul II's Moral Encyclicals.* Grand Rapids, Mich.: Eerdmans.

HUXLEY, H. D. (1894). *Evolution and Ethics and Other Essays.* New York: D. Appleton and Co.

JOHN PAUL II (1986). Address to the Academy of Sciences, no. 1, *L'Osservatore Romano*, Eng. edn. (24 Nov.).

——(1987). *Sollicitudo Rei Socialis: On Social Concern*; repr. in O'Brien and Shannon (1992), 393–436.

——(1991). *Centesimus Annus: On the Hundreth Anniversary of Rerum Novarum*; repr. in O'Brien and Shannon (1992), 437–88.

——(1993). *The Splendor of Truth: Veritatis Splendor.* Washington: United States Catholic Conference.

——(1995). *The Gospel of Life: Evangelium Vitae: On The Value and Inviolability of Human Life.* Washington: United States Catholic Conference.

——(1996). Message to Pontifical Academy of Sciences, 22 Oct.

KEENAN, JAMES F., SJ and SHANNON, THOMAS A. (eds.) (1995). *The Context of Casuistry.* Washington: Georgetown University Press.

McCabe, Herbert, OP (1994). 'Manuals and Rule Books', in Wilkins (1994), 61–8.

McCormick, Richard, SJ (1989). *The Critical Calling: Reflections on Moral Dilemmas since Vatican II.* Washington: Georgetown University Press.

McInerny, Ralph (1982). *Ethica Thomistica: The Moral Philosophy of Thomas Aquinas.* Washington: Catholic University of America Press.

——(1992). *Aquinas on Human Action: A Theory of Practice.* Washington: Catholic University of America.

MacIntyre, Alasdair (1981). *After Virtue.* Notre Dame, Ind.: University of Notre Dame Press.

——(1988). *Whose Justice? Which Rationality?* Notre Dame, Ind.: University of Notre Dame Press.

——(1999). *Dependent Rational Animals: Why Human Beings Need the Virtues.* Chicago and La Salle, Ill.: Open Court.

McKeon, Richard P. (ed.) (1941). *The Basic Works of Aristotle.* New York: Random House.

Mayr, Ernst (1988). *Towards a New Philosophy of Biology: Observations of an Evolutionist.* Cambridge, Mass.: Harvard University Press.

——(2001). *What Evolution Is.* New York: Basic Books.

Midgley, Mary (1978). *Beast and Man: The Roots of Human Nature.* Ithaca, NY: Cornell University Press.

Murray, John Courtney, SJ (1960). *We Hold These Truths: Catholic Reflections on the American Proposition.* New York: Sheed and Ward.

Niebuhr, Reinhold (1979 [1935]). *An Interpretation of Christian Ethics.* New York: Seabury.

——(1941). *The Nature and Destiny of Man: A Christian Interpretation,* 2 vols. New York: Charles Scribner's Sons.

Nitecki, Matthew H. and Nitecki, Doris V. (eds.) (1993). *Evolutionary Ethics.* Albany, NY: SUNY Press.

Noonan, John T., jun. (1995). 'Development in Moral Doctrine', in Keenan and Shannon (1995), 188–204.

O'Brien, David J. and Shannon, Thomas A. (eds.) (1992). *Catholic Social Thought: The Documentary Heritage.* Maryknoll, NY: Orbis Books.

O'Hear, Anthony (1997). *Beyond Evolution: Human Nature and the Limits of Evolutionary Explanation.* Oxford: Clarendon Press.

Pinckaers, Servais (1995). *The Sources of Christian Ethics,* trans. Sister Mary Thomas Noble, OP. Washington: Catholic University of America Press.

Pinker, Steven (1997). *How the Mind Works.* New York and London: Norton.

Plato (1961a). *Gorgias,* in Hamilton and Cairns (1961), 229–307.

——(1961b). *The Republic,* in Hamilton and Cairns (1961), 575–844.

Polkinghorne, John (1987). *One World: The Interaction of Science and Theology.* Princeton: Princeton University Press.

Pope, Stephen J. (ed.) (2002). *The Ethics of Aquinas.* Washington: Georgetown University Press.

Porter, Jean (1999). *Natural and Divine Law: Reclaiming the Tradition for Christian Ethics.* Grand Rapids, Mich., and Cambridge: Eerdmans/Novalis.

Rahner, Karl (1985). *Foundations of the Christian Faith: An Introduction to the Idea of Christianity,* trans. William V. Dych. New York: Crossroad.

Rose, Steven (1998). *Lifelines: Biology beyond Determinism.* New York: Oxford University Press.

SPOHN, WILLIAM C. (1995). 'Morality on the Way of Discipleship: The Use of Scripture in *Veritatis Splendor*', in Allsopp and O'Keefe (1995), 83–105.

—— (1999). *Go and Do Likewise: Jesus and Ethics*. New York: Continuum.

SUSSMAN, R. W. (ed.) (1977). *The Biological Basis of Behavior*. New York: Simon and Schuster.

TAYLOR, CHARLES (1989). *Sources of the Self: The Making of Modern Identity*. Cambridge, Mass.: Harvard University Press.

TRAINA, CRISTINA L. H. (1999). *Feminist Ethics and the Natural Law: The End of Anathemas*. Washington: Georgetown University Press.

TUTU, DESMOND MPILO (1997). *No Future without Forgiveness*. New York: Random House.

WEBER, MAX (1958 [1919]). 'Science as Vocation', in H. H. Gerth and C. Wright Mills (eds.), *From Max Weber: Essays in Sociology*, New York: Oxford University Press, 77–156.

WILKINS, JOHN (ed.) (1994). *Understanding Veritatis Splendor*. Cleveland: Pilgrim Press.

WILLIAMS, GEORGE C. (1988). 'Huxley's Evolution and Ethics in Sociobiological Perspective', *Zygon: Journal of Religion and Science*, 23, 383–408.

CHAPTER 10

EXPERIENCE

DOUGLAS F. OTTATI

THEOLOGICAL ethicists often refer to experience as one source of knowledge among others. Sometimes, the reference is explicit, as when Max L. Stackhouse lists Scripture, tradition, reason, and experience as 'principles' or 'touchstones of authority' for a 'public theology' that examines what Christians believe and also 'gives guidance to the structures and policies of public life' (1987: pp. xi, 4). Stackhouse says that Scripture refers to sacred texts accepted as normative. Tradition points to the insights of forebears who also endeavoured to understand their lives and practices in the light of Scripture, while reason involves criteria for coherence and consistency that make human communication possible. 'Experience', according to Stackhouse, 'has particularly to do with emotion and feeling and with that kind of knowledge that is directly built up through doing something.' It puts theology in touch with 'the wisdom already present in the sensibilities and practices of life' (1987: 13).

Sometimes, the reference to experience is implicit. For example, Lisa Sowle Cahill identifies 'four complementary reference points' for a Christian ethics of sexuality. They are 'the foundational texts or "scriptures" of the faith community—the Bible; the community's "tradition" of faith, theology, and practice; philosophical accounts of essential or ideal humanity ("normative" accounts of the human); and descriptions of what actually is and has been the case in human lives and societies ("descriptive" accounts of the human)' (1985: 5). Experience is most closely associated with the fourth reference point, which includes factual information furnished by empirical sciences as well as personal stories. Indeed, these 'descriptive resources', says Cahill, 'serve as corrections to biblical, traditional, and normative accounts that simply do not correspond to the realities of human experience' (1985: 10).

CLARIFYING THE QUESTION

Allowing for differences of vocabulary as well as for substantive disagreements over how to understand one or another source of knowledge, we might conclude that the question before us is simply this: How does experience function as one of a number of sources for theological ethics? This is accurate as far as it goes, but it obscures important complications that follow from a signal feature of the field.

Consider Stackhouse's insistence that his public *theology* is 'ethical in nature' (1987: p. xi). Again, Cahill's inquiry into foundations for a Christian *ethics* of sexuality delves quite deeply into theology—something that becomes apparent as she discusses the law of nature in Thomas Aquinas as well as doctrines of creation and the Fall in Luther (1985: 105–7). Consider, too, the subtitles of the volumes of James M. Gustafson's magisterial work, *Ethics from a Theocentric Perspective*: 'Theology and Ethics' (1981) and 'Ethics and Theology' (1984). The field of theological ethics combines the disciplines of theology and ethics. It brings theology into conversation with ethics, and vice versa, so it involves a complex set of interactions between a vision of God and world and important elements of moral reflection.

More specifically, and like a number of other writers, I contend that our moral stances, arguments, debates, and deliberations are informed by four elements (Potter 1970: 23–4; Dyck 1977: 33–51; Swezey 1978: 5–20). Our theological visions interact with our understandings of these elements. One element comprises a *situational analysis*, a reading of circumstances calling for moral involvement. Here we make judgements about what is going on, as well as predictions concerning the outcomes of alternative responses and courses of action. Another element is comprised of *anthropological assumptions*. These are assumptions about the capabilities of human agents, communities, and institutions, their motives, possibilities, and limits within the courses of nature and history—e.g., the range of human freedom, our abilities to predict and control outcomes and events, our need for institutions of coercion and restraint. A third element is made up of *norms* and *guidelines* as well as the reasons we give for them. This is the place where things such as particular understandings of love, justice, fairness, and care for the weak and dependent enter in. The fourth element specifies the *causes* or *goods* to be served by our practices, actions, and policies. The focus here is on centres of loyalty and commitment, such as the well-being of children, a society, a nation, or an ecosystem.

Suppose, then, that we envision God as creator, judge, and redeemer, and world as good creation subjected to consequences of human corruption but also benefiting from instances of redemptive renewal. This particular theology will condition our ethics. It will influence our understanding of worthy causes and goods. It will contribute to our assumptions about the possibilities and limits of persons, communities, and institutions. It will affect how we understand moral norms and the ways they function. It will influence how we construe different circumstances and situations calling for moral involvement. At the same time, however, our specifications of the elements of ethics hardly derive from theology alone. Other inquiries and perspectives also contribute relevant insights into our readings of circumstances, assumptions about human beings, understandings of norms, and judgements about whose well-being or good is at stake. So, for example, my theology may dispose me towards attending to the needs of the poor with special seriousness, but it cannot by itself supply an interpretation of specific circumstances calling for moral involvement. An argument in favour of improving housing for the poor in Rio de Janeiro by giving them the land on which their current dwellings stand will therefore depend in part on empirical studies as well as reports concerning poverty and political and economic prospects in that city. And this illustrates a general point—the practical moral relevance of our theological vision of God and world is influenced by the bearing of other inquiries, reflections, and perspectives on the elements of ethics.

If we take these interactions seriously, then it follows that theological ethics is not merely 'applied theology'. Neither is it simply a matter of identifying the theological implications of an ethical stance that has been formulated entirely apart from theological input. We may also observe that a theological ethicist does not merely deploy a theological vision that she obtains from somewhere else. Minimally, she chooses and approves the particular theological vision that she brings into conversation with ethics, and is therefore responsible for defending the choice. Maximally, she will be actively involved in formulating her own theological vision. And, of course, similar things should also be said for her understanding of ethics.

The fuller question before us, then, is this: How does experience function as a source of knowledge and insight for a field that brings together theology and ethics? And, the answer must be that experience functions as a source in two related but distinguishable ways: it contributes to the formulation of a theological vision, and it contributes to specifications of the elements of ethics.

EXPERIENCE AND THEOLOGY

The church's pastoral aim is to help people order their lives, or their interactions with other persons, objects, situations, and realities (e.g., their families, the state, their natural environments), in a manner that is appropriately responsive to God. However, this aim cannot be pursued without some understanding of how God relates to us as well as to the many objects and others with which we interact. In the service of its pastoral aim, then, the church endeavours to interpret or envision in relation to God the many objects and others with which its members interact. It generates interpretations of current *experiences*. This is the point of a good deal of preaching and teaching, and it is also where theology comes in. A Christian community's theological vision interprets the present experiences of the community and its members, and so informs their efforts at faithful living.

The imaginative resources of the Christian community play an indispensable role in the formulation of a theological vision. Images, symbols, and ideas drawn from the community's scriptures and traditions are used to interpret the many objects, others, situations, and realities with which the community and its members currently interact. The result is an interpretation, vision, or construal of current interactions in relation to God. Consider, for example, an interpretation of human life in relation to a good creator who is responsible for the gift of embodied life in this good material world. Such an interpretation works with images of God as creator and world as good creation. The images are drawn from the Bible and developed by the church's theological traditions. They are employed here in order to envision important aspects of our experiences in the midst of natural and social environments. The resultant interpretation is also practically relevant, as it disposes us more positively toward realities such as human generativity and childbirth than does a theology that works with the image of an evil creator who ensnares good immaterial human souls in a bad material world.

Interestingly, however, this amounts to a specific instance of a more widely distributed interpretative process. Imaginative resources furnished by our communities and cultures often help us to interpret objects, others, situations, and realities. Our interpretations, in turn, orient and dispose us toward these things in certain ways. Thus, the church's imaginative resources are not the only resources available for interpreting our experiences. Additional resources—e.g., images and interpretations of embodied human life, sex, children, and parenting—are proffered by other communities, enquiries, practices, and artefacts—e.g., biological sciences, ethnic groups, interactions with one's own parents, films, literature. We should therefore say that the Christian community makes use of its own imaginative resources to interpret experiences that are also interpreted with the aid of other imaginative resources. For this reason, it is entirely possible that, as our current experiences of embodiment, sex, and family are interpreted with the aid of these additional resources, they will influence or even challenge the ways in which we have understood these realities with the aid of the church's traditional imaginative resources. Current interpretations may even lead us to adjust and revise the way we organize, arrange, and understand important biblical symbols and traditional doctrines.

Walter Rauschenbusch's 'social Christianity' is a case in point (1991). Rauschenbusch was formed in an evangelical piety that emphasized the sin, conversion, and salvation of individuals. However, his ministry in New York City during an age of industrialization, his participation in political efforts at progressive reform, and his attention to recent studies in sociology and economics gave him an appreciation of current injustices, the interdependence of persons in society, and the importance of institutions. When he joined this appreciation (or these appeals to experiences) with contemporary approaches to Scripture, Rauschenbusch was led to formulate a different understanding of the heart of the gospel: namely, Jesus' prophetic ministry and message of God's kingdom. And this supported emphases on social justice as well as social dimensions of sin and salvation—signal revisions of Rauschenbusch's received evangelical theology that he used, in turn, to reinterpret the social and institutional realities of his time.

Some liberation theologians also have stressed the point that our experiences may form in us rather distinct perspectives on the gospel and the Christian tradition. Thus, in his classic work, Gustavo Gutierrez claimed that his theology of liberation is 'a theological reflection born of the experience of shared efforts to abolish the current unjust situation and to build a different society' (1973: p. ix). James H. Cone (1997) pointed to the relationship between a social location characterized by oppression and hopes for deliverance and an emphasis on God as liberator of the oppressed, while J. Deotis Roberts said that recurrent oppression of blacks in America has generated distinct insights into the gospel (Roberts 1974: 47–73). More recently, James H. Evans, jun., notes that the encounter of the black church with the Bible has been shaped by the convergence of an African-derived world-view and the experiences of slavery and oppression (1992: 2). Again, for Rosemary Radford Ruether, the uniqueness of feminist theology lies in its appeal to 'women's experience', a criterion and source that leads her to radicalize prophetic biblical traditions, reinterpret Jesus' salvific significance, and also revisit contributions made by counter-cultural, marginal, and dominant strands in Christian theological traditions (1983: 12–46).

When 'experience' is referred to in this way, it means a complex set of factors, including the distinctive circumstances, practices, sufferings, and interests of ethnic and sexual groups, the poor, and so on, as well as the psychological and emotional dynamics of struggle. These are both expressed and interpreted or construed in personal stories, communal memories, artefacts, records, art, literature, and historical, sociological, and economic analyses of persistent conditions. Such materials, in turn, constitute resources that dispose persons and groups to take up distinct perspectives on the imaginative resources of the Christian movement. Recently, they have encouraged many to regard the Bible as the story of God's call of the people from slavery to freedom, and so to construe redemption primarily as liberation.

One may raise a variety of critical questions. How shall we both check and correct for potentially distorting idiosyncrasies in the stories of specific persons and communities? (Part of the answer, one suspects, is by comparing them with empirical studies, as well as with other stories and accounts.) How shall we correct for the sometimes emotionally distant character of some empirical studies? (Partly by considering them together with personal stories and accounts.) How can we determine whether a specific interpretation, construal, or account of a community's experiences enriches, corrects, or distorts our take on the Christian symbol system? (It may be impossible to answer with certainty, as one Christian sub-community's orthodoxy is often another's heresy. But at least we may offer detailed and self-critical accounts of how we make use of appeals to experience, biblical texts, and traditional doctrines.)

A further question also arises: Is a Christian image or symbol that has been selected as central and interpreted in conjunction with some particular readings of a community's distinctive experiences actually being understood in a manner that accords with other readings, accounts, and studies of our experiences? Peter C. Hodgson criticizes some liberation theologies because they appear to require, or at least imply, what communities in history never actually experience: namely, a definitive event of liberation. By contrast, says Hodgson, we should recognize that there is 'only a plurality of partial, fragmentary, ambiguous histories of freedom'. These sometimes issue in ' "livable humane balances or fragile" syntheses ... that achieve a momentary liberation from the chaos and tyranny of human affairs' (1994: 82).

Questions such as these indicate some of the difficulties that attend appeals to experience as a source of insight for theology. In particular, they underscore the fact that these appeals inevitably involve us in a dynamic process of interpretation that entails complicated interactions among the church's imaginative resources, current experiences, and interpretative resources furnished by other communities and enquiries. These considerations encourage us to exercise caution, but they do not negate the point that appeals to experience contribute to our theological visions. Indeed, whether explicitly and critically or implicitly and uncritically, appeals to experiences appear inevitably to form an integral component of the theological visions we bring into conversation with the elements of ethics.

EXPERIENCE AND ETHICS

Experience also functions as a resource for specifying the elements of ethics. Consider the following illustration. For the past few days, letters and articles in the *New York Times* have listed some objections to legal acceptance of same-sex couples (31 July: A1, A10; 1 August: A1, A14, A22). Although the objectors have been relatively diverse, a generalized version of their case looks something like this.

Those who object tend to view our current *situation* as one in which the 'sanctity' and/or special standing of the institution of marriage between a woman and a man is eroding. They judge that the legal recognition of alternative unions will further diminish the social and cultural esteem for 'traditional marriage'. In addition, they believe that sex between a woman and a man is natural (partly because it may lead to offspring), and that procreation and child rearing are among the most important purposes of marriage. Some also say that allowing gays and lesbians to adopt will put children in 'unhealthy' environments. *Assumptions about our capacities for action or intervention* that accompany this situational analysis generally include the idea that we are able to manipulate or control at least some social outcomes. Specifically, it is assumed that we can predictably influence social patterns and attitudes by manipulating legal policies. It is assumed, too, that we can predictably influence the psychological and personal development of adopted children by placing them with 'traditional' married couples. It is also assumed that we can enhance the well-being of society by supporting the placement of children in 'traditional families'. These points are often combined with appeals to the *moral norm or guideline* of care for dependent children. In addition, some who object to same-sex unions add that they oppose unjust discrimination against homosexuals, so the norms of justice as fairness and respect for persons also come into play. Most also voice a commitment to the *good* or well-being of 'traditional families', which they understand to be closely tied to the well-being of children and also the well-being of society at large.

These specifications of the four elements interact to build an argument about legal recognition of same-sex couples and also to suggest a more general moral stance concerning children, family, sex, and society. Thus, the claim that social esteem for 'traditional marriage' is eroding helps to support the contention that the well-being of the 'traditional family' is at stake. The judgement that heterosexual relations are natural because they may lead to offspring lends support to a strong connection between 'traditional marriage' and the moral norm of caring for dependent children. And the judgement that alternative contexts will be unhealthy for children supports the contention that the well-being of children and society is also at stake. Moreover, by making changes in the specification of one or another element, we may significantly alter the overall stance. Suppose, for example, we agree that attitudes toward 'traditional marriage' are changing, but we attribute this to the erosion of historic limits placed on women. We may then judge it unlikely that esteem for 'traditional marriage' will be enhanced by withholding legal recognition from same-sex couples. Again, suppose that we judge a relationship of mutual help and companionship to be a fundamental characteristic of marriage, and that we also believe that such a relationship goes a long way toward furnishing a healthy environment for raising children. It then becomes considerably less clear why same-sex unions should threaten the well-being of marriage, children, or society.

INTERPRETING CIRCUMSTANCES

In any case, the question before us here is how experience functions as a source of knowledge and insight for specifications of the elements of ethics. Not surprisingly, there are a number of ways in which appeals to experience may count for and against claims concerning current circumstances. For example, empirical studies of the number of people who get married as well as the number of unmarried couples living together seem relevant to the judgement that the social standing of traditional marriage is eroding. Studies of the ways in which marriage is portrayed in television programmes and films may also be relevant, as may be demographic interviews and personal stories that touch upon attitudes toward and experiences of marriage. And, of course, in order to judge whether esteem for marriage has eroded, it will be necessary to compare what we learn from resources such as these with studies of past patterns and attitudes. The judgement that heterosexual relations are natural because they may lead to offspring may reflect the emphasis of evolutionary biology on the role of sex for the survival of species. It may also reflect an appreciation for the story of God's blessing of (fish, birds, and) humans, in Genesis 1: 'Be fruitful and multiply.' Even so, empirical studies of sexual acts among animal and human populations, their frequency and their relation to possibilities for procreation may also be relevant. Personal stories on this point might also be consulted. And, it is possible that these resources will move us to ask whether sexual activity also has highly important and natural functions other than reproduction: e.g., play, gratification. Again, empirical studies, communal histories, and personal stories seem relevant when it comes to determining whether marriage serves important purposes in addition to procreation and raising children, such as mutual help and companionship. (After all, not all marriages result in children, and a marriage of 30, 40, or 50 years seems unlikely to be entirely consumed with having and rearing offspring.) Finally, a host of empirical studies and personal narratives will surely be among the factors that influence our answers to complicated questions surrounding families and the healthy development of children.

Note that the theological ethicist does not appeal to raw or uninterpreted experiences, but only to experiences that have also been interpreted in empirical studies, personal narratives, artistic productions, and so on. The use of these resources in order to build an interpretation of current circumstances requires that ethicists weigh and interpret different texts and results that already represent interpretations of experiences. And, of course, this is another place where theology comes in. Consider, for example, that all of the points presented above regarding sex, children, and marriage fit rather comfortably within a theological vision of embodied life, generativity, and children as good gifts. Nowhere have we assumed (as another theological vision might have encouraged us to do) that embodied life, generativity, and the birth of children amount to the entrapment of good imma-terial spirits in bad material bodies. Theologically speaking, we may say that the way our analysis of circumstances makes use of empirical and other materials has been framed by a particular understanding of the doctrine of creation. We may also wonder whether a theological portrait of marriage and family as covenantal societies of mutual help and companionship will influence the way one regards some of the evidence mentioned above concerning the purposes of marriage and sex (Baxter 1990: 431–57; Breward 1970: 416–39; Ottati 1995: 130–1). These are ways in which a theological vision (in which interpreted experiences are already ingre-dients) may interact with other resources in building a situational analysis without simply overrunning their relative independence.

ANTHROPOLOGICAL ASSUMPTIONS

A number of factors count for and against relevant specifications of our capacities for action and intervention. For example, the assumption that we are able to influence social attitudes and consequences by manipulating legal policies will be bolstered by a theological vision of divine governance which recognizes that persons and groups are able to predict at least some outcomes with success. (It does not accord with a theology that envisions history as entirely in the hands of a hidden providence and therefore maintains that we cannot accurately predict consequences of our interventions.)

Of course, this question need not be decided by appeals to theology alone. Appeals to experience in the form of historical and empirical studies of past laws, their intended and actual consequences, may also count. Relying on information of this sort, we may be encouraged to maintain a more or less measured confidence in our limited capacities to manipulate the attitudes and practices of persons and groups by means of the law. The assumption that we can successfully predict the consequences for children of allowing gays and lesbians to adopt may also be informed by a wide array of philosophical, theological, and experiential-empirical resources. Ditto for the assumption that we can successfully predict the consequences of such practices for the well-being of society at large.

As a further illustration, consider the assumption of earlier Christian realists that persons and groups have need of institutions of coercion and restraint, as well as for balances of power. The assumption gained support from important imaginative resources drawn from Scripture and tradition. For example, the story of human corruption, cycles of violence, and the emergence of civilization in Genesis 4–11: 9, as well as the recovery of Augustine's interpretation of sin or the radical and

universal human fault. Indeed, Reinhold Niebuhr favoured a Pauline and Augustinian approach to the doctrine of sin, because of 'its ability to throw light upon
complex factors in human behavior which constantly escape the moralists' (1941:
248–9). At the same time, however, the assumption was also strengthened by more
recent interpretations of experiences—e.g., relations between capital and labour,
the courses of two World Wars, and the horrors of the Holocaust. Thus, D. R.
Davies suggested that war reveals human nature as well as the error of 'modern
man's proud faith in himself', and he connected these points with an interpretation
of sin and the Fall (1940: 25, 57, 64).

Norms and Guidelines

Experience is also important for identifying and understanding moral norms and
guidelines. Take the norm of caring for dependent children. Many Christian
theological visions suggest that, just as God and Christ care especially for the
poor, the weak, and the dependent, so should we (Hauerwas 1974: 187–94). It
may also be important to recognize the influence of the idea that, in Christ, we
become God's children and recognize God as our benevolent and caring Father
(Gerrish 1993: 87–123). In addition, a number of Reformed and Puritan theologians
envision parents as having special covenantal duties and responsibilities to children
(Baxter 1990: 449–54). Nevertheless, the norm of care for dependent children also
gains strong support from a consideration of the social benefits of the practice in
the experiences of many human communities. Where children are cared for, they
are educated into a community's distinctive social pattern and cultural heritage.
They are also more likely to feel an obligation to care for the ageing parents who
cared for them. Not to mention the negative consequences of not caring adequately
for children: poor education, the disruption of a community's heritage and pattern
of living, an erosion in the felt obligation to respect and care for elders, and (in
extreme instances) disease, physical endangerment, and death. (In the context of
some theological visions, these might be understood as consequences of corruption
and as divine judgements.) Perhaps we should say that, in the experiences of many
persons and groups, caring for children appears to be a moral requisite or con-
stituent for a flourishing community. Again, one may argue that the norm of caring
for children gains support from the felt obligation that many people experience
toward their children, the remorse that they feel when they fail to uphold this
obligation, as well as from their outrage when it is flagrantly violated.

Similar points can be made about truth telling in public contexts, including
courts of law. Here is a guideline that receives broad theological support from the

idea that God is truthful and just. It has direct biblical support in Exodus 20: 16 and Deuteronomy 5: 20, which Brevard S. Childs translates: 'You shall not testify against your neighbor as a lying witness' (1974: 424). Indeed, the setting of the commandment is the courtroom, where it functions as 'a safeguard of the judicial process' (Miller 1990: 93). We may also point to the inherent sense of obligation to tell the truth that many of us experience when others are depending on us to do so. There appear too to be considerable benefits to communities when they uphold relatively just and truthful courts of law rather than rely on more haphazard and violent means for settling disputes. And one might argue that a relatively just and fair judicial system seems a moral requisite for flourishing human communities. This, in fact, is how the moral philosopher Arthur J. Dyck interpreted the Mosaic Decalogue.

> If one is to have community at all, and if there is to be some kind of cooperative association among individual members of a group, all of whom will have their peculiarities, needs, and aspirations, certain moral obligations to form community and to refrain from acts or policies that would be evil because they are destructive of human associations or institutions would need to be identified, acknowledged, and, for the most part, acted upon. (1977: 93)

Interestingly, one might argue that a similarly experiential (and possibly also consequentialist) appeal seems implicit in the text of Deuteronomy, where long life in the land is often cited as a result of obedience to all the provisions of the law (Miller 1990: 85). For example, Deuteronomy 5: 33: 'You must follow exactly the path that the Lord your God has commanded you, so that you may live, and that it may go well with you, and that you may live long in the land that you are to possess' (NRSV). And this raises an important critical point. We recognize the Bible as a codified set of texts, or canon. As such, it both can and should be distinguished from appeals to experiences as these are interpreted in non-canonical personal stories, communal histories, and empirical studies. Nevertheless, we may also judge that, as literary products, biblical texts themselves often represent interpretations of past experiences with the aid of received imaginative resources. Indeed, Gustafson suggests 'that what is given in the Bible is itself reflection on the meanings of common human experience in light of an experience of the presence of God' (1981: 146).

CAUSES AND GOODS

This brings us to the contributions of experience as a source of insight when it comes to specifying relevant causes and goods to be served. Consider the stances of many environmentalists. Most emphasize that humans often take too narrow a view of the relevant causes and goods at stake in many policy decisions. Most argue that we should take into account, preserve, and enhance not just the well-being of our human communities but also the well-being of the wider natural-social ecology of which we are a part. So, for example, Holmes Rolston III calls us away from an anthropocentric view of value toward an ecocentric view that extends ethics to the planetary level (1994: 177, 204–5). Obviously, this emphasis reflects the considerable enlargement and complexification of our modern scientific picture of a vast, interrelated world. That is, an ecological expansion in our interpretation of the relevant causes and goods at stake in our actions is responsive, at least in part, to appeals to experience in the form of empirical studies.

Resources other than appeals to our experiences may also contribute to this emphasis and expansion. Thus, H. Richard Niebuhr's radically monotheistic theological vision upheld a commitment 'more inclusive than humanism', or even than Albert Schweitzer's 'reverence for life', that also accords with an ecological expansion of the community of value and concern. For Niebuhr, the identification of the principle of being ('the Maker of heaven and earth') with the principle of value ('God the Father') supports the expansion of moral commitment and concern beyond all partial and closed societies toward the universal community of being with God at its head (1993: 36–7). At the same time, however, an expansion of the field of moral concern beyond isolated human communities is supported by our experiences of the plainly deleterious and destructive consequences for us and for other creatures of *not* taking wider ecologies into account as we make social, economic, and political decisions. Indeed, we sometimes say that such consequences *demand* that we take wider contexts into account. For example, Rosemary Radford Ruether claims that 'the interrelation of all things' is a basic lesson of ecology for ethics, and that, 'in addition to recycling, sustainable ecosystems demand diversity, and a balance of interdependency' (1992: 48, 53). Here again, we find ourselves appealing not only to personal narratives, group and social histories, but also to quite extensive empirical studies of the expansive web of interdependent social and natural interrelations in which we stand.

In the illustration above concerning our stance toward same-sex couples, the causes to be served are the well-being of children, the well-being of 'traditional families', and the well-being of society. Appeals to experience may count for and against the rather crucial contention that these three are closely (and perhaps also somewhat exclusively) linked (Steinmetz 2003: 9A). Thus, on this point, we are not surprised to encounter arguments that make use of personal narratives, social histories, and empirical studies. And if it can be shown that the well-being of children is sometimes threatened in 'traditional families', while alternative families sometimes enhance it, then the linkage might need reconsidering or even revising. All sorts of instances will be relevant here. But consider the case of a young mother who comes to recognize that she is a lesbian. She and her husband subsequently divorce. Can we be certain that it is not in the best interests of the children to be placed in their mother's household? And if we are uncertain, might it be possible to link the well-being not only of 'traditional families' but also of alternative ones with the well-being of children and society?

A CONCLUDING CONSIDERATION

Appeals to experience in theological ethics function on two related and interacting levels. They come into play as we formulate our theological visions and also when we specify our readings of circumstances, assumptions about human agents, conceptions of moral norms, and understandings of causes or goods to be served. Moreover, important critical questions emerge as we make appeals to experience in all of these areas. These are the most important and general points I have tried to make in this essay. But there is an additional question, and the way we answer it influences the way we understand all of these appeals: What is experience?

One answer takes its understanding of experience from a logical positivist picture of scientific theory and experiment. The claim is that true theories are statements derived by formally logical means from incorrigible data supplied by repeatable experiments (Cook 1991: 81; Lewis 1971: 171–2). Experience, then, is understood on the model of repeatable experiences that supply invariant data and information. Experience = neutral sensory perceptions. We may therefore regard human experience as a single, generally available and invariant court of appeal on the basis of which we may formulate universal truths: e.g., universally recognized understandings of the human situation, universally approved moral norms. These universals, in turn, may become standards for what is true and false in the received religious, moral, and cultural traditions of particular communities. They may also serve as foundations for true theologies and valid ethics.

This essay has moved in a different direction. I have claimed that a theologian makes use of the Christian community's imaginative resources, e.g., images of God as creator and world as good creation, to interpret experiences, e.g., sex and childbirth, which both she and others interpret with the aid of other resources as well, e.g., biological studies, current cultural practices. She may take the dynamic play of interpretations to bolster some classical Christian understandings of these realities. She may come to the conclusion that some classical Christian understandings of them are superior to some contemporary interpretations. Then again, she may adjust, revise, or even reject some classical Christian understandings of these realities, as well as the ways in which some Christians and their communities have arranged and understood their own symbols and doctrines. I have claimed, too, that ethicists appeal to experiences which are also interpreted by empirical studies, personal narratives, philosophical statements, artistic productions, and so on. The ready implication, then, is that experience, as I have used the term here, indicates a complex set of occurrences, factors, circumstances, and accounts. It includes disciplined accounts of the regular consequences of certain actions, policies, and procedures, as well as methodologically explicit explanations of why these consequences occur. It includes the distinctive circumstances, practices, sufferings, and interests of particular ethnic, sexual, and economic groups (of the poor, the privileged, the oppressed, and so on) as these come to expression in personal narratives and communal histories. Indeed, my own judgement is that, in theology and ethics, we never appeal or have access to raw or 'pre-linguistic' experiences. Whether we consult disciplined empirical studies or more passionate and anecdotal personal narratives, the language, images, concepts, interests, commitments, practices, and social locations of particular persons and groups are always involved. Thus, my entire discussion pushes me to press a point that logical empiricist understandings of experience neglect. What if the experiences of interested, linguistically and socially conditioned subjects are never simply a collection of neutral sensory perceptions?

Consider a constructivist answer: experience is shaped definitively by the beliefs, interests, images, ideas, and practices of socially conditioned subjects. That is, the experiences of persons are influenced radically, or perhaps even constituted, by their socially furnished (and sometimes passionately affirmed) imaginative resources. Indeed, people may be said to *construct* their experiences in accord with their different social locations, communal practices, vocabularies, concepts, interests, and so on. So we may say that, in North America today, poor Catholic, Hispanic women have different experiences than do wealthy Protestant, Anglo men, because their experiences are definitively shaped by different socially located interests, beliefs, concepts, and practices. We may then conclude that, as appeals to experiences are always to the socially constructed experiences of different persons and groups, there is not one generally available and invariant court of appeal called human experience. There are only disparate human experiences, and they do not form a basis for identifying universal truths. We may also claim that we cannot get back behind our particular socio-linguistic constructions to a more general vocabulary that might either adequately or helpfully describe objects, situations, and realities as they are experienced by different persons in different social locations.

This need not mean that appeals to experiences in theology and ethics are unimportant. An appeal to the socially constructed experiences of any particular group (say in the form of slave narratives) can at least keep us from mistaking the constructed experiences of another group (say in the form of plantation owners' memoirs) as simply normative and universally valid. Again, we might claim that the constructed experiences of feminist women expose the allegedly universal experiences and norms put forward by male-dominated hierarchies for the interested, power-preserving, and ineluctably particular social constructions that they are. A constructivist answer to the question of experience suggests that appeals to the experiences of persons and groups serve the important critical function of exposing false objectifications and false universals (Fulkerson 1994: 50–8).

Appeals to socially constructed experiences may also help us to articulate the viewpoint of our own particular social-ethnic-sexual group. We might then bring this viewpoint into conversation with viewpoints articulated by other particular groups, although, at a deep level, we may assume that the experiences and viewpoints of different groups are unique and incommensurable. Even so, an additional constructive move seems possible. We might contend that, in the context of the imaginative resources of the Christian community, the social locations, interests, viewpoints, and constructions of some persons and groups are radically privileged, i.e., a strong epistemological option for the constructions of the poor and oppressed.

Although I do not wish to revive a logically empiricist picture of experience, I think that constructivist responses to the question of experience too easily dismiss, obscure, or neglect the matter of reference. (To what, if anything, do our experiences refer?) I therefore favour a third position that is neither logically empiricist nor constructivist: experience = sensory input + interpretation. This third position accords with much that Martin L. Cook says about the relevance for theology of the 'new' historicist philosophy of science associated with Thomas Kuhn and others—a philosophy that recognizes a role for socialization and tradition in our perceptions and reflections (Cook 1991: 11). Here, the experiences of socially located and conditioned subjects are thought to be responsive to *both* internalized frameworks for interpretation *and* sensory inputs. If this is so, then we never have access to neutral sensory perceptions (as the logical empiricists assume). However, we need not conclude (as some constructivists seem to) that our experiences are simply constituted by our internalized beliefs, interests, images, and practices, and that, at bottom, the experiences of different communities must be incommensurable.

For proponents of this third position, the high confidence of the logical positivists in our ability to identify universal truths is unavailable, and, at times, appeals to experiences may take on something like the critical functions emphasized by constructivists. As all accounts of experiences are interpretations or construals offered by historically and socially conditioned persons, all are subject to critiques that highlight the specific interests, practices, and vocabularies involved in arriving at the particular interpretative accounts in question. Thus, one reason why proponents of this third position compare different interpretative accounts of experiences is to highlight and expose their ineluctable particularities and biases. Nevertheless, if we take up this third answer to the question of experience, then we may believe that the interpreted experiences of different persons and groups are often responsive to relatively common situations and realities. We may compare diverse interpretative accounts offered by different persons and groups to see whether we can identify and articulate significant commonalities. Moreover, there is nothing to prevent us from concluding that two different interpretative accounts of a situation or reality are mutually correcting because they contribute to a third interpretative account that is (in some respects) more adequate. In these ways, we may try to formulate critical generalizations about important aspects of human life in the world, as well as of circumstances, assumptions about human agents, goods, and moral norms on which more than one community may agree.

These formulations might be called 'almost universals'. They will not have the force or status of classic universals because, on this third position, we cannot assume a strict or simple correspondence with the order of reality. But neither will they be understood as pure constructions. Instead, they will resemble relatively high-level generalizations and inferences that are subject to emendation and revision as we consider additional interpretations and accounts (Gustafson 1975: 158).

So, for example, having studied a variety of narratives and accounts, I may conclude that very many persons and communities experience life as a compelling and (most often) good reality dependent on circumstances and interdependencies beyond their own control. This conclusion, in turn, may help to support Christian theological statements about God as creator, the world as good creation, and life as a gift. Or I may infer from a broad range of experiences expressed in varied studies and accounts that highly destructive consequences very often attend certain sorts of attitudes and actions on the part of both persons and groups. Particularly when understood in the light of some traditional Christian symbols, this inference may help to support theological statements about God as judge. Again, I may infer from a broad range of human experiences expressed in narrative accounts, communal histories, empirical studies, and more, that persons and groups have significant but none the less limited capacities to foresee and control the consequences of their actions and interventions. Or I may hazard the generalizations that very many communities recognize critical benefits of caring for children and also of maintaining some relatively just and fair system for settling disputes. And I may infer that these generalizations indicate moral values and practices that provide needed conditions for human social life.

The generalizations and inferences are subject to qualification. I may observe that, for compelling reasons, some people do not experience life as a good gift. Moreover, cultures and communities often have somewhat different understandings of childhood and whether or not persons of a certain age still qualify as children. Again, different judicial systems are notoriously varied both in their procedures and in the penalties they may exact for specific offences. Nevertheless, the generalizations and inferences point to significant commonalities that the qualifications do not render insignificant. True, the commonalities and agreements that may be identified in this way are likely to remain too few and too thin (or at too high a level of abstraction) to form the entire basis for an actual or full theology and ethics. True, they remain subject to emendation and revision in the light of further investigations. Even so, they may help us to articulate how our theological statements are responsive to something more than merely the received imaginative resources of our communities and traditions. They may indicate that at least some of our traditions are responsive to important commonalities in human experiences. They may also point to circumstances, human possibilities and limits, goods, and norms that our particular communities and traditions ignore at some cost to the intelligibility of their theologies and ethics.

In sum, for proponents of this third position, appeals to experiences may function critically as important checks on received theologies, moral views, and philosophies that seem out of touch with experienced realities. They may encourage us to revise or even reject some of the symbols, concepts, and interpretations put forward by our particular communities and traditions. At the same time, however, they may also function positively. They may help us better understand, articulate, and deepen the distinct symbols, concepts, and interpretations put forward by our particular community or tradition. They may help partly to confirm our traditions by showing how at least some of these symbols, concepts, and interpretations refer to relatively common situations and realities. And this, in fact, is the range of functions of appeals to experiences that I have associated with theology and ethics in this essay.

References and Suggested Reading

Baxter, Richard (1990). *The Practical Works of Richard Baxter*, I: *A Christian Directory*. Ligonier, Pa.: Soli Deo Gloria Publications.

Breward, Ian (ed.) (1970). *The Work of William Perkins*. Appleford: Sutton Courtenay Press.

Brown, Harold I. (1977). *Perception, Theory, and Commitment: The New Philosophy of Science*. Chicago: University of Chicago Press.

Cahill, Lisa Sowle (1985). *Between the Sexes: Foundations of a Christian Ethics of Sexuality*. Minneapolis and New York: Fortress Press and Paulist Press.

Childs, Brevard S. (1974). *The Book of Exodus: A Critical Theological Commentary*. Philadelphia: Westminster Press.

Cone, James H. (1997). *God of the Oppressed*. Maryknoll, NY: Orbis Books.

Cook, Martin L. (1991). *The Open Circle: Confessional Method in Theology*. Minneapolis: Fortress Press.

Davies, D. R. (1940). *The Two Humanities: An Attempt at a Christian Interpretation of History in the Light of War*. London: The Religious Book Club.

Dyck, Arthur J. (1977). *On Human Care: An Introduction to Ethics*. Nashville: Abingdon Press.

EVANS, JAMES H., jun. (1992). *We Have Been Believers: An African-American Systematic Theology.* Minneapolis: Fortress Press.

FULKERSON, MARY MCCLINTOCK (1994). *Changing the Subject: Women's Discourses and Feminist Theology.* Minneapolis: Fortress Press.

GERRISH, B. A. (1993). *Grace and Gratitude: The Eucharistic Theology of John Calvin.* Minneapolis: Fortress Press.

GUSTAFSON, JAMES M. (1975). *Can Ethics be Christian?* Chicago: University of Chicago Press.

—— (1981). *Ethics from a Theocentric Perspective,* I: *Theology and Ethics.* Chicago: University of Chicago Press.

—— (1984). *Ethics from a Theocentric Perspective,* II: *Ethics and Theology.* Chicago: University of Chicago Press.

GUTIÉRREZ, GUSTAVO (1973). *A Theology of Liberation: History, Politics and Salvation.* Maryknoll, NY: Orbis Books.

HAUERWAS, STANLEY (1974). *Vision and Virtue: Essays in Christian Ethical Reflection.* Notre Dame, Ind.: Fides/Claretain.

HODGSON, PETER C. (1994). *Winds of the Spirit: A Constructive Christian Theology.* Louisville, Ky.: Westminster John Knox Press.

LEWIS, C. I. (1971). *An Analysis of Knowledge and Valuation.* LaSalle, Ill.: Open Court Press.

MILLER, PATRICK D. (1990). *Deuteronomy.* Louisville, Ky.: Westminster John Knox Press.

The New York Times (31 July, 2003).

The New York Times (1 August, 2003).

NIEBUHR, H. RICHARD (1993). *Radical Monotheism and Western Culture, with Supplementary Essays.* Louisville, Ky.: Westminster John Knox Press.

NIEBUHR, REINHOLD (1941). *The Nature and Destiny of Man,* I: *Human Nature.* New York: Charles Scribner's Sons.

OTTATI, DOUGLAS F. (1995). *Reforming Protestantism: Christian Commitment in Today's World.* Louisville, Ky.: Westminster John Knox Press.

—— (1996). *Jesus Christ and Christian Vision.* Louisville, Ky.: Westminster John Knox Press.

POTTER, RALPH B. (1970). *War and Moral Discourse.* Richmond, Va.: John Knox Press.

RAUSCHENBUSCH, WALTER R. (1991). *Christianity and the Social Crisis.* Louisville, Ky.: Westminster John Knox Press.

ROBERTS, J. DEOTIS (1974). *A Black Political Theology.* Philadelphia: Westminster Press.

ROLSTON, HOLMES III (1994). *Conserving Natural Value.* New York: Columbia University Press.

RUETHER, ROSEMARY RADFORD (1983). *Sexism and God-Talk: Toward a Feminist Theology.* Boston: Beacon Press.

—— (1992). *Gaia and God: An Ecofeminist Theology of Earth Healing.* SanFrancisco: Harper.

STACKHOUSE, MAX L. (1987). *Public Theology and Political Economy: Christian Stewardship in Modern Society.* Grand Rapids, Mich.: Eerdmans Publishing Co.

STEINMETZ, DAVID C. (2003). 'Episcopalian Changes Not Over', *The Star-News,* 14 August, Wilmington, NC.

SWEZEY, CHARLES M. (1978). 'What Is Theological Ethics? A Study of the Thought of James M. Gustafson' (Ph.D. thesis, Vanderbilt University).

WALZER, MICHAEL (1994). *Thick and Thin: Moral Argument at Home and Abroad.* Notre Dame, Ind.: University of Notre Dame Press.

PART III

THE STRUCTURE OF
THE CHRISTIAN LIFE

CHAPTER 11

....

VOCATION

....

MAX STACKHOUSE

THE doctrine of 'vocation' (from the Latin *vocatio*) or 'calling' (related to the Greek *kaleō*) has many implications. The Semitic root *qr*, the ancient biblical correlate, like the old German 'Ruf', indicates an announcement of a message, sometimes shouted to all, but usually directed to a specific audience and intended to evoke specific responses. Thus, the Hebrew *qārā*, is used to denote the acts of crying out as in joy or pain or fear, but also calling in the senses of hailing someone, summoning to duty, announcing a command or telling insight able to elicit a response of obedience (obviously related to the later Islamic '*Qur'an*'). In all these uses there is a 'caller' and a 'callee', and an active relationship established between them by communication.

BIBLICAL BACKGROUND
....

In the ways in which these terms are used from the creation stories at the beginning of the Bible on, we can see that the terms and their derivatives have specialized uses as well as general meanings. In Gen. 1: 5, God 'called' the light 'day' and the darkness 'night', and in Ps. 147: 4, God 'calls' the stars by name. This 'calling' by naming indicates, in classic Hebraic thought, a sovereignty over, as well as a caring for, that which is created and 'named'. The one who has the power to create, of course, has the power to name; and the one who can name what is created has, in principle, also the authority to deploy what is named. Thus, according to Gen. 1: 27 ff., God called humanity, male and female, into existence and commissioned them to be fruitful, to fill and subdue the earth; and according to Gen. 2: 19 ff., God presents the animals to humanity so that the beasts could be given the names by which they were to be called. Humans are given a stewardly dominion over the creatures and a vocation to create culture from the beginning of existence.

There are other uses of the root ideas that bear on religious ethics and social life. Not only is all humanity called in a general sense, but a particular people, Israel, is called by name, and is 'chosen' from all the peoples of the world to be witnesses to God. This people does not always remain faithful to the covenanted responsibilities to which they are called, but the faithful God renews that covenant again and again. When, after the Exodus, the name of God is revealed to the reconstituted people called into covenant through the offices of Moses, Israel is expected to call upon the name of God in times of distress, in thanksgiving, and in worship. This too becomes the basis of their vocation, their purpose for being. Thus, Israel is periodically 'called together' (*miqrā'*) for feast, fellowship, instruction, or offering, or for battle in self-defence (*qᵉrāb*), and, above all, to be a witness to God's righteousness and faithfulness.

Further, other people in the community were called, or 'elected', to perform specific duties for the well-being of the people. Priests, for example, had a special role to play in conducting the worship. And the prophet Samuel, in some ways following the example of Moses, was called to be a prophet to the people of Israel. He was also called to anoint the earliest kings of Israel, and by the time that David's rule is established (I Kgs. 1: 38 ff.), prophets, priests, and kings were all 'anointed' as those called to special responsibilities under the laws of God, for the glory of God, to guide the people in the common life. There were others clearly named, to be sure—scribes, judges, heads of tribes, etc.—and they had duties under God's watchful eye; but the anointed were the primary officers with special callings. Much later, when the leaders forsook their vocation and the people became unruly and impious, God even called a foreign ruler, Cyrus, to chastise the wayward people (Isa. 45: 1–3). They were later taken into captivity in Babylon and awaited a messiah who would redeem them.

These ancient themes are adopted, adapted, developed, and refined in the Christian New Testament. Most importantly, Jesus was recognized as the expected Messiah, the Christ, the anointed one—the one who was not only the Son of God, but the fulfilment of the offices of the previous biblical record. Matthew begins by tracing Jesus' legal lineage from the royal house of David and stresses the moral and spiritual illegitimacy of the ethnarch, Herod. Mark begins his gospel by stressing the continuity of Jesus with John the Baptist, the last and greatest of the prophets until Christ. And Luke opens his gospel by showing Jesus' continuity with the priestly family—Zechariah and Elizabeth. The 'set-aside' three offices of the ancient tradition of special calling are seen as fulfilled in Christ—the *munus triplex*, as the later tradition named it.

The Fourth Gospel adds another accent. It begins by identifying Christ with the Logos—the 'creative and reasonable word of wisdom', if one may put it that way. This Logos is seen as intrinsic to the divine life, at least partially discernible by the learned and and recognized as important even by the simple. The scribe, the scholar, the rabbi, the scientist, and the student all live by engagement with creative and reasonable words of wisdom; yet the reality they can almost discern does not remain abstract and 'conceptual-spiritual' only, but is held to have become enfleshed in a 'son of man' who is like all men—an accent that acknowledges that the model of true religion resists the temptation of any called to follow Christ to become 'Gnostic', ignoring the presence of divine intent in the fabric of material life, finding the connection of revelation with historical event unreasonable, or denying that prophetic, priestly, and political roles in society can be Godly.

Moreover, not only is Christ the fulfilment of these ancient callings, in him is also given the possibility of salvation from the perils of sin and death. Several texts in the New Testament speak of an intended universal salvation: e.g., 'God . . . desires everyone to be saved and to come to the knowledge of truth' (1 Tim. 2: 3 f.: NRSV). Other texts, to be sure, suggest that only 'those whom [God] predestined are called; and those who are called are also justified; and those who are justified are also glorified' (Rom. 8: 30). Still, it is affirmed by all parts of Scripture that Jesus was and is the Christ, '*the* anointed one', inaugurating the movement that was eventually to become the church (*ekklesia*), the company of those 'called out', a term borrowed by the early writers from the assembly of the Greek *polis* and one that has parallels in *synagōgē*, a term from Hellenized Judaism referring to those brought together outside the normal pattern of the workaday world to worship, pray, and form a witnessing community. This church was called to be a new, wider, covenanted people, no longer ethnically defined, that honoured the heritage of Israel, but pointed more emphatically to the final fulfilment and judgement of life that Christ made actual.

The disciples were called to the special tasks of preaching and teaching this good news—and in the process both casting out those malicious forces that are destructive of personal and communal life and conferring the blessings of faith, hope, and love on those who received the Spirit of Jesus. These activities shaped a new community, which sought to discern where the promises of the new age were already active within and among them, and so to clarify the meaning of human life and history and to point to a realm of divine life beyond present possibilities.

It was, however, in the other writings of the New Testament that the idea of 'calling' was more fully developed. The call to enter the church is a call that comes to people through the word of preaching, which is not merely a human word, but the word of God (1 Cor. 1: 9; 2 Pet. 1: 3), and those called have a 'heavenly calling', and are to be saints (Rom. 1: 7; 1 Cor. 1: 2). Thus, the call into communion with

Christ and the fellowship of the church also involves a moral change, 'not for uncleanness, but for holiness' (1 Thess. 4: 7). It involves a change that brings with it 'the more diligence to make your calling and election sure'. Yet many passages also recognize that people have earthly obligations, and the calling is closely identified with one's responsibilities in life, which one is to fulfil dutifully (1 Cor. 7: 20; Philemon).

Those who became members of the church, and thus members of the body that lives toward a New Jerusalem not of this world, were advised not to leave the positions of ordinary responsibility to which they were 'called'—as husbands or wives, parents, workers or owners, and members of civil communities. At the same time, some were also set aside in the church to assume particular ecclesial offices— elders, supervisors (e.g., bishops = *epi-scopos*), deacons, preachers, evangelists, and apostles (Acts 6), and, elsewhere, teachers, guides, and pastors (1 Cor. 12: 28). All these officers were to be examined by the community to see if their sense of calling was authentic and their character sufficiently formed by the Spirit of Christ that they could nurture and model life in exemplary ways. Gradually rituals were developed to publicly signify that those called to these vocations were held to be gifted for and dedicated to their special responsibilities (1 Tim. 4: 14; 2 Tim. 1: 6).

This biblical heritage had within it a number of possible directions, with the main ones prompting several diverse, but highly intertwined, later developments. We can perhaps identify these by tracing key elements of the following four developments, and thus revising one of the older, now almost classical, treatments of vocation (Holl 1928): the medieval formation of the clerical ideal; the Reformation understanding of the vocation of the laity, the Puritan emphasis on social democracy; and the current patterns of leadership in the modern professions.

THE DEVELOPMENT OF THE MONASTIC IDEAL

In the midst of both a Hellenized Judaic culture and a Roman Imperial political order that largely ignored or repudiated the early church, the ideas that appear in Scripture about the emerging community of faith and its leaders being 'set aside' were embraced and applied in particular ways. Being baptized or being ordained involved a sense of being called by Christ into his company of disciples and, for some, elected to the leadership of the body of Christ. The commissioning of the disciples was early taken as a model, and the title of 'the Twelve' was given, echoing memories of the tribes of Israel. Later 'the Seventy' was noted, anticipating the mandate to preach to the seventy peoples who were, symbolically, thought to constitute the peoples of the earth. Baptism set believers apart from the surrounding culture, and ordination began to separate clergy from laity in ways that had far-reaching consequences. Increasingly the laity were expected to continue to be a part of the common social life—marrying, working in their occupations, participating in the economy, serving in the military if required to do so, and selectively enjoying the fruits of cultural life. But the clergy, especially the bishops and the monks, were to focus their attention on the spiritual life as distinct from familial, occupational, economic, political (certainly military), and cultural life—except that the life of learning was to be engaged, also selectively. Clerical status came to be the primary model of having a vocation. It defined the emerging priesthood and augmented efforts to establish a stratified model of organization in the church as a model for, but also a model of, the world.

Several influences shaped this development. The biblical image of the priesthood of ancient Israel stood ever in the background, and parts of it had been taken as normative in the New Israel of the church. The idea of a 'royal priesthood' (Exod. 19: 6) reappears in 1 Pet. 2: 4–9 (and elsewhere), and focuses attention on those who officiate at the atoning sacrifice. Christ, of course, is the sacrificial lamb who takes away the sins of the world, and the priest is the one who ritually re-enacts that event in the sacerdotal liturgy. To be called to such a holy responsibility was held to demand a kind of unblemished spiritual purity. Moreover, the Roman government had laws governing who could approach 'the gods', regulations as to what kinds of religious groups could be formed, and rules about what sorts of rituals could be enacted for or among the people by what kinds of religious leadership. Some of the church's development of the rites of the priesthood were conditioned by these contextual factors, well before Constantine proclaimed establishment privileges for the church.

Internal developments also shaped the stratified character of the church's hierarchy. One of these was the growing influence of Neoplatonic philosophy on the development of theology. Influential Fathers of the Church saw the world, and thus the society and the Church within it, as a vast 'chain of being', a graded ladder ranging from the very lowest form of materiality to the highest form of pure spirituality, with many rungs in between. Some clergy—the 'secular priesthood'—would, of course, have to deal with ordinary people in their daily, and inevitably earthly, materialistic problems. Others entered an order of specialized ministry—education or missions or care for the needy—that supplemented the work of the secular priests. But some felt called to a life of contemplation and prayer that accumulated benefits in heaven. In this case, particularly, the materialist levels should be renounced or a rather intense asceticism adopted to keep those earthly needs and desires under spiritual control. Pachomius, the founder of the first recorded monastic community, required of novices that they know how to read, learn how to pray, and accept the discipline of ordered labour to sustain the monastery—all marks of a new asceticism—if they were to have their sense of 'calling' ratified by acceptance into the monastery. Others, following Gregory, took contemplation as the chief end of the holy life, sustained by donations. But Benedict established 'The Rule' that one with a 'vocation' was obligated to spend his life in communal prayer and work, assuming vows to this end. This set the dominant pattern for a large number of subsequent orders.

Of course, laypersons did not feel called to keep their lives free of economic, sexual, or political concerns, although they were expected to place these concerns under moral constraint. By contrast, those who took the monastic vows of poverty, chastity, and obedience (to the 'rule' of the order, thus not to political authority) became established as embracing the higher ideal. To have a vocation came to mean that one entered either the secular priesthood or, if one were more genuinely spiritual, one of the orders of monks or nuns, many of whom later became increasingly sacramental or contemplative, less focused on work as an ascetic discipline and more dependent on the support of others. As we shall see, the three vows were later required of secular priests also.

A key problem turned out to be one that endured for at least a millennium. It was the relationship of the authority of the priesthood to that of the political order—and to the question of how believers should honour their parents. As secular priests were increasingly bureaucratized and organized into a stratified hierarchical system, they and the 'prophetic' monastics grew in social influence. Which of those with special vocations—the priesthood *or* the rulers—had the higher authority became a contested matter. That debate turns on whether religion or politics best supplies the comprehending and organizing principles for civilization, on what precisely God has called these two 'set-aside' leaders to do, and, indirectly, on what role parental authority plays in the formation of persons and determination of their station in life. Is political succession by heredity, or must political authority be blessed or anointed by religious authority? Is Aaron or Samuel the normative model, or is it David?

In many ways, the medieval period in the West, deeply influenced by these developments, did not differ greatly from what could be found in other parts of the world where complex civilizations developed, each with an internal differentiated structure of occupations and something of a contest between the relative dominance of political force and the rule of the wise. The ancient traditions of Confucianism, Hinduism, and Buddhism, for example, formed distinct patterns of relationship between the priestly-literary class, with popular followings, and the political-ruler class, with subjects. The medieval, Christian West has had moments that roughly correlate with each of these patterns; yet the Christian traditions were substantially influenced by a theology of 'vocation' that altered, in various degrees, the organizing principles of the dominant modes of social order in European lands. Those called to the higher levels of the church, particularly to the monastic orders or to the role of bishop, were in principle neither under nor over the political authorities, as the literati of China were 'under' the Emperor, the Brahmins of India were 'over' the Kshatrya princes, or the Buddhist monks were 'jewels in the crown of the kings'. Instead, their relative independence was stated in a number of ways— e.g., the 'right' and 'left' hands of God, which wielded the 'two swords', the sword of *regnum* (as manifest in war and the administration of law) and the sword of *verbum* (as manifest in the penetrating interpretation of holy texts and performance of sacerdotal liturgies). Both were seen as under divine scrutiny, and each side was expected to exercise its vocation with dutiful diligence. And both were to give guidance to life in this temporal world in accord with the truths that could be known about the spiritual world.

Among those who wielded the 'sword' of *regnum*, some orders of knights took vows of celibacy during periods of their sacrificial service. Further, those called to monastic orders forsook their families for life (the historical significance of the vow of chastity can be overestimated only with difficulty). In the High Middle Ages the requirement of a vow of celibacy was extended to the secular clergy, more clearly cutting off the 'core' of the religious community from familial obligations as well as from political ones. 'Vocation' came to mean the taking of 'religious' vows and entering an order of monks, the priesthood or an order of nuns or brothers, or, indeed, an order of knights. The effects of this can be recognized if we remember that in most highly stratified societies family and regime determine the social status and occupational duties of most people. This 'religious' vocation established a third centre of identity and authority outside hereditary patterns of ranked status and usually outside the exercise of coercive power. Indeed, the vow of poverty also cut the bonds to claims of ownership and responsibilities with regard to the economic wealth of both the family and the rulers, who often owned the land on which the hereditary peasantry had the duty to work.

Of course, there are instances in which the monasteries became wealthy, where clergy (or knights) did not remain celibate, where bishops also became princes (and practised nepotistic succession), or relatives of the princes became bishops beholden to the princes. But a historic shift had taken place. The inevitably pluralistic structures of a complex society were, to be sure, organized in a vertically stratified way, which we often call 'hierarchical'. Nevertheless, especially after the Cistercian order was centralized by St Bernard, establishing a model that others adopted, the independent organization of the 'vocations' brought a new horizontal pluralization of the centres of authority and identity. Some of the orders of monks or nuns became centres of medical care and healing, orphanages and schools, or specialists in brewing or wine-making (which became quite profitable). They began to shape the whole civilization of the West, as church and state, on the one hand, and church and family, on the other, were institutionally separated in law, practice, and consciousness, even if influences flowed between them (Berman 1991).

One other highly significant development grew out of this institutional reordering of the common life and remapping of social 'ethical' living. The church, in its cathedral and monastic schools, and later its universities, became the centre of education and learning. To be sure, there were also court schools attached to royal palaces, and, later, 'city' schools and universities were developed in the independent towns. In many of these, however, clergy were appointed as professors, and in all the centres clergy became the custodians of learning, philosophy, arts, and the sciences—the intelligentsia of society. And in the academic centres to which many gave their lives, a sense of the proper response to one's calling was cultivated. The *vocatio* with its divine origins required a human response—a *professio*, most especially as a profession of faith, but also as a dedication to develop excellence in a specific area of study in which one was gifted with talent and to cultivate practices that would glorify God and benefit humanity. Thus, it was in church-based organizations that the so-called modern professions were conceived—the professors of higher education and the applied professions of ministry, law, medicine, and the 'mechanical arts' (today's engineering) (Noble 1997). These became specialists, called by God to be set aside in church and society for indispensable and critical roles in a more differentiated civilization.

Of course, there have been lawyers and judges, doctors and nurses, teachers and wise men, 'engineers' and warriors, in every complex civilization, and they all had traditions of disciplined training for excellence long before the theological view of the *vocatio–professio* connection was established, but they were almost always in the employ of the imperial, princely, or theocratic rulers or were able to use their skills to form privileged urban élite families. Naturally, therefore, some of these new specialists become more dedicated to serving the interests of their family or of political authorities than to serving God, and some found the constraints that the church put on their scholarship or professional practice much too restrictive. Nevertheless, the seeds of an 'independent' set of professions having their own integrity under God, organized outside family and regime, had been planted and watered by the theological baptism that the 'vocational' monastic movements gave them.

THE REFORMATION

In the cities of the late medieval and early modern period a more egalitarian citizenry and the growing independent professions met in an extraordinary mix, with new classes of artisans seeking opportunities to ply their trade and labourers fleeing the peasantry that bound them in perpetual poverty and obedience to land-holding petty royalty and landlords. There were, of course, more wealthy burgers and less wealthy guild members, and poor workers or apprentices, but there were also prospects for a change of status. It was in these cities that the new religious stirrings manifested themselves—in Wycliffe's London, Hus's Prague, Luther's Wittenberg, Zwingli's Zurich, and Calvin's Geneva—in many ways the heralds of 'modernity'. These brought many changes, including a refined definition of 'vocation'.

The German sociologist Max Weber engendered a century of debate about these matters in a series of essays in the early twentieth century, later woven into a book, *The Protestant Ethic and the Spirit of Capitalism* (1935). He and his friend, the social historian Ernst Troeltsch, argued that repudiation of the monastic ideal in the Reformation and application of the doctrine of vocation to the laity working in many fields inaugurated a social and economic revolution (especially in the retrieval of the biblical notion that all who are called into Christ's church become part of a 'royal priesthood'). This did not destroy the notion of ascetic discipline for those set aside, but it transferred that discipline from the monastery to the hearts of individual believers and to the spheres of ordinary life more dramatically than even the earlier cultivation of the professions had begun to do. Weber accented the ways in which life was brought under a this-worldly asceticism that enhanced the rationalization of the economy, the bureaucratization of politics, and the routinization of ethical prophecy. Troeltsch accented the stimulus given to democratic forms of polity and a new appreciation of familial life. Both pointed to the ways in which Luther in Germany, Calvin in Geneva, and the later Puritans in England and New England not only abolished celibacy as a mark of holiness but also intensified ethical discipline over sexuality while fostering affectional intimacy. They held that most believers had a calling to be married, and they demanded a new ethical discipline in social and political life. A telling slogan of Protestantism, 'the priesthood of all believers', may not have been fully implemented in the internal authority structure of the Reformation churches, but it was seized on by lay believers, and indirectly and unintentionally promoted the disciplined ordering of everyday life.

Weber compared these developments to those in ancient Judaism, China, and India, while Troeltsch compared them to early church, medieval, and modern teachings in the West. The degree to which Weber's and Troeltsch's accounts are accurate has been debated in great detail now for a century. Some of their views have been laid to rest by subsequent research; others remain suggestive but without adequate evidence. Still others have led to highly probable conclusions, and many seem to be confirmed. They probably did not emphasize sufficiently the Reformers' primary understanding of the idea of 'calling', as first of all the call to become a disciple of Christ and a member of the community of faith established by the power of the Holy Spirit. And if we try to trace the implications for society, economy, and politics of the Reformers' understanding of vocation, we should note that the core of their protest against monasticism was theological—centred on the relationship of God to the world, of spirituality to materiality. They did not believe that either the Scriptures or reason taught that the natural, material world could be perfected only by the supernatural spirituality of sacramental practice, prayer, and contemplation. They also did not think that the sacraments were in any sense made pure by priests who abstained from contamination by property and wealth, sex and family, power and politics.

Instead, the Reformers held that nature is not only imperfect but is also fallen from the state intended by God in creation, and that it could not be restored or brought to fulfilment by any human spiritual activity. It could be redeemed and transformed by God's grace alone. Further, they believed that human spirituality was as much flawed and fallen as the material world. Hence, to think that vows of poverty, chastity, and obedience were signs of spiritual superiority seemed to them to be moral and spiritual pretence. In fact, living and working in one's ordinary station in life with a heart renewed by the love of Christ, and showing forth there a pattern of life that glorified God and served humankind, enacted a more faithful life of prayerful discipleship. Those with a true vocation are not to remove themselves from the common fabric of life to form an alternative community. They are to live, move, and have their being in the common life—filling it, and perhaps transforming it, with a new spirit from within. So the Reformers closed monasteries, aided monks and nuns to find marriage partners, allowed confiscation of monastic lands, and honoured city magistrates above the Holy Roman Emperor. They promoted a work ethic and the rise of industry. On the Continent they wrote 'confessions' as national creeds. In later English and American Puritan developments they wrote new 'constitutions' for the political order, in the form of 'covenants', believing that it was their calling to do so.

The Protestant movement was not, however, unified in its redefinition of the callings of believers or the vocation of the church. The early Protestant tradition tended to follow Luther directly for many years, envisioning society as pre-structured by God-given 'orders of creation' in which believers should remain (as the text in 1 Cor. 7: 20 says: let all persons stay in their 'assigned station' in life). One's *Beruf* (calling) was understood in terms of one's *Stand*—one's social position (*Stellung*), trade (*Gewerbe*), or office (*Amt*)—given in the created order of things. True, one's calling may have become distorted by greed, lust, or pretence, but these could be overcome by the spirit of love conveyed through God's grace to the human heart, accepted in trust, and nurtured by 'the Word rightly preached'. This could lead to a recovery of the primal possibilities given by God in creation, and could make possible restoration of the human capacity to be in communion with God and to serve the neighbour by diligently engaging the given daily tasks of life together, properly obedient to authority in family, church, and state. For some interpreters this seemed to imply a conservative legitimation of an established social cosmos of ranked order, each level doing its proper job in an organic solidarity. Luther was, on this view, still a medieval man. Some scholars have disputed this view of Luther, but it does seem true that such a view was historically influential in shaping certain features of North European life, and in the later, Nazi period was used by Hitler to evoke passivity in the face of his edicts (Wingren 1958; Lazareth 2001).

This Lutheran view is often contrasted with a later Reformed, Calvinist view, in spite of the fact that much of what Calvin taught was in continuity with older traditions as modified by Luther. Both gave strong approval to the development of professional excellence, for example. At three points, however, there are differences in the way the concept of vocation was developed. First, Calvinists applied the text from Romans 4—that in Christ 'we can become what we are not'—to the concept of 'calling'. One who is among the elect is not only transformed in heart and renewed in mind, and called into the church by the new relationship with God made possible in Christ and by the action of the Holy Spirit, but also, in the common life, one who is born a peasant or a craftsman may be called to a vocation and given the gifts of talent to become a scientist, an artist, a business leader, or a city council member. Indeed, the son of a magistrate might well be called to become a good street-cleaner. One's status is not given by one's original location in a predetermined social order. Second, the pre-given structure of labour, the ranks and orders of classes in society, are not fixed by a creational order in the past; rather, God's ongoing creative activity is constantly bringing about new possibilities in social history. Thus, the manufacturer and the merchant, the banker and the international trader, were able to see what they were doing as genuine vocations—something that was not imagined in earlier periods and was still under suspicion by Luther. Third, Calvin's earlier legal training gave his theology a high appreciation of the role of law in framing the sanctification of the moral life—a motif that gave a more dialectical understanding of the relation of Law and Gospel than Luther's views, which were at points dualistic.

SOME PURITAN ACCENTS

These teachings found fertile ground in the new, more technologically complex life of the growing Reformed cities: in Geneva, to which unnumbered Protestants fled from French persecutions; later in Amsterdam, to which both Protestants and Jews fled; and later still in New England, to which Puritans fled from England, Scotland, and Holland. These new contexts opened doors of occupational reconstruction that could also be seen as providential signs of a person's new vocational possibilities. The occupational order was malleable, not fixed, and it was increasingly held that nature itself was subject to radical change. Since nature was seen as fallen, the use of technology to reconstruct it became a moral duty and an honoured vocation.

It is only sometimes noted that the argument of Weber about the Calvinist reconstruction of vocation that reshaped, especially, modern economics takes its primary evidence not from the continental Reformers, but from popular Puritan preachers (such as Baxter, a century later) and from Arminian pietists (such as Wesley, two centuries later). But it was Troeltsch's study of Anabaptist and other sectarian groups that traced more fully the manner in which the multiple strands of Protestantism influenced developments in the doctrine of vocation. These sects often saw their entire communities as 'set aside' and called to be witnesses to another way of life—one of non-violence, simple living, and self-governance.

The host of smaller Protestant movements that developed with the breakdown of earlier Catholic unity were not all alike, but they were influenced by both the earlier tradition of vocation and Reformation emphases. They were like the monastics in thinking that the church established by imperial power or by the later Lutheran princes or Calvinist magistrates was too enmeshed in the world of political power, too accommodating to the many goats among the sheep in Christ's flock. Both the earlier monastics and many of the newer sectarian groups believed that church and society were filled with unrighteous half-believers. For some, this necessitated both withdrawal from the world in the name of following Jesus and formation of 'free' and 'holy' churches made up of believers only. They marshalled biblical texts, especially the Sermon on the Mount, to support their notion that the true community of faith is to be a community 'called out'—out of the world of coercion and politics, and out from technological complexity for the sake of simple living governed only by an ethic of love. From this root come the Mennonite, Quaker, and other notable 'peace churches', and—even if faith was thin in some quarters—the utopian communitarian movements of modern history.

Another branch saw vocation as a calling to be a reforming instrument of God's righteousness and justice in the world, by the use of force if necessary. The 'Peasant Revolt' against which Luther railed, the 'Prophets of Zwickau' whom the Reformed opposed, and the 'Chaplains' of the New Model Army, and the 'Diggers' and 'Levellers' of the Puritan period in England anticipated the movements later known as 'Christian socialism' and still later as 'liberation theology'. They were among the radical reformers of modernity, and some in recent centuries, seeing nothing gained for the workers by turning to the faith, turned instead to a secular hope for a new, revolutionary, classless society.

For most of these smaller Protestant movements the doctrine of vocation is more collectivistic in character than in the other Protestant traditions, and more given to a new social solidarity of dedication that can actualize God's laws and purposes on earth—for the more pietistic wing without violence, and within the church but not society; for the more puritanical wing with force if necessary, and for the salvation of the society. Over time both wings have tended to modulate and blend into other branches of the tradition—with the quietism of the one finding a deep affinity with strands of Methodist and Lutheran pietism, and the socially transformative impetus of the other finding affinity with repeated efforts at reform and renewal in a prophetic church committed to mobilization for social and political engagement.

CONTEMPORARY DEVELOPMENTS

The impact of these several movements prompted modern developments in the West, including the complex differentiation of society, the development of an emerging, global civil society, and a wide range of professional groupings that are unaware or (even) critical of any notion of a God-given 'vocation'. The development of a post-agricultural society, in which higher and higher percentages of the population are engaged in craft, manufacturing, technical, service, or helping occupations, rather than the extraction industries of farming, fishing, or mining, has brought an increasing accent on job skills. By the turn of the twentieth century three trends were already noticeable, trends that continued through the century in spite of the disruption of World Wars, the Depression, the Cold War, and a host of lesser conflicts. One had to do with populist movements, which advocated 'vocational training' for those who were not destined for college education. Carpentry, metal-working, mechanics, plumbing, and other crafts were seen as the 'callings' of those who were gifted with an ability for skilled labour but who lacked interest or capacity for theoretical studies. The rationale behind this specialized training was not only to equip a new generation of craftsmen to be self-supporting in the booming new cities that were developing, but also to provide these workers with a sense that God had called them to these indispensable tasks, so necessary in a growing society. Parallel to this movement, however, was a highly secular understanding of work that was often tedious and dull, demanding few skills and offering few rewards, materially or spiritually. Here the worker was seen as the actual builder of society, but one likely to be alienated from his tools and from the fruits of his labour.

Marxist thought was the epitome of this mode of thinking, and it played a tremendous role in forming a consciousness of solidarity in the working classes. Through consolidated class action, specifically against the capitalists who owned the means of production, alienation was to be overcome through the abolition of private property and the advent of a new system of sharing based on humanist and materialist grounds alone. What was, with respect to the topic of vocation, remarkable about this proposal was that workers were given—not by any god but by 'the logic of history'—if not precisely a 'vocation', at least a scientifically discerned 'destiny', to carry out a revolutionary programme in history aimed at producing a classless society. Any notion of a divine calling was seen as a mystifying and idealistic ideology designed to manipulate the motivations of the worker, although this logic of history seemed to many observers to be a secularized version of radical Christian thought (Hardy 1990).

During the twentieth century the complexity and variety of occupational opportunities increased, bringing with it a new set of issues. The skills of the elders were soon obsolete, and while many young people followed in the footsteps of their family's trade, a new question became common, often posed to even younger children: 'And what do you want to be when you grow up?' When we remember that for most of human history the lot in life of most people has been determined by birth and social location, this must strike us as an amazing question. For now it turns out that one can 'choose' one's vocation—or, at least, one can choose a kind of job training for a career path, possibly through many positions. Higher and higher percentages of the population were able to receive advanced education, and thereby to increase their options. To be sure, these options were sometimes limited by race, gender, class, and structural opportunities in the social environment, but in principle the number of possibilities multiplied greatly. Over the last 100 years remarkable gains were made in these areas in developed and developing countries, while, at the same time, the overtly Christian theological sense of vocation was reduced, in part because it was covertly incarnated into the fabric of the culture. Everyone wanted to be seen as skilled, dedicated, and responsible in their work—in part because the educational and job opportunities were, in fact, increasingly open to people of all faiths. Aptitude tests were introduced to uncover unacknowledged potentialities and unrecognized interests in order to match these with occupational possibilities in the environment. The result was less the nurturing of a sense of vocation than a prelude to job placement.

Perhaps nowhere is this double effect of incarnation into common cultural expectations and overt secularization more evident than in the classical 'high' professions and the imitation of them by a host of 'new' professions. Since the Middle Ages, the cleric, the doctor, the lawyer, and the professor had high status and certain privileges that accompanied their specialized training. They were often seen by the communities they served, and by themselves, as providing indispensable services to humanity, and they felt responsible for upholding standards of excellence in their practice and personal behaviour. The professional levels of education for these positions have, on the whole, risen in modernity, and other professionals have joined the ranks of the highly trained and highly regarded—scientists and engineers, architects and accountants, diplomats and military generals, journalists and managers. Further, a host of 'lesser' occupations have come to call themselves and be seen by others as 'professionals'—from pharmacists and school teachers to hairdressers and major league athletes. But it is not clear that all is well in these areas in spite of their growth. Many complaints can be heard that these professions have forgotten their basic responsibility before God to the neighbour and the society, and are becoming another form of commercialized expertise for hire (May 2001). Indeed, while the overwhelming majority carry out their duties with dedication and skill, and many in fact love their work, little cultivation of a sense of calling is found in professional circles. And some argue that the absence of an overt sense of vocation within the fabric of instruction in modern professional education leads to a spiritual and ethical void in practice.

In response to this situation a number of scholars and church leaders have attempted to recover and, where necessary, revise the doctrine of vocation as a guide to the renewal of the world of work under the changed conditions of a post-industrial society and a globalizing economy. Gordon Preece, for example, has re-examined twentieth-century theologians who have sought to bring the understanding of vocation into renewed focus. He explicitly compares and contrasts the Lutheran theologian Gustaf Wingren's creational view, the Reformed theologian Karl Barth's Christological view, and the Baptist theologian Miroslav Volf's pneumatological view of the concept of vocation, and argues for a fuller Trinitarian understanding (Preece 1998). Three compendia of resources regarding the practices of medicine, law, and business as vocations have recently appeared (Lammers and Verhey 2001; McConnell *et al.* 2001; and McCann *et al.* 1994). Douglas Schuurman has also recently treated the vocations of the laity, arguing that all aspects of life are potentially holy. And this author has sought to explore the new directions of vocation and professionalization in view of the globalization of international law, educational standards, technological developments, medical care, environmental awareness, and certain moral ideals, as well as economic regulatory organizations such as the World Bank, the International Monetary Fund, and the World Trade Organization. (Stackhouse *et al.* 2001).

Whether such efforts will be fruitful in the future is, as yet, quite uncertain, but failure to develop an effective understanding of vocation is likely to leave much of the world in moral drift or subject to various kinds of ideological fanaticism. On the whole, given the pluralistic and dynamic global environment in which we live, and given the need to recover and recast the deepest core of our values, we might best turn again to the doctrine of the 'three offices of Christ'—so that every believer will understand that being in Christ involves for them a calling to be prophetic advocates for justice, priestly care-givers to their neighbours, and politically wise participants in the ordering of all the spheres of the common life.

REFERENCES AND SUGGESTED READING

BARTH, K. (1961). 'Vocation', in *Church Dogmatics*, III/4, Edinburgh: T. & T. Clark, 595–646.
BERMAN, H. (1983). *Law and Revolution: The Formation of the Western Legal Tradition.* Cambridge, Mass.: Harvard University Press.
HARDY, L. (1990). *The Fabric of this World: Inquiries into Calling, Career Choice, and the Design of Human Work.* Grand Rapids, Mich.: William B. Eerdmans.

HOLL, K. (1928). 'Die Geschichte des Worts Beruf', in *Aufsätze zur Kirchengeschichte*, III. Tübingen.

LAMMERS, S. and VERHEY, A. (2001). *On Moral Medicine*. Grand Rapids, Mich.: William B. Eerdmans.

LAZARETH, W. H. (2001). *Christians in Society: Luther, the Bible, and Social Ethics*. Minneapolis: Fortress Press.

McCANN, D., STACKHOUSE, M., and ROELS, S. (1994). *On Moral Business*. Grand Rapids, Mich.: William B. Eerdmans.

McCONNELL, M. W. *et al.* (2001). *Christian Perspectives on Legal Thought*. New Haven: Yale University Press.

MAY, W. F. (2001). *Beleaguered Rulers: The Public Obligation of the Professional*. Louisville, Ky.: Westminster Press.

NOBLE, D. (1997). *The Religion of Technology: The Divinity of Man and the Spirit of Invention*. New York: Alfred Knopf.

PREECE, G. (1998). *The Viability of the Vocation Tradition in Trinitarian, Credal and Reformed Perspective: The Threefold Call*. Lewiston, NY: Edwin Mellen Press.

SCHUURMAN, D. (2004). *Vocation*. Grand Rapids, Mich.: Eerdmans.

STACKHOUSE, M. *et al.* (2000, 2001, 2002). *God and Globalization*, 3 vols. Harrisburg, Pa.: Trinity Press International.

TROELTSCH, E. (1932). *The Social Teachings of the Christian Churches*. New York: Harper.

VOLF, M. (1991). *Work in the Spirit*. New York: Oxford University Press.

WEBER, M. (1958). *The Protestant Ethic and the Spirit of Capitalism*. New York: Charles Scribner's Sons.

WINGREN, G. (1958). *The Christian's Calling: Luther on Vocation*. Edinburgh: Oliver & Boyd.

CHAPTER 12

....

VIRTUE

....

JEAN PORTER

REFLECTION on the virtues has been central to Christian ethics from its inception. This might have surprised theologians in the early part of the twentieth century, when the idea of virtue played at most a secondary role in both Protestant and Catholic ethics. However, by the middle of the last century Protestant as well as Catholic theologians, especially but not only in the English-speaking world, began once again to turn to the idea of virtue as an organizing motif for theological ethics. It has become something of a commonplace to regard the virtues as *the* proper expression of the Christian life, in comparison with which the language of law and duty is regarded as derivative, excessively philosophical, or in some other way sub-Christian.

Yet it is far from obvious that the virtues should play a central role, or indeed any role, in a theologically sound Christian ethic. If Scripture is the touchstone for theology, then it would seem that Christian theological ethics should be pre-eminently an ethic of law. As even a cursory examination of the texts will confirm, the way of life proper to the faithful is depicted throughout Scripture in terms of obedience to law, or to God's commands. The language of virtue as such is absent from the Hebrew Scriptures, and the virtues are mentioned only in passing in the New Testament. Moreover, there is a theological case to be made against a Christian virtue ethic, on the grounds that such an approach encourages a false sense of one's own goodness and a reliance on that goodness rather than on God's grace. This line of argument has been especially prominent in Protestant circles, but there is a different case to be made against virtue ethics within a distinctively Catholic context. That is, a properly developed moral theology should focus on setting forth the prohibitions and duties that men and women must observe in order to attain salvation. The language of the virtues has pastoral value, but on careful analysis the core virtues are simply dispositions to observe the moral law. Anything beyond this is properly the province of spirituality or the theology of mysticism, not moral theology as such.

None the less, in spite of these criticisms, reflection on the virtues emerged early in Christian ethics, and has flourished more or less continuously ever since. In its earliest stages, this reflection was mostly unsystematic and pastoral in orientation. It focused especially on identifying and encouraging traits of character which serve as remedies for the besetting sins of the Christian life—for example, humility is approached as an antidote to pride (Wenzel 1974). This approach continued to dominate pastoral reflection, preaching, and literature throughout the Middle Ages. But, in addition, a more theoretically focused approach to the virtues emerged with the writings of Augustine in the fifth century, and in the early twelfth century this approach began to be transformed by the scholastics into systematic theories of the virtues. The language of the virtues has played a central role in theology ever since.

Why should this be the case? In this essay, I would like to explore one reason for the continuing importance of the virtues for theological ethics. As I will try to show, the language of the virtues builds in a kind of flexibility, even ambiguity, that is not so evident in the languages of law and duty. (I believe that these latter are in fact comparably flexible and ambiguous, but this is not so obvious.) This is a fruitful ambiguity, because it enables the theologian to hold together two seemingly inconsistent yet compelling perspectives on the moral life, and even to begin to integrate them in a systematic way—although the terms of this integration will of course vary from one theologian to another.

THE FRUITFUL AMBIGUITY
OF THE VIRTUES

The virtues are generally regarded as praiseworthy traits of character—for example, courage, generosity, and fairness. We also sometimes consider admirable or valuable traits of intellect to be virtues—for example, wit or keenness of perception. None the less, early Greek philosophical reflection on the virtues focused on those traits of character that are praiseworthy and not simply valuable, and the association between the virtues and moral approval has persisted ever since (Annas 1993: 47–134).

Yet, in another respect, the moral status of the virtues is not so clear as we might assume. Even those virtues which would seem to be clearly moral traits turn out on closer inspection to be morally ambiguous. A pirate can show great courage in pursuing his trade, and a soldier can fight valiantly in what he knows to be a vicious war. A parent can be generous to the point of spoiling a child, rendering the adult incapable of making an independent living. Even fairness can have a dark side; scrupulous fairness between the claims of two children, without regard to the needs and the distinctive personalities of each, can have the effect of hurting both and turning them against each other.

These examples raise what might be described as the problem of the (seemingly) instrumental character of the virtues. That is, it seems that men and women can draw on their virtues in pursuit of all kinds of ends, including the ill-considered and the vicious, as well as those that are praiseworthy. Yet, if the virtues are morally good in themselves, how can they be expressed through morally bad actions? This need not present a problem, if one has no particular stake in defending the independent moral value of the virtues themselves. Yet it seems counter-intuitive to regard courage, generosity, and fairness as qualities which are morally neutral in themselves, however valuable or even (non-morally) admirable they may be—as if they were, after all, equivalent to non-moral qualities such as perception or wit. Yet, if the virtues are morally good in themselves, how can they be expressed through morally bad actions?

This problem is distinct from, yet related to, the more familiar question of the connection or the unity of the virtues (Hursthouse 1999: 153–60 is especially helpful on this point). Is it possible to have one virtue and not others, to be courageous but unjust, generous and fair but imprudent? Or should we say that anyone who has one virtue necessarily has all the major virtues (the connection thesis), or even more strongly, that the virtues rightly understood are all expressions of one fundamental virtue (the unity thesis)? On its face, this question seems to be less worrisome than the instrumentality problem. After all, experience seems to confirm that it is not only possible, but almost inevitable, to lack some virtues while possessing others, to be brave, generous, or fair, yet also to be unjust, imprudent, or callous. Yet the theses of the unity or connection of the virtues gain force because they suggest one way of addressing the more exigent problem of the instrumentality of the virtues. If someone is capable of acting unjustly, imprudently, or callously, then this at least suggests (admittedly, it does not prove) that the person lacks the opposing virtue. Most versions of the unity or connection theses would suggest that in such a case, someone's actual good qualities are not genuine virtues. By the same token, we might argue that the seeming courage of the pirate is not true courage, and so for the rest of the examples. Thus we would avoid the problem of the instrumentality of the virtues, since these and similar cases would not represent the use of genuine virtues in pursuit of bad ends.

Clearly, there are better and worse ways to develop this line of argument. Without some independent criteria for distinguishing true from seeming virtues, we would in effect be stipulating that any seeming virtue expressed through a bad act cannot count as a true virtue. In its stronger forms, this argument turns on a claim that true virtues presuppose some kind of capacity for wise judgement or perception of the genuinely good, which will inform the individual's whole life if it is present at all. I myself find a version of this argument to be persuasive, but my purpose here is not to defend it. Rather, I want to point out that the fundamental claim that the virtues are all one, or are all connected, depends for much of its plausibility on the ambiguity of the language of the virtues. The virtues are not only correlated with vices, which we know to be bad; they are also associated with similitudes, which also turn out to be bad, even though in some ways, and especially as expressed in particular acts, they closely resemble virtues. To the extent that these distinctions are plausible, they lend credibility to claims that true virtues are all connected, or are all expressions of one fundamental quality.

And in fact, distinctions among virtues, vices, and similitudes are not just philosophical expedients; they run through our ordinary moral judgements, albeit not in those terms. Very often, we find ourselves asking whether some seemingly admirable trait really is such, and in at least some instances, it makes good sense to decide that it is not. Teenagers play chicken on country roads because they want to prove their courage, but this does not mean that courage is in fact what they are exhibiting. ('Chicken' is a game in which two persons in automobiles speed towards each other, and the first one to swerve away loses.) What looks like courage may turn out to be rashness or foolhardiness, or someone may simply be too slow to recognize a dangerous situation when he sees one. What looks like generosity may turn out to be an indiscriminate profligacy or an overly sensitive reluctance to say no to any demand, and seeming fairness may actually stem from a desire to keep up appearances. This line of analysis, in turn, lends plausibility to the proposal to draw a similar distinction in other, more problematic cases. If we can agree that rashness is a similitude of courage, then it is perhaps not so strange to regard the seeming courage of the pirate or the wicked soldier as being likewise similitudes of courage.

At the same time, it would be a mistake to conclude that the distinction between true virtues and their similitudes serves to eliminate the ambiguity of the language of the virtues. Not every seeming virtue is truly good, but, correlatively, similitudes of virtue are not always wholly bad or without value. Even the more obvious similitudes of virtue have something attractive about them—after all, teenagers play chicken for a reason: namely, to show that they do possess an admirable indifference to danger. And even if we regard a quality such as the (seeming) courage of the pirate or the wicked soldier as another kind of similitude, the bravery of bad men and women can still move us to deep admiration. A profligate inability to say no can call forth tender sympathy, and even an unbending regard for respectability can call forth a grudging respect, even when we recognize the relevant qualities for what they are, as vices rather than virtues. We can recognize that a particular quality is bad, yet find it admirable or attractive—this is perhaps the most telling indication of the ambiguity of virtue language.

Seen from the standpoint of Christian ethics, this has proved to be a fruitful ambiguity. Because the language of the virtues can be given both positive and negative values, and sometimes both together, it provides a uniquely helpful framework for formulating and reflecting on similar problems arising within Christian thought. Similar, not identical—while the problems discussed above have played an important role in Christian ethics, theologians since (at least) the time of Augustine have focused on another problem, arguably still more funda-mental from a Christian standpoint, which we might describe as the ambiguity of morality itself.

Augustine: Admirable Vices and Flawed Virtues

To my knowledge, Augustine was the first to develop an extended critique of his society's ideals of the virtues from the perspective of Christian theology. As is well known, he argued that the seeming virtues of the Romans, splendid though they might be, are in the last analysis better described as vices, rather than virtues:

> For however praiseworthy the command of the soul over the body and the reason over the vices may appear to be, if the soul and reason itself do not serve God as God Himself has commanded that He is to be served, in no way do they rightly command the body and the vices. For what kind of mistress of the body and the vices can a mind be which neither knows the true God nor is subject to His command, but is prostituted to the corrupt and vicious demons? Hence, whatever virtues it seems to itself to have, by which it commands the body and the vices in order to attain or to hold onto anything whatever except God, are themselves vices rather than virtues. For granted that the virtues are thought by some to be true and upright when they are referred to themselves and not sought on account of something else, even then they are puffed up and proud, and should not be judged to be virtues, but vices. (De Civ. Dei, 19. 25; all translations from Augustine are my own; however, I have checked my translations against W. C. Greene's translations in the Loeb editions)

On a first reading, this passage would appear to reflect a complete break with classical ideals of the virtues. Yet, seen in context, Augustine's characterization of the Roman virtues as vices is not so radical as it seems. What he offers is, rather, a critique of popular ideals of virtue developed with tools taken from the philosophy of his day. Specifically, he appropriates the Stoic version of the line of analysis discussed above, according to which seeming virtues are to be evaluated in terms of the aims that they serve. Augustine refers explicitly to this line of argument in *City of God* (*De Civ. Dei*, 5. 20), and as John Rist has pointed out, it is central to his accounts of virtue throughout his works (1994: 168–73). On this view, only those seeming virtues which are directed to genuinely good ends are to be counted as true virtues. To return to an earlier example, someone who is scrupulously fair only because she wants to be respectable cannot be said to be genuinely just.

More importantly, when we place these remarks in the context of Augustine's overall critique of Roman virtue in *City of God*, we find that his assessment of the Roman virtues is more complex than we might at first assume. The virtues of the Romans cannot be dismissed as vices without qualification, because it is possible to distinguish between better and worse, more and less genuine and admirable forms of these qualities. Roman virtue at its best was directed towards glory; quoting Sallust, he says of the ancient Romans that they were 'avid for praise and liberal with money, desiring great glory and honest wealth'; glory, as Augustine goes on to say, 'they loved most ardently, on account of it they wished to live, for its sake they did not hesitate to die. They repressed every other desire for the sake of this one great desire' (*De Civ. Dei*, 5. 12).

Thus, for Augustine, virtue at its human best is integrally bound up with the desire for glory, rooted in a desire for praise. Unsurprisingly, he regards this love of praise as a vice, even though he admits that it does at least restrain the baser vices (*De Civ. Dei*, 5. 14). Even those few Romans who despised glory, seeking virtue for its own sake, do not escape criticism. In Augustine's view, they too were seeking human praise, since they sought the approval of their own conscience (*De Civ. Dei*, 5.20). In short, Roman virtue was inextricably bound up with the love of human praise, and, as Augustine memorably says, human praise was its fitting reward:

To these, therefore, to whom God was not to give eternal life with the angels in his heavenly city . . . if he had not conceded to them this earthly glory of a most excellent empire, he would not have rendered to them a reward for those good works, that is to say, those virtues through which they endeavored to come to such glory. For it was concerning such persons, who do some good that they might be seen and glorified by others, that the Lord said, 'Amen, I say to you, they have received their reward.' So these also despised their private interests for the sake of the common interest, that is to say, the republic and its treasury; they resisted avarice, they advised the fatherland with frank counsel, and they were not guilty of any crime against its laws, or any evil desire. By such arts, as by the true road, did they strive for honor, power, and glory; they were honored among nearly all the nations, they imposed the laws of their empire upon many nations, and to this day they are glorified by the literature and history of almost all the nations. Hence they have no grounds to complain against the justice of the highest and true God: 'They have received their reward.' (*De Civ. Dei*, 5. 15)

None the less, as these words suggest, the Roman ideal of glory is not ignoble. On the contrary, it is deeply admirable, as Augustine recognizes. The Roman Empire was a fitting reward for what were in some sense good works, stemming from virtues that, while not genuine, were not without value either. Christians do not do as much for their salvation, Augustine says, as the Romans did for glory in the city of Rome *(De Civ. Dei, 5. 18)*. What is more, the love of glory at its best is something other than a desire for praise or fame on any terms. The ancient heroes of Rome sought glory through genuine devotion and extremes of self-sacrifice, and they would have scorned to attain it by false pretences. They did not seek popular acclaim but, rather, hoped to win the praise of those who are themselves praiseworthy *(De Civ. Dei, 5. 12)*. Everlasting honour in the society of the honourable—this is something better than popular fame, finer than dominion, and very far removed from the desires for security and pleasure which govern most people's lives.

More to the point, the ancient ideal of glory and honour, and the virtues stemming from it, are far better than the simulated virtues and the frank vices that came to dominate Roman society in its latter years—so Augustine believes, here again sharing in a widespread view of the intelligentsia of his time. The ardour for honourable renown that informed Roman virtue at its best has given way to a vulgar desire for fame on any pretext, and the austerity and self-restraint bound up with the classical ideal have been supplanted by lasciviousness, greed, and especially cruelty, as Augustine notes—although he also points out that even in ancient times, the Romans did not always live up to their own best ideals (*De Civ. Dei*, 5. 7).

At this point, we can begin to appreciate the originality and theological significance of Augustine's critique of Roman virtue. We have already noted that Augustine took his theoretical analysis of virtues in terms of their governing aims from Stoic philosophy, and, like the Stoics, he uses this analysis to distinguish between true and seeming virtues. But at the same time he also develops this line of analysis in the opposite direction. That is, not only does he claim that the seeming virtues of the Romans are not true virtues, because they are directed to false ends; almost immediately, he goes on to argue that at their best, the false virtues of the Romans none the less resemble true virtues in some important ways. They reflect a genuine integrity and self-restraint which are humanly admirable, and Christians can acknowledge them as such; indeed, Augustine seems to regard the virtuous heroes of ancient Rome as models for Christian imitation (*De Civ. Dei*, 5. 18). Even more importantly, these forms of virtue can be distinguished from what we would ordinarily regard as their similitudes, as well as from frank vices. The Roman desire for honourable glory is not a true virtue; yet there is a real difference between this and a vainglorious desire to be praised by anybody, at any cost. Perhaps we want to say that in the final analysis—that is to say, the Christian analysis—both are to be regarded as forms of vice; none the less, in another sense vainglory is a vice in a way that honourableness is not. The latter is a vice in the sense of being a defective virtue, but there is no plausible sense in which vainglory can be described as a virtue.

The ambiguity of the language of the virtues can be turned to advantage philosophically because it allows us to distinguish between true virtues and their similitudes, which turn out to be vices. Augustine's example shows that this ambiguity can be exploited theologically as well—through a distinction between diverse forms of goodness: well-ordered, perfect, or complete goods, on the one hand, and disordered, imperfect, or incomplete forms of goodness, on the other. This is important, in turn, because it offers one way of formulating and addressing what turns out to be a recurring problematic in Christian theology. That is, seen from the perspective of God's perfection and holiness, any form of human goodness will appear to be a shabby pretence, and evaluated by the ideals of the Church, the limits and even the viciousness of the ideals of secular society become manifest. (One of the strengths of Augustine's analysis stems from the fact that he compares the ideals of the Church with the ideals of secular society, rather than comparing the ideals of the Church with actual secular practice— on the contrary, he suggests that actual Christian practice does not always compare favourably with life in pagan Rome.)

Yet, if we take the doctrine of creation seriously—if we regard everything that exists, including ourselves, as creations of a good God—then it is problematic, at best, to claim that human virtue is altogether and without qualification false and evil. Moreover, theologians, like philosophers, must come to terms with their intuitions, and it is strikingly counter-intuitive to claim that there are no meaningful distinctions among what are generally regarded as virtues, their similitudes, and the vices opposed to them—no real distinctions among honourableness, vainglory, and cravenness, or among courage, rashness, and cowardice. Finally, it is important to remember that Christians are also participants in a secular society, informed by its ideals and shaped by its practices. Paul himself frankly appropriates the ideals of the Hellenistic world around him in developing his ideals of the Christian life (see, for example, Phil. 4: 8–9), and Christians ever since have followed his example, with more or less criticism and self-conscious distancing thrown in. How could it be otherwise? We cannot reflect on how we ought to live, or much less criticize accepted mores and propose alternatives, except in terms of the moral vocabulary that we actually have—and to a greater or lesser extent, this will be the vocabulary that we share with those around us, whether Christian or not.

The perennial value of Augustine's critique of classical virtue lies in the fact that he exploits the ambiguity of the language of the virtues as a way of formulating and reflecting on a different, though related, theological ambiguity. The ambiguity of the language of the virtues, as it is manifested in ordinary moral language and embedded in philosophical reflection, is located in the space between moral goodness and diverse forms of vice and corruption, at least some of which ineradicably retain marks of goodness. Augustine draws on this ambiguity in order to formulate a different ambiguity, located in the space between the humanly good and the infinite Goodness that is God. Seen from this latter perspective, moral goodness even at its best falls so far short as to appear to be another form of vice. Yet, even from this perspective we can still distinguish among the virtues, humanly understood as such, and both frank vices and similitudes of virtue.

The continuing salience of these distinctions, in turn, suggests that even seen from the perspective of God's supreme goodness, human morality retains something of its value and force. And this poses a further problem. As Augustine brilliantly shows, we cannot attribute supreme or unmixed goodness to human virtue, even at its best. But if this is so, then what kind of value should we to ascribe to humanly attainable virtues and, by extension, to the moral life generally considered? I believe that Augustine is aware of this issue, even though his sense of the continuing value of human virtue has been obscured by the slogan of 'splendid vices' that came to be attached to his work. At any rate, this problem becomes central for later theological reflection on the virtues. While we cannot trace later discussions of this problem in any detail, it will be helpful to see how it is addressed by one of Augustine's greatest interpreters, Thomas Aquinas.

Aquinas: The Complexity
of the Virtues

We are accustomed to regard Aquinas's treatment of the virtues as a restatement of Aristotle's theory and, as such, to contrast it with Augustine's (supposedly) more theological account. But Aquinas's theory of the virtues was developed in a context of ongoing theological speculation on the virtues, within which Aristotelian and Augustinian elements had already been synthesized in complex ways (for this background, I rely on Lottin 1949: 99–150).

When theologians began to reflect systematically on the virtues in the early twelfth century, they had two starting-points from which to choose. Peter Lombard offered one such starting-point, in the form of an appropriation (and, I would suggest, an over-simplification) of Augustine's doctrine of virtue. Specifically, he interpreted Augustine's claim that genuine virtue is impossible without God's grace in such a way as to identify virtue with grace. This identification is reflected in his well-known definition of virtue: 'Virtue is a good quality of the mind, by means of which one lives rightly, of which no one can make bad use, which God brings about in us, without us' (II *Sentences*, 27. 5). His contemporary Peter Abelard provided the alternative, in the form of a philosophical sketch of the virtues developed out of the Aristotelian doctrine of the mean (see Nederman 1991 on the availability of Aristotelian ideas in the early twelfth century). True virtue is possible without grace on this view, and, correlatively, we can develop a fully adequate account of virtue in purely philosophical—which is to say, non-Christian—terms.

Unsurprisingly, later theologians were reluctant to adopt either of these alternatives without qualification. They recognized that, without grace, the human person cannot please God or attain salvation—this was by now regarded as orthodox doctrine—and this lent support to Peter Lombard's equation of virtue with grace. None the less, intellectuals in the twelfth and thirteenth centuries tended to have a high regard for the wisdom and probity of the philosophers of classical antiquity, and they also recognized that their own Jewish and Muslim contemporaries sometimes attained high standards of learning and uprightness of life. Hence, they were not prepared to deny the value of purely human virtue out of hand, or to equate virtue with grace *tout court*.

They attempted to hold these two perspectives together by appropriating a set of distinctions grounded in Scripture and already well ensconced in Christian tradition. On the one hand, they argued, the distinctively Christian virtues of faith, hope, and charity identified by Paul are both necessary and sufficient for salvation, and these depend on grace. On the other hand, they claimed that a lesser, yet genuine form of virtue is possible without grace. Virtues of this sort, which can be attained through human effort alone, are not sufficient for salvation, but they are none the less genuinely good because they are directed towards a good end: that is to say, the well-being of civic society. Hence, these virtues were described as political virtues, and they were identified with the four cardinal virtues of classical antiquity—prudence, justice, courage, and temperance.

When we turn to Aquinas's analysis of the virtues as developed in the *Summa theologiae*, we immediately see that he does not draw on the distinction between theological and political virtues as an organizing principle, although he does comment on it (I-II 60. 5, I-II 61. 5; these and all subsequent references to Aquinas are taken from the *Summa theologiae*; the translations are my own). Rather, Aquinas's theory of the virtues is structured around what seems at first to be an unnecessarily complex twofold distinction, between infused and acquired virtues, on the one hand, and between virtues directed to God and those directed to the rational good, on the other. Yet, as we will see, this complexity offers a key to understanding Aquinas's distinctive theological approach to human morality.

This distinction, and the motivation behind it, are both signalled early on in Aquinas's account of the virtues. Aquinas begins his analysis of the virtues as such with Peter Lombard's summary of Augustine's conception of the virtues, which he restates in correct logical form and defends as the most adequate definition of the virtues. However, he immediately qualifies this defence by adding that the last clause, according to which 'God brings about [the virtues] in us, without us', applies only to the infused virtues, since we can attain the acquired virtues (as the name suggests) through our own powers (I-II 55. 4).

Reading further, we find that for him this distinction takes the place of the more usual distinction between political and theological virtues as an organizing principle. At the same time, we see that the resultant analysis is more complicated than the theological/political distinction which Aquinas rejects. He does retain one key element of the earlier structure: namely, its identification of three theological and four cardinal virtues (I-II 61, 62). We might expect that he would map his infused/acquired distinction on to this division, in such a way as to identify the infused virtues with the theological virtues, and the acquired with the cardinal virtues. Up to a point, that is what he does. The theological virtues, he says, can only be infused by God; they can in no way be acquired by human effort (I-II 62. 1). This distinguishes them from the cardinal virtues, which can be understood either as general qualities of moral goodness or as specific virtues with their own characteristic forms of expression, and which can in either case be acquired by human effort (I-II 61. 1). However, the infused virtues include not only the theological virtues, but also infused cardinal virtues (I-II 63. 3, 4). While no one can attain salvation without the infused virtues, on Aquinas's view, he nevertheless regards the acquired virtues as genuine virtues, albeit in a qualified sense (I-II 62. 1, 2).

One of Aquinas's professed aims in writing the *Summa Theologiae* (as stated in his introduction to the work as a whole) is to prune and simplify the exuberance of contemporaneous theological discussion. Why, then, does he introduce complexities that his interlocutors did not appear to need? In my view, Aquinas adopts this complex structure in order to accommodate a twofold analysis of the virtues in terms of their aims and their causes. The theological virtues are distinguished from the cardinal virtues, in so far as the former have God as their direct object, whereas the latter are directed towards some aspect of the human good as grasped by reason (I-II 62. 2). The diverse objects of the two kinds of virtues, in turn, imply two kinds of causation. The cardinal virtues are aimed towards various aspects of human flourishing—indeed, Aquinas endorses an ancient view that the naturally attainable form of human happiness consists in the practice of the virtues (I-II 5. 5). Hence, the cardinal virtues are integrally related to our existence and flourishing as creatures of a specific kind, and as such, they can be attained through the proper development of our own natural powers (I-II 61. 2). By contrast, the theological virtues have God as their direct and immediate object, and infinitely exceed the natural capacities of any creature. Precisely because natural principles of operation would not be necessary to attain a supernatural end, Aquinas argues, we stand in need of a distinct principle of operation in order to attain salvation. This principle is grace, which works in us through the infused virtues, including pre-eminently the theological virtues (I-II 63. 3, I-II 110. 3).

So far, Aquinas's analysis fits within the framework of the division between theological and political virtues. However, he adds a third category, in the form of infused cardinal virtues (I-II 63. 3). The cardinal virtues are infused together with charity, and while they cannot exist without charity, neither can charity exist and operate without them (I-II 65. 2, 3). Aquinas is not saying that charity subsumes and reorients the acquired virtues. While the infused cardinal virtues are analogous to their acquired counterparts, they are specifically different—that is to say, different in kind—because directed towards a different end (I-II 63. 4). Whereas the acquired virtues are directed towards a connatural form of human happiness, the infused cardinal virtues are directed towards the attainment of supernatural happiness, union with God in the Beatific Vision, even though they are directed towards this end indirectly, via the proper pursuit and enjoyment of the diverse objects and activities proper to human life (I-II 65. 3).

Why does Aquinas find it necessary to postulate infused as well as acquired cardinal virtues? Why does he not simply say that charity directs us to our final end in and through directing the other virtues, infused and acquired, in such a way as to give their proper acts the required orientation? Aquinas replies to this question by pointing out that God does not act less perfectly through grace than through nature, and since natural principles of motion require intermediate and instrumental capacities (for example, the principle of life requires capacities for nutrition), so the supernatural principle of grace requires intermediate principles of operation, in addition to the primary and architectonic principles conferred by the theological virtues, and above all by charity (I-II 65. 3, especially ad 1). In order to appreciate the force of this argument, we need to see it in the context of Aquinas's overall analysis of virtue.

Near the beginning of that analysis, he asks whether the faculties for passion—the concupiscent and irascible parts of the soul—can be the subjects of virtue. He replies that this is not only possible but necessary if the human person is to be capable of good actions: 'For an act which proceeds from one potency subsequent to being moved by another cannot be perfect, unless each of the potencies is well disposed with respect to the act' (I-II 56. 4). For this reason, he goes on to explain, an act involving the passions cannot be rendered good through reason alone; rather, the passions themselves must likewise be well disposed through the appropriate virtues. At the same time, as we read further on, the virtues of the passions cannot exist or function apart from the relevant virtues of reason and will—that is to say, prudence and justice (I-II 58. 4). Hence, a virtuous disposition cannot be attained through either a rational control of the passions or an unreflective sensibility; reason, will, and passions must all be well disposed and appropriately oriented, in themselves and in relation to one another, in order for the human person to act well. By the same token, neither can charity and the other theological virtues result in actions directed towards our salvation unless reason, will, and passions are likewise disposed towards salvation, albeit indirectly, through an appropriate orientation towards particular ends.

At this point, we begin to appreciate why Aquinas felt it necessary to complicate, rather than simplify, his interlocutors' analysis of naturally available and divinely bestowed virtues. Only in this way can he do justice to the complexity of human nature. The human creature can act only through the co-ordination of a diverse set of capacities, and she can act well only if each of these capacities is well disposed in itself and well ordered to the others. This is a basic requirement of the integrity of human nature, and, as Aquinas repeatedly reminds us, grace does not destroy nature, but rather perfects it (see, for example, I 60. 5).

This brings us to a further point. Aquinas consistently maintains a clear distinction between nature and grace (see, for example, I-II 109). This distinction has sometimes seemed to reflect a denigration of nature, but I believe that it is motivated (in part) by the opposite concern. Aquinas insists on the distinction between nature and grace, not only to preserve the gratuity of grace, but also to safeguard the integrity and intelligibility of nature, which operates through comprehensible principles in order to produce finite and attainable ends (again, see I-II 109, especially articles 1–3). The integrity of nature is important, in turn, because every creature is good in so far as it approaches the full perfection of the intelligible nature in which it has been created (I 5. 1, 4). Sub-rational creatures cannot attain any higher form of perfection. The rational or intellectual creature is capable of attaining a kind of perfection transcending its natural capacities, albeit only through a distinctive kind of divine assistance (I-II 1. 8, 5. 5). But if this supernatural perfection were to obviate the natural goodness of the creature, this would mean that two expressions of God's wisdom and love would be at odds, and for Aquinas this would be an intolerable conclusion.

This brings us to the issue at hand, because it indicates how Aquinas deals with the ambiguity among different forms of moral and divine goodness. Augustine's rich and complex distinctions among different ways of falling short of divine goodness are transformed by Aquinas into a distinction between two principles of operation, nature informed by reason, and grace, aimed towards two distinct ends, naturally attainable happiness, and the supreme happiness of personal union with God. Aquinas agrees with Augustine that acquired virtue is virtue only in a derivative sense. Seen from the perspective of the final end of union with God to which we are in fact called, the acquired virtues, which cannot bring us to that end, can be regarded as virtues only in a qualified sense (II-II 23. 7). At the same time, this judgement does not seem to carry the same negative connotations that it does for Augustine. Aquinas makes explicit what Augustine (to my knowledge) only suggests: namely, the real distinction between genuine virtues, whose proper goods can be oriented towards our final end through charity, and similitudes of virtue, which are vicious even humanly considered and in no way consistent with a charitable life (ibid.). Even more importantly, the exigencies and rational considerations informing the acquired virtues continue to have force within the life of grace. To be sure, the infused cardinal virtues are distinct from their acquired counterparts, not only because they are oriented towards a distinct end, but also because their proper objects are transformed accordingly (I-II 63. 4 ad 1). None the less, the infused cardinal virtues have the same fields of human need and action as do their acquired counterparts, and they dispose the human person with respect specifically to those fields, in a way that is responsive to a particular set of rational exigencies (see, for example, his treatment of infused temperance, II-II 141, especially 6 ad 1). Similar exigencies inform even the theological virtues; most strikingly, Aquinas argues that charity does not obviate the claims of justice generated by our particular relationships to family members and other close associates, since these are generated by reason, and grace is not less reasonable in its operations than is nature (II-II 26. 6).

Aquinas thus follows Augustine in holding that, even at its best, humanly attainable virtue falls short of the ideals set by divine perfection and God's grace. But for Augustine, the chasm between human and divine goodness appears always to imply some taint on humanly attainable virtue, which even at its best is never too far from outright sin. Aquinas likewise insists on the infinite distance between divine and human perfection, but this does not seem to imply for him that the latter is in itself tainted or corrupt. The goodness proper to a creature does not cease to be goodness simply because it is not the goodness of its Creator; indeed, to suggest otherwise might appear to dishonour the Creator, rather than the contrary. Undoubtedly, Aquinas lacks Augustine's deep sense of the ambiguity of lived morality, but in compensation, he makes a point that Augustine did not express so clearly. That is, the abyss between God and the creature is not simply a distinction between God's goodness and human sinfulness. Even at its highest and uncorrupted best, created nature cannot attain the supreme end of direct union with God. 'It is impossible that any created intellect should see the essence of God through its natural capacities,' he says (I 12. 4). As he goes on to explain, in order for anything to be raised to a state beyond its proper nature, it must receive a disposition which is above that nature,

and so, when some created intellect sees God through God's essence, the very essence of God becomes the intelligible form of the intellect. Hence, it is necessary that some supernatural disposition be added to it, in order that it be elevated to such a sublime height. Since therefore the natural power of a created intellect does not suffice to see the essence of God, as has been shown, it is necessary that a power of understanding be added to it from divine grace. (I 12. 5)

By our standards, and certainly in comparison to Augustine's writing, this is dry language. Yet, Aquinas makes a point that Augustine did not make so clearly, but which none the less needs to be made: that is, the distance between the Creator and creatures cannot ultimately be expressed within a scale of moral values. God exceeds every standard of comparison; yet this supreme transcendence has the effect of safeguarding, rather than undermining, the genuine integrity and value of created natures and their corresponding finite forms of goodness.

Space does not permit further comparisons between Augustine and his interpreters. I think it could be shown that most of them reflect a similar sense of the ambiguity of human morality, and resolve that tension in a way that would fit, roughly, on a scale between Augustine's tempered pessimism and Aquinas's sober optimism. But making that case is a project for another day.

References and Suggested Reading

ANNAS, JULIA (1993). *The Morality of Happiness.* Oxford: Oxford University Press.

AQUINAS, THOMAS (1888–1906). *Summa theologica,* in *Opera omnia jussa edita Leonis XIII, p.m.,* vols. 4–12. Rome: Ex Typographia Polyglotta S.C. de Propaganda Fide.

AUGUSTINE, *City of God, II: Books IV–VII,* Loeb Classical Library 412, and *City of God, VI: Books XVIII.36–XX,* Loeb Classical Library 416 (Cambridge, Mass.: Harvard University Press, 1963, 1960).

CATES, DIANA (1996). *Choosing to Feel.* Notre Dame, Ind.: University of Notre Dame Press.

CESSARIO, ROMANUS (1991). *The Moral Virtues and Theological Ethics.* Notre Dame, Ind.: University of Notre Dame Press.

HAUERWAS, STANLEY (1981). *The Peaceable Kingdom: A Primer in Christian Ethics.* Notre Dame, Ind.: University of Notre Dame Press.

——and PINCHES, CHARLES (1977). *Christians among the Virtues.* Notre Dame, Ind.: University of Notre Dame Press.

HURSTHOUSE, ROSALIND (1999). *On Virtue Ethics.* Oxford: Oxford University Press.

LOMBARD, PETER (1916). *Libri IV Sententiarum.* Florence: College of St Bonaventure.

LOTTIN, ODON (1949). *Psychologie et morale aux XII et XIII siècles,* III: *Problèmes de morale, seconde partie.* Louvain: Abbaye du Mont César.

MACINTYRE, ALASDAIR (1984). *After Virtue,* 2nd edn. Notre Dame, Ind.: University of Notre Dame Press.

MEILAENDER, GILBERT (1984). *The Theory and Practice of Virtue.* Notre Dame, Ind.: University of Notre Dame Press.

NEDERMAN, CARY (1991). 'Aristotelianism and the Origins of "Political Science" in the Twelfth Century', *Journal of the History of Ideas,* 52, 179–94.

RIST, JOHN (1994). *Augustine: Ancient Thought Baptized.* Cambridge: Cambridge University Press.

WENZEL, SIEGFRIED (1974). 'Vices, Virtues, and Popular Preaching', *Medieval and Renaissance Studies,* 6, 28–54.

YEARLEY, LEE (1990). *Mencius and Aquinas: Theories of Virtue and Conceptions of Courage.* Albany, NY: SUNY Press.

CHAPTER 13

RULES

RICHARD B. MILLER

A TAXONOMY OF RULES

RULES behave oddly in Christian ethics no less than in philosophical ethics, perhaps more so. As used in this essay, *rules* refer to normative regulations of individual or corporate behaviour. In Christian ethics, rules allow one to evaluate the conduct of individuals, the practices of intentional Christian groups, and the procedures and policies of complex institutions, some of which may have clear religious commitments. The commandment against theft is an example of a rule for individuals; the Rule of Saint Benedict is an example of a rule for an intentional Christian group; the just war doctrine's principle of discrimination is an example of a rule for military planners; and a policy in a Catholic hospital that prohibits physicians from practising abortion on demand is an example of a rule for a complex organization. The product of cultural processes and human reasoning, rules provide moral direction and terms for judging practice, identity, and policy.

In part, rules are made odd by the fact that they do not track human conduct in the way that scientific laws track the behaviour of physical bodies. Such laws cover the behaviour of physical bodies much like money can cover an expense: precisely and comprehensively, without remainder. But moral rules provide neither of these

I wish to thank Karen Boeyink and Mark Wilson for research assistance with this paper, and Nigel Biggar, Jennifer Girod, Terence Martin jun., Gilbert Meilaender, Jean Porter, William Schweiker, Charles Wilson, and Mark Wilson for comments on an earlier draft.

forms of coverage. That is because the behaviour to which moral rules refer is the result of human freedom and is embedded in chance and contingency. Moreover, the coverage provided by moral rules is relatively indeterminate in part because the language of moral rules is open-textured, requiring interpretation and clarification in the process of connecting them to facts or cases.

At one level, rules in Christian ethics embody many of the more general features of rules in philosophical ethics because both kinds of rules provide normative terms for assessing human behaviour. Rules have three forms of normativity: they prescribe, permit, or prohibit conduct. In addition, rules have several general features that involve important terms and distinctions. These include rules' time-less dimension, proper subject matter, grammar, function, grounding, range, and stringency. Attention to these features enables us to generate a taxonomy of rules as one step toward understanding their role in the moral life and the peculiarities of their work.

Rules have a timeless dimension in that they are applicable *prospectively, contemporaneously,* and *retrospectively.* As a contemporaneous or prospective guide, rules direct current or future conduct. As a retrospective guide, rules provide the basis for judging past conduct. But beyond being applicable to present, future, and past action, rules inform our sense of how we should routinely behave, and expect others to behave, in social interactions. Rules thus 'fix the future' in a loose sense by setting the terms according to which we can anticipate how people are to conduct themselves on a regular basis.

Both *conduct* and *character* are regulated by rules. Such regulations provide direction for how we should act (or should have acted), and shape how we ought to order (or should have ordered) our dispositions toward others and the world. As *prescriptions of acts,* rules function as action-guides and provide a basis for assessing behaviour or policy as right or wrong. As *prescriptions of character,* rules provide the basis for assessing personal dispositions or corporate ethos as good or bad.

Rules differ in how broadly or narrowly they are formulated. They can be relatively *general*—e.g., the rule to grant the benefit of the doubt to others—or they can be relatively *specific*—e.g., the rule prohibiting cheating on examinations. However, as I have noted, all rules are open-textured and thus have a measure of indeterminacy. One purpose of rules is to identify not a single, unique action but a class of similar actions that deserve approval, permission, or disapproval. Questions about the meaning and applicability of a rule to human conduct are a function of the inevitable gap between rules (however general or specific) and particular, concrete experience. *Whether* a rule applies to me or my act is a fundamental question for moral deliberation.

The difference between *substance* and *procedure* likewise affects the shape of rules. Substantive rules identify concrete actions or dispositions to be avoided or adopted. Such rules provide direction for conduct or character. Although the distinction between substance and procedure is not always sharp, procedural rules are more formal and contain less content than substantive rules. Procedural rules step back from the particulars of the moral life to regulate how substantive rules ought to be conceived or applied. Substantive rules indicate *what* to do or feel; procedural rules indicate *how* we are to act, dispose ourselves, apply more specific rules, or achieve certain values. The rule to avoid calumny is a substantive rule about respect and friendship; the rule to cut a birthday cake in identical sizes is a procedural rule about how to distribute equal shares.

Rules can also differ in their relationship to practices. They function to *set the terms* for initiating conduct or to *assess* human action. Thus we distinguish between 'ground rules' and other, more familiar sorts of rules. Ground rules make possible certain practices and conventions by defining the terms for social interaction. Such rules provide foundations for action and make possible one or another sphere of activity; they are internal to a role or institution and constitute it as such (Rawls 1967). Such rules have no meaning outside the sphere to which they apply. The rule to move one's king in check makes no sense outside the game of chess. In contrast, rules of assessment can hover over a series of related practices and stand independently of them. The rule not to harm extends across a range of activities, e.g., medicine, education, research, social etiquette, and the like.

Certain practices or institutions incorporate ground rules and rules of assessment. Thus we speak of 'rule-governed activities', such as a just war. In such instances, rules indicate how to prevent the activity in question from degenerating into amorality. Rule-governed activities rely on rules to define an institution's moral aims as well as to assess the behaviour of persons within that institution. Rules provide rule-governed activities with an internal structure according to which behaviour in an institution is justified and constrained.

The fact that rules can function internally to an institution points to another aspect. Rules can be *explicit*, when they are codified and promulgated, or *implicit*, analogous to grammar in language. In this latter capacity, rules are embedded inconspicuously in one's identity or social customs. Indeed, as I hope to make plain below, rules are much more implicit in our practices than we typically assume. Moreover, rules can be *instrumental*, guiding our quests to meet a goal or value, or informing our judgements of action. Rules can also be *constitutive*, functioning to shape the identity of an individual or group through ongoing habituation.

The social and institutional dimension of rules suggests an important distinction between *primary* and *secondary* rules, as helpfully described by H. L. A. Hart. Primary rules assign rights or duties to members of a community. Rules that prohibit theft or killing are this sort of rule. Secondary rules indicate how, and by whom, primary rules are to be developed or modified. Rules that establish how a legislative body is composed and is to enact legislation are of this latter sort (Hart 1961: 91–6).

The bases of rules in Christian ethics reside in *reason* and *revelation*. Reason constructs rules that apply to Christians and non-Christians alike. Within Christianity, such rules have typically rested on a theory of human nature and the human good, as in natural law reasoning. Revelation grounds rules that are specific to Christian attitudes and perspectives, and often indicates what makes Christian life distinctive.

Social context can also affect rules. They can be *universal* in that they apply always and everywhere, irrespective of context. Rules of this sort tend to be vague or general, e.g., the rule to respect others. Rules can also be *role-specific*, and thus pertinent only to a specific set of circumstances or role relations. The duty of parents to attend to their children's medical welfare, or to create a warm and affectionate home environment, is the latter sort of rule.

Finally, rules vary according to stringency. There are *absolute rules, prima facie rules,* and *rules of thumb.* An absolute rule binds always and everywhere; it is indefeasible. A prima facie rule is presumptive, and may be overridden by a conflicting obligation. A rule of thumb rule is instructive and provides a general guideline, but is more illuminating than prescriptive of action (Childress 1996: 210).

THEOLOGY AND RULES

Rules are a ubiquitous feature of the Christian life, and their ubiquity derives chiefly from theological ideas about God as One. That idea implies a basic unity and regularity to all that issues from God. The divine communication of rules or laws is an expression of this more fundamental regularity of God's being and activity. Christians believe that God's sovereignty over creation has been made evident in part by the revelation of commandments in both Scripture and the created order—two 'books' which make explicit God's ordering and regulative design. Those commandments provide clear directives for action and disposition. The Decalogue and Covenant Code are conspicuous features of the Bible; Jesus speaks of two great commandments; and the Christian tradition has borrowed from Greek and Stoic sources to clarify how God's interest in creation directs humanity to the right and the good by way of clear ordinances. The overall sanction for using rules in Christian morality draws from the idea that Truth has communicated clear regulations of human conduct. The Christian believer is called to assume responsibility for his or her behaviour, to exercise freedom as one feature of reflecting the divine image. Human freedom is to be guided by God's commandments across a range of personal, social, and cultural activities.

Rules not only model the communication of divine regularity and sovereignty, they acquire depth of meaning when interpreted in light of theological symbols and images. The rule against killing, for example, derives not only from a respect for persons or bodily integrity, but from the idea that God is sovereign over matters of life and death, and that taking another's life is prima facie to usurp a divine prerogative (cf. Barth 1961: 324–470). On that account, killing might exhibit disrespect or lack of love, as well as disregard for one's place in the larger order of things. It can reveal not only moral callousness but *superbia*, the sin of pride.

Theology also imposes constraints on how tensions between rules should be viewed. That is to say, *methodological* features surrounding the interpretation and application of rules depends in some measure on wider *substantive theological* claims. Of particular relevance is the belief in theodicy, the idea that the cosmos is justly ordered. Theodicy means that conflicts between rules are only apparent—that there may be moral conflicts that require adjudication, but that there are no *real* moral dilemmas (Santurri 1987). If the cosmos is governed by a rational and just sovereign, then in principle Christians should be able to find reasonable ways to settle conflicts of conscience and justify particular plans. Attempts to provide a decision procedure for settling such conflicts, about which I will say more below, are driven (if only implicitly) by the need to eliminate doubts about the fairness of divine sovereignty. A God who leaves humanity without a basis for being confident about resolving moral disputes—or who leaves moral decisions to personal whim—seems inconstant and unworthy of allegiance.

Belief in theodicy also means that there is a strong basis for moral motivation in the Christian life. The belief that the cosmos is on the side of justice means that the right will always be joined to the good, that the unjust enjoy no advantage over the just. For the Christian, obedience to rules should finally come at no ultimate cost. However much one might suffer for obeying a rule, the good has been promised to those who follow righteousness.

Yet theological beliefs include an understanding of human fallibility that opens up more troubling features of rules within a belief system premised not only on divine constancy and justice but also on the freedom and graciousness of God. Such beliefs point to rules' limits and highlight some of their odd behaviour in Christian ethics. Of special importance is the idea that obedience to rules does not guarantee righteousness and may even tempt one toward unrighteousness. From the teaching of Jesus' anti-Pharisaism to Augustine's anti-Pelagianism, rules enjoy an uneasy place in Christian thought and practice. That uneasiness turns on the distinction between the spirit and the letter of a rule, a distinction that has two formulations.

The first, drawing on Jesus' anti-Pharisaism, insists on the need to interpret and apply rules in light of their deeper rationale. In saying, 'The Sabbath was made for man, not man for the Sabbath', Jesus cautions against mechanical or rigoristic applications of rules—applications that are uninformed by a wider understanding of a rule's purpose and limits. Rules may be put aside when their literal application impedes the realization of their deeper aims or purposes. The letter of a rule may give way when we need to conform to broader values toward which the rule imperfectly points.

A related problem is that rules are typically too general to apply to unusual or unanticipated circumstances. Given the contingency and particularity of experience, we cannot expect rules to anticipate all cases. For that reason, Christians have seized on various methods for handling ambiguous or conflicting rules. Christians emphasize the Greek virtue of *epieikeia* in the discernment of rules, the importance of analogical reasoning when interpreting and applying rules, the merits of specifying rules as a way of eliminating conflicts, or the challenge of weighing and balancing conflicting norms, principles, or rules. *Epieikeia* aims not to abandon justice or right action but to ensure that human conduct is directed to the values and purposes that 'lie behind' specific rules (Aristotle 1941: 1137^{a}31–^{b}30). Analogical reasoning seeks to address less familiar moral experience by building a bridge to more familiar moral paradigms and taxonomies (Jonsen and Toulmin 1987). Specification attempts to qualify a rule by limiting its scope, often with reference to specific circumstances that restrict the range of a rule's application (Ramsey 1968; Richardson 1990). Weighing and balancing seeks to ascertain which of two conflicting norms, principles, or rules applies to a case (Childress 1996). In all of these modes of practical reasoning, the core idea is that a rule requires interpretation in order to ascertain its true meaning, often in relation to other rules or values.

Jesus also spoke against vain or hypocritical obedience, giving rise to another set of worries about rules in Christian morality. This second line of thought, developed more fully in Augustine's anti-Pelagian writings, insists on the need for proper motives for obeying rules, motives that are empowered and graced by God's love. Here the challenge turns not on how to interpret a rule's rationale but on how to determine the quality of one's character when following a rule. A rule must be obeyed out of love rather than fear of divine punishment or the desire to secure divine favour (Augustine 1955). Obedience premissed on anything other than a loving will draws from selfish motives. Adhering to a rule thus 'kills' if it is done without due understanding of humanity's dependence upon and subordination to God's gracious love and inspiration. Fidelity to rules must be moved by a will that is shaped by the virtue of humility and infused by a delight in doing good for its own sake.

One reason why rules behave oddly in Christianity, then, is that they present the temptation of self-justification and the corresponding danger of works-righteousness. In Christian ethics a firm tension between religion and morality exists. More specifically, that tension is between the moral and salvific dimensions of Christian belief and practice. On the one hand, Christian tradition cautions against the idea that morality is instrumental to salvation. Christians are taught that they cannot justify themselves before God, even if they seem justified before each other. On the other hand, Christian tradition includes clear moral proscriptions and prescriptions of acts and character. Christian morality is ineluctably suspended between acknowledging humanity's dependence on divine grace and power, and recognizing the requirements of moral responsibility.

JUSTIFYING RULES

Rules state what a person or group should, should not, or may do. Although they regulate behaviour, they do not *establish* that one should, should not, or may do something. For that, we need to justify rules, to link them to a set of reasons.

Justifying rules can be conceived in one of two ways. The first—what I will call the deductive account—argues that a rule's correctness is a function of its connection to a more general principle. Although the distinction between principles and rules is not always sharp, principles are more general than rules, and identify broad values or norms—e.g., equality or respect for persons. Rules, in contrast, are more directive and prescriptive of actions or dispositions.

On the deductive account, when we are challenged to find support for a rule, we may turn to a higher-order principle or concept on which the rule is based. Doubts about the merits of a higher-order principle or concept are to be addressed by examining that principle's relation to an even higher-order value or concept against which the principle is measured. Echoing Plato's account of how truth is discovered in reason's ascent from particulars to illuminative Forms, this view holds that rules are justified by principles, which are in turn justified by more general ideas, which rely on even more comprehensive notions, in an ascending order of abstraction. Naturally this line of reasoning raises questions about what justifies increasingly higher-order concepts, leading to a potentially infinite regress, a leap of faith, or the intuitive self-evidence of a rule or higher-order principles, values, concepts, and the like (Aiken 1962: 65–87).

In theological ethics, however, this problem might be countered by an appeal to divine purposes as the final arbiter of a rule's, principle's, or concept's justification. Such an approach to justification can generate an overly hierarchical and top-down approach to moral reasoning, although it need not. For reasons I will make clearer below, a better alternative exists. Suffice it to say here that rules in Christian ethics find their justification by connecting them to more general accounts of God's sovereign will or reason, or by connecting them to the implications of divine symbols. The justification of rules in a theistic ethic is interpretive. The key point is that because God has moral qualities, Christian ethics possesses resources for justifying rules and for deflecting the problem of generating an infinite regress of higher-order appeals.

A second way to justify a rule is to proceed in a horizontal rather than a vertical direction, by measuring a rule's merits in light of its connection to intersubjective habits and practices. Whether a rule makes sense, what it means, whether it is humanly possible to meet its demands, or whether it actually fits a case to which it putatively applies—these are all questions to which the testimony of prior and contemporary experience can speak. On this account, determining the correctness of a rule depends on something other than whether it connects with higher-order and increasingly abstract ideas, or whether it enables us to assess action and character by applying a rule in a top-down manner to experience. Indeed, we fail to understand rules if we see them as providing an algorithm for morality. Instead, rules sharpen and extend fundamental moral ideas that derive from paradigmatic instances of good and bad, right and wrong (Kirk 1948: 107; Jonsen and Toulmin 1987; Miller 1996). A rule is thus justified immanently and pragmatically—that is, in light of its place within a wider set of intersubjective meanings and uses that constitute a common life.

INTERPRETING AND APPLYING RULES

To understand how this is so, it will help to examine the grammar or structure of rules. Rules include imperative sentences (do this, don't do that) that rely on a prior set of classifications. The prohibition of murder relies on a concept according to which we classify specific actions as 'unjustified killing'. Equally important, as J. M. Brennan writes, rules (and the concepts on which they rely) are 'open-textured' (Brennan 1977; cf. Hart 1961: 123–32). Brennan calls attention to the fact that moral ideas (concepts, rules) are open rather than closed sets. Like all terms, they do not admit of strict definitions or an unequivocal scheme for classifying actions. Moreover, rules are taxonomic; they refer to *types* of actions or people. For that reason, rules are necessarily general. They are unable to foresee all the circumstances to which they might be relevant.

Rules, then, apply to a class of actions and not to one action alone. An action that purports to be unique cannot fall under a rule that aims to cover a cluster of instances. Owing to the fact that rules apply to types of acts rather than to isolated or unique instances, we should understand them as covering a range of acts or people that are similar enough to be bundled together under a common rubric. In order for a rule to work, it must presuppose a group of data to which it refers. As Paul Ramsey notes, rules serve in part to classify actions as actions *of a sort* (Ramsey 1968: 76, 94). Rules thus pertain to instances that are judged to be sufficiently similar to fall within a common genus and sufficiently different from instances that require another genus.

How far a rule's jurisdiction extends—what acts or persons it covers—is a matter of interpretation and judgement. Rules are both fixed and indeterminate. They are fixed in so far as they focus moral attention on a circumscribed set of facts about human action. In this way rules classify our conduct. They are indeterminate in so far as we cannot know in advance of applying them how far they can extend (Porter 1995: 22). Consider the commandment in the Decalogue against killing. How far this rule should apply—which actions it includes and excludes within its range—is a fundamental question of practical reasoning. For most Christians and many non-Christians, the rule against killing does not forbid certain forms of lethal self-defence—for example, defending one's life against a violent aggressor. Whether that rule forbids all cases of voluntary euthanasia or suicide is considerably more controversial. Thus we are led to consider whether (or how) a rule should be crafted to allow for certain borderline cases. Interpreting and applying a rule involves determining which actions it includes and excludes. Whether a rule 'fits' a case is not always self-evident. Rules thus generate doubts about how far they reach. Applying rules to cases requires a prior act of judgement about the appropriateness of a rule's connection to experience. There is an irreducible element of discretion involved in co-ordinating a rule with a case or problem.

Whether that judgement is reliable is a function, as Ludwig Wittgenstein argues, of a rule's place within a wider set of social practices (1958: 80–8). Rules are not mental constructs that reside in the mind, independent of a way of life. Rather, rules are social and cultural artefacts that express a practical understanding of acts or characters deemed laudable or condemnable. How to connect a rule to a particular case depends on a reservoir of inchoate common sense regarding the fit between rules and experience. That rules are uncontroversial in many areas of the moral life should remind us that their application relies on an unarticulated background of shared agreement regarding their applicability to one or another instance. As John Rawls puts the point about applying a rule, there is a 'background of circumstances under which it is expected to be applied and which need not—indeed cannot—be fully stated' (Rawls 1967: 157).

This means that we do not understand a moral rule prior to cases, as if cases were instances that merely illustrate conformity to or departure from a more general prescription. Rules derive from paradigmatic cases that fix our moral perceptions about conduct or character that is clearly laudable or condemnable. Whether a rule applies to a problematic case, then, often depends on analogical reasoning. For that, we ask how a borderline or questionable case compares with the paradigmatic instance on which a rule relies. To what extent does applying a rule reflect the inchoate wisdom that shapes the background of habit and common sense on which a rule depends for its intelligibility?

Viewing rules against the background of habit means that interpreting and applying moral rules should not be understood as producing an algorithm of practical reasoning or an ironclad decision procedure for the conscience. This fact seems strange, because we typically condemn a person who violates a rule and commend a person who obeys a rule. The idea that rules are algorithms suggests that rules apply deductively to experience, that they easily and unequivocally subsume cases. It is more accurate to say that rules are institutions that, like all institutions, rely on a settled set of convictions and shared agreements that reflect a tradition of development, experience, and ongoing reflection and revision.

Whether a specific act falls within a rule's jurisdiction depends on how similar or different it is from the paradigmatic features of a case about which a rule fixes our moral perceptions.

If rules are to be understood as a set of social practices and institutions, then their justification in a theological ethic of the Platonic sort I described must be rejected. Rules in a theistic ethic find their justification not by connecting them with higher and more abstract concepts that finally rest in ideas about the will or reason of God. Stated differently, rules are not justified by deducing specific imperatives from more general theistic concepts. The connection between rules as social and cultural artefacts, on the one hand, and religious beliefs and concepts, on the other, is more indirect, interpretive, and phronetic. Rules that rest on paradigmatic cases and help to fix moral perceptions are given depth and meaning by attaching them to fundamental understandings about how life should be ordered, about what confers meaning and purpose to human experience. Religious concepts justify rules by providing an organizing framework or horizon according to which a rule makes sense to a community as it moves in dialogue with other communities across time and space.

This is not to say that the justification of rules entails merely appealing to 'how we customarily do things'. It is rather to say that the reasons we invoke when a rule is challenged aim to articulate what is otherwise an inchoate set of customs and shared understandings that help constitute a way of life. When we are questioned about the merits of a rule, we try to spell out how and why that rule embodies an understanding of right or good action. Challenges to a rule thus require us to proceed from an implicit, immanent grasp of a rule to one that reflexively opens up to reasoned articulation and argument.

ADJUDICATING CONFLICTS BETWEEN RULES

Rules often conflict when we try to extend or apply them. How does one rule, such as not to harm or injure others, stand up to other rules, e.g., to relieve discomfort or respond to unjust aggression? As I noted earlier, the belief in theodicy suggests that moral conflicts are not irresolvable—that actions can be justified and conflicts adjudicated upon due consideration of relevant concepts, values, principles, and the like.

Understanding the roots of moral conflict returns us to the relatively open-textured character of rules. Rules must be general enough to subsume a cluster of similar actions, and specific enough to mark off one class of actions from another. One of the challenges of rule making is to craft rules so that they provide reliable direction for the conscience while heeding the complexity of ordinary moral experience. Allowing for an excessive number of exceptions or qualifications will provide little practical guidance; failing to acknowledge conflict reinforces the self-deceptive view that moral experience is uncomplicated.

In addition to discerning the deeper meaning of a rule (*epieikeia*) and analogical reasoning, there is another widely discussed model for handling moral conflicts, namely, *specification*. This model aims to take a broad, general rule and sharpen its meaning by indicating more precisely when and on what terms it applies. In an important article on the subject, Henry S. Richardson describes specification as seeking to resolve moral conflicts by 'qualitatively tailoring norms to cases' (1990: 283). Specification sets out 'substantive qualifications that add information about the scope or applicability of the norm or the nature of the act or end enjoined or proscribed' (ibid. 296). The model of specification begins with the idea that norms allow for latitude in their interpretation and application. Richardson thus presupposes the open-textured quality of rules, their relative indeterminacy. The key to specification is to take what casuists traditionally understand as the circumstances that surround an act and incorporate those facts into the rule's formulation. On his model, we specify rules 'by adding clauses indicating what, where, when, why, how, and by what means, by whom, or to whom the action is to be, is not to be, or may be done or the action is to be described, or the end is to be pursued or conceived' (ibid. 295–6). Amended in this way, a rule is 'tightened up' so that potential conflicts and the need to anticipate possible exceptions are eliminated from moral deliberation. By specifying a rule, we can turn it from a broad formulation, one that applies 'generally and for the most part', into one that is exceptionless.

Richardson sees specification as adding an important dimension to a pragmatist approach to moral theory. Pragmatists such as John Dewey ask us to deliberate about the moral life by considering how to bring a broad norm to bear on experience in a way that 'preserves the initial meaning of the norm while it is being modified in the course of its application' (ibid. 291). But pragmatists have done little to identify conditions according to which we can say that a general norm is being respected in the course of connecting it to experience. Richardson sees the model of specification as providing pragmatist ethics with this missing link.

In addition, Richardson presents specification as a better alternative to two other approaches to practical reasoning: subsuming a case under a rule, and weighing and balancing conflicting norms. On his view, these models are vague or excessively subjective when it comes to connecting general rules to specific cases. In fact, they are not two distinct models, Richardson observes, because the former inevitably generates a conflict of duties that must be weighed and balanced in the course of determining how best to act. For every norm that involves a complex action—the staple of moral reflection and everyday experience—we meet an array of conflicting possibilities. The duty to care for a patient who refuses a treatment that has few risks and great benefits generates such a conflict. Does care mean respecting the patient's wishes or seeking the patient's medical benefit? Applying the duty of care to such a case quickly produces the need to weigh and balance one obligation against another.

For Richardson, the problem with weighing and balancing norms, rules, or duties consists in the fact that there are no rational decision procedures for resolving conflicts. Specification, in contrast, has the advantage of claiming 'discursive rationality' (ibid. 283). For Richardson, a stable theory of moral reasoning turns on what he calls the 'coherence standard for the rationality of specification', carrying the Rawlsian idea of 'wide reflective equilibrium' all the way down to cases. The advantage of this model is that it 'makes intelligible logical connections among the norms to which one is committed that . . . explain some of them in terms of others'. Unlike intuitive approaches, the model of specification is 'fully subject to discursive statement and criticism' (ibid. 300).

To illustrate this model's rational aspects, Richardson asks us to consider how one might decide whether to withhold nutrition and hydration from a severely defective newborn, thereby allowing it to die. The case presents a conflict between the general prohibition of directly killing innocent persons, the duty to respect parental wishes, and the duty to benefit persons for whom one has medical responsibility. Assuming that the first principle is not resolved with reference to the principle of double effect or on act-omission grounds, we are left with what appears to be a serious moral quandary.

Those who use the model of specification to resolve this case assume that principles are not fixed and clear, but general. According to Richardson, resolution rests on specifying the second of the three competing principles. 'In this case', he writes,

> there is a specification readily available in the ethical tradition which will lessen the practical conflict . . . by restricting the range of the principle of respect for parental choices to choices that themselves express respect for their children. . . . Accordingly, [one] may specify this principle as requiring that one respect the reasonable choices of parents regarding their children so long as they respect the children's rights. (ibid. 305)

This process commends itself as rational, Richardson avers, because specification overcomes a conflict of principles by appealing to the deeper meaning of the relevant norms or principles. The specification enhances the fit among our principles, 'at least in this limited domain'. Richardson adds: 'Their grounds are not some kind of private and nondiscursive perception or intuition. Rather, they rest on grounds open to rational public debate and assessment, such as those arguments resting on the underlying theory of respect for persons' (ibid.).

Note two things about this case. First, it is not clear why the second of the three principles is the most relevant. Richardson indicates that the third is too general and indeterminate, but indeterminacy characterizes all norms according to the model of specification. Selecting the second norm as applicable to this case seems no less intuitive than the models that Richardson rejects. Moreover, and second,

Richardson's specification proceeds by way of introducing not circumstances of the sort that he says enable us to tailor principles to cases, but substantive moral concerns: namely, children's rights. The effect of the argument is to specify respect for parental authority only by weighing it against the value of a child's basic interests. In cases when parental decisions put their children at risk, parental authority is trumped by values that surround a child's welfare.

The problem, in other words, is that it is sometimes difficult to describe specification as a clear alternative to weighing and balancing. Often one cannot know how to qualify a norm unless one has already determined how and why it should be obeyed, and that it outweighs (or is not outweighed by) a competing norm, value, or principle. Consider again Richardson's example. He tailors the general duty to respect parental authority by introducing additional moral concerns regarding children's rights. One norm is 'specified' by saying that it does not apply when it conflicts with another.

Perhaps a clearer illustration is provided by those who seek to satisfy the general duty to respect a patient's wishes in medical settings. That duty is too general to provide much guidance, for the wish may be expressed in haste, under coercion, or in ways that ignore the needs of others. Moreover, it may mean heeding a patient's demand for treatment that has no medical benefit. Thus we specify the rule by saying that we have the duty to respect a patient's wishes when the patient declines (rather than demands) treatment, when the wish is voluntarily and competently expressed, and when heeding that wish does not put a third party at risk. The general norm is 'trimmed' by limiting the circumstances in which it will be heeded. In the course of specifying the norm, we have considered instances in which the duty to consider the needs of others would outweigh the duty to respect a patient's competent wish. We have specified the latter norm so that it does not include circumstances of putting other parties in danger. We have thus weighed and balanced competing norms—respect for persons, and the duty not to harm others—as a prior condition for specifying one of them. In this instance, specification is not an alternative to the model of weighing and balancing norms, but is dependent on it.

Practical reasoning thus includes *weighing* rules against each other, either before or after specifying norms when we seek to connect them to cases. The model of 'weighing and balancing' is premissed on the view that rules are not absolute but prima facie. The term 'prima facie' indicates that there are strong but not indefeasible reasons for honouring a rule or duty. Such rules are binding unless they conflict with weightier rules or duties under clearly defined conditions. When another rule prevails, the overridden rule may leave 'moral traces', requiring the agent to abide by the overridden rule as closely as possible along with feeling regret for the loss of value in question.

One problem with this model of moral reasoning is that, as Richardson notes, it appears overly subjective in the face of moral conflicts. W. D. Ross, the progenitor of this model, appeals to what appears to be a subjective notion when seeking to clarify a decision procedure for practical reasoning. Ross's answer relies on Aristotle's account of *phronēsis*: 'The decision rests with perception' (Ross 1930: 42).

James F. Childress has addressed Richardson's challenge to provide discursive rationality by attaching a more precise set of conditions to the model of weighing and balancing. In order justifiably to override a prima facie duty, Childress writes

there must be a realistic prospect of realizing the moral objective that appears to justify the infringement; the infringement of a prima facie principle must be necessary in the circumstances; the infringement should be the least possible, commensurate with achieving the primary goal of the action; and the agent must seek to minimize the negative effects of the infringement.

Beyond this point, nothing more can or should be added. Childress writes: 'Neither moral experience nor moral theory warrants a stronger decision procedure for resolution of conflicts between prima facie principles in concrete cases' (Childress 1996: 213).

If I am correct about how the model of specification might rely on the model of weighing and balancing, then we can see why the difference between these models is easily exaggerated. Both strategies attempt to accommodate rule making to the exigencies of conflict and complexity. Specification tends to build in its 'exceptionalist' clauses by way of circumscription: rule X applies to this range of actions that, by definition, excludes consideration of actions whose moral claims may generate a conflict. Exceptions, often informed by substantive moral concerns, are incorporated into the formulation of the rule. The overall effect is to craft rules that are absolute by dint of their delimitations. The narrower a rule is, the more stringent it can be. In contrast, weighing rules makes moral conflict explicit. This second strategy makes public the complex ways in which obligations weigh on the conscience.

Still, Richardson's worries about the rationality of moral deliberation are real. One alternative to Childress's line of response is to ask why the model of weighing and balancing is not subject to the same kind of test for coherence that Richardson applies to specification. It is not clear, in other words, why the model of weighing and balancing necessarily excludes the sort of coherence model of moral reasoning that he imputes to the model of specification.

A more promising route is to say that Richardson's quest for rationality is insufficiently pragmatist. We can resolve conflicts between rules, in other words, on the same terms as we justify them. In the final analysis, we test the rationality of our claims in light of intersubjective meanings. In the case of how far to honour the duty to respect parental authority in the medical treatment of children, we specify that duty in light of substantive moral concerns, e.g., children's rights. Those rights make sense in light of a broader set of intersubjective meanings and practices that rejects the notion that children are property, that recognizes how hierarchy sometimes creates tyranny, and that understands how it is difficult to make sense of life-sustaining treatment for individuals whose physical life is disconnected from the enjoyment of a wider cluster of goods and values. This last judgement is clear given the esteem we place on self-awareness, the value we assign to interpersonal relationships, and the corresponding importance of communication—all of which can be absent in individuals who are severely and permanently impaired.

When discussing the idea of following and justifying rules, Charles Taylor puts the point well: 'Reason giving has a limit, and in the end must repose in another kind of understanding' (1995: 179). This understanding is not a matter of subjectivity or intuition, as Richardson suggests. It is, rather, the kind of embodied understanding according to which we inhabit the world and comport ourselves in a 'natural', unreflective way. As Taylor remarks, such understanding reposes in the 'inarticulate familiarity with a certain environment, enabling us to get around in it without hesitation, on one hand, and a map of this terrain, on the other' (ibid. 176).

Crisp models of practical reasoning tempt us to overlook the dynamic relationship between rules and practices. What Taylor describes as true of general concepts pertains to rules as well: namely, that they 'are only islands in the sea of our unformulated practical grasp of the world' (ibid. 170). Given that fact, rules cannot be viewed simply as codes that are externally imposed to assess our behaviour. That is because rules not only regulate our practices, they acquire meaning in their very application. This aspect of rules is a function of their indeterminacy—the fact that they gain meaning as they are connected to particular cases. But it is also a function of the fact that rules acquire their sense in the practices they guide. Rules are to unarticulated intersubjective understandings, our 'practical grasp of the world', as *parole* is to *langue*. The former is possible only because of the pre-existence of the latter. At the same time, Taylor notes, 'the acts of parole are what keep the langue in being. They renew and at the same time alter it. Their relation is thus reciprocal' (ibid. 178).

Understood in pragmatic terms, rules help to articulate a society's sense of itself, its embodied practices and ways of life. Efforts to express, sharpen, or revise the meaning of a rule reflect wider social changes and embodied understandings. The practice of altering a rule reflects and disciplines wider patterns of social and intersubjective change. When rules are revised, a society or community is modifying its inchoate sense of who or what counts as one of its legitimate members or what counts as important and worthy of moral concern.

CONCLUSION

A pragmatist account of how rules are justified and their conflicts adjudicated enables us to handle some basic problems in moral theory, as I have noted above. It also invites us to revisit some theological problems in a new light. Viewing rules as an open-textured set of cultural artefacts and institutions enables us to handle the traditional problems of Pharisaism and Pelagianism from a modern point of view. The relatively indeterminate quality of a rule requires us to ascertain its core value and underlying rationale when connecting it to concrete cases. Legalistic or mechanistic application of rules to experience—the target of Jesus' anti-Pharisaism—hardly coheres with an understanding of rules as open-textured. Rules must be interpreted as a condition of their use. Moreover, the open-textured quality of rules mitigates the temptation toward works-righteousness. Viewing rules as open-textured means that their proper application to experience is often in doubt. Rules' open-textured quality leaves them subject to revision and development in the course of applying them to new or uncertain cases. Hence a spirit of inductivism and fallibilism surrounds the use of rules, contrary to the moral certainty (and related issue of pride) to which Augustine addressed his anti-Pelagian writings.

If I am correct that rules are not mental constructs that reside independently in the mind but are cultural artefacts that acquire their correctness against a backdrop of embodied understandings and a practical grasp of the world, then we are in a position to revise what is typically understood as the task of ethicists. On this pragmatic account, the role of an ethicist is as much to articulate and critically participate in the social dialogue within which rules acquire their meaning and intelligibility as it is to address the theoretical aspects of rules as normative directives of acts and character. Knowledge of rules without an understanding of the cultural processes and habits within which rules function as 'islands in a sea' is deficient. Such knowledge overlooks the fact that rules depend no less on the transcendent qualities of moral reasoning than on the immanent aspects of rules' social embodiment. Failure to note rules' relationship with society and culture, in short, means that we will continue to underestimate the complexities, limits, and oddness of their work.

References and Suggested Reading

AIKEN, HENRY DAVID (1962). *Reason and Conduct: New Bearings in Moral Philosophy.* New York: Alfred Knopf.

ARISTOTLE (1941). *Nicomachean Ethics,* trans. W. D. Ross, in Richard McKeon (ed.), *The Basic Works of Aristotle,* New York: Random House, 935–1112.

AUGUSTINE (1955). 'The Spirit and the Letter', in John Burnaby (ed.), *Augustine: Later Works,* Philadelphia: Westminster Press, 195–250.

BARTH, KARL (1961). *Church Dogmatics,* III/4. Edinburgh: T. & T. Clark.

BRENNAN, J. M. (1977). *The Open-Texture of Moral Concepts.* New York: Barnes and Noble Books.

CHILDRESS, JAMES F. (1996). 'Moral Norms in Practical Ethical Reflection', in Lisa Sowle Cahill and James F. Childress (eds.), *Christian Ethics: Problems and Prospects,* Cleveland: Pilgrim Press, 196–217.

CURRAN, CHARLES and McCORMICK, RICHARD A. (eds.) (1979). *Readings in Moral The-ology*, I: *Moral Norms and the Catholic Tradition*. New York: Paulist Press.

D'ARCY, ERIC (1963). *Human Acts: An Essay in their Moral Evaluation*. Oxford: Clarendon Press.

GARVER, NEWTON (1967). 'Rules', in *Encyclopedia of Philosophy*, New York: Macmillan, VII. 231–3.

GUSTAFSON, JAMES M. (1971). 'Context versus Principles: A Misplaced Debate in Christian Ethics', *Harvard Theological Review*, 58, 171–202.

HART, H. L. A. (1961). *The Concept of Law*. Oxford: Clarendon Press.

JONSEN, ALBERT, R. and TOULMIN, STEPHEN (1987). *The Abuse of Casuistry: A History of Moral Reasoning*. Berkeley: University of California Press.

KIRK, KENNETH (1948). *Conscience and its Problems: An Introduction to Casuistry*, 4th edn. London: Longmans, Green and Co.

MILLER, RICHARD B. (1996). *Casuistry and Modern Ethics: A Poetics of Practical Reasoning*. Chicago: University of Chicago Press.

PORTER, JEAN (1995). *Moral Action and Christian Ethics*. Cambridge: Cambridge University Press.

RAMSEY, PAUL (1968). 'The Case of the Curious Exception', in Gene H. Outka and Paul Ramsey (eds.), *Norm and Context in Christian Ethics*, New York: Charles Scribner's Sons, 67–135.

RAWLS, JOHN (1967). 'Two Concepts of Rules', in Philippa Foot (ed.), *Theories of Ethics*, Oxford: Oxford University Press, 144–70.

RICHARDSON, HENRY S. (1990). 'Specifying Norms as a Way to Resolve Concrete Ethical Problems', *Philosophy and Public Affairs*, 19, 279–310.

ROSS, W. D. (1930). *The Right and the Good*. Oxford: Clarendon Press.

SANTURRI, EDMUND, N. (1987). *Perplexity in the Moral Life: Philosophical and Theological Considerations*. Charlottesville, Va.: University Press of Virginia.

SOLOMON, WILLIAM DAVID (1978). 'Rules and Principles', in Warren T. Reich (ed.), *En-cyclopedia of Bioethics*, New York: Free Press, I. 407–13.

TAYLOR, CHARLES (1995). 'To Follow a Rule', in Taylor, *Philosophical Arguments*, Cambridge, Mass.: Harvard University Press, 165–80.

WITTGENSTEIN, LUDWIG (1958). *Philosophical Investigations*, trans. G. E. M. Anscombe, 3rd edn. New York: Macmillan Co.

CHAPTER 14

RESPONSIBILITY

GERALD P. McKENNY

RESPONSIBILITY is a relatively new concept in ethics. Many have noted that it makes its first significant appearance in late nineteenth-century moral thought. Its relative novelty raises questions as to its status in Christian ethics. Did modern moral philosophers and theologians discover in the concept of responsibility something heretofore concealed, a feature of moral life that had eluded the traditional conceptual apparatus of act, will, and conscience? Or did modern morality bring something genuinely new into being, something which these older concepts were inadequate to express?

This essay is an argument for the latter view. The entry of the concept of responsibility, and the primacy it assumes in some theories of ethics, signals an expansion or an intensification of the role of the human subject in ethics correlative to the modern withdrawal of God from the world. The very notion of responsibility draws attention to the sense in which a matter of morality or the whole thereof is 'up to us'. Of course, every ethics presupposes that *something* is up to us; moral discourse would be pointless and moral practice impossible if this were not the case. Nevertheless, the appeal to responsibility, and the role it has come to play, indicate an intensification and expansion of what is up to us. At the same time, however, theologians and philosophers also appeal to responsibility for the explicit purpose of opposing certain features or implications of this modern trend without returning to pre-modern ethics. The concept of responsibility, then, embodies a struggle over the status of the human subject in modern moral theories. This essay explores that struggle in Christian ethics by tracing it through two kinds of appeal to responsibility. One kind of appeal treats responsibility as a substantive principle, the other kind as a way of characterizing the moral self.

Responsibility as a Substantive Principle

H. Richard Niebuhr opened his classic exposition of the ethics of responsibility by observing that in his day responsibility and its cognates were increasingly doing work once done by terms like 'moral' and 'good' (1963: 47). This observation points to a widespread use of responsibility as an ethical principle that was prevalent in twentieth-century Christian ethics. During the middle decades of the century responsibility was frequently invoked in relation to claims of freedom from traditional authority. In such contexts responsibility served two purposes: namely, (1) to subject to moral evaluation an area of life in which latitude is given to human freedom, and (2) to provide a substantive principle for that area of life. In short, responsibility was invoked in relation to matters that are morally significant yet for which either there are no determinate norms or it is unclear which norms should determine choices.

For mid-century writers in Christian ethics, matters that fit this description were becoming increasingly prominent. Among the most prominent were issues in sexual ethics. Decades-long controversies over birth control in various Christian communions had raised questions about the scope of legitimate human freedom in matters of procreation. Within certain constraints—procreation as at least a necessary good of marriage and, in the Roman Catholic tradition, the prohibition of contraception—Christian ethics during this period increasingly acknowledged a positive sphere of human freedom in choices about when to have children and how many to have. The appeal to responsibility served both of the purposes identified above. Against tendencies to reserve this sphere for an amoral freedom, it affirmed that choices in these matters are subject to moral evaluation. To declare that couples must choose responsibly is to say that choices regarding the number and spacing of children are subject to considerations beyond mere preference, even though they are not subject to any determinate norms. The second purpose was to indicate, however roughly, certain factors or interests that such choices should take into consideration. Here responsibility serves as a substantive principle, doing the work done by practical wisdom (*phronēsis* or *prudentia*) in non-formal theories of moral reasoning: it identifies, in the absence of definitive norms, considerations relevant to a moral choice.

These two purposes characterized both Catholic and Protestant appeals to responsibility in the context of procreation in the mid-twentieth century. This is illustrated by both the Vatican II document *Gaudium et Spes* and the *Church Dogmatics* of Karl Barth. Both explicitly acknowledge the legitimacy of the claim to freedom in this domain, stress the responsibility in which this freedom must be exercised, and go on to list various interests that couples must consider in deciding the number and spacing of children (*Gaudium et Spes*) or factors they must consider in decisions regarding whether to practice birth control and which form to choose (Barth) (Abbott 1966: 254; Barth 1961: 268–76).

This kind of appeal to responsibility is now out of fashion in Christian ethics. Why? Perhaps the recovery of virtue ethics has made it obsolete. Much of virtue ethics appeals to the same phenomenon that motivated the turn to responsibility: namely, the recognition that certain areas of life (or perhaps the whole of it) are not easily brought under determinate norms, yet are still morally significant. The appeal to responsibility was useful for reining in the exaggerated claims on behalf of freedom that sometimes accompanied this recognition (the first purpose), but it proved less fruitful in articulating the morally significant features of the area of life that is declared free of such norms (the second purpose). The older language of virtue provides a much richer moral vocabulary for discharging the latter task. It is now *phronēsis* or *prudentia* in conjunction with a virtuous character that identifies and weighs the morally relevant features of situations. The concept of responsibility is too thin to compete in this task with the well-elaborated conceptions of the moral and intellectual virtues that have appeared in recent decades. Moreover, the task for which the concept of responsibility is arguably better suited—affirmation of the moral seriousness of an area of life not governed by determinate norms—is less urgent today than it was when exaggerated claims for freedom were more frequent in Christian ethics. Indeed, the very turn to virtue to illumine these areas of life itself implies that more is at stake in them than unqualified freedom. It follows that both as a marker of moral seriousness and as a substantive principle the concept of responsibility has been in decline in Christian ethics.

For some Christian ethicists of the mid-twentieth century, not only particular regions of the moral life but the whole of it was taken to be outside the authority of norms. For them responsibility served as a comprehensive principle of Christian ethics. Two important contemporary theories also treat responsibility in a comprehensive sense. However, they differ over which of the two purposes responsibility in this comprehensive sense serves—i.e., over whether it serves the purpose of bringing something under moral evaluation or that of establishing a substantive principle. The first of these purposes is served by William Schweiker (1995). In contrast to his mid-century predecessors, Schweiker advocates responsibility as the solution to the problem posed not by the expansion of human freedom but by the expansion of human power. The question is not how freedom can be exercised morally in the absence of determinate norms, but rather how power can be exercised for the sake of the good without becoming itself the good. Responsibility, then, governs the relation between power and the good in an era when the expansion of human power through technology, combined with the loss of confidence in a divine agency working in the world on behalf of the good, renders the good vulnerable. Responsibility means that human power is subject to moral evaluation, that it is not exercised for its own sake but for the sake of the good—a good whose source and end is God. Schweiker explicitly denies that responsibility is itself a substantive principle. The substantive moral principle—namely, the integrity of life—is defined independently of responsibility. Responsibility nevertheless assumes a privileged position for Schweiker, precisely because human power looms so large; the realization of the good is critically dependent on whether human beings exercise power to respect and enhance life or to demean and destroy it. Here responsibility is the antidote not to the absence of norms in the face of human freedom but rather to the vulnerability of a norm in the face of human power.

In contrast to Schweiker, Kathryn Tanner (1993) seeks to establish responsibility as a substantive principle. She seeks to replace predominant conceptions of the divinely created moral order as a set of natural or moral constraints with a conception of that order as supportive of human capacities for self-development. The divine moral order, on this view, empowers self-development rather than supplying determinate norms for it. Since this order imposes few natural *or* moral constraints on self-development, human beings are responsible for determining what constitutes fulfilment. It follows that responsibility, as that whereby one undertakes one's self-development, functions as a substantive principle, albeit a thin one. Its thinness, however, renders Tanner's ethic of responsibility vulnerable to the same fate that befell mid-century sexual ethics: it seems to be an inadequate substitute for a missing theory of virtue. Theories of virtue also depict moral life in terms of self-development towards a fulfilment that is underdetermined by fixed ends or rules. But the often rich articulations of the moral and intellectual virtues that specify this fulfilment and the self-development leading to it contrast sharply with the thinness of the bare notion of responsibility.

Before leaving this first kind of appeal, we must examine H. Richard Niebuhr's ethics of responsibility (1963). Designating self-knowledge as the first task of ethics, Niebuhr points out that, morally, we have traditionally understood ourselves either as makers who shape our lives and our world in view of one or more ends, or as citizens who exist under moral legislation. He then proposes a third image in which we understand ourselves as answerers who respond to actions on us. On this account, moral selfhood and agency unfold in our responses to events around us as we interpret these events and anticipate responses to our own response, all of this occurring in, and helping to form, a social context. The moral question—the point at which selfhood and agency are not merely respons*ive* but respons*ible*—arises when we ask to whom or to what we are accountable in all the actions on us. Our answer to this question affects how we respond to and interpret all the actions on us. For example, do we respond to the sack of Rome as a barbarian attack on Roman honour, as the judgement of God on an arrogant empire, or as an act of divine providence beyond the illusory grandeur of the nations? Moral evaluation of an action consists less in asking to which end(s) it is oriented or under which law(s) it falls than in asking into which ordering of actions and responses it fits.

Does responsibility function here as a substantive principle? Niebuhr himself presented his notion of the fitting action as an alternative or supplement to notions of good (i.e., end-oriented) and right (i.e., law-governed) action. Moreover, because judgements as to whether or not an action is fitting depend on to whom or what one is accountable, the notion of the fitting is subordinate to that of responsibility. Which response to the sack of Rome is judged as fitting depends on whether one's ultimate accountability is to God or to country, and whether the God to whom one is accountable is ultimately a God of judgement or of providence. But this means that responsibility itself is only formal; it is the principle of accountability. The substantive moral question is: to whom or to what is one accountable? For Niebuhr, as for Augustine, one is accountable to a God who acts in all actions and events, and whose action is ultimately, even if not always visibly, providential. Human actions are therefore fitting in so far as they respond in a universal social and temporal framework and do so in the confidence that a universal good is being accomplished. Thus, while Niebuhr argues that we should treat the entire moral life, and not just certain parts of it, as at least to a large extent undetermined by norms expressive of the right or the good, responsibility itself is not a substantive principle but is rather the formal principle of accountability, which is the condition of the ethical itself. Responsibility is what constitutes selfhood and agency as moral.

Niebuhr, then, leads us to our second kind of appeal to responsibility. But before following him there, we can summarize our findings regarding the first kind of appeal. Responsibility gains currency as a moral principle in contexts in which the traditional authority of norms is challenged by claims of human freedom or assertions of human power, and in which moral guidance must be given in the absence of determinate norms. The ethics of virtue has proved itself superior in discharging the latter task and may also suffice for the former task, at least in the case of freedom. In the case of power, Schweiker makes a strong case for the continuing necessity of responsibility. Aside from this case, however, responsibility seems to have articulated the expansion of what is 'up to us' without supplying the corresponding qualifications or limits of this newly discovered or asserted human freedom. It follows that the appeal to virtue has largely replaced the first appeal to responsibility in Christian ethics.

RESPONSIBILITY AND THE MORAL SELF

In their efforts to map the field of responsibility, Albert Jonsen (1968: 5) and William Schweiker (1995: 55–8) describe three modes of responsibility which can be designated *imputability* (that actions can be ascribed to one), *accountability* (that one is answerable to someone), and *liability* (that one is answerable for something or someone). These three modes interrelate and overlap in significant ways, so that at best we can distinguish three aspects of a single reality. The three aspects and the single reality can be expressed schematically in a single sentence: *x is responsible to y for z.* What follows is an analysis of the three aspects of this single reality.

Imputability: *x is responsible*

Imputability involves the distinction between what one does and what happens to one or in one. We may distinguish weak and strong theories of imputability in Western philosophical and theological traditions. Aristotle offers a weak theory. That the agent, rather than something external, is the cause of an action, and that the action is performed in knowledge of the circumstances and objects of the action, are for Aristotle sufficient to impute that action to the agent (1976: 111–15). The critical question for Aristotle and for other weak theories of responsibility is whether the action originates in the agent's power to act or not act. It does not matter whether this power is expressed in a rational judgement, a desire, or an irrational feeling; all of these originate in the agent rather than in the coercion of an external force or agency. Imputability, on this kind of theory, does not require the conception of a subject who chooses in abstraction from desires and inclinations.

Weak theories of responsibility are evident in much Christian thinking about the bondage of the will. The question is how human beings can be responsible for sin if they are in bondage to sin. Weak theories of responsibility can explain how sinful actions are voluntary even if the sinner is not free to act in a sinless way. Thus, for Augustine, sinful acts are imputable to agents on the grounds that they are chosen freely (*liberum arbitrium*) rather than coerced by an external agency, even though the agent is bound by perverse self-love and therefore has no freedom (*libertas*) to act without sin—i.e., to choose good rather than evil actions. Similarly, in his debate with Erasmus, Martin Luther argued that the sinner acts voluntarily even though he or she is inwardly moved by the evil spirit and has no will over against the evil spirit—i.e., no volitional power to choose otherwise than as the evil spirit chooses. Indeed, the very absence of such a will to the contrary means that the sinner acts voluntarily—i.e., is not coerced (Luther 1969: 139–43). But what about the perverse habit of self-love or the evil spirit within? Is the sinner responsible for that? Neither Augustine nor Luther answers this question in a way that satisfies their critics. Augustine argues that each human being has already sinned in Adam, since all are Adam in the sense that their nature is in Adam's seed (Augustine 1998: 555 f.). Luther avoids this explanation, but it remains a mystery exactly how one is responsible for the displacement of the Holy Spirit by the evil spirit.

Immanuel Kant offers a strong theory according to which responsibility entails a subject who is capable of choosing in abstraction from desires, inclinations, etc. The question for him is not simply whether the agent has the power to act (i.e., is not coerced by an external force or agency and is not ignorant), but whether the agent has the power to act otherwise than his or her desires or inclinations dictate. Responsible actions are not merely voluntary, but free; i.e., they are not merely uncoerced, but are spontaneous. Responsibility requires a subject whose will is capable of being determined by an abstract principle, namely the moral law. For Kant the question of the bondage of the will presents its own difficulties. Because imputable acts must be free from determination by desire or inclination, Kant is unable to locate the bondage of the will in a perverse orientation of desire. Rather, the will is bound by an act that is freely chosen (and thus imputable), but which is prior to, and the ground of, all actions chosen in time. By deriving the bondage of the will from a free choice, Kant avoids the problems that Augustine and Luther had in accounting for the imputation to us of that by which we are bound. However, he avoids these problems only by removing from time the choice whereby one binds oneself.

Within this general framework strong theories can be understood in two differ-ent ways. From one standpoint they simply give a more ambitious account of the necessary and sufficient conditions for imputing actions, requiring that these actions be not only voluntary (uncoerced) but also free (spontaneous). Understood in this way, strong theories of responsibility stand under a mixed verdict in most contemporary philosophy. Many hold that while such theories preserve imput-ation, and the practices of praise and blame which provide the rationale for imputing actions, in the face of reductionist accounts of desire and inclination, they are unnecessary, either because these reductionist accounts are false (the will is not determined by empirical factors) or because they are true (the will is deter-mined by empirical factors) but not in a sense that is incompatible with respon-sibility. This verdict is reflected in much Anglo-American moral philosophy, in which theories of responsibility increasingly exhibit weak (Aristotelian) rather than strong (Kantian) characteristics.

From another standpoint, however, strong theories of responsibility involve a different understanding of imputation and its rationale. Imputation is a factor not of social practices of praising and blaming, but of an act in which one is constituted as a moral subject in distinction from the empirical subject of desire, inclination, etc. Understood in this way, strong theories of responsibility again face a mixed verdict, depending on how the constitution of the moral subject is understood. For Kant, one constitutes oneself as a free subject in obedience to the moral law. Fichte, however, realized another possibility inherent in strong theories of responsibility, in which responsibility is the act of a subject who makes himself responsible or asserts responsibility. Here one posits the moral law by which one realizes oneself as a subject distinct from one's desires and inclinations. Responsibility is an act of self-assertion by which one posits or constitutes oneself as a subject over against what is other. Here we have a profound instance of the expansion and intensification of the human subject referred to above.

The notion of responsibility as asserted in an act of will by which one constitutes oneself as a moral subject is poignantly captured by Nietzsche in his *Genealogy of Morality*. By attempting to show how the responsible subject is not realized in a transcendental act of self-positing, but is rather the product of a long history of often violent social practices, Nietzsche attacked the pretensions of the modern moral subject (1994: 38–42). Nietzsche marks a turning point in the problem of imputability. After his deconstruction of the modern moral subject, the question is how to impute actions to a self whose moral identity is no longer stable. Theories of imputability must now confront two kinds of dispersal of the subject: one in time and one in space. In Christian ethics narrative theories of responsibility address the diachronic fragmentation of the self, while theories of responsibility as singularity address the spatial diffusion of agency in the Weberian bureaucracy and the Foucauldian apparatus.

For Kant the relation of the moral subject to the moral law entails that time is not a factor in imputability; reason considers only whether it is one's own deed, however long ago it was committed (1996a: 219). But for Stanley Hauerwas (1981: 129–52) the dissolution of the Kantian moral subject means that the continuity of moral identity over time is now a problem and a task. How can we make past actions our own when the temporal distance which separates us from them makes them now appear as something that happened to us rather than something we did? Moral identity over time is essential to responsibility; to be able to claim one's past actions as one's own is a necessary condition for claiming one's present actions as one's own. However, the terms in which Hauerwas posed this question in his early work indicate that, at this stage, he remained in the orbit of the modern moral subject. For him, the task was to make one's actions one's own; imputation is still, as it is for the modern subject, an act whereby one constitutes oneself as a moral subject over against what is other. In his case the otherness is the estrangement of the self from itself involved in temporal distance. Narrative replaces the act of will as what constitutes the subject, and time replaces desire and inclination as the other; but the result is the same. In his insistence on the temporality of the self, then, the early Hauerwas only seems to challenge the modern notion of responsibility.

In his recent work, however, Hauerwas explicitly denies the existence of a subject who exists prior to the story which forms her and who chooses which story will form her. The shift here is subtle yet profound. It is no longer the self that constitutes itself as a moral subject over time through narrative, but rather narrative that constitutes the self as responsible, that imputes past actions to the present self. However, the most significant shift is not this reversal in the mutual relation of self and narrative. Rather, the most significant shift is from the Kantian theme of responsibility as the constitution of a subject distinct from desires and inclinations to the Aristotelian theme of responsibility as a factor of social practices of praise and blame. Aristotle was right after all: for Hauerwas there is nothing more to say about moral identity beyond character formation. It is precisely by referring to character that we understand how choices or decisions made without our knowing what we were doing can nevertheless be our own, for character expresses the truth that moral selfhood is constituted by such choices and decisions. The question is whether one's character is formed by practices and narratives that are capable of making such choices and decisions one's own.

For many, the greater threat to imputability today comes not from the temporal fragmentation of the self but from its spatial diffusion in the relentless bureaucratic organization of human acts which characterizes modern societies. The ethical urgency that often accompanies this recognition of collective action follows from the demonic form it took in the Nazi administration of mass murder. Less urgent, but still of great concern, are the forms it takes in nations, corporations, and other institutions. Two questions arise in the face of this phenomenon. One question is whether actions can legitimately be imputed to collective entities such as corporations and other organizations. This question has received most of the attention in recent theories of responsibility, especially in Anglo-American philosophy. The other question is not whether a collective entity can be responsible in this sense, but whether the individual hears a call to responsibility that sets her apart from her identification with such an entity. In an age when moral identities are easily subsumed into the magnetic pull of nation and ethnicity or diffused throughout the bureaucracies described by Weber or the knowledge–power configurations described by Foucault, to articulate the summons that calls one out from such an identification is at least as important as the effort to justify imputing actions to such collective entities.

This summons is formulated, in different versions, by Kierkegaard's Johannes de Silentio in *Fear and Trembling*, by the philosopher Emmanuel Levinas, and by Karl Barth, for whom the summons to responsibility is issued by the Word of God. Like Hauerwas's early theory of narrative responsibility, this theory remains within the horizon of Kantian responsibility. But this form of responsibility is neither a factor of one's narrative-formed character nor is it asserted by an act of will. Rather, responsibility is inaugurated by an address or call which constitutes one as a subject to whom acts can be imputed, as one who is summoned to assume responsibility for oneself precisely as *this* one. Responsibility entails singularity, which means that morally speaking one is irreplaceable, required to answer for oneself, singled out, unable to evade responsibility or transfer it to someone else. To be responsible is to be designated in this way, to be appointed as one who will be held accountable. We are already encroaching on responsibility *to*, and for good reason: one point of this alternative is that imputability and accountability are inseparable even if they can and must be distinguished. Accountability here is the ground of imputability. If, for

Aristotle, acts are imputed in the third person, by the community of praise and blame, and if, for Kant, imputation involves the first person, the act of spontaneity, we may say that for this alternative, imputation is established in the second person, as one is addressed as one to whom acts can and will be imputed. The Kantian theme remains in the constitution of the responsible subject, in distinction from the socially formed subject of desire and inclination, and in obedience to the moral law (here reformulated as the address or summons). But, as the latter point makes clear, in this case responsibility limits rather than authorizes the self-asserting subject. Thus, while this alternative retains the sense, essential to responsibility, that it's up to us, here the 'up to us' is not that of a self-asserting subject, but of an obedient one.

Accountability: *responsible to y*

Responsibility *to* plays a role in every ethic. Indeed, we were unable to discuss theories of imputability without referring to the community (the source of social praise and blame, honour and punishment, as in Aristotle) and to God (who summons one to responsibility) as those to whom one is answerable. The Latin *respondeo* and the German *Verantwortung* point to answerability to someone or something as the root sense of responsibility. Answerability is also the first element that F. H. Bradley identifies in his enquiry into the common person's understanding of responsibility. To be morally responsible involves 'the idea of a man's appearing to answer'. Answer to whom? To a 'moral tribunal', i.e., 'the court of conscience'. The judge in this court could be 'divine or human, external or internal' (Bradley 1927: 3). Answerability, then, brings us into the domain of conscience, but, as Bradley points out, the judge in the court of conscience may be external or internal. Modern theories of responsibility coincide with the internalization of conscience, signalling once again the relation of responsibility to the modern subject; while recent theories of responsibility counter with an emphasis on an other who inaugurates responsibility by calling the self into question. We will now trace these trends.

For both Thomas Aquinas and Kant, conscience, while internal, is unintelligible without an external dimension. For Aquinas, conscience involves reason proposing an act to the will. And in its comprehension of the moral law through *synderēsis*, reason participates in the eternal law of God (1964: 182–4). For Aquinas, then, reason, participating in eternal law, commands the choosing subject. Thus, while conscience is internal, Aquinas recognizes a kind of alterity in the relation of reason to the choosing subject, and in the notion of reason as participation in the eternal law of God. This alterity is radically intensified by Kant. For Kant also, conscience is internal, 'the business of a human being with himself', but 'one constrained by his reason sees himself constrained to carry it on as at the bidding of *another person*' (italics original). Kant emphasizes the other person because conscience for him is less reason proposing acts to will than judgement before a tribunal. Given this view, to think of the one who is accused as the same person as the judge is absurd; on that assumption, Kant wryly notes, the prosecutor will always lose. The conscience, then, must think of its judge as another person, ideal or actual. Moreover, this person must be thought of as capable of scrutinizing the heart (since the court is internal), as one in relation to whom all our duties are his commands, and as one who is able to give effect to his laws. Such a person, of course, is called God, so that 'conscience must be thought of as the subjective principle of being accountable to God for all one's deeds' (1996b: 560 f.). Thus conscience, though still internal, involves a robust form of alterity. However, as Kant immediately goes on to say, this requirement supplies no ground for one to assume that God exists outside oneself. This idea of God is a practical, not a theoretical, idea, and is thus a principle of action rather than of belief.

In Kant, then, the reason which conscience commands has ceased to be reason which participates in the law of a God who exists apart from the subject. In terms which Karl Barth applied to a parallel development in the transition from the Protestant Reformers to orthodoxy and rationalism, accountability to God is on the way to becoming a dramatization and (with the demise of Kant's notion of God as a rational moral idea) mythologization of our relation to a law that is really within ourselves (Barth 1957: 372 f.). Standing at the end of this process, Paul Ricoeur can refer to conscience as 'surely the most internalized expression of the responding self' (1995: 271). At this point the modern subject reigns, and the very notion of answerability is threatened.

This internalization of responsibility, and with it the intensification of the role of the human subject, who replaces God as the lawgiver and judge to whom one is accountable, has provoked a reaction in the form of various ethics of alterity. The most important philosophical version is that of Emmanuel Levinas, but answerability to an other external to oneself is also central to Barth's theological ethics. For Barth, God decides on our conduct, measuring it by the criterion of electing grace and questioning it as to its fulfilment of this criterion. It follows that our conduct, and we in our conduct, constitute a continuous reply (*Antwort*) to the Word of God as command. Barth can therefore refer to the notion of responsiveness (*Verantwortlichkeit*) as 'the most precise description of the human situation in the face of the sovereign decision of God'. The decision of God regarding our conduct gives our conduct the character of a reply or response to the question posed to us by the command of God as the witness to, or expression of, God's decision on us and our conduct. In this responsiveness consists our accountability (*Verantwortung*) to God: we are placed in the position of having to render an account to God (1957: 641). This alterity that pertains between the command of God and the subject governs Barth's conception of conscience. Etymologically, conscience involves a co-knowledge (*conscientes*, *suneidotēs*) of the command of

God. But to know the command of God through conscience in this way would erase the alterity between the command of God and the knowing subject. Barth therefore identifies conscience as an eschatological, rather than an anthropological, concept; the Word of God that commands us is the promise that we *will* become co-knowers with God (1957: 667). Barth thus combines the alterity of Kant with the participation in the law of God of Aquinas—now understood eschatogically. Responsibility no longer entails a subject who is responsible only to herself, but rather a subject who is constituted by her responsibility to a gracious God.

Liability: *responsible for z*

Responsibility *for* is also a critical element in any moral theory. Here we encounter the notion of liability in the sense of that for which one is answerable. We may distinguish two senses of responsibility *for*. The first has to do with care: one is answerable for the safety or welfare of something or someone that falls under or makes a claim on one's care. To cite the classic paradigms, statesmen are responsible in this way for their nations, and parents for their children. To these paradigms Hans Jonas (1984) famously added responsibility to the future existence of humankind, which becomes an object of care due to the prospect of nuclear annihilation and ecological destruction. In each case responsibility means that something under one's power becomes an object of one's care. Jonas illustrates the point made in this essay that the modern concept of responsibility both signals an expansion of the subject—in this case the expansion of human power over the future—and places a limit on this subject—in this case an imperative to preserve the conditions for the future existence of humankind.

In Christian ethics Dietrich Bonhoeffer (1955) identified care as the basic structure of the moral subject. Referring to the father, the statesman, and the teacher, Bonhoeffer defines responsibility *for* as 'deputyship', which means that one acts on behalf of others and combines in oneself the selves of the others for whom one acts. The moral subject is therefore not the isolated individual of modern ethics, but is constituted by relations to those for whom she acts. For Bonhoeffer, this form of responsibility is grounded Christologically: 'Jesus ... lived in deputyship for us as the incarnate Son of God, and that is why through him all human life is in essence a life of deputyship. Jesus ... was not the individual, but he lived only as the one who has taken up into himself ... the selves of all men' (1955: 225). Responsibility *for*, then, is, a non-identical imitation of Christ. It is grounded in responsibility *to* God, understood in terms similar to those of Barth described above. Responsibility, for Bonhoeffer, therefore retains the focus on the subject that characterizes the modern turn to responsibility, while also countering the expansion and intensification of the subject.

A second sense of responsibility *for* concerns liability for the consequences of one's actions. An important question in moral theology is whether an agent is liable for the evil effects of an action that is permissible by virtue of its intention and object. This question takes a peculiarly modern turn in Max Weber's lecture on 'Politics as a Vocation' (1978). Weber's political theory lies between moralism and realism: politics is not subordinate to any higher law, but neither is it merely the exercise of power. Rather, it is an arena in which political actors try to realize self-chosen causes through political means, which involve power backed by violence. Devotion to a cause and the power inescapably connected with its pursuit constitute politics as the scene of an ethical tension. In this context Weber considers two principles: intention and responsibility. Under the principle of intention, the politician focuses exclusively on the cause, refusing to take account of, or to assume liability for, the effects that follow from the attempt to realize it, and ignoring or denying the moral danger intrinsic to political action as the exercise of power backed by force. For Weber, adherents of the ethics of intention simply refuse to face the moral ambiguity inherent in politics as the exercise of power backed by violence. By contrast, the principle of responsibility faces this ambiguity, taking account of the effects that follow from the pursuit of a cause by political means, and accepting the moral danger that accompanies those means.

This does not mean, though, that Weber treats responsibility as a normative theory that resolves the ethical tension of politics. He asserts repeatedly that no theory can determine which causes are worthy of choice, or whether or when a cause justifies the morally problematic means that are endemic to political activity. It follows that no theory can tell one whether or when to act in accordance with the principle of intention or that of responsibility. Instead, Weber appeals to the nobility of character exhibited by those who take responsibility for the means and effects of their political actions and to the false nobility usually exhibited by those who refuse to do so. The nobility in responsibility lies in facing up to an ethically irrational world in which all causes are matters of choice, and in which one cannot trust divine providence for the effects of one's actions or for a coincidence between morally good causes and morally acceptable means. In the end, responsibility is the self-limitation of a political actor who understands a certain kind of character to be demanded by politics as a vocation. Once again, then, responsibility occupies a space no longer governed by moral norms. It is up to the subject to choose a cause and to decide what limits, if any, evil means and effects place on its pursuit. This means that responsibility is less a principle governing this space in the absence of norms than a choice to assume liability for the implications of acting in that space. Echoes of this ethic of responsibility resound in Christian realists, who adopt both the warning about the moral ambiguity of causes and the recognition of, and willingness to accept, the moral danger of political means.

The third sense of responsibility *for* has to do with blame or guilt: one may be answerable for actions done by others. A corporate officer may be liable, morally or legally, for the actions of those under her authority, and in some cases may have to resign because of their actions, taking the blame for them. A strong version of responsibility as liability for the blame or guilt of others holds that each person is responsible for the deeds of every other human being. Hannah Arendt defines the idea of humanity as the view 'that in one form or another men must assume responsibility for all crimes committed by men and that all nations share the onus of evil committed by all others' (1991: 282). This idea, she argues, is the necessary basis of politics in light of the discovery, in the Nazi Holocaust, of the evil of which human beings are capable.

For Arendt, universal responsibility is mediated through the conception of a common humanity; both the guilt itself and the assumption of it are collective. Fyodor Dostoevsky (1993) offers a different formulation, one that also has political implications but is carried out by individuals. In *The Brothers Karamazov* the narration of the death of Father Zossima is followed by biographical notes and exhortations attributed by the narrator to the revered monk. In the biographical notes Father Zossima tells of the illness and death of his elder brother, Markel, whose late adolescent experiment in atheism suddenly gives way during a terminal illness to a deep saintliness. His relations with his family, servants, and even the birds outside his window are radically transformed as Markel confesses that he has sinned against all and proclaims that 'everyone is really responsible to all men for all men and for everything' (1993: 41). Years later a profound experience brings Father Zossima himself to the same conviction, which becomes the central theme of the exhortations recounted by the narrator after his death.

Two things are worth noting about Father Zossima's universal responsibility. First, it is a matter of imputation: one imputes to oneself the blame for the sins of others. Father Zossima exhorts his hearers to 'take yourself and make yourself responsible for all men's sins'. Nor is this a morally or spiritually useful fiction or an exercise of self-assertion, 'for as soon as you sincerely make yourself responsible for everything and for all men, you will see at once that it is really so, and that you are to blame for everyone and for all things' (1993: 76). Why? Because of one's failure to be a light of goodness to others. 'If you had been a light, you would have lightened the path for others too, and the evildoer might perhaps have been saved by your light from his sin' (1993: 78). Second, Dostoevsky sets Father Zossima's universal responsibility against Ivan Karamazov's moral despair. His 'I am to blame' contrasts directly with Ivan's assertion that 'no one is to blame' in a nihilistic, mechanistic world where there is suffering and no one is guilty, where effect simply follows cause in a moral vacuum (1993: 14). Ivan is morally sensitive enough to want justice—compensation for all suffering—in this world, but enlightened enough to know that justice in this sense is inconceivable in this-worldly terms. The result is moral despair. It is precisely against moral despair that Father Zossima counsels universal responsibility. 'Fly from that dejection, children!', he exhorts, then urges his hearers to take responsibility for all and for everything (1993: 76). For Ivan desire for justice combined with an amoral, mechanistic world produces moral despair. Father Zossima opposes to this the fraternity of universal responsibility in a world that is not a dead mechanism but an 'ocean' in which 'all is connected', where 'a touch in one place sets up movement at the other end of the earth' (1993: 76).

Father Zossima's universal responsibility goes beyond the singularity of the subject called out from identification with her desires and inclinations and with the narratives and practices in which the latter are formed. It raises a difficult question: is imputing to oneself the blame for the sins of others a way of imitating Christ, or is it a way of substituting oneself for Christ? Suspicion that it is the latter is fuelled by Father Zossima's frequent insistence that in those who embody universal responsibility, earth is heaven (his indirect answer to Ivan's rejection of the world) and by his identification of Russia as the agent of salvation. If these suspicions are justified—if it is the universally responsible Russian monk who brings heaven to earth—then for Dostoevsky, too, the turn to responsibility signals expansion of the self. Responsibility in this case is not the imitation of Christ but the substitution for Christ of a subject who knows it is 'up to us'. In his non-identical repetition of Christ that does not substitute for Christ but remains in, and follows from, responsibility *to* God, Bonhoeffer avoids this danger that in one's liability for the guilt of others one will not imitate Christ but replace him. Once again, then, we find responsibility both setting and resolving the problem of the moral subject.

CONCLUSION

If attention to responsibility is associated with the expansion and intensification of the human subject and with the absence or retreat of moral norms in areas such as sexuality and politics, how should Christian ethics treat responsibility? Our examinations of sexual ethics and political ethics indicate that, in these areas at least, responsibility is inadequate, or at least insufficient, as a substantive principle. One alternative is to attempt to assert or reassert norms in areas of life left open by modern developments. Another alternative is to apply theories of virtue to these areas. In the case of the responsible self or subject, some would argue that Christian ethics should abandon strong notions of the self and return to Aristotle in the case of imputation, Aquinas in the case of conscience, and to more limited versions of responsibility *for* that characterize pre-modern theories. While these critics may continue to use the term 'responsibility', they in effect seek to return to notions that preceded the rise of responsibility. However, the examples of Barth and Bonhoeffer show us that strong notions of the self can also be countered by direct deployment of the concept of responsibility. Responsibility can serve just as effectively to limit the ambitions and self-assertion of the modern moral subject as it has served to fuel those ambitions and that self-assertion. Moreover, the concept of responsibility is also necessary to address the paradoxical coincidence of expanded human power and diffusion of moral agency characteristic of contemporary societies. Used in these ways, responsibility is the best concept we have to illuminate the senses in which morality is up to us and the senses in which it is not.

REFERENCES AND SUGGESTED READING

ABBOTT, W. (ed.) (1966). *The Documents of Vatican II.* New York: Herder and Herder.

AQUINAS, THOMAS (1964). *Treatise on Happiness*, ed. J. A. Oesterle. Notre Dame, Ind.: University of Notre Dame Press.

ARENDT, H. (1991). 'Organized Guilt and Universal Responsibility', in L. May and S. Hoffman (eds.), *Collective Responsibility: Five Decades of Debate in Theoretical and Applied Ethics*, Savage, Md.: Rowman & Littlefield, 273–83.

ARISTOTLE (1976). *Ethics.* London: Penguin.

AUGUSTINE (1998). *The City of God against the Pagans*, ed. R. W. Dyson. Cambridge: Cambridge University Press.

BARTH, K. (1957). *Church Dogmatics*, II/2: *The Doctrine of God.* Edinburgh: T. & T. Clark.

—— (1961). *Church Dogmatics*, III/4: *The Doctrine of Creation.* Edinburgh: T. & T. Clark.

BONHOEFFER, D. (1955). *Ethics.* New York: Macmillan.

BRADLEY, F. H. (1927). *Ethical Studies.* Oxford: Clarendon Press.

DOSTOEVSKY, F. (1993). *The Grand Inquisitor.* Indianapolis: Hackett.

GUSTAFSON, J. M. and LANEY, J. T., (eds.) (1968). *On Being Responsible: Issues in Personal Ethics.* New York: Harper.

HAUERWAS, S. (1981). *A Community of Character.* Notre Dame, Ind.: University of Notre Dame Press.

HUBER, W. (1990). *Konflikt und Konsens: Studien zur Ethik der Verantwortung.* Munich: Kaiser.

JONSEN, A. R. (1968). *Responsibility in Modern Religious Ethics.* Washington: Corpus.

KANT, I. (1996a). 'Critique of Practical Reason', in *Practical Philosophy*, trans. and ed. M. J. Gregor, New York: Cambridge University Press, 133–271.

—— (1996b). 'The Metaphysics of Morals', in *Practical Philosophy*, trans. and ed. M. J. Gregor, New York: Cambridge University Press, 353–603.

LUTHER, M. (1969). 'On the Bondage of the Will', in E. G. Rupp and P. S. Watson. (eds.), *Luther and Erasmus: Free Will and Salvation*, Philadelphia: Westminster Press, 101–334.

NIEBUHR, H. R. (1963). *The Responsible Self: An Essay in Christian Moral Philosophy.* New York: Harper & Row.

NIETZSCHE, F. (1994). *On the Genealogy of Morality.* Cambridge: Cambridge University Press.

RICOEUR, P. (1995). 'The Summoned Subject in the School of the Narratives of the Prophetic Vocation', in *Figuring the Sacred*, Minneapolis: Fortress Press, 262–75.

SCHWEIKER, W. (1995). *Responsibility and Christian Ethics.* New York: Cambridge University Press.

TANNER, K. (1993). 'A Theological Case for Human Responsibility in Moral Choice', *Journal of Religion* 73, 592–612.

WEBER, M. (1978). 'Politics as a Vocation', in *Weber: Selections in Translation*, ed. W. G. Runciman, trans. E. Matthews, Cambridge: Cambridge University Press, 212–25.

CHAPTER 15

DEATH

DARLENE FOZARD WEAVER

CHRISTIAN life is one of dying and rising with Christ. What is the relationship between this dying and rising and our death? What does this relationship mean for facing death and for our care for the dying? This essay considers these questions with respect to (1) death's 'natural' dimension as the separation of body and soul, (2) death's 'personal' dimension as the end of our earthly life, and (3) death's 'moral' dimension as a wager of love. Drawing on Paul Ramsey and Karl Rahner, this essay sketches a theological moral anthropology; the person is a unity of body and soul who lives by the love of God. This anthropology appears in Christian construals of death as the bodily manifestation of, and punishment for, our wilful alienation from God in a misplaced or self-withholding love for life. Ramsey finds in the Christian fusion of sin and death a critical resource for facing death and for care for the dying—namely, that death is a personal indignity. Rahner insists on the difference between dying in sin and dying in Christ. Together, they lead us to a Christian insight into human biological death: the sovereign and perfect efficacy of Christ's redeeming death destroys us in our alienation by establishing us in love. This good word, since it comes to us in death, is also a hard one, and it points to guidelines for Christian care for the dying.

DEATH AS NATURAL

Is death natural? Human beings are finite, bodily creatures, and as such are subject to death. Death is natural to human beings in the sense that we are mortal. What does this mean, and how ought we human beings to live before it in our living before God? Does our mortality indicate that death is natural to us in a second sense, as 'proper' to us?

In 'The Indignity of "Death with Dignity"' Ramsey rejects the claim that death is natural to human beings in any way beyond biological necessity. He does this to distinguish a proper 'acceptance' of death (which grounds resistance to undue medical interventions to prolong life) from campaigns for 'death with dignity'. These campaigns only add insult to injury, because they remove the 'human countenance' from death, thwarting our efforts to 'convey dignity to the dying', inasmuch as they fail to encompass '—nakedly and without dilution—the final indignity of death itself' (Ramsey 1998: 210). Death is an indignity because it contradicts 'the unique worth of an individual human life' (Ramsey 1998: 209). Ramsey rejects a common consolation used to support death with dignity, that 'death is simply a part of life'. This appeal is unpersuasive. We regard other parts of life—suffering, murder, congenital defect, for example—as 'enemies and violations of human nobility' (Ramsey 1998: 210); why believe that death is not (or need not be) among these? Is it, perhaps, because death is an 'evolutionary necessity', a part of life as the succession of generations? Ramsey argues that the human being is not reducible to the human species; man's 'dis-ease in dying' is evidence of his transcendence over the species (1998: 211). A second warrant for death with dignity is that death is *not* a part of life. Granted, 'we never experience the experience of the nothingness which is natural death' (Ramsey 1998: 212). Life and death are 'sequential realities' that 'never *meet* in direct encounter', and thus there is an 'incommensurable contrast' between them (Ramsey 1998: 219). Yet it is a small consolation to say that as long as you are, death is not, and when death is, you are not. The claim that death is not a part of life fuels dread of death, because 'the dread of death is the dread of oblivion, of there being only empty room in one's stead' (Ramsey 1998: 212). In short, both supports for death with dignity comprise futile attempts to manage our proper dread of death through strategies of self-distancing objectification. In one case, we are to evade our own death by way of a generic mortality; in the other, we evade it with reference to some postulated objective 'experience' of death that we by definition can never experience. These efforts effectively work against a true understanding of an individual person's irreplaceable worth; for the more acceptable death is in such terms, the more we attenuate the unique worth of one who dies, the one who truly comprehends that and how it is that he will be no more.

In contrast to these 'death with dignity ideologies', Ramsey describes a Christian humanism which perceives rightly that death 'is an enemy, surely, and not simply an acceptable part of the natural order of things' (1998: 218). Death is an enemy because it brings to oblivion our one and only earthly life as a punishment for sin. The Christian gospel announces our redemption in Jesus Christ from sin and death. Importantly, in 'Indignity' Ramsey is less concerned to proclaim this good news than to offer an apology for the human condition it presupposes, that the person will die, and *knows* it. Death may be a 'conquered enemy', but it is 'in the natural order—and as long as the generations of mankind endure will remain—an enemy still' (Ramsey 1998: 220). Ramsey invites us to consider Christianity's insight into our predicament, since our impending death and awareness of it give the lie to the self-distancing objectifications of death considered above. So Ramsey says that 'death is a natural fact of life', but only as a biological necessity, not as proper to human beings. He insists that 'no man dies "naturally" nor do we have occasions in which to practice doing so in order to learn how' (Ramsey 1998: 211). The reason behind this latter assertion is clearer in Ramsey's 1961 sermon *Death's Duell* than in 'Indignity' (upon which Ramsey draws for 'Indignity'). No one dies naturally, because human beings 'no matter how they try will never learn to perish like things' (1961: 5). The wish to do so deprives oneself 'of the essential grandeur of manhood' (1961: 3). The view that death is an enemy does more justice to our psychosomatic unity; human nature is a coinherence of body and soul, thus bodily death ends the person's unique and non-interchangeable life.

In his response to 'Indignity', Leon Kass shares some of Ramsey's concerns that our practices *vis-à-vis* the dying may weaken 'respect for life' (Kass 1987: 201). But he sharply disagrees with Ramsey that death itself is an indignity, chiefly because '*death is natural and necessary and inextricably tied to life*. To live is to be mortal; death is the necessary price for life' (Kass 1987: 206). While Ramsey (Kass says) personifies death as an enemy, and thereby treats it as an 'external agent', Kass insists that it is part 'of the *life cycle*' (1987: 206). Unlike suffering, murder, and congenital defects, 'which *occur* in life, decline and death are a *part* of life, an integral part which cannot be extruded without destroying the whole' (Kass 1987: 206). Moreover, Kass wonders, 'is there really dignity ... in railing against the inevitable? Is there not more dignity in facing up to such things and in facing them nobly and bravely' (Kass 1987: 206)? Indeed, according to Kass, Ramsey is wrong to say that human beings have no occasion for learning to die naturally. We can 'habituate our sentiments and feelings, so that we may live properly before [death], without undue fear or anxiety ... if we reflect on the fact that we were once not here and that we will again not be here, and that this is the way things are and must be' (Kass 1987: 207). Kass goes on to say that Ramsey 'speaks as if the really *proper* condition for a being such as man is immortality, that man fell to a merely mortal, merely natural condition. He speaks as if man had a chance for immortality but squandered it' (1987: 207). This is because Ramsey assents to the teaching that death is the wage of original sin. While Kass grants that 'there is Hebrew biblical support for this view', he argues that 'the most traditional Jewish view on the necessity of death' holds death 'to be part of the order of the world since creation. God made man from the dust of the earth, and to dust he must return' (1987: 208). For Kass, the naturalness of death indicates that it is an 'evil good', especially in view of generational succession. Death is ' "natural" or "proper to man" ' (Kass 1987: 209).

Claims about whether or not death is natural locate death in the economy of salvation and index our creatureliness—our spiritual, embodied existence in the world with others—to some understanding of God's creative and saving work. If the proper human condition is immortality, lost in the Fall, we may, by comparison, denigrate mortal human life, and thus undermine the claim that death is an indignity for human beings. Moreover, we imply some original human nature that is intrinsically fit for immortality (O'Donovan 1998: 229). Death then necessitates resuscitation, not resurrection, restoration of a native capacity, not transfiguration. If death is proper to human beings as part of a natural life cycle, we may affirm the value of bodily human life (by avoiding a comparative denigration), but this move locates our value in view of generational succession, not in our unique life spans. Moreover, if death is natural—proper to us—Christ's death does not and need not redeem ours, because death is not a fallen reality (Alison 1998: 272). Either way we betray Christian faith's revelation of our radical need for salvation, and fail to appreciate the import of our body–soul unity—we devalue bodily life in relation to a spiritual potential for immortality or devalue the unique worth of individual human life in favour of human interchangeability.

Like Ramsey, Rahner explores death's natural dimension with regard to the person's psychosomatic unity. David H. Kelsey rightly notes that, for Rahner, death is natural to us as such a union, but he may err in concluding that for Rahner this means that biological death is in some way a 'good' (Kelsey 1997: 348). Rahner describes death as an event universal to all human beings. As an empirical observation, the statement that death is universal does not tell us why human beings die, or what the essence of death is. As an affirmation of faith, the universality of death is not ultimately a matter of biological necessity, but the divine–human relationship (Rahner 1961: 14). Whatever death's natural causes may be, they can be traced to 'the moral catastrophe of mankind in its first parents' (Rahner 1961: 15).

Christian faith also affirms that death is the separation of body and soul. Rahner considers two features of this separation. First, in death, the soul assumes 'a new and different relation to what we usually call the body' (1961: 17). According to Rahner, 'this separation results in a new relation between the soul and the material universe, of which the body is a part' (1961: 18). The soul becomes 'pancosmic' in death; 'surrendering its limited bodily structure', it becomes 'a co-determining factor of the universe precisely in the latter's character as the ground of the personal life of other spiritual corporeal beings' (Rahner 1961: 22).

Second, Rahner considers the separation of body and soul as the process of bodily dissolution. According to Rahner, the person has a transcendental orientation toward grace and 'the supernatural goal of sharing in the life of God' (1961: 37). Moreover, 'this orientation gives him a dynamic tendency towards a fulfilment of the whole man through a transfiguring change in which the bodily constitution remains intact' (Rahner 1961: 38). Death as a natural *process*—the phenomenon of bodily dissolution—contradicts this ontological feature of human existence. It is unnatural to us.

Although death is a natural process, it is not merely that. Death has a natural *essence*, which consists of more than the natural process of bodily dissolution. Rahner gives two reasons for this assertion. First, the natural process of death was set in motion by Adam. Second, because each individual dies a death which is either the consequence and culmination of sin or a dying with Christ, and since death cannot be both simultaneously, there must be a natural essence to death in virtue of which it may be either damnation or salvation. Although death's natural *process* is unnatural to us as psychosomatic creatures meant for embodied communion with God and others, death's natural *essence* is a consequence of our body–soul unity:

In death the soul achieves the consummation of its own personal self-affirmation, not merely by passively suffering something which supervenes biologically, but through its own personal act. Death, therefore, as the end of man as a spiritual person, must be an active consummation from within brought about by the person himself, a maturing self-realization which embodies the result of what man has made of himself during life. . . . At the same time, death as the end of the biological life is simultaneously and in a way which affects the whole man, an irruption from without, a destruction . . . so that man's own death, from within, through the act of the person, is at the same time an event of the most radical spoliation of man, activity and passivity at once. (Rahner 1961: 30–1)

Death's natural essence is its 'obscure, hidden' character, death's irreducible unity as activity and passivity, fulfilment and end, self-completion and destruction. It is a consequence of our body–soul unity because the person as a free, conscious spirit consummates his life—himself—in the act of death, which is simultaneously an event that he suffers, passively, the end and dissolution of his bodily life. According to Rahner, Adam in his original integrity would have died a death without dying, 'attaining a perfection of an embodied kind yet open to the world in its totality' (1961: 34). His death 'would not have been hidden in darkness' (Rahner 1961: 42). It is precisely because death is an event of personal consummation, whereby the soul becomes pancosmic, that the natural essence of death is not itself sin, but a consequence of the person's body–soul unity in time, wherein our bodily constitution has been changed by sin and by Christ's redeeming death. So, death as consummation is natural to us. Death as the phenomenon of bodily dissolution is not natural to us. The obscurity of death itself permits each individual death to be an event of salvation or damnation, depending on how the individual person 'sustains this feature of his nature', by surrendering himself in the darkness of death to God's judgement, or by autonomously refusing to so give himself (Rahner 1961: 36).

Ramsey, Kass, and Rahner agree that death is natural to human beings, in that it is biologically necessary. Kass takes this first sense of 'natural' to imply a second, that death is 'proper' to human beings. Ramsey rejects this; death is an enemy, a personal indignity. Rahner provides a third alternative. By positing a natural essence of death, Rahner may honour our embodied individuality in and for the world, as creatures made for communion with God. The obscurity of death as activity and passivity takes seriously our human psychosomatic constitution, meant for communion with God of an embodied kind open to the world. Sin penetrates our bodily constitution, such that the person's self-consummation—his death as a personal act—occurs post-lapsarianly under the violence of bodily dissolution, even as his death pancosmically finalizes who he is in relation to the world. As we will see, Rahner's insistence on the natural essence of death permits him to connect more closely than Ramsey the Christian's dying and rising in Christ and his physical death. Yet Ramsey's argument points to a theological ethical problem in Rahner's: inasmuch as Rahner construes our appropriation of Christ's death as our own act, and as a process culminating in our physical death, he may compromise the sovereignty and independent efficacy of grace.

DEATH AS AN END

Human death has a personal dimension, as the end of our earthly life. At the end of biological human life the *person* comes to an end. In keeping with their respective understandings of death as (un)natural, Ramsey and Rahner consider the person's appropriation of death, taking up one's death as one's own. For both, a rightful appropriation of death involves facing death's indignity (Ramsey) or obscurity (Rahner) and apprehending from such a point the unique value of individual human life.

For Ramsey, death is an indignity, because it assaults the unique worth of a person, whose individual life span has irreducible value. For such creatures, 'death means *finis*, not itself *telos*. Certainly not a telos to be engineered, or to be accomplished by reducing both human life and death to the level of natural events' (Ramsey 1998: 214). Rather than 'thing-ify' death, we do better to recognize death as a temporal limit we live toward and up against. Death 'bears on us while still alive' (Ramsey 1998: 212) as a limit 'to an individual's inward desire, effort and hope' (Ramsey 1998: 211).

According to Ramsey, 'if the "bodily life" is neither an ornament nor a drag but a part of man's very nature; and if the "personal life" of an individual in his unique life-span is accorded unrepeatable, noninterchangeable value—then it is that Death the Enemy again comes into view' (Ramsey 1998: 221). Christian humanism rightly perceives death as an enemy. Whereas 'Hebrew consciousness' understood the basic human problem as sin, and 'Greek consciousness' understood it as death,

Christianity brought a new awareness of personal existence into the Western world, that the sting of death is sin. The fusion of sin and death yields insight into the human condition—the person dies and knows that he will die, and death is thus a 'threatening limit that begets evil'. Just as Reinhold Niebuhr recognized that anxiety over death is the source of human destructiveness and creativity, Ramsey too argues that 'without death, and death perceived as a threat, we would . . . have no reason to "number our days" so as to ransom the time allotted us, to receive life as a precious gift' (Ramsey 1998: 218; Niebuhr 1964). Awareness of one's death may prompt one person to eat, drink, and be merry, and another to seek wisdom, but 'both are lifespans enhanced in importance and in individuation under the stimulus of the perceived evil of death'. So 'death may be a good evil or an evil evil, but it is perceived as an evil or experienced indignity in either case' (Ramsey 1998: 218).

The contemporary preference for a sudden death exemplifies how modern ideologies of death permit fear of death to undermine our acknowledgement of the individual's dignity (cf. Ariès 1974). This preference crystallizes the above ideological objectifications of death, since it equates death with dignity—or at least without indignity—with an '*unknowing* death' (Ramsey 1998: 215). It expresses our wish to evade the responsibilities associated with facing our own dying and death, for ourselves and others. By contrast, Ramsey notes that the Anglican prayer book includes a petition for deliverance from sudden death. 'Such a petition bespeaks an age in which dying with dignity was a gift and a task . . . a liberty to encompass dying as a final act among the actions of life, to enfold awareness of one's self dying as the finale of the self's relations in this life to God or to fellowman—in any case to everything that was worthy' (Ramsey 1998: 215). For Ramsey the person appropriates death as the end of one's own and only life of relationships and value by responsibly assuming death's indignity in reverence, gratitude, and love to God and others.

By insisting that death in itself is an indignity, Ramsey, Kass argues, fails to give nature her due. Recall Kass's argument that death is part of the created order, and his charge that Ramsey speaks as if the proper human condition is immortality, lost in the Fall for a 'merely mortal, merely natural condition' (1987: 207). Ramsey's appeal to the Christian connection between sin and death implies, for Kass, that the proper human end is immortality, which, by comparison, denigrates mortal, *bodily* life. Kass also criticizes Ramsey's argument for the worth of *individual* human life. Inasmuch as Ramsey ties the person's worldly dignity to his awareness of the evil of death, death paradoxically becomes 'the "great individualizer," and hence . . . the source of all worldly dignity' (Kass 1987: 211 n. 6). Kass insists that death is neutral with respect to dignity. Dignity is displayed in the character of the one who dies. Mortality is the 'necessary condition for the display of at least *some* aspects of a human being's dignity' (Kass 1987: 201). Death is part of the good of life, and, moreover, death 'becomes good because of generation, continuity and renewal' (Kass 1987: 209).

Kass and Ramsey agree that human dignity is not found in dying, but must be brought to dying (O'Donovan 1998: 224). For Kass, death's *neutrality* is the condition for the display of human dignity, contingently actualized in the life one lives and by accepting death's inevitability, which appears as good in view of generational succession. For Ramsey, death's *indignity* occasions the appearance of human dignity. But Ramsey's appeal to *awareness* of death's indignity as the source of human dignity points to a *generic* feature of humanity that does not in itself secure the value of individual life, and, paradoxically, makes death the source of worldly dignity. Thus Ramsey's appeal to psychosomatic unity seems insufficient to affirm the value of human life as bodily and individual.

Oliver O'Donovan suggests that Ramsey is vulnerable to Kass's criticisms because Ramsey isolates the principle of body–soul unity from 'its context in the Christian gospel' and specifically from consideration of the Resurrection (1998: 228). Ramsey errs by beginning his account of Christian humanism with the connection between sin and death, because this connection is secondary to

the way death is understood in the light of the vindication of life. To see death as the emblem of divine judgment requires that we have first seen life as an emblem of divine acquittal. Because God has said his final 'Yes' to the world, we may understand the mysterious and world-denying absurdity of death as God's penultimate 'No', the No which supports the Yes by refusing all forms of uncreation and destruction in the human will. The assertion that Christ's *death* is redemption comes second . . . to the assertion that his *resurrection* is redemptive. (O'Donovan 1998: 233)

Death is not the source of human dignity or the *telos* of human life. God vindicates life in the Resurrection, grounding the worth of bodily human life. Although Ramsey's affirmation of the individual's irreplaceable value stands 'somewhat apart' (O'Donovan 1998: 233) from this claim, the Resurrection contextualizes Ramsey's link between psychosomatic unity and the individual's value by virtue of its 'eschatological affirmation that each person is to be recalled to an irreplaceable presence before the judgment seat of God'. Moreover, the Resurrection grounds the individual's unique value, 'not by backing the claim of the individual against the community but by doing away with the notion of replacement as applied to any part of the human community' (O'Donovan 1998: 235). As we will see, Ramsey's sermon *Death's Duell* more successfully argues for the worth of individual bodily life, and the Christian address to our existential fear of death as it obstructs proper love for life. However, Ramsey's argument there compromises his insistence that death itself is an indignity.

For his part, Rahner explicitly construes death's personal dimension as the end of the person's earthly pilgrimage. Human death must include this personal dimension, because the person is a body–soul unity (1961: 13). 'The fundamental moral decision made by man in the mundane temporality of his bodily existence . . . is rendered definite and final by death. This doctrine of the faith involves taking this earthly life with radical seriousness. It is truly historical, that is, unique, unrepeatable, of inalienable and irrevocable significance' (Rahner 1961: 27). Rahner locates the individual's unique value in the fact that the person is a history; moreover, he does so from an eschatological perspective. The individual and the created world (of which he is a part and which is part of him) move toward a definite end, the transformation of all creation before God (Rahner 1961: 28). Death is a 'personal self-fulfillment', not only a biological event passively undergone, but 'an act that a man interiorly performs. Moreover, rightly understood, it must be death itself which is the act, and not simply an attitude the human being adopts towards death but which remains extrinsic to it' (Rahner 1961: 30). The person's free self-determination is an 'intrinsic, essential constitutent of death' (Rahner 1961: 29) that occurs in dialectical unity with death's natural process of bodily dissolution and will 'again find expression in concrete bodily form in the resurrection of the body' (Rahner 1961: 33). Importantly, the person's appropriation of his death must include and culminate in his physical death. Physical death finalizes his decision for or against God not simply because it ends the earthly life during and with which he makes that decision, but because his death itself is either a participation in Christ's death or not.

Human death's natural essence, its obscurity, permits each individual death to be either salvation or damnation; *which* it is depends on how the individual 'sustains this feature of his nature'. *Every* 'man is enacting his death, as his own consummation, through the deed of his life, and in this way death is present... in each of his free acts, in which he freely disposes of his whole person' (Rahner 1961: 44). An *individual* rightly faces death only 'when [death] is entered upon by man as an act in which he surrenders himself fully and with unconditional openness to the disposal of the incomprehensible decision of God, because, in the darkness of death, man is not in a position to dispose of himself unambiguously' (Rahner 1961: 44). The person's rightful appropriation of his own death consists in a free and full surrender of himself to God's judgement, in an appropriation of Christ's death which makes his death a dying with Christ.

Our appropriation of Christ's death is possible by virtue of the similarity and difference between Christ's death and ours. In the Incarnation Christ entered into 'human life in a situation in which that life reaches its fulfillment only by passing through death in all its obscurity' (Rahner 1961: 61). Christ dies our death, the death of fallen human beings; the similarity between Christ's death and ours is the dialectical unity of death's natural essence. The difference between his death and ours consists in the grace and absolute liberty with which he lived and died. 'It is precisely in its darkness that the death of Christ becomes the expression and embodiment of his loving obedience, the free transference of his entire created existence to God. What was the manifestation of sin, thus becomes, without its darkness being lifted, the contradiction of sin, the manifestation of a "yes" to the will of the Father' (Rahner 1961: 62). Christ's death is 'axiologically present in his entire life', and since the person's free self-determination becomes final only in death, only Christ's death (versus some other moral act) could redeem us. 'By that death his human reality and grace, definitively ratified by the real concrete human freedom of his death, became a determining feature of the whole cosmos' (Rahner 1961: 66). Christ dies a human death, in a way in which no other human can. Christ's *death* redeems us, because his free and total self-disposal in the obscurity of death changes death from sin to life. Christ's death changes the ontological possibilities for ours. Thus, Rahner may adopt what George Hunsinger designates as a 'middle soteriology'.

We are saved by the effect *in us* for which the work apart from us functions as little more than the precondition for its possibility.... What took place spiritually in Christ is what now takes place spiritually in us, i.e., the same *sort* of thing is to be repeated, regardless of all difference in degree. Although the Savior is the source of our salvation...the difference between the Savior and the saved would seem to be both relative and provisional. (Hunsinger 2000: 265–6)

Both Rahner and Ramsey recognize that only God can solve the problem of sin and death, yet O'Donovan's appreciative criticism of Ramsey points to a difference between Ramsey and Rahner. Rahner construes salvation in terms of the person's actualization—in physical death—of the possibilities that Christ's death effects, such that grace empowers the person to surrender himself in the darkness of death as a wager of faith, hope, and love, which transform the reality of his death. Ramsey construes salvation in terms of the person's present relationship to God in Christ, which frees him from fear of death and for responsible love for others.

Death as a Wager of Love

Why describe death's moral dimension as a wager of love? The person, as a body–soul unity, cannot and ought not to endeavour to die as a thing. Thus, human death's natural dimension as the separation of body and soul points to its personal dimension, the end of earthly life. As Ramsey and Rahner grasp, the person is a centre of self-consciousness and freedom, and as such must (implicitly or explicitly) confront his death. This confrontation of one's own death entails an interpretation of the meaning and value of one's life, and of what and whom is worthy in it. Thus, the person's appropriation of his death is a wager, an act of faith whereby the person entrusts himself to some source of meaning and value. Hence, we may rightly call this devotion of oneself a wager of love.

In 'Indignity' Ramsey draws on the First Epistle of St John: 'perfect love casts out fear', and 'where fear is, love is not perfected'. These verses offer a standard for 'unflinching care of a dying fellow man, or short of that of any fellow mortal any time', a standard cut to the perfect benevolence of God. They refer human love and care in faith to an 'ultimate righteousness beyond the perceptible human condition' (Ramsey 1998: 217). 'Indignity' suggests that 'behind the perception that death brings lovelessness after it, there lies the proclamation that by faith in divine love we may overcome the lovelessness that death brings' (O'Donovan 1998: 226–7). So Ramsey argues: 'perfect care of the dying casts out fear of one's own death or rejection of [another's] dying because of fear of ours. . . . Where fear of death and dying remains, medical and human care of the dying is not perfected' (1998: 217). Fear of death is fear of the 'properly dreadful' (Ramsey 1998: 219), and Ramsey argues that we ought not to repress those feelings of awe and dread (1998: 220). We have already considered Ramsey's discussion of the mistaken ways in which we endeavour to reduce or evade this dread. But if fear of death obstructs perfect care for our neighbours, how might we bear dread of death in morally fitting love and care for others?

Ramsey's sermon *Death's Duell* offers some help by distinguishing two Christian connections between sin and death. First, death begets sin. As Ramsey puts it, 'From the power of death in us flows bitterness of spirit and alienation from God and man and from the common life. . . . [Death] induces permanent anxiety at the roots of personal existence, which we can scarcely share or acknowledge, and which turns every man a stranger to his neighbor' (1961: 4). As we saw above, 'Indignity' emphasizes this connection between sin and death, that *death* draws *sin* after it; but *Death's Duell* notes and favours a second connection: namely, that *sin* draws *death* after it. According to Ramsey, the biblical account of the Fall locates sin in a 'wrong-headed and wrong-hearted' desire for life (1961: 6). More basic than anxiety over non-being is the desire for true life, and in particular the human's desire to be oneself the giver of true life. Our attempt to live by our own powers causes us to 'blunder into death' (Ramsey 1961: 6). 'Death is our last enemy, not the first' (Ramsey 1961: 5).

By placing sin before death, biblical tradition radically redefines life and death, relocating 'where true life and real death are to be found' (Ramsey 1961: 5). True death results from the vain attempt to live by our own powers, to live according to the flesh. The Christian gospel proclaims our redemption from both sin and death. 'Jesus the Christ is the Act of God with which no man cooperates to bring it to pass. Living out of faith in Him requires a decisive giving up of all attempts to live according to our fleshly powers, and hereby we all are made alive. Dying to the world, we are raised with Christ. Receiving life from him, we cease trying to give ourselves life' (Ramsey 1961: 6). The biblical redefinition of life and death crucially concerns the person's present relationship to God in Christ. 'Those who in this life already *have* eternal life have it because, whether we live or whether we die, we are the Lord's' (Ramsey 1961: 7). Since the primary human problem is that of wrong love, and 'precisely because life is so great a good we need daily to appropriate our redemption in order to love life properly' (Ramsey 1961: 5). Love that flows from faith permits 'respect for the shadow of death upon the face of another' (Ramsey 1961: 5).

Recall that, for Kass, Ramsey's argument in 'Indignity' implies a proper human condition of immortality, and thus may, by comparison, denigrate bodily, mortal life. Moreover, Ramsey's appeal to human awareness of death's indignity concerns a generic human capacity, and makes death the source of individual human worth. Kass regards individual, bodily human worth in terms of the individual's actualization of dignity, and in view of generational succession. In contrast to individual achievements or species membership, Kass argues, 'notice where dignity lies on Ramsey's view of nature and man. Man, the mortal sinner, has *only* an alien dignity bestowed upon him by God' (1987: 207, my emphasis).

Does *Death's Duell* affirm the value of individual bodily life? On the one hand, Ramsey argues that the new creation which Christ makes of those who believe in him 'restores to us that old creation under which man lived before ever he sought to become himself the giver and sustainer of his life' (1961: 6). On the other hand, he insists that eternal life is not immortality, not a quality of human spirit or a human potentiality. 'Eternal life belongs to Christ and to us only derivatively as we belong to Him' (Ramsey 1961: 7). These claims are compatible, because the restoration of creation which grace effects is restoration to God's life-giving Spirit, not the renewal of some native human capacity. This point challenges both Kass's account of human dignity and Rahner's account of death. The dignity that God confers on the person may appear to be 'only' an alien dignity in contrast to Kass's emphasis on actualizing one's dignity through one's choices and actions. But if, as Kass puts it, 'the secret is to transcend one's selfish attachments' (1987: 209), in order to understand how death might become good, then these attachments arguably include one's own achievements as well as one's progeny. Ramsey understands better that only trust in, and devotion to, God's love for creation in its unity and particularity frees the person *from* the futile attempt to secure his life and worth for himself, and thereby frees him *for* genuine love of neighbour. Moreover, Jesus Christ's death and resurrection accomplish our salvation *extra nos*, not by way of our interior self-disposal in free surrender to God. Ramsey thus emphasizes the sovereignty and independent efficacy of grace more clearly than Rahner's argument may allow.

We saw above that Rahner understands Christian death in terms of the person's total surrender to God's incomprehensible decision regarding him. The person enacts this surrender or its opposite, a self-withholding refusal, through his life. Importantly, Rahner cautions against dissolving our earthly dying with Christ 'into an idealistic ethical conception' that loses contact with physical death. Physical death in the state of grace is a saving *event*, the 'culmination of both the reception and the effecting of salvation' (1961: 69), because it is also the person's *act*, which gathers together and finalizes the wager he makes in and with his life in a total self-disposal to God's judgement. Death, says Rahner, always includes the character of divine judgement (1961: 55). Death is judgement, because, post Adam, it is the consequence, manifestation, and punishment for sin; it is 'remoteness from God' (Rahner 1961: 70), 'guilt made visible' (Rahner 1961: 49). Because of sin a person can come to his proper end—communion with God of an embodied kind open to the world—only by passing through the obscurity or darkness of death, its unity as active self-consummation and passive subjection to the violence of bodily dissolution. Christ's death changes the reality of human death into the 'advent of God in the midst of that empty loneliness' (Rahner 1961: 70). Through Christ's grace the Christian dies a different death from the sinner; he dies in Christ, not only because he has lived in Christ, but because his death is itself a participation in Christ's death (Rahner 1961: 69). In Christian death, faith, hope, and love transform death, but not as extrinsic attitudes accompanying it. Rather, precisely because they enter the darkness of death, its character as remoteness from God, they constitute the reality of the Christian's death as 'the highest act of believing, hoping, loving' (Rahner 1961: 71). In the obscurity of death, 'we are to hear the good news of death, which is life, and of the coming of the Lord who is that life which knows no death, although it comes to us in death' (Rahner 1961: 80).

Hunsinger's 'middle soteriology' indicates the theological stakes of Rahner's argument. 'Salvation essentially encounters us as a *possibility* that is not actual for us *until* it is somehow actualized in our spiritual and social existence, and the *process* of actualization proceeds by degrees. Though primarily a divine gift, salvation is always *also* a human task' (Hunsinger 2000: 266). In *Death's Duell* Ramsey implies a higher soteriology, in which 'salvation encounters us as *a finished and perfect work* so that... neither its *actuality* nor its *efficacy* depends on our acceptance of it,... our accepting it depends rather on its *prior* actuality and efficacy *precisely* for us, and indeed for the whole world' (Hunsinger 2000: 267). Rahner has no quarrel with Ramsey's claim that eternal life belongs to us only derivatively as we belong to Christ. The difficulty is that for Rahner salvation seems to be a process worked out in human life, the full efficacy of which waits on our actualization of it in physical death.

Yet Rahner's resolute link between biological death and dying in Christ highlights a difficulty in Ramsey's approach. *Death's Duell* addresses the central concern of 'Indignity', concerning fear of death and care of the dying (and for neighbours generally). But it compromises Ramsey's insistence that physical death is itself an indignity. The Christian redefinition of life and death may imply that biological death no longer matters, such that Christian life becomes one more ideology for denying our dread of death. To be fair, in 'Indignity' Ramsey says that death may be a conquered enemy, but in the natural order it is an enemy still. Hence, we need daily to appropriate our redemption. But Ramsey explicates this in *Death's Duell* in a way that distances the person's dying in Christ from physical death itself. This risks what Rahner cautions against, making dying with Christ an 'idealistic ethical conception'.

The task is to maintain the decisive and perfect accomplishment of our salvation in Jesus Christ, but identify better the place of our biological death in it. God's life-giving grace reaches into the event of death, the wage of sin. We are saved not only from fear of death, but death, the bodily and spiritual consequence, manifestation, and punishment for our wilful alienation from God and others. As Ramsey grasps, fear of death prompts us to love the wrong things or love things in the wrong way. Death begets sin. Yet death is also already the embodied expression of human sinfulness, our alienation from God, the giver of life and ground of meaning and value. Death is an enemy *because* death is enmity. As Rahner's account of Christian death suggests, faith in divine love not only overcomes 'the lovelessness that death brings' (O'Donovan 1998: 226–7), it overcomes the lovelessness that *brings death.*

Hence, an adequate Christian account of death must proclaim that Christ's death and resurrection change death itself. For those who participate in Christ's death through their own, what is the real manifestation of sin becomes life. We can say with Rahner that the Christian's physical death is a culmination of his dying and rising in Christ, not because the efficacy of Christ's death awaits our enactment of it, but because its efficacy (apart from and for us) transforms our bodily constitution. The grace of Christ's death redeems us not *in spite* of our death but *in* it. Thus we may also say with Ramsey that eternal life is ours only derivatively, as we belong to Christ. We do not co-operate with salvation; rather, Christ's grace enfolds us in judgement and mercy as the particular individuals we are. In this dark intimacy the 'act' of death we 'perform' is a purely responsive wager that God's 'no' to who we are in our sinful alienation is already God's redeeming love, a divine self-gift that gives us to ourselves and the world.

CHRISTIAN CARE OF THE DYING

Faith that God changes death rightly makes death's indignity more acute, since God's decisive vindication of life displays the full scope and efficacy of God's rejection of human sinfulness. Thus, Rahner's theology of death affords a negative contribution to Ramsey's argument against 'death with dignity' ideologies: Christian faith ought not to supply another self-distancing objectification of death. Since grace transforms human biological death from enmity to love, Christian care of the dying crucially involves discerning this good word through concrete practices of keeping company with the dying.

Two relevant and interrelated guidelines for such care, which we can only sketch here, are reverence for human bodies and respect for personal histories (cf. Smith 1986). Reverence for human bodies entails responsible use of medical resources to resist and cure threats to bodily flourishing and prohibits direct, intentional killing.

It also limits our medical care; when cure-oriented treatment proves burdensome and merely prolongs dying, we rightly eschew it in favour of palliative care. Reverence for human bodies enjoins Christian care-givers to provide ordinary forms of care—for example, feeding versus artificial nutrition and hydration (ANH). In cases where direct feeding is impossible or burdensome to the dying, reverence for human bodies warrants a presumption in favour of ANH. Ordinary care for human bodies not only meets the patient's physiological needs, it provides human contact and includes the dying person in powerful forms of human community. When offered with patience and generosity, such bodily care may counter medical objectification of the dying person's body. It creates a space where we may, with the dying person, grapple with the loss and deterioration of bodily functions, countering our and their possible alienation from their bodies with a loving hospitality. Respect for the personal histories of the dying is not reducible to respect for their autonomy. It includes regard for relevant wishes the dying person may have expressed concerning end-of-life care, but resists taking cover in the provisions of advance directives that may not accord with his best interests (Meilaender 1991). Respect for personal histories enjoins medical professionals, family, and friends to provide information and opportunity for the dying to prepare for death. This means enabling the dying person to remain as conscious as is compatible with managing their pain, prudent involvement in decision making, and providing material and spiritual support for them, their care-givers, and mourners.

In short, in their reverence for dying human bodies Christian care-givers keep company with the dying, a company that witnesses to the divine transformation of bodily destruction by a love that overcomes alienation. Likewise, respect for the personal histories of the dying involves material forms of honouring the dying person's unique worth in community. Christian care for the dying must be patient of diverse attitudes toward death that the dying person may have, avoiding platitudes that, if well-intentioned, nevertheless presumptuously seek to dispel the darkness of death. Christian care-givers ought to enable the dying person to confront his death by accompanying him into that darkness as they can, through concrete forms of care alert to and trusting in the perfect efficacy of Christ's grace, divine love's thoroughgoing transformation of our spiritual and bodily life.

REFERENCES AND SUGGESTED READING

ALISON, J. (1998). *The Joy of Being Wrong: Original Sin through Easter Eyes.* New York: Crossroad.

ARIÈS, P. (1974). *Western Attitudes toward Death from the Middle Ages to the Present,* trans. Patricia M. Ranum. Baltimore: The Johns Hopkins University Press.

AUGUSTINE (1984). *City of God.* New York: Penguin.

BALTHASAR, H. URS VON (1990). *Mysterium Paschale*, trans. A. Nichols Edinburgh: T. & T. Clark.

—— (1994). *The Moment of Christian Witness*, trans. R. Beckley. San Francisco: Ignatius Press.

FAGAN, A. (ed.) (2004). *Making Sense of Dying and Death*. Amsterdam and New York: Rodopi.

GUROIAN, V. (1996). *Life's Living Toward Dying*. Grand Rapids, Mich.: Eerdmans.

HUNSINGER, G. (2000). *Disruptive Grace: Studies in the Theology of Karl Barth*. Grand Rapids, Mich.: William B. Eerdmans.

KASS, L. R. (1987). 'Averting One's Eyes or Facing the Music?—On Dignity and Death', in S. E. Lammers and A. Verhey (eds.), *On Moral Medicine: Theological Perspectives in Medical Ethics*, 1st edn., Grand Rapids, Mich.: William B. Eerdmans, 200–11. Originally published in *Hastings Center Studies*, 2 (May 1974), 67–80.

KELSEY, D. H. (1997). 'Two Theologies of Death: Anthropological Gleanings', *Modern Theology*, 13/3, 347–70.

McCORMICK, R. A. (1984). *Health and Medicine in the Catholic Tradition*. New York: Crossroad.

MEILAENDER, G. (1991). 'I Want to Burden my Loved Ones', *First Things*, 16 (Oct. 1), 12–14.

NEUHAUS, R. J. (2000). *The Eternal Pity*. Notre Dame, Ind.: University of Notre Dame Press.

NIEBUHR, R. (1964). *The Nature and Destiny of Man*, I. New York: Charles Scribner's Sons.

O'DONOVAN, O. (1998). 'Keeping Body and Soul Together', in S. E. Lammers and A. Verhey (eds.), *On Moral Medicine: Theological Perspectives in Medical Ethics*, 2nd edn., Grand Rapids, Mich.: William B. Eerdmans, 223–38. Originally published as 'Ne pas séparer l'âme du corps', trans. M.-B. Mesnet, *Ethique*, 11 (1994), 64–89.

RAHNER, K. (1961). *On the Theology of Death*. New York: Herder & Herder.

—— (1982). *Foundations of Christian Faith*. New York: Crossroad.

RAMSEY, P. (1961). *Death's Duell*. University Park, Pa.: Pennsylvania State University Press.

—— (1978). *Ethics at the Edges of Life*. New Haven: Yale University Press.

—— (1998). 'The Indignity of "Death with Dignity"', in S. E. Lammers and A. Verhey (eds.), *On Moral Medicine: Theological Perspectives in Medical Ethics*, 2nd edn., Grand Rapids, Mich.: William B. Eerdmans, 209–22. Originally published in *Hastings Center Studies*, 2 (May 1974), 47–62.

SMITH, D. H. (1986). *Health and Medicine in the Anglican Tradition*. New York: Crossroad.

TOLSTOY, L. (1981). *The Death of Ivan Ilych*. New York: Bantam.

WOLTERSTORFF, N. (1987). *Lament for a Son*. Grand Rapids, Mich.: Eerdmans.

PART IV

THE SPIRIT OF THE CHRISTIAN LIFE

CHAPTER 16

....

FAITH

....

GENE OUTKA

'IT is God himself who called you to share in the life of his son Jesus Christ our
Lord; and God keeps faith.' 'As God in his wisdom ordained, the world failed to
find him by its wisdom, and he chose by the folly of the gospel to save those who
have faith' (1 Cor. 1: 9, 21, REB). These two passages indicate that the term 'faith'
(*pistis* in the New Testament) can refer both to God's action and to ours. Yet the
two sorts of action present features that we can neither blend wholly together nor
separate entirely. Differences obviously obtain. God calls us to share in the life of
God's Son with a fidelity on which we may utterly rely; we do not call God to any
such thing, nor do we prove to be, *de facto*, similarly reliable. God ordains in a
wisdom that confutes ours. God chooses to save, and our faith is in God's action,
not in our own. Still, points of correspondence obtain as well. Although no one of
us is so steadfast, trustworthy, truthful, reliable, or sure as God, we are called to
share in the life thus patterned. At a minimum, our faithfulness to God and our
neighbours corresponds to this pattern, on our own level, with our own capacities.

Saying even this much throws open a range of questions that enquiries in
theological ethics keep central. In the case of 'faith' under the rubric of 'The Spirit
of the Christian Life', how specifically do features of God's keeping faith and
features of our keeping faith differ and correspond? That is, how do we get their
interplay right? These are our ordering questions here. Let us accept that the
magnitude of this subject can dizzy us, and the fragmentariness of our replies
can chasten us. Yet, given that the term 'faith' has a family of uses in the Bible and
tradition (Jones 2002: 519–30), such questions, for all of their vastness, shape one
type of enquiry. And we may set limits. One is to focus on faithfulness as *human*

intentional activity. This fits an enquiry in theological ethics, although we must refer sufficiently to God's faithfulness to allow our particular enquiry to go forward. Another limit is to bypass accounts of faith as a general human phenomenon, a mode-of-being-in-the-world, while acknowledging that these accounts can be deep. Kant's account is a case in point: if our *moral faith* is *truly* serious, we *must* postulate God, freedom, and immortality. Other accounts may instruct us about conditions for human authenticity, and in some cases about basic attitudes that go from faith in idols or implicit faith to conscious faith in God (Niebuhr 1960: 114–26). In short, we start now with faith in God's action, without exploring paths that persons do or should take to arrive there.

Let us conduct our enquiry under four claims that assume and in various ways lead us to specify differences and points of correspondence.

FAITH IS BASED ON GOD'S ACTIONS
AD EXTRA

This first claim identifies the object of faith, and offers a realist interpretation of God's relation to the world. As the object of faith, God is external to us. While 'external' signifies irreducible otherness, it does not signify non-involvement or imperviousness. We depend on God's transcendence *and* immanence, and distinguish these from 'four quasi-theistic faiths, polytheism, pantheism, deism, and emanationism' (Fern 2002: 110–16). Faith in God is construed on traditional Christian reckonings within the second half of a distinction which theologians draw between the Godhead in itself (the immanent Trinity) and God's actions *ad extra* (the economic Trinity, which is first in the order of knowledge). We specify thematically the shape of God's self-disclosure and governance in our existential and historical reality, and thereby attend to creation, the history of Israel, and the coming of Jesus, the contest with sin and moral evil, our life in the Church and in the world, between the times, before the last things. There are convictions that identify this shape, constituting an inclusive framework that is, straightforwardly, the structure of credal belief. This structure is composed of a narrative, the basic elements of which are found in the Bible, and also in Christian creeds, forms of worship, preaching, and teaching. In the course of time, theologians attached technical names to the basic units of this narrative, which constitute an outline of Christian belief. A common scheme is creation, fall, the covenant with Israel, incarnation, the Church, salvation, and last things.

Briefly, *creation* refers to the divine origin and preservation of the world, and whatever order and coherence we find there. *Fall* refers to the onset of sin and evil, and the distortions and derangements they bring into the world. *The covenant with Israel* refers to God's particular relationship to a people God chooses, a people in whom the history of redemption stays rooted, and by whom all of the nations will bless themselves. *Incarnation* refers to the life, death, and resurrection of Christ, and the gift of the Holy Spirit. The *Church* refers to the Christian community in its corporate life and in the lives of persons who identify with it, and in its relationships to surrounding social worlds. *Salvation* refers both to justification, as God's utterly free love that rescues human beings, and the consequent freedom and love they are to show in human interaction; and to sanctification, as God's action in and through the Holy Spirit that works to regenerate and transform human beings, both in the characters they develop and the quality of community they realize. *Last things* refer to the final state of the world when God's purposes are fulfilled, the promise of which warrants a manner of life in the present dominated by hope.

To have faith in the God who undertakes such *ad extra* actions includes ascribing a certain status to the basic units of this narrative. The narrative is judged to be true, to be in need of promulgation, and to be comprehensive. We start with claims embedded in the credal structure, and sources of our knowledge of them, which offer a view of the human condition. The structure summarizes a way of seeing the world, the panorama of human history and the meaning of creaturely life in the present, that purports to be true. No part of the structure is thought to stand outside a biblical world, though the credal elements are theologically conceived. The Bible and the tradition thus remain indispensable for the comprehensive convictions that the creed registers. Without these sources, the convictions lack determinateness. Of course we know vast numbers of things from other sources. But we do not thereby cease to need to return to these particularist points of departure. Moreover, *ad extra* actions tell us things that we cannot simply tell ourselves, and the narrative about them has to be promulgated. It is thought to be available by virtue of God's gracious unilateral initiatives resident for Christians in Word and Spirit that we may not sunder and that we need to hear and receive. Finally, all of the convictions serve as necessary points of reference. It is a mistake to seize upon one and pay it exclusive heed. Taken together they furnish parameters that test the adequacy of more detailed proposals put forward.

Although this structure is not something we should attempt to get behind, we should also beware of getting things too pat. Those whose faith is based on God's *ad extra* actions are called upon to interpret each of the convictions so far noted and to estimate how the convictions relate to each other. Each of the credal elements affords interpretive leeway, and an interpretation of one element may have implications elsewhere. Disputes arise when certain credal convictions, though they do not logically entail each other, none the less cohere as a determinate constellation. Some constellations fail to harmonize sufficiently with others to foreclose debate. In addition to intramural disputes, extramural disagreements arise that reflect more radical departures that jettison certain credal elements, or at least alter them so thoroughly that they are more discontinuous than continuous with anything recognizably traditional. Assumptions about inherited sin, for example, under interpretations of the Fall, are sometimes rejected *tout court*, on extramural scientific and/or moral grounds. Even here, however, we may assess more clearly questions posed from outside the credal structure when we expressly identify what is being criticized and in some instances left behind. In any event, those who retain faith in the comprehensive structure delineating God's *ad extra* actions face an intramural amalgam of more specific possibilities to sift and weigh.

Consider one example of a determinate constellation that moves between and relates creation, fall, incarnation, and church in a characteristic way. It addresses matters that those in theological ethics are bound to weigh, as they think within the structure, draw on its elements, and focus on cumulative implications for our life in the Church and world, between the times.

Moral pessimism is associated with the Fall; yet the latter remains parasitic on a good creation. One indication is that appeals to justice retain their intelligibility. They lead us to lament what we actually find on the basis of considerations some of which make at least partial sense to an open-ended audience. Augustine under-scores what we know even now about theft.

Theft receives certain punishment by your law (Exod. 20: 15), Lord, and by the law written in the hearts of men (Rom. 2: 14) which not even iniquity itself destroys. For what thief can with equanimity endure being robbed by another thief? He cannot tolerate it even if he is rich and the other is destitute. I wanted to carry out an act of theft and did so, driven by no kind of need other than my inner lack of, or feeling for, justice. Wickedness filled me. (Augustine 1998: 28–9)

We can discern that theft is forbidden and liable to censure. We can also discern hypocrisy when thieves who rob others without scruple rage against others who rob them. We can recognize that a pattern of inconsistency—we unwillingly suffer what we willingly do—pervades ordinary interactions.

But some of the pessimism goes deeper. The last part of Augustine's own observation takes us further down. Even here he does not break with creation and become an ontological pessimist or a nihilist. Still, he grows more mysterious to himself, and more profoundly disquieted about his impulse to iniquity. These movements arguably ally themselves with a recognition that *bondage* to sin afflicts him, and that without God's *grace* he cannot avoid sinful action, and in any case, he cannot satisfactorily redress by his own efforts the past wrongs he has done. Something further is glimpsed, and casts more light on his impulse. The import of contempt for well-doing is shown in certain paradigmatic events, for Christians, in contemplating the cross. Revealed *there* is the fact that matters are far worse than we imagined. The contempt for well-doing is not simply that, bad as it is.

Something insidious displays itself; our enmity not only takes in others, it reaches God. We meet the possibility of a 'permanent revolt' against God. But we need to be told this in the first instance; our resources for flattering ourselves are sufficiently adept that *we* may perpetually miss it. And we depend on the Church and tradition, here on its communal transmission of convictions that the enmity goes deeper than we know. The theft we can see and censure is now the tip of the iceberg. This standard metaphor instructs us both ways. The initial censuring is not overturned. What we learn from the cross, and must learn, does not transport us elsewhere, perhaps to a place where the opposite might be true, where theft is judged to be a good thing, that we should all now practice. What is below the tip does not break away. Yet the depth of our antagonism we do not see initially. It must be disclosed to us.

This constellation affirms a distinctive interplay. Differences between God and ourselves include God's grace and our reliance on it, and God's disclosure of the depth of our enmity that we cannot know alone. Points of correspondence include our recognition that appeals to justice retain their intelligibility and our discernment of inconsistency and hypocrisy.

In this brief space, we can hardly canvass each unit of the narrative structure, though we assume here that faith appropriates them all, or multiple constellations. We focus on God's creating action, and on the distinction between Creator and creature. Yet, again, we should interpret even this distinction as necessarily in circuit with other credal convictions. We err when we pay it exclusive heed, or accord it a unique epistemic status, or leave it unaffected by the full range of such convictions. We then jeopardize its interpretive reliance on divine self-attestation, including God's actions *ad extra* as first in the order of knowledge, and we rely instead on a dispassionate reading of data that seeks to found an independent case for a creator. Given the circuit among credal convictions, how we focus shows myriad effects from other convictions to which we nevertheless cannot attend now.

FAITH IS BASED ON A DISTINCTION BETWEEN CREATOR AND CREATURE

'*The basic ontological distinction in Christian theology is that between the Creator and the creature: this is radical and incommensurate*' (Jones 2002: 252–3). Our account of differences and points of correspondence should abide by the distinction. When we heed this radical distinction in context, two of the other claims that follow are these.

God as Worthy of Worship

Augustine writes that God is 'utterly good, utterly powerful, most omnipotent, most merciful and most just, deeply hidden yet most intimately present' (Augustine 1998: 4). These attributes have been elucidated and debated through the centuries, and we must content ourselves with saying only this. Predicated of God, 'good' and 'powerful' combine to point to something like utterly *right power*. To ascertain the sense of right power, we associate God's goodness with God's love and God's power with God's freedom. So Barth depicts God as 'the being of... the one who loves in freedom' (Barth 1957: 257). God's love and freedom, always distinct, always connected, to be interpreted together, without one being more basic than the other, constitute the attributes that shape our understanding of all others. And for Christians, the final warrant for concluding that God's relation to the world is that of 'loving dominion' (Morse 1994: 127) is the Christological paradigm. We take the actions of Jesus to be the enacted intentions of God.

Right power, so construed, disallows two moves that gathered strength in the twentieth century. The first *identifies* the power of God with all of the powers we encounter in nature and history. This move brings indiscriminateness: it allows us to deify whatever occurs in the world (Barth 1957: 531, 533). We may include attitudes and actions that we hardly trust or laud, so that lies, flattery, forgetting promises, etc. become possibilities for God, and not only for us. Against this move, God would not be the One who loves in freedom if God could be anything at all, among the powers we know that violate divine love and freedom—e.g., if God could deceive, be hypocritical, or break a covenant divinely established. We retain a place for sin and moral evil and refuse to attribute these to God. They are not ultimately tolerable or necessary parts of what God wills. They do not contribute to the universe's ultimate perfection. Rather, they genuinely conflict with the fulfilment of God's will. God does not transform them into something other than what they are, and we do not escape responsibility for setting them in motion (Outka 2002: 106).

The second move *restricts* the power of God to *persuasive* actions only. This move avoids indiscriminateness. But it narrows God's actions to an extent that collides with too many biblical witnesses. While love's quintessential movements may prove persuasive or at least remain non-coercive, we stipulate unwarrantably when we limit God's dominion to persuasive action, exhaustively and without remainder. We then do justice neither to creation as God's act nor to the awesomeness and holiness of God as worthy of worship (Neville 1993: 140–53). Against this move, we refuse to domesticate God, either between the times or with reference to last things. We do not take sin and moral evil in our present reality as beyond the reach of God's governance. God may intervene at every juncture, and may use our good *and* our evil deeds. We believe (as Abraham Lincoln did) that 'the judgments of the Lord are true and righteous altogether' (Ps. 19: 9, KJV). Although their justice is partly hidden between-the-times, and God's ways exceed human powers fully to calculate, we have faith that God guides and guards all that is good and right. Eschatologically, we believe that God's dominion governed by love will finally triumph over all that opposes it (Morse 1994: 127). Before this triumph, the tenacity of sin prevents the removal of all contradictions in human interaction. Eschatological transformation derives from grace. Nothing in our history demands, and no turn of events in the present assures, such transformation. Thus God's promise regarding the future transcends any solely humanly trans- formed world. To be sure, our wills interject their own freedom into human history. Meaning is granted to present history under providential guidance, and significance to relative good and evil. History is ultimately fulfilled rather than annulled. Still, the modalities of God's action that secure the triumph of God's love are God's to determine, in accordance with right power.

The Goodness of Creation

'The good God made everything good,' Augustine declares (1998: 116). The status of the world as a whole is positive, not negative. It is real, not a fiction. God is the world's-creator, and faith in God is world-affirming. Human creatures are made in the image of God. This means among other things that we are capable of inten- tional activity, moral accountability, and friendship, in relation both to God and to one another. To believe that we resemble God by virtue of these capabilities does not deny the differences so far canvassed, but it prompts us to set our 'being able to carry on intentional activity'—for example, 'our ability to envisage and work toward the achievement of goals...in the context or arena of divine activity' (Plantinga 1999: 17). This vast undertaking yields, *inter alia*, two injunctions that pertain to our faithfulness to what God gives us in creation. The injunctions signal two wide normative boundaries within creation in terms of which we should strive faithfully to make our way.

FAITH DISALLOWS 'TEMPTING GOD'

The first injunction is: we should not 'tempt God', or 'You are not to put the Lord your God to the test' (the latter is Jesus' answer to one of the temptations that the devil presents to him, that Jesus throw himself down from the parapet of the temple in

Jerusalem and trust that the angels will support him in their arms (Matt. 4: 5–7; Luke 4: 9–12, REB)). An extended example helps to clarify this unusual locution. Luther offers a set of judgements during a plague in Wittenberg in 1527 about what Christians should do and forbear. When our stricken neighbour needs us, we should go at once and succor freely. But if we cannot confer actual benefits on another in this way, we should not expose ourselves pointlessly. Sometimes we simultaneously serve our neighbour (we survive to help in the future) and preserve our own body and life by seeking deliberately to avoid contamination. What Luther opposes in particular is the stance of those who disregard all of *our own* attempts to counteract the plague, who light-heartedly disparage the use of medicines, and who demonstrate their own independence from worldly entanglements by entrusting everything to God, immediately, passively. 'This is not trusting God but tempting him. . . . By the same reasoning a person might forego eating and drinking, clothing and shelter, and boldly proclaim his faith that if God wanted to preserve him from starvation and cold, he could do so without food or clothing. Actually that would be suicide' (Luther 1968: 131; Gaebler 2003: 115–23).

We may conclude that *honouring our agential powers* is one ingredient in showing faithfulness to God. God has right power as previously described; it is not all the power there is; God gives us creaturely powers. *That* we exercise the latter, and *how* we exercise them, matter *coram Deo* and *coram hominibus*. So faithfulness to what God gives us in creation implies, as the example from Luther attests, that we should not cast aside ordinary prudence in the expectation of miraculous intervention. This faithfulness also implies that we should not permit the capabilities and possessions given to us to lie fallow (Matt. 25: 14–30; Luke 19: 11–23). More generally, it implies that our human interactions have their own integrity and exigencies. Pervasive interdependence reigns here, yet *how* energetically we act, as well as *what* we do and forbear, may affect our creaturely sphere, for good or ill. Not all historical outcomes are forgone. Drama persists, things could have been otherwise: paths taken and avoided, promises kept, fidelity shown, treachery displayed. (We may say in Jesus' case that he could have sinned but did not, rather than that he could not have sinned: the temptation stories are real, in that he could have succumbed.) And we should not denigrate the stakes for us. How we contribute to actual degrees of relative good and evil counts, as it were non-soteriologically; even dubious virtues can produce better cultures.

This ingredient of faithfulness to God—that we should honour our agential powers—shows that culpability can attach to inaction as well as to action. Yet this is so in three distinguishable ways. We may characterize each as a kind of faithlessness. Thus culpability pertains in each case to the God-relation as well as to human interaction. One kind violates the first injunction directly. The other two kinds have less to do with putting God to the test, yet indicate other ways in which we may fail to honour agential powers.

Neglecting created freedom and expecting miracles   Let us go to this first kind. Here Luther's judgement about tempting God serves as a central illustration. It assumes the possibility of created freedom and its appropriate use among the goods of creation. Faithlessness is interpreted accordingly. Something presumptuous animates us when we refuse to do or to forbear from doing what lies well within our power and expect God *then* to rescue us by miraculous intervention or else. By neglecting operations that our created freedom makes fittingly ours, this refusal fails to keep faith with God's creative action. (We may say this, moreover, without having to deny the possibility of miracles as such, albeit shorn of presumptuous expectation. To consider Jesus' response to the devil in light of Jesus' life, death, and resurrection suggests that to reject putting God to the test is not to reject interventionist accounts of God's activity. We may affirm, for instance, in the time between the times that 'if it is a main part of God's purposes for us to foster a personal relationship with us, God has a reason to intervene *sometimes*, and perhaps to work miracles *occasionally*, even if divine purposes regarding our freedom require that miracles should be infrequent' (Adams 1994: 39).)

Harbouring created freedom and failing to be other-regarding enough   A second kind of faithlessness does not violate the first injunction, yet constitutes a further instance where culpability attaches to inaction. The focus shifts in two ways. We move from putting God to the test by our inaction to neglecting our neighbour's weal and woe by our inaction. And we move from praiseworthy prudence that we recklessly set aside to blameworthy apathy or self-absorption that we indulgently retain. Such a dual shift departs from what Luther assumes in the particular judgement we have considered, that faithful prudence and other-regard can *coincide*. We dwell instead on *conflict*, where we *harbour* our agential powers on our own behalf, frequently at our neighbour's expense. Culpable inaction now refers to failing to be other-regarding enough. Such harbouring is faithless by virtue of normative links between dedication to God and dedication to neighbours, where the latter is a necessary and appropriate measure of the former (Outka 1972: 44–54). It is also a subject in moral and legal debates about how far, e.g., a 'duty to rescue' extends. Many claim that even the apathetic and self-absorbed should give other-regarding assistance that involves no disproportionate inconvenience to themselves (Outka 1992: 17–44). In general terms, we reach judgements of faithlessness of the second kind when we can plausibly pose the alternatives starkly. That is, we envisage neither immoral nor risky actions from those who are able to rescue, only generous ones, and we contrast these with inaction rooted, again, in apathy and self-absorption.

Dispersing created freedom and lacking determinate character   A third kind of faithlessness also does not violate the first injunction, yet constitutes a further instance where culpability attaches to inaction. We may locate it by depicting 'sloth'. This refers here not to laziness but to failure to become a focused self. The dynamics of sloth assume agential powers as part of the goodness of creation that undergo deformation. The signs include an absence of intra-psychic vitality, a want of personal decisiveness, prizing determinate character too little, and taking our cues from others too much. Narratives over lifetimes lack definite shapes, consistent views, abiding aims, permanent loyalties. The focus shifts now in three ways. While we assume the possibility of created freedom and its appropriate use, we consider not a sequence of events where we should use medicines and the like, but the importance of having a determinate character across our personal history. We spend less time on evaluating apathy and self-absorption as blameworthy, as self-referential indifference to others, and more on the dangers of passivity and torpor. And while we recognize that conflicts between ourselves and neighbours recur, we believe that we may expand coincidences, in relationships where neither side abnegates or dominates.

In recent decades feminist writers above all have explored the corruptions of sloth in ways that exert wide influence (Saiving 1979: 100–12; Plaskow 1980; Dunfee, 1982: esp. 318–24; Keller 1986: 40; McFadyen 2000: 131–66; cf. Thistlethwaite 1989; West 1995: esp. 1–7, 38–47, 62–73). Important questions widely canvassed exceed the reach of our enquiry: e.g., whether sloth bedevils women particularly and pride bedevils men particularly, or whether such a generalization falls victim to excessive gender stereotyping. Feminist writers play a prominent role, however, in pressing a consideration that is fully germane. It is that when we accord to the corruptions of sloth the importance that is their due, we come to see that we need not try to reduce sloth to pride or pride to sloth. Certain features of sloth we have described above; certain features of pride connect not only to the second kind of faithlessness also described above, but to more Promethean sorts of inordinate self-aggrandizement. And now the following theological appraisal suggests itself. We should view *faithlessness as an explanatory and evaluative key to both pride and sloth* (Outka 1992: 48–60).

The verdicts are these. We are faithless when we suppose in our pride that we matter more than our neighbours, and that we may dominate and control them, or regard them as merely our audience or our willing instruments. And we are faithless when we suppose in our sloth that we matter less than our neighbours, and that we are not basically imperilled when we become careless about matters concerning our own integrity and determinate character, and allow ourselves to become endlessly distractable and suggestible. To the extent that this diagnosis proves correct, it supports one side of an ancient theological dispute concerning the relationship between unbelief and pride: namely, that unbelief, here, faithlessness, is prior to pride as the paramount sin. Faithlessness remains the common source of pride *and* of sloth, without reducing the different patterns that each assumes in human interaction.

FAITH DISALLOWS 'PLAYING GOD'

The second injunction is: we should not 'play God' 'Playing God' has many senses, some of which are discussed instructively in recent bioethical literature. We invoke the phrase both to condemn and to extol expanding scientific knowledge and technological innovations in areas such as genetics. Much depends on what we examine and what perspective we bring. Those in theological ethics rightly engage in these debates (Ramsey 1970; Fletcher 1974; Cahill 1995; Peters 2003). Here we appropriate them within a larger framework. Three negative senses amplify kinds of faithlessness, and permit comparisons with the other normative boundary previously drawn, that we should not put God to the test.

Idolatry

We begin with traditional usage. It makes sense to say that we wrongly play God when we aspire to a standing and seek to usurp powers that are properly God's. Ezekiel announces to the prince of Tyre: 'In your arrogance you say, "I am a god; I sit enthroned like a god on the high seas." Though you are a man and no god, you give yourself godlike airs' (Ezek. 28: 2, REB).

When our putting on godlike airs becomes our settled practice, we can overreach to an extreme point. This could be ridiculed were it not so dangerous. Ezekiel censures the prince of Tyre for arrogance; the latter aspires to merge his standing with God's. This aspiration is integral to what Augustine sees as the perverse imitation of God. It is perverse because it is impossible. Yet this is not all. It can nevertheless wreak havoc elsewhere. Its futile dynamics set in motion destructive effects within us and between us. We seek, for example, to 'lord it over' others.

That a certain imitation is impossible, and that bad things follow as we attempt to deny this, disposes us often to employ the category of *idolatry* to describe and evaluate what goes wrong. This category refers more and less ambitiously. It ranges from false worship to farcical pretensions to immoderate attachments. The falsity consists above all in ascribing God's own attributes to entities of this world. A sensible general rule is this: 'any nonabsolute value that is made absolute and demands to be the center of dedicated life is idolatry' (Halbertal and Margalit 1992: 246). Within this range, we concentrate now on ways we simultaneously overreach and menace. The more we seek to merge our standing with God's, the more we aggrandize in our own world. Others take notice as they realize that they stand in our way and must resist us or flatter us. If they resist, conflict occurs that can turn deadly, especially if we have the power to dominate, like the prince of Tyre or countless other tyrants. If they flatter, they provide the assurances we crave, but crave insatiably, for we seek more than human beings can give each other. Nothing stabilizes; such encounters leave no one unthreatened.

This idolatrous overreaching imperils promotion of human dignity, not only by the self-deception it manifests and the callousness toward others it induces. It also imperils in the opposite direction by encouraging us to denigrate the goodness of our actual standing as creatures (Tanner 1992: 160–1). By attempting what is impossible, we may grow careless about or contemptuous of the possible. Yet our creaturely goodness *is* real. We are to celebrate and correspond to the ways our world resembles God, participates in God, rather than becomes God. When we do not transmute resembling or participating into merging, and thereby do not deny God's transcendence, we may affirm that whatever is, is good, including our natural sociality, the beauty we apprehend, the stages of life through which we go. We should neither divinize nor depreciate the creaturely constituents of human dignity. Rather, we should cherish, protect, and enhance them. To say that idolatry cuts against them in both directions overlaps importantly with a fear of domination and control in *human interaction.* For again, the more we seek to merge our standing with God's, the more we aggrandize in our own world. Still, the deepest attitude toward *God* comes out when Augustine sees something else in idolatry as well. He believes that our enmity toward God goes deeper than we know. Even the aspiration to merge that is doomed to frustration, and the consequent destructive imitation of God elsewhere, yield a crucial but incomplete diagnosis. When we thus aspire, Augustine adds, we actually *prefer* ourselves to God. And it is our own obstinacy more than our ignorance that leads us astray (Augustine 1950: 385). In brief, even to *collude* with God's lordship in some pattern of mutual reinforcement would leave us dissatisfied. We *oppose* such lordship altogether.

Playing God in accordance with the diagnosis of idolatry recounted here displays a set of possibilities more akin to pride than to sloth. We do not neglect our created freedom and wait passively on God; rather, we strive mightily, if vainly, to overturn the distinction between Creator and creature. We do not simply harbour our created freedom by not being other-regarding enough; rather, we arrogate ourselves over, and not merely ignore, our neighbours' weal and woe. We do not disperse our created freedom in too many directions; rather, we focus and concentrate with a vengeance, but in patterned arrogance that renders ourselves the centre of a dedicated life. Neither trust in God nor obedience to God as features of faith make an appearance. For that to happen, we must restore an honouring of differences and points of correspondence between God and ourselves that avoids perverse imitation or attempted merger.

Responsibility for Final 'World-historical' Outcomes

Another instance of perverse imitation qualifies as playing God, when we mistakenly aspire once more to govern all we survey, but plausibly claim to have other-regarding more than self-aggrandizing motives. Contemporary examples abound; we are now tempted not as monarchs but as sovereign social engineers. The possibility of perverse imitation arises in bioethical discussions of genetics when we shift from talk of affirming our responsibility *to* God, to talk of affirming our responsibility *apart from* God. Indeed, the shift means that we dwell exclusively on *our* responsibility, quite self-consciously, *instead of* God (Verhey 1995: 355). This shift connects with a readiness to form our moral judgements only with reference to world-historical consequences and states of affairs, to adhere entirely to consequentialist normative theories. The end of all things is no longer God's in any sense that counts with us.

That this instance of playing God deserves to be circumscribed becomes clear when we recognize that to affirm our responsibility *to* God is to support a host of human interventions on behalf of life and flourishing and against death and disease. Our earlier account of not putting God to the test and Luther's *reductio ad absurdum* supports actively honouring our agency as integral to such an affirmation. Fidelity to God may include endorsement of many technological developments, the use of lightning rods and of anaesthesia during childbirth, etc. It backs an ethic of stewardship generally and may even invite us to ' "play God" in the correct way' (Ramsey 1970: 256). It requires discriminating judgements rather than indiscriminate warnings and indiscriminate benedictions. These judgements seek to honour differences and points of correspondence in distinctive combinations.

We may play God incorrectly, however, when we cease to locate spheres of responsibility or to entrust overall outcomes to God. Faithlessness occurs especially when we no longer *refuse* to do some things that lie within our power to do. Such refusals engage our agential powers in a way not considered so far. Central considerations at stake come out in the ancient narrative of Joseph in Egypt, recorded in Genesis. Joseph displays personal virtues and social commitments that are widely admired. He trusts in God. He is free of vindictiveness. He is sexually self-controlled. Early on he refuses to commit adultery and suffers for his refusal. We may suppose that the prohibition against adultery serves as an agent-relative deontological restriction on his actions and attitudes (Nagel 1986: 175–80). And this restriction specifies Joseph's own relation to the prohibition's normative truth. 'Agent-relative' means here that *he* cares what he himself *does*, and not only about what *happens overall in the world*. (There can be community-relative restrictions, such as those the Church may make, where the particular relation of the community to the outcome is also essential.) There are restrictions that serve as criteria of faithfulness.

But we should go on to connect this deontological restriction to Joseph's sense of providential governance. The latter sense warns us against premature foreclosures. For Joseph discerns that as part of a providential pattern God may override the evil that people do to one another. He alludes to this as the Genesis narrative ends. He replies to his brothers who dread his wrath for the evil they did to him: 'Do not be afraid. Am I in the place of God? You meant to do me harm; but God meant to bring good out of it by preserving the lives of many people, as we see today' (Gen. 50: 19–20, REB). His earlier conviction that adultery is a wicked thing, a sin against God, does not block his discernment by the end of the narrative that God puts various events to use. These include in his case the evil actions of his brothers. It seems that Joseph is responsible for what he does and forbears, but that he is not similarly responsible for what his brothers do and forbear, and that later he is simply content to marvel at what God has done. We may interpret Joseph's sense of providential governance as affirming that no human wickedness finally defeats such governance. Yet we are also goaded to mark spheres of responsibility. In the case of human life in interaction with other human life, Joseph's responsibility remains distinct from that of his brothers. In the case of human life before God, he asks his brothers, 'Am I in the place of God?' He is primally responsible for what *he* does and forbears. But he does not confuse his responsibility with God's. Rather, he leaves it to God to settle the balance of overall human goods and human evils. In this instance, the final outcome that God brings about includes material blessing even for his brothers. But this is God's doing. Joseph does not presume to bring about such an outcome on his own. True, he aids and abets it in the ways open to him, by the concrete help he gives to his father and brothers, help made possible by the position of power he comes to occupy. Yet this position is itself viewed under the canopy of providential governance; his own talents are themselves put to use. In any event, he continues to act within the limits of what God enjoins and permits. What God may do still differs relevantly from what he, in faithfulness to God, may do.

These central considerations reappear. Christians perceive Judas's betrayal as heinous, yet taken up mysteriously into a larger outcome God brings about. That evil deeds may become God's instruments, does not mean, however, that we should seek to emulate God here. There are forces that God can and does govern and defeat, but that we ourselves cannot and ought not to engage as God does.

Presuming Zero-sum Relations

We may play God in a last way that takes us more directly into metaphysical thickets. The wrong turn comes when we assume that between God's action and ours there is competitiveness in principle—that is, when we assume that strictly zero-sum relations obtain. In modernity and postmodernity the assumption of zero-sum relations typically manifests itself in claims that God's power, as either domination or benevolence, must collide with human liberation. For we presume that God's action and ours are sufficiently commensurable that they may directly compete, that they belong on a continuum of degrees, and that we may treat them as rivalrous and adjudicate their respective legitimacies. And we must alter and harness God's action in order to enhance and empower our own. To accomplish this requires that we assume a superior vantage point.

We may avoid this turn by refusing to exempt human agency from total dependence on God and by articulating 'a metaphysics capable of formulating that dependence in ways that respect all of the modalities of creatures, including freedom' (Burrell 1994: 109; cf. Tracy 1994). On this understanding, God's transcendence is not antithetical to, or necessarily contrastive with, either God's immanence or our created exigencies. 'If it makes sense to say that God can call forth a nondivine being with an integrity of existence of its own, then it makes sense to say that God can call forth nondivine beings with real powers of their own to influence other creatures' (Tanner 1994: 117; see also Tanner 1988). A key realization, then, is that our created freedom *owes itself* to God's creating action. Difficult questions remain about the paradox of double agency. But we may address these without having to posit zero-sum relations that mingle who God is and who we are. The understanding in question is more radical than many suppose, and has been forgotten more often in the last centuries than many realize. Kierkegaard captures something of the radicality:

[O]mnipotence can not only bring forth the most imposing of all things, the world in its visible totality, but it can create the most delicate of all things, a creature independent of it. Omnipotence which can lay its hand so heavily upon the world can also make its touch so light that the creature receives independence. It is only a miserable and worldly picture of the dialectic of power to say that it becomes greater in proportion as it can compel and make things dependent. . . . Creation out of nothing is once again the expression of omnipotence for being able to make things independent. It is to him who made me independent, while he nevertheless retained everything, that I owe all things. If in order to create man, God had lost any of his power, then he could not have made man independent. (Kierkegaard 1959: 180–1)

We are given a context for saying that we should neither blend God's faithfulness and ours wholly together nor separate them entirely. Our discussion suggests the following: from an active God we should not infer a passive creature; from an active creature, we should not infer an absent God.

Afterword: On the Eschatological Status of Faith

The foregoing remarks on faith and faithlessness refer to the time between the times, as I indicated. Two of the ways in which we combine certain credal convictions to depict this time we must assume without pausing to specify. The first goes to creation and fall. That Joseph confronts how to respond to the evil actions of his brothers, that how we take the figure of Judas tells us much about the profundity of a particular Christian age, suggest things we do not welcome. A good world has *gone* wrong; our faith now grants no clear and present space between a good world and 'gone' in the past tense. The prohibitions of the Decalogue themselves assume this, in a fashion we often miss. The second way goes to the time between the times and last things. We ask how closely the most transformed life it is given us to know in this world corresponds with celestial life. Let us take celestial life to include *unimpeded* communication and communion. If, for example, we grow, learn, and change, it is never at the expense of others, but in unrelieved harmony with them. If this is right, we face an instructive tension. On the one side, some of the prohibitions and injunctions that promote constructive dimensions of our relationships here and now are tied to matters that threaten these dimensions. The second table of the Decalogue, for instance, forbids certain actions and exchanges that typically do harm. But in forbidding them it acknowledges them, and has its force in relation to what it acknowledges. Similarly, forgiveness makes sense only when a *bona fide* wrong has occurred. These conditions suggest that there are some religious and moral concepts that we need only after the Fall. One of the things we say about a person who lives a transformed life here and now is that he or she does not violate the prohibitions and is disposed to forgive. Yet it is hard to see how the Decalogue or forgiveness have a place in celestial life. On the other side, we long for unimpeded communion, and perceive it to correspond to transformed life even in the present.

These considerations leave us with the following recognitions. In the eschatological state, faith and hope *open a way* to sight and vindication (while eternally abiding in the outcome). Love is *fulfilled*, so continuity ends in consummation. Despite these differences, faith features indispensably in the time between the times.

References and Suggested Reading

ADAMS, R. M. (1994). 'Theodicy and Divine Intervention', in Thomas F. Tracy (ed.), *The God Who Acts: Philosophical and Theological Explorations*, University Park, Pa.: Pennsylvania State University Press, 31–40.

AUGUSTINE (1950). *The City of God.* New York: Modern Library.

—— (1998). *Confessions.* Oxford: Oxford University Press.

BARTH, K. (1957). *Church Dogmatics*, II/1. Edinburgh: T. & T. Clark.

BURRELL, D. B. (1994). 'Divine Action and Human Freedom in the Context of Creation', in Thomas F. Tracy (ed.), *The God Who Acts: Philosophical and Theological Explorations*, University Park, Pa.: Pennsylvania State University Press, 103–9.

CAHILL, L. S. (1995). '"Playing God": Religious Symbols in Public Places', *Journal of Medicine and Philosophy*, 20/4, 341–6.

DUNFEE, S. N. (1982). 'The Sin of Hiding: A Feminist Critique of Reinhold Niebuhr's Account of the Sin of Pride', *Soundings*, 65/3, 316–27.

FERN, R. L. (2002). *Nature, God and Humanity: Envisioning an Ethics of Nature*. Cambridge: Cambridge University Press.

FLETCHER, J. (1974). *The Ethics of Genetic Control*. Garden City, NY: Anchor Books.

GAEBLER, M. D. (2003). *Retrieving Luther's Ethic: Christian Identity and Action*. Ann Arbor: UMI Dissertation Services (Ph.D. dissertation, Yale University).

HALBERTAL, M. and MARGALIT, A. (1992). *Idolatry*. Cambridge, Mass.: Harvard University Press.

JONES, J. R. (2002). *A Grammar of Christian Faith: Systematic Explorations in Christian Faith and Doctrine*. Lanham, Md.: Rowman and Littlefield.

KELLER, C. (1986). *From a Broken Web: Separation, Sexism, and Self*. Boston: Beacon Press.

KIERKEGAARD, S. (1959). *The Journals of Kierkegaard: 1834–1854*. London: Oxford University Press.

LUTHER, M. (1968). 'Whether One May Flee from a Deadly Plague', in *Devotional Writings*, ii, Philadelphia: Fortress Press, 113–38.

MCFADYEN, A. (2000). *Bound to Sin: Abuse, Holocaust and the Christian Doctrine of Sin*. Cambridge: Cambridge University Press.

MORSE, C. (1994). *Not Every Spirit: A Dogmatics of Christian Disbelief*. Valley Forge, Pa.: Trinity Press International.

NAGEL, T. (1986). *The View from Nowhere*. New York: Oxford University Press.

NEVILLE, R. C. (1993). *Eternity and Time's Flow*. Albany, NY: State University of New York Press.

NIEBUHR, H. R. (1960). 'Faith in Gods and in God', in *Radical Monotheism and Western Culture*, New York: Harper, 114–26.

OUTKA, G. (1972). *Agape: An Ethical Analysis*. New Haven: Yale University Press.

——(1992). 'Universal Love and Impartiality', in Edmund Santurri and William Werpehowski (eds.), *The Love Commandments: Essays in Christian Ethics and Moral Philosophy*, Washington: Georgetown University Press, 1–103.

——(2002). 'Theocentric Love and the Augustinian Legacy: Honoring Differences and Likenesses between God and Ourselves', *Journal of the Society of Christian Ethics*, 22, 97–114.

PETERS, T. (2003). *Playing God? Genetic Determinism and Human Freedom*. New York: Routledge.

PLANTINGA, A. (1999). 'Augustinan Christian Philosophy', in Gareth P. Matthews (ed.), *The Augustinian Tradition*, Berkeley: University of California Press, 1–26.

PLASKOW, J. (1980). *Sex, Sin and Grace: Women's Experience and the Theologies of Reinhold Niebuhr and Paul Tillich*. Lanham, Md.: University Press of America.

RAMSEY, P. (1970). *The Patient as Person: Explorations in Medical Ethics*. New Haven: Yale University Press.

SAIVING, V. (1979). 'The Human Situation: A Feminist View', in Carol P. Christ and Judith Plaskow (eds.), *Womenspirit Rising: A Feminist Reader in Religion*, San Francisco: Harper, 100–12.

TANNER, K. (1988). *God and Creation in Christian Theology: Tyranny or Empowerment?* Oxford: Blackwell.

——(1992). *The Politics of God: Christian Theologies and Social Justice*. Minneapolis: Fortress Press.

TANNER, K. (1994). 'Human Freedom, Human Sin, and God the Creator', in Thomas F. Tracy (ed.), *The God Who Acts: Philosophical and Theological Explorations*, University Park, Pa.: Pennsylvania State University Press, 111–35.

THISTLETHWAITE, S. B. (1989). *Sex, Race, and God: Christian Feminism in Black and White*. New York: Crossroad.

TRACY, T. F. (1994). 'Divine Action, Human Causes, and Human Freedom', in Thomas F. Tracy (ed.), *The God Who Acts: Philosophical and Theological Explorations*, University Park, Pa.: Pennsylvania State University Press, 77–102.

VERHEY, A. (1995). '"Playing God" and Invoking a Perspective', *Journal of Medicine and Philosophy*, 20/4, 347–64.

WEST, A. (1995). *Deadly Innocence: Feminism and the Mythology of Sin*. London: Cassell.

CHAPTER 17

HOPE

JOHN WEBSTER

I

CHRISTIAN hope is a moral phenomenon; but it is so derivatively, and the derivation is one of the clues to its Christian character. For, on the one hand, to speak of Christian hope is most properly to speak of the object of Christian hoping, that for which the Christian hopes: namely, the personal divine subject 'Jesus Christ our hope' (1 Tim. 1: 1; RSV). Hope is this one, before it is a set of attitudes or undertakings on the part of those who hope in him. And, on the other hand, hope shares with other Christian virtues—most of all, faith and love—the fact that its human exercise is at the same time a work of God the Holy Spirit, and so cannot be described in a comprehensive way simply by talking of creaturely operations. Nevertheless, the hope which Jesus Christ constitutes and which the Holy Spirit engenders is of necessity bound up with moral activities and moral judgements. To abound in hope by the power of the Holy Spirit (Rom. 15: 13) is not only to look to a prospective benefit but also to receive appointment as a certain kind of agent. The presence of Christian hope is therefore visible in, amongst other things, the particular activities and abstentions by which members of Christ's fellowship dispose themselves in the world.

Christian hope is thus one of a cluster of spacious and internally complex theological realities which serve to provide moral orientation. The hope of Christian people is part of what is involved in envisaging the world in the light of the Christian gospel. Through this primary feature of Christian moral vision, the

Christian agent is schooled into steady, disciplined knowledge of certain moral realities and ends, and is thereby instructed in action which is fitting—that is, action which is in accordance with the way in which the Christian gospel declares the world to be. In particular, hope enables the Christian moral agent to clarify and act out a way of life within the historical character of created existence—that is, existence in time. To exist in Christian hope is to trust that in all its dissipation, complexity, and misery, human history is by the mercy of God on the way to perfection. History is not random, unformed occurrence, but an ordered reality moving towards the fulfilment of its given nature in the coming manifestation of the immeasurable greatness of Christ's power (Eph. 1: 19–21). The life and activity of the Christian fellowship are, therefore, life and activity in the knowledge of his coming reality, a reality of which the New Testament speaks in irreducibly personal terms as 'our blessed hope': namely, 'the appearing of the glory of our great God and Saviour Jesus Christ' (Titus 2: 13). This knowledge is both the church's joy and its affliction: joy, because hope for coming perfection exalts; affliction, because to wait is to suffer imperfection. Further, hope is both prospective and retrospective. It is rooted in faith's trust in a *future* perfection which *has been* promised and secured. Hope arises from the divine promises—that is, from authoritative divine enactments and declarations in the past which are sufficiently commanding and persuasive in the present that they can direct the Christian fellowship's actions towards the future. Emerging from the promises of God, hope shapes the actions of the Christian fellowship by instructing it about its true condition. Hope sees the world as a particular kind of place, one which moves along a specific historical trajectory, and which makes possible and necessary action in a particular direction.

Accordingly, an enquiry into Christian hope as a moral phenomenon asks a number of related questions. Are the world and its history such that hope is not a fantasy but a truthful estimation of our situation? What kind of person is the Christian who hopes, and in whose company does she live and act? Existing within that world and history, with a particular given identity and a particular set of companions, to what kind of hopeful action is the Christian summoned, equipped with what resources and for what ends? Taken together, answers to these questions would form an account of the conditions and modes of Christian hope. But they would do so only if they rested upon an answer to the fundamental question concerning Christian hope: namely, the identity of God as the object and ground of Christian hope, the one by and towards whom all hopeful action is directed. A moral theology of Christian hope, that is, must start from the Christian confession of God.

Before turning to theology proper, however, three observations about this way of approaching the moral theology of hope ought to be recorded. First, one test of adequacy for a theological account of Christian hope as a moral phenomenon will be whether it asks all those questions, and asks them in their proper sequence and order, in such a way that the range and structure of its account are shaped by the

Christian confession. Thus, for example, answers to the question of the ethical forms of hope are derivative from answers to the question of the human historical condition, which are in turn dependent upon theological teaching about God. Second, a theological account of Christian hope will give priority to biblical and theological description, and will not invest heavily either in a phenomenology of hope as human attitude and disposition or in the self-descriptions of contemporary culture. Often, indeed, it will find that the matter of its own enquiry requires a rather free and sometimes critical attitude to such preoccupations, believing that the persuasiveness of Christian hope is demonstrated more satisfactorily when it is allowed to emerge with its own inherent clarity and profile than when it is commended or defended comparatively. Third, a theological account of Christian hope is especially concerned with given moral nature and ends. This means that it is an exercise in moral ontology, though of a distinctively theological kind. Christian hope concerns the phenomenon of human action. But, as we shall see, it is not action as pure, spontaneous world making, but action ordered to the world and its history as an *economy*, a shaped sphere in which God's creative, reconciling, and perfecting acts precede, enclose, judge, vindicate, and consummate the works of creatures.

With this in mind, we examine (1) theology proper, that is, the triune God as the object and ground of Christian hope; (2) a Christian understanding of the nature of creaturely history as the theatre of the works and promises of God which engender hope; (3) the nature of the human subject and agent of hope within the divine economy; (4) the particular character of hopeful human action in relation to the coming perfection of all things in Christ.

II

Christian hope is hope in God, for the God confessed by the Christian fellowship is 'the God of hope' (Rom. 15: 13). Christian hope and its activities have to be explicated out of faith's apprehension of God and God's ways with the world as its maker, reconciler, and consummator. In formal terms, this is simply an application of the rule that Christian moral theology ought not to exist in independence of Christian doctrine. In material terms, it is an application of the rule that all Christian teaching, including teaching about the moral life, is an extension of the doctrine of the Trinity, which is the Christian doctrine of God. Christian hope is hope in this God; and the doctrine of the Trinity can therefore rightly be said to furnish 'the environment of Christian behaviour' (Lehmann 1963: 117). How is this so?

The Christian confession of God as Trinity attempts to indicate that the sovereign majesty and perfection which is God's life is that of the eternal and perfect relations of Father, Son, and Spirit. God is the relations of these three persons; his being is his eternal fullness as the Father who begets the Son, the Son who is begotten of the Father before all worlds, and the Spirit who proceeds from them. In these relations, fully achieved and lacking nothing, God is one; his unity is the repleteness and blessedness of the fellowship of the three.

This repleteness of God's life includes within itself, as an integral aspect of its perfection, a turn to that which is not God. In this turn there occurs a movement in which the fellowship of the immanent life of God creates a further object of love. This turn is free, self-caused, wholly spontaneous, original to the divine being; its necessity is purely the necessity of God's own self-determination to be in fellowship with that which is other than himself. As such, it is not a turn which completes or extends the divine life; it is a turning out of fullness, not out of lack. More simply: it is gift, love. This turning or act of love is the work of the triune God as the world's creator, reconciler, and consummator. It takes historical form in the simple yet staggeringly complex work of God's majesty in the entire scope of the economy, as God brings creaturely reality into being, redeems it and ensures that it will arrive at its perfection.

As Father, God purposes that in its abundance the divine love should be directed to bringing creation into being, bestowing upon it life, order, and direction. Because it is rooted in the Father's will, this purpose is unshakeable. That is, God's relation to what he makes is not simply an act of origination, but an act which ensures the creation's *destiny*, and therefore one which oversees, directs, and protects the creation so that it attains that destiny. As Son, God intervenes in the history of creation when, by its own perversity, the creature seeks to struggle free from the Father's purpose, refusing to be a creature, and in so doing exposing itself to mortal peril. Only as creature can the creature have life; and it is the work of the Son to reconcile, and therefore to recreate, what has brought destruction upon itself. Through the person and work of the Son, gathering created being to himself and bearing in himself its alienation from the source of its life and well-being, creation is reintegrated into the Father's purpose. Lastly, as Spirit, God acts to bring to completion that which the Father purposes and the Son secures against all opposition: namely, the identity and integrity of the creation in fellowship with God. God the Spirit perfects, bringing creaturely being and history to their completion.

What is the significance of this for Christian hope? Hope is that creaturely disposition which corresponds to the fact that all occasions of human history, including its future, are caught up within the economy of the triune God's mercy. Because God is to the depths of his eternal being triune, and because he acts in the world as the one he is in himself, then the entire scope of human history and action is embraced by God's purpose. God is not simply originator (setting the creation in motion), nor simply end (tying up the loose ends of history at its terminus). Rather, as Father, Son, and Spirit, God is infinite—no time or space is apart from or beyond his presence and action—and thus steadfast—his purpose has been, is, and will be at all times constantly and reliably at work. And it is as this one that God is the ground of hope, for hope trusts that, because the Father's purpose has been accomplished in the Son and is now at work in the world in the Spirit's power, then human history is God's economy. Within the space which the triune God creates, hope is neither a fantasy nor a gesture of defiance, but a fitting, truthful attitude and shape for action. In sum: hope rests upon God's faithfulness, and God's faithfulness is triune.

One immediate effect of rooting a theology of Christian hope in the doctrine of the Trinity is to prevent an exclusive orientation towards eschatology. Hope is not simply a correlate of the divine futurity or the coming of God; it is, rather, a disposition which is related to the entirety of God's dealings with his creatures, past, present, and future. Within this, hope undoubtedly has an especial regard for the future horizon of human history. But this future quickly becomes isolated when not adequately related to a theological account of God as the world's creator, and as its reconciler in the person and work of Christ. An isolated eschatology accords little weight to created nature, and often has only a pale theology of incarnation and atonement, precisely because the preponderant doctrinal weight is placed on the future of God. This imbalance within the structure of Christian teaching orients hope not to the fulfilment of God's eternal purpose, but to an absolute eschatological *novum*. The corrective to the imbalance is achieved by relating hope not simply to the future but also to the triune eternity of God— that is, to God's sovereign and purposive presence to, and action within, all creaturely time. Christian hope, and therefore hopeful Christian action, rests not simply on what will be, but on what will be as the fulfilment of God's steadfastness as Father, Son, and Spirit, his already enacted, present, and promised constancy to the creature. Hope is hope in God's steadfast love (Pss. 33: 18, 22; 130: 7; 131: 3; 147: 11).

A Christian moral theology of hope begins thus with the perfection of the triune God. This suggests a further consequence: namely, that because hope is hope in God, it has no grounds and no capacity in itself. Not only does this mean that hope is, as Aquinas puts it, *totaliter ab extrinseco* (IaIIae, q. 63, a. 1), since it is that to which we have been 'born anew' (1 Pet. 1: 3). It also means that hope relies upon the fulfilment of the promise of divine grace, and that only as such is it active engagement in the works of hope. 'The hoping person looks gladly, willingly, and joyfully beyond the present and away from himself,' writes Barth (1981: 515). And so:

As faith is real faith only by being finally transcended in demonstration of the faithfulness of God, and as love is the good work of faith only inasmuch as we are loved by God before we ever love him ... so the question of whether we really hope can be answered with ultimate clarity and certainty only as we give up the dignity of being subjects and admit that we can hope only in and by God himself, and that the overwhelming certainty and clarity of Christian hope rests upon its being hope not at all on the basis of its own hope, but wholly and utterly for the sake of what is hoped for... Yet we do not plunge into an abyss here, for if we want to stand, then again we finally have to lose all ground beneath our feet save the one. (Barth 1981: 515)

Starting in this way from the doctrine of the Trinity shows how far back we must reach in enquiring into the practices of Christian hope. In order to reflect upon ourselves and our acts, we must talk of the perfection of God. But because God's perfection is his perfection as this one—the triune Lord, saviour, and finisher of creation—then it is not a perfection indifferent to human history, absorbing it and robbing it of its proper substance; rather, God's perfection includes his perfecting of his creatures. The arena of this perfecting is human time; hope is among the virtues which correspond to God's perfecting work. Rightly to discern the character of Christian hope, therefore, we need to turn next to consider its historical conditions. In what kind of historical sphere do we exist? How does this condition shape the practices of Christian hope?

III

Christian hope requires for its exercise a particular sense of our historical condition; the explication of that condition is one of the tasks of Christian moral theology. As it elucidates the historical condition of Christian hope, theology seeks to develop a moral ontology. That is, it attempts to understand the kind of place the world is, and the kind of beings that we are; and what it says both about the world and about ourselves derives from what theology hears in the gospel about who God is. Christian moral theology thus depicts the historical situation of Christian hope by talking of 'natures' and 'ends'. It portrays, first, the given identities ('natures') of the agents in history—the triune God, as the origin, ruler, sustainer, judge, and redeemer of created time, and human persons, as those created by God for fellowship with himself. And, second, theology depicts the historical situation of Christian hope by portraying the 'ends' of history: that is, the *telos* of created reality and persons in which their natures will be perfectly realized. Such a reflective portrait of the nature and ends of created history furnishes the frame for a Christian ethics of hope, offering a theological description of the moral field within which the practices of Christian hope take place.

Fundamental to such an account is an affirmation that it is possible to speak of history as a whole, as an integrated reality which has form and direction by virtue of the purpose of its creator and lord. History of a field of hope, because it is part of the divine economy, God's orderly administration of all things by which they are brought to fulfilment. History is not simply random, indecipherable, endlessly redescribable; it has shape, order. Shape and order are given; that is, they precede all our human attempts to bestow a unity upon history. Of course, history's shape and order are not given in such a way that history is from the beginning a finished product, established by a pre-temporal decree. History is real; its shape and order are attained through a historical process of perfecting; they are that which history *becomes* as it moves towards its end. Nevertheless, that which history becomes is in accordance with the divine purpose: it moves to its end.

To speak thus is certainly to invite reproach for ideological imposition, or for detaching hope from the broken miseries of time. The danger certainly exists, and protest against it is proper. But a gesture of protest, however necessary, ought not to be allowed to become a first principle; when it does, it inhibits thought, and may relieve theology of its responsibility to give an account of the Christian confession that our times are in the hands of God. Much will depend upon how theology sets about the task of giving such an account—whether it succeeds in avoiding heartless serenity, whether it retains a sense of its own corrigibility, whether it speaks of the end of history with fear and trembling. Yet not to speak of history as God's ordered economy is to fail to articulate a primary condition of Christian hope, for hope arises from discernment of our place in God's history with us.

What is it that hope discerns? It sees human history as the history of fellowship between the triune God and his human creatures. That history is a fellowship which is purposed by the eternal will of God the Father, who creates and gives destiny to that which he creates. History is therefore embraced by 'the purpose of his will' (Eph. 1: 5) or his 'plan for the fullness of time': namely, 'to unite all things in [Christ], things in heaven and things on earth' (Eph. 1: 9 f.). By virtue of the Father's will, history has a destiny. Yet this history does not unfold flawlessly; the history of fellowship includes—and appears to be broken by—the contradiction of sin in which the creature refuses to be satisfied with its given nature and end as a creature made for fellowship, seeks to create its own destiny, and so unleashes the dreadful episode of human depravity. But it remains an *episode*; it may not be rendered absolute and all-consuming so as to annul the constancy of the creator. To the estrangement of creatures from their own good there corresponds the work of God the reconciler through whose saving work sinful, self-destructive creatures are reintegrated into the divine purpose, so that the Father's will to fellowship triumphs. 'In him we have redemption' (Eph. 1: 8)—that is, human history is liberated from bondage to sin, falsehood, and disorder and set free to attain its end. That it is even now moving towards perfection is the work of the Spirit, by whom history is pointed to its consummation, in which the purpose of the Father will be vindicated and the creation glorified.

Christian hope knows itself to be in this historical condition. Grasping the fact that human creatures are caught up in the economy of God's grace, embraced by the Father's purpose, the Son's redemption, and the Spirit's promised consumma-tion, Christian hope is a stance within this history. Most of all, it is a stance towards our future, which regards the incompleteness and imperfection and bleakness of history not with terror or resignation but with trust that, because God has made himself known as creator and reconciler, he will also demonstrate himself to be consummator. The triune God has been, and is now, for his creature, and so he will also prove himself to be in what is to come. This means, once again, that it is not quite correct to relate Christian hope only to the eschatological element of history. Christian hope is expectation; but it is expectation which is instructed by past and present mercy. Certainly it is oriented to 'the expected future of God's kingdom' (Moltmann 1999: 286). But Christian hope anticipates the future as consummation, not only as contradiction of the present order; what is anticipated is the destiny purposed by God the Father and secured in the Son's reconciling work. The experience of Christian hope is not simply an intrusive 'sabbath' moment in which 'the laws of this world are suspended and only the righteousness of God counts' (Moltmann 1999: 280). Rather, it is based in a judgement that the true 'law' of the world is God's plan for the fullness of time, which is now at work and which will receive its consummation in the future for which the church hopes.

As it takes stock of its circumstances, Christian hope does not see itself situated in a history of decline, still less in a tragic situation in face of which hope is simply protest or contradiction. It finds itself in the time of grace, in that space in human history which follows the death and resurrection of Jesus Christ and the outpour-ing of the Spirit. Thus, for the writer of Ephesians, knowing 'the hope to which [God] has called you' (Eph. 1: 18) is inseparable from knowing 'what is the immeasurable greatness of his power in us who believe, according to the working of his great might which he accomplished in Christ when he raised him from the dead and made him sit at his right hand in the heavenly places, far above all rule and authority and power and dominion, and above every name that is named, not only in this age but also in that which is to come; and he has put all things under his feet and has made him the head over all things for the church' (Eph. 1: 19–22). This is not to dismiss the reality of sin and suffering, or to turn from its victims: to wait in hope is to groan (Rom. 8: 22 f.). But the situation in which hope finds itself remains—solely by the merciful judgement of God—one in which grace is super-abundant, and therefore one in which the possibility of a tragic reading of our history has been taken away. Jesus Christ rules, and Christian hope finds in his rule the enactment of the Father's purpose which will be fully manifest in the coming of 'our blessed hope, the appearing of our great God and Saviour Jesus Christ' (Titus 2: 13).

To draw the threads together: a moral theology of Christian hope generates a moral ontology, an account of hope's historical condition. Looking back to God's work of creation and reconciliation, Christian hope also looks for the coming consummation of all things. The present time is not an empty space to be filled with dread, or perhaps with dread held at bay by projects of self-making and self-defence. It is the arena of promise. To hope is to exist in trust that God's constancy is such that the present is on the way to perfection.

This moral ontology finds both its norm and its content in the Christian gospel, from which it acquires its rather distinctive picture of human history and of the nature of hope. Beginning from the gospel and governed by it throughout its enquiry, a Christian moral theology of hope is not much disposed to take its bearings from prestigious readings of our cultural situation developed without the gospel's tutelage. Partly this is because the gospel outbids other interpretations of human history; partly it is because the gospel is the principle of its own explanation and defence. Little is to be gained (and a good deal may be lost) by expounding Christian hope as a counterpart to some philosophical or cultural-theoretical presentation of the human condition. Apologetic advantage is always short-lived, and frequently won by succumbing to the temptation to believe that our historical situation is transparent to us—that we know, as it were, what it is to be without hope, and need only to be furnished with the hope for which we long. Similar difficulties attend attempts to frame a theology of hope in terms of theodicy: how can we hope in face of this or that monstrous evil? But even—especially—our experience of evil is not self-interpreting: evil lies about itself. A theology of hope does not hang upon a satisfactory answer to the question of theodicy (satisfactory to whom, and to what ends?), but vice versa: only on the basis of faith's confession of the God of hope, of his ways with the world in the history of fellowship in which we now live and for whose consummation we wait, is it possible to develop anything like a responsible Christian theodicy.

IV

Having remarked on the God of hope and on hope's historical condition, we turn to the anthropological question: what kind of person is the Christian who hopes? By way of a brief answer, the Christian who hopes is one who knows in faith that in the economy of God's grace, enacted in the resurrection of Jesus and the giving of the Spirit, and lived out in the company of the saints, his or her future is secure; and so the Christian who hopes is one who turns to that future and acts in its light, confident because in the Spirit, Jesus Christ is our present help and the pledge of our coming consummation.

The question, what kind of person is the Christian who hopes?, is an ontological question before it is an ethical one. The answer which it invites is a description of human nature formed by the purpose and action of God. The Christian who hopes is not engaged in an act of self-formation; he or she makes history only because in a deep sense history has already been made, and because only on that basis is it possible to be a hopeful person and agent. A Christian anthropology of hope is decidedly non-voluntarist. Hope is a correlate not of freedom (understood—degenerately—as radical self-government) but of nature (that is, of the reality which the work of the triune God establishes and which the gospel announces with joy). The Christian who hopes is one whose being is enclosed, determined, and protected by Jesus Christ our hope.

Such an anthropology of hope is not readily available to us in late modernity. The disruptive effects of its absence can be illustrated from Rubem Alves's *A Theology of Human Hope*. 'Only as the creator of history does man find his authentic life; only where man is the creator of history is there hope for the world' (Alves 1969: 141). By conflating hope with human self-actualization, the book falls victim to the agonistic habits of modern conceptions of freedom in which the primal form of free human consciousness is 'the consciousness of being dominated by a power which does not allow it to create its own history' (Alves 1969: 10). On this account, hope is freedom, and therefore power (not, note, trust in being helped). Hope is thus not to be set in the economy of grace, for any such economy could only be repressive and alienating: all perfection is at the cost of human liberty. Rather, as Alves puts it, the person who hopes 'is experimentation' (Alves 1969: 137): 'when man's hope informs his action, man thrusts himself upon the world as power' (Alves 1969: 138). The problem here is not simply that this remains entangled in modern dualities of freedom versus nature, divine versus human action, though they are ruinous enough and scarcely compensated for by a muddled theology of grace in which 'creation is a joint enterprise' (Alves 1969: 144). It is more that Alves cannot conceive of a genuine anthropology of hope based on what he dismisses as 'a non-historical, dogmatic idea' (Alves 1969: 87). Therefore he cannot satisfactorily distinguish his 'messianic humanism' from secular political humanism, since the entire metaphysical-theological apparatus of Christian anthropology has to be discarded in order to respect the basic principle for an account of the ethics of hope: 'When nature or any sort of order becomes the context which man elects for his life, history comes to an end. At least man loses his openness to the future since the future is to be the imitation of the values once given in the past' (Alves 1969: 83). A Christian anthropology needs to move beyond this acute historical responsibility, and allow the gospel to introduce us into a more spacious and relaxed world. It will do so by starting, not from human indeterminacy, but from faith's confession of God's works of creating and preserving persons for fellowship and therefore for hope. This—material—starting-point will then be reflected in the order of exposition, so that the anthropology of hope is derivative, not fundamental. Here, too, it is a matter of removing 'the last possibility of a surreptitious resort to anthropology in Christian ethical reflection' (Lehmann, 1963: 120).

The Christian who hopes exists in an 'eschatological situation' defined not by self-realization but by the judgement of God. This is a matter of being

a person under the promise and in the expectation of new life. Under this promise one is called, one is inserted into the new situation before God that is opened up by God's condemning and saving judgement. One is inserted into the hidden history of Jesus Christ in the world. That *is* the living space in which our human history is 'located' and 'takes place'. 'For you died, and your life is hidden with Christ in God'... That is a categorical indicative, the content of the judgement of God upon our existence and at the same time the communication of new life. (Sauter 1996: 197–8)

This new life determining the Christian is a life towards the future in which God's purpose will be completed. To hope as a Christian is to hope as a creature— one who has been formed and appointed by God to live a specific history, reach a specific destiny, and so attain perfection. It is also to hope as a sinner who has been redeemed from self-destruction—one whose evil tendency away from creaturely good has in Christ been authoritatively intercepted and put away. It is to hope as a saint—one who, because elect and redeemed, is also directed and empowered to live towards a certain perfection. And it is to be all this in a fellowship of persons gathered by God as the communion of saints. Christian hope has its roots in our common participation in the reality of grace extended to us; to be a person of hope is to partake in this history in this company.

All of this rests, however, upon the fact that God's merciful judgement upon lost creatures in which their human vocation is restored is the gift of *being*. God's judgement is not a conditional offer, contingent upon the completion of a task: it is a mighty work of creation. For the Christian who hopes, this is who she and her fellows are. Hope is thus an aspect of that 'conformity-to-being' (Spaemann 2000: 79) in which consists the goodness of our acts and our blessedness. To hope is to be the person one is and will be, a person for whom hope is 'natural'—that is, a disposing of oneself in accordance with the nature and vocation bestowed by God. Two consequences follow.

First, the Christian who hopes is one who knows his or her future. Such knowledge comes from the 'spirit of wisdom and of revelation' by which 'the eyes of the heart are enlightened' and we come 'to know what is the hope to which God has called us' (Eph. 1: 18). To the Christian who hopes there is revealed that we are reconciled creatures of God directed by him to our coming blessedness; so hope includes knowledge. This knowledge, because it is the gift of the Spirit, is 'spiritual'. It is not sight or possession: 'who hopes for what he sees?' (Rom. 8: 24). We have hope as we have God, as gift, not as material or psychological condition. Yet spiritual knowledge is for all that no less certain. Christian hope is 'fully assured' (Heb. 6: 11) of the coming perfection. Hope is not 'nescience' which fears to go beyond 'the unfinished narrative of history' (Lash 1986: 195). It is the knowledge of our future good given by the Spirit who is 'the guarantee of our inheritance until we acquire possession of it' (Eph. 1: 14). And such knowledge is sufficiently robust, offering a sufficiently persuasive account of our condition and our identity, that it forms the basis for action which is not timid or calculative but a free, bold, and generous move towards the future to which we have been appointed.

Moreover, because hope includes knowledge given in the Spirit's work of 'revelation in the knowledge of [Christ]' (Eph. 1: 17), it is inadvisable to speak of the cognitive dimension of hope in terms of imagination (see Bauckham and Hart 1999). 'Imagination' suggests something too projective or poetic, too little oriented to what has been accomplished and what is now being made known in the Spirit's revealing work. A natural counterpart of a strongly futurist eschatology, imagination is oriented more to possibility than to actuality; and it can make hope's envisaging of the future into a task to be undertaken, rather than the hearing of an authoritative divine judgement which has already been announced.

Second, Christian hope is a mode of personal existence (though not *private*, since I hope in company with my fellow members in the body of Christ) in which the Christian, having been turned by God to her future good, turns to that good. God's turning to his creatures, his self-communicative presence and promised constancy, evokes a corresponding turn on the part of the creature; Christian hope is an aspect of that turn. The creaturely movement of hope is entirely and astonishingly a matter of grace—'It is very difficult to keep in mind the fundamentally incomprehensible fact that hope, as a virtue, is something wholly supernatural' (Pieper 1986: 35). The Christian turns to the future only because that future has already been secured, has already made itself our good and the condition of our being. Above all, that to which the Christian turns—this 'future good'—is Jesus Christ himself. Because he is not only the first but also the last, because he is alive for evermore (Rev. 1: 17 f.), then the Christian may—must—turn to him. To be without hope is for the Christian an impossibility, excluded by the promise of Jesus Christ; to turn to him in hope is the only way forward.

Yet hope is *hope*, not delight. The object of delight is 'a good that is present' (Aquinas 1964: IaIIae, q. 40, a. 8); the object of hope is future: 'we do not hope for what is at present within our grasp' (IaIIae, q. 40, a. 8). Further, the object of hope is 'something arduous, attainable only with difficulty' (IaIIae, q. 40, a. 8). Hope is therefore a particular disposition which, in knowledge of our coming good, turns to that good. Hope lies between despair and the delight of possession. It is not despair, because Jesus Christ has already turned to us and secured our future; it is not delight, because our fellowship with him awaits consummation. Hope is, rather, confident longing for the full realization of life with Christ. The Christian who hopes is confident. Because hope is conformity to being, because it is knowledge, because it is active turning to the future which has already turned to us at the resurrection of Jesus Christ, then hope 'does not disappoint' (Rom. 5: 5), and leads to boldness (2 Cor. 3: 12) and steadiness (Heb. 6: 19). Accordingly, the Christian who hopes is free and assured, and can venture what Paul Ramsey calls the 'immoderate life' (Ramsey 1993: 226–31), living and acting beyond the demonstrable and actual, with an intemperance grounded in the reality of the one who died, is risen, and will come again.

V

What has been offered so far is a sketch of the moral domain of Christian hope: Christian hope is part of the movement of reconciled life in which redeemed creatures look for and tend towards their end. But to exist in this moral domain, as this kind of person in covenant with this God, is to be quickened to action. The economy of grace is also *law* (that is, being in its imperatival force) to those who exist within its blessing. To what acts are we quickened? To what are we summoned by the law of our eschatological being?

In answering this question, moral theology has to guard against the drift towards either eschatological moralism or eschatological passivity. The first was much promoted by Kant: 'the Kingdom of Heaven can be interpreted as a symbolic representation aimed merely at stimulating greater hope and effort in achieving it' (Kant 1992: 161). But eschatology is not mythological incitement to action; nor is that for which the Christian *hopes* identical with that which the Christian *makes*. Action is action in a field of reality, and makes sense only as a response to a condition. Hope, courage, and effort require a sense that the world has certain qualities which make such action possible and offer it a reasonable chance of success. 'Eschatology'—the objective grounds of Christian hope—is the attempt to depict these qualities; without them, Christian hope is moralistic and profoundly ungracious.

This does not, however, entail passivity. To hope is to act in conformity with being. Is hope a help or a hindrance to action?, asks Aquinas (IaIIae, q. 40, a. 8). It seems to be a hindrance, for 'hope brings a sense of security, but this feeling leads to carelessness, which frustrates action'. But 'of its very nature hope is an aid to action, intensifying effort in two ways. First, in terms of its object, which is difficult, possible, and agreeable, awareness of difficulty calls forth concentration; the judgement of possibility certainly does not stifle effort. Hope, then, will inspire a man to earnest action. Second, in terms of its effect we have seen that hope causes delight, and that makes for more effective operation. Therefore hope is a help in acting' (IaIIae, q. 40, a. 8). Hope does not generate *negligentia* but *operatio, conatus*. Because hope has this object and engenders delight, it leads to action. Put more concretely, hope is an aspect of the fellowship with God for which we have been created and reconciled and in which our perfection lies; and that fellowship is a differentiated fellowship of action. Elected to this end, we are summoned to hope in its direction. The divine Word which promises our end is also the divine command which summons us to move actively towards that which is promised. But with what kind of action?

Christian action is hopeful when it is oriented to the future consummation of all things in the Kingdom of Christ. Hopeful Christian action is undertaken in the trust that Christ's coming Kingdom is present and promised with such axiomatic certainty that it outweighs all discouragement, opposition, and counter-testimony. In such trust (to which courage is closely akin) the Christian extends herself towards that which has been promised. Hope refuses a moral calculus based on what, apart from the gospel, is taken to be our present condition; it incites action which is obedient to the true law of our being: namely, that the creation 'will be set free from its bondage to decay and obtain the glorious liberty of the children of God' (Rom. 8: 21). Hopeful Christian action stems from the judgement which has been declared to the believer: namely, that 'the sufferings of the present time are not worth comparing with the glory that is to be revealed to us' (Rom. 8: 18). On the basis of that judgement, the Christian reaches towards the coming consummation and glorification, acting in and upon the world as the reality which it will be. That reaching towards—what Aquinas calls magnanimity, *extensio animi ad magna* (IIaIIae, q. 129, a. 1)—is action which seeks the fullest possible anticipation of our end.

Hopeful Christian action extends towards the world's coming judgement and vindication. The eschatological dimension of Christian action is sometimes stated by speaking of hope as essentially critical—oriented not to the present but to the overcoming of the present in the future. Hope thereby opens up a distance from the present which inhibits the kind of stasis in which history is already considered to have achieved its perfection. In his *Theology of Hope*, for example, Moltmann speaks of 'hope which sets about criticizing and transforming the present because it is open towards the universal future of the kingdom' (1967: 335). In concrete terms, this means that hope engenders a highly mobile attitude to the orders of social existence: hope does not seek to preserve or stabilize but 'historify' (Moltmann 1967: 330). This reaches towards one moral consequence of the last judgement. But Christian hope does not look only for the overthrow of present disorder, but also for the vindication of present righteousness. 'Hope', says Calvin, 'awaits the time when [God's] truth shall be manifested' (Calvin 1960: III. ii. 42). The manifestation to which hope looks, and towards which it acts, will also be the vindication of present action—that is, the declaration that such action has been in conformity with the good order of God. To act in the light of that coming vindication is to trust that acts whose end is not yet evident, and which may therefore appear vulnerable, even futile, will bear fruit. Charity which receives little or no reciprocation, resistance to powers which oppose Jesus Christ, sponsoring forms of civic courtesy and respect for strangers: such things are hopeful, not simply because they 'historify' (which they do not always do; often they are caught in moral gridlock), but because they anticipate a coming revelation of their obedience to the law of our being. And in that lies their authority as hopeful actions which bear witness to the true end of the human world. Hopeful Christian action is action which is both realistic and unafraid of its own limits. All action in history is necessarily limited—by lack of competence or knowledge, by the un-availability of resources of time, energy, wisdom, and political and economic power. Such limits do not undermine Christian action, however, because Christian hope confesses that we do not need to be infinite in order to act well now and to survive in the future: we are and will be *helped*. Incapacity and limitation do not inhibit, because Jesus Christ has undertaken for our future. And so the Christian agent, hoping in him, is relieved of final responsibility, and called instead to steadfastness, alertness, and expectancy.

Such are some of the characteristics of hopeful Christian action. If the description risks vagueness, it is because hope is primarily a matter of orientation or general moral policy. Hope is not so much a separate act as a quality of other acts; in one sense it is adjectival. The determination of the particular moral configuration of Christian hope will depend upon a number of factors: the depth and seriousness with which Christian agents have come to read themselves and their situation in the light of the gospel; a developed capacity for truthful attention to particulars; the existence of intelligent and worshipful forms of Christian common life to enable such training in Christianness. Above all, however, formation in hope, and discernment of which acts of hope are fitting and prudent, are the works of the Spirit; and prayer for his coming is the first and last act of the hopeful Christian.

REFERENCES AND SUGGESTED READING

ALVES, R. (1969). *A Theology of Human Hope*. Washington: Corpus.
AQUINAS (1964–). *Summa theologiae*. Oxford and New York: Blackfriars and McGraw-Hill.
BARTH, K. (1962). *Church Dogmatics*, IV/3. Edinburgh: T. & T. Clark.
—— (1981). *Ethics*. Edinburgh: T. & T. Clark; Grand Rapids, Mich.: Eerdmans.
BAUCKHAM, R. and HART, T. (1999). *Hope against Hope: Christian Eschatology in Contemporary Context*. London: Darton, Longman, and Todd.
CALVIN, J. (1960). *Institutes of the Christian Religion*. London: SCM Press; Philadelphia: Westminster Press.
ELLUL, J. (1977). *Hope in Time of Abandonment*. New York: Seabury.
GENOVESI, V. (1982). *Expectant Creativity: The Action of Hope in Christian Ethics*. Washington: University Press of America.
KANT, I. (1992). *Religion within the Limits of Mere Reason*, in A. W. Wood and G. di Giovanni (eds.), *Religion and Rational Theology*, Cambridge: Cambridge University Press, 39–215.

LASH, N. (1986). 'The Church's Responsibility for the Future of Humanity', in *Theology on the Way to Emmaus*, London: SCM Press, 186–201.

LEHMANN, P. (1963). *Ethics in a Christian Context*. London: SCM Press.

MOLTMANN, J. (1967). *Theology of Hope: On the Ground and the Implications of Christian Eschatology*. London: SCM Press.

—— (1999). 'The Liberation of the Future and its Anticipations in History', in R. Bauckham (ed.), *God Will Be All in All: The Eschatology of Jürgen Moltmann*, Edinburgh: T. & T. Clark, 265–89.

PANNENBERG, W. (1998). *Systematic Theology*, III. Edinburgh: T. & T. Clark.

PIEPER, J. (1986). *On Hope*. San Francisco: Ignatius Press.

RAMSEY, P. (1993). *Basic Christian Ethics*. Louisville, Ky.: Westminster John Knox Press.

SAUTER, G. (1996). *Eschatological Rationality: Theological Issues in Focus*. Grand Rapids, Mich.: Baker.

SCHWÖBEL, C. (2000). 'Last Things First? The Century of Eschatology in Retrospect', in D. Ferguson and M. Sarot (eds.), *The Future as God's Gift: Explorations in Christian Eschatology*, Edinburgh: T. & T. Clark, 217–41.

SPAEMANN, R. (2000). *Happiness and Benevolence*. Notre Dame, Ind.: University of Notre Dame Press.

VOLF, M. and KATERBERG, W. (eds.) (2004). *The Future of Hope: Christian Tradition amid Modernity and Postmodernity*. Grand Rapids, Mich.: Eerdmans.

CHAPTER 18

LOVE: A KINSHIP OF AFFLICTION AND REDEMPTION

AMY LAURA HALL

You shall not wrong or oppress a resident alien, for you were aliens in the land of Egypt.

Exod. 22: 21, NRSV

Be merciful, just as your Father is merciful.

Luke 6: 36, NRSV

I had my abortion on June 30th, and I was a mess. I was weeping all the time . . . We were watching the parade on Main Street in Hamlet, at my in-laws' cottage, and a family with a kid with Down's was standing in front of me. Right there at the parade, honest to God, like a sign direct to me. And the thing was, I really looked at the kid, how she dripped her ice cream all over, how she couldn't be made to do what the other kids wanted. I looked at her and thought, 'she doesn't belong in that family.' She didn't look like them, she looked like someone else. Like a lot of someone elses, not quite from the same race, if you know what I mean. And it made me feel, well, that I'd done the right thing, that the one I aborted wasn't quite from my family, either.   Emily, 37, white antiques restorer

(quoted in Rapp 1999: 274)

INTRODUCTION

ANDERS NYGREN incited a barrage of scholarship when in 1953 the English translation of *Agape and Eros* appeared as one volume. In this long but somewhat
unsubtle defence of sacrificial, non-appraising love, Nygren presented what was to
be a 'type of scientific analysis' whereby the matter of love's essential essence could
be settled (1953: 38). Many beautiful secondary works emerged, suggesting that
Nygren had ill-described *agapē* or misdiagnosed *eros*. Consistently problematic and
confusing was Nygren's supposedly Lutheran claim that 'the Christian can be
likened to a tube, which by faith is open upwards, and by love downwards' (1953:
735). This seemed a singularly inept metaphor. Nygren's work thus, and in other
ways, began a renaissance of love, sending four generations of theological ethicists
back to Scripture and the formative saints to revisit the characteristics and concomitant tasks of Christian love.

In my own early attempt to complicate the debate (Hall 1999), I drew on the
complexity of Scripture, noting that the Septuagintal *agapē* replaces Hebrew words
as disparate as *ahav* (passionate intimacy), *rechem* (maternal mercy), and *dodh*
(delight). *Agapē* carries from one testament into the next echoes from stories and
commands, a cacophonous memory that cannot be distilled into one meaning. It
should neither surprise nor disconcert that the attentive saints found warrant for
different, even divergent, melodies. As love appears in the tradition, embedded in
whole systems of theological enquiry, some scriptural voices are amplified over
others. I concluded in that essay that a faithful explication and gesticulation of love
requires continued engagement with the undistilled scriptural tradition. I have
come further to sense that the moral theologian may best offer apt, scripturally
responsible renditions of love, suggesting plausibly helpful answers to questions. If
Nygren and some of his interlocutors are over ambitious to generate *the one*
definition of love, the theological ethicist must still craft a catechetically *useful*
description. Such is this aim of this essay.

I will here assume a Nygrenian distinction between formulations of love that
sound in the register of the *imago Dei* and those in the register of *theologia crucis*—
between formulations that emphasize the worth of each individual as created by
and destined for God and those that revolve around the crucified Christ who saves
sinners. *Contra* to Nygren, I wish to note that Scripture attests to both emphases.
To set both as legitimate poles on a continuum is still to over-simplify. Also, it is
not possible for Christians to say something about the *imago Dei* without some
reference to Christ, or to say something about Christ without saying something
about the *imago Dei*. But we may emphasize one constellation of doctrinal affirmations when talking about love. With these caveats, it is useful to examine the strand
in the tradition that depicts our sense of kinship in affliction and redemption. I will
first call attention to love as such kinship by reading Thomas Aquinas's discussion

of mercy as it relates to charity (particularly in the *Prima Pars* 20–1 and the *Secunda Secundae* 30 of the *Summa Theologiae*) and then read two authors who elicit love by attention to the cross: Julian of Norwich and Martin Luther.

A question prompts these readings. The subtitle of this essay reiterates a term used by anthropologist Robert Edgerton regarding the mentally retarded. Anthropologist Rayna Rapp develops this theme of a 'kinship of affliction' or even a 'tribe' of suffering to which people with Down's syndrome belong, drawing on testimony from women like the one quoted above, to justify prenatal testing and abortion (1999: 40). For Christians, the *theologia crucis* may be useful catechetically in response to this failure of moral imagination exacerbated by advances in biotechnology. With the capacity to detect disability and other traits of difference *in utero*, there is a growing phenomenon—sometimes called 'selective abortion'—whereby a potential mother or parents determine, based on foetal characteristics, to terminate the pregnancy. The potential mother or parents often want *a* child, but not *this* child. The social shame of bearing a 'defective' child, and concomitant exposure or abandonment, are not new. New to this generation is the capacity to detect 'defects' and to terminate with efficiency, scope, and anonymity. To evoke a sense of *cruciform consanguinity* may possibly serve (1) to rectify the failure of the currently able-bodied and independent to recognize kinship with people who are neither, and (2) to reverse the currently growing practice of detecting and aborting foetuses who are overtly different and vulnerable. I do not suggest that this is the only way to describe or elicit love, but rather that to think along these lines may be helpful in relation to this crisis.

'Some Costly Delicacy'

In the *Prima Pars* 20, 4 of the *Summa Theologiae*, Thomas Aquinas discusses love as an attribute of God and asks 'Whether God Always Loves More the Better Things'. In order to understand the difference between mercy and charity later in the *Summa*, we may back up to this point. Thomas relates several passages (Rom. 8: 32; Heb. 2: 16; Luke 15: 7) that seem to provide evidence that God does not love more those who more fully exhibit the excellence of their species. If God loves the better things, then why did God deliver unto death the sinless Christ for the sake of sinful man? For that matter, why was Christ not sent in the form of an angel rather than in the form of a man? And finally, how can God both love the better things and rejoice more fully over the penitent sinner? Thomas counters, drawing from Ecclesiasticus 13: 15, that it must be the case that God loves the better things, because 'everything loves what is like it', and 'the better a thing is, the more like is it to God'. The apparent discord within Scripture must be only *apparent*, and we are to view the question from different perspectives in order to perceive the coherence.

When viewed 'as to natural condition', an angel is better than a man. But we need not view God's assumption of human nature in Christ only in terms of how God, 'absolutely speaking', loves his creatures. When viewed in terms of *need*, it is clear that 'the needs of man were greater'. Thus God assumed human nature 'as the master of a house may give *some costly delicacy* to a sick servant, that he does not give to his own son in sound health' (20, 4, emphasis added). Similarly, 'other things being equal', innocence is 'the nobler thing and the more beloved', but 'the gifts of grace ... are more as conferred on the penitent ... just as a hundred pounds are a greater gift to a poor man than to a king'. The gift to the penitent is greater, and she is thus more likely to 'rise from sin more cautious, humble, and fervent'. Viewed from the perspective of need, God's gift to the penitent exceeds that given to the innocent, as the master's gift of a costly delicacy is a sign of the greater love.

The relationship among God's justice, God's liberality, and God's mercy is similar, in that what seem like paradoxical contrasts become consistent when viewed as different 'aspects' of God's activity toward humans. The contrast between the deserving and the needy returns as, in the third article of question 21 of the *Prima Pars*, Thomas explains that mercy should be seen not as a 'relaxation of justice', but as 'the fullness' of justice. Again using the imagery of gift, he suggests that we view differently what is given in 'proportion' (justice), what is given 'only on account of [God's] goodness' (liberality), and what is given as 'more than justice' (mercy). In his subsequent discussion of mercy, Thomas notes that one 'who pardons an offense committed against him ... may be said to bestow a gift'. Deepening this insight, Thomas continues in the next article to consider whether all of God's works, when viewed from a certain perspective, are mercifully gratuitous:

God out of the abundance of His goodness bestows upon creatures what is due to them more bountifully than is proportionate to their deserts: since less would suffice for preserving the order of justice than what the divine goodness confers; because between creatures and God's goodness there can be no proportion. (21, 4)

We may read Thomas as implying in this section that to speak about proportion, justice, desert, and due measurement between God and humans is potentially to lose sight of a more fundamental, merciful, *dis*proportion.

In the *Secunda Secundae*, Thomas sets charity as a virtue within this context of gratuity. The goodness that God confers through charity is distributed 'not according to our natural capacity, but according as the Spirit wills to distribute His gifts' (II-II, 24, 3). God's friendship is bestowed through the infusion of the Spirit, and as such, it is not a matter of 'acquisition by the natural powers' (II-II, 24, 2). This distribution of infused gift is the work of divine goodness on which 'every virtue depends', Thomas explains in 23, 4, and we may read him here as explaining the fundamental, gratuitous context that makes virtue itself possible. 'Charity is in-cluded in the definition of every virtue', Thomas explains in the same question, and continues in article 8 to explain that charity 'directs the acts of all other virtues to the last end' and is the virtue on which 'all other virtues draw their sustenance and nourishment'. This 'foundation or root' of love (23, 8) is distinguishable from the context of justice, wherein 'works done in respect of another person' are 'under the aspect of the legal due' (23, 3). Drawing on Aristotle's account of friendship, Thomas describes charity in article 3 as eliciting works performed in the context of 'a friendly or moral duty, or rather *that of a gratuitous favor*' (23, 3, emphasis added).

Regarding our own works of love, we must ask whether works that are more gratuitous and disproportionate are better fruits of this root, or foundation, of divine charity than works that are more proportionate? Put differently, if God's decision to become incarnate, rather than angelic, is akin to an occasion when 'the master of a house may give some costly delicacy to a sick servant, that he does not give to his own son in sound health' (I, 20, 4), is it a better approximation of charity when a master of the house gives an extravagant gift to an ill servant than when he gives one to his own healthy son? Or would such an act be more properly *mercy*, rather than charity?

When Thomas explains how charity works its way into the details of human love, he draws on an embedded sense of proportion. There is a kind of 'due' related to affinity, nearness, and kinship that is set within the context of God's gratuitous and blessedly disproportionate work on and for humanity. Although for Thomas charity is gratuitously given, through this gift God draws us nearer in friendship and, enkindling love of neighbour, makes us worthy of love. As we grow closer to God in charity, we also grow closer to God's friends, our neighbours, as they are moved toward their and our ultimate *telos*. Thus there are relevant ways that human works of love will properly draw on the importance of proximity and the evaluation of goodness. In 44, 7 on the 'Precepts of Charity' Thomas explains that 'the reason why we ought to love others out of charity is because they are nigh to us, both as to the natural image of God, and as to the capacity for glory'. Through God's work, we become nearer to every human as he or she bears the image of God and is capacitated for friendship. But within that broader relation of grace, relations of nearness and gradations of goodness are applicable. With this in mind, it may make sense that we are to love more those who are nearer to God through their greater goodness (26, 6), but that we are to love those who are nearer to us in kinship more than those who are, due to their goodness, nearer to God (26, 7). We may further understand that, while we are to love sinners out of charity (25, 6), only those who are close to God should risk association with those who are far from goodness. Thomas addresses the most obviously disproportionate work of love—love of one's enemy—in 7, 7. It is more fitting, more characteristic of goodness, he explains, to love a friend who is more nearly good due to love of you than to love an enemy who hates you.

This preliminary explanation is necessary if we are to note the subtle difference that Thomas makes between the fittingness of charity and the logic of mercy. Falling under the heading of charity—as a virtue integrally related to charity—mercy is different in that it involves relating to another primarily due to his and our *need*, not due to his goodness, nearness to God, or proximity. Whereas the preceding questions on the order of charity consider the love due to another on the continuums of goodness and proximity, mercy involves in the merciful one and in the one to be shown mercy a common 'defect', or at least a vulnerability to defect (30, 2). We may read mercy as the virtue corresponding to distance from, rather than proximity to, blessedness. It is worth quoting Thomas at length on this question:

[S]ince sorrow or grief is about one's own ills, one grieves or sorrows for another's distress, in so far as one looks upon another's distress as one's own. Now this happens in two ways: first, through union of the affections, which is the effect of love. For, since he who loves another looks upon his friend as another self, he counts his friend's hurt as his own, so that he grieves for his friend's hurt as though he were hurt himself... Secondly it happens through real union, for instance when another's evil comes near to us, so as to pass to us from him. Hence the Philosopher says that men pity such as are akin to them, and the like, because it makes them realize that the same may happen to themselves. This also explains why the old and the wise who consider that they may fall upon evil times, as also feeble and timorous persons, are more inclined toward pity; whereas those who deem themselves happy, and so far powerful as to think themselves in no danger of suffering any hurt, are not so inclined to pity. (30, 2)

To take pity, to show mercy, is to become involved in another's suffering rather than to eschew the danger of such association. The impetus behind this incautious proximity may be friendship, natural inclination toward pity, or a kind of merciful wisdom born of age and/or virtue. This latter impetus—mercy born of wisdom—is important to Thomas's explanation, in that it is the virtue contrary to unmerciful pride. He elaborates further on the vice by which a person misunderstands her own freedom from suffering and/or her relation to goodness, explaining, 'the proud are without pity, because they despise others, and think them wicked, so that they account them as suffering deservedly whatever they suffer' (30, 2). Quoting Gregory the Great, Thomas names this 'false godliness'.

Reading charity through mercy complicates an interpretation of Thomistic charity that relies on the logic of proximity, natural kinship, and excellence. Reading charity through mercy reveals a *veritable* godliness involving the wisdom that one is the recipient of God's disproportionate grace. Charity may thus most rightly beget not a cautious calculation of proper relations, but holy risk. Consider again how Thomas discusses love for sinners, in II-II, 25, 6. We may read his answer to the question from two perspectives. We may read it as advice to the Christian to avoid the unfaithful—for those who are becoming more proximate to God to avoid those whose lives are marked more by distance from than proximity to God.

His suggestion that we love sinners on the basis of their ineradicable participation in the *imago Dei* may involve a least common denominator approach; we love the imperfect inasmuch as they are still, at the very least, human. Or, alternatively, we may read Thomas's answer with mercy in view. Growth in charity will bring with it the capacity to show mercy without fear of being tainted by association. To consider the next larger concentric circle, we may view mercy as a gift born of charity born of the *dis*proportionate grace shown through Christ. As one grows in grace, one may become more aware of the larger, fundamental *kinship of neediness and giftedness* in grace. One may become cognizant of the elemental need and dependence in which the saint and the sinner are held in common. If, as Paul Wadell beautifully puts it, 'for Aquinas charity is a virtue of vulnerability, a virtue of abiding, extreme openness to God', this openness may issue forth in a merciful openness to the suffering and vulnerability of others (Wadell 1991: 78).

There are resources in Thomas's account of the ordering of charity on which to draw when considering selective abortion. We may form an argument about the maternal love due to a foetus, given the undeniable proximity between the woman and the life she carries. We could make the case that a foetus with a detectable disability is not only like the ill servant in Thomas's example but is specifically an ill daughter or son, doubly due love through proximity *and* need. But the conversation would be richer if we considered the ordering of charity with Thomas's discussion of mercy in view. Because the phenomenon of selective abortion involves fear of association with dependence and fear of those whose suffering deepens our own dependence, it seems fruitful to concentrate on the wisdom of mercy. I wish to spend some time considering how a love born of a wise regard for our common dependence may contribute to the conversation about selective abortion. Rather than discussing our worth as sharers in the *imago Dei*, or the ordered love due to the proximity of natural kinship, I now draw on two theologians who sense that we are knit together in sin and redemption.

'A Great Union between Christ and Us'

At this point I wanted to look away from the cross, but I dared not, for I well knew that while I contemplated the cross I was safe and sound; therefore I was unwilling to imperil my soul, for beside the cross there was no safety, but the ugliness of fiends. Then a suggestion came from my reason, as though a friendly voice had spoken, 'Look up to his Father in heaven.' Then I saw clearly with the faith that I felt, that there was nothing between the cross and heaven which could have distressed me, and either I must look up or I must answer. I answered and said, 'No, I cannot, for you are my heaven.' (Julian of Norwich 1998: Short Text (hereafter ST), 11, 17)

Julian's text is dedicated to 'all those who wish to be lovers of Christ'. For the reader who wishes to enter the 'revealing' of this love, the initial task is to receive a 'vivid perception of Christ'. As the text opens, Julian asks for wounds, for sickness, and for participation in the pain of Christ's death. And at 30, she receives this strange gift. On her bed, she anticipates her own death, and a priest sets the cross in front of her. While propped up on pillows, she tries instead to keep her eyes affixed toward heaven. She then supposes it perhaps easier to look straight ahead at the crucifix and, in the interest of basic convenience, she accepts the priest's suggestion and looks into the face of Christ. This simple decision is blessed. She is granted, 'suddenly', the blood of Christ pouring from his brow, 'all hot, freshly, plentifully and vividly', the fruit of this 'same who suffered for me' (ST, 3, 6). Through this vision, shown to her 'without any intermediary', Julian receives bodily assurance that she and 'every creature living that would be saved, could have strength to resist all the fiends of hell and all spiritual enemies' (ST, 3, 7).

How can this be so? How can a mere human have the strength to resist evil, particularly a dying, merely female human? In Julian's 'bodily sight', she is intertwined with suffering, pain, and safety. While enduring grief and approaching death, she embodies the Fall, but she also comes into contact with the one whose fall is our safety. Her whole being is immersed in the 'vivid' blood of Christ, and she receives the 'bodily sight' of Christ 'our clothing'. 'Hanging about us in tender love', he becomes so much a part of his beloved faithful that 'he can never leave us' (ST, 4, 7). The vision abruptly changes again, and Julian beholds a 'little thing' in which all that is, is held in God's palm. Draped with Christ as her garment, soaked in Christ's blood, held as a tiny thing on a little thing that is all that is made, Julian is brought to see that she is 'really nothing' and that she is 'in oneness of love' with all that God loves (ST, 6, 10).

What about sin? How can we be rolled together in a little ball the size and with the smooth texture of a hazelnut, given the rampant ramifications of the fracture? She receives another vision at the point of this question; she watches as not the brow but the whole body of Christ begins to bleed, 'so abundantly that it seemed to me that if at that moment it had been natural blood, the whole bed would have been blood-soaked and even the floor around' (ST, 8, 12). She reflects here on the strange fittingness that God gives us 'holy blood to wash away our sins', given that 'it is so plentiful and it shares our nature' (ST, 8, 13). Yet what about sin? Does it remain? How does his blood conquer the sin passed down through our own? She receives the words 'By this is the Fiend overcome'. This, the abundant, plentiful blood of Christ's body in distress and darkness is the way that God 'holds fast all the Devil's power', 'scorn[s] his wickedness and set[s] him as nought' (ST, 8, 13).

As she gropes toward the significance of this vision, she receives the assurance that, through this blood, 'all manner of things shall be well', and that through this blood those beloved by Christ are 'filled with compassion' for others (ST, 13, 22). For, as Christ enters her, washes her, and clothes her, she is made compassionate—part of his passion and part of Christ's love for all others.

Julian returns repeatedly to the problem of sin. How can sin be nought until it is brought to nought at the end of time? Is sin not real in suffering and willed ignorance and vice? In answering, God grants a confusing temporal collapse, as all time prior and hence meets instantly in the cross: 'for this atonement is incomparably more pleasing to God and more glorious in saving mankind than Adam's sin was ever harmful' (ST, 14, 22). The atonement forms the present; sin and suffering collide with the safety wrought by Christ's work. We are told in the longer text that it takes her twenty years to understand how this can be so, given our undeniable culpability: 'For I knew through the universal teaching of Holy Church and through my own experience that the guilt of our sin weighs us down continually' (Long Text (hereafter LT), 50, 114). It is only in the parable of a fallen servant and a loving, gracious lord that she is able to make some sense of Adam's guilt, our predicament, and the safety of the Crucifixion. In an extensive meditation, Julian discovers that Adam and Christ have been united in the person of the servant: the suffering of Adam's fall and Christ's dutiful suffering become mixed so as to be undistinguishable. 'And thus our good Lord Jesus has taken upon himself all our guilt; and therefore our Father neither may nor will assign us any more guilt than he does to his own son, dearly loved Christ' (LT, 51, 122). By Julian's vision, we cannot understand the *imago Dei*, the fall of Adam, sin, or suffering without seeing Christ. The doctrines are bled together in the bleeding of the new Adam. In this way, she comes to realize how 'wretched sin' is, truly, *nothing*.

By asking for the wounds of Christ, a woman comes to receive his blood directly, 'without an intermediary'. Through the profligate, redeeming blood, she receives bodily assurance of her safety and indeed the safety of all that is. Laughing at the devil himself, knowing him now to be nothing, she is granted the word 'that the love of God unites us to such an extent that when we are truly aware of it, no man can separate himself from another' (LT, 65, 150). Her revelation is significant even out of historical context. But in order to comprehend the full significance, it is helpful to note a few features of the turn from the fourteenth to the fifteenth century.

First, Frederick Bauerschmidt explains that the Eucharist at this time in England was by no means a celebration of the profligate blood of Christ. Rather, the Mass was 'a complex rite that depended on the participants properly performing their distinct functions', which included details such as a strictly hierarchical reception of the body and, even more notably, the restriction of the blood to the clergy (1999: 18–19). Julian receives profligate, abundant, floor-soaking blood, directly from the brow and side of Christ. Second, at the time when Julian received her revelation, people maintained a kind of obsessive control of blood itself—fearful precisely of the mixing of blood lines, contamination through bodily humours, and the transgression of boundaries both individual or corporate. There was a cultural consensus that the present was fragile and therefore in need of regulation. Bauerschmidt suggests that, by stark contrast, Julian's 'images of the human body seem to exploit that fragility's capacity for openness and generativity' (1999: 64).

With peasant revolts, ruptures in the political body, and plagues spread by the unruly fluids of individual bodies, fear of others and the desire precisely for a man to 'separate himself from another', seem reasonable. Yet Julian receives Christ's blood and envisions the world held safe in such a way that 'sin is not shameful to man, but his glory' (ST, 17, 26). In this passage, Julian touches upon one of the most radical implications of her text, the glory of those who are obviously fallen. Naming David, Peter and Paul, Thomas and Magdalene, Julian concludes that 'it is no shame to them that they have sinned . . . for there the badge of their sin is changed into glory' (ST, 17, 26). Fear of the suffering brought on by sin, and even fear of sin itself, is consumed as Christ pulls all near to his own proximity to sin. Drawing on this passage, Bauerschmidt believes that, in Julian's vision, 'the structure of the social body of Christ gives pride of place not to those who possess the most power, but to those who have been most in need and received the greatest mercy' (1999: 123).

If we bring these revelations into contact with Thomas's explication of mercy and charity, we may suspect that Julian's vision makes the *dis*proportion of divine grace the logic of an order that redefines consanguinity, proximity, and excellence. At a time when blood lines and kinship were enforced by law and by custom, Julian's vision bleeds the boundaries into kinship with Christ. At a time when fear of sin and suffering led to suspicion of blood and of unruly bodies, Julian receives the word that Christ's suffering and unruly blood are the means of safety. The task is thus not to sort through the orders of proximity and goodness, but to live in the risk-taking faith that God has poured out Christ's blood. We are all kin, and in such a manner that those on the margins of goodness and coherence are God's favoured ones. The work of the faithful is not to remain sufficiently free of suffering and sin, but to risk both with the bodily knowledge that God has conquered the fiend. For, as she says, 'although a man has the scars of healed wounds, when he appears before God they do not deface but ennoble him' (ST, 17, 26). Bound up with Christ, we may be enabled to risk mercy, to the point of physical and even spiritual danger. The blood of the Crucified One does not grant impermeability, but instead enters through our permeability to create hope, merciful wisdom, and courage. For, as she reminds us, 'He did not say, "You shall not be tormented, you shall not be troubled, you shall not be grieved," but he said, "You shall not be overcome"' (ST, 22, 34).

'SATURATED AND INTOXICATED' BY GRACE

Since these promises of God are holy, true, righteous, free, and peaceful words, full of goodness, the soul which clings to them with a firm faith will be so closely united with them and altogether absorbed by them that it will not only share in all their power but will be saturated and intoxicated by them. (Luther 1989: 601)

In *The Freedom of a Christian*, Martin Luther begins by working through 1 Corinthians 9: 19 and Romans 13: 8: 'For though I am free from all men, I have made myself a slave to all', and 'Owe no one anything, except to love one another'. The servitude that marks Christian love requires a radical freedom, a freedom owing to Christ's payment for our iniquity. Luther intertwines these Pauline verses in order to weave together justification and love; for Luther, our sin and Christ's gift become united such that the sinner becomes a servant. The Christian life is distinguished as radically freed for selfless service, and all that is worthy of our doing is worthy only inasmuch as it is saturated and intoxicated by the promises of God.

The rhetoric of the text involves, first, the nothingness of our own work, in order that we might become receptive to the work of another. This condition of nothingness is ubiquitous, not occasional. Whether we look to the Old or the New Testament, the one who seeks to love will find the same thing—'As we fare with respect to one commandment, so we fare with all, for it is equally impossible for us to keep any one of them' (Luther 1989: 600). Luther's felicitous evocation of the law brings us to the point of sheer receptivity to the grace that intoxicates:

Now when a man has learned through the commandments to recognize his helplessness and is distressed about how he might satisfy the law—since the law must be fulfilled so that not a jot or tittle shall be lost, otherwise man will be condemned without hope—then, being truly humbled and reduced to nothing in his own eyes, he finds in himself nothing whereby he may be justified and saved.

We would misread Luther if we saw merely forensic condemnation, for through being 'reduced to nothing' we are opened to receive the 'One thing, and only one thing', that is 'necessary for Christian life, righteousness and freedom'. The law teaches the soul that there is no longer any point to striving, so that one may receive the only thing needful: 'for if it could be justified by anything else, it would not need the Word, and consequently it would not need faith' (1989: 598). As Luther puts it in another treatise, *Concerning the Letter and the Spirit*, 'Grace is only given to those who long for it' (1989: 85).

Luther makes beautiful use of the Song of Solomon to evoke the 'royal marriage' between the sinner and Christ. This metaphor makes law itself like a love song by which God brings the soul closer and closer to Christ and all his benefits. If it were not for the theological use of the law and our openness to grace, there would be no 'blessed struggle and victory and salvation and redemption'—there would be no 'communion' (1989: 603). Drawn to Christ, knowing that he is the only thing needful, the Christian receives all that is Christ's, and Christ receives all that is ours. 'Sin, death, and damnation' become through this union Christ's own, and we are united with all of the 'grace, life, and salvation' that is Christ (1989: 603).

Clinging to the one who saturates us with grace, the longing soul becomes a lover. But the longing is not a once-satisfied longing. The longing and the freed servitude are intermingled. His use of the Aesop's fable about a dog running along the stream with a steak in its mouth provides a helpful entrée (Luther 1989: 608). Found at the crux of the text, the fable of the relinquished steak and the lost reflection illumines a central concern for Luther. The dog loses the steak and the image of the steak, because the image remains only inasmuch as the dog resists the illusion that the reflection is an entity by itself. The image of the meat glistening in the water is not a false impression; but neither is it real in and of itself. Works of freed, self-giving love are not ephemera; but neither do they exist apart from union with Christ.

As we are bound to Christ, opened in receptivity, we are made capable of love. Passionate longing allows the soul to receive the form of Christ our lover. Here Luther joins Paul's Letter to the Romans, with which he began the treatise, to Paul's Letter to the Philippians (1989: 617). Through our condemnation before the law, we are enabled to open ourselves to Christ, taking on the form of 'nothing' in order that we can receive everything. This 'emptying' is crucial. Our graced receptivity becomes the recurring pattern for love—our reflection, if you will, of the meat of faith. In order for us to love our neighbour, we must come to that neighbour as one who perpetually longs for Christ. As Luther puts it, we become 'Christs to one another', inasmuch as we know ourselves saved only by Christ. By this kind of faith, the Christian 'descends' to love her neighbour as he is also in need (1989: 623). The creation of obedient servants has the form of *kenosis*, and the emptying results in joyful abundance, enabling 'the freest service, cheerfully and lovingly done' (1989: 619). Because Christ gives all that a soul needs, the life of a Christian is a 'surplus', an act of doxology (1989: 617). Through *kenosis*, receptivity, and union with Christ, our lives become gift, and hardly ours to hoard or navigate with precision. Love for another becomes, quite literally, gratuitous—the Christian life one that is freely given. 'Caught up beyond himself into God' the Christian is freed to consider 'nothing except the need and advantage of the neighbor' (1989: 617).

One spot where such gratuity hits the ground is in Luther's meandering but insightful letter *Whether One May Flee from a Deadly Plague*. Written over several months, while the plague was spreading across Germany, the letter links Christ's work and our willingness to risk death to tend the suffering. Luther begins the second half by observing frankly that 'a man who will not help or support others unless he can do so without affecting his safety or his property will never help his neighbor' (1989: 743). Simply to have a neighbour means to be in proximity to another; logistically, we are bound and endangered by one another. My neighbour's house may catch fire and spread to my own, for example. To live with one another is to be exposed to the suffering around us. How we will deal with that risk is the question.

He asks the reader to recall continually that 'Christ shed his blood for me and died for me', and thus, 'why should I not expose myself to some small dangers for their sake and disregard this feeble plague?' (Luther 1989: 745). Calling God the ultimate physician, and Christ the 'far greater medicine', Luther asks why we would fear suffering?

Friend, what are all the physicians, apothecaries, and attendants in comparison to God? Should that not encourage one to go and serve a sick person, even though he might have as many contagious boils on him as hairs on his body, and though he might be bent double carrying a hundred plague-ridden bodies! What do all kinds of pestilence or devils mean over against God, who binds and obliges himself to be our attendant and physician? (1989: 746)

Anyone who has read Jean Giono's novel about the nineteenth-century cholera epidemic *The Horseman on the Roof* (or who has seen the film) cannot sneeze at the repellent task to which Luther calls his brethren. Luther writes this section while the plague is running through Wittenberg, knowing that he is asking people to risk their lives for the sake of not only their kin, but anyone who is in need. He suggests that to do so is to lash out at the devil himself: 'Just because you hate it, I'll spite you by going the more quickly to help my sick neighbor' (1989: 745). On the other hand, if we fail to go to our neighbour, the stakes are high: 'what you do or fail to do for your neighbor means doing the same to God' (1989: 747). If word spread that Mary or Jesus himself were afflicted, 'nobody would flee but everyone would come running'. Fumigate, he concludes, use medicine, do not recklessly tempt sickness, but be ready and willing to risk for others because Christ risked all and continues to be our safety even to death.

Although Luther himself tragically misread the plight and blessing of children born with disabilities, we may read him beyond his own interpretation. It is possible to interpret his advice to be outrageously merciful as directed straight to the question of prenatal testing. With the God who redeems us in Christ as the 'attendant and physician', the medical news that a foetus carries an 'abnormality' may strike us differently. Luther's texts may intermingle our understanding of the *image of God* that marks us as human and our drastic *need for Christ* that marks us as children of God. We may, reading Luther alongside Julian, set the questions of human 'normality' firmly within the framework of theological normality. For Julian and Luther, human beings are somatically related inasmuch as we are knit together physiologically by Christ's work on the cross. Saved in this way, we are bound to run toward, rather than away from, those who most obviously need physical care. Like Julian, Luther does not underestimate the courage required for such work, or the demands that a strange, Christian sense of safety will bring, but he affirms that God will not abandon those who risk.

CRUCIFORM CONSANGUINITY

When Thomas Aquinas discusses mercy, he appeals to the wisdom that we are each privy to suffering, and suggests that to view the suffering of others as their punishment is to court ungodliness. To read mercy and charity together in the *Summa* is to know the possibility of a graced and merciful disproportion that forms all wise love—the knowledge that we are knit together in need and grace. Both Julian and Luther write to redefine sin so that the task of love is not to avoid proximity with those whose needs are conspicuous but to see ourselves bound up in need and in Christ—particularly with those whose need is overt. Being bled into Christ, being wed to Christ, we are freed from our fear of entanglement, for we know ourselves to be already thoroughly entangled *and also* lovingly freed to care in proximity for those whose vulnerability or supposed 'defect' cannot be denied.

In the third epigraph to this essay, the woman who fled from mothering a child with Down's syndrome named a set of related assumptions running through the Western world. In the USA, women who discover Down's syndrome abort at a rate of 90 per cent. Nine out of ten women in the USA deem the task of mothering a child with need and difference to be more than they can bear. Because Down's syndrome marks a child in a way we desire to avoid, whole cultures have deemed that they are not, ultimately, our kin—that they belong to a race distinguishable due to their dependence and incapacity for what we count as excellence. With our increasing demand for efficiency and productivity, it is hardly surprising that many women find themselves not up to the task of bearing a child who drastically does not fit. She may soberly predict that she will go it largely alone. If we enter the default perspective and attempt to sort through the implications, it is hard to deny that our society is involved in a quiet, efficient genocide.

There are resources in Thomas, Julian, and Luther to quicken one's imagination for a kind of loving and faithful courage to risk. There is ample reason to do so. Rayna Rapp's text has itself become a standard for excellence in the field of reproductive bioethics, read in academies across the country. In the book, it becomes clear that Rapp is herself incapable of thinking within the disproportionate logic of mercy. She cannot make sense of the willed decision to bring to life a baby marked by need, in part due to the fact that, as she reveals in the conclusion to the book, she believes herself justified in aborting the Down's syndrome foetus that occasioned her research. The choice *for* affliction seems in Rapp's context to be arbitrary, a reckless endorsement of suffering. The decision to eliminate suffering through the use of selective abortion seems the most reasonable answer to the defects of nature.

At the risk of specifying what cannot be named, I will suggest one systematic implication of my reading. By becoming interwoven with Christ's suffering, we may view disability and nature in a particular way. We may come to view disability as always also a blessed sign of the Word broken for our sakes, never merely as a sign of the Fall from the ideal of nature. To view 'the natural' or the marks of normative humanity with Julian and Luther, we may not look at creation, the Fall, or signs of overt need without Christ's redemptive work as our focal point. The Word through whom the world was spoken is also the Word through whose wounds we are healed. That same Word, after the Resurrection, still bears the marks that are our redemption. It is possible that Christians may use this logic in a way that makes the choice to receive a child marked by need seem newly *reasonable*, a sign of our kinship of affliction in need and redemption in Christ. To receive gratefully and mercifully the gift of such a child may become a *natural* witness to our common need, our proximate consanguinity in suffering, and our marriage to Christ. So to choose may testify to a different kind of safety and a different kind of love.

REFERENCES AND SUGGESTED READING

AQUINAS, THOMAS (1948). *Summa Theologica*. New York: Benziger.

BAUERSCHMIDT, F. (1999). *Julian of Norwich and the Mystical Body Politic of Christ*. Notre Dame, Ind.: University of Notre Dame Press.

GIONO, J. (1996). *The Horseman on the Roof*, trans. Jonathan Griffin. New York: North Point Press.

HALL, A. L. (1999). 'Complicating the Command: Agape in Scriptural Context', *Annual of the Society of Christian Ethics*, 19, 97–113.

JULIAN OF NORWICH (1998). *Revelations of Divine Love*, ed. E. Spearing and A. C. Spearing. New York and London: Penguin.

LUTHER, M. (1989). *Martin Luther's Basic Theological Writings*, ed. T. Lull. Minneapolis: Augsburg Fortress.

NYGREN, A. (1953). *Agape and Eros*, trans. P. Watson. Philadelphia: Westminster Press.

RAPP, R. (1999). *Testing Women, Testing the Fetus: The Social Impact of Amniocentesis in America*. New York : Routledge.

WADELL, P. (1991). *Friends of God: Virtues and Gifts in Aquinas*. New York: Peter Lang.

PART V

SPHERES OF THE CHRISTIAN LIFE

CHAPTER 19

CHRISTIANS AND GOVERNMENT

ROBERT BENNE

THE well-known Christian ethicist Stanley Hauerwas and I were once part of a panel discussion on how Christians should relate to politics. (In this chapter I will use 'politics', 'the state', and 'government' as equivalents. *Random House Webster's College Dictionary* (1991) defines government as 'the political direction and control exercised over the actions of the members, citizens, or inhabitants of communities; direction of the affairs of a state'. The same dictionary defines 'state' as 'the body politic as organized for civil rule and government'.) The question came up: Ought a Christian to be a senator? As a Lutheran, my answer was clear: 'Of course, politics is an honourable vocation in which a Christian can serve his fellow human beings by seeking temporal peace, order, and justice.' Hauerwas had quite a different answer: 'I suppose a Christian could be a senator if his career lasted only one term.' This meant that a Christian senator would propose so many radical pieces of legislation that his constituents would immediately vote him out of office, if they didn't impeach him first.

This small example of controversy among Christians about their relation to government is a microcosm of a debate that has taken place in Christianity since its inception. There are many contemporary manifestations of this age-old disagreement. Some Christians belonging to Mennonite traditions believe, like Hauerwas, that all politics is so caught up in coercion and violence that Christians must shun it. (Or at least take one brief turn in it!) Many more Christians believe that Christians should sequester their religious convictions in their private lives. They, like many of their American secular counterparts, seem to think that 'separation of church and state' means that neither religious institutions nor persons should express religious rhetoric or values in public life.

However, a much larger contingent of Christians believe that churches and individual Christians should involve themselves vigorously in political life. Most churches in the United States have 'advocacy offices' through which they try to persuade elected officials to adopt their preferred policies. To the great consternation of Europeans, American Christian political leaders use religious rhetoric in their speeches and employ religious ideas in shaping their policies. American Christians expect candidates to speak about their religious commitments. Indeed, half of American voters would not vote for an atheist, and more than half of them believe that journalists should quiz candidates about how their religious convictions will affect their policies (Pew Forum on Religion in Public Life).

What is the origin of these differences among Christians with regard to their involvement in government? What are the significant issues involved in these differences? Are there good reasons to opt for one or another of these Christian positions? In this chapter I will examine the biblical sources for Christian reflection on Christians' relation to politics, examine the classic, historical Christian traditions on these matters, and finally offer my own conclusions.

BIBLICAL SOURCES

Christian attitudes toward politics are invariably based on biblical sources, though it is clear that different church traditions interpret those sources in different ways. However, they all start with the Scriptures.

On the face of it, the Old Testament does not seem to offer much help in shaping Christian views on government. In the Old Testament, government, religion, economics, family, and society were fused into one organic whole, just as they were in all ancient societies. So there was no room for religious people to stand over against their government; it was all of a piece. (A small group of Christians called 'Reconstructionists' or 'Dominionists' believe that Christians should adapt the Old Testament model and apply it to modern circumstances. In their view Old Testament Law would then become the law for American society. There are obvious parallels here between Reconstructionists and Muslims who believe that Islamic law should become the law of the land wherever Muslims prevail.)

Even though there is a vast difference between our modern Western societies and that of ancient Israel, there are fundamental themes from the Old Testament that affect Christian views of government. One such theme is the affirmation that God created the world and humans in his image. Humans are the crown of creation and to be deeply respected. However, immediately following the account of creation is the story of the Fall, which is central for all Christian views of government. No human escapes the stain of sin, and this sin is compounded in collective life, which obviously includes government. This means that all humans and their institutions are tainted by sin, though there is disagreement among Christian traditions about the extent and comprehensiveness of sin, as well as about the possibilities of its being overcome.

Though the creation is fallen, God did not abandon the world to its own devices or to Satan, but has continued to sustain it in order that he might recall it to himself. God elected Israel to carry out his purposes in the world. He liberates Israel from its bondage in Egypt and leads it toward the Promised Land. Even the world beyond Israel is under the providence and sovereign will of God. For example, God uses King Cyrus to liberate Israel from its Babylonian captivity (Isa. 44: 28 and Ezra 1). God is sovereign over the world and its history, including its governments.

Another crucial theme is that of covenant. Israel believed that God had made a number of covenants with them (the promissory ones to Abraham and Noah, for example, and the law covenant with Moses). The Mosaic covenant is the most important for our purposes, because it laid out a vision of peace and justice (shalom) that was ordered by God's commandments. These commandments were not viewed as a burden. Rather, they were a gift of God's grace that enabled the community to live in harmony. That grace was continuous with the grace that had elected them and had freed them from bondage.

The covenantal existence of Israel was characterized by a number of important features that remain relevant to contemporary Christians. One is that the covenant binds the people together in a moral community in which they have continuing responsibilities to and for one another. Each member owes each other just treatment. Each person counts in the covenant. The covenant goes beyond contracts (rational bargaining about rights and duties) to more open-ended commitments. It includes the wayfarer, the sojourner, and other vulnerable persons. The community of the covenant is held accountable to God, and he blesses or judges according to the standards he has established (Allen 1984: 49 ff.).

The great prophets were called by God to make clear his commands as well as Israel's failure to live up to them. They reminded Israel of its covenant with God and communicated both judgement and hope. The prophets held Israel accountable to something that transcended them: God and his commandments. Judges, kings, and high priests were all subservient to God's will.

By the time of the New Testament the kingdoms of Israel were long gone, and the Roman Empire governed the areas of the world where Christianity began. Now there was an 'over-against-ness' of Christian believers with regard to the state and government. Both the Jews and the early Christians had to come to terms with the Roman political reality.

However, ancient Hebrew ideas about the purposes of government were not forgotten by Jesus and the early Christians. When the Pharisees try to stump Jesus with a difficult question about whether it is lawful for Jews to pay taxes to Caesar, he wisely retorts: 'Render to Caesar what is Caesar's, and to God the things that are God's' (Mark 12: 17; New Oxford Annotated RSV). This has had continued meaning for Christians. For one thing, Jesus does not counsel disobedience or rebellion against the Roman tax laws, as some of his followers wanted him to do. He also recognizes that Caesar does important things, and that it is lawful for Jews to pay taxes to support those things—order, security, and a semblance of justice. However, he also makes it clear that believers' first loyalty ought to be to God, not to Caesar. Though it would be hazardous to parse Jesus' meaning on these matters too finely, these basic meanings have been significant for Christians throughout the ages.

Paul follows Jesus' teaching that the state has important functions that Christians should honour. But he is less enigmatic than Jesus. Paul advises:

Let every person be subject to the governing authorities. For there is no authority except from God, and those that exist have been instituted by God. Therefore he who resists the authorities resists what God has appointed, and those who resist will incur judgment. For rules are not a terror to good conduct, but to bad. Would you have no fear of him who is in authority? Then do what is good, and you will receive his approval, for he is God's servant for your good. But if you do wrong, be afraid, for he does not bear the sword in vain; he is the servant of God to execute his wrath on the wrongdoer. Therefore one must be subject, not only to avoid God's wrath but also for the sake of conscience. (Rom. 13: 1–5, RSV)

Paul then counsels Christians to pay their fair portion of taxes. In the First Letter of Peter we find very similar directives to early Christians in the Roman Empire (1 Pet. 2: 13–17).

Paul is clear that the Roman authorities have proper authority over Christians, but that authority is an authority derived from God. The state has important purposes: to keep order by punishing the wrongdoer. Indeed, it does this in God's stead. This favourable assessment of Rome is counterbalanced by Peter's famous statement in Acts 5: 29: 'We must obey God rather than men.'

The letters of John present a more emphatic and systematic rejection of life in Roman culture in general and participation in politics in particular. While Christians are enjoined to love one another, since God is love, they are not to love the 'world'. 'Do not love the world or the things of this world. If any one loves the world, love for the Father is not in him' (1 John 2: 15). The 'world' appears as a realm under the power of evil and darkness; citizens of Christ's kingdom must not enter it. Rather, Christians are to gather into enclaves of love until the end comes, when they shall be rescued from a world that is dying.

The writer of Revelation follows a similar tack, but is even more graphic in his portrayal of Rome as an idolatrous power. Rome is the 'Whore of Babylon', who demands that Christians must worship it. When Christians refuse to bow to it in worship, the Beast ravenously devours them. Christians are bound to resist it by suffering. The Rome in Revelation is a demonic power that will finally be crushed by the power of God, which will vindicate the Christians who have suffered under it. These images from Revelation have resonated throughout the ages among Christians who have been oppressed by violently hostile states.

Both Old and New Testaments contain powerful, but often contradictory, ideas of how Christians should relate to politics. Taken by themselves, they provide no systematic approach to Christians and government, because they are fragmentary, and because they were written in dramatically different times. In the Old Testament there is no distinction between religion and politics, and there are obviously no Christians. In the New Testament Christians are a small and sometimes oppressed group that has little responsibility for the political order, which is dominated by Rome. More careful reflection on Christianity and the political order emerged only after the Church became a power to be reckoned with and therefore accepted some responsibility for worldly affairs.

Yet, Christians throughout the ages have drawn on these ideas and themes to develop more systematic accounts of the Christian churches' role in government, which then affect how the individual adherents of particular churches see their relation to politics. In the following section I will show how these biblical themes have been organized by specific Christian traditions into more coherent interpretations of Christians and government.

DIFFERENT CHRISTIAN TRADITIONS AND THEIR ACCOUNTS OF CHRISTIANS AND GOVERNMENT

Christ against Politics

H. Richard Niebuhr's perennially helpful book, *Christ and Culture* (1951), is a good place to begin sorting out these varied traditions. The first response to the question of how Christianity should relate to politics—which is definitely a part of culture in Niebuhr's account—is given by the 'Christ against culture' tradition. This tradition picks up the negative posture depicted in the letters of John and Peter and in Revelation, and develops them into a coherent viewpoint and ethos. It had important representatives in the early Church—the authors of *The Teaching of the Twelve* and Tertullian—as well as in radical monastic movements in the Middle Ages. It resurfaced in the so-called Radical Reformation among the followers of Menno Simons. It gained a powerful spokesman in the nineteenth century in Count Leo Tolstoy, who in mid-life rejected all his literary achievements and his wealth, organized a radical Christian commune, and left 'the world'. It continues to this day in the more conservative Mennonite communities and among many Christians of other traditions who are persuaded by its uncompromising stance toward the world, its simplicity, and especially its pacifism.

This tradition views 'the world' as radically fallen, particularly in its institutional life. Politics is perhaps the worst of institutions, because it is based on coercion and the threat of violence, if not violence itself. This is contrasted with the teachings of Jesus in his Sermon on the Mount (Matt. 5–7), which enjoins a radical obedience to his teaching. This radical obedience is possible to follow and necessary for salvation. The Beatitudes blesses those who show a simple but firm obedience, who cast their existence on the grace of God. Later, Jesus' moral injunctions require 'turning the other check', 'loving one's enemies', and refraining from oaths, anger, lust, vengeance, and hypocrisy.

Living according to Jesus' teachings will create a community of love like that depicted in the letters of John. Likewise, followers of this tradition believe that there can be no compromise with the world, as so many other Christians do. When Jesus enjoins these radical behaviours, he intends them simply and straightforwardly for Christians to live by, not as some interim or future ethic, but one for right now.

This stance has often meant that adherents of this Christ against culture tradition retreat to Christian enclaves. For those who do not retreat, it means a reluctance to participate in public institutions such as government. The injunction of Peter to obey God rather than men rings loudly in their ears. Adherence to this tradition means pacifism and a refusal to serve in the military. Members of this tradition may be farmers and craftsmen, but never mayors or senators. Yet there are contemporary representatives of the tradition—the late John Howard Yoder and Stanley Hauerwas, for example—who are neither reclusive nor passive. They believe that Christians should bear witness to Jesus' radical teachings by living them out publicly and by demonstrating the stark contrast between the 'peaceable kingdom' of Jesus and a political world built on coercion and violence. Such Christians are called to the prophetic task of helping the world understand what it really is. But as for becoming a senator, only one term please! (Hauerwas 1983; Yoder 1972).

While this tradition has an important witness to make—it reveals the many compromises with the world that other Christians make—it ultimately seems to deny that the sovereign God calls Christians to responsibility in and for the world. Its refusal to participate in the political process reneges on the divine requirement to love the neighbour through that process, even though the political process requires the use of coercion and threat of force. While it is willing to 'bind the wounds' of the world in various charitable enterprises, it is unwilling to participate in political efforts to maintain order and justice.

By contrast, the three great magisterial traditions of mainstream Christianity—Catholic, Lutheran, and Reformed—all have theologies that allow and even encourage participation in the political world. They do this by affirming Christian participation in the fallen world, including its politics. Though the world is fallen, it is still God's world, and Christians in churches and as individuals are called to serve their neighbour through government. These three great traditions recognize the tension between the radical teachings of Christ and politics, but do not spurn participation in the political process like the Christ against culture Christians do. Rather, they embrace that tension, but manage it in different ways. The Christ above politics tradition is a good place to begin, because it was the dominant model for many centuries—from the time of Constantine in the fourth century to the time of the Reformation.

Christ above Politics

Though the rapidly growing Christian movement was persecuted sporadically throughout the first three centuries after Christ, an astounding reversal took place when Constantine the Great became emperor. During his struggle to become the sole governor of the Roman Empire, Constantine experienced a vision in which Christ told him to put the symbol of Christ on the shields of his soldiers. He converted to Christianity and became the unchallenged emperor in 311. He arranged the Edict of Milan in 313, which granted toleration to Christianity. As his reign progressed, he increasingly favoured Christianity and began to suppress paganism. He called the Council of Nicaea in 325, which issued in the Nicene Creed, a great ecumenical creed that defines the key doctrines of Christianity (Walker 1959: 101).

However, the remarkable thing was that the emperor was now a Christian and began to work some Christian teachings and values into his governing. He gathered bishops as advisors, and he died in the baptismal garb of a Christian neophyte in 337. For the first time the Christian Church and Christian individuals were in the highest governing roles. Though some early theologians, such as Clement of Alexandria, provided a rationale for this new Christian role, it took a long time before Christians came to terms with their new position of political dominance.

The Christ above politics model was constructed throughout the early and medieval Church. The full realization of this model took place in the High Middle Ages (twelfth to thirteenth centuries) and was given its most systematic articulation in the theology of Thomas Aquinas (1225–74). One of Thomas's great intellectual achievements was the synthesis of the classical philosophy of Aristotle with the Catholic theology of the Church.

What Thomas synthesized intellectually was reflected in the practical life of the High Middle Ages, which featured a grand synthesis between Christ and culture, the Church and politics. It is a hierarchically ordered fusion that features one God, one Son of God, one Vicar of Christ on Earth, one Church, and one king over one kingdom. A grand unity—called Christendom—is presided over by the supernatural wisdom and grace of the Church. Indeed, this Christendom carries interesting parallels with the Old Testament kingdoms, though there was obviously no Church to direct things in the Old Testament.

In contrast to the Christ against politics tradition, Christ above politics distinguishes Christ from politics without separating the two. Put another way, Christ and politics are combined without confusion, something unthinkable to Christ against politics adherents.

The Church and the Christian king who is tutored by the Church are now responsible for the earthly institution of government. But the king, as well as the citizens who live below him in the earthly realm, are directed by something quite other than the Sermon on the Mount. They are guided by the cardinal virtues of courage, justice, prudence, and moderation, which were recognized and nurtured by the classical civilizations of Greece and Rome. These virtues, which enable both king and subject to live according to natural law, orient them both to the worldly ends of temporal happiness. The king governs according to these virtues, laws, and ends. Subjects are called to obedience to the Christian king, who also is responsible for protecting the Church and hearkening to its guidance. In all these activities he is allowed and, at proper times, even obligated to use coercive force to enforce temporal justice and peace.

Indeed, the Church of Christendom developed authoritative teaching on when and how lethal force can be used by the king. The doctrine of a 'just war' is an important sign that the Christian sovereign and Christian soldiers can participate in warfare that protects the Church and fellow Christians from unjust attack. The direct injunctions of the Sermon on the Mount can be laid aside in the service of love for the neighbour in this fallen world.

However, all these earthly goods are merely preparatory to something higher. While the earthly *polis* can bring humans to the natural level, only the Church can bring them to their supernatural destiny. Through its sacramental system the Church can channel all Christians to their final end, the Beatific Vision of God. Indeed, the Church is directed by a Pope and a priesthood that transcend the religious and moral level of the laity, including the king. Those who enter priestly and monastic orders are expected to live according to the radical teachings of the Sermon on the Mount. They are to live lives of poverty, chastity, and obedience. Thus, the Catholic synthesis incorporates the radical teachings of Jesus while at the same time taking responsibility for the temporal world, especially its governance.

This synthesis is presided over by the Church, which is given power over the 'earthly sword' (the king) by Christ, and whose vicar, 'the Pope', guides the Church. Since the world is fallen and its guidance by fallen men may falter, the Church is given the final authority in matters of governance. Though the Middle Ages were characterized by constant jousting between king and Church, it was clear that worldly matters of politics were finally subservient to the Divine Will as interpreted by the Church.

This synthesis of Christ and politics had an enormous impact upon the Western world. It shaped the landscape of Europe by elaborating its laws and various other social institutions. The Western world is still living on the moral capital of this synthesis. However, the synthetic model had grave shortcomings, which have led to its abandonment. The Church itself became so enmeshed in politics that its religious activities tended to become politicized, and its political activities were given religious legitimation. The Church became one more political entity among other contenders and lost its transcendence over politics. Its monopoly over religion also tended to corrupt its religious character. Above all, its involvement in political and military power distorted its proper task, the transmission of the Gospel, which cannot be realized authentically by coercive means. Perhaps the Church did the responsible thing in taking up political power when the ancient world crumbled, but later centuries proved that the Church is on perilous ground when it wields political power.

In the last half-century the Roman Catholic Church has distanced itself from the Christ above politics model. The Church no longer claims to wield direct political power, though it still holds that religious values should deeply influence political life. Popes John XXIII and John Paul II have led the Church to accept liberal democracy and religious freedom. But the Church still encourages a robust role in politics for the Catholic laity, and it offers guidance to both its members and society with its social teachings.

Christ and Politics in Paradox

One of the issues that sparked the Reformation was the Roman Catholic Church's enmeshment in politics. Martin Luther argued that its entanglement in politics led to the corruption of its teaching and mission, as well as its involvement in the oppression of many peoples. One of the first initiatives of the Reformation was to reduce the direct political involvement of the Church. For the Lutheran Reformers the Church's mission was the proclamation of the Gospel, and this central task could be achieved only by the 'weapons of the Spirit', not through political power.

However, the Christ and politics in paradox tradition had its inception long before Luther. Its biblical progenitor was St Paul, who, as noted earlier, advised Christians to honour the emperor, obey the Empire's laws, and be good citizens.

Following Jesus, Paul teaches that Christians should give to Caesar what is Caesar's, but to God what is God's. And to God Christians owe their ultimate loyalty. But in this current time they live between two aeons—one in which Christ will reign and the current one in which Caesar reigns (Rom. 5). They must be accountable and responsible in both kingdoms, though their final home is not in the earthly kingdom. Paul opens the way for Christians to participate in politics and the military, though in Paul's time Christians collectively were neither strong enough nor large enough to make much of a political impact.

St Augustine in the fourth and fifth centuries continues this tentative dualism. Christians participate in and are finally loyal to the city of God, which is closely identified with the Church, provisionally in its earthly form but ultimately in its heavenly. The rich covenantal existence of the Church is enabled by the grace of God. But, Christians also live in the earthly city, which is oriented toward mutable and often perverse goods. Its peace is based on strife. Yet, Augustine argued, Christians must be responsible citizens within it. They can make use of and participate in the provisional, marred peace of the earthly city, which is shared by good and bad alike. Christians can participate in the provisional goods of the earthly city without forgetting that their final destiny is destruction. Indeed, the two cities co-mingle until they are finally winnowed out at the end of history.

In the meantime, Christians can take part in 'giving and taking commands', which is the essence of government. 'When Christians undertake governmental responsibilities, which they should be willing to do out of love for their neighbors, they do so with a restraint born of repugnance, for they understand the inherent tragedy in the need for coercive justice. This modifies their severity and makes them seek opportunities for constructive love to the offender: emperors take vengeance only for unarguable reasons of state' (1958: 5); 'warriors are peacemakers even at war' (Letter 189); 'judges are tormented by the limitations of their ignorance; slave-owners make themselves the servants of those they appear to command' (Letter 10).

Christians—informed by the love of Christ—do indeed participate in political life. And as Christians they mitigate its harshness. But there is little confidence that the fundamental logic of the earthly city will change. The recalcitrance of sin will always dictate that the desires of the earthly city will remain fundamentally disordered. As Christians participate, then, they live paradoxically 'in' but not 'of' the world. They live 'in' it in a responsible way, because even in its fallen state they are enjoined by God to love their neighbours in many ways, including the political. But they are not 'of' of it, because they realize that its destiny is not theirs. Theirs is the heavenly city.

Luther does not spatialize the two cities as does Augustine; the Church is not simply the city of God, nor is the world simply the earthly city. Rather, Luther emphasizes that God acts or rules in two different ways. He rules through his 'right hand', the Gospel, which is proclaimed to all persons. (The Gospel is proclaimed in and through the Church, but is not identified with the Church.) Those who receive the Gospel—the grace of God in Christ—are then 'free lords of all; subject to none'. Their direct relation to God in Christ makes them immediate participants in God's reign through the Gospel. However, those same Christians are 'servants of all, subject to all'. They are sent into a world that is governed by God's 'left hand' through his law, i.e., the creating, sustaining, limiting, and judging actions that maintain this fallen world.

Like Augustine, Luther does not expect the left-hand kingdom to approximate the kingdom of God. It is fully permeated by sin, death, and the Devil, which contend with God for allegiance of the world and all its inhabitants. This realism about the recalcitrance of sin in politics and society is a reflection of the Lutheran teaching that even justified Christians remain sinners until the end of their days. Thus, pessimism about Christians living a sanctified, perfected life on the individual level is paralleled by the Lutheran conviction that full transformation cannot be realized on the political and social level. The Lutheran tradition is profoundly anti-utopian.

But God has not given up on the world. He has established certain orders of creation that are instruments of his law and serve as 'dikes against sin'. Family (which included economic life in Luther's view), Church, and state are all such orders. Though their function is certainly negative, there are positive possibilities within them, especially if they are filled by Christians who, responding to the Gospel, live out their callings in these places of responsibility.

In Luther's view Christians can be princes, mayors, magistrates, lawyers, and above all responsible subjects who not only do what God's law and their roles require, but in addition serve their fellow human beings in their callings by expanding and stretching their duties. In this way, Christians become conduits of God's love in their callings, including their political callings. However, their deeds of love cannot run roughshod over the obligations they have in their places of responsibility. The individual Christian may follow the Sermon on the Mount if he is accosted by robbers in the forest, but as a sheriff or governmental official, the Christian is obligated to resist and arrest the robber, using lethal force if necessary.

Early Lutheranism built up its own society after its initial sharp rejection of the older Catholic model (Witte 2002). One of its features was that all the 'orders of creation', including the Church, were placed alongside each other rather than in the hierarchical order of the Christ above politics model. But institutions mutually influenced each other, mainly by Christians within them exercising their callings. The priest or Pope was no higher before God than the king, and neither was higher than the Christian lay person. However, the early Lutherans made the fateful decision to place the Church under the care and governance of the prince. This entailed a fateful dependence of the Church on the state, which in turn often produced a quietistic Church with regard to political matters.

Though early Lutheranism featured a lively dialectical relation between the Lutheran Church and the political order, over time this lively tension diminished as the Church became more passive before a strengthening government. On the other hand, individual Lutherans continued to exercise worthy and effective vocations in government. But for the larger mass of Lutherans the government's commands took on the status of strict obligation and blind duty, sometimes leading to tragic political consequences. Modern Lutheranism, by contrast, has generally overcome this passivity, partly due to its interaction with the fourth tradition of Christ and politics, to which we now turn.

Christ Transforming Politics

The final tradition with which we will deal is the one preferred by H. Richard Niebuhr himself, Christ transforming culture. (Niebuhr included a fifth type of Christ–culture relation, which he called 'Christ of culture', that we will not elaborate. This tradition relaxes the tension between Christ and politics not by withdrawing from the latter, as does the Christ against politics tradition, but by so immersing itself in politics that political ideology and activity replace religious identity and activity. Christians of this sort adapt so fully to political imperatives that they soon lose any Christian distinctiveness.) While he affirmed that the other traditions held important insights for the Christian role in the world of politics, he argued that this 'transforming' or 'conversionist' perspective most honours the whole counsel of God as creator, redeemer, and sanctifier. Certainly Old Testament affirmations of the sovereignty of God over all creation and history are crucial for this perspective, as is the responsibility to conform Christian action to God's sovereign will. Likewise, the notion that God is pressing history toward his kingdom, a dynamic kingdom that embodies his covenant love and promotes covenantal existence in all the world. Further, the requirement to obey Jesus in all callings, including the political, adds additional dynamic to this perspective. Indeed, Niebuhr wrote a book entitled *The Kingdom of God in America* (1959), in which he argues that one cannot understand America without grasping the idea of the kingdom of God. It is a story of 'constructive' Protestantism, which is animated by the theological themes of the sovereignty of God, the kingdom of Christ, and the coming kingdom. This tradition calls the Church and Christians to a robust relation to the political world, one that intends to transform the world toward God's kingdom.

If the Lutheran Reformation expressed an ambivalent attitude toward the Christian and politics, the Calvinist version did not. It aimed at creating a Christian society through politics, not one directed by a hierarchical Church, but one directed by godly magistrates formed by the Church. God's reign in and through worldly institutions is not something negative, but expansively positive.

While the conversionist perspective is just as realistic in its assessment of the pervasiveness of human sin in the world, it is more likely than the paradox perspective to believe that fallen structures can be transformed to approximate the kingdom of God, with all its covenantal characteristics. This transformation is first of all the work of God, but it proceeds with the obedient co-operation of Christians. Politics is a crucial instrument in this transformational process.

The Calvinist Reformation had much more confidence in its capacity to shape a Christian society than did the Lutheran. It believed that the Bible reveals a discernible pattern—called the 'Third Use of the Law' in Reformed theology—for a holy life. Christians informed by the Holy Spirit have the capacity not only to discern this pattern but to construct an approximation of the kingdom of God on earth. This 'constructive' approximation takes place in politics, economics, culture, and social institutions (Witte 1997).

This Christian belief in the possibility of political transformation is reflective of a deep theological conviction about the Christian life. Reformed Christianity has a strong doctrine of sanctification, which stipulates that the Holy Spirit can lead to a robustly sanctified life in the faithful Christian. Such Christians can then become the spearhead of transformative projects that can 'Christianize' society. Confidence in personal sanctification leads to confidence in political transformation.

The Puritans went to America from England not only so that they could worship freely, but also because they would then have the opportunity to construct a pure and holy church, government, and society. Their 'errand in the wilderness' was to follow God in his desire to give the world a new start in the New World, free from the corruptions and inertia of the Old World.

Thus, the 'conversionist' tradition was transplanted to America, where it became the dominant religious perspective. It has produced a robust Christianity that has been both institutionally and individually involved in political life. It has expended great energy in transformationist projects—abolition, prohibition, women's suffrage, unionization, and civil rights, among many others. God is doing new things in America; as Christians respond to his will, they participate in building the kingdom.

American life is replete with the many voluntary associations spun off by the Church that are devoted to the betterment of society. Some are charitable, some are cause-oriented, and some are directly political, but a significant proportion are fuelled by Christians who have been influenced markedly by a Reformed Christianity that has convinced them that they must take up the responsibility to contribute to the expansion of God's kingdom on earth.

While many Western nations have been blessed by this 'constructive' Protestantism, it also has weaknesses that can lead to deformation. Undue confidence in discerning God's will can lead to arrogance and legalism. The original belief in God's sovereignty can be domesticated into confidence that humans can build God's kingdom. The exaggerated estimate of the possibilities of politics can lead to cynicism and despair when politics fail to bring in the kingdom. Perhaps most seriously, the fascination with politics as an instrument of transformation can lead to a replacement of genuine religious interest and conviction by political immersion and ideology. Politics can replace religion as the religious vitality of the conversionist tradition wanes. Thus, there can be a subtle transition over time into the Christ of culture posture. Such can be the fate of Reformed Christianity without its deeper confessional conviction.

CONCLUDING REFLECTIONS ON CHRISTIANS AND GOVERNMENT

H. Richard Niebuhr ended his *Christ and Culture* with a chapter title borrowed from Kierkegaard called 'A Concluding Unscientific Postscript' (Niebuhr 1951: 230 ff.). In that chapter he reflected on what these different and sometimes conflicting Christ–culture traditions might contribute to God's whole truth. Though he seems to argue for the 'conversionist' tradition, he admits that none of us can assess these traditions from God's point of view. However, he offers hope that the partial truths in all of them may converge over time to make a more complete and accurate picture of how Christ relates to culture. In this concluding section I will synthesize the most compelling themes into a framework that I hope will be useful to Christians in relating to government. In that framework I will make a theological assessment of government, define some crucial marks of the Church, and summarize briefly my view of the proper relationship of Christians with government.

It is important to note that these reflections assume the kind of governments characteristic of Western democracies, which share certain features—consent of the governed, an independent judiciary, civil rights, and limits on the scope and power of government. These governments do, however, exercise power which is coercive, and can rightfully engage in violence in just causes. It is certainly true that governments can become terribly oppressive, but here I am assuming more positive examples.

The first theme in this theological assessment of government is that it should *be rightly honoured by Christians*. As St Paul argued in Romans 13, government is part of the created order, given us by God to establish order, security, and justice. Without such political achievements at home and abroad, life in all its forms cannot flourish; with them it can. Above all institutions on earth, government can command resources for the worthy purposes for which it is constituted. Therefore, Christians can and ought to participate in the functions of government.

This affirmation distinguishes my approach from the Christ against politics tradition, which seems to view government as so inevitably and thoroughly fallen that Christians ought not participate in it. That view implies that God has abandoned the political world to evil powers, which simply ought not to be engaged. This negative judgement is mainly due to that tradition's making non-coercion a moral absolute. It makes the Sermon on the Mount the centre-piece of Christian faith and life, ignoring many of the other biblical and theological themes mentioned earlier. Since governments do employ coercive methods, it argues, Christians cannot participate in them.

Yet, it is certainly not clear that coercion is absolutely prohibited in the Bible. The Old Testament has God commanding Israel to use coercive force against her enemies. Jesus cleanses the Temple with emphatic force: 'And making a whip of cords, he drove them all, with the sheep and oxen, out of the temple' (John 2: 15).

Moreover, there is in this tradition a certain reluctance to come to the realistic defence of the neighbour who is under threat. The other traditions affirm that it is justifiable to use coercive force, even lethal force, to keep predators from harming innocent persons.

This first theme—that Christians ought to regard government highly—also differentiates my perspective from the cynicism of some parts of the Lutheran tradition, which sees government as hopelessly corrupt and therefore acts with cold self-interest in political affairs. Similarly, this perspective denies that government has only negative functions, as Lutheranism sometimes held in its image of the state as a 'dike against sin'. Certainly, government does have important negative functions in maintaining order and security, but it can and does go beyond them. The Reformed and Catholic traditions are more wholesome here, the Reformed suggesting that government can move the political community toward covenantal practices that expand and deepen justice, and the Catholic suggesting that government policies that pursue the common good can lift humanity to its full 'natural' level. Christian love working through principles of justice can enable governments to do positive good.

A second theme in my assessment of government is that *it is necessarily accountable to God's will, which transcends it.* While the state indeed has authority, it is a derived and conditional authority. For Christians, then, there is always the possibility of conscientious objection to the policies of the state, for when those policies conflict with the demands of God, Christians 'must obey God rather than men' (Acts 5: 29). Though the Christ against politics tradition is too absolutist in its rejection of coercion, it nevertheless is an important witness to the transcendence of God's will over the will of the state. The option of conscientious objection has been exercised frequently in history, and will continue to be exercised as long as there are authentic Christians around.

Moreover, Christian faith denies any salvific power in the policies and actions of government. The state is to seek order and justice, but it can never save souls. It has the task of seeking penultimate goods. It will be fortunate to achieve a modicum of justice in this turbulent world. This sense of the limits of politics differentiates my position from that of Christians who are tempted to conflate the saving grace of God with revolutionary action or who believe that they can use politics to build the kingdom of God on earth.

These seemingly negative contributions of the Christian faith are exceedingly important at this time in history. The state, above all other earthly centres of power, has the capacity to claim godly power. Since the rise of the nation-state as the central political unit, it has constantly been tempted to proclaim itself *the* centre of value, demanding that ultimate loyalty be given to it by its citizens. The totalitarian states of our time—both Communist and Fascist—made and violently enforced such idolatrous claims in a pervasive way. The most powerful democracies of our time—including the United States—are not immune to idolatrous temptations, though they carry within them important checks and balances. Here the great prophetic tradition of the Old Testament provides a resource for Christians to resist idolatrous tendencies, no matter what their source.

The mission of the Church is to proclaim the Gospel in word and sacrament and to gather through the Spirit a community that responds to that Gospel. No other institution on earth is called to such an ultimately important task. As it nurtures Christians in the Church—the Body of Christ—so it forms them in the Christian virtues of faith, love, and hope and implants in their minds a vision that is made up of centuries of Christian reflection on the biblical narrative, which includes many of the biblical insights explored earlier. This vision is comprehensive and central. It is comprehensive, in that it applies to all of life, not just to the inner recesses of the heart. It is central, in that it assesses the world of politics with compelling biblical and theological insight. Christians who 'have been transformed by the renewal of their minds' (Rom. 12: 2) go into the world of politics with a perspective that will make a difference. They will be salt and leaven in the political process. The greatest political calling of the Church is to prepare the laity for their worldly callings.

Moreover, the Church is to carry out its mission using only the 'weapons of the Spirit'—proclamation, education, protest, and address. It is not to become directly enmeshed in the power plays of government. The corrupting tendencies of such involvement for both Church and society have been clearly evident throughout history.

Given this assessment of government and the mission of the Church, it seems clear that Christians are called to active involvement in political life. God has established government for the benefit of the human community. Though it is a fallen institution, it nevertheless carries great possibilities as well as great dangers. Christians should grasp their political responsibilities and *participate critically* in political life. This means bringing their perspectives and actions to bear on the dynamic of political life. They should hold government in high esteem, but not idolatrously so.

Above all, it is important that lay persons carry their Christian values right into the heart of the political process. Such witness will be far more effective than the sometimes necessary social statements or advocacy efforts of the institutional Church, because those lay Christians will be in the decision-making centres of political life in a way that the institutional Church cannot be. Such indirect ways of political involvement are far more appropriate for an institution that is charged to proclaim a radical and universal Gospel.

REFERENCES AND SUGGESTED READING

AHLSTROM, S. (1975). *A Religious History of the American People.* New York: Doubleday.

ALLEN, J. (1984). *Love and Conflict.* Nashville: Abingdon Press.

AUGUSTINE (1958). *City of God.* Garden City, NY: Image Books.

—— (1992). *Letters of St Augustine,* ed. J. Leinenweber. Tarrytown, NY: Triumph Books.

AULEN, G. (1948). *Church, Law and Society.* New York: Charles Scribner's Sons.

BENNE, R. (1995*a*). *The Paradoxical Vision: A Public Theology for the Twenty-First Century.* Minneapolis: Fortress Press.

—— (1995*b*). 'The Paradoxical Vision: A Lutheran Nudge for Public Theology', *Pro Ecclesia,* 4/2, 212–23.

—— (2003). *Ordinary Saints: An Introduction to the Christian Life.* Minneapolis: Fortress Press.

BERGER, P. and NEUHAUS, R. J. (1977). *To Empower People: The Role of Mediating Structures in Public Policy.* Washington: American Enterprise Institute for Public Policy Research.

BILLING, E. (1951). *Our Calling.* Rock Island, Ill.: Augustana Book Concern.

BRAATEN, C. (1990). 'God in Public Life: Rehabilitating the Orders of Creation', *First Things,* 8 (December), 32–8.

BROWN, C. (1992). *Niebuhr and his Age: Reinhold Niebuhr's Prophetic Role in the Twentieth Century.* New York: Trinity Press International.

CENTER FOR CONCERN (1989). *The Road to Damascus: Kairos and Conversion.* Washington: Center for Concern.

CHILDRESS, J. and MACQUARRIE, J. (eds.) (1986). *The Westminster Dictionary of Christian Ethics.* Philadelphia: Westminster Press.

DAVIS, H. and GOOD, R. (eds.) (1960). *Reinhold Niebuhr on Politics.* New York: Charles Scribner's Sons.

DUCHROW, U. (1977). *Two Kingdoms: The Use and Misuse of a Lutheran Theological Concept.* Geneva: Lutheran World Federation.

ELSHTAIN, J. B. (1998). *Augustine and the Limits of Politics.* Notre Dame, Ind.: Notre Dame University Press.

FORELL, G. (1954). *Faith Active in Love.* Minneapolis: Augsburg Publishing House.

—— (1960). 'Luther and Politics', in *Luther and Culture,* Decorah, Ia.: Luther College Press, 3–69.

HAUERWAS, S. (1981). *A Community of Character.* Notre Dame, Ind.: University of Notre Dame Press.

—— (1983). *The Peaceable Kingdom.* Notre Dame, Ind.: University of Notre Dame Press.

LAZARETH, W. (2001). *Christians in Society: Luther, the Bible and Social Ethics.* Minneapolis: Fortress Press.

LUTHER, M. (1985). *Christian Liberty.* Philadelphia: Fortress Press.

—— (1962). *The Christian in Society,* in *Luther's Works,* XLV, Philadelphia: Fortress Press.

MARTY, M. E. (1960). *Righteous Empire: The Protestant Experience in America.* Fort Worth: Dial Press.

NEUHAUS, R. J. (1991). 'To Serve the Lord of All: Law, Gospel and Social Responsibility', *Dialog,* 30 (Spring), 140–9.

—— and BERGER, P. (1977). *To Empower People: The Role of Mediation Structures in Public Policy.* Washington: American Enterprise Institute for Public Policy Research.

The New Oxford Annotated Bible (1977). New York: Oxford University Press.

NIEBUHR, H. R. (1937). *The Kingdom of God in America.* New York: Harper & Brothers.

—— (1946). 'The Responsibility of the Church for Society', in K. S. Latourette (ed.), *The Gospel, the Church and the World,* New York: Harper & Brothers.

—— (1951). *Christ and Culture.* New York: Harper & Brothers.

NIEBUHR, R. (1944). *The Children of Light and the Children of Darkness.* New York: Charles Scribner's Sons.

—— (1949). *The Nature and Destiny of Man,* 2 vols. New York: Charles Scribner's Sons.

—— (1962). *Reinhold Niebuhr on Politics,* ed. Harry Davis and Robert Good. New York: Charles Scribner's Sons.

NOLL, M. (1992). 'The Lutheran Difference', *First Things,* 20 (February), 31–40.

PERRY, M. J. (1991). *Love and Power: The Role of Religion and Morality in American Politics.* New York: Oxford University Press.

PEW FORUM, <http://pewforum.ore/publications/surveys/Green/pdf>

Random House Webster's College Dictionary (1991). New York: Random House.

STACKHOUSE, M. (1987). *Public Theology and Political Economy.* Grand Rapids, Mich.: Eerdmans.

SVENSBYE, L. (1967). 'The History of a Developing Social Responsibility among Lutherans in America from 1930 to 1960' (Th.D. diss., Union Seminary).

THIEMANN, R. (ed.) (1991). *The Legacy of H. Richard Niebuhr.* Minneapolis: Fortress Press.

TINDER, G. (1989*a*). 'Can We Be Good without God?', *Atlantic Monthly,* 264, no. 6 (December), 69–85.

—— (1989*b*). *The Political Meaning of Christianity.* Baton Rouge, La.: Louisiana State University Press.

TROELTSCH, E. (1941). *The Social Teaching of the Christian Churches.* London: George Allen & Unwin, Ltd.

VON DEHSEN, C. and KLEIN, C. (1989). *Politics and Policy: The Genesis and Theology of Social Statements in the Lutheran Church in America.* Minneapolis: Fortress Press.

WALKER, W. (1959). *The History of the Christian Church.* New York: Charles Scribner's Sons.

WEBER, M. (1958). *The Protestant Ethic and the Spirit of Capitalism.* New York: Charles Scribner's Sons.

WINGREN, G. (1957). *Luther on Vocation.* Philadelphia: Muhlenberg Press.

—— (1961). *Creation and Law.* London: Oliver & Boyd.

WITTE, J., jun. (1997). *From Sacrament to Marriage.* Louisville, Ky.: Westminster John Knox Press.

—— (2002). *Law and Protestantism.* New York: Cambridge University Press.

YODER, J. (1972). *The Politics of Jesus.* Grand Rapids, Mich.: Eerdmans.

CHAPTER 20

CHRISTIANS AND FAMILY

SONDRA WHEELER

A MIXED INHERITANCE

A PERSON who had only the common currency of modern Western culture to draw upon could come away with the impression that the relationship between Christian faith and the social institution of the family was uncomplicated and entirely positive. Families arise from the given facts that human reproduction is sexual and human offspring are dependent and slow to mature. Thus, they are anchored in nature and, theologically, in creation. Moreover, the story of Adam and Eve is one of the few biblical narratives known to the majority of contemporary adults. In that story, the human couple recognize each other as of one bone and substance, partners in fulfilling the imperative to 'be fruitful and multiply', and they cleave together to form a unity that Genesis 2: 24 declares to be 'one flesh'. So the primal social structure of husband, wife, and children is pictured as springing forth immediately from the basic nature of male and female. The declaration that husband and wife are to 'become one flesh' has both powerful ethical and theological implications, as well as poetic resonances that have fuelled the imaginations of writers for millennia. This image and its implications undergird serious work on the ethics of marriage and family life, but in a fashion less reflected upon they have also found their way into the popular culture of churches and secular society at large.

The alliance between Christian theological commitments and the 'sanctity' and stability of families is so taken for granted in public discourse that phrases like 'Christian family values' roll off the tongues of participants and pundits alike. The most significant embarrassments suffered by prominent Christian leaders, ranging from Presidents Reagan and Clinton to evangelist Baker and civil rights leader Jesse Jackson, have been occasioned not by failures of charity to the poor, or lack of a serious life of prayer and discipleship, or even by lapses in basic financial integrity. They have been the result of their being publicly charged with failure to honour the marital and parental obligations taken to be so near to the heart of Christian morality. Extravagant life-styles and financial improprieties could be overlooked or rationalized away, but too-ready divorce and remarriage, allegations of parental neglect or marital infidelity, these call into question their Christian leadership. Except for the special, and shrinking, class of Roman Catholic clergy who are excused from these obligations for the sake of serving the Church (and increasingly even these are suspect), to be a good Christian is taken to be inseparable from being a good family man or a good wife and mother.

One would hardly want to present the Christian religion as an apologist for irresponsible or immoral conduct toward spouses and children, or as insensitive to the richness and challenge of family life as a context for personal spiritual formation. But it is important to recognize that this easy confluence of Christian ethics and familial duty is something of an anomaly historically. Moreover, it is an anomaly for good reasons: reasons rooted deep in our moral and theological traditions, in the texts that form us and the practices that sustain our communities. To make this case, I will start with a broad sketch of the biblical material dealing with family life, from the primeval histories down to the explicit moral teaching of the pastoral epistles. From here I will scan (more briefly yet) some of the complicated strands of early Christian teaching about the relationship between faithfulness and family life, and the preaching, teaching, and pastoral advice of the classical Reformation theologians. Finally, I will hazard some interpretation of the roots of the modern sacralization of family life, and suggest something about the insights it costs us and the moral perils to which it exposes us. In the end, I want to offer a constructive proposal for reclaiming the sphere of family life under the aegis of discipleship, and to suggest that such a strategy depends upon the conversion of natural loves.

THE OLD TESTAMENT ON FAMILY

One of the regular features of Bible-as-literature surveys for undergraduates, or even basic Bible courses in churches, is the students' discovery that the Bible is pretty racy stuff. One doesn't get very far into Genesis before the pristine picture of familial unity that closes chapter 2 is rent by jealousy and murder. Brother becomes an enemy to brother, as intimacy and proximity help turn bare difference into enmity. As the narrative continues, so does the conjunction of closeness and violence. Families are fractured by rape and incest, by theft and deception, by intrigue and betrayal and the desire for revenge. The Abraham cycle is home to every sort of 'family dysfunction', from the early competition between Abram and Lot (Gen. 13: 5–7) to the fissure between Sarah and Hagar and their sons (Gen. 16: 6 *et passim*). Perhaps no sibling conflict in history is more famous than that between Jacob and Esau (Gen. 25: 22 *et passim*), and no scene of reconciliation more moving than theirs (Gen. 33: 4–11). But over time, it turns out, as had been the case with Abram and Lot, that 'their possessions were too great for them to live together' (Gen. 36: 7), and one comes away with the impression that familial harmony requires a great deal of land!

The narrative moves on to the story of the rape of Dinah, in which family solidarity finds its expression in conspiracy and massacre, as brothers take revenge on a whole people for the wrong done to their sister (Gen. 34). The cycle continues with Joseph and his brothers, where arrogance and a remarkable lack of judgement combine to make Joseph so odious to his brothers that they barely manage not to kill him, instead merely selling him into slavery. While that drama is off-stage for a while, Judah's son Er provokes God so greatly that 'The Lord killed him' [!] (Gen. 38: 7), and when his second son Onan refuses to give his bereaved sister-in-law Tamar a child in accordance with the law, he suffers the same fate. Judah likewise fails to fulfil his duty to his daughter-in-law by providing her with a husband and children; he must be tricked into impregnating the young woman himself, while she is disguised as a prostitute. Although at the dénouement Judah wisely declares Tamar 'more righteous than I' (Gen. 38: 26), clearly even the strategies for ensuring family continuity are problematic.

It would be easy to go on, but we are only midway through Genesis, and a summary in similar detail of the disturbances in family life and relationships in the successive books of the Old Testament would occupy more space than is allotted for this whole essay. Suffice it to say that the ongoing canonical narratives are laced with stories of rape and abuse between siblings, adultery and abandonment between spouses, and violence and even war between parents and children. Families are torn apart by jealousy and greed, by lust and ambition, and by long-smouldering hatred. Conversely, elsewhere in the saga they are kept together by deception and by the lure of inheritance.

Covenant law, with its intensive regulation of sex, marriage, and family life, and its dire penalties for offences between close relatives, suggests that these stories are not just anomalies of ancient history. Likewise, the books of the prophets and the Wisdom writings give evidence of the long, sorry record of grief and destruction at the heart of intimate relationships. The sons of true prophets are faithless and self-serving (1 Sam. 2: 12–17, 8: 1–5), and the enemies of a man are those of his own household (Mic. 7: 6–7). The bitterness of domestic strife and the folly of children makes the writer of Proverbs long for solitude (Prov. 17: 1–2, 17: 25, 19: 13, 21: 19), and the unfaithfulness of Israel is mirrored by a wife's infidelity in an enacted metaphor that cannot avoid cutting both ways (Hos. 1–3). Of course, the record is not all one-sided. There are also moments of aching tenderness, acts of extraordinary loyalty, stories of forgiveness and reconciliation that still have power to move us centuries later. The Book of Psalms affirms what the narratives make clear, that children are indeed a gift from God, and the Book of Proverbs closes with a poem in praise of the blessing of a good wife. But it is plain that the Hebrew Bible is neither naïve nor romantic about family ties. It presents forcefully the evidence that they can bind so as to entangle and kill as well as give life.

FAMILY IN THE NEW TESTAMENT

Turning to the New Testament moves us forward in time, and into a world whose political organization is somewhat more familiar. Instead of the basically familial structures of household, clan, and tribe as the ordering patterns of society, by the first century we find an empire occupying Palestine as conquered territory. Here we see a thoroughly bureaucratized government of Roman officials, with soldiers serving as both defence and law enforcement. But if the role of the family is less all-pervasive than in earlier eras, it remains central to all social life, and to the transmission and reinforcement of cultural and religious heritage. Thus, its strength is indispensable to the survival of Israel as a people under Roman domination. That essential role, and the profound stake in family belonging as the linchpin of individual identity and status, ensure that family remains a recurrent theme in the New Testament.

But if we expect to find there an unmixedly positive evaluation of family ties and obligations, we will be disappointed. From the first, the picture of the family in the synoptic narratives is complex and clouded. Matthew's genealogy of Jesus incorporates by allusion the stories of adulterous liaisons and forbidden foreign wives (Matt. 1: 1–17), and Joseph's natural pursuit of the 'family values' of purity and respectability in his wife must be deflected by a dream sent from God (Matt. 1: 18–21). In Luke, already at age 12 Jesus flouts his parents' authority and ignores their natural concern by remaining in Jerusalem without notice, offering in explanation only the faintly offensive query, 'Did you not know I must be about my father's business?' (Luke 2: 49: NRSV). At a point of intense conflict, where his family appears in doubt about his sanity, Jesus denies the relevance of family bonds altogether, absorbing them entirely into the duties and affinities created by his mission and message. In one of the few sayings appearing in all three synoptic gospels, he asserts flatly, 'Whoever does the will of God is my brother and sister and mother' (Mark 3: 35; Matt. 12: 50; Luke 8: 21).

Nor is this uneasy relationship between faith and family peculiar to the Messiah, with his unique mission and unparalleled 'family of origin'. There are throughout the gospels frank and alarming acknowledgements of the opposition between loyalty to family and the demands of discipleship to Jesus. Matthew includes striking warnings about family members turning believers over to death (10: 21), warnings which appear in Luke as well (21: 16), and both of these gospels borrow Micah's picture of families cloven by the divisive message of the gospel (Matt. 10: 34–6; Luke 12: 51–3). In Luke, Matthew's apocalyptic prediction about 'two in a field, one taken, one left' (Matt. 24: 40) is sharpened to 'two in one bed, one taken and one left' (Luke 17: 34), clearly envisioning an eschatological division which cuts between husband and wife, parent and child. In Matthew, Jesus explicitly gives to his disciples the warning that 'whoever loves father or mother more than me is not worthy of me, and whoever loves son or daughter more than me is not worthy of me' (10: 37), which Luke renders more fiercely yet as, 'Whoever comes to me and does not hate father and mother, wife and children, brothers and sisters, and yes even his own life, cannot be my disciple' (14: 26). And Jesus turns away two would-be followers who attempt to place family obligations, however temporarily, between hearing and heeding the call to discipleship (Matt. 8: 21–2; Luke 9: 59–62).

In fact, doubt is cast upon the normative status of marriage and family life altogether. While Jesus' own singleness is notable enough in his context, one is astonished to hear this Jewish rabbi speak with evident approval of those who have 'made themselves eunuchs for the sake of the Kingdom' (Matt. 19: 14). Additional examples could be offered, but the point is made. With varying degrees of subtlety or directness, the family is called into question throughout the synoptic narratives.

But here, as in the review of Old Testament texts, the picture offered so far is one-sided and not fully representative. Alongside these disturbing sayings and stories are others that press the other way. For example, there is Jesus' challenging teaching on the permanence of marriage, including the equation of divorce and remarriage with adultery, anchored firmly in God's creative intention (Mark 10: 2–12). This is highlighted by its placement at the centre of Jesus' exposition of the costs of discipleship (Mark 8–12), and by its repetition and development in parallel and related texts (Matt. 5: 31–2, 19: 3–12; Luke 16: 18; 1 Cor. 7: 10–15). More comforting examples are the multiple depictions of devotion between parents and children in gospel narratives and parables (e.g., Matt. 9: 18–25; Mark 5: 22 ff., 7: 26–30, 9: 17 ff.; Luke 7: 12–15; 8: 40 ff.; 15: 11–32). Even Jesus' ironic reference to parental care in Matt. 7: 11 ('If you, who are evil, know how to give good things to your children . . .') presumes parental benevolence as a background experience common to all. There is also the exemplary faithfulness of Jesus' own mother at the cross, and his consignment of her care to the beloved disciple at his death (John 19: 25–7).

Most significant of all in the New Testament witness is the wholesale adoption of kinship language to convey the centrality and warmth of relationships between God and God's people, and among Jesus' followers. The familiar and intimate 'Daddy' ('Abba') of the Lord's Prayer speaks volumes about the immediacy of the communion between Jesus and God the Father, and about the character of the relation into which we are invited as his followers. So do Jesus' repeated remarks about the duties owed between 'brothers' and 'sisters' united solely by their common calling to discipleship. Such analogies, which draw deeply upon human experiences of trust and care, are dependent for their intelligibility upon these primary human connections. These are the contexts in which we learn the grammar of relationship.

Therefore, to frame the question as one of whether the family is good or bad from the gospels' point of view is to mistake the meaning of the gospels' treatment altogether. The family as it exists is neither approved nor disapproved of; it is a fact of human existence, rooted deep in human nature as created and embodied, fundamental and inescapable. It is directly and powerfully tied to the creative design and will of God, as the original context for the giving and protection of life. But there is a counterpoint: according to the logic of Christian faith, the life thus given is fallen and in need of redemption, and fallen with it are these primal attachments. Therefore, this matrix of human connections must be reclaimed and taken up into God's redemptive purposes. The gospels insist that this claiming of family relationships is key, and to be claimed is also to be constrained and challenged and redefined. Ultimately, it is to be decisively relativized in accord with the overwhelming priority of God's reign. This is the source of what appears as the gospels' deep ambivalence about the family.

There are parallels to this complex and tensive witness in the epistles. Here, however, it is possible to be briefer, because the most notable feature of epistolary teaching on the family is that there isn't all that much of it. Moreover, what teaching there is does not appear to be central to the aims of the letters in which it appears. In the authentic Pauline correspondence, teaching on family life and duties appears mainly in response to specific questions or controversies, notably in 1 Corinthians 5 and 7. In the pastoral and general epistles, it comes in closing paranetic sections, often in the form of conventional codes of household behaviour. These address both family members and servants or slaves, and are part of admonitions to good order for the sake of a positive witness among the 'Gentiles', a term used for outsiders even in address to non-Jewish communities (Eph. 5: 22 ff.; Col. 3: 18–22; Heb. 13: 4; 1 Pet. 3: 1–7).

That said, the content of the epistles' teaching is broadly consistent with the tenor of the gospels, including their reservations. Family duties are, on the one hand, affirmed as binding and serious; so Paul makes an almost unique direct reference to the command of Christ when he admonishes married partners not to separate, or to remain single if they cannot be reconciled (1 Cor. 7: 10–11). On the other hand, Paul's counsel in view of the 'impending distress' is that all who find themselves able to restrain sexual desire remain single, and those who already have wives and families are advised to 'live as though they had none' (1 Cor. 7: 25–35).

It is important, in view of the long history of powerful and significant misreadings of these passages, to be clear about what Paul's concerns here are, and what they are not. Both of these admonitions are part of Paul's advice to keep from being entangled in the world that is 'passing away'. They are offered with a view toward being single-hearted in devotion to the gospel, particularly in a context of persecution and eschatological expectation, rather than with an ascetic ideal of celibacy in view. In fact, Paul displays here the matter-of-factness about sex that is characteristic of Jewish treatments of marriage in the period. He admonishes married couples directly not to suspend sexual relations with each other (1 Cor. 7: 2–5), and offers the power of sexual desire as a reason *for* marriage, not a reason against it (1 Cor. 7: 36). It is not the lure of sensuality which causes his reservations about marriage, but the power of distraction, and the danger of capture by the everydayness of domestic obligations. How well this corresponds to the real spiritual challenges of married life, those who are married can testify.

The general epistles, taking up a form of moral instruction commonplace in their era, provide guidelines for members of households according to their role in the family (Eph. 5: 22 ff.; Col. 3: 18–22; 1 Pet. 3: 1–7). The models of family here taken for granted are all hierarchical, and these codes are noteworthy in their social context mostly for including in their address the subordinate partners (wives, slaves, and children) rather than solely the paterfamilias, as was customary at the time. Ephesians in particular contrives at once to uphold and to subvert the patriarchal household by likening the relationship of husband and wife to that between Christ and the church, with the model of authority being that of Christ whose lordship is expressed in his self-sacrifice for his bride. In various ways, then, even when the model of family is consonant with that of the prevailing social order, the character and duties of family life are distinctively shaped by the demands of fidelity to the gospel. Thus it is fair to say that in the New Testament canon, the social institution of the family is assumed, affirmed, resisted, and co-opted by turns, in accord with its relationship to the Kingdom whose priority that canon proclaims.

VIEWS OF FAMILY IN EARLY AND MEDIEVAL CHRISTIANITY

It is perhaps no wonder that a community developing in conversation with this textual tradition comes to have a complex and not fully coherent view of the moral and spiritual meaning of family. Moreover, Christian experience of the relationship between family and life in the community of faith was by no means uniform. Particularly in the centuries before the social acceptance of the Christian religion in the late Roman Empire, many in the early church were likely to have all-too-vivid reminders of the potential for conflict between family loyalties and the compelling claims of the new faith. In their case, the price of conversion might include disinheritance and the loss of social location and status in a relatively static social order. That the loss of primary social and emotional ties was keenly felt, we know from writings of the period (e.g., Felicitas 1972). For such converts, the gospel warnings about the scandal and division occasioned by Christ's proclamation must have provided a grim sort of comfort, a means of understanding and enduring their new situation. Conversely, women and slaves in particular might have practical reasons to embrace a shift in their loyalty and identity from the patriarchal structures in which they were so firmly subordinated, to the quasi-familial ties of the church, in which they might experience an alternative social self that was 'neither bond nor free, neither male nor female'. But the New Testament also bears witness to the endurance of family bonds and loyalties. Families not uncommonly converted together, and the personal greetings that close Paul's letters in particular frequently make reference to married couples or to whole families who are united in service to the church (e.g., Rom. 16: 3–5, 10–15; 1 Cor. 16: 15–20).

Apart from this diversity, the views of the early church were shaped not only by Scripture and the distinctive experience of Christians, but also by pagan culture and philosophy, and that in both directions. Family continued to serve throughout the patristic period as the bearer of individual identity, that which conferred belonging and status, determinative to a large extent of a person's education (if any), profession, and marriage prospects. In this cultural setting, it would be impossible to think of oneself primarily as a solitary individual. (Indeed, this is what made familial fractures caused by conversion so deeply painful.) On the other hand, along with the elevation of reason and the unchanging and incorruptible realm of ideas in Graeco-Roman philosophy went a corresponding devaluation of the changing world and all that was bound up in time and decay. Family was a realm of non-rational passion and the connection of high-status men to lower-status women and children and to the cycle of bearing, nurturing, and dying. Sex itself was frequently regarded with a kind of contempt among the educated élite. Either it was trivialized, devalued as unimportant, or it was degraded as a sort of folly, an attitude summed up later in Thomas Browne's influential description of intercourse as 'the most foolish act a wise man will commit' (1909: 45). Family life was not always held in high esteem.

Stoicism, with its deep distrust of the disorder in a soul ruled by passion and appetite rather than by reason, responded to the troubling character of sexuality by resolutely harnessing sex and marriage to the production and nurture of offspring. It found a value for family in the orderly handing down of status, culture, and property to legitimate heirs, and in the sustenance of the civil polity built upon domestic order. This, however, was not a fully viable strategy for the church, which placed its emphasis rather on spiritual kinship within the church, and aimed to produce not citizens but saints.

As a result, what develops in the period of late antiquity is an uneasy comprom-ise between Christian commitments to the affirmation of family life in a context of sexual discipline and a developing ascetic tradition that prized virginity in itself. This moral tradition is shaped partly by the rigorous subordination of earthly to spiritual kinship found in the New Testament, and by the ideal of single-hearted devotion to God. However, it also partakes deeply of the Graeco-Roman (or even Gnostic) distrust of passion and the body itself. This is most clearly evident and most influential in Augustine, whose Manichaean rejection of the body is con-verted more successfully to a Christianized Stoicism than to a true Hebraic appreciation for the unity of the human person. The result is the development within the early Catholic Church of a purely procreative ethic of sexual intercourse within marriage, and a distinct preference for virginity as a more elevated spiritual state. So pronounced is this preference that Augustine, *contra* any reasonable reading of 1 Corinthians, regards a married couple who abstain from sex as morally and spiritually more advanced than one that continues to have sex 'beyond the necessity of bearing' (1887: 401).

At the same time, constrained by the inherited doctrine of a good, embodied creation, as well as the pastoral text which identifies the prohibition of marriage as an aberration (1 Tim. 4: 3), the Church never takes its prizing of sexual continence to the point of condemning marriage or sexual union within it. In fact, even in the twelfth century, at the height of medieval monasticism, the Albigensian and Catharist heresies are banned largely on the strength of their condemnation of marriage and sexual union. The Church throughout this time adheres firmly to the standard of permanence in marriage, and the norm of sexual fidelity within it is clearly taught (however unevenly it may have been observed, then as now). Procreation is affirmed as a good gift of God, and part of the human work of sustaining human society. Moreover, there are a few early patristic sources such as Clement of Alexandria (1971) and St John Chrysostom (1986) who liken the care exercised by parents over their children to the comprehensive providence of God, and insist (in line with the pastoral epistles: 1 Tim. 3: 12; Titus 1: 5–6) that family life is a proper school for church leaders. Unhappily, their witness is lost to much of the Western Church in the medieval period, overwhelmed by the turn towards ascetic spirituality, which thought of Christian vocation as a call away from the ties and constraints of family life, to a celibate life alone or in a community united by faith and service rather than kinship ties.

The limitations and distortions of prevailing Christian views in this period, with their treatment of marriage and family life as a distinctly inferior and secular form of life suited only to those without a call to holiness, must be acknowledged. Still, there are insights made available by the development of the monastic tradition which we should keep in view. Its elevation of ties of faith and vocation over the socially, politically, and economically decisive bonds of kinship provided an important counter-current in a society where not only property but social station and life possibilities were rigidly fixed by inheritance. Monastic orders, in their existence and their missional activities, asserted the priority of service to humanity in general over loyalties to clan and kindred, and pressed universal duties over against those confined within existing social networks. They constituted a standing critique of the cultural dominance of familial self-interest, and were the origin and first institutional form of care for the sick, the destitute, the insane, and the abandoned. In many cases, religious orders were the only alternative for women otherwise confined entirely within structures of social and economic power controlled exclusively by men. In effect, they created within the Church an alternative family of great power, indeed so great that it in turn, and repeatedly, had to be purged of its own pretensions and corruptions. This model had its failures, and its characteristic distortions, including denigration of natural family life from which the Church has had to recover. But it kept a foothold in the practical world for a claim greater than those of blood and filial duty, and a witness to One who could, and did, call some to leave home and family and kindred to become bearers of the gospel and servants to the world.

FAMILY AS A CHRISTIAN VOCATION AND A SCHOOL OF HOLINESS

Prominent among the debts owed by the whole Christian world to the Protestant Reformation is its recovery of marriage and care of the family as a concrete Christian vocation. Although Luther's public writings on this topic are often marred by the vehemence of his polemical style, there is still in them a crucial core of truth. This is particularly the case as his experience moves him beyond the rhetorical defence of marriage as counterweight to medieval distortions, into a frank and sometimes eloquent appreciation of married life as a school of holiness and a realm of Christian service.

In the first instance, Luther's motives were negative. In his earliest treatments of the topic, he was driven by what he saw as a rejection of the divinely given blessing and mandate of procreation, and a perverse prizing of sexual abstinence as an end in itself. Seeing the command to 'be fruitful and multiply' as inscribed in our very flesh (1962: 18), Luther makes some problematic assertions about the irresistible character of sexual desire, which can only give rise to 'fornication and secret sins' when thwarted of its natural object by ecclesiastical impositions of celibacy (1962: 19). Luther does make some provision for the possibility of celibacy as a divine gift, even calling it a 'higher' gift (1958: 135), but he regards it as a rarity (1962: 21), and commends marriage to all others.

Complicating the situation which Luther addressed in the early sixteenth century was the Catholic Church's claim to exclusive jurisdiction over the social institution of marriage. Citing the status of marriage as a sacrament (a position that was contested in the Western Church until its formal definition in 1563), the Church exercised control not only over the pastoral and spiritual dimensions of marriage, but also over marriage as a legal state affecting property, social status, and inheritance. A lengthy and detailed body of canon law specified who could lawfully be wed, and what conditions would invalidate an ostensible union. Luther regarded this proliferation of regulations as a cynical grab for power on the part of the clergy, especially since dispensations from many of the rules could often be obtained by payment of a fee.

Apart from the issue of corruption in the system governing access to marriage, and the politics of Catholic versus Protestant Church power in the era, Luther had a theological reason for resisting the notion of marriage as a sacrament rightly administered by the Church. He understood marriage and family (along with work and civil government) to belong under the rubric of 'the orders of creation', the basic governing structures instituted by God to sustain the world. These stand apart from and prior to God's particular covenantal relations with Israel and the Church. The ordering of men and women to partnership with one another in the generation and rearing of children is fundamental, and forms the basis of all human societies, whether pagan or Christian. For this reason, Luther argued that the regulation of marriage was properly the business of the civil order, which had legitimate authority over conduct of all citizens in general. It was the state which was charged with the maintenance of peace and order in the ordinary affairs of life. All of these concerns are visible in Luther's treatise 'The Estate of Marriage', written in 1522, while Luther himself, despite his encouraging vowed religious to leave their communities and marry, was still single.

The tenor of his conversation about marriage changed subtly after his 1525 marriage to Katherine von Bora, a shift evident in a comparison of 'The Estate of Marriage' with his later *Commentaries on Genesis* (1535–7). From an emphasis on marriage as a remedy for lust and a prevention of fornication, Luther moves to a frank appreciation of the gifts and challenges of home-making and child rearing, of the burdens of domestic life and the heroism it evokes. His teaching about marriage is no longer primarily an insistence upon the freedom of Christians to find here a refuge from sin. It is a call to the joys and tasks of parenting and partnership as a school of virtue, as a good and holy work that calls upon all our physical and spiritual energy as we take on responsibility for the temporal and spiritual welfare of the children whom God entrusts to us. This is an authentic calling of God, a vocation which Luther calls 'noble and great' (1962: 46).

LATER INHERITORS

This Lutheran inheritance has enriched the whole Church, and renewed the vision suggested by Jesus' teaching on marriage: that faithful marriage is to be understood as an aspect of discipleship, and the family life that flows from it as a form of Christian service and a witness to the gospel. But in the hands of later Lutheran interpreters, the stress upon the orders of creation, with its accent on the continuity between natural and redeemed life, reinforced some problematic and troubling aspects of human culture. For example, it baptized the presumptive patriarchy of early modern Europe, and did so without even Luther's own careful distinction between the equality of male and female at creation and the present inequality which he regarded as the mark and burden of sin. It has also blunted the sharp edge of cultural criticism that makes the body of New Testament teaching on the family both rich and troubling.

An example of this tendency to flatten the complex witness of Scripture and tradition can be found in the writings of the German church historian Ernst Troeltsch. Writing in 1912 on the social teachings of the Church, he attributes to Jesus a kind of untroubled enthusiasm for family bonds and loyalty that reflects nothing at all of Jesus' sometimes harsh language toward his own mother and brothers, or his fierce rejection of anything that compromised the claims of the Kingdom, including duties to family. (Unsurprisingly, neither has he any ear for the power and appeal of celibate life as a means of freeing individuals for Christian service.) Instead, Troeltsch finds that 'the idea of family may be regarded as one of the most fundamental features of [Jesus'] feeling for human life', and speaks of the 'nobler result of the Christian idea being the personalizing, individualizing and deepening of the family ideal' (1992: 61). Whether or not one finds his vision appealing, it seems clear that it partakes rather more of the ethos of Germany at the start of the twentieth century than of the teaching attributed to Jesus in the gospels.

There is nothing unique about this decisive influence of culture on Christian understandings of the family, and in fact it may be a bit unfair to single out such a text for criticism. It stands merely as a convenient example of the compelling power of our own moral visions of family, deeply shaped as they are by the ideas and norms of our own societies, to blind us to aspects of the biblical and traditional teaching, and even to cause us to attribute our own rather different convictions and ideals to the One whom we profess to follow. Certainly Lutherans are neither the first nor the last to engage in this kind of unselfconscious reinterpretation of an ambivalent and uncomfortable biblical witness. Others have written critically of similar trends in the tradition of Catholic social teaching (Cahill 2000), in the heirs of Calvin, and (in a different key to be sure) in the inheritors of evangelical and Anabaptist theological thought (Bunge 2001: 329–64). It is therefore no surprise to find that the current American Christian ethos of 'family values', both in its more liberal and its more conservative forms, offers its own amalgam of faith and culture.

THE FAMILY IN CONTEMPORARY AMERICAN CHRISTIANITY

It is, of course, incumbent upon Christian communities in successive times and diverse places to find a way to proclaim and embody the gospel in the new contexts in which they find themselves. The challenge is in the process of critical adaptation. Wisdom lies in the judgement about what is essence and what accident in the patterns of thought and conduct we inherit from our shared texts and traditions, and likewise in judging what may be accommodated and what must be challenged or rejected of the contemporary social and moral systems within which we operate. Contemporary Western Christians are conscious of many points of tension between the societies they inhabit and the form of life to which they are called by their faith. The realm of sex and family life is simply one such area, one that has received a great deal of attention in recent years.

Without unanimity in detail, Christians nevertheless have as a common inheritance a broad moral consensus. This has traditionally called for the restriction of full sexual intimacy to committed partnerships, an intention (at least) for permanence in such partnerships, and a norm of parental responsibility that expects long-term investment of both parents in the nurture and education of offspring. To say this much is already to place Christians on the conservative end of a contemporary spectrum whose other end is permissive of essentially any form of sexual activity that takes place between consenting adults, and where expectations regarding parental responsibility are minimal.

In the past decade or so, a great deal of time and effort has gone into reclaiming all or most of this broad Christian consensus for the mainstream churches, many of which had drifted with our culture toward a sexual ethic based primarily on personal fulfilment and individual flourishing. A large body of writing, some academic and more of it semi-popular in style, has been produced across a wide span of the theological and social spectrum of American Christianity, making a case for the recovery of a family-based ethic of personal conduct. It lifts up the norms of sexual responsibility, marital permanence, and commitment to child rearing. (For a sampling: Browning *et al.* 2000; Cahill 2000; Post 1994, 2000.) This is a move animated by a growing sense of responsibility on the part of Christian leaders for the maintenance of reasonable social functioning, and by a new recognition of the costs of the sexual revolution for America's children, which has been documented in numerous social-scientific studies. Its result has been a renewal of the Church's role as the upholder of the family, and of the norms that support its social function as a context for child rearing.

BEYOND FUNCTIONALISM

To avoid misunderstanding, I will say what is obvious: that responsibility is morally preferable to irresponsibility, and that there are in fact good and compelling reasons for sexual restraint and marital permanence, reasons bound up with the real needs of children and the real requirements of stable societies. On the other hand, none of these motives or imperatives are distinctive to the Christian community; nor do these observations in themselves provide a theological rationale for a Christian understanding of the status and duties of family life. They provide, if you like, a natural foundation for the family, which may appropriately be enshrined in civil law and public policy. But such treatments of the family do not undertake either to warrant or to limit the claims of our duties to family by appeal to the confessions that unite Christians as such. They connect us only very tenuously to our biblical and theological traditions, so they do not provide us with either the vigour to support or the critical leverage to challenge and revise our cultural constructions of the family. They remain open to co-optation, easily made captive to the aims of a consumer economy, whose stake in family responsibility may have as much to do with households as purchasing units as it does with the moral meaning of commitment or the well-being of children (Matzko-McCarthy 2001).

For the sake of our own identity, as well as the integrity of our witness to our society, we need a full and serious recovery of the depth and breadth of our moral and theological resources in Scripture and tradition. This includes a notion of Christian marriage as a distinctive theological vocation based in discipleship, a call to embody in our faithfulness and forgiveness toward one another, in our patient nurturing and bearing with one another, the endless forbearance shown us by God in Christ. Only such a full-blown call to fidelity and permanence in marriage can offer something beyond the practical calculation of generic social functionality, the claim that *in general* it is better for children and for society if married partners remain together. Such a general acknowledgement will never outweigh the burdens of pain and difficulty with which the lives of particular individuals in struggling families are marked (Hays 1996: 370–2). Likewise, only a vision of parenting that is clearly and intentionally modelled on the love, patience, and honour bestowed on us by God can sustain us through all the storms and struggles of nurturing another full-fledged human being into the freedom and responsibility of adulthood. If we are to enter into family life as Christians, we must recover a vision of marriage and parenting as aspects of Christian discipleship, concrete forms of the imitation of Christ.

But the point is not primarily that only a more vigorously *theological* ethic of family life can have the desired effect on family health and stability, although I think that is true. More fundamentally, I contend that in order to remain genuinely Christian, an ethic of the family must include significant reservations about familial claims and loyalties. Such reservations are rooted in the Christian insistence that our duty to God's reign must trump every other duty: that indeed we are first bound to love God with all our heart and soul and mind and strength. Clarity about such theological premisses is key, not solely because such pre-eminence is rightly due the God we worship, though this Christians must affirm. Nor are these premisses to be retained only because some of us are called to forgo family life for the sake of our vocations, or even to reject its constraints when they compete with a vision of our true identity as disciples, although that too is true. We need to recover a vivid sense of the call to love God first because only then will we be able to love our neighbours (including our spouses and children) as ourselves, or know how.

Rooted deep in the Christian tradition is the conviction that only those deeply schooled in charity, those whose lives are reordered by the primacy and sufficiency of divine love, can inhabit the field of natural loves without peril. It sometimes appears that the popular notion of the 'sanctity' of the family is so prized because it represents the only flicker of the transcendence of self left in a secularized world. But in truth the family is not holy in itself, nor is it any guarantee of holiness. The whole history of the human race teaches us that human belonging and intimacy are no proof against corruption, but rather a distinctively dangerous occasion for it.

The death of unconstrained patriarchy, the end of the status of wives and children as chattel, and the prohibition of child labour hardly signal that family life in twenty-first-century America is now morally safe. Where once we faced the temptations associated with hardship and poverty, we are now surrounded by the more insidious temptations afforded by comfort and affluence. American culture offers a full range of corruptions, shaped by its distinctive features of consumer capitalism and technological self-confidence. Marriage is now explicitly a life-style choice, an economic strategy, and courtship is more and more overtly conducted in a marketplace complete with advertising, both veiled and direct. In similar vein, we are offered a thousand subtle abuses of parental power by which we can make our children means to our ends, the vindication of our self-worth, or the vicarious fulfilment of our thwarted desires. Their methods range from the expensive grooming provided the children of the rich in private academies, to the various uses of genetic tests and techniques to ensure that the children born to those who can afford these interventions will be desirable and rewarding. Luther's 'children of God entrusted to our care' are readily converted into one more category of the possessions by which we mark our achievement of the American dream, and demonstrate our success in the economic competition that so pervades our consumer society by purchasing for them every advantage (Wheeler 2001, 2002, 2003).

Now, as in every age, 'sin crouches at the door' of the household, and we need the full range of our moral and spiritual resources to recognize and resist it. It is in the heart of family, as we confront spouse and sibling, son and daughter, so nearly images of ourselves, that the true otherness of the other—their final belonging to God and not to us—is hardest to see, and hardest to honour. Only when our own hearts are converted, only when our natural loves are disciplined by charity and reordered to the priorities of disciples, can we learn to see and to turn from all the subtle distortions of family life. These take their particular shapes in the matrix of a particular society, but this does not make them either new or less potent. It only makes them harder for us to recognize.

REFERENCES AND SUGGESTED READING

AUGUSTINE (1887). 'On the Good of Marriage', in *St Augustine: On the Trinity, and Doctrinal and Moral Treatises, The Nicene and Post-Nicene Fathers of the Church*, III: ed. Phillip Schaff, Buffalo, NY: Christian Literature Company, 397–413.

BROWNE, T. (1909). *Religio Medici*, The Harvard Classics, 4, NewYork: Collier Press.

BROWNING, D. S., McLEMORE, B., COUTURE, P., LYON, K. B. and FRANKLIN, R. (2000). *From Culture Wars to Common Ground*. Louisville, Ky.: Westminster/Knox Press.

BUNGE, M. (ed.) (2001). *The Child in Christian Thought*. Grand Rapids, Mich.: Wm. Eerdmans Publishing.

CAHILL, L. (2000). *The Family: A Christian Sociological Perspective*. Minneapolis: Fortress Press.

CLEMENT OF ALEXANDRIA (1971). 'Stromata', in II: *Fathers of the Second Century, The Ante-Nicene Fathers*, ed. Robert Alexander and James Donaldson, Grand Rapids, Mich.: Wm. B. Eerdmans Publishing, 381–402.

CHRYSOSTOM, JOHN (1986). *On Marriage and Family Life*. Crestwood, NY: St Vladimir's Seminary Press.

FELICITAS (1972). 'The Martyrdom of Perpetua and Felicitas', in *The Acts of the Christian Martyrs*, trans. Herbert Mursurillo, Oxford: Clarendon Press, 107–31.

HAYS, R. B. (1996). *The Moral Vision of the New Testament*. San Francisco: HarperCollins.

LUTHER, M. (1958). *Commentaries on Genesis*, in *Luther's Works*, I, ed. Jaroslav Pelikan. Saint Louis, Mo.: Concordia Publishing House, 3–236.

——(1962). 'The Estate of Marriage', in *Luther's Works*, XLV, ed. Walter Brandt. Philadelphia: Muhlenberg Press, 17–49.

Matzko-McCarthy, D. (2001). *Sex and Love in the Home: A Theology of the Household*. London: SCM Press.

Post, S. (1994). *Spheres of Love*. Dallas: Southern Methodist University Press.

——(2000). *More Lasting Unions: Christianity, the Family, and Society*. Grand Rapids, Mich.: Wm. Eerdmans Publishing.

Troeltsch, E. (1992). *The Social Teaching of the Christian Churches*. Lousiville, Ky.: Westminster/John Knox Press.

Wheeler, S. (2001). 'Contingency, Tragedy, and the Virtues of Parenting', in Ronald Cole-Turner (ed.), *Beyond Cloning*, Harrisburg, Pa.: Trinity International Press, 111–23.

——(2002). 'Power, Trust and Reticence: Genetics and Christian Anthropology', in Ronald Cole-Turner: (ed.), *New Conversations*, New York: United Church of Christ Press, 17–35.

——(2003). 'Parental Liberty and the Right of Access to Germline Intervention: A Theological Appraisal of Parental Power', in Audrey R. Chapman and Mark Frankel. (eds.), *Designing Our Descendants: The Promises and Perils of Genetic Modification*, Baltimore: Johns Hopkins University Press, 238–51.

CHAPTER 21

CHRISTIANS AND ECONOMICS

HARLAN BECKLEY

CHRISTIANS affirm, in different ways, the inviolable and equal dignity of each human person. Economic theory and practice often seek—either explicitly or implicitly—to maximize the common good conceived as the aggregate satisfaction of individual preferences. Christian ethics, of course, considers the common good, but always in its relationship to individual human dignity, not merely in relation to individual preferences. The commonplace assumption that Christian views of human dignity and economists' efforts to maximize the common good are incompatible should not surprise us.

This essay challenges that assumption. I argue that the increasingly authoritative use of cost–benefit analysis (CBA) for evaluating public policies and practices can maximize respect for the equal dignity of persons. The argument begins with a particular theological and ethical conception of human dignity and its relation to the common good, and depends on revisions of Paretian welfare economics. It further proposes ways in which this theologically informed respect for dignity and

I am grateful to Union Theological Seminary and the Presbyterian School of Christian Education in Richmond, Virginia, and to *Societas Ethica* for invitations to present versions of this essay before audiences that provided helpful comments. James M. Gustafson and Meredith McNabb, a student research assistant funded by the Washington and Lee University Law School, have also contributed significantly to the preparation and revision of this article. In addition, I have benefited from editorial comments by Gilbert Meilaender.

a revised CBA can inform each other to maximize respect for dignity. I use CBA to designate a general procedure of 'explicit valuation' of 'broadly consequentialist' net benefits determined by a form of 'additive accounting' that may include both qualitative and quantitative measurements (Sen 2000: esp. 931–8). These 'incompletely theorized' 'foundation principles' of CBA admit 'considerable plasticity' and ample room for controversy (Sen 2000: 935; Sunstein 2000: esp. 1060–1). However, they exclude 'cost-effective analysis' (CEA) (Beauchamp and Childress 2001: 195–9; Gewirth 1990: 209–10), which rejects all comparative measurements of benefits from investments for different ends, and therefore provides no means of assessing the overall worth and the opportunity costs of a project. Inasmuch as the resulting use of CBA reflects theoretical and empirical practice in economics, this exploration of one significant segment of the boundary between Christian ethics and economics functions as a synecdoche for the relationship between these disciplines.

ENGAGING AN UNDERSTANDABLE SCEPTICISM

CBA is gaining an increasing role and authority in the USA. Since Ronald Reagan's Executive Order 12291 in 1981, US presidents have issued a series of executive orders requiring CBA studies. State statutes and gubernatorial directives have followed suit, and a constitutional requirement for CBA has entered the legal discussion (Adler 2003). Economics and other disciplines have developed and promoted these 'additive accounting' procedures for evaluating policies and practices. Less formal procedures for evaluating decisions and policies by weighing costs and benefits pervade our culture and civic life. Many Christians criticize this intrusion of economics into moral reasoning for injecting consequentialist reasoning that weighs the inviolable value of individual human dignity in relation to costs and benefits. They think that Christians should keep CBA at bay and oppose its practice where we can. Many economists are equally leery of all normative thought, including Christian ethics, that is not based on individual tastes.

In his monograph, *On Ethics and Economics*, Amartya Sen contends that this separation of economics from ethics has impoverished both. Ethics, Sen asserts, can correct 'the narrow consequentialist welfarism used in standard welfare economics'. Conversely, economists' appreciation for 'logistical issues of interdependence and interconnection' can revise 'some deontological approaches used in moral philosophy, involving inadequate consequential accounting' (1987: 78; see also 7–10, 78–9). My claim is a species of Sen's generic contention. Respect for equal dignity, informed by Christian theology, can be brought into a mutually corrective relationship with CBA. Both formal CBA and a less formal consequentialist weighing of costs, risks, and benefits will, if rightly conceived, enhance respect for the equal dignity of persons.

A Dubious Harmony: The Common Good and Absolute Rights

John A. Ryan, the twentieth-century American, moral theologian most knowledgeable about economics, represents an important kind of scepticism about CBA precisely because he forged compatible and mutually informative relations between what he called the science of economics and respect for equal human dignity. In 1942, near the end of a long career of bringing economic policies into compliance with respect for human dignity, Ryan asserted to a group of Catholic economists that 'economics should be treated as a positive science', offering 'a full description of economic phenomena, pointing out the laws or uniformities involved'. He simultaneously averred that economics 'is in large part also a normative science', offering 'a moral evaluation of the economic practices and suggest[ing] remedies for bad practices' (1942: 3–5). Catholic economists should evaluate economic practices, Ryan held, according to the inviolable and sacred dignity of every human. Respect for dignity entails that every person has an absolute right to the means indispensable to fulfil her proximate end in life. Economics should adopt this normative standard from ethics. However, the informing influence also runs from economics to ethics with regard to norms instrumental for respecting human dignity. Major portions of Ryan's writings offered economic justifications for a legal minimum wage and other policies as indispensable means to secure the decent livelihood demanded by respect for human dignity. Justification for the right to private property, Ryan held, is 'obviously empirical, drawn from consequences' (1916: 60–1 n. 1; 1996: 175 n. 4). Economic consequences count.

Despite his interdisciplinary approach to evaluating policies, moral theology alone, according to Ryan, stipulates the absolute rights required for human dignity. Economics offered Ryan no reason to doubt the feasibility of these absolute rights. He never wavered in believing that sound economic policies can provide the rights indispensable for every person's dignity. Sound economics challenges presumptive rights instrumental to respect for human dignity, rights that some consider absolute, e.g., the right to private property. Ryan even considered sound economics indispensable for respecting the sacred, equal dignity of persons, but good economics never caused him to doubt that respect for dignity is sacred and attainable.

Cost–Benefit Analysis and Absolute Rights: An Incompatible Pairing

Two features of Ryan's moral theology are incompatible with almost all CBA. First, he derived the absolute rights that safeguard human dignity from a teleological and perfectionist understanding of the person (Beckley 1992: 130–1). These rights are the indispensable means for persons to be physically stronger, intellectually wiser, and spiritually nearer to God, rather than means for persons' freedom to pursue their own conception of the good (Ryan 1916: 361–2; 1996: 115). Both modern welfare economics, based on aggregate satisfaction of preferences, and political liberalism, for which respecting dignity entails freedom to pursue different ends in life, reject Ryan's neo-Thomist perfectionism.

This essay defends a form of CBA and a conception of dignity that incorporate respect for freedom as proposed by some forms of political liberalism. On the other hand, it challenges reliance on preferences as the normative basis for CBA. In these claims, I stand in good and large company. Martha Nussbaum, Aristotelian influence notwithstanding, argues for views of dignity and rights that both leave 'a great deal of latitude in determining what goals to pursue' (2000: 1022–3) and reject aggregated preferences as the value to maximize in CBA (2000: 1028–9).

Second, Ryan believed, on theological grounds, largely independent of other sources of knowledge, that God ordered the universe so that no right indispensable for human dignity needs to be denied on consequentialist grounds (Beckley 1992: 161–4). He did not restrict moral theology to deontological absolutes. Ethics includes attention to the welfare of society as something immediately and formally different from the dignity of its members. However, faith that the divinely created order is always good for individual human dignity led Ryan to consider the good of society, at least over the long run, only for the purpose of securing the dignity of *all* of its component parts (Ryan 1919: 78). As a result, economic reasoning considers how the common welfare satisfies absolute rights, but never whether satisfying these rights is unfeasible. For Ryan, good economics never requires a trade-off among rights essential for human dignity.

CBA also focuses on a conception of the common good. Indeed, E. J. Mishan, one of its influential advocates, differentiates CBA from accounting only because the former asks 'whether society as a whole will become better off by undertaking' a project under evaluation (1976: p. xii). However, CBA, unfettered by constraints for respecting individual dignity, considers the common good as maximizing aggregated satisfaction of individual preferences. Ryan persistently and vigorously distinguished how sound economics promote the common good from maximizing aggregate economic welfare. The common good, he frequently reiterated, considers the social welfare 'distributively as well as collectively' (Ryan and Boland 1940: 145; Ryan 1937: 174–6), meaning that prudent accounting for economic consequences always secures respect for the full dignity of every person.

My argument, like Ryan's, is informed by a theology affirming ethical respect for the dignity of every individual. However, the theology and correlative ethics allow for consequentialist reasoning that raises doubts about whether the common good can sustain respect for all aspects of dignity for all persons.

An Alternative View of the Common Good and Dignity: Reciprocity without Harmony

Ryan is not alone in asserting both a necessary and a fully harmonious relationship between the common good and respect for human dignity. David Hollenbach, in his recent book on the common good, offers a superb account of how justice for disadvantaged peoples requires a strong commitment to the common good and, like Ryan, assumes total harmony between individual dignity and the common good (2002: esp. 173–244).

On the other hand, James Gustafson disputes this assumption on theological grounds. 'The relationship between the good of the individual parts and the common good', Gustafson contends, 'is reciprocal, but is seldom, if ever, harmonious.' The divine ordering of the universe reflects purposes that surpass and sometimes restrict the good of individuals. 'Restraints and denials of interests, even those that have considerable justification, are simply part of the ordering of life' (1984: 19, 22). Gustafson's view of the divine ordering, a theology backed by CBA, denies compatibility between the common good and absolutist respect for every aspect of human dignity. This challenge is especially pertinent to the robust conceptions of human dignity defended by both Ryan and Gustafson.

Gustafson's conception of dignity also undercuts classical CBA on two fronts. First, he rejects valuations based on aggregate welfare without independent regard for equality and respect for persons. Second, he rejects the assumption that the common good has no value apart from the aggregate good of persons (1984: 109–10). These criticisms of utilitarians and welfare economists move consequentialist-sensitive moral reasoning in the direction of Ryan's economics, but they permit a version of CBA that fosters the equal dignity of humans while requiring trade-offs among values that sustain dignity.

CONCEPTIONS OF HUMAN DIGNITY: WHY THEY MATTER

Human Life as Sacred

Both mutuality and harmony between respect for dignity and the common good depend on the operative conception of dignity. Human dignity, and the duty to respect it, may be understood narrowly. Paul Ramsey sometimes even eschewed the term 'dignity' in favour of the God-bestowed sanctity of human life (1970: p. xiii). Ramsey did not assert the absolute value of human biological existence: many values are worth dying for. Nevertheless, he confined the intrinsic value of the person commanding respect to the integrity of biological life combined with informed consent. Ramsey based this intrinsic worth on creation in the image of God in a person-to-person covenant relationship with God, independent of humans' rational or other natural capacities (1950: 249–84).

The contrast with Gustafson is dramatic. Ramsey drew almost exclusively on biblical sources for an understanding of creation limited to God establishing a covenant with individual humans. Human worth is 'derivative from God's appointment'. It is not 'something about man *per* se' (1950: 277). Gustafson understands creation based on scientific accounts of human agents, as well as the biblical accounts, and does not view creation as God establishing a covenantal relationship with persons. A biblically informed doctrine of the *imago Dei*, so crucial for Ramsey, is inadequate without a construal of human life in continuity with 'nature' (Gustafson 1981: 269–70, 282). Consequently, for Ramsey, respect for dignity focuses narrowly on the integrity of biological life and informed consent, and neglects other aspects of human agency—cognitive, affective, and physical capacities—that are crucial to respect for dignity from Gustafson's perspective.

Prudence notwithstanding, respect for the integrity of biological life combined with informed consent may be considered a near deontological absolute. Although Ramsey once wrote—and never retracted—that Christian love considers the good only after a 'right relation to neighbor has been established' (1950: 116; cited by Gustafson 1984: 85), his developed ethics considered circumstances, consequences, and the common good. Care for the dying and consent to experimental medicine, for example, require knowledge of both the consequences and the common good. The key to Ramsey's near deontological absolutism was his narrow view of human dignity. The consequences of practices need to be considered only in so far as they impinge on the integrity of biological life combined with informed consent. Ramsey acknowledged at least one exception. In an extreme situation when life-saving therapies must be rationed, treating a person whose life is indispensable for saving many lives may be justified without the consent of others whose lives are of equal intrinsic value. In such rare circumstances, absolute respect for the integrity of biological existence combined with informed consent undermines respect for dignity of all others. One life must be valued more than others to preserve the common good required to maximize equal respect for the intrinsic worth of all. Having acknowledged this exception, Ramsey immediately insisted that this consequentialist thinking is only for the 'restoration of conditions of there being any good', and should never become the 'rule of practice' (1970: 257–9).

On Ramsey's narrow view of human dignity, trade-offs of dignity for dignity are extremely rare. The systematic practice of CBA need not, and should not, intrude into the territory of respect for dignity. The ' "sanctity" of human life' commands an 'awesome respect' that withstands 'engineering' for the sake of others except in 'the sacredness of their bodily lives' (Ramsey 1970: p. xiii).

Ramsey demonstrated that absolute respect for the dignity of persons as ends in themselves need not be naïve about the consequences and the common good. Given his narrow view of human dignity, rejecting CBA is not imprudent. However, human dignity that entails the worth of cognitive, affective, and physical capacities precludes prudent absolute respect for human dignity. If, for example, we understand dignity in terms of Amartya Sen's concepts of human capability and effective freedom, we need to consider whether securing the safety of some persons jeopardizes minimal provision for the health and education of others. A more robust conception of dignity requires much greater attention to both the reciprocity and the disharmony between individual human dignity and the common good (see Gustafson on his differences with Ramsey in this regard, 1984: 84–93, esp. n. 166 and 92–3).

Human Autonomy as Sacred

Some ethicists contend that respect for human dignity as autonomy, ostensibly an even narrower conception of dignity than Ramsey's, rules out consequentialist intrusions requiring trade-offs. Conceptions of dignity as autonomy vary, but their proponents frequently view respect for dignity as absolute. Hence, autonomy should never be a means to other ends, including trade-offs among aspects of autonomy. However, the claimed harmony of absolute rights necessary for autonomy turns out to be naïve.

Ironically, proponents of minimalist negative rights, adamant about respect for persons as ends in themselves, are often the most naïve about consequentialist considerations requiring trades-offs among purportedly absolute ends. Robert Nozick, for example, places absolute 'side constraints' on actions or practices that curtail the right to private property for the purpose of maximizing good or minimizing harm (Nozick 1974: 28–35, 171–4). This rejection of consequentialist reasons for overriding negative rights withers before criticism from a bevy of moral philosophers. Amartya Sen, among others, challenges imprudent neglect of 'consequence-sensitive reasoning' about negative rights. Sen demonstrates the implausibility of exclusively deontological reasoning about negative rights, and criticizes Nozick in particular for 'inadequate consequential accounting'. Even moral reasoning 'dealing with intrinsically valuable objects', Sen concludes, should make use of the 'consequential reasoning of the type standardly used in economics' (1987: 70–8).

Henry Shue, in his widely read book *Basic Rights*, vividly reveals how negative rights entail heavy costs. The duty to protect persons from violations of their negative rights requires resources comparable to the duty to satisfy positive rights such as the right to subsistence (Shue 1996: 35–46, 153–6). The cost of Homeland Security in the USA serves as a dramatic example. Money is only one cost of protecting this negative right to life. The costs include serious inconveniences and some civil rights. Recent guidelines for regulatory analysis from the US Office of Management and Budget acknowledge these costs by inviting commentary on how 'to more effectively evaluate the costs and benefits' of Homeland Security proposals (2003: 5499). At what point should one minimal negative right be partially sacrificed for another? Can CBA help calculate this trade-off among rights?

Alan Gewirth proposes a more robust conception of dignity as individual autonomy. He locates dignity in an understanding of purposive action that all free and rational human agents must acknowledge. Dignity, so conceived, entails positive rights necessary for generally successful action (Gewirth 1996: 16–26, 38–44; 1992). Not surprisingly, this understanding of respect for dignity precludes a harmony of absolute rights, a conflict Gewirth acknowledges. He then proffers his own version of 'moral cost–benefit analysis' (MCBA), which he contrasts with 'economic cost–benefit analysis' (ECBA) (1996: 45–6 n. 16; 1990). MCBA, unlike Gewirth's depiction of ECBA, recognizes that human dignity transcends the value of productive activity measured in monetary terms alone. It never calculates rights in monetary terms. Rather, it calculates trade-offs among a hierarchy of rights when they intractably conflict with each other—for example, health therapies that divert resources from other more effective health measures (1990: 223).

Although Gewirth's view of dignity expands on views proposed by Ramsey and negative rights theorists, it mostly assumes uniform, naturally given human capacities for purposive action. In so far as this assumption is valid, positive rights to an equal set of resources in food, health care, education, and job opportunities secure respect for dignity. Gewirth largely neglects significant differences in individuals' capabilities to convert these resources into productive action. To his credit, Gewirth recognizes some exceptions. '[A]sthmatics and the elderly' have a right to cleaner air than others (1990: 224), and addicted persons have a right to efforts to remove obstacles to their purposive action so that their 'potentialities for agency may be actualized' (1992: 27). However, Gewirth does not incorporate these rights to specialized help into his MCBA, and he even implies that these rights will never conflict with the rights of persons without special needs (1990: 224–5).

We should not be surprised, then, to discover Gewirth's optimism about avoiding tragic trade-offs among rights. He assumes, for example, that using MCBA, rather than ECBA, prevents 'forced choices between polluting or carcinogenic jobs and no jobs at all' (1990: 225). In the end, Gewirth's MCBA establishes a lexical ordering of the hierarchy of rights so that no rights crucial for generally successful action need to go unsatisfied. MCBA avoids tragic inabilities to satisfy values associated with dignity entailed by CBA.

Human Dignity in Equal Capability

Both Amartya Sen and some theologically informed conceptions of human dignity challenge Gewirth's assumption of a standard set of capacities for converting external resources into purposive action. Sen's capability approach to dignity assumes what he calls '*inter-individual* variation' in human nature (1992: 85). He contends that 'variations related to sex, age, genetic endowments, and many other features give us unequal powers to build freedom into our lives even when we have the same bundle of [instrumental goods]' (1990: 121). Equal external resources and opportunities for self-development will not equalize individuals' capability for functioning. If we consider variations in rates of metabolism, susceptibility to malaria or asthma, or learning disabilities, the goods required for equal dignity vary for persons with these distinguishing features. Respect for dignity cannot be limited to forbearance from interfering with autonomy or to supplying resources and opportunities instrumental for purposive action. Respect for dignity entails attention to the multi-dimensional variations in persons' agential capacities: variations, such as a learning disability, that can pose obstacles to persons' 'effective freedom' for functioning. It requires that society compensate for the unequal capacities of some persons to convert resources into productive action if all persons are to have at least minimal freedom to choose from among an 'alternative combination of functionings' suitable for pursuing a variety of ends in life (Sen 1993: 31).

Douglas Hicks's recent work on inequality builds on Sen's capability approach, and further escalates the demands entailed by respect for human dignity. Hicks argues that equal dignity before God is not normatively meaningful without an empirical account of how unequal capability shapes selfhood. Significantly unequal capabilities marginalize persons from participating in society, and thereby degrade human dignity. Hicks's distinctive theological understanding of equal dignity before God entails '*some level of relative equality of economic power, or at least the limitation of extreme inequalities*' (Hicks 2000: 186). To the extent that Hicks is correct, respect for dignity demands relative equality as well as a threshold of minimal resources and capability.

Human Dignity in the Potential for Renewal

The operative conception of common grace in James Gustafson's theocentric ethics further broadens the scope of respect for dignity. We have seen that, for Gustafson, dignity in relation to God depends on cognitive, affective, and physical development consonant with what Sen and Hicks call equal capability. Gustafson's understanding of divine redemption goes further. It extends the significance of equal capability to include possibilities for partially overcoming limits of the self due to both finitude and sin. Capability diminished by misfortune, injustice, and even by habituated irresponsible behaviour may sometimes be renewed by divine grace mediated through actions such as therapeutic care and forgiveness (1981: 247–50). Hence hope in God's redemptive powers moves us to undertake prudent efforts to restore freedom lost by the 'sort of persons' we have become (Gustafson 1981: 222–3). Provision for diagnosis and therapeutic care for persons abused, addicted, or physically and psychologically impeded, and second chances for education become part of respect for dignity (see Beckley 2002: 123–32).

A Robust Conception of Human Dignity

This robust conception of human dignity cannot be confined to the sanctity of human life, to autonomy as negative freedoms, or even to an array of positive rights. As Gustafson observes, in light of his understanding of human agency, 'respect for only autonomy can be viewed as denigrating' (1981: 291). Respect for dignity responds to traits that limit persons' capacity to convert resources into effective freedom, mitigates inequalities that marginalize persons, and renews those hindered by their personal histories.

Thus understood, human dignity incorporates plural and even incommensurate values that must be weighted differently: for example, minimal income, opportunities for productive agency, healthiness, cognitive development, and life itself. Some of these values have priority. For example, life itself, although not an absolute value, is the 'indispensable condition' for all other values, as well as an intrinsic value. It has 'high priority' (Gustafson 1971: 140–4). Henry Shue claims that basic rights to human security, liberty, and subsistence are necessary pre-conditions for other rights and values (1996: 18–29). It follows that statistical lives should have great value in CBA, but not that they should never be risked at any cost in order to save other lives or other important values likely to be realized for an infinitesimally small risk to life. Entitlement to therapy for the psychological trauma resulting from physical abuse has less value than the right to physical security. In sum, respect for human dignity is not a seamless standard.

Two matters relevant to CBA follow from these conclusions. First, provision for the common good inevitably requires sacrificing or risking some essential aspects of respect for dignity for the sake of protecting and fostering others. CBA can help to preserve the common good and determine what costs, risks, and benefits will maximize respect for dignity. Second, the multi-dimensional values associated with respect for dignity cannot properly be measured either by their market value or by aggregated individual preferences. For example, restoring addicts to capability for functioning cannot be appropriately valued by their future earning power or by the willingness of individuals to pay for this benefit to addicts. Hence, CBA based on market valuations or preferences cannot preserve respect for human dignity.

Respect for Dignity Requires Trade-offs

John Ryan and others notwithstanding, the common good, as Gustafson contends, is incompatible with absolute respect for all aspects of every person's dignity. We need a method for evaluating trade-offs among the values for respecting individual dignity. CBA offers a method. It shows that the good of the whole sometimes requires sacrifices of human dignity, and, properly conceived, it does so without pitting the common good against respect for dignity. The trade-offs are ultimately between dignity and dignity. When, for example, the cost of protecting life for a few prohibits provision for this and other aspects of human dignity for many, choices and sacrifices must be made.

Ironically, contrary to those who contend that CBA undermines absolute respect for dignity, it can maximize respect for human dignity. Cass Sunstein, defending CBA for policies affecting human health, concludes not only 'that balancing is far better than absolutism', but also that 'absolutism [i.e., rejecting calculations that place a statistical life at risk] may actually be counterproductive and hence far from what it seems'. CBA, Sunstein contends, would not only save 'billions of dollars unnecessarily wasted on current programs, but also . . . save many thousands of lives' (1997: 381). His conclusion fits Gustafson's assertion that '[t]he relationship between the good of individual parts and the common good is reciprocal' (1984: 19).

CBA bears on respect for human dignity in two ways. First, it undercuts an absolute deontological respect for individual dignity that unintentionally, but foreseeably, subverts respect for human dignity. Second, it maximizes respect for human dignity.

Types of CBA

This conclusion depends on revising the value assumptions of strictly economic versions of CBA. As Sunstein notes, 'abstract ideas of "cost" and "benefit" need above all to be specified by some theory of value' (1997: 380). How would my theologically informed conception of human dignity revise traditional and some current versions of CBA? We can begin with misperceptions about the traditional economic version of CBA and then consider Sunstein's critique and revision of this economic version. Sunstein takes us some way in incorporating the intrinsic and equal value of human dignity into CBA.

Beyond cost accounting   We should not confuse CBA based on welfare economics with calculations based only on the market costs or, even worse, the legal costs of doing business. The shocking internal memorandum made public by the legal case involving the Ford Pinto abuses even the most flat-footed CBA methods. The memorandum valued human life primarily in terms of market costs—for example, for funeral expenses and the loss of victims' future productive labour. These calculations of aggregate social costs may have been no more than a CBA ruse to veil an internal (mis)calculation that the cost to Ford of placing lives at risk would be less than the cost of diminishing those risks (see Birsch and Fielder 1994). We should not confuse such crass calculations with CBA based on Paretian theory. Pareto improvement seeks to maximize aggregate satisfaction of preferences, not to minimize costs to a firm or direct market costs.

CBA routinely moves beyond mere market calculations to measure preferences in terms of willingness to pay (WTP), which may be expressed by market analogies or by surveys. Nor are preferences limited to self-interests. Although some economists collapse preferences into self-interests or pursuit of interests within the market, CBA may account for preferences to advance another's well-being at some cost to oneself (see Sen 1987: 15–22). Beginning with preferences, CBA has the purported advantage of leaving the valuing to individuals. They are presumably free to express whatever they value. Although this 'subjective welfarism' entails normativity, it claims not to impose values on others and to respect persons' autonomy.

Beyond Pareto improvement   Economists do use WTP to express and compare preference valuations in monetary measurements of aspects essential to human dignity such as life, health, or other functionings (Sunstein 1997: 139–43). Some ethicists, Gewirth included, reject these preference-based valuations, because the values of dignity and associated rights are established by rational arguments that override mere preferences. Sunstein's and Sen's criticisms of CBA take a different approach. They show why individual choices, whether expressed in the market or by surveys, fail to reveal true preferences. Sunstein says that no surefire method exists for knowing individual preferences. He doubts the entire 'edifice of social science based on notions of "preference" or "metapreference"' (1997: 51), a conclusion that leads to his significant revision, but not abandonment, of CBA inherited from welfare economics. He turns to democratic deliberation as a necessary, but insufficient, means for determining the values in CBA.

Both empirical and theoretical analyses undermine the hope for accurately establishing values based on preferences. Internal contradictions defeat 'subjective welfarism', even if we were to accept value theory based on aggregating individual preferences, which respect for human dignity does not. Four of many inadequacies will suffice to demonstrate this self-contradiction. All four show that preferences are endogenous—that is, adapted to various contexts (Sunstein 1997: 14).

First, actual choices depend on social norms (Sunstein 1997: 15, 38–41). The choices which persons express, whether in markets or in surveys, vary with different sets of social norms. Nor can we know for certain if different social norms free persons to choose according to their preferences. For example, does a social norm for safe driving free a teenager to act on her preference to minimize risks to herself and others?

Second, choices we make for ourselves differ from our choices for collective action (Sunstein 1997: 22–3, 141). Sunstein cites a citizen who does not recycle but votes for mandatory recycling (1997: 34). Our preferences for collective actions cannot be determined by market behaviour or WTP for private goods; they can only be discovered in the choices we make in deliberations about public goods.

Third, Sen and Sunstein observe how unequal distribution of economic resources and capability distorts both utilitarian theory and empirical conclusions about WTP. Poor persons choose willy-nilly what they need to survive. Their revealed preferences would change with more equal capability and resources (Sunstein 1997: 140, 25–8; Sen 1987: 45–7, esp. n. 17; see also Gewirth 1990: 214), and hence do not adequately measure what they value for themselves. Sen adds that increases in the freedom to choose following from greater capability are valuable independently of what persons actually desire (Sen 1987: 47–51; 2000: 944–5). For example, increasing a less-skilled worker's freedom to choose reduced risks in her workplace is valuable to that person even if she chooses not to reduce those risks. Persons value freedom as well as the goods they choose. Hence, CBA should value opportunities and rights that augment effective freedom, in addition to valuing the new goods that might be preferred in a changed context.

We should not confuse this criticism of the internal coherence of CBA based on revealed preferences with the more typical criticism of Pareto optimality for ignoring distributive justice. This second, ethical argument obtains independently of how unequal distribution distorts preferences. Respect for dignity requires that an acceptable CBA attend to this ethical argument as well as adjust for how unequal distribution skews revealed preferences. (See Gewirth 1990: 213–15 for an account of these distinct criticisms of strictly Paretian CBA.)

Sen exposes a fourth fatal flaw in CBA preference theory. Persons often prefer other-regarding values that diminish their well-being. They may, for example, sacrifice fulfilment of their own desires in order to pursue justice. Gandhi and Martin Luther King illustrate this tension between agency goals and well-being. The sacrifices they willingly made in pursuit of justice detracted from the good they almost certainly would have preferred in more just circumstances. CBA based on WTP is unlikely to account for these other-regarding preferences, but even if it collects accurate empirical data about other-regarding preferences, satisfaction of these preferences does not maximize satisfaction of the well-being that these agents would have chosen under different circumstances (Sen 1987: 40–5, including n. 15).

Democratic deliberation to specify cost–benefit values   Neither Sen nor Sustein claim, as Gewirth does, that valuations for CBA follow directly from a rational moral argument that overrides values based on preferences. However, they preclude weighing costs and benefits on preferences alone, because no method exists for a fully accurate measurement of rational preferences. Respect for an agent's rational preferences, Sen concludes, does not accept whatever the person happens to value prior to her deliberation (1987: 42). Deliberation, private and public, is necessary in order to respect the freedom of individual agents and avoid arbitrary or expert specification of values for CBA. '[D]emocratic choices should reflect a process of reason-giving . . . rather than a process of [mere] preferences satisfaction' (Sunstein 1997: 310–11). Only deliberation in a democratic context of relative equality can yield values approximating considered preferences. Moreover, this deliberation, according to Sen, can include an objective ethic—for example, an ethic that defends the intrinsic value of human dignity—if that objective ethic gives an important role to what persons do in fact value (1987: 42).

Incommensurate values   This deliberative process, according to Sunstein, should not be circumvented by calculations based on valuations in a single metric. Intrinsic values differ in kind, and cannot be rendered commensurate by money or any other single metric (Sunstein 1997: 80–3). Accurate descriptions of goods and harms respect this incommensurability. If, for example, we value children for their joy in appreciating literature, their affection and sheer existence in a family, and their potential as citizens, we should not describe money spent on their education as investing in children (Sunstein 1997: 86–9). See Jonathan Kozol's *Ordinary Resurrections* for poignant illustrations of valuing children and criticism of economic distortions of the value of children (2000: esp. chs. 16 and 11).

Sunstein employs non-monetary metrics to help measure values of a like kind. CBA can, for example, compare risks to life with alternative risks to life without monetary calculations, at least on the benefit side. Such calculations can maximize risk reduction given a limited investment for safety. But even life itself is not a unitary metric for valuing life. Rational persons often value one life more than another, due to age, distribution of risks, voluntariness of risk, dread of a particular type of death, and pain associated with death. The currently widely used measurement of 'quality-adjusted life years' (QUALYs) successfully encapsulates many, though not all, of these different valuations of life (see Beauchamp and Childress 2001: 210–12). Even if QUALYs accurately measured life benefits to life benefits, to evaluate from investments in safety and health care, they could not measure commensurate benefits from equal investments in non-subsistence consumption goods (e.g., travel for many) or in cognitive development of children. Consequently, CBA respecting incommensurate rational preferences must surrender hope for fully quantitative calculation. CBA has no means of 'producing an algorithm for decision' (Sunstein 1997: 306, 310–11, 143–5).

Sunstein's alternative   How, then, may CBA proceed? Some argue that it has no role to play in public policy. Elizabeth Anderson, in her philosophical examination of *Values in Ethics and Economics*, concludes that CBA has no place 'in choices involving human lives and environmental quality [its current principal uses] because these goods are not properly regarded as commodities' (1993: 195). Anderson admits the necessity for trade-offs among non-monetized intrinsic values, and proposes 'reason giving' in democratic deliberation as an alternative to CBA. Her rejection of CBA seems to be founded on two considerations. First, 'economic opportunities' and 'gains' are extrinsic values, in a different domain from intrinsic values, and have 'no weight at all' in deliberations about valuing human life and the environment. Second, although consequences have a role in democratic 'reason giving', a systematic 'additive accounting' of cost and benefits has no place in deliberations regarding human life and environmental values (1993: 190–216, esp. 208–9, 215–16; see above, 361, on 'additive accounting').

Sunstein takes a different path. 'Incommensurability need not entail incomparability,' he writes (1997: 81). We routinely weigh costs and benefits among intrinsic values in different domains, without relying on a single metric—for example, when we risk life to enjoy time with a distant family member. More systematic comparisons, including a role for monetary calculations, should figure in our deliberations about reducing one risk to life against opportunities to reduce other risks to life or to expand individual freedoms or physical and cognitive development (see Sunstein 1997: 84). Sunstein concurs with Anderson that weighing of values should rely on reason giving in democratic deliberation. However, systematic CBA can facilitate democratic deliberation and reduce intuition in making trade-offs (Sunstein 2000: 1092–3).

Sunstein illustrates his claim by examining government safety regulations that reduce risks to some workers while increasing ancillary risks to the health of others due to opportunity costs entailed by regulatory allocation of funding (1997: 298–317). Under these circumstances, overall risks to life and health cannot be reduced by investing more money in safety, thereby trading economic efficiency for worker safety. Trade-offs must be made among different risks to life and health; health and life must be weighed against health and life. Informative CBA measures both monetary costs and the value of the lives and health of one group against other groups vulnerable to different safety hazards. But lives, health, and economic productivity are not the only values at stake. Sunstein proposes that CBA also consider other values entailed by respect for dignity: the distribution of risks, the voluntariness of accepting risks, and so forth (1997: 299). The often cited *Johnson Controls* case, dealing with the right of fertile women to work in an environment with slightly increased exposure to lead (cited by Sunstein 1997: 302), addresses circumstances in which these values conflict. The various court opinions illustrate how CBA could be used—but was not used in Justice Blackmun's majority opinion—to combine qualitative and quantitative accounting of both instrumental economic and intrinsic human and moral costs and benefits in a deliberative process about workplace safety and opportunities (*International Union* v. *Johnson Controls* 1989, 1991). Sunstein demonstrates how CBA that factors economic costs into an analysis can add precision to evaluating the trade-offs bearing on respect for human dignity. CBA can save both lives and money (Sunstein 1997: 381), although its primary purpose should be to maximize respect for human dignity.

Beyond Sunstein: theological and ethical qualifications   Sunstein (and others) have moved CBA theory and (to a lesser extent) practice toward compatibility with respect for human dignity. Notwithstanding these positive contributions, Sunstein's proposal for CBA should be revised and expanded based on a theologically informed conception of human dignity. CBA as a theory and an authoritative practice remains open to modification from ethical perspectives. Christian ethics has a potential role in this process.

Sunstein's method for specifying values for CBA accounting leaves room for ethics, but he shies away from ethical thought. He shows that satisfying preferences is an inadequate basis for either a positive science or a norm for CBA. Values for CBA must be specified from beyond a theory of preferences. Nor should CBA rely solely on values specified by expert analysts. Sunstein, in a chapter written with Richard Pildes, turns to lay judgements in democratic deliberation in combination with WTP and to expert judgements (see Sunstein 1997: 130–8). Although he occasionally offers ethical arguments to specify CBA values (see, e.g., 2000: 1080–4, 1086–7), Sunstein grants ethical enquiry a severely limited role. CBA experts informed by the deliberative democratic process have almost ultimate authority in specifying values. Although Sunstein acknowledges the need for 'an inquiry that is frankly normative and defended as such', 'an understanding of what people's ends *should be*', he promptly adds that this enquiry would 'take us far afield from positive economics and social science' (1997: 54).

Christians concerned with human dignity should not be so reticent. Ethics experts need not replace CBA experts in order for ethical discourse to be a part of democratic deliberations about values for CBA, and, as Sen notes, ethics can grant an important role to what persons do in fact value (above, 373). Christians and others for whom respect for individual dignity is paramount should test the specification of values in CBA, as currently practised, by that principle. The current US Office of Management and Budget guidelines for CBA heavily favour monetized valuation based on WTP, but leave room for qualitative values, including fair distribution of risks and benefits. They do not incorporate respect for human dignity as proposed in this essay, but they retain openings for discussion (2003: esp. 5516, 5525). Ethical enquiry may conclude that authoritative CBA is incompatible with respect for dignity. Neither CBA experts nor democratic deliberation ensure respect for a robust conception of human dignity. However, nothing intrinsic to the process of CBA necessitates withdrawal from deliberations about its authoritative use.

I shall open more explicitly ethical enquiry into CBA with three criticisms of Sunstein's proposal. First, Sunstein's proposal for health–health trade-offs can be expanded to consider capability–capability trade-offs. Sen's conception of capability extends to education and to choices about participation in society. Systematic efforts to account for capability–capability trade-offs in the areas of education, special education, public assistance programmes, and improvements in opportunities for disabled persons—as well as for health care and safety—could account for a more robust conception of human dignity. Trade-offs are required within each domain—for example, between the costs and benefits of investments in special education for physically disabled children and investments in education for economically deprived children. A capability approach also calls for considered trade-offs in even more apparently unrelated domains—for example, education for disadvantaged children and some forms of homeland security.

Second, these trade-offs should also account for equality of capability more explicitly and emphatically than Sunstein's does. Hicks's theological and empirical argument for linking a sense of selfhood with equal capability and Sunstein's and Sen's sensitivity to equal distribution in the formation of rational preferences accentuate the role of equal capability in respect for dignity. CBA, thus understood, would of course go beyond considering whether Head Start (HS) or State Children's Health Insurance Programs (SCHIP) investments, for example, save taxpayers money or produce more economically productive citizens. It would also measure educational achievements, healthy reproductive practices, and engagement in civic life; but even more, it would measure whether investments in HS and SCHIP equalize these capabilities by comparison with economically well-off children. It would consider incremental capability improvements, but it would also measure whether these programmes narrow the capability gap among children.

Third, current CBA, focused on regulations, neglects the effectiveness and potential benefits of therapies, policies, and programmes designed to renew the capability of persons whose functioning has been impeded by some combination of misfortune, injustice, or wrongful behaviour. Respect for human dignity informed by Gustafson's view of grace requires considering benefits from public funding intended to help persons overcome barriers to functioning such as addictions or the effects of physical abuse, neglected education, and imprisonment. Since respect for dignity discounts merit as a basis for proportional distribution, and accentuates equal capability, benefits for these groups should be weighted heavily. The beginnings of CBA studies focused on these cohorts may come from unexpected sources. President Bush and the White House Office of Faith-Based Initiatives have declared that grant awards to anti-poverty organizations should be based on quantifiable data showing that their programmes succeed in turning lives around (see McNabb 2003: 4–9).

Systematic CBA expanded to incorporate human capability, its equality, and its renewal would be even further from offering an algorithm for trade-offs than the CBA proposed by Sunstein. Nevertheless, it could play a constructive role in democratic deliberations and government decisions about the value of current and proposed programmes. It would also be more compatible with respect for human dignity.

GOOD ECONOMICS MAXIMIZES HUMAN DIGNITY

John Ryan once quipped that 'in the matter of social institutions, moral values and [economic] expediency are in the long run identical' (Ryan and Hillquit 1914: 58). He believed that the best economics of his day, informed and revised by moral theology, improved Catholic social ethics. Although this essay disputes Ryan's optimism that economics and ethics combined can support absolute rights, I concur that good economics can advance overall respect for human dignity.

Systematic CBA based on the right values assumes and confirms that attention to the common good requires trade-offs of dignity for dignity. Respect for equal human dignity as an absolute intrinsic value will be, in Sunstein's word, 'counterproductive' (see above, 370). In so far as relations between the common good and the dignity of individuals are reciprocal but not perfectly harmonious, CBA can enhance the reciprocity and maximize respect for human dignity. However, this reciprocity does not allow Christian ethics to be absorbed by good economics.

Since CBA and respect for dignity do not lead to identical conclusions, as Ryan's assertion assumed, economics and ethics, even as they inform each other, must remain in tension. Ryan correctly refused to subsume individual dignity into the common good. Violations of individual dignity indicated by calculations of economic necessity should not be blithely accepted by suspending the principle of respect for dignity. When CBA calls for overriding absolute respect for dignity in order to maximize respect for dignity, the continuing relevance of rights associated with human dignity elicits lament for the moral tragedy of this decision, as Sunstein asserts (1997: 102–3). Martha Nussbaum goes further. CBA, she observes, does not 'enable us to represent' this sense of moral tragedy and regret. For that, 'we badly need an independent ethical theory of basic entitlements' (2000: 1032–6, esp. 1036). This sense of tragedy, Nussbaum and Sunstein concur, spurs us on 'to use our imaginations, thinking how we might construct a world in which such conflicts... confront [citizens] as rarely as possible' (Nussbaum 2000: 1036; see also Sunstein 1997: 102–3). Christian ethics should help sustain this persistent insistence on respect for dignity, impelling us to envision possibilities beyond the circumstances in which CBA-indicated trade-offs between dignity and dignity assist us to diminish, but never to eliminate, this tragedy.

Respect for dignity informed by Christian theology and ethics requires revisions of CBA grounded in economics. Even revised, CBA can never full incorporate respect for dignity independently of ethics. Nevertheless, Christian ethics should learn from economists, as Sen proposes that ethics generally should. CBA, as an authoritative tool for administrative, judicial, and legislative policies, and as an instrument for advancing democratic deliberation and moral discourse in churches, can advance Christians' respect for the equal dignity of persons.

REFERENCES AND SUGGESTED READING

ADLER, M. D. (2003). 'Rational Choice, Rational Agenda-Setting, and Constitutional Law: Does the Constitution Require Basic or Strengthened Public Rationality?', University of Pennsylvania Law School, Public Working Paper 21: U of Penn, Inst for Law & Econ Research Paper 03–01. <http://ssm.com.abstract_id=371161: 1–68>.
——and POSNER, E. A. (eds.) (2001). *Cost–Benefit Analysis: Legal, Economic, and Philosophical Perspectives*. Chicago: University of Chicago Press.
ANDERSON, E. (1993). *Values in Ethics and Economics*. Cambridge, Mass.: Harvard University Press.
BEAUCHAMP, T. L. and CHILDRESS, J. F. (2001). *Principle of Biomedical Ethics*, 5th edn. Oxford: Oxford University Press.
BECKLEY, H. (1992). *Passion for Justice: Retrieving the Legacies of Walter Rauschenbusch, John A. Ryan, and Reinhold Niebuhr*. Louisville, Ky.: Westminster/John Knox Press.
——(2002). 'Capability as Opportunity: How Amartya Sen Revises Equality of Opportunity', *Journal of Religious Ethics*, 30/1 (Spring), 107–35.
BIRSCH, D. and FIELDER, J. H. (eds.) (1994). *The Ford Pinto Case: A Study in Applied Ethics, Business, and Technology*. Albany, NY: State University of New York Press.

GEWIRTH, A. (1990). 'Two Types of Cost–Benefit Analysis', in Donald Scherer (ed.), *Upstream/Downstream: Issues in Environmental Ethics*, Philadelphia: Temple University Press, 205–32.

—— (1992). 'Human Dignity as the Basis of Rights', in Michael J. Meyer and William A. Parent (eds.), *The Constitution of Rights: Human Dignity and American Value*, Ithaca, NY: Cornell University Press, 10–28.

—— (1996). *The Community of Rights*. Chicago: University of Chicago Press.

GUSTAFSON, J. M. (1971). 'God's Transcendence and the Value of Human Life', in *Christian Ethics & The Community*, Philadelphia: Pilgrim Press, 139–49.

—— (1981). *Ethics from a Theocentric Perspective*, I: *Theology and Ethics*. Chicago: University of Chicago Press.

—— (1984). *Ethics from a Theocentric Perspective*, II: *Ethics and Theology*. Chicago: University of Chicago Press.

HICKS, D. A. (2000). *Inequality and Christian Ethics*. Cambridge: Cambridge University Press.

HOLLENBACH, DAVID, SJ (2002). *The Common Good and Christian Ethics*. Cambridge: Cambridge University Press.

International Union v. *Johnson Controls* (1989). 886 F. 2d 871 (7th Cir., reversed).

International Union v. *Johnson Controls* (1991). 499 U.S. 187.

KOZOL, J. (2000). *Ordinary Resurrections: Children in the Years of Hope*. New York: Harper-Collins.

MCNABB, M. (2003). 'Gatekeeping between Government and Religion: Faith-Based Initiative Competition and Supervision'. Unpublished paper at <http://www.shepherd/wlu.edu/academics/student_papers.htm>.

MISHAN, E. J. (1976). *Cost–Benefit Analysis*, new and expanded edn. New York: Holt, Rhinehart and Winston.

NOZICK, R. (1974). *Anarchy, State, and Utopia*. New York: Basic Books.

NUSSBAUM, M. C. (2000). 'The Costs of Tragedy: Some Moral Limits of Cost–Benefit Analysis'. *Journal of Legal Studies*, 29 (June), 1005–36. See also Adler and Posner 2001: 169–200.

RAMSEY, P. (1950). *Basic Christian Ethics*. New York: Charles Scribner's Sons.

—— (1970). *The Patient as Person*. New Haven: Yale University Press.

RYAN, J. A. (1916). *Distributive Justice*. New York: Macmillan.

—— (1919). *The Church and Socialism and Other Essays*. Washington: The University Press, 1919.

—— (1937). *Seven Troubled Years, 1930–1936: A Collection of Papers on the Depression and on the Problems of Recovery and Reform*. Ann Arbor: Edwards Brothers.

—— (1942). 'Two Objectives for Catholic Economists', *Review of Social Economy*, 1/1 (Dec.), 1–5.

—— (1996). *Economic Justice: Selections from 'Distributive Justice' and 'A Living Wage'*, ed. Harlan R. Beckley. Louisville, Ky.: Westminster/John Knox Press.

—— and BOLAND, F. J., CSC (1940). *Catholic Principles of Politics*. New York: Macmillan.

—— and HILLQUIT, M. (1914). *Socialism: Promise or Menace?* New York: Macmillan.

SEN, A. (1987). *On Ethics and Economics*. Oxford: Blackwell.

—— (1990). 'Justice: Means versus Freedoms', *Philosophy & Public Affairs*, 19/2 (Spring), 111–21.

SEN, A. (1992). *Inequality Reexamined.* New York: Russell Sage Foundation; Cambridge, Mass.: Harvard University Press.

—— (1993). 'Capability and Well-Being', in Martha Nussbaum and Amartya Sen (eds.), *The Quality of Life*, Oxford: Clarendon Press,

—— (2000). 'The Discipline of Cost–Benefit Analysis', *Journal of Legal Studies*, 29 (June), 931–51. See also Adler and Posner 2001: 95–116.

SHUE, H. (1996). *Basic Rights: Subsistence, Affluence, and U.S. Foreign Policy*, 2nd edn. Princeton: Princeton University Press.

SUNSTEIN, C. R. (1997). *Free Markets and Social Justice.* Oxford: Oxford University Press.

—— (2000). 'Cognition and Cost–Benefit Analysis', *Journal of Legal Studies*, 29 (June), 1059–1101. See also Adler and Posner 2001: 223–67.

US OFFICE OF MANAGEMENT AND BUDGET (2003). 'Report to Congress and Costs and Benefits of Federal Regulations'. 68 Fed. Reg. (3 Feb.): 5491–527.

CHAPTER 22

CHRISTIANS AND CULTURE

VIGEN GUROIAN

I

T. S. ELIOT once commented that Matthew Arnold 'set up Culture in the place of Religion, and . . . [left] Religion to be laid waste by the anarchy of feeling' (1932: 351). His observation prompts one to consider whether Arnold, the quintessential Victorian, was also the prototypical modern who, unable to muster belief in the biblical God, embraces culture as a faith substitute. And that consideration certainly can lead to the larger questions of what is culture and how Christianity ought to be disposed toward it.

We are here concerned with answering these latter questions. Nevertheless, it is expedient to enter this enquiry through the special case of Matthew Arnold. For even if Eliot was correct that Arnold made culture, and duty to it, stand for religion, the great Victorian was sufficiently sympathetic to the spirit of historic Christianity that his vision of culture was neither atheistic nor thoroughly secularist. He was a transitional figure from whom we can learn a lot about the late modern context of our discussion.

In his own day, Arnold was in the company of a broad range of critics who believed that high culture is not the product of mere inquisitiveness or experimentation, but is deeply related to historical religion and religious piety and who worried that the contemporary spirit of innovation was shading into a crass new barbarism. Arnold expressed that concern as follows:

The danger now is, not that people should obstinately refuse to allow anything but their old routine to pass for reason and the will of God, but either that they should allow some novelty or other to pass for these too easily, or else that they should underrate the importance of them altogether, and think it enough to follow action for its own sake, without troubling themselves to make reason and the will of God prevail therein. (1961: 46)

Arnold had caught the scent of a rising new secularity and a practical atheism, driven by the spirit of utility and fuelled by popular passions. In this respect, Eliot probably unfairly accused him of opening the gates to 'an anarchy of feeling'. Furthermore, I would argue that Arnold did not so much 'set up Culture in the place of Religion' as overstate the case for culture. That is because he confounded religion and culture. In this regard, Arnold, absolutely, was a fish who swam and breathed in the brackish waters of late Christendom.

Symptomatic of that location, Arnold valued biblical religion in mainly anthropological terms as educative, inspirational, and supportive of culture. 'Religion is the greatest and most important of the efforts by which the *human race* has manifested its impulse to perfect itself' (my emphasis), he opined. Religion 'comes to a conclusion identical with that which culture,—culture seeking the determination of this question [of the nature of perfection and how to achieve it] through all the voices of human experience which have been heard upon it, of art, science, poetry, philosophy, history, as well of religion, in order to give a greater fullness and certainty to its solution,—likewise reaches' (1961: 47).

Here Eliot rightly objected. Art, literature, or poetry that conveys religious ideas and sentiments is no substitute for, or equivalent of, faith and dogma, ecclesiastical authority, and corporate worship. Religion, and Christianity in particular, must never be collapsed into culture or studied as a subset of culture. 'Man is man because he can recognize supernatural realities, not because he can invent them,' wrote Eliot in criticism of the New Humanism that gained attention and stirred a controversy in the 1920s and 1930s. 'Either everything in man can be traced as a development from below, or something must come from above. There is no avoiding that dilemma: you must either be a naturalist or a supernaturalist' (1932: 485). Not by its own power or on the basis of naturalism or a secular humanism could culture rescue or repair a fraying and disintegrating civilization and hold back the emerging, dehumanized mass society, the 'Wasteland' of Eliot's own poetry.

Eliot also rejected Arnold's claim that culture is a guide to perfection, and maybe even its ultimate embodiment. 'Now, then, is the moment for culture to be of service', Arnold had written, 'culture which . . . believes in perfection . . . [and] is the study and pursuit of perfection' (1961: 46). Pursuit of perfection through culture is at the very least a path to disappointment, Eliot admonished. It may even lead to its dark opposite, nihilism, when disappointment sours into disillusionment and despair. Nevertheless, the inverse of Arnold's proposal, that religion is a useful means to perfection, is not true either. In his essay 'The Idea of a Christian Society',

Eliot argues against valuing the Christian faith on instrumental or social utilitarian grounds. 'And what is worst of all is to advocate Christianity, not because it is true, but because it might be beneficial. . . . To justify Christianity because it provides a foundation of morality, instead of showing the necessity of Christian morality from the truth of Christianity, is a very dangerous inversion' (1949: 46).

Many of Arnold's generation who no longer believed in the biblical God, but continued to be sympathetic to the cultural legacy of faith, welcomed Arnold's analysis and found comfort in it. His vision supported the easy Victorian, and the increasingly less comfortable Edwardian, assumption that high Western culture could carry all of the valuable Christian truths about human nature and human possibilities without subscription to formal religion or faith in the supernatural.

Twentieth-century theologians and philosophers corrected this assumption. They maintained that culture grows from the religious cult. 'Culture is the development of the religious cult, of its differentiation and the unfolding of its content' (1936: 212), wrote the Russian religious philosopher Nicholas Berdyaev. When the cult's vitality diminishes, the culture becomes exhausted, turns brittle, and hollows out; although even after the well of faith has dried up, a pragmatic, instrumental, and objectivistic use of religion that props up culture may continue for some time in the course of civilization.

II

Lay and learned people alike often make pronouncements about culture with wild inexactitude as to its meaning. I have not stopped to define my use of the term, either. So let us pause to do that. In point of fact, the definition given here is much nearer to Arnold's understanding than to the familiar description of contemporary social science.

Arnold embraced culture as wholly positive and well-nigh redemptive. That is not acceptable. Christian orthodoxy regards culture as religiously and morally ambiguous, and more is said about this below. On a strictly descriptive level, however, Arnold could subscribe to this definition:

Culture is the cultivation, development, and exercise of certain distinctively human capacities of freedom, reason, conscience, and imagination. It is embodied in manners and mores and is promoted by education: producing art, craft, music, literature, science, and the like.

That is what I mean by culture here. Thus, I am putting aside the reigning definition of the social sciences that now strongly influences even the liberal arts, including religious studies and academic theology. This anthropological and sociological definition arose in the latter half of the nineteenth century and has dominated the higher learning since at least the second quarter of the last century. According to it:

Culture is a distinctive way of belonging to a particular group or a historically formed people. This way of belonging is grounded in social tradition and values, expressed through a variety of symbolic forms, rituals, and activities, and embodied in institutions, art, literature, religion, and the like.

This definition is considerably broader and more encompassing than the one I have offered. Culture, in this sense, is virtually equivalent to the whole human social world. In this meaning it is interchangeable with society and civilization. H. Richard Niebuhr adopted this usage in his modern classic *Christ and Culture*, where he describes culture as 'the "artificial, secondary environment" which man superimposes on the natural. It comprises language, habits, ideas, beliefs, customs, social organization, inherited artifacts, technical processes, and values.' This '"social heritage"', Niebuhr adds, is what 'New Testament writers frequently had in mind when they spoke of the "world," which is represented in many forms but to which Christians like other men are inevitably subject' (1975: 32).

Beneath this broad umbrella, Niebuhr gathered, classified, and interpreted a host of important historical thinkers' views on Christianity and culture. Yet, whether one speaks of Clement of Alexandria or Tertullian, John Chrysostom or Augustine, Dante or Thomas More, Kant or Kierkegaard, Tolstoy or F. D. Maurice, none understood culture as Niebuhr defines it. And, of course, this can become confusing, if not plainly misleading, when he then goes about describing and analysing some of their Christian outlooks on 'culture'.

Niebuhr states that when the New Testament writers used the word 'world' (the Greek is *aeon*), they meant culture. According to this thesis, St John meant culture when he wrote, 'It was not to judge the world (*aeon*) that God sent his Son into the world (*aeon*), but that through him the world (*aeon*) might be saved' (John 3: 17; REB). But this is not so. In this passage, the evangelist is contemplating far more than mere human existence and its artefacts, but rather the whole creation that in its fallen condition is in need of salvation. Neither the New Testament authors nor their ancient audience conceptualized culture and distinguished it from world in the manner of the modern social sciences. They did not have at their disposal a word equivalent to culture in Niebuhr's sense.

The early Christian apologists and Greek Fathers, however, gradually adopted a word into their vocabulary that did come to mean culture in the first sense that I have identified above. The word is *paideia*. Werner Jaeger explains that *paideia* originally applied to education, or the process of educating. But, as with the Latin 'cultura' and English 'culture', which began with a similar meaning, *paideia* came to refer not just to the process of education but to its content, issuance, and endurance as intellectual and artistic tradition. After the fourth century, Greeks (and

Greek speakers) were using *paideia* regularly 'to describe all the artistic forms and the intellectual and aesthetic achievements of their race, in fact the whole content of their tradition' (1939: 303).

In his *Panegyric on St Basil*, St Gregory of Nazianzus employs *paideia* with mixed meaning as both education in the strict sense and as culture when he writes:

I take it to be admitted by men of sense, that the first of our advantages is education; and not only this our more noble form of it, which disregards rhetorical ornaments and glory, and holds to salvation and beauty in the objects of contemplation; but even that external culture which many Christians ill-judgingly abhor, as treacherous and dangerous, and keeping us afar from God. . . . [So] from secular literature we have received principles of inquiry and speculation, while we have rejected their idolatry. . . . Nay, even these have aided us in our religion, by our perception of the contrast between what is worse and what is better, and by gaining strength of our doctrine from the weakness of theirs. We must not then dishonour education, because some men are pleased to do so, but rather suppose such men to be boorish and uneducated, desiring all men to be as they themselves are, in order to hide themselves in the general, and escape the detection of the want of culture. (1978: 398–9)

The meaning of the English word 'culture' is near to its etymological source. The Latin *colere* means 'to till'. The verb 'to cultivate' is derived from the past participle *cultus*. 'Cult' comes from the same. The Roman Stoic Seneca is instructive about this etymology of culture when he writes: 'As the soil, however rich it may be, cannot be productive without culture, so the mind, without cultivation, can never produce good fruit' (Edwards 1954: 111). Culture, so conceived, means much the same as *paideia*.

III

Just as classical liberal political philosophy makes a strong distinction between state and civil society, so I propose something similar for culture and society. Culture grows in society, where it may or may not flourish, just as the political state functions within society, where it may or may not prosper. But culture, like the state, is more discrete and limited than the broad and general society. This analogy between state and civil society and culture and society is not exact, however. As with most analogies, it can be taken only so far. Culture and society overlap and interpenetrate in ways that, according to liberal theory, state and society do not, or, at least, should not.

Society exists in animal nature as well as in human history. In the natural world society is determinate. It is the product of what, for lack of greater precision, we sometimes call instinct or laws of nature. Natural society is repeated without significant innovation. The beehive is essentially the same in form and function time and again, according to the life cycle of that insect. There is in it no trace of freedom, personality, or self-transcendence. By contrast, human society entails reason, imagination, memory, and, most significant for our purposes, freedom and creativeness. Thus, human society varies considerably, despite the fact that it does not wholly transcend natural determinacy. As man is comprised of both nature and spirit, so is human society.

Society may be historical or natural, but culture is distinctively historical, and exclusively human. Human art is qualitatively different from even the intricately woven and otherwise remarkable spider's web. Human art does not necessarily serve a 'useful' purpose. It may simply express form and beauty. Human music is qualitatively different from the purely imitative, but otherwise impressive, repertoire of the mocking-bird. It expresses sadness or joy, conscious memory or sentiment, emotions and capacities that we do not ascribe to the mocking-bird. There may be similarities of movement between the mating gesticulations of the bird of paradise and human dancers. Yet human dance, even when man and woman perform it romantically, is much more than an instinctive mating ritual. It expresses rhythm and story. A human home may include a complex of 'rooms', as in a rabbit warren, and provide shelter from the elements, as does the warren also. But a human home may also include architecture, decorative art, and furnishings that express the personal tastes, histories, and expectations of the family members.

In addition to having historicity, culture is also personal, inasmuch as it is an expression of freedom and not determinate laws of nature. It manifests the human spirit, freedom, and self-transcendence more freshly and with greater immediacy than society. It is nearer than social order and organization to the well-spring of creative inspiration. Culture helps form and shape human society, but it is not reducible to society; just as human personality, which expresses itself through culture, is not reducible to mere individuality as member and number of the species *Homo sapiens*. Individuality belongs solely to material, spatial, and temporal existence, while personality pertains to spirit. It is the human being created in the image and likeness of God. Spirit may exist without individuality, as the Godhead is triune personality but is not individuated.

IV

During the period in which *paideia* came to mean culture, Christian attitudes toward classical culture ran the full spectrum from highly positive to strongly negative. Yet this spectrum reflects opinions about pagan culture, and not necessarily culture *per se*. Tertullian and John Chrysostom, who speak harshly of contemporary culture, agree no less than Clement of Alexandria, who is more sympathetic to it, that Christians should create their own culture.

Niebuhr's *Christ and Culture* is famous for its five-fold typology ranging from 'Christ against Culture' to 'Christ of Culture'. Whatever one's judgement about that typology, it is indisputable that Christians have differed, sometimes dramatically, in their estimates of the value of the culture in which they lived and whether or not it is compatible with Christian faith. As I have said, my principal concerns here are to define culture, and in view of that definition render a normative account of the relationship between Christianity and culture.

Thus, in the latter half of this essay I set forth briefly a normative theology of culture. The historical source of this theology is the ancient fourth- and fifth-century synthesis of faith and culture that Jaroslav Pelikan brilliantly analyses in his Gifford Lectures of 1992–3 entitled *Christianity and Classical Culture: The Metamorphosis of Natural Theology in the Christian Encounter with Hellenism*. The principal subjects of Pelikan's study are the three Cappadocian churchmen and theologians St Basil of Caesarea, St Gregory of Nyssa, and St Gregory of Nazianzus, along with St Macrina, the sister of Basil and the first Gregory. All four lived and wrote in the Greek East during roughly the same time as St Augustine of Hippo, who in the Latin-speaking West was developing his own account of culture and the Christian faith, most notably in his monumental *The City of God*.

Pelikan argues that the Cappadocians negotiated and defined the terms on which Byzantine Christianity continued to engage the classical cultural heritage, and that their influence is central even to Orthodox theology today (1993: 6). The Cappadocians 'stood squarely in the tradition of Classical Greek culture', Pelikan writes, 'and each was at the same time intensely critical of that tradition. Each was in constant interchange, and in less constant controversy with the monuments of that culture and with contemporary expositors of the monuments' (1993: 10). Each of the Cappadocians carried on his or her criticism of classical culture in a somewhat different key from the others. Together, however, they presented a broad view of Christianity and culture that permitted a range of defensible responses to culture.

Gregory of Nazianzus was the least critical of classical culture and learning. He saw very little inconsistency between its best wisdom and the Christian gospel. Gregory of Nyssa had the broadest and most penetrating insight into Greek *paideia*. Yet he was also attuned to 'the cultural differences between more cultivated and "more barbarian people"'. He warned 'that sin and vice were universal'. In his profound work of spirituality *The Life of Moses*, Gregory argued that the great Hebrew patriarch was the best example of 'how to properly benefit from pagan learning … [He] had, according to the Book of Acts "received a *paideia* in all the *sophia* of the Egyptians"'[Acts 7: 22]. Basil emphasized more than Gregory of Nyssa, even, the desultory effects of sin on human learning and conduct. He refused to elevate Moses as high as his brother had, remembering that Moses, too, was a member of the fallen race of men. 'Macrina ... drew on the ideas of the pagan philosophers' (1993: 10; see also Jaeger 1961) and writers, whom she regarded as wise men, though we know less about her thought and its nuances. But it is noteworthy that both she and her brother Basil founded monastic communities.

The Cappadocians grounded their synthesis of Christianity and culture in the doctrine of the image of God (*imago Dei*) that their great predecessors Irenaeus, Origen, and Athanasius propounded. This belief in the human person as *eikon* of God is at the centre of Cappadocian anthropology. It is a reason why none rejected classical culture outright. For however 'disfigured' by ancestral (original) sin the image of God in man is, it is not erased. What is more, because Christ restored the *imago Dei* in his own person for the whole of humanity, culture itself may be positively understood as sacramental, soteriological, and eschatological image (*eikon*) of the kingdom of heaven. The twentieth-century Russian Orthodox theologian Paul Evdokimov carries this tradition when he states, 'If every human being in the image of God is His living icon, culture is the icon of the Kingdom of God' (2001: 132).

V

Culture elevates society above and beyond its natural form to a truly human status of personality and communion. 'Culture indicates the fashioning of material by the action of spirit, the victory of form over matter. It is ... closely connected with the creative act of man' (1944: 122–3), writes Berdyaev. This creative act of man expresses the *imago Dei*. 'The Creator gives to man, to his own image and likeness, free creative power. Man's creativity is like that of God—not equal and identical, but resembling it' (1954: 136), Berdyaev explains. And Evdokimov adds: 'God is the creator, poet or maker of the universe and man, who resembles him is also creator and poet in his own way' (2001: 196). If 'art is the signature of man', as G. K Chesterton once said (1993: 34), then culture is man's letter to God.

In their best moments, human beings reach toward divine similitude. In their worst moments, they demonically parody God. The Book of Genesis in chapters 4–11, especially, explores these opposite potentialities. God created human beings in his own image so that they might grow into his likeness (Gen. 1: 26). The descendants of Adam and Eve, whom God intends to live in community, create culture and technology. They practice agriculture, invent music, make tools, and fashion artistic artefacts (Gen. 4: 17–22). All of these, when used properly, increase human stature and well-being, as God intends. The builders of the Tower of Babel (Gen. 11: 1–9), however, abuse their freedom and creativity. With Promethean pride and ambition, they perversely endeavour to fashion their city to equal heaven. They would steal God's glory to further their own power and reputation among the rest of humankind.

My own Orthodox tradition builds upon all of these biblical insights for its understanding of culture. It rejects categorically the Gnostic or Manichaean outlook that denies the goodness of the material creation. Were Christians wholly to reject culture as evil, they would deny also the divine image within themselves and the Incarnation through which God has set human existence back on a trajectory of blessed and eternal life. Instead, Orthodox Christianity embraces the profound wisdom of the Prologue to St John's Gospel. Significantly, it recapitulates the Genesis account of creation in the new key of the Divine Word made flesh (John 1: 14). This Divine Word is co-creator with the God the Father (John 1: 3). By becoming a human being, the Divine Word and Only Begotten Son (John 1: 18) reaffirmed the Father's original blessing that the creation coming from his hands was good and beautiful (Gen. 1: 29). (The Greek of the Septuagint has not the expected *agathos*, but *kalos*: which may be translated beautiful. The Hebrew *tob* is properly rendered good or truly perfect.)

Thus, by his divine power and through his perfected humanity, Jesus Christ transforms fallen human life and culture into a new creation that is good and beautiful. This passage of the old *aeon* into 'a new heavens and a new earth in which righteousness dwells' (2 Pet. 3: 13, NKJV) is symbolized by John's account of Jesus' transformation of the poorest water into the finest wine at the marriage in Cana of Galilee (John 2: 1–11). Temporal human marriage is itself revealed as an eschatological sign of the great 'marriage supper of the Lamb' (Rev. 19: 9, NKJV) at the dawn of the new creation.

Berdyaev states that 'the appearance in the world of the God-man marks a new moment in the creativity of the world, a moment of cosmic significance. In the revelation of the God-man begins the revelation of the creative mystery of man. *The world is being created not only in God the Father but also in God the Son.* Christology', he continues, 'is the doctrine of continuing creation' (1954: 137–8). The Holy Spirit's descent upon the apostles and disciples at Pentecost, and every person whom the Church baptizes, breathes new life into man and reignites the ecstatic flame of creativeness in the human spirit. Inside the Church, the Spirit proleptically perfects the *imago Dei*, so that it may be magnified in the world.

In his Letter to the Colossians, St Paul writes that Christ 'is the image of the invisible God' (Col. 1: 15, NKJV). This means that the visible humanity of the Son is itself the image and symbol of God's invisible divinity. In the Incarnate Son's human face, we see the face of God that was hidden from Moses even on Mount Sinai. We also see the face of sanctified humanity. For in Christ they are the same.

Traditional Christian iconography expresses this 'realism' about the divine image in man and the humanity of God. It is not interested in naturalism, in depicting the so-called natural human being that Christian faith knows to be fallen and sinful. Instead, iconography represents Christ and the saints in their divinized humanity, in the perfect humanity that God intended for his creation from eternity.

This image of perfection in Christ inspires the Christian ideal of culture. Just as Christ and the saints embody and confirm the biblical truth about the human being as the image of God, so human culture may become an expression and extension of that divine image in the world. This humanization of the world is also its divinization. In other words, through culture, humanity imprints the image of God upon the world: it enstamps upon the world Christ, who is 'the brightness of [God's] glory and the express image of His [the Father's] person' (Heb. 1: 3, NKJV).

VI

In this light, culture is humanity's artistic response to God's redemptive act in Jesus Christ to renew the world in and according to the divine image detailed by Christ in the Beatitudes (Matt. 5–7). St Paul writes: 'For we are God's fellow workers; you are God's field, you are God's building' (1 Cor. 3: 9, NKJV). This is the high calling of culture, to be an icon of the kingdom of God. 'At the great moment when the world passes from time into eternity', Evdokimov writes, 'the Holy Spirit will touch this icon lightly with His fingers, and something of the Spirit will remain in it forever. In the "eternal Liturgy" of the age to come, it is by means of all such elements of culture as have passed through the fire of purification that human beings will sing the praises of the Lord' (1994: 132–3). All the externalities of civilization and the political state will pass away with the old *aeon*, but the human spirit embodied in culture, 'this treasure in earthen vessels' (2 Cor. 4: 7, NKJV) shall not pass away, but be 'transformed ... from glory to glory' (2 Cor. 3: 18, NKJV).

Thus, even a fallen culture is not discontinuous with the new creation. We will look to the Christian Eucharist for insight and illumination on this profound matter. But it is important to state at the start that human beings, since time immemorial, have recognized and affirmed this positive value of culture when they have worshipped divinity and in so doing celebrated the goodness of creation.

VII

In his modern classic *Leisure: The Basis of Culture*, the Roman Catholic philosopher Josef Pieper makes a stunning phenomenological analysis of the connection between the worship of divinity and the rise of culture. He extends that analysis to make some very particular claims about Christian worship. That analysis is the bridge to my closing comments. I am less concerned, however, with Pieper's powerful and persuasive thesis that leisure, which he defines as 'everything that lies beyond the utilitarian world', is the basis of culture, the pre-condition for its birth, as his correlative claim that 'culture lives on religion through divine worship' (1963: 61).

In other words, Pieper says that worship is the basis of leisure, which, in turn, is the source of true culture. In a similar vein, Berdyaev writes: 'Philosophy, science, architecture, painting, sculpture, music, poetry and morality are integrally comprised in the ecclesiastical cult in undifferentiated form' (1936: 212). Pieper insists that true leisure is not 'killing time'. It is not 'idle' time. It is not 'wasted time'. It is none of these, because it is not a state of existence the value of which is measured over and against time spent in economic labour or work the aim of which is to produce goods external to the actual performance. Religious worship—in this case not limited to the Christian Eucharist—is the quintessential home of leisure, because it is nothing less or more than a freely performed celebration of the divine presence and thanksgiving for the good of that presence in the lives of those who participate.

During this worship, time ceases to tyrannize human existence, because there are no 'in order tos', 'wherefores', or 'whyfores' in worship-*full* time. Liturgical time is liberation from time as necessity, and is, instead, a proleptic participation in the freedom and creativeness of the divine nature (2 Pet. 2: 4). In this manner, worship marks off the difference between *artes liberalis* and *artes serviles*. From its sacred ground and in its time, one recognizes that a play of Shakespeare, or the study or performance of it, belongs to the realm of the *artes liberalis*. The value and purpose of the play lies within the creative act. This is culture, and may be contrasted with business marketing. Business marketing, whether it is taught as a subject in the university or practised in the marketplace, belongs to the realm of *artes serviles*. It is not culture—although culture can potentially elevate and humanize it. Business marketing's purpose to sell products is external to it. The value of such economic activity and organization is mainly instrumental.

The pragmatic or utilitarian mind has a hard time grasping this account of the birth and nature of culture or the distinction between it and other 'necessary' forms of human activity, much as it can hardly fathom C. S. Lewis's observation that joy is a 'surprise' that cannot be conjured by well-planned recreational events. 'Celebration of God in worship cannot be done unless it is done for its own sake', says Pieper (1963: 62). Yet, if this is so, then culture itself is at least as much a gift from divinity as a human achievement, more a surprise than something that can be secured by government grants to the humanities.

Culture is among humankind's highest expressions of freedom. For genuine worship is not compelled; it is 'done' voluntarily. The human person, created in the image of God, makes culture in a manner analogous to how God brings all things into being from nothing, not from necessity but perfectly freely. 'The object of God's creativity, the world, is not only a universe', writes the Orthodox theologian Sergius Bulgakov, 'but an artistic work, the *kosmos* in which the artist rejoices'

(1999: 195). Human beings dwell in a 'divine culture', a divine milieu, even before—I mean this ontologically, as state of being, not temporally—they make human culture. Indeed, divine culture is the pre-condition of human culture. Divine culture is paradise before the Fall; it is forgotten and lost through ancestral (original) sin; it is remembered and regained through prayer and sacrament.

The notion of 'the origin of arts in worship, and of leisure derived from its celebration', says Pieper, 'is given [by Plato] in the form of a magnificent mythical image: man attains his true form and his upright attitude "in festive companionship with the Gods"' (1963: 61). In our epoch, however, the world of economically driven labour and the market makes claim to being the whole field of valuable human existence and activity. This state of mind (or habit of being) may be described as 'secularism', Pieper continues. 'What in our days is called "secularism" represents perhaps, not so much the loss of a Christian outlook, as rather the loss of some more fundamental insights that have traditionally constituted humanity's patrimony of natural wisdom' (1989: 142). If the Cappadocians were alive today, they, no doubt, would agree with Pieper.

Something more, however, needs to be said about the specificity or singularity—even the uniqueness—of Christian worship and, therefore, Christian culture. Bulgakov states the crux of the matter when he observes: 'Man is the son of eternity plunged in the stream of time, the son of freedom' caught in a fallen world. The Church in its liturgy calls upon human beings to ' "lift up your hearts" ', whereas the modern spirit beckons ordinary humanity to think that the answer to the mystery of its origin, nature, and destiny is no mystery at all, but a fact found beneath human existence in animal and inanimate nature. 'It cannot with impunity be dinned into a man's ear that he is a two-legged brute, that his nature is purely animal, and that therefore the only thing left him is to recognize this and to worship his own brutishness. . . . One cannot deprive man of the ideal of personality and hide Christ's image from him without devastating his soul' (1976: 63).

Bulgakov has also identified the crisis of human meaning that we call modernity and postmodernity. The current condition of Western culture is inextricably and unavoidably intertwined with the decline of Christian orthodoxy, and the future of Western culture with the future of the Christian faith. This is, of course, contrary to contemporary conventional wisdom.

VIII

For two millennia, through sacraments and liturgy, Christians have remembered the divine image. Out of this worship they have drawn the hope and inspiration to build up culture in a world that modern science tells them is doomed to end in ice and fire. Christians have understood the Eucharist as God's gift to humanity and the whole world for health and renewal. God calls upon human beings to act as priests of his creation, to recollect and return the entirety of it with whole heart and mind to God as matter and subject (Rev. 5: 13) of the 'eternal Liturgy' (Heb. 8: 1–2; Rev. 4: 1–8), in which the old creation is transformed into a new one. 'And I saw a new heaven and new earth, for the first heaven and the first earth had passed away' (Rev. 21: 1, NKJV).

The sacred and hallowed death that the Eucharist commemorates is not only the last bloody sacrifice acceptable to God; it is the ultimate sacrifice that sanctifies and renews the entire creation. For Christ gave not only himself as a sacrifice, but rendered to God, through his body and blood, all of creation as one holy oblation transformed into his resurrected body.

In light of this sacramental character of the world, revealed in and fulfilled by the Christian liturgy, the true value of culture comes to light. Indeed, it needs to be said that the Eucharist renders human beings fit to create culture as sign and image of the kingdom of heaven. This creation may be a great cathedral, the work of many, or the simple prayer of one small child.

'Three exclamations of the celebrant and three short replies from the gathering comprise an introductory dialogue by which the sacrament of the [Byzantine] anaphora begins'(1988: 166), writes Alexander Schmemann in his last work, on *The Eucharist*. The three exclamations are: 'The grace of our Lord . . . be with you all', 'Let us lift up our hearts', and 'Let us give thanks to the Lord'. The three responses are assent to and affirmation of these declarations as right and appropriate. Thus, in Eucharistic worship, by the holy oblation offered, Christians realize that their words, actions, and achievements participate in the goodness, truth, and beauty of the divine life that is all three in unity. They remember that all of their words, deeds, and creations attain value only in so far as they themselves dispose their whole self to that which is 'high' and 'heavenly'. And they express gratitude to God that in and through this holy sacrifice their lives and the life of the world are redeemed, renewed, and sanctified. These are the three liturgical movements of the soul that mystically (hidden from unbelieving eyes) have given birth to the culture of the West.

IX

In his criticism, Matthew Arnold proved himself a true, late child of nineteenth-century liberal Christianity and of modernity. He could leave creed and dogma and prayer and worship behind, yet remain paradoxically (perhaps contradictorily) attached to Christendom and convinced that culture would continue. Today, we are living at the end of that self-contradictory and self-delusory modern legacy. Against this backdrop, postmodernity rises up to reject Christendom and, with no qualms, to leave it behind completely.

A path, which I cannot walk here, may be followed from the Arnoldian belief in culture to the aggressive, monolithic secularism of today. This secularism asserts the absolute autonomy of man and experiments with a new Prometheanism. The twentieth-century Roman Catholic theologian Romano Guardini once described modernity 'as a movement that in its beginning denied the Christian doctrine and a Christian order of life even as it usurped its human and cultural effects'. In the midst of this, Christian men and women 'found ideas and values, whose Christian origin was clear, but which were declared the property of all'. Guardini predicted that the new coming age 'will do away with [even] these ambivalences; ... [and] declare that the secularized facets of Christianity are sentimentalities. This declaration will be clear', he continues. 'The world to come will be filled with animosity and danger but it will be a world open and clean' (1998: 105). No one will be able to doubt any longer what is at stake.

Guardini tendered these penetrating observations more than half a century ago. The term 'culture wars', which has gained such wide usage in the past two decades, can be misleading, and is an inadequate description of the choices that contemporary society is making for the future of humanity. None the less, it registers a widening gap of disagreement between secularists and the religiously orthodox about the meaning and value of culture. Secularists are believers in progress through education, economics, social science, multi-culturalism, feminism, and deconstructionism. They reject transcendental reality, or at least regard the possibility that it exists as irrelevant to human endeavour. They are persuaded that the perfect or best of all possible worlds is a strictly human and historical project. Whatever the secularists' precise definition of culture, culture is the 'end game' without closure or fulfilment in final meaning. 'Culture is opposed to eschatology, to the apocalyptic. . . . [It] is opposed to an ending, its secret hope is to remain in history', Evdokimov writes (1994: 127).

Christianity defines culture not merely in anthropological and sociological terms but, more importantly, soteriologically, sacramentally, and eschatologically. For two millennia, this religious vision supplied Western society with a unifying image of human excellence. Culture was understood as the expression and concretization of the spiritual element of human nature writ large, the *imago Dei* growing out into the world and transforming it. Because this was a fallen world, deeply, ontologically, rooted in the habit of sin, culture was also understood as profoundly ambiguous. On the one hand, it was the manifestation of the godlike creative capacities of human beings, owing to the fact that they were endowed with the divine image. On the other hand, culture could express the most destructive proclivities of human beings, owing to the Fall and ancestral (original) sin. Culture was neither man's perfection nor his salvation. Culture was historical and finite, and not an end in itself. 'Culture, in its essence ... [was] the search in history for what is not found in history, for what is greater than history and leads outside its boundaries' (Evdo-kimov 1994: 132). No culture, however 'Christian', could convert the sinful human being and render the human condition blessed. The perfection of culture, like that of humankind, was dependent completely upon God's initiative in and through the Incarnation.

I have put this account in the past tense to emphasize that this vision is rejected by postmodernity. I do *not* mean to suggest that the vision has completely vanished, however. For it continues to reside in the 'cult' that gave birth to it and infused it into the decadent, hollowed-out culture of late antiquity, and trans-formed that dying world into what we call Christendom.

'Every culture has its spiritual origin in a cult, from which little by little it becomes detached, until it is entirely cut off and self-contained, even perhaps the reserve of an elite,' observes the contemporary Orthodox theologian Olivier Clém-ent. Ironically, as it enters its decadent phase, a culture may achieve 'high refine-ment, subtlety and consciousness', Clément adds; but there is a loss of focus, wholeness, and spontaneity. With higher consciousness comes objectification, 'skepticism, tolerance of diversity, a dislike of sharp distinctions, a readiness to see shades of grey, rather than black and white' (2000: 132).

Because of Western culture's Christian past, growing indifference to the Incar-nation and rejection of it spell the decadence and ultimate demise of this culture. 'In its decadent phase (using the phrase with no pejorative intent) a culture becomes accessible and in a way that simultaneously enfeebles and enriches it, when it spreads beyond its traditional organic community,' Clément writes. It is like a dying sun, growing weaker and more diffuse until it implodes. 'This accessibility and openness are accompanied by a certain predilection for the unknown, what Spengler called "secondary religiosity"' (2000: 132–3), after which complete secularity follows.

An agnostic or atheistic culture, however, 'can only be a parasite plant on an alien stock, and one which kills the tree upon which it is feeding', Bulgakov insists. 'Self-deification [through culture] is not life-giving but ... death-bringing' (1976: 62). Some will make comparisons between contemporary Western civilization and the late Roman Empire into which Christianity entered. Social scientists and historians might accept or reject these comparisons on so-called objective grounds. But in all of this, a fundamental claim of the Christian faith does not figure. It is that the course of human history, and so this culture too, has been altered fundamentally and irreversibly by the Incarnation.

Post-Christian society cannot be like pre-Christian society; it cannot return to its pagan past, because God has unveiled his face as the face of man in Christ. It cannot remain agnostic indefinitely either. New gods may be invented. But that is just it; they would be inventions. After Christ, 'there is only *one* true and finally valid form

of cultic worship, which is the sacramental Sacrifice of the Christian Church'
(Pieper 1998: 59). On the cross, Jesus Christ ended ritual sacrifice and the pre-
Christian cult for ever. 'For the student, Christian or non-Christian, of the "history
of religions"', Pieper argues, 'it really is not possible to meet with any actually
established cult other than the Christian, in the world-wide European culture'
(1998: 59).

Our 'post-Christendom civilization' might turn aggressively atheistic, but this
atheism can only be in reference to biblical faith also. Thus, postmodernity is not a
new culture. It is the rotting corpse of a thoroughly descralized Christendom or,
alternatively, the empty shell of the Christian cult inhabited by alien ideologies.
I must conclude that an institutionalized postmodernity inside the old Christendom, lately called modernity, would be the 'incarnation' of the Antichrist. It would
be culture that is anti-culture.

Guardini says that such a future would entail two phenomena: 'the non-human
man and the not-natural nature'. In such an unexperienced and unnamed heathen or
atheistic future, man would 'face an existence in which' he exercises absolute lordship
of creation with no recognized limitations: 'the freedom to determine his own goals:
the freedom to dissolve the immediate reality of things, to employ its elements for the
execution of his own ends. These things will be done without any consideration for
what had been thought inviolate or untouchable in nature' (1998: 73–4).

In such a future, humanity will be ignorant of, or defiant toward, the religious
sense 'of the sacredness of nature which had endured within mankind's earlier
vision of the world' (1998: 740). Humankind might carry all of this 'to the last
consequence' (1998: 73), says Guardini, by which I take him to mean the complete
destruction of the world by man's own hands through a diabolic parody of the
divinity.

Guardini presents an alternative that, due to his optimism born of his Christian
faith, he regards as the more likely possibility. 'The faith of the Christian will . . .
take on a new decisiveness . . . strip itself of all secularism, all analogies with the
secular world, all flabbiness and eclectic mixtures', he writes, (1998: 103–4). Dogma
and worship will also revive as Christians 'are forced to distinguish' themselves
'more sharply from a dominantly non-Christian ethos' (1998: 106). A new Christian
culture might then arise from the renewed cult, although where it arises may be a
surprise.

References and Suggested Reading

ARNOLD, M. (1961). *Culture and Anarchy.* Cambridge: Cambridge University Press.
BERDYAEV, N. (1936). *The Meaning of History.* New York: Charles Scribner's Sons.
—— (1944). *Slavery and Freedom.* New York: Charles Scribner's Sons.
—— (1954). *The Meaning of the Creative Act.* New York: Harper & Brothers.

BULGAKOV, S. (1976). *A Bulgakov Anthology*, ed. J. Pain and N. Zernov. Philadelphia: Westminster Press.

—— (1999). *Sergii Bulgakov: Towards a Russian Political Theology*, ed. and introduced by R. Williams. Edinburgh: T. & T. Clark.

CHESTERTON, G. K. (1993) *The Everlasting Man*. San Francisco: Ignatius Press.

CLÉMENT, O. (2000) *On Human Being*. New York: New City Press.

EDWARDS, T. (Compiler) (1954). *The New Dictionary of Thoughts*, rev. C. N. Catrevas and J. Edwards. New York: Standard Book Company.

ELIOT, T. S (1932). *Selected Essays*. London: Faber & Faber.

—— (1949). 'The Idea of a Christian Society', in *Christianity and Culture*, New York: Harcourt, Brace and World, Inc., 1–77.

EVDOKIMOV, P. (1994). *Women and the Salvation of the World*. Crestwood, NY: St Vladimir's Seminary Press.

—— (2001). *In the World, of the Church*, ed. and trans. M. Plekhon and A. Vinogradov. Crestwood, NY: St Vladimir's Seminary Press.

GREGORY OF NAZIANZUS (1978). Oration 43: 'The Panegyric on S Basil', in *A Select Library of Nicene and Post-Nicene Fathers of the Christian Church*, VII, Grand Rapids, Mich.: Wm. B. Eerdmans, 395–422.

GUARDINI, R. (1998). *The End of the Modern World*. Wilmington, Del.: ISI Books.

JAEGER, W. (1939). *Paideia: The Ideals of Greek Culture*, I. New York: Oxford University Press.

—— (1961). *Early Christianity and Greek* Paideia. Cambridge, Mass.: Harvard University Press.

NIEBUHR, H. R. (1975). *Christ and Culture*. New York: Harper & Row.

PELIKAN, J. (1993). *Christianity and Classical Culture*. New Haven: Yale University Press.

PIEPER, J. (1963). *Leisure: The Basis of Culture*, trans. A. Dru. New York: Random House, Mentor-Omega Books.

—— (1989). *Josef Pieper: An Anthology*. San Francisco: Ignatius Press.

—— (1998). *Leisure: The Basis of Culture*, trans. G. Malsbary. South Bend, Ind.: St Augustine's Press.

SCHMEMANN, A. (1988). *The Eucharist*. Crestwood, NY: St Vladimir's Seminary Press.

CHAPTER 23

CHRISTIANS AND THE CHURCH

PAUL J. GRIFFITHS

THERE is no shortage of figural language for the Church. Much of it is biblical, and still more is woven into the fabric of the Church's hymnody and prayer. The Church is, according to her own account, wife and mother, city and garden, kingdom and diaspora, people and body, sign and sacrament, warrior and peace-maker, seed and harvest, pure and defiled, virgin and whore, lover and taskmistress, lamb, eagle, hen, and doe. Feminine figures predominate, in part because of the grammatical gender of the ordinary Greek and Latin words for her, and in part because Christian talk about the Church has always shown a deep elective affinity for talk about the archetypically female functions of nurturing, protecting, birth giving, and educating. This is the primary language of Christians about the Church: it is poetic, associative, suggestive of endless meanings that cannot be reduced to precise technical formulations without significant loss.

Such reduction is what ecclesiologists, those who theorize about the Church, attempt. Their works are many, some of them profound and of great use to ecclesiologists-in-training, of which the Church always needs some; but they are too often predicated upon the assumption that the florid proliferation of Christian figural talk about the Church needs to be knocked into conceptual shape, pruned, trimmed, and cultivated. For some purposes, no doubt, this is true. This essay, however, attempts no such thing. It is not ecclesiology, and its purpose is not to survey or to provide waymarkers through that vast and heavily tracked field. It is, instead, an attempt to state a particular understanding (and thereby to prompt other, fuller understandings) of what the primary Christian figures for the Church suggest about her significance for the moral life of Christians.

Figure—metaphor, synecdoche, metonymy, and so on—is language's dream-work, as the philosopher Donald Davidson (1991) elegantly puts it. Such linguistic forms work as do dreams, reveries, and soulful gazes into the beloved's eyes, which is to say by provoking a shift of the gaze through, behind, and beyond what is immediately before the eyes toward a deeper noticing. Linguistic figures provide intimations that exceed what is apparent on their surface. In this they are like icons, which also reconfigure and redirect the gaze (see Marion 2001). Linguistic figures understood in this way cannot be paraphrased or translated without remainder into non-figural language. They are provocations whose results, in action and thought, cannot be fully predicted, in much the same way that (as Dante tells us in *Inferno*, v. 127–42) Paolo and Francesca's reading provoked, unpredictably, the look, the kiss, and the love-making. What figural language will provoke cannot, then, easily be foretold from the meanings of the words in which the figure is given. Analysis of linguistic figures proceeds best by paying attention to the effects that the use of particular figures has (or might have) upon those who use them.

Christians are of course not formed morally only, or even principally, by the language they use. They are formed morally by the practices they perform, among which the deep and repeated use of figural language is only one. None the less, thought (non-paraphrastic thought, of course) about what Christian figural language for the Church might provoke and intimate by way of understanding the Church as a theatre of moral formation may itself be an instrument of importance in furthering and deepening the conformation of Christ's body to Christ. Such thought is what I hope to offer in this essay. If the figure is language's dreamwork, this essay offers an interpretation of dreams whose goal is to help those who dream the ecclesial dream to do so more fully, and perhaps also more interestingly. The interpretation of dreams here offered is prescriptive rather than descriptive. That is, it commends what should be, rather than describes what is. The picture given here of the significance of the Church for the moral formation of Christians will be only partly and fitfully evident in the formation of actual Christians by actual churches. It may serve, perhaps, as a set of regulative ideas and images.

The essay is written under the assumption that properly and fully Christian thought about any topic whatsoever should begin by consulting and deploying the primary language of the tradition as its first and last tool of thought. There are, of course, circumscribed and particular topics for which there is no relevant primary language: these include most questions answerable by empirical investigation (what are the syntactical principles of Sanskrit?), and most questions in areas of theory of no direct and explicit interest to the tradition (is it true that every even number greater than 2 can be expressed as the sum of two primes?). In such cases there will be no primary Christian language to consult and deploy. But our question—what is the significance of the Church for the moral formation of Christians?—is very much not of this sort. Treatment of it by Christians must therefore begin in the way I've suggested. Any other mode of approach will be sub-Christian.

I begin, then, with the body.

BODIES

'Body' is a fundamental figure for the Church. To say that the Church is Christ's body is deeply scriptural, and the elaboration of this claim lies at the heart of Christian theological thought. The grammar of this claim is a complex one, however, as is the syntax of ordinary, non-Christian and non-theological talk about bodies. The complexity of the latter is in large part an offshoot of the complexity of the former, and certainly Christian thought about bodies and the grammar of the term 'body' must begin with thought about Christ's body.

Christ's body is, first, the most real of all bodies: it belongs to the second person of the Holy Trinity, and the difficulty of stating precisely the nature of the relation (identity? possession? property?) between Christ's body and Christ is mirrored exactly by the difficulty of stating exactly the relation between my body and me or your body and you. The fundamental syntax of Christian talk about Christ's body oscillates between two poles: one pole is the Eucharist, on which more below; the other is the Church, of direct concern here. The two poles are always related, of course: when the Church as Christ's body celebrates the Eucharist, it eats what it is, as Augustine's frequently repeated formula has it. Among other bodies, it is this one that for Christians is of primary and unsurpassable significance, this one in terms of which all other bodies must be thought about and understood.

This primary point of reference for body-talk provides at least the following: all bodies are social as well as individual, intimately and essentially related to and constituted by the bodies of others, as well as being (sometimes) a particular person's embodiment. The social constitution of Christ's body is given first by the triune nature of God, within which trinity he is a person identified by his relations to other persons. It is also given by the fact that Christ's body is eaten by, and thus constitutes as a body (his own body), a multitude of particular human bodies—perhaps one and a half billion of them at the beginning of the second millennium after Christ's incarnation. But it provides more than this: it gives also the beginnings of a criterion for distinguishing between imaginary and real bodies.

If, as is axiomatic for Christian thought, the supremely real body is Christ's, the reality that any other body has must be derivative from and dependent upon the reality of his. It is then theoretically (and to some degree actually) possible to assess the degree of reality that particular bodies have by assessing the degree to which they participate in Christ's body. Individual bodies of flesh, mine and yours, all have reality in virtue of the fact that they are creatures; and since creation is a work of the triune God, not of any one of the three persons alone (I assume here an approximately Augustinian trinitarianism, according to which the only predicates proper to just one of the divine persons are those that designate that person's relations to one or both among the other two), fleshly reality, like every other reality, is given by participation in the Trinity. But since the ordinary first connotation of body-talk for Christians is Christ's body, and since Jesus Christ is embodied in ways that the other divine persons are not (the risen Christ continues to be embodied), it is reasonable to say (though there are complications here) that all human fleshly bodies participate in the divine Trinity through the act of creation under the mode of participation in Christ's fleshly body. This is a specification of what it means to say that human physical bodies are creatures. But some fleshly bodies participate in Christ's fleshly body more fully by being, publicly, members of Christ's own social body by baptism and (what follows upon such public membership) by becoming conformed to him through the consumption of his fleshly body in the Eucharist. These individual fleshly bodies have moved closer to their final perfection, a perfection not to be realized fully until the eschaton, because of their membership in the Church.

If, as I think, moral realism of a teleological sort is the properly Christian way to think about ethics (also, of course, the truth—this follows from its being properly Christian), then it follows at once that the increasing conformity of the individual Christian's fleshly body to Christ's body that is given by membership in the Church has direct moral relevance. Being and goodness are convertible transcendentals, as the tradition at least from Augustine to Aquinas has argued. On this view, to be more is to be better. Incorporation into Christ's body already makes the one so incorporated morally better than she would otherwise have been, just because (and in the same sense as) she is more than she would otherwise have been. Fleshly membership in Christ's body is, then, morally transformative. This is an abstract, theoretical understanding; flesh will be put on its bones in what follows.

There are social bodies as well as individual, fleshly bodies. Another name for these social bodies is 'communities', groups of individual persons ordered to some end. A half-understood remnant of Christian talk about communities as bodies is to hand in the English-speaker's ease with such phrases as 'the body politic' and 'the student body'. These modes of expression and understanding have pagan roots as well as Christian ones, but their genius is Christian. For Christians, the Church, because it is Christ's body, is the paradigm of community: all others are understood to be such in terms of this paradigm, and assessed as to their goodness in terms of their approximation to it. Once again, this mode of approach provides criteria for distinguishing between real and imaginary social bodies or communities, and for commending or requiring degrees of loyalty to (and so also formation by) particular communities based upon such a distinction.

The picture sketched so far suggests that the Church is the primary social body for Christians, and is so because its reality exceeds that of any other. This is because the Church is brought into being by the self-emptying of God into its founding events. These events include not only the incarnation, crucifixion, resurrection, and ascension of Jesus Christ (though these are crucial); they comprise also the call and covenanting of the Jewish people, from which it follows, though not without a chain of reasoning too long and involved to be given here, that the social body of the Jewish people is the only one whose reality can approach that of the Church (there are difficulties for Christian thought about the social body of Islam, the *ummah*; but these can't be explored here). The Jewish people and the Christian Church are, then, the pre-eminently real social bodies, constituted by election, covenant, and sacrament; their reality is directly and distinctively given and guaranteed by God.

Also real, though not in the same way nor to the same extent, are the social bodies brought into being by sex (though not only by sex). These are families, and their reality is given by the procreative acts that most clearly distinguish them from other social bodies. Heterosexual partners are made into a social body by marriage, the distinctive feature of which is potentially procreative sex; and their offspring are made into a social body with their parents and with one another by blood (as older generations would have said) or by genetic inheritance (as we would say). These—the Church and the family—are the two real communities, the two real social bodies. The reality of both is given by God, the one by graceful election and the other by graceful creation.

Every other community—the nation, the city, the village, the sports team, the professional association, the wrecking crew—lacks the reality of Church and family. None is rooted in God's elective choice and sacramental gift, as is the Church, and none is constituted by blood and sex, as is the family. The reality they do have (and of course they are not entirely unreal) is imaginary. Those who belong to them and order their lives or parts of their lives by that membership must imagine their worth and meaning, must imagine that about them which constitutes them as communities. These acts of imagination, together with the narratives that accompany them and give them shape, provide the only reality such communities have: they are not founded and given by God, and blood does not flow through their veins. What is imagined can of course assume the appearance of what is not, and can become the principal shaping force of a life. The nation is the best example in recent centuries of the power an imagined body can come to exercise over those who have imagined it; the abundant literature provoked by Benedict Anderson's (1991) study of the nation precisely as an imagined community provides a plethora of examples of how the imagination's power can be harnessed to this end. Church and nation are alike in requiring acts of imagination to elaborate the narratives that depict them and order the thoughts of those who inhabit them. They differ in what those imagined narratives respond to: in the case of the Church to God's gift; in the case of the nation, only to more of the same: imagination all the way down.

Real bodies require a degree and depth of loyalty and commitment not properly given to imaginary bodies. This means that Christians' loyalty to all social bodies other than Church and family is secondary to and derived from their loyalty to Church and family (the family is treated elsewhere in this volume). And this in turn means that the Church is, for Christians, the primary theatre of moral formation and transformation. In it, the individual's body of flesh is written upon by corporate worship, made a member of the Church as social body by liturgical habituation. The fundamental moral fact about a Christian, then, is that she has become habituated to non-idolatrous worship of the God of Abraham, Isaac, Jacob, Mary, and the saints. This makes her into the kind of person whose fleshly body is no longer hers but Christ's, which in turn means that she is an icon of God's presence both to the world's body that lies outside and around the Church's body, and to the very body of the Church. Christ's real corporate body writes itself upon the individual Christian's real body: it makes her holy.

This is to say that the Christian is a saint, a *hagios* or *sanctus*, just because she is a member of Christ's body, the body of those who worship God in the name of Jesus Christ. This is good Pauline usage, of course: the First Letter to the Corinthians is addressed 'to the church of God in Corinth, to those who have been made holy in Christ Jesus, who are called to be holy [a phrase, *klētois hagiois*, that could just as well be rendered "to those called holy"] along with all those everywhere who invoke the name of our Lord Jesus Christ'. Holiness is, for Christians, the fundamental moral category, because it denotes conformity to God, becoming the kind of person who is transparent to God's will because her body has been conformed to God's. This is given by incorporation into the supremely real and (therefore) supremely holy body, and by habituation to the practices, corporate and individual, of that body.

In considering the figure of the body it is important to emphasize, perhaps against the inclinations of our time, that the moral formation that is sanctification proceeds principally by embodied habituation and not by any activity of the intellect. Pascal, as so often, saw this with great clarity:

You want to arrive at faith and you don't know the way; you want to be cured of lack of faith and you ask the remedy: learn of those who've been bound like you and who now bet everything they have; these are the people who know the way you'd like to follow, who've been cured of the illness of which you want to be cured. Do the kind of thing they began with, which is doing everything as if they believed, taking the holy water, having masses said, and so on. Precisely this will bring you naturally to belief and will make you like a beast. (Translated from Kaplan 1982: 143)

On this view, in order to arrive at faith, the only human action necessary is to learn from those who have it, and to learn by doing what they do, performing the practices they perform. People who have faith began by performing liturgically as if they believed in what they were doing, and thereby came to believe. The examples of liturgical performance that Pascal provides—taking holy water, having masses said—may not be equally to the taste of all Christians; but he means them as only a sample, to be expanded *ad libitum*. But it is the last sentence of the quoted extract that is most striking and most importantly correct: 'Precisely this [performing what those who have faith perform] will bring you naturally (*naturellement*, in the sense of automatically, inevitably) to belief and will make you like a beast.' The force of the last verb *abêtir* is often muted in English renderings of this section of the *Pensées*: it really does mean, for Pascal, that our liturgical actions should be like the habituated automatism of animals, and should not be a demand or result of reason. He has, just before the passage I've quoted, been extremely critical of the demands of reason for proof and understanding. And this is just right: the moral formation (which is also sanctification) of the body by what liturgical action writes on the body proceeds without any necessary connection to ratiocination, and will often be hindered by it.

This is not to say that liturgical action will inevitably bring those who perform it to holiness (or even belief); if Pascal means this (and I don't think he does: the argumentative context of the extract quoted suggests otherwise), he is wrong. It is to say that liturgical performance is among the conditions necessary for holiness, though not a condition sufficient for it. If it were the latter, worship would become theurgy. Pascal's worry is not about theurgy, but about an excessive emphasis on understanding, rationality, and motivation. These he thinks, rightly, much less important for sanctification than liturgical performance.

How then does the body become morally habituated by performing the actions proper to Christ's body? A full account of that would be impossibly long. It would require, above all, analysis of what the worshipper becomes habituated to when she becomes habituated to the liturgy, which is to say to the worship undertaken by Christ's body. Suggestive comments are all that's possible on that large subject.

The Sunday assembly of Christians has a single overarching purpose: to adore God. Adoration (worship, confession, praise—the lexicon is large and multi-faceted), some Christians have thought, is the fundamental purpose of every Christian act in every sphere of life. Augustine, for example, in a comment on Psalm 99: 5, claims that adoration is not only sufficient for the avoidance of sin, but also necessary for it: *non solum non peccemus adorando, sed peccemus non adorando* (Migne 1844–64: vol. 37, col. 1264). Whether or not this is true (my own inclination is to say that it is), it is certainly the case that adoration is the distinctive feature of what Christians do at their assemblies. This corporate adoration is what defines Christ's social body as such: it is a body that adores, and the members of that body have their moral bodies written upon by adoration.

Adoration as the Church practises it in its Sunday assemblies (and not only in them; but they will here have to serve as the archetype of what the Church does) is a complex activity. It typically comprises four modes of adoration, present to differing degrees and with different understandings in different Christian communities, but typically all present. Each of these modes of adoration writes something on the worshipper's moral body, thus conforming her more closely to the body of which she is, in her fleshly body, a member. What is written gets progressively more deeply incised by repetition, rather as the fleshly bodies of spouses are deeply written upon—which is to say morally formed—by repeated love-making over the years.

The first mode of adoration is confession. By it, the Christian acknowledges her sinfulness and unworthiness to receive God's blessings; she does this by claiming responsibility for that in her which is ontological and moral lack, rather than fullness. A scriptural focus of a peculiarly intense kind for this mode of adoration is 1 Timothy 1: 15, where Paul (or whoever wrote the letter) wrote that it is a truth worthy to be believed that Jesus Christ came into the world to save sinners *ōn prōtos eimi egō*, 'among whom I am the first'. To confess oneself the greatest of sinners is a Christian reflex action, an embodied habit (one may kneel, strike one's breast, bow one's head) given voice, and a habit that at once establishes a moral relation between the worshipper and God, as well as between the worshipper and all others—all others within and outside the assembly. It is a moral relation that dissolves self-righteousness into humility, and thereby checks the tendency to grasp and display one's virtues and rights assertively. Such habituation ramifies rapidly into particular modes of presence to and action in church and world.

The second mode of adoration is praise, performed in the assembly with psalms and hymns. Praise is explicit acknowledgement of, dependence upon, and participation in the giver of all gifts, including the gift of the capacity to praise. It is a performance that recognizes and acknowledges the condition of its own possibility, and in so doing forms the one who does it into someone whose mode of being in the world is one of responsive gratitude. As the worshipper's body is increasingly conformed to this mode of being, she becomes one who takes no credit for what is good, but who celebrates it. This is a mode of being complementary to that formed by confession: responsibility for lack entails praise for gift, and each is framed by awareness of the saturated excess of what is given (for a phenomenological explication of this language see Marion 1997: 251–342) and the echoing nullity of what is lacking. These responses of confession and praise, when deeply written upon the worshipper's body, order his actions and attitudes as much without as within the assembly's worship. Praise for gift and confession of lack inform, for example, the worshipper's moral interactions with human others, whether or not they are explicitly members of Christ's body.

The third mode of adoration is listening. Within the assembly's corporate worship the principal forms of this are attentive hearing of Scripture and of its exegesis and application in sermon or homily. This attitude embodies and represents the need for moral formation and inspiration by instruction; what the worshipper needs to know and become cannot be had by introspection, by merely social formation, or by the use of reason to discern and act upon duty. It is not that these modes of learning and formation are useless or bad; it is rather that in order to have the use and goodness they ought to have, they must be framed and preceded by attentive hearing of the word that is given. The content of what is heard, and the particulars of the formation produced by hearing it, cannot be pursued here, and are in any case profoundly varied. More important for the purposes of this essay is that attentive hearing is inextricable from confession and praise: confession of one's own lack implies the necessity of instruction *ex auditu*, and impels the one who confesses to become a hearer; and praise for gift is the natural and proper response to the particular gift of the word heard. As with confession and praise, the embodied attitude of attentive listening incises the worshipper's body with a habit that informs her actions and relations outside the assembly. She becomes, against the grain, less prone to garrulous self-assertion and more prone to attention to what others say and do. Silence, over time, becomes more attractive than speech.

The fourth mode of adoration is both more controversial among Christians and more difficult to expound than the other three. It is incorporation-by-eating (or: consuming) that to which the other three modes of adoration are responsive. Christians confess lack to the triune God; they praise the triune God for his excessive gift; they attentively listen to words given by the triune God; and they incorporate (and are incorporated by) that self-same God by eating his body and drinking his blood. Doing this is, some Christians think, the most intimate and fullest expression of adoration possible for the corporate body and its individual members; it may be, to return to the Augustinian tag already mentioned, aphoristically summarized by saying that when Christians do it, they eat what they are. Its intimacy is indicated by one of its names: communion; that it is a mode of adoration is indicated by another: eucharist. How is incorporation-by-eating to be understood as a moral formation of the body? This too is a vast subject, full address of which would require entrance into some deeply disputed metaphysical questions. If, as the dominant tradition of Christian thought from the fourth to the sixteenth century asserts, the Christian's fleshly body has been made (by baptism) into an explicitly participatory member of the supremely real body, which is Christ's, then a fuller conformity to that body can be described as an increase in the reality of what is thus conformed. And, if being and goodness are convertible, an increase in reality is also (equivalently) an increase in moral goodness. This way of thinking explains, conceptually, how incorporation-by-eating can be an instrument of moral transformation. It does not explain, substantively, what that transformation is like. All that can be said here is that the principal substantive aspect of that transformation is the formation of the communicant's body as one who is lovingly invited and then lovingly accepted by the God to whom he confesses, praises, and listens. Repeatedly hearing and responding to God's graceful and winsomely cajoling invitation to eat what you are in spite of your unworthiness will, among many other things, transform your body in the direction of becoming one who invites others as he is invited.

So much, inadequately, for attention to what 'body' as ecclesial figure provokes by way of thought about the Church. Most immediately, it provokes theologians to think about the liturgy, the corporate worship of Christ's body, as of primary importance in the Church's moral formation. The spectacle of Christian worship, when participated in rather than observed, is morally transformative in opposition to the transformations wrought by secular spectacles such as sport, the liturgies of war, or the liturgies of money. Both Christian moral theology and Christian formation should have the liturgy as their point of first worship, and there is no better focus for thought about it than thought about the Church under the figure of body.

But 'body' is not the only ecclesial figure that properly provokes thought about the moral formation of Christians by the Church. There is also the city, and to that I now turn.

CITIES

Calling the Church a city has almost as good a scriptural and traditional pedigree as calling it a body. But this figure is more often questioned, rejected, transfigured, and erased by Christians than is that of the body, as Graham Ward's (2000) study of cities in the Christian imaginary and in late modern actuality shows. Cities are ambiguous and problematic in Christian thought, in ways that bodies are not: there is no credal affirmation of, or any prayer for the resurrection of, an earthly city. It is different with bodies. Whence the difficulty with cities?

Cities have walls, defended by armies: they are the authorized users of violence within their boundaries. Cities demand loyalty of their citizens, and in return dispense the largesse of protection, education, and (thus) identity: they issue passports, to tell you who you are and to guarantee safe conduct beyond the defended walls. Cities have laws and norms of conduct, the former enforced by punishment's violent sanction and the latter by ostracism's cold exclusion. Cities tend always to seek extension of authority both within and without their walls: authority within the walls is expanded by the (often violent) suppression of rival claimants to allegiance; and extension without the walls is pursued ordinarily by conquest and colonial expansion. Cities are places of civilization, without which, their defenders tend to think, there is only barbarism, the barbarism of those who do not speak Greek—and, therefore, Latin and its European successor languages as bearers of the only culture that counts. And, of course, cities are places of indulgence and luxury, in which the virtues of civilization tend to be coupled with an endlessly imaginative multiplication of the possibilities of vice: in them, God's voice is obscured, and the illusion that we are self-sustaining fostered. That is why they must often be abandoned for the deserts and the mountains, in which God's voice may be heard more clearly.

Four cities, actual and symbolic, have shaped the Christian imagination. The first is Jerusalem, in whose earthly form the Temple was built and twice destroyed, whose streets Jesus walked and lamented, and outside whose walls he was killed. Thinking about Jerusalem in its heavenly form became for Christians, at least from the Book of Revelation onward, among the principal ways of thinking about heaven, and of differentiating their ecclesial city from other earthly cities—including, often with distressing results, the continuing earthly city that is the community of the Jewish people. Among cities, the symbolic associations of Jerusalem are most closely connected with thought about what the Church will become as she is finally purified before God at the end of all things.

The second city is Babylon, Jerusalem's antitype, a place of linguistic and conceptual confusion (the Hebrew word rendered 'Babel' in most English versions of Genesis 3: 9 is the same as the Hebrew word for Babylon), of exile, of mourning, and of the corruptions and distractions of luxury and imaginative viciousness. A splendid visual representation of this aspect of Babylon's symbolism can be seen in the Babylon segment of D. W. Griffith's 1916 film *Intolerance*. Christian thought about the Church as city proceeds in significant part by imagining the Church as the anti-Babylon, and there is, in general, no deeper accusation of perverse and dangerous otherness than the epithet 'Babylonian'.

The third city is Athens, in whose gift lies philosophy, literature, theatre, and all the gifts of thought and culture. This city, too, is typically imagined as alien to the Church, but not, as is the case with Babylon, as inevitably hostile. It may be classified by extremists like Tertullian as simply alien to the Church-as-Jerusalem; and Jerome can tell, in his twenty-second letter, of a vow (rapidly broken) to stop reading Cicero and his like, whom he thought of as the literary representatives of the Athenian heritage, and whose prose he took to be alluringly distractive from the plain truths of Scripture. But, more often, Athens has been for the Christian imaginary a city to be respectfully borrowed from (or, sometimes, pillaged) with the intention of ornamenting more gorgeously the walls of the ecclesial city. In commendation of such borrowing, Augustine the bishop fondly recalls his inspiration by Cicero's *Hortensius* and the shaping of his mind by Aristotle's categories; Aquinas spends a good portion of his life and intellectual energy reading and commenting upon the Aristotelian corpus; and Jonathan Edwards draws gratefully (though with mixed results) upon John Locke's philosophical psychology.

The fourth city is Rome. Athens's inheritor and despoiler, Rome is the secular city that killed Jesus and shed the blood of the martyrs. But it is also the city of

Peter and of the Roman Church, which for all Christians, Catholic, Protestant, and Orthodox, holds a special symbolic place. The Roman Church in its visible institutional form is never imagined as simply identical with the Church as such, not even by conservative Catholic ecclesiologists; much less can it be thought of as identical with what the Church will become. But among all earthly institutions and all earthly cities, the city of Rome and the Church of Rome remain, for Christians, those in terms of which identity must be construed. Such construal may be negative, as when the Pope or the Roman Church is called the whore of Babylon, and particular Christian practices accepted or rejected according to the degree to which they are 'Romish'; or it may be expropriative, as when successive cities— Constantinople, Moscow—take to themselves the name of the new (the second or the third or the fourth) Rome (on this see Brague 2002: esp. ch. 1; the whole book is essential reading for the relations between the idea of Rome and the idea of Europe, a set of relations which is itself a subset of the Christian imaginary of cities). But the metaphorical and actual city of Rome remains an utterly central point of reference for imaginations of the Church.

The figures woven around all of these cities are for the Christian imaginary ambiguous and subject to unweaving almost as soon as woven. The figure of the city, in general or in any of the four particular forms mentioned, is so fraught with difficulty that it can never be used as positively for the Church as has been the figure of the body. The Church-as-city is an unavoidable figure for Christians, nevertheless, at least since Augustine's magisterial and weighty play with it in *City of God*; but the ambiguities with which it is instinct in Christian thought mean that when the Church is depicted as a city, and when Christians are formed (as they are) by thinking of themselves as citizens of God's city here below, this thought and this formation occur most often in the mode of contrast and erasure. The Church is a city very unlike actual earthly cities; and so citizenship in it must be understood largely by contrast with and rejection of the requirements of earthly citizenship. The Church is a counter-city, a city-under-erasure, and the fact that this is the dominant grammar of Christian thought about the Church as city means that Christians are formed by their citizenship in the Church into some very particular relations with actual earthly cities. This is, none the less, a properly moral forma- tion, for it constitutes (or should: recall that I write here not in the indicative but rather in the ideal mood) Christians as agents of a particular kind *vis-à-vis* earthly cities. I'll conclude this essay by considering two central aspects of this moral formation.

The first is erasure of primary loyalty to any earthly city. Christians are as a matter of course citizens of earthly cities: of nations, of towns, of villages, and of all manner of other political communities from trades unions to lobbying groups. They do and should exercise full citizenship in these polities. But such citizenship is always a matter of secondary loyalty and secondary interest, always questioned and partly erased by the primary loyalty and primary interest, which is citizenship in the Church. This relegation of all non-ecclesial citizenships to a level of secondary importance is grounded first of all upon the distinction aready made between imagined and real communities. Non-ecclesial polities are all given the reality they have by an act of the imagination, whereas the Church, like the family, has reality independently of anyone's imaginations. It follows immediately that someone who has been formed in such a way as to think this—and it is certainly the direction in which moral formation in and by the Church tends—will understand, whether explicitly or not, the duties of earthly citizenship as insignificant when contrasted with the gifts of ecclesial citizenship. The radical version of this erasure is evident in martyrdom. Martyrs witness to the reconfiguration of their political loyalties with their blood, and they do so joyfully. A useful index of the extent to which the Church has failed to form its citizens in this attitude is the extent to which martyrdom seems unattractive to them. It should serve as a governing paradigm of erasure of primary loyalty to any polity but that of the Church; and at various times and places it has done so.

Formation in primary loyalty to the ecclesiastical polity is signalled pre-eminently in baptism. Baptism is death: it drowns the old Adam (and Eve) in its waters, so that the reborn Christian, now named and sealed as such, may emerge with a new set of loyalties established even if not yet understood. And baptism is also renunciation: the catechumen renounces, as the ancient triple formula has it, allegiance to world, flesh, and devil, a renunciation marked, once, as a kind of exorcism by a triple exsufflation—outblowing—of these false allegiances by the one performing the baptism. These loyalties are replaced with loyalty to Christ and the Church as Christ's city on earth, and this is so even if the replacement is not yet understood by the newly baptized. Baptism is, then, among other things an instrument used by the Church for the moral formation of Christians in their relations to non-human cities. It kills that allegiance as primary, and then permits it to live in a secondary way, to be abandoned whenever it contradicts or etiolates the primary loyalty to the Church's polity.

This hierarchical ordering of political allegiances is also an ordering of desires, and to describe it in this way makes even more obvious that it is an instance of moral formation. Desire has weight: it moves the one who desires toward what is desired, often with what seems like an irresistible impetus. The weight of citizenship's desires is heavy upon us; it masters us easily, and it is plastic: it can be shaped, directed, and ordered. Imagined political communities—the nation, the earthly city—deploy a massive technology precisely in order to direct political desire toward themselves. May Day parades in the old Soviet Empire, July Fourth festivals in the United States, recitations of the pledge of allegiance in American public schools, flag-waving greetings to the monarch as she makes her way through the streets of London to open a new session of the House of Commons—all these are instances of the technology of desire at work. The Church's moral formation of its citizens toward erasure of primary loyalty to any polity but itself is a counter-technology of desire.

It begins with baptism, proceeds through the moral formation provided by worship (sketched above), and is always eschatological in orientation—which is to say that it turns its citizens away from exhaustive engagement in imagined polities by ordering their political desire toward a polity not yet fully known, a polity most fully foreshadowed by the Church but evident even there only in chiaroscuro. The political formation of Christians by the Church in these ways not only erases primary loyalty to imagined communities, but also turns its citizens' gaze beyond itself toward the New Jerusalem, which is the only finally and fully real *polis*.

This aspect of the moral formation of Christians by the Church makes them into unusual political agents. They act politically, often with passion and vigour. But they tend to act with a deep sense of the inevitable failure of their actions. Since imagined political communities are by definition not perfectible, a point constantly underlined by the Church's moral formation of her citizens, action without this sense would be an idolatrous error. There is, so Christians tend to think, no finally successful political solution to systemic injustice, to violence inflicted upon the weak, to the corruptions of wealth and power, and to all the other difficulties to which earthly cities are always subject. Political action in the earthly city is therefore more likely to be understood by Christians as an attempt to alleviate and reduce unavoidable horrors than to create a world order in which such horrors will cease to be. This attitude underlies and explains the second fundamental aspect of the Church's formation of its citizens in their relations to earthly cities: training in lament.

Lament is not despair; it is, instead, public evidence of hope. It is the response to violent injustice characteristic of those who see it for what it is, which is an inevitable work of all imaginary polities; who see, too, that it can and must be alleviated, opposed, and challenged; and who understand, regretfully, that all such attempted alleviations and challenges will not fully succeed but must none the less be attempted, ever and again. Christian liturgy has lament as one of its dominant tones: I've mentioned confession already, and it is one note in this tone of lament. But more important is the Church's use of the Psalms. These are, predominantly, cries of lament. Their cry (like that of Job) is one that combines incomprehension of violent injustice with knowledge that it is violent and unjust, with hope that there will be a time and a place in which there is no more of it, and with certainty that that time and place is not now and not here. It is a cry that, as Gillian Rose (1992, 1996) showed so precisely and eloquently before her untimely death in 1995, can only be uttered in the broken middle between the delusory dream of a perfectly just earthly city and the desert of despair that abandons hope and rejects the city without remainder. Rose made this argument in the service of a particular construal of Judaism; but this is something that Christians and Jews share, and they share it principally because of the Psalms and their liturgical use.

Formation in the ecclesial city is thus a counter-formation to that given by the earthly city. It is a catechesis of erasure, aporia, and lament. Primary loyalty to imagined communities is erased, and as a result they are given just the kind of allegiance they deserve; the aporetic contradiction between what is hoped for and what is actual is constantly pressed upon the Church's citizens, and increasingly deep awareness of this contradiction fosters both political action and lament for its failure. The former without the latter is an inevitably violent perfectibilism; the latter without the former is a quietist withdrawal. The joining of the two, in a gesture of mourning that becomes the law, is most fully possible for those whose bodies and whose citizenship have been given them by the Church.

References and Suggested Reading

ANDERSON, BENEDICT (1991). *Imagined Communities: Reflections on the Origin and Spread of Nationalism*, rev. edn. London: Verso. First published 1983.

BRAGUE, RÉMI (2002). *Eccentric Culture: A Theory of Western Civilization*. South Bend, Ind.: St. Augustine's Press. Translated by Samuel Lester from *Europe, la voie romaine*. Paris: Éditions Critérion, 1992.

DAVIDSON, DONALD (1991). 'What Metaphors Mean', in *Inquiries into Truth and Interpretation*, Oxford: Clarendon Press, 245–64. First published 1978.

DULLES, AVERY (1987). *Models of the Church*. Garden City, NY: Doubleday.

HÜTTER, REINHARD (2000). *Suffering Divine Things: Theology as Church Practice*. Grand Rapids, Mich.: Eerdmans.

KAPLAN, FRANCIS (ed.) (1982). *Les Pensées de Pascal*. Paris: Cerf.

MARION, JEAN-LUC (1997). *Étant donné: essai d'une phénoménologie de la donation*. Paris: Presses Universitaires de France.

——(2001). *The Idol and Distance: Five Studies*. New York: Fordham University Press. Translated by Thomas A. Carlson from *L'Idole et la distance*. Paris: Grasset, 1977.

MIGNE, J.-P. (ed.) (1844–64). *Patrologiae cursus completus series latina*, 221 vols. Paris: Garnier.

MILBANK, JOHN (2003). *Being Reconciled: Ontology and Pardon*. London: Routledge.

ROSE, GILLIAN (1992). *The Broken Middle: Out of Our Ancient Society*. Oxford: Blackwell.

——(1996). *Mourning becomes the Law: Philosophy and Representation*. Cambridge: Cambridge University Press.

STERN, JOSEF (2000). *Metaphor in Context*. Cambridge, Mass.: MIT Press.

VOLF, MIROSLAV (1998). *After Our Likeness: The Church as the Image of the Trinity*. Grand Rapids, Mich.: Eerdmans.

WARD, GRAHAM (2000). *Cities of God*. London: Routledge.

PART VI

THE STRUCTURE OF THEOLOGICAL ETHICS: BOOKS THAT GIVE SHAPE TO THE FIELD

CHAPTER 24

....

ERNST TROELTSCH'S

THE SOCIAL TEACHING OF THE CHRISTIAN CHURCHES

....

WILLIAM SCHWEIKER

INTRODUCTION

....

BOOKS that have decisively shaped theological ethics inevitably have their own peculiar history. That is certainly the case with Ernst Troeltsch's magisterial *Die Soziallehren der christlichen Kirchen und Gruppen* ([1912] 1992). The massive work began as a book review. In trying to engage Martin von Nathusius's *Die Mitarbeit der Kirche an der Lösung der sozialen Frage* (1904), Troeltsch realized that an adequate response required a thorough study of Christian social teaching. No such study was available. Troeltsch set about the task. Over the course of some years, he produced studies which, when collected, eventuated in the book as we

Throughout this chapter reference to *The Social Teaching of the Christian Churches and Groups* will be given in the text by volume and page number of the most recent English edition (1992). The text is also referred to by an abbreviated, somewhat incorrect, but none the less widely used title, namely, *The Social Teachings*. I would like to thank Aimee Burant, Kelton Cobb, Michael Johnson, and K. Kevin Jung for helpful comments on the argument of this essay.

now have it. But Troeltsch's enterprise was not only historical. His aim was also to articulate the *theological* aspect of the social problem. He was convinced that the modern world was a new situation 'in which old theories no longer suffice, and where, therefore, new theories must be constructed, composed of old and new elements' (I. 25). *The Social Teachings*, as they are often called, aimed to understand and respond to the new situation by exploring 'the Christian Ethos in its inward connection with the universal history of civilization' (I. 25). This is a grand work of astonishing magnitude by a brilliant and committed thinker.

In appreciation for being awarded both the *Doctor philosophies honoris causa* and also the *Doctor juris honoris causa*, Troeltsch dedicated the book to the philosophical faculty at Greifswald and the faculty of law at Breslau. From the moment of its publication, Troeltsch's work had considerable effect on a variety of fields of study, ranging from law to sociology to theology and Christian ethics. By the mid-twentieth century, theologians like Paul Tillich and H. Richard Niebuhr were acknowledging their debt to Troeltsch. Tillich dedicated his early 'systems of the sciences' to Troeltsch, while Niebuhr wrote his Ph.D. thesis on him as well as developing the typological method throughout a long career. The trend continued in the works of German theologians Trutz Rendtorff and Friedrich Wilhelm Graf, as well as thinkers in the USA, including James Luther Adams, Brian Gerrish, and James M. Gustafson and critics of Troeltsch such as John Howard Yoder. The way in which Troeltsch posed and then answered the questions of Christian social ethics has decisively influenced Christian thought. What is one to make of such a book?

This chapter does not examine in every detail the development and argument of this famous and complex text. There is already plenty of scholarship on Troeltsch's thought, and I am not a 'Troeltsch scholar' in any technical sense. Besides, some books simply must be read on one's own. The purpose of the following pages is the attempt to capture the enduring importance of *The Social Teachings* for anyone interested in theological and ethical reflection on cultural and social life. My judgement is that in many ways contemporary theological ethics really cannot reject the Troeltschian legacy, even if, as we will see, important and profound revisions in that project are necessary (see Schweiker 2004). Thinkers who try to reject this legacy and rely solely on the discourse of the tradition in the name of Christian uniqueness too easily fail to grasp the real complexity of the age in which we think and live.

TROELTSCH'S PROJECT

Born in 1865 in Augsburg, Germany, Troeltsch studied theology at Erlangen, Göttingen under the influence of Albrecht Ritschl, and also Berlin. At the age of 29 he became professor of theology at the University of Heidelberg, where he served until 1915. There he wrote *The Social Teachings*. He also worked closely with the famous sociologist Max Weber. In fact, while in Heidelberg the Troeltsch and Weber families lived for several years in the same house on different floors. The two men also travelled together to deliver lectures at a meeting held in conjunction with the 1904 World's Fair in St. Louis. From 1915 to 1923, Troeltsch was professor of philosophy in Berlin, where he was a renowned lecturer. At various times he held political offices in Baden and Berlin. After World War I he was Secretary of the Prussian Ministry of Public Worship, from 1921 until his death in 1923. Troeltsch was what is nowadays called a public intellectual. He experienced the stress and strain of social existence in a direct and powerful way. Problems of nationality and also modernity were basic to his thought and found expression in his leading ideas.

Troeltsch is usually now identified as a 'liberal theologian', a term coined by critics that he rarely used himself. Hardly as homogeneous a group as critics claim, these thinkers did share some basic convictions. These convictions are many, but included at least the following.

1. The conviction that Christians must strive to make sense of their piety in terms understandable to the present age. This requires, at a theoretical level, a distinction between theological method (how one thinks in a disciplined and coherent way) and the substance of Christian conviction, so *revisions* in how to express those convictions are possible. Liberals believed, against their critics, that Christian communities have always been involved in this work of revision.
2. A criticism of traditional structures of authority and the critical revision of confessions of faith mindful of real religious pluralism within churches and societies. Liberals focused on the practical, as opposed to the dogmatic and theoretical, in the religious life, and so the need to highlight moral action, individual existence, and personal experience.
3. Liberals desired to specify a 'cultural synthesis' wherein the coherence or unity of a culture might be manifest. They believed that 'liberal religion'—practical, pluralistic, personal, progressive—was important for democratic societies.
4. The truth of theological claims about social, moral, and political matters must, liberals insisted, be public in nature, as opposed to relying on the authority of confessions or appeals to divine revelation.

Of course, each element of 'liberal theology' has been challenged or revised. But one can summarize by saying that for liberal theologians the focus of theological thinking is not on church doctrine and authority but on developing theologies of culture.

Part of the brilliance of Troeltsch's work is that it subtly weaves together a multidimensional argument about the Christian moral outlook and the social conditions of Western life. Unlike churchly theologians who assume that a neat line can be drawn between the 'church' and the 'world', he understood that both the 'church' and the 'world' are complex realities, and that their existence and manifold interactions change throughout history. Troeltsch thought that the critical thinker must be a historian and a philosopher. One needs to understand the historical dynamics of a period, but also to define norms and value judgements to orient human action. He was thus preoccupied with the challenge that 'historicism' (*Historismus*) put to the churches. 'Historicism' is the realization that *all* human realities are subject to time, and therefore that the meaning of basic beliefs change, and even moral norms and values are relative to their historical period. As will be shown below, Troeltsch did insist on the importance of moral absolutes. But, given the realization about history, he and others were convinced that a historical method was inescapable, and this constantly endangered his ability to articulate normative standards. As he wrote about the historical method (Troeltsch [1898] 1991: 16), 'All our investigations regarding nature and goals of the human spirit must be based on it. Goethe's words still apply:

> Those who will not account
> To themselves for the past thirty centuries
> May continue to live
> In the dark, day-by-day, grossly ignorant.'

In *The Social Teachings*, Troeltsch accounts in vast detail for past centuries, moving with stunning breadth of analysis from Jesus and the early church to the Stoics, medieval Catholicism, the Reformers, pietists and Anabaptists, and a range of mystical thinkers. In the course of his career the force of *Historismus* provoked Troeltsch, unlike many other progressive Protestant German theologians, to admit the relativity of his culture and Christianity in the West (see Troeltsch [1923] 1999).

Troeltsch was also absolutely clear that one must be specific about what one means by 'the social problem'. His idea of the 'social' is what is now meant by 'civil society', that is, arenas of associational life between the state and the individual. 'The social question' so defined was debated throughout the nineteenth and early twentieth centuries, ranging from the social encyclicals of the popes to the advocates of the 'Social Gospel' in the United States. One of the difficulties regarding the reception of *The Social Teachings* is that too often present-day critics have a definition of the 'social' different from that of Troeltsch. In his words, 'the idea of the "Social" means a definite, clearly defined section of the general sociological phenomena—that is, the social relations which are not regulated by the State, nor by political interest, save insofar as they are indirectly influenced by them' (I. 28). The 'social problem', accordingly, consists in the *relation* between sociological phenomena (e.g., economic life, education, tension among social groups, division of labour, class, and (we would now add) race and gender) and the political community, or the state.

Troeltsch knew well that with modernity 'the State and Society are conceived as quite distinct from each other, and the characteristic conception of Society only arises out of the contrast with the modern, formal constitutional conception of the State' (I. 31). The modern differentiation of the political from the social, and so constitutional forms of human association from others, poses the 'social problem'. How should the churches, organized, in his words, 'from the viewpoint of the religious idea of love to God and man', relate to purely secular non-political forms of organization, to the state, and to the relation between them? In so far as Troeltsch's interest is in the *theological* aspect of the social problem, the question becomes how a religious aim is related to social theory.

Few other thinkers have been as bold, intelligent, and theologically persistent in trying to respond to the social problem. Troeltsch's response was to write a history of the reciprocal impact of the Christian ethos and Western civilization. This was to advance a liberal concern: 'How can the Church harmonize with these main (political and social forces) in such a way that together they will form a unity of civilization?' (I. 32). Of course, this concern could lead to a tragic and unfaithful identification of the Church and social powers. But while many 'liberal' German theologians of his time seemed to have assumed that the 'unity' of culture could be found only in a version of Protestantism and its powerful belief in freedom, Troeltsch, also deeply Protestant, was more subtle. In his reflection on the relativity of values and norms he foresaw, but did not answer, the challenge of 'pluralism' that beset later twentieth- and, now too, early twenty-first-century thought. In the current situation, one must, for good theological as well as social reasons, reject the assumption that Protestantism, or any expression of any religious tradition, alone can or should serve as the force of a cultural synthesis.

The history which Troeltsch provides in *The Social Teachings* interweaves methodological, ethical, and theological reflection. We can usefully trace the impact of his work on theological ethics by isolating these dimensions.

TYPOLOGICAL THINKING
AS HISTORICAL METHOD

Writing during the high point of modern conceptions of 'science', Troeltsch, along with Max Weber, believed that 'society' could not be studied in the same way as natural realities. There is at best an analogy between the *Naturwissenschaften*, the natural sciences, and the *Geisteswissenschaften*, the human sciences. Natural phenomena can be submitted to theoretically developed and empirically tested 'laws'.

Social dynamics, composed of a wild array of individual factors and developing through time, cannot be grasped in the same way.

More precisely, the natural sciences aim to provide a causal *explanation* of some reality, in which all instances of that reality are seen in the light of an overarching law. We expect, for instance, that a valid theory of particle acceleration will generate a specific 'law' which explains the movements of all relevant particles. The human sciences, conversely, seek to *understand* the meaning of some domain of individual or social human behaviour, not in their likeness but in their distinctiveness through time. What is more, the perspective of the interpreter will necessarily be involved in a historical method. This requires that one seek to curtail bias in research and thereby practice what Weber somewhat unhappily called 'value-free inquiry'. Of course, there has been considerable debate about this conception of science and enquiry. Given developments in the philosophy of science since Troeltsch's time, contemporary use of his method might need some revision. We cannot pursue that question here.

The reason why Troeltsch and Weber insisted on the distinction in method between the natural and human sciences is that sociological factors are the stuff of human action, and thereby include the values that motivate behaviour. The centrality of action and value meant the priority of practical over theoretical reason in cultural and religious studies. This emphasis on practical reason is found among many liberal, neo-Kantian thinkers, especially Albrecht Ritschl, with whom Troeltsch studied. Religion, on this account, is fundamentally practical rather than speculative or dogmatic in nature. In terms of social analysis, the point is that one cannot understand historical social realities by trying to reduce them to non-human, causal forces—say, the material dialectics of history that the late Marx championed. Indeed, Weber and Troeltsch were adamant that ideals and values were not the ideological superstructure of a social order arising out of the economic substructure. Ideas and values are motivating forces in social life, and thus must be related but not reduced to economic factors. Troeltsch went so far as to connect this insistence on human action and values with a basic element in Christian faith: the importance in the Gospel of personal existence, faith, and redemption. We return to the question of 'personality' and value in a moment. At this point the question is about Troeltsch's historical method, the concern for *Verstehen*, or understanding.

Social realities are historical things. They must be understood via their changing faces through time. Yet, if all the scholar does is to record historical changes, no real insight into the meaning of social realities is attained. Troeltsch, along with Weber, therefore sought to isolate within the welter of historical materials certain ideal types, or general patterns of social life, which, while not 'law-like', would help us understand these changing social realities. These 'types' do not exist in any empirical sense; they are ideal. Any actual historical reality—say, any real Christian church or any real individual—will have features not specified by the 'type'. One might think of an ideal type as a conceptual portrait. Like any portrait, the artist must select, order, and present features of a living reality in some compelling way, in order to communicate something about the subject. The portrait is not a strict replica of the subject; it is not a one-to-one correspondence of their every element, a simple reduplication. From the perspective of a strict replica, a portrait might seem distorting, and it certainly reveals something about the artist. Yet, precisely for these reasons, a fine portrait discloses distinctive insights about its subject. It is not simply an expression of the artist's impressions and desires; a portrait tries to capture something true about the subject. An ideal type, then, is a scholarly, conceptual construct or portrait that aims to reveal patterns of social life in and through the history of some community, like a church. The method is a way of doing history and philosophy together.

Troeltsch argued that there are in fact some very basic Christian responses to the 'social problem' in the West. The 'Church-type' seeks to harmonize political and social reality under the domination of the Church. It is found in medieval Catholicism, and also in different ways in strands of the magisterial Protestant Reformation. It is superior to the other types in terms of its inclusiveness and ability to accommodate other social forces. The 'Sect-type' denies the possibility of any harmony on theological grounds, and thereby retreats from the attempt to provide a unified civilization. This type is a portrait of a host of movements ranging from the Franciscans to elements in the Radical Reformation. The Sect-type is superior to the others in maintaining Christian identity and confession. The 'Mystic-type', emerging with the modern world, is a challenge to any form of social cohesion. It places emphasis on the individual's religious experience. The strength of the Mystic-type is its capacity to renew vital religious passions. The fact that Troeltsch was critical of the Mystic-type demonstrated that his form of 'liberalism' was not individualistic. Yet he thought that most modern theologians—including himself—were 'mystical' in the sense of not being ecclesio-centric. As he noted, 'My own theology is certainly spiritual' (II. 985).

As shown below, each type focuses on some element of Christian conviction about the natural moral law as it is found within different historical situations. Under the conditions of modernity what is needed is a tensive interaction of the strengths of each type within the Church's structure. The Church-type, specifically, must be strengthened, because it has the best chance structurally of meeting the demands of the modern world and its social problem. Later we will explore why Troeltsch reaches this normative judgement.

The method of typological thinking practised in *The Social Teachings* has been used by other theologians but has also been the subject of much debate and confusion. Some thinkers, like H. Richard Niebuhr (1951) and James M. Gustafson (1968), applied the method to the relations between Christian communities and culture, and also to beliefs about Christ and moral theory. These thinkers expanded the range of 'social realities' beyond the politics considered in Troeltsch's own work. Other thinkers attacked Troeltsch's method. John Howard Yoder and others working within the 'Radical Reformation' tradition argued that Troeltsch's Sect-type does not capture the empirical reality of their communities (1984). Challenging any identification of the Christian community with the 'political agenda' of the state, these thinkers argued that the Church must offer a contrasting political vision of life. This criticism, it seems, works with a different conception of the 'social' than Troeltsch's, and so is somewhat wide of the mark. The emphasis on the nation-state leaves open precisely the question that Troeltsch hoped to explore: namely, how churches are deeply historical and so must respond to the 'social problem' that emerges in the *interaction* between social phenomena and political entities. Troeltsch's typology is not just about the stances which churches take to political power. It is about the teachings of these communities on the 'social', and therefore about domains of life that are related to, but also outside, political authority.

There is another criticism of the typological method. Some theologians argue that the Church is an absolutely unique, eschatological reality defined by a message of peace, and so unlike any other community in a world marked by violence (see Milbank 1991). An 'ideal type' that would *compare* religious communities is theologically illegitimate. The Church cannot be classified like other communities; it is a treasure, but not in an earthen vessel (2 Cor. 4: 7). There is therefore no analysis of a social problem that a variety of communities must address, let alone an attempt to engage in comparative thinking about communities and 'religions'. Reflection is oriented by the specific mission of the Church. The confusion here is to assume that a 'type' is like a scientific law, so all instances of it must be the same, and, further, that the 'social problem' can be answered in theological terms alone. On both of these points, Troeltsch would differ. In the modern world, and now global age, social thinking must be comparative and multi-dimensional if one wants to understand the present situation. This means that a thinker must have the courage to see his or her own convictions and community in reflexive and comparative relations with other cultures and traditions. There is also an irony in the criticism. Those thinkers who challenge the idea of types nevertheless work according to its presupposition: historical and social change is driven by acting human beings and the values that motivate their behaviour, rather than by suprahuman natural, economic, or political systems.

At the level of *historical method*, Troeltsch's book review continues to influence the field of Christian ethics. The array of responses to it takes us deeper into the volumes with respect to basic presuppositions about human behaviour and association.

VALUES AND PERSONALITY

Some social theorists, Marxist and otherwise, believe that the origins of Christianity can be found in class struggle, economic choice, or other social dynamics. Troeltsch was sure that from the very beginning the religious impulse was basic.

'The central problem is always purely religious, dealing with such questions as the salvation of the soul, monotheism, life after death, purity of worship, the right kind of congregational organization, the application of Christian ideals to everyday life, and the need for severe self-discipline in the interests of personal holiness' (I. 39). For Troeltsch and other liberals, 'religion' was intensely personal and centred on the Kingdom of God, which they envisaged as the reign of love. Indeed, 'personality', as the task of self-cultivation (*Bildung*) through reflexive practices, was a central concept in so far as growth in consciousness of relation to God's Kingdom was seen as the core of the Christian message (Troeltsch [1923] 1999: 37–130). Troeltsch argued that the greatness of the Gospel 'lies in the postulate—disregarding state and society—that the personality be infused with eternal life and that people be united in a transcendental communion of love' (Troeltsch [1910*a*] 1991: 160). This focus on personality, experience, and the inner life meant several things for Troeltsch.

Like other 'liberals', Troeltsch insisted that Christianity is mainly about life and action, rather than dogma. In order to understand Christian faith, one must explore it through time and through the various practical responses that Christian communities make to their situation. That is, of course, the task of *The Social Teachings*. The contemporary interest in praxis, moral identity, spiritual practices, and faith as a way of life finds its roots in this 'liberal' practical account of religious conviction. Yet, while most forms of contemporary Christian reflection are in this respect heirs of post-Enlightenment thinking like that of Troeltsch, there is a decided difference.

Troeltsch and other neo-Kantians held that it was possible to isolate a connection to the divine in human subjectivity. This connection could be specified outside of the language and symbols of the faith community. By 'religious a priori' Troeltsch meant, in a revision of Kant, the synthetic function of consciousness in the formation of a unified personality. He tried to specify a rational core and fundamental unity of personality that lies *before*, a priori to, any experience, action, or psychological working. According to Troeltsch, more like Ritschl than Kant, this unity of personality in its dynamic operations is bound to values and ideals, and not simply to the law-giving power of pure practical reason. The *religious* a priori is how the unity of personality is related to God and God's reign. Given this, it was possible, and maybe required, to revise Christian discourse in light of this more basic, rational, and shared religious principle (see Troeltsch [1909] 1991). The conviction of a religious a priori seems to motivate the work of *The Social Teachings*, which Troelstch intended not only as a historical survey of Christian social theory, but also as a resource for the revision of the expressions of the religious a priori in modern times.

Already in the 1920s and continuing throughout the twentieth century, this claim about a formal a priori religious principle of consciousness has rightly been submitted to many forms of criticism. The famous 'linguistic turn' in philosophy and theology made everyone aware of the ways in which thought and experience are saturated with the narratives, symbols, beliefs, and values of specific communities. In one respect this merely continues the 'historicist' insight about the temporal and social relativities of human existence. Yet it also marks a departure from Troeltsch's project. The idea of religious experience is rejected or radically revised. Neo-orthodox theologians like Karl Barth (1957) insisted that Christian discourse must be understood on its own terms. Arguments about any 'religious a priori' replace God's revelation with reflection on human subjectivity. Other theologians, like Rudolf Bultmann (1934) but also Paul Tillich (1952), and philosophers such as Martin Heidegger (1962) rejected the language of an 'a priori rational unity of subjectivity'. They argued that human life is defined by an existential decision, ultimate concern, or care amid the anxiety of finite life. In this way they revised the rationalism of the Kantian project in existential ways.

Recently, so-called post-liberal and narrative theologians, like Stanley Hauerwas (1988) and George Lindbeck (1984), insist that the Christian tribe has its own unique story. The task of the moral life, Hauerwas insists, is to form a people able to live truthfully by that story. Christian moral discourse is necessarily limited to the confession of the community, and thereby entails a radical rejection of the Troeltschian project. Other thinkers likewise criticize the idea of a general religious a priori, yet do not limit their ethical discourse to the resources of the Church. Wolfgang Huber (1990) in Germany, Johannes Fischer (2002) in Zürich, and some Americans, including Jeffrey Stout (1988), Max Stackhouse (1987), and others, try to show the resources of the Christian tradition for addressing widespread moral problems. While differing among themselves, these thinkers deny the assumption, basic to post-liberal theology, that different communities speak incommensurable languages. There is also now, thankfully, renewed interest in the inner life, after the strident turn to language. Various ethical thinkers, religious and not, are reclaiming reflection on the complexity of personal life. They do so in ways different from Kantian rationalism and the kinds of existentialism seen in the twentieth century. More attention is paid to the role of the emotions, loves, and modes of perception, as well as the ways in which individuals are distinctive and peculiar, rather than defined by the same 'synthetic operation' or existential concern (see Gaita 2000).

These reactions to Troeltsch's philosophical project do not challenge his diagnosis of the historical situation in *The Social Teachings*. In fact, this work seeks to specify the range of responses to the social order found among Christian churches and groups. The various 'types' of Christian social teaching demonstrate the connection between communal resources and moral formation. The Sect-type, as Troeltsch noted, wants to keep Jesus' 'laws and organize a tightly-knit congregation according to the principle of love and the idea of holiness'. The Church-type 'saw in the community the institution of salvation and redemption', and therefore 'renounced organization according to the law of Christ in favor of the monergism of grace'([1910*a*] 1991: 160). And even his claims about the Mystic-type show the deep connection between a way of life, communal organization, and moral identity.

One can conclude that Troeltsch the historian has more enduring significance than Troeltsch the philosopher of the 'religious a priori'. As a historian, he was able to explore the complex connection between the values and norms of historically contingent and distinctive communities without the need to isolate a single religious 'principle' supposedly manifest in different forms throughout history. His philosophical reflections on religion, steeped in German Idealism and neo-Kantian theory, must be reconsidered in so far as one hopes to explore the connection between moral identity and communal norms and values. This does not necessarily mean rejecting altogether the idea of a 'religious a priori'. Troeltsch himself noted later in life that he would like to rethink the idea along more phenomenological than idealistic lines. Clearly, more work is necessary on the theme of moral identity, work that will reach beyond the resources at Troeltsch's disposal.

RELIGION AND CULTURAL SYNTHESIS

Part of the enduring importance of Troeltsch's *The Social Teachings* is that it deploys a method of historical thinking deeply connected to long-standing Christian convictions about human action. It also specifies the ways in which communities inhabit the world differently, even within the same religious tradition. Prominent criticisms of Troeltsch's typological method of *Verstehen* have been noted, along with problems about his conception of a 'religious a priori'. Yet in these ways too, Troeltsch's work continues to cast a long shadow across the field of Christian ethics. It is probably too much to say, as James Luther Adams did, that Troeltsch's corpus 'stands as the twentieth century's most thorough and systematic attempt to come to terms with the historical character of culture, knowledge, and religion' (Adams, in Troeltsch 1991: p. vii). Nevertheless, his reflection on historical method as well as on religious experience and communal identity are of singular importance for Christian ethics. This brings us to Troeltsch's deepest theological and philosophical concern.

Like many of his contemporaries, Troeltsch was captivated by the problem of religion and modernity. With modernity comes the decay of traditional structures of authority and the rise of differentiated and rationalized social structures, as Weber argued. The modern world is one in which a single, overriding authority, usually religious and developed through lineage or charisma, has decayed due to the differentiation of politics, society, religion, morals, education, media, law, and the like. Each of these 'spheres' is increasingly rationalized in and through its own logic, discourse, norms, and values. Troeltsch, Weber, and other social theorists agree on this point. The question then becomes how to articulate the unity or functional coherence of the social order. Further, what role do cultural and social forces, including the churches, that exist alongside political and economic realities, have in that order?

Theologically understood, something else is at stake in the modern rationalization of spheres and a social order that works politically through constitutional authority. Troeltsch was convinced that human existence transpires in an irresolvable tension. Life is defined by the struggle of existence from the most basic biological level, captured in Darwinian thought, to the will to power that too often marks social existence. On this level of his argument, there is a deep engagement by Troeltsch with the works of Nietzsche and Schopenhauer, who, in his judgement, insist on the struggle for existence and thereby rightly challenge modern optimism about progress. The struggle for existence in which life competes with life means that human communities, if they are to endure, must develop an inner-worldly ethics that limits conflict and focuses on secular goods and achievements.

This lower stage of morality, as Troeltsch called it, is a presupposition of distinctly Christian ethics. In fact, the work of Christian piety 'cannot begin until nature's raw drives, instinctive group loyalties, and the jungle of the struggle for existence have either been broken or transformed and ennobled through cultural work and organization, through law and order, through intellectual and social discipline' ([1910b] 1991: 353). In addition to the relative goods and the ordering of the struggle of life, human beings aspire to absolute values. Human beings strive toward 'a supreme, purely personal morality, where people are inwardly united by a mutuality of disposition and by a community of free, inner understanding that transcends law, power, coercion, and struggle' (ibid.). Christian ethics is just such a supreme ethics: 'its individual morality is, accordingly, an ethics of self-sanctification for God, and its social morality is an ethics of the community of all the children of God, in God' ([1910b] 1991: 351–2). The challenge placed before every Christian community is how, in what way, and to what degree the lower morality is related to this higher moral vision. One might see this problem in terms of how to mediate the distinction Weber drew, in his famous essay 'Politics as Vocation', between an ethics of absolute conviction and an ethics of responsibility. However, Troeltsch casts the problem on a wider historical and social plane.

The conceptual tool with which to undertake the task of relating lower and higher moralities traditionally in Christian thought had been the idea of 'natural law', found also in classical Stoicism. Troeltsch distinguishes with the Stoics between an *absolute natural law*, the law of the primeval age or pre-fallen (pre-lapsarian) existence and also future redeemed existence, and the *relative natural law*, 'with its harsh order of state and law, the protection of property' that developed into the 'law of nations' ([1910a] 1991: 160). Early Christians identified the *relative natural law* with the Decalogue as the theological warrant for political laws, and then had to relate the Christian ideal of love to this law. The various social ethics found in the Christian West either seek to hold fast to the distinctly Christian vision, and thereby fail to address those factors in the struggle of life that are its presupposition (the Sect-type), or attempt to fashion a compromise, a 'cultural synthesis', that mediates and accommodates lower and higher morality (the Church-type). Even within the Church-type there are differences. The idea of natural law and its implications for addressing the 'social problem' are different in medieval Catholicism, Lutheranism, and especially the link between the Reformed, Calvinistic churches and their relations to the emergence of the modern nation and capitalism.

Modernity on Troeltsch's account is an intensification of the secular this-worldly domain of life and thereby the ruthless struggle that characterizes existence. Cultural productivity, the rise and development of capitalism, advances in the natural sciences, political revolutions, the force of historical consciousness, and (we would now add) global cultural and economic flows all mean that 'modernity' is defined by an immanentalism and virtual 'deification of the actual'. This immanentalism is a value scheme, an ethos, which propels the cultural synthesis called 'modernity'. The modern intensification of the secular threatens to overwhelm the human drive for absolute values. It is a challenge root and branch to Christianity. In fact, this is precisely the 'modern' social problem for the churches. How are Christian communities to relate to a civilization in which society and state are functionally differentiated yet share an increasingly ardent immanentalism that denies or thwarts the human drive for absolute values?

It is in this light that Troeltsch, after more than 1,000 pages, concludes *The Social Teachings*. He writes that Christian social work is in a problematic condition. 'It is problematic in general because the power of thought to overcome brutal reality is always an obscure and difficult question; it is problematic in particular because the main historic forms of the Christian doctrine of society and of social development are today, for various reasons, impotent in face of the tasks by which they are confronted.' New forms of thought are needed, beyond the traditionalism of doctrinaire theology. This new thought must 'be evolved out of the inner impulse of Christian thought, and out of its vital expression at the present time' (II. 1012). It must specify absolute values, but ones that can also be accommodated to the modern ethos.

In Troeltsch's mind, this process of adjustment or accommodation to the struggle of existence and inner-worldly goods, with all its risk of betraying Christian convictions, has always been the task of Christian ethics. He judged that among the various 'types' of traditional social teaching, the Church-type held together the tension between pure Christianity and the social world in which it existed. With modernity and its deification of the actual, something like the

Church-type is needed, but without its traditional, pre-modern structures of authority or dogmatic rigidity. It must also be infused with elements of the Sect- and Mystic-types. This is, of course, just how Troeltsch described the enterprise of 'liberal Christianity', a form of life and thought that meets the modern world and seeks to mediate the Christian ethos and modern secularity without resolving the antitheses.

Troeltsch thought that commitment to this 'liberal' enterprise was a necessary consequence of one of the main truths to emerge from the journey of *The Social Teachings*. 'There is also no absolute ethical transformation of material nature or of human nature; all that does exist is a constant wrestling with the problems which they raise' (II. 1013). It is important to realize in this light that many so-called liberal theologians, beginning with Schleiermacher, had conceived of the *summum bonum* as the harmony of reason and nature, the virtual fashioning of natural and human existence in and through the highest ideals of reason. Troeltsch's conclusion in *The Social Teachings* is a break from that mode of thought, and this break puts him closer to the kinds of 'Christian realism' seen in the United States. In his mind only 'doctrinaire idealism' and 'religious fanatics' deny that moral ideals can never be fully realized in history yet also must continue to inspire human action.

A realistic attitude demands that one meet the unending need to respond to new situations by mediating and even accommodating 'pure Christian morality' to the realities of life. This attitude, Troeltsch intimates, is not without its theological aspect. 'Faith', he writes, 'is the source of energy in the struggle of life, but life still remains a battle which is continually renewed upon ever new fronts' (II. 1013). The purity of Christian piety confronts the ever-changing reality of historical and social life with the confidence that God's reign is the ultimate good of all things. And so he ends *The Social Teachings*: 'The truth is—and this is the conclusion of the whole matter—the Kingdom of God is within us. But we must let our light shine before men in confident and untiring labor that they may see our good works and praise our Father in Heaven. The final ends of all humanity are hidden within His Hands' (II. 1013).

The impact of these conclusions about the accommodation of the Christian ethos and the struggle of existence have deeply marked the field of Christian ethics. In the United States, various thinkers identified with Christian realism, from Reinhold Niebuhr (1996) to, more recently, Robin Lovin (1995) and Douglas Ottati (1999), have insisted with Troeltsch that the Kingdom of God will not be built on earth. Nor is the Church an outpost of redeemed people free of the struggles of existence. H. Richard Niebuhr (1999) argued even more explicitly that the problem of human life is to move from an 'ethics of death' marked by defensiveness in the struggle of existence to an ethics of faithfulness and responsibility. This requires, he was sure, an ongoing revolution of heart and mind never finished in history. Other thinkers, moving towards what Troeltsch thought was idealism or fanaticism, have argued that the Christian community is an eschatological reality defined by peaceableness free from the ontology of war that besets 'the world'. For these theologians, the Christian ethic is about transcending the tooth and claw of existence. It is not about 'natural law', but, rather, about the formation of a community defined by pacifism in discipleship to Christ. At this level, there is a debate, then, in moral ontology or metaphysics—that is, a debate over the claims about reality entailed in Christian faith.

These ontological questions are deeply bound to how a thinker and community understand the goodness or fallenness of the structures of existence. If one assumes that the 'world' is nothing but the domain of sin, then the 'Church' is called and empowered to witness to that reality. This would seem to be a denial of the goodness of creation that endures even under conditions of sin, human travail, and violence. Conversely, one can affirm, along with Troeltschian liberals and Christian realists, an attitude of grateful acceptance for life in all its turmoil, which sparks ardent service to transform its brutishness. If Troeltsch is right, these options are just a further working out of the basic types of Christian social teaching. Yet only a realistic, liberal spirit has any lasting chance of meeting the challenges of the present age. In a time of ecological endangerment and worldwide threats to the human species—say, in the globalization of disease—what is needed is some affirmation of the fragile goodness of life and a dedication to respect and enhance the integrity of life (see Schweiker 1998).

Whatever theological judgement one reaches about the 'secular intensification of life' and also the acknowledgement of the struggle for existence within an ethics, Troeltsch's project is none the less flawed on one point. The age of 'globality' has been called 'modernity at large' (see Appadurai 1996). We daily witness the spread of market economies, political freedoms, and rationalized social systems that threaten and overturn traditional cultures and authority structures. As everyone knows, this has sparked conservative and even fundamentalist revivals worldwide and the hatred of the 'modern world'. What has also become obvious is that the worry of Troeltsch and many other social theorists about the eventual domination of 'secularity' and the eclipse of religion is simply wrong (see Stackhouse *et al.* 2000). The so-called secularization theory has proved inadequate in helping us to understand the postmodern or global age. Perhaps Troeltsch should have anticipated these developments, given his insistence on an enduring religious impulse in human life, the so-called 'religious a priori.' And in all fairness, in an early lecture and again near the end of his life, especially the last work, *Christian Thought: Its History and Application* (1923), Troelstch was concerned with the confrontation among the religions.

Still, the fact remains that for Troeltsch the challenge to Christian social ethics was 'secularity' (the deification of the actual), not the interaction among religions in and through shared global problems and horrible legacies of conflict. Even now, only a few thinkers are addressing this problem in any deep and compelling way through ideas about a 'global ethics' or 'comparative religious ethics'. This work, or some version of it, is the demand of the near and distant future. It is the reality of religious and cultural struggle on a global scale, rather than the will to power arising in natural forces, that must now be related to Christian claims. Yet, on this point as well, Christian social ethics is in a problematic situation. Too many thinkers and communities focus on their Christian identity, rather than seeking to respond with others to the emerging global reality.

Conclusion

What, then, are we to make of this massive book? *The Social Teachings* and the various strands of Troeltsch's thought that it encompasses continue to help define issues in Christian ethics, ranging from questions of method to claims about human action, moral norms, and the relation between religious communities and social as well as political realities. Various criticisms of his work have been noted in this chapter, as well as those points in which new directions for thought are needed. These include renewed attention to questions about religious experience, undertaking the labour of comparative religious and ethical reflection, and extending the pluralistic impulses of his project beyond assumptions about the cultural importance of the many forms of Christianity to Western social life.

None of this would surprise Troeltsch. The historical condition of thinking requires that new ideas and theories meet new situations while drawing on old resources. In this respect, Troeltsch's enduring impact on the work of Christian ethics is less in terms of his 'answers' to the social problem. It is to be found more in his manner of articulating the moral, social, and religious condition or space within which people live and work. If anything should be obvious, it is that the present forces structuring the postmodern, global world continue, intensify, and also radically alter those features of 'modernity' that Troeltsch so skilfully and deeply analysed. It is for this reason that the 'effects of a review' continue to reach into the present work of all who labour in the field of theological ethics.

References and Suggested Reading

Adams, J. L. (1991). 'Preface', in E. Troeltsch, *Religion in History*, Minneapolis: Fortress Press, pp. vii–viii.
Appadurai, A. (1996). *Modernity at Large: Cultural Dimensions of Globalization.* Minneapolis: University of Minnesota Press.
Barth, K. (1957). *Church Dogmatics.* Edinburgh: T. & T. Clark.

BECK, U., GIDDENS, A., and LASH, A. (1994). *Reflexive Modernization: Politics, Tradition and Aesthetics in the Modern Social Order*. Cambridge: Polity.

BULTMANN, R. (1934). *Jesus and the Word*. New York: Scribner.

CHAPMAN, D. (ed.) (2002). *The Future of Liberal Theology*. Burlington, Vt.: Ashgate Publishing.

FISCHER, J. (2002). *Theologische Ethik: Grundwissen und Orientierung*. Stuttgart: W. Kohlhammer.

GAITA, R. (2000). *A Common Humanity: Thinking about Love and Truth and Justice*. London: Routledge.

GRAF, F. W. (2002). 'Ernst Troeltsch: Theologies als Kulturwissenschaft des Historismus', in P. Neuner and G. Wenz (eds.), *Theologen des 20. Jahrhunderts: Eine Einführung*, Darmstadt: Wissenschafftliche Buchgesellschaft, 53–69.

GUSTAFSON, J. M. (1968). *Christ and the Moral Life*. New York: Harper & Row.

HAUERWAS, S. (1988). *Christian Existence Today: Essays on Church, World, and Living in Between*. Durham, NC: Labyrinth Press.

HEIDEGGER, M. (1962). *Being and Time*. New York: Harper & Row.

HUBER, W. (1990). *Konflikt und Konsens: Studien zur Ethik der Verantwortung*. Munich: Chr. Kaiser.

KELSAY, J. and TWISS, S. B. (1994). *Religion and Human Rights*. New York: The Project on Religion and Human Rights.

KUNG, H. and KUSCHEI, K.-J. (eds.) (1995). *A Global Ethic: The Declaration of the Parliament of the World's Religions*. New York: Continuum.

LINDBECK, G. A. (1984). *The Nature of Doctrine: Religion and Theology in a Postliberal Age*. Philadelphia: Westminster Press.

LOVIN, R. W. (1995). *Reinhold Niebuhr and Christian Realism*. Cambridge: Cambridge University Press.

MILBANK, J. (1991). *Theology and Social Theory: Beyond Secular Reason*. Cambridge, Mass.: Basil Blackwell.

NIEBUHR, H. R. (1951). *Christ and Culture*. New York: Harper & Row.

—— (1999). *The Responsible Self: An Essay in Christian Moral Philosophy*. Louisville, Ky.: Westminster/John Knox Press.

NIEBUHR, R. (1996). *The Nature and Destiny of Man*, 2 vols. Louisville, Ky.: Westminster/John Knox Press.

OTTATI, D. (1999). *Hopeful Realism: Reclaiming the Poetry of Theology*. Cleveland: Pilgrim Press.

SCHWEIKER, W. (1995). *Responsibility and Christian Ethics*. Cambridge: Cambridge University Press.

—— (1998). *Power, Value and Convictions: Theological Ethics in the Postmodern Age*. Cleveland: Pilgrim Press.

—— (2004). *Theological Ethics and Global Dynamics: In the Time of Many Worlds*. Oxford: Blackwell.

STACKHOUSE, M. L. (1987). *Public Theology and Political Economy: Christian Stewardship in Modern Society*. Grand Rapids, Mich.: W. B. Eerdmans Publishing Company.

—— et al. (2000). *God and Globalization*, 4 vols. Harrisburg, Pa.: Trinity Press International.

STOUT, J. (1988). *Ethics after Babel: The Languages of Morals and their Discontents*. Boston: Beacon Press.

TILLICH, P. (1952). *The Courage to Be*. New Haven: Yale University Press.

TROELTSCH, E. ([1898] 1991). 'Historical and Dogmatic Method in Theology', in E. Troeltsch, *Religion in History*, Minneapolis: Fortress Press, 11–32.

——([1907] 1991). 'The Essence of the Modern Spirit', in E. Troeltsch, *Religion in History*, Minneapolis: Fortress Press, 237–72.

——([1909] 1991). 'On the Question of the Religious a Apriori', in E. Troeltsch, *Religion in History*, Minneapolis: Fortress Press, 33–45.

——([1910*a*] 1991). 'Christian Natural Law', in E. Troeltsch, *Religion in History*, Minneapolis: Fortress Press, 159–67.

——([1910*b*] 1991). 'On the Possibility of a Liberal Christianity', in E. Troeltsch, *Religion in History*, Minneapolis: Fortress Press, 343–59.

——([1923] 1999). *Christian Thought: Its History and Application*. Eugene, Ore.: Wipf and Stock.

——([1912]1992). *The Social Teaching of the Christian Churches*. Louisville, Ky.: Westminster/John Knox Press.

——(1998). *Kritsche Gesamtausgabe*, ed. Friedrich Wilhelm Graf, Volker Drehsen, and Trutz Rendtorff. Berlin: Walter de Gruyter.

Troeltsch-Studien, ed. H. Renz and F. W. Graf. Gütevsloh: Mohn, *c.* 1982–   .

WEBER, M. (1958). *From Max Weber: Essays in Sociology*. Oxford: Oxford University Press.

YODER, J. H. (1984). *The Priestly Kingdom: Social Ethics as Gospel*. Notre Dame, Ind.: University of Notre Dame Press.

CHAPTER 25

ANDERS NYGREN'S *AGAPE AND EROS*

WILLIAM WERPEHOWSKI

I

IN the opening paragraphs of *Agape and Eros*, Anders Nygren states that his purpose is 'to investigate the meaning of the Christian idea of love', and 'to illustrate the main changes it has undergone in the course of history' (1953: 27). The investigation is devoted to an explication of the 'specifically Christian conception' of *agapē* both in its integrity and in its opposition to a form of love that 'originally' has nothing to do with it—the Platonic conception of *eros*. While these two 'fundamental motifs' or 'general attitudes to life' offer thoroughly different approaches to moral and religious existence, 'they have nonetheless become so thoroughly bound up and interwoven with one another that it is hardly possible for us to speak of either without our thoughts being drawn to the other' (1953: 30). Moreover, theological ventures which seek some combination or positive ordering or synthesis of these two kinds of love have corrupted the account of divine *agapē*, which itself lends full coherence and meaning to the Christian faith. Given that, on Nygren's terms, the motifs *contradict* one another, corruption is inevitable. His historical analysis intends to expose how Christian love, announced and embodied

I wish to thank James M. Gustafson, Kevin Hughes, Gilbert Meilaender, David Schindler, and Darlene Fozard Weaver for their generous help with this essay.

in the Synoptic Gospels, brought to its highest expression in Paul, and formally stated in 1 John, has been embattled and then purified in a pattern of synthesis and renewal culminating in the Reformation theology of Martin Luther.

Nygren also remarks in the early going that his topic, though perhaps the most central for theological work, is among the most neglected by contemporary theologians (1953: 27). It is safe to say that *Agape and Eros* turned out to be one hearty remedy for any such neglect. Since its publication in two parts in 1930 and 1936 (and then in English translation in 1932 and 1938–9), the question of the meaning of Christian love has received extensive attention, and Nygren's study is an abiding point of reference. The book's conceptual clarity has prompted similar efforts in its wake, as Christian thinkers take up Nygren's fourfold analysis of God's love for humanity and humanity's for God, self-love, and the love of neighbour. Students of Christian ethics have done well to try to match in their responses the author's sharpness of vision and capacity for theologically substantive historical interpretation. We find here a revealing and focused thesis about the character of Christian love that deserves careful consideration.

There are also conceptual quandaries and historical lapses in the book, and theologians reflecting on Christian love have attended to them. Thus a revealing and focused thesis is taken to risk in its oppositions an unenlightening severity concerning, for example, the status of creation in the divine economy (D'Arcy 1956). John Burnaby sees in Nygren 'the embarrassment of the anti-mystic', that special pleading which continually resists the idea that the human love of God commended in Psalms and the Gospel of John is really... well, *love* (1938: 6–7). These specific sites of controversy display how *Agape and Eros* poses an uncompromising either/or, *agapē or eros*, that images the sorts of either/or's often associated with theological divisions between Protestant and Roman Catholic Christianity. In the divide between the two loves we would discover the confrontation of 'two religious standpoints which differ in principle—that of Catholicism in which fellowship with God is won by our uplifting with the support of divine grace to the level of God's holiness, and that of the Reformation, where fellowship with God comes to pass through God's bringing himself down to the level of our humanity and sin' (Burnaby 1970: 185, quoting Nygren).

One may contextualize such a sweeping judgement somewhat by referring it to the specific theological movement that *Agape and Eros* reflects. While a professor at the University of Lund, Anders Nygren co-founded with Gustaf Aulen the 'Lundensian system' which began to capture the theological thinking of Sweden in the early 1920s. For them, according to Nels Ferre, the 'basic motif underlying Christianity... became a transcendent unmotivated love, the knowledge of which is through and through supernaturally disclosed', and which preserves 'the purity of the Pauline-Lutheran theme: *sola gratia-sola fides*'. *Agape and Eros* 'draws out the Lundensian thesis to the sharpness of a razor's edge' (1967: 32–3, 108). It also engages a tradition of research on Martin Luther that draws a direct line from the Bible to him, and that takes him to be 'the restorer of original Christianity, the restorer of the primitive Church in the midst of a corrupt and deviationist medieval Church' (Johnson 1967: 248–9).

At this point we ought not to let our enquiry be determined within the confines of the sweeping judgement and the kind of choice it would demand; and while we may pause, with Karl Barth, over Nygren's tendency to suggest 'that all the ways of God can and must end with Luther', we would be foolish to linger (Barth 1958: 738). I will attempt to analyse some major themes in *Agape and Eros* on their own terms, and consider whether those terms can bear the fullness of the Gospel vision to which Nygren would be faithful. Many of the issues I will present have been presented before (e.g., Outka 1972). Given its long, venerable, and contested run, an author can fairly wonder what more there is to say about this volume. I hope, in any event, to bring forth something of the power and the limits of this classic in Christian ethics.

II

For Nygren, *agapē* is the fundamental motif of the Christian faith, because he finds it to be a decisive and concentrated expression of the Christian Gospel: *God's sovereign and gracious self-disclosure in Jesus Christ for us and for our salvation*. We can understand his interpretations of *agapē* and *eros* by considering the terms of this description.

God is the *sovereign* Lord who rules all creation with absolute authority (Nygren 1953: 45). Such free independence apart from us implies that God alone establishes and enacts the conditions of fellowship with God; hence there is no legal framework that mediates them and to which God is bound. Neither an independent measure of human righteousness nor its retention in conditioning appeals to the good works of the *unrighteous* (e.g., repentance and humility) is compatible with divine sovereignty. So, too, with identification of God as humanity's 'highest good', inasmuch as this renders the One who is 'Good-in-Itself' measurable by human standards of value and just a means for the satisfaction of human desire (Nygren 1953: 91–2). It is impossible, moreover, to construe God's sovereign act as *seeking* some good or value that God needs for self-completion and upon which God is therefore dependent.

The sovereign Lord is *gracious*. God's freedom apart from us ratifies how God may act freely for us. 'God does not love in order to obtain any advantage thereby, but quite simply because it is His nature to love, with a love that seeks, not to get, but to give', 'freely and generously', from the divine superabundance (Nygren 1953:

201, 212). Thus the sovereign and gracious God *discloses* or *reveals* himself, as Karl Barth (1957: 184) regularly insisted, with a message that we cannot tell ourselves, and that 'transcends everything that can be made an object of human desire and longing' (Nygren 1953: 213). In his discussion of Augustine, Nygren goes after a eudaemonism that reduces the divine to 'the only right and natural correlate' of a general structure of human desire, a structure in which 'God' is an answer to the human 'erotic' question and quest for a source of *rest* and a satisfaction of *need* which increases creaturely being and may be permanently possessed (1953: 486–93). He also criticizes theologies which *pass by* the specific bond between God and God's beloved through 'rational explanations' which appeal abstractly and universally to the 'reciprocal sympathy' bonding, say, the Creator to his creation, or to the creaturely bearer of a 'divine spark' (1953: 79; cf. Balthasar 2004: 68). Moves of this sort evade the fact and character of divine revelation.

God's self-disclosure is *in Jesus Christ*, who served and called sinners through a freely giving and forgiving love (Nygren 1953: 68–70). The Apostle Paul attains to the 'sublimest conception of God's Agape ever given or capable of being given' in identifying it with the cross of Jesus Christ. The cross attests that in Christ God reconciles us to himself with a love 'that gives itself away, that sacrifices itself, even to the uttermost' (Nygren 1953: 119, 118). This reconciling work is *for us*—for our right relation with God—and *for our salvation*, our being saved from the estrangement of sin and death.

The characteristic aspects of God's *agapē* for Nygren move into focus. It is strictly spontaneous (1953: 75–6), springing sovereignly from God's nature and not from anything extrinsic to it. As such, God's love is the exclusive source, condition, and meaning of fellowship with God. Divine *agapē* is not motivated by the discovery of 'value in the beloved along the lines of human motives for a good that completes the self'. 'Indifferent to value', it nevertheless creates it in the bestowal of a free gift to those who lack it. Our saving relation with God consists in grateful submission and devotion to the One unveiled in the suffering love of Jesus Christ. *Agapē* alone 'is the initiator of fellowship with God . . . there is from man's side no way at all that leads to God' (Nygren 1953: 80).

Nygren works out his vision of the other, aforementioned loves accordingly. Human love for God is a response to the divine love, and hence not totally 'spontaneous'; but it is so relatively, in that it is not motivated by the self's desire for some good for itself. This claim of 'relative spontaneity' protects against supposing that the responding human subject has an 'independent life of his own apart from God'. The heart's 'free surrender' to God must be an outcome of a love that 'flows by inescapable necessity from the fact of belonging unreservedly to God'. There can be no thought of gain, even the thought of gaining God, for when God loves freely, 'there remains nothing for man to gain by loving God' (1953: 125, 94). In order to preserve the priority of grace for sinners and our own pure reception of it, Paul, says Nygren, aptly *resists* the language of 'love of God', while still capturing its 'spiritual reality' of devotion and response with the better name of 'faith' and its consequence in 'obedience' (1953: 126–7).

Christian love of neighbour is distinguished entirely from humanistic ideals of altruism and sympathy, as it is rooted in fellowship with God and the experience of divine love. It reveals its spontaneous and unmotivated essence in a love of enemies that 'creates fellowship even where fellowship seemed impossible' (Nygren 1953: 102). Neighbour love is free of the self's bondage to itself, and hence gives of itself, sacrifices itself, for the other who is regarded 'in his concrete condition and concrete situation' for his own sake, independently of relative worth or attractiveness (Nygren 1953: 98). In truth, this *agapē* is 'an outflow of God's own life', such that the 'stream of love' infused in the Christian heart flows forth to the neighbour (Nygren 1953: 140, 141). One may even say that the subject of this love is God alone, with the Christian serving as a tube or channel through which divine blessings drop forth.

Nygren's image of the 'tube' or 'channel' is often derided by critics, who seek, as we shall see, a more integral account of human moral agency. One finds three related reasons for its use. Nygren wants, first, to stress the work of the Holy Spirit in giving a new life of love to the Christian. Not our own doing, *agapē* becomes a kind of 'pneumatic fluid' shed abroad in our hearts and counted as pure grace (1953: 129). 'I live; yet no longer I, but Christ liveth in me' (Gal. 2: 20). The notion of a channel can also express a parallel pattern of neighbour love being 'freely given' in virtue of receiving the free gift of God's love. But all of this concern about grace and gift appears to be governed by an idea of the unimpeded motion of divine love to which the self, and the self's love of itself, affords no barrier and provides no medium. *Agapē* 'excludes all self-love'; for 'in self-love it finds its chief adversary which must be fought and conquered. It is self-love that alienates man from God, preventing him from sincerely giving himself up to God, and it is self-love that shuts up a man's heart against his neighbor' (Nygren 1953: 217). Hence the unimpeded motion through the tube that is the Christian flows 'up' and 'down', upward in faith and obedience by the inescapable necessity of being mastered by God's love, and downward in love to the neighbour (Nygren 1953: 735).

The opposite of *agapē*, eros exists in contradiction to the good news of Jesus Christ. Attending to its Platonic core, Nygren deems it an acquisitive love, constituted by 'a desire, a longing, a striving'. It is driven by a motivation to gain what one lacks because of its value to oneself. This value is no small thing, but the highest thing, and so *eros* reaches heavenward as humanity's way to the divine. *Eros* is therefore an *egocentric love*, 'for all desire, or appetite, and longing is more or less egocentric', and because desire's religious quest is 'to gain possession of an object which is regarded as valuable and which man feels he needs' (Nygren 1953: 175–80).

In Jesus Christ God's love is *free grace*. *Eros* grasps out of need, and renders a conception of a God who is either incapable of love (for God needs nothing) or who seeks only himself and not the beloved in the grasping. God's *agapē* is offered *to sinners. Eros* pursues value present, rather than creating value where none exists. What is more, the sinner's love for God is a matter of *unreserved surrender*. It cannot be made good through an acquisitive desire or appetite 'which as such strives to obtain advantages' in the assessment of and ascent to its own greatest good. Christian love of neighbour must not be distorted into a regard that would *use the beloved* as a meritorious means to God, or that otherwise intends acquisitively to *possess the beloved* for one's own needs and purposes, or that *bypasses the neighbour* in directing itself to some 'divine spark' in her. *Eros* distorts in these ways. The worm at the heart is that *eros* is essentially self-love, that very barrier and impediment to God's love descending for us and for our salvation, that needy craving that conforms God to itself and then in self-congratulation counts itself holy in its more or less successful 'ascent'. With all respect to Nygren's Lutheranism, let us add that for him theologies of *eros* lay a trap for the religiously serious woman or man. For example, in its supposed 'synthesis' with an *agapē* that seemingly enkindles our love for God, it lays a dreadful burden upon the sinner who now, looking upward, is to purify her desire and seek a holiness that attains to God through a process of salvation that engenders either arrogance or despair.

III

Critics of the historical studies in *Agape and Eros* commonly complain that the strict, governing contrast between these two forms of love impedes fair and accurate examination. Bernard McGinn, for example, writes that the interpretation of the Neoplatonist Plotinus's notion of 'descending love' misrepresents him, 'in order to get him to fit the Procrustean bed of Nygren's theory' (1996: 198). John Burnaby questions how far Nygren, 'by approaching Augustine's work with ready-made definitions of the motifs of agape and eros...may have condemned himself in advance to failure in understanding the doctrine he is to examine' (1970: 180). Henri de Lubac, while believing that Nygren 'has successfully brought to light the originality of the Christian idea of love and, in so doing, the idea of Christianity', still finds himself unable 'to escape the impression that Mr. Nygren is defending a thesis rather than engaging in a truly historical inquiry'; why else does he rule out 'as coming from Hellenism, all idea of desire, where so many biblical texts express precisely the thirst for God?' (1989: 87). This problem of a posited opposition that is defended come what may, I believe, also impedes investigation of dimensions of theology and ethics that hold a prominent place in the very vision of the Christian Gospel which Nygren takes to ground the *agapē* motif. One may 'admit just as readily as Mr. Nygren the antithesis of eros and agape in the terms in which he defines it', and deny with him that *eros* so defined 'can be understood as a preparation for and commencement of agape' (Lubac 1989: 89). Nonetheless, this specific campaign against *eros* appears insufficiently discriminating of theological matters we ought not to ignore or jettison.

Recall that Nygren's idea of *agapē* is connected with the comprehension that God is *sovereign* and *gracious*. Free and independent apart from us, God completely and concretely determines the basis of fellowship with humanity. This basis is nothing other than God's generous love, which is not a means to obtain some needed advantage, but simply expressive of the divine nature. God's *trinitarian* nature, we might say, is constituted by the self-gift of the Father to the Son and the Son's corresponding kenosis in thanksgiving, represented as absolute love by the Holy Spirit (Balthasar 2000: p. viii). Divine sovereignty is confirmed and established in the being of the one who loves with this supreme freedom of self-giving in Jesus Christ and his work of reconciliation for sinful humanity (Balthasar 2000: 79–83; cf. Barth 1957: 257–321). God's *agapē* simply is not an egocentric, acquisitive desire, but only a glorification, or bringing to light, of God's merciful being for us.

Yet it is necessary to go on to say, if the preceding is to remain theologically intelligible, that God is an *agent* whose *purposes*, expressive of God's nature and in which God is 'interested', include a desire for the good of God's beloved for his or her own sake. In fact, what is desired for its own sake is *fellowship* with the beloved. It would be odd to claim that God desires this (egocentrically) for God's own sake, as if out of need for completion; but it would be odd as well simply to hold that God desires fellowship for 'our good', as if somehow this was distinct from God's gracious and faithful embrace. No, the good that God desires for us 'gratis, for its own sake', *is* fellowship with God. And *that* desire for good may well be termed 'erotic'. 'The central case of Eros', writes Robert Merrihew Adams, 'is a passionate desire for a personal relationship. . . . It is the lover's desire for relationship with the beloved. It may be self-interested, but it need not be.' Hence 'Agape includes a sort of Eros—not every sort of Eros, for there are certainly selfish, sick, and destructive forms of Eros that have no place in the Christian ethical ideal. One of the distinguishing characteristics of Agape is the kind of Eros that it includes: the kind of relationship that is desired in Agapē' (1987: 187, 190).

Perhaps the central element for ethics in Nygren's vision of *agapē* is the way it is an implication of God's *self-disclosure in Jesus Christ*. In this respect he finds an unlikely comrade of sorts in the Roman Catholic Hans Urs von Balthasar. The basis of fellowship with God is God's self-revelation 'in—and *only* in—the kenosis of Christ', in which 'the *inner* mystery of God's love comes to light, the mystery of the God who "is love" in himself and therefore is "triune"' as sketched above (2004: 87). The divine love, moreover, is decisively identified with the cross and given to sinners. 'Indeed, it is in the God-forsakenness of the Crucified One that we come to see what we have been redeemed and saved from: the definitive loss of God, a loss we could never have spared ourselves through any of our own efforts outside of grace' (2004: 93). Nygren might have quarrelled with the sort of appeal to 'efforts' here, but leave that aside for now. God's merciful love in Jesus Christ is offered us in our *concrete condition* of absolute need; it is unconditional, not grounded in our relative worth, including the self-deceiving worth *we* may cite as being God's good creation—still!—and just so *in possession* of *possibilities* for the divine.

A question remains concerning the nature of God's love for the *individual* beloved, in his or her 'concrete condition' *and full reality.* Consider this philosophical posing of the question. In our attempt to present an understanding of love 'which recognizes the individual *qua* individual', 'the individual frustrates our efforts by a maddening transparency. Insofar as I love him for his qualities, the qualities seem to constitute the proper object of my love; insofar as I love him irrespective of the particular qualities, it becomes unclear in what sense I may be said to love, specifically, *him*' (Kosman 1976: 57). In a Christian idiom, the puzzle suggests that God's love may yet be an *affirmation* or *approval* of the human person (1) unconditionally (independently, in spite of sin, 'nevertheless'), (2) *for* himself or herself ('I love you for *yourself*'), and (3) for the beloved's *own sake* (Pieper 1997: 166–72). Nygren leaves out the middle term, since that drives, he thinks, to some independent value for God in the beloved that the sinner lacks by definition, and focuses on the first and third in contrast with an *eros* that is conditional on value and egocentric.

The account of Christian love need not and should not go that way. It may lead us to overlook the goodness of the sinner *as he or she stands before God in Jesus Christ.* It may also, as Gilbert Meilaender argues in his contribution to this volume (Chapter 5), stress divine grace as favour toward sinners to the exclusion of grace as a gift of love poured into our hearts by the Holy Spirit, one that truly offers us a *new life* with and for God and neighbour.

'How', von Balthasar asks, 'can an enemy be reconciled while he is still an enemy?' While we were yet sinners, Christ died for us, he answers, with a love 'which surpasses us and anticipates us.... The decisive thing is that the sinner has heard of a love that could be, and really is, there for him; he is not the one who has to bring himself into line with God; God has already seen in him, the loveless sinner, a beloved child, and has looked upon him and conferred dignity upon him in the light of this love.' Even in our sinful condition, this is (also) what we really are, and we may become what God takes us to be in the light of Christ (2004: 101, 103–4). And if the Christian's response is not only trust in divine mercy but also, as Nygren clearly admits, gratitude, then it appears to be a response that presupposes an interest in *one's own good*, given by and to be offered to God, in praise and thanksgiving and fellowship (Adams 1987: 186–7).

I will turn to this last point below. Now I wish to lay bare the implication that God's *agapē* includes not only an 'erotic' desire for a bond with us for its own sake, but also a desire for communion with that 'beloved child' God sees and makes true in Christ. *Agapē* is creative of value, as Nygren claims; but the claim now appears to draw near to or overlap with a feature of Platonic *eros*: i.e., the way love *recognizes* and *bids* the beloved to be what he or she truly is. God's love may be seen to be 'the condition ... of asking the other that he be himself ... even perhaps in the mode of non-presence' (Kosman 1976: 64). To that extent, *pace* Nygren, who takes the language of 'beauty' in the context of *agapē* to sound 'very much like blasphemy' (1953: 224), divine love creates and affirms the beauty, the realest self, of the beloved, graciously given and called forth. It promises our glory before God, our coming to the light and into God's delight 'as an artist delights in his work or a father in a son' (Lewis 1949: 10).

God's self-revelation *is for us and for our salvation*. It is, after all, for our good accomplished through a work of redemption that reconciles us with God. Our good should not be construed as the satisfaction of a kind of *eros* that Karl Barth also describes as antithetical to *agapē*, a 'grasping, taking, possessive love' that fabricates God out of the 'compulsion and impulsion' to one's own 'self-enclosed and self-inflated being'. It consists, rather, in a life-act of self-giving love, a will to live from and to God 'simply because He is God, and as such worthy to be loved' (1958: 735, 744). Still, Barth goes on to argue that 'agape-love takes place in affinity, *eros*-love in opposition to human nature' created by God (1958: 743). Note that Nygren is reluctant to make the first claim, and is perhaps a bit too eager to replace the second with an ambiguous identification of *eros* with our *sinful nature*; the latter may be inferred, for example, from his remark that 'when man has fallen away from God, he is wholly lost and has no value at all' (1953: 222). For Barth, neither *agapē* nor *eros* rests on a 'possibility of human nature as such'; neither alters our created nature, and both are 'historical determinations' of it. It is just that *agapē* does in fact correspond to our being from God and to God, and *eros* contradicts it. Loving fellowship with God (and neighbour) objectively fulfils us; it is our *highest good* in that there our God-given nature is both expressed and by grace transcended (1958: 744).

IV

I dare next to ask: may our love include *desire* for God and for our right relation with him? Divine grace effects reconciling fellowship, and *agapē* includes, recall, an 'erotic' desire for this relation for its own sake. Surely we may be grateful for God's *agapē* and the bond it forges; gratitude, as we have seen, includes an appreciation of the gift as freely given for our own greatest good, which includes both our being ransomed from God-forsakenness and our new life in God. One may draw from these matters appreciation of how our love for God is rejoicing over the existence of the beloved one; it is the desire that he be rather than not be; it is longing for his presence when he is absent; it is happiness in the thought of him; it is profound satisfaction over everything that makes him great and glorious. Love is gratitude; it is thankfulness over the existence of the beloved; it is the happy acceptance of everything that he gives without the jealous feeling that the self ought to be able to do as much; it is a gratitude that does not seek equality; it is wonder over the other's gift of himself in companionship. (Niebuhr 1956: 35)

It is also the case that the desire, rejoicing, and longing concern a fellowship in which one gives oneself to God in a losing of oneself as one's own. It has to do with a renunciation of wilfully seeking after oneself, in a 'chase in which he is both the hunter and the hunted, and which for this reason can be utterly futile' (Barth 1958: 749). One comes to oneself in a self-giving that responds in love to the love of God. Similarly, gratitude and wonder are made good in an 'offer of one's whole being to the God of Jesus Christ, so that he can use this being according to his loving pleasure for the work of salvation' (Balthasar 1994: 113).

A theologically adequate conception of our loving desire for God our highest good, a desire for fellowship with God that brings us to ourselves in self-giving, must be, then, along the lines of what H. Richard Niebuhr straightforwardly names a 'nonpossessive *Eros*' (1951: 18). This would be, repairing to Adams, the kind of *eros* that *agapē* includes. But for Nygren, and for Barth in virtually all of his explicit remarks about the 'antithesis' of *eros* and *agapē*, the idea of a non-possessive *eros* amounts to a contradiction in terms.

Can and should we redeem the idea? Barth gives grounds for why we may and perhaps must, even if in spite of himself. First, and formally, he writes that the act of love brings 'exaltation, gain, and joy'. Christians do not perform it for this reason; 'the one who loves does not want anything except to love, except more fully and seriously and perfectly to give himself, to enter into relationship with the loved one' (1958: 788). Loving as one loved by God, one is *joyful* in an 'arrest' of one's movement in desire, 'in which man experiences himself in the fulfillment of this movement' (1961: 376). Barth cautions that 'it is only with the most stringent reservations, and in the last resort not at all, that we can say the same of *eros*', holding that its self-enclosing cycle of 'enthusiasm and disillusionment' is a 'melancholy business' (1958: 788). That cycle, however, refers to an *egocentric eros*, and the references here to a *desire to enter a relation that fulfils one joyfully in self-giving response to God's love* looks a whole lot like a *non-possessive eros*. So, for the sake of theological clarity and precision, why not *make* the stringent reservations, and *deny* the necessity of the 'last resort'?

Better, why (else) should we? Second, Barth discusses our love for God in a manner that explicitly departs both from Nygren and from the 'embarrassment' he himself expressed (recalling Burnaby) in his earlier work (cf. Outka 1972: 214–16). *We may love God in freedom.* Nygren, however, 'has even decreed that there can be no question of a spontaneous love of man for God', and that Paul's stress on obedience and faith 'happily overcomes' an unfortunate ambiguity in the great commandment to *love* God and neighbour. Barth finds in the biblical witness to love God and Jesus 'too strong and explicit' an emphasis to permit this move. He believes that it courts a 'rationalistic moralism' that reduces the work of the Holy Spirit to 'the management of an eternal working day', and removes any room for prayer (1958: 795). It is far better to rid oneself of embarrassment and restore the love of God to its central place as source of obedience and service to the neighbour, even to the point of risking some 'religious eroticism'. Otherwise we create a theological and spiritual vacuum into which an excessive and mistaken response of 'eroticism' will hurry. The authority of Scripture, the dangers of moralism, the life of prayer, and even the battle against egocentric *eros* itself seem to permit and demand affirming our non-possessively erotic love for God.

Third, our Spirit-quickened love for the God who first loved us in Jesus Christ will be followed by obedience. But 'a puppet does not obey. It does not move itself. . . . But to be quickened by the Holy Spirit is to move oneself, and to do so in obedience.'

[Our act of love] cannot be understood as a prolongation or effluence of the divine action, of the love of God. . . . Nor can we describe as a covenant relationship the kind of relationship in which God alone is really at work and man is only the instrument or channel of the divine action . . . [Divine] initiative aims at a correspondingly free act, at genuine obedience as opposed to that of a puppet, on the part of the man with whom the covenant is made. (1958: 800)

Recall my earlier comments about the imagery of tubes and channels. Karl Barth ends up questioning Nygren's suppositions about human agency in the name of the conditions for relation with God, conditions which Nygren himself seems to need. The former does not shrink from the fact that such agency is the work of divine grace in the power of the Holy Spirit. He matches Nygren in non-stop attention to the way in which human love is freely given as God's love is received in Christ. Barth will not accept God's mastery of the human subject to amount to God's being a master puppeteer (cf. Outka 1972: 234–5).

I said that what governs Nygren's preference for the tube depiction is an idea of an unimpeded movement of gracious love to which the self and its love of itself afford no barrier or medium. The 'medium' of the self as agent, however, is necessary for an act of fellowship. In its non-possessive desire for relation with God, moreover, the self would of itself afford no barrier, unless one ruled out of court the very possibility of this desire by requiring that *all* desire is 'more or less egocentric' and seeks 'to gain possession of an object' (Nygren 1953: 175–80). To say this is to suppose that loving desire for some good is always and only a matter of the person's reaching and grasping hand, which posits the good for oneself in a subjective choice for it (O'Donovan 1980: 16–17, 28–9). Desire of this sort, moreover, comes to grief spiritually and theologically if we suppose, in turn, that it operates within a view of salvation as some synergistic sequence, in which what God graciously 'does' for us calls for an 'answer' on our part that is reckoned as 'our own' apart from grace (however much grace affords the means to it). Thus the (sinful) subject's desire can be taken only to appropriate grace for itself arrogantly in the effort to 'ascend' to God. Alternatively, the subject despairs of what he or she is called to do because of the honest knowledge of his or her thoroughgoing fallenness.

The first idea places desire within a theological anthropology. The second bears on soteriology. We find the first informing Nygren's analysis of Augustine, whose 'caritas-synthesis', it is proposed, runs together contradictory 'theocentric' and 'egocentric' emphases. Augustine's 'anti-moralism' demands God's sovereign, prevenient grace in Jesus Christ. Without this free divine love, nothing in who we are and what we do affords right relation with God. Augustine's 'eudaemonism' allows that when love is infused in the human heart, one 'still continues to seek the satisfaction of his desire, though he seeks it no longer in the things of sense, but in a supernatural bonum. Here our gaze is turned unwaveringly upon our own self and what can satisfy its needs' (1953: 530). However, and as Oliver O'Donovan has shown, an objective or 'realist' interpretation of eudaemonism removes the implication of egocentrism; for in this version the end that fulfils a human being is in the order of reality an absolutely supreme being who as such stands over against and lays a claim on her. 'Desire itself is understood not simply as an affect of the subject, but as a decisive confrontation between subject and object. Where then', O'Donovan rightly challenges, 'is the egocentricity?' (1980: 156). God, the highest good, is certainly *not* a being chosen by the grasping hand for oneself. One may answer that for Augustine and others human nature is *oriented* to its highest good in virtue of God's creation of it; yet, as we saw in Barth, this proposal *of itself* is patient of the strongest affirmations concerning God's utterly gracious self-disclosure in Jesus Christ, a self-disclosure not reducible or corresponding to any human potency for God. Augustine's own reliance on the authority of revelation, in addition, leaves us unpersuaded by the proposal that the divine is for him a mere correlate of desire (O'Donovan 1980: 157–8).

The soteriological issue gets to the heart of Nygren's commitment to 'the purity of the Pauline-Lutheran theme: *sola gratia-sola fides*'. He is correct in maintaining this commitment. An adequate soteriology, however, may *deny* that our salvation is a gradual process or sequence conditioned by human contributions to it, *affirm* that it is accomplished once and for all *extra nobis* in and through the reconciling work of Jesus Christ, and still *launch enquiry* into how it is we may *participate*, in the mode of our reception of that salvation accomplished for us without us, in the new life in Christ we are given. Not merely granting, but demanding first and foremost, that nothing whatever affords us God's fellowship but God's merciful, descending love to sinners whose temporal lives will always display their sin, one may yet ask after the 'movement effected by seeing what God has shown' us in that descending love. What is shown us is who the living God is, for us. In the work of salvation, we are offered a bond of love with God, and the offer is for participation in God's life 'in such a way that man can see it, understand it, make it his own, and live from it in keeping with human nature' and in spite of oneself in one's fallenness (Balthasar 1982: 121).

Nobody should say that this enquiry is easy. It has to avoid the idea that our new life is 'our own' inherent and self-available possession. It must eschew a notion of 'holiness' in which we seek to ascend to 'God's level', in so far as such a notion rules out the central denial and affirmation about our justification before God stated above. Yet God's promise to us includes a promise that we may be holy, not as a tube or channel, but as agents and non-possessive lovers of God who are *transparent*, bringing God and God's love to light in worship and service. We may press on to make the righteousness from God that depends on grace and faith our own, because Christ has made us his own (Phil. 3: 12). Our sanctification is, then, our transfiguration to this transparency, our coming ourselves to light as God's beloved children 'beholding the glory of the Lord', 'changed into his likeness from one degree of glory to another', 'from the Lord who is the Spirit' (2 Cor. 3: 18). One should retreat from any sweeping judgements about 'religious standpoints' which 'differ in principle', and put in their place a conversation relating the sovereignty of grace to 'how the human self is brought to eschatological glory as self, i.e., as a self-moving and responsible agent' (Root 2004: 18). Recent theological work has mined rich resources in Luther, Thomas Aquinas, and others for this purpose (e.g., Meilaender, this volume (Chapter 5); Root 2004).

It would also be good to continue a conversation after Nygren that reassesses his interpretation of 'self-love' as 'entirely pernicious' (Weaver 2002: 48; cf. Outka 1972: 56–63). In this essay I have identified (1) a form of concern for self that corresponds to a non-possessive desire for fellowship with God, our highest good; (2) an interest in one's own good as it is given by God that makes sense of our responses of joy and gratitude to God. 'It is a self-interest already satisfied, rather than a striving self-interest that is required' (Adams 1987: 187). Finally, there is (3) a will to become in self-giving that 'realest self' brought to light by grace in Christ, a self that as such works for the divine love without counting its works, that approaches God with 'empty hands', and addresses to God the wish, in the words of St Thérèse of Lisieux, 'to be clothed in your own *justice* and to receive from your *love* the eternal possession of *yourself*' (*Catechism* 2000: para. 2011). To describe these stances as an 'egocentric' seeking of one's own 'wholly under the dominion of sin' (Nygren 1953: 722–3) is a mistake. They appear, rather, to reflect self-acceptance, 'an affirmation of oneself in the way one is affirmed by God' (Tillich 1954: 34).

V

Consider again Nygren's approach to the religious source and normative content of Christian love for the neighbour. It is bound to the context of fellowship with God, and springs from the experience of God's *agapē* freely given and gratefully received. The neighbour is every human being, whose well-being is sought for its own sake independently of judgements of comparative value or merit. The positive basis of this regard is a love of enemies grounded in God's love for sinners, with and for whom fellowship may be created where none seemed possible. Delivered from egocentric motives, the lover may give herself freely to the neighbour, without interests in using her as a means to ascend to God, or in otherwise acquisitively possessing her for her own needs or purposes. There is deliverance, too, from loving the neighbour for the sake of her created potential for or likeness to God, or in virtue of the lover of God that she may become. These motives look for the source of the God-relation elsewhere than in the suffering love of Christ, depend on some 'return' to one's love in bringing souls to God, and/or generally restore neighbour-love to the terms of the self's own futile, acquisitively erotic search for value. The upshot is that *agapē* apprehends the neighbour in her concrete condition of need, a need answered by what after all is God's own *agapē* pouring down and out through the Christian.

We may affirm and also revise this statement in keeping with conclusions reached in sections III and IV above. These are (1) that *agapē* generally includes a self-concerned but non-egocentric desire for loving relation with another, for its own sake; (2) that God's love for the sinner in her real individuality is also for a beloved child who lives in Christ and is called as such to participate in the divine life; (3) that this participation may be an object of non-possessive desire fully encompassed by God's gracious mercy and power; and (4) that the sinner as real covenant partner may respond out of that desire in self-giving love for God that corresponds to her God-given nature and thus to her good.

Love of neighbour, then, is based upon God's unconditional and abiding mercy. Our experience of it enables and patterns Christian moral life. The pattern may include, however, a desire and a hope to forge relations of loving communion with others, for their own sake, without prejudice to *agapē*'s faithful, self-giving core (Outka 1992: 88). This hopeful attention and attending hope is part and parcel of a human agent's (non-possessive) zeal for God's glory and all human life within it, even as one remains prepared freely to find one's kindness 'thrown away and lost' (Nygren 1953: 733). Also, our love for others aims at the neighbour's concrete condition as created, fallen, redeemed, and destined in promise for God. Recognizing our sinful self-estrangement from God and God's costly gift of reconciliation and peace, we may hold fast the beloved as a sufferer in need and a recipient of the grace to which we witness. Faithful service to the neighbour will not fail to respond to her creaturely needs in consideration of her dignity before our Creator and Redeemer; it may also creatively and appreciatively seek and elicit the neighbour's eternal validity, her beauty, as authorized by life in God. These appeals to creation and eschatological destiny do not presuppose evasion of God's self-disclosure or a self-glorifying 'use' of the neighbour as a means to God. They are expressions of love for 'the God and Father of our Lord Jesus Christ, who has blessed us in Christ with every spiritual blessing ... even as he chose us in him before the foundation of the world, that we should be holy and blameless before him. He destined us in love to be his sons through Jesus Christ ... through his blood ... [and] has made known to us in all wisdom and insight the mystery of his will ... to unite all things in him, things in heaven and things on earth' (Eph. 1: 3–5, 7, 9, 10).

REFERENCES AND SUGGESTED READING

ADAMS, R. M. (1987). *The Virtue of Faith.* Oxford: Oxford University Press.

—— (1999). *Finite and Infinite Goods.* Oxford: Oxford University Press.

BALTHASAR, H. URS VON (1982). *The Glory of the Lord,* I: *Seeing the Form.* San Francisco: Ignatius Press.

—— (1994). *The Moment of Christian Witness.* San Francisco: Ignatius Press.

—— (2000). *Mysterium Paschale.* San Francisco: Ignatius Press.

—— (2004). *Love Alone is Credible.* San Francisco: Ignatius Press.

BARTH, K. (1957). *Church Dogmatics,* II/1. Edinbugh: T. & T. Clark.

—— (1958). *Church Dogmatics,* IV/2. Edinburgh: T. & T. Clark.

—— (1961). *Church Dogmatics,* III/4. Edinburgh: T. & T. Clark.

BURNABY, J. (1938). *Amor Dei.* London: Hodder & Stoughton.

—— (1970). 'Amor in St. Augustine', in C. W. Kegley (ed.), *The Philosophy and Theology of Anders Nygren,* Carbondale and Edwardsville, Ill.: Southern Illinois University Press, 174–86.

Catechism of the Catholic Church, 2nd edn. (2000). Rome: Libreria Editrice Vaticana.

D'ARCY, M. C. (1956). *The Mind and Heart of Love.* New York: Meridian Books.

FERRE, N. F. S. (ed.) (1967). *Swedish Contributions to Modern Theology.* New York: Harper & Row.

JOHNSON, W. A. (1967). 'Developments in Swedish Theology, 1932–66', in N. F. S. Ferre, *Swedish Contributions to Modern Theology.* New York: Harper & Row, 242–95.

KOSMAN, L. A. (1976). 'Platonic Love', in W. H. Werkmeister (ed.), *Facets of Plato's Philosophy,* Amsterdam: Van Gorcum, 53–69.

LEWIS, C. S. (1949). *The Weight of Glory.* Grand Rapids, Mich.: William B. Eerdmans.

LUBAC, H. DE (1989). *Theological Fragments.* San Francisco: Ignatius Press.

McGINN, B. (1996). 'God as Eros: Metaphysical Foundations of Christian Mysticism', in B. Nassif (ed.), *New Perspectives on Historical Theology,* Grand Rapids, Mich.: William B. Eerdmans, 189–209.

NIEBUHR, H. R. (1951). *Christ and Culture.* New York: Harper & Row.

—— (1956). *The Purpose of the Church and its Ministry.* New York: Harper & Brothers.

NYGREN, A. (1953). *Agape and Eros.* London: SPCK.

O'Donovan, O. (1980). *The Problem of Self-Love in St. Augustine*. New Haven and London: Yale University Press.

Outka, G. H. (1972). *Agape: An Ethical Analysis*. New Haven: Yale University Press.

—— (1992). 'Universal Love and Impartiality', in E. N. Santurri and W. Werpehowski (eds.), *The Love Commandments*, Washington: Georgetown University Press, 1–103.

Pieper, J. (1997). *Faith, Hope, Love*. San Francisco: Ignatius Press.

Root, M. (2004). 'Aquinas, Merit, and Reformation Theology after *The Joint Declaration on the Doctrine of Justification*', *Modern Theology*, 20, 5–22.

Tillich, P. (1954). *Love, Power, and Justice*. Oxford: Oxford University Press.

Weaver, D. F. (2002). *Self-Love and Christian Ethics*. Cambridge: Cambridge University Press.

CHAPTER 26

KENNETH KIRK'S
THE VISION OF GOD

DAVID H. SMITH

THE main point of Kenneth Kirk's learned but too little read book *The Vision of God* is that worship is prior to ethics. Worship is the key to the unselfishness required of all morally serious persons. Unselfishness is attained not through valiant attempts but through discovery and acknowledgement of something more valuable than the self. That happens in worship. Worship should focus the Christian's thoughts on God. 'To look towards God, and from that "look" to acquire insight into both the follies of one's own heart and the needs of one's neighbors...this is something very remote from the quest for "religious experience" for its own sake' (Kirk 1931: 445).

Ethics or service that is not rooted in worship will inevitably be egoistic and self-righteous. Worship roots moral action and service in humility, in the recognition that one is a servant, not God, and therefore fallible and dependent. Without roots in worship even the best social programme and reform succumbs to what Kirk called the 'service of patronage' in which those providing service imagine themselves superior to the recipient of their service. Kirk finds that posture of moral superiority deeply repugnant and fundamentally un-Christian.

I am grateful to the editors and to Professor Timothy Sedgwick for helpful comments on an early draft of this essay, but my greatest debt is to James Swan Tuite, who, as a colleague at the Yale Bioethics Project for six months, has read, discussed, questioned, and edited in ways far beyond the call of duty. Work on this project was partially supported by the Yale Bioethics Project's Donoghne Initiative.

SETTING THE STAGE

The Vision of God is the culmination of a series of four books written over the span of a decade. The first, *Some Principles of Moral Theology,* is a Thomistic introduction to the field; most of Kirk's recurrent themes are clearly stated in it. 'The standing problem of all ethics is the reconciliation of two apparently opposed principles, which may be called respectively the principles of law and liberty, or of authority and individualism' (Kirk 1920: p. ix). On Kirk's reading, Protestantism stands for liberty, Roman Catholicism for authority. The objective of moral theology is to assist free souls that seek perfection; moral theology assumes that persons can't make it on their own. Ethics requires a religious or spiritual foundation. 'The service of others...can only be truly performed by the man who is aspiring to personal holiness', but this should not mean shifting 'the soul's attention from Christ to itself'. As souls reach spiritual maturity, rules and laws may be 'discarded little by little' (Kirk 1920: 19–22). In true Anglican fashion, he sought a *via media* between what he saw as the Roman and Protestant mistakes.

In *Ignorance, Faith and Conformity* and *Conscience and its Problems* Kirk developed two central ideas. First was the Thomistic concept of invincible ignorance. For Kirk it is very clear that if someone is responsibly in error—is not wilfully or negligently in error—her conscience binds. She must follow the dictates of her conscience, even if she is objectively wrong; the moral error is not her fault. In this sense, invincible ignorance secured Kirk's 'liberty' commitment without advocating an unrestrained individualism.

Kirk further argued that in the Church of England custom had significant moral authority, but customs in the UK are diverse and inconsistent (1999: 147). A legitimate custom must be reasonable, but 'reasonable' is hard to define. That difficulty led Roman Catholicism mistakenly to substitute canon law for custom (Kirk 1999: 155–8). That was their great mistake. Individuals must decide for themselves among conflicting customs, he thought, but they should be cautious. 'Whatever "holds the field" of a man's life—law, custom, or non-observance—may, and (except in the last instance) should, be left in possession until conscience gives a further ruling' (Kirk 1999: 159). In other words, only change when the arguments clearly favour departure from custom or habit.

Kirk's discussion of practical reasoning, or *casuistry,* in *Conscience and its Problems* complements his account of custom. The constructive thesis in *Conscience and its Problems* distinguishes the kinds of issues facing a conscientious person who wants to be virtuous. For example, one may face a straightforward conflict between a clear teaching of the Church and the individual's conscientious conclusion. On both sides of the dispute the conclusion and reasoning processes are clear. This is *error*; some party to the dispute—not necessarily the individual, as Kirk is clear that the Church is fallible—must be mistaken in moral reasoning. Eventually, this should probably lead to a parting of the ways, but only *eventually*, because one or other party may have second thoughts.

In fact, communities where a custom has the force of law rarely encounter conflict marked by *error*. Two kinds of conflict are much more common: doubt and perplexity. We may, for example, be uncertain whether a given customary rule applies to a particular situation—perhaps because the situation is novel. We say that genetic fathers are the 'real fathers' of children, but what about adoptive fathers? Children conceived through AID? What about surrogate mothers? We may, in short, be in doubt about which rule to apply, or in doubt about the significance of new facts—for instance, facts about the process of the fertilization of human eggs. These are situations of *doubt*. We are in doubt about what principle or customary practice to apply.

Doubt can be resolved by permissiveness or by always taking the morally most cautious option. In either case I give up on reasoning and follow a path of least resistance. Kirk rejected these options out of hand. The live options for him were *probabiliorism*, which meant that one must act on *the most reasonable option at a given time*, or *probabilism*, which meant that it was legitimate to act on *any one of a (relatively short) menu of reasonable and therefore morally legitimate options*. Although the seventeenth-century Church of England moralists had favoured the more stringent of these options, Kirk preferred the more flexible probabilism.

The third kind of conflict is a true moral dilemma in which two clearly binding rules or customs compete for conscience's allegiance; this is *perplexity*. Debates over abortion and euthanasia involve many individuals in perplexity. They want to respect life and maintain a robust prohibition on killing, but they take respect for individual liberty and the relief of suffering with comparable seriousness. Kirk characterizes their kind of uncertainty as perplexity, not doubt. They know the facts well enough, they know the relevant rules or customs, but they have a very hard time settling conflicts among these rules. Kirk thinks that such situations call for much soul searching, attempts to find courses of action that will honour both moral demands, and patience to see if a way through can be found. But if none of this works, he falls back on utilitarian reasoning and pursuing a course of action that does the least harm.

THE ARGUMENT OF *THE VISION OF GOD*

The general objective of *The Vision of God* is to put Kirk's prior reflections on morality into a larger theological context. Practical reasoning, integrity of conscience, loyalty to authority—these concepts of morality are only a part, and a consequent part, of Christian life. For Kirk, attaining the vision of God is the proper goal of the Christian life. 'Blessed are the pure in heart for they shall see God' (Matt. 5: 8). Thus, Kirk's discussion of the vision of God develops around the problem of disciplining for the true end of Christian life.

Kirk begins by surveying conceptions of the vision in the Hebrew Bible, Jewish, philosophical, and other religious writers up until the time of the New Testament. Despite the disparate viewpoints of these writers, Kirk identifies the common commitment of each to the ideal of a vision of God as the goal of religious life. Beginning with an idea of literally seeing God—which leads to death—and ending with the view that God was best known by faith, mystic or ecstatic experience, Kirk claimed that the central presupposition of the diverse writers was a 'moral affinity' between God and the person; that affinity made the vision possible. Virtually all the writers he surveys contend that God is knowable more fully after death.

Discipline, or moral guidance, the main subject of Kirk's prior writing, is important, he thought, as an aid to attaining the vision. In a theological context, discipline is a means to an end, but it goes without saying that discipline can go wrong. In advising Christians on how to lead a life centred on the vision of God, the tradition has faced two possible pitfalls: institutionalism and formalism. 'Institutionalism' arises from Christian communal formation. Aware that the Church as a collectivity should stand for something, early Church leaders quickly found themselves trying to enforce a set of moral commitments on all members. Thus they mistakenly came to stress practices of excommunication and public penance that clearly and definitively marked Christian communal boundaries. Those practices were explicable as strategies for maintaining the public face of the Church, but were pastorally unhelpful in assisting persons to grow in the faith. Church leaders, on Kirk's account, increasingly thought of principles as necessary to assure external conformity, rather than as means for individuals to secure purity of life.

Moreover, preoccupation with image misled the Church to focus on conspicuous and major sins, glossing over the smaller and less visible betrayals and harms that comprise the daily life of most Christians. Many average Christians thought they had no need of repentance and discipline, because they were not guilty of the gross sins on which the Church focused. The Church was right to see that trying to be faithful entailed moral demands, but it found itself taking a stand on the wrong thing—perhaps better, on the wrong kind of thing—on social conformity rather than the requirements of spiritual growth.

'Formalism' goes hand in hand with institutionalism. It is the formulation of general rules of discipline. The sense that the Christian life requires self-denial was right, and the limited amount of codification that can be found in the New Testament is all to the good. But the early Church was wrong to depart from St Paul's obvious resistance to systems of codification. Formalism runs many risks: it tends to focus on behaviour rather than motivation; it shifts the fulcrum of ethics to a focus on the human subject. But focus on one's own moral status leads to self-righteousness, scrupulosity, and eventually despair. A focus on general rules by-passes the key fact that the first move in Christian ethics is not action but receptivity, awaiting the transforming grace of God.

When grace is shifted into the background in this way, God can appear only as judge and lawgiver. The result is a moral irrationalism that stresses obedience for its own sake, or a 'religion sublimated into etiquette, although an etiquette attended by formal sanctions' (Kirk 1931: 138). The core problem of formalism, of a Christian ethics based on rules, is that it mistakenly assumes that once one really hears the Gospel of grace, one's only problem is figuring out what the requirements of altruistic witness are.

To the contrary, there is a prior task or calling: putting oneself in a position to be renewed in spirit. A process of growth in character orientation must accompany the intellectual task of morality. Forgetting or minimizing the importance of the spiritual health of the agent is rooted in a notion that even thinking about one's own joy and fulfilment is corrupt. Kirk thinks that Jesus *helped* persons forget themselves by stressing the importance of seeking joy and blessedness in the vision of God. Christians who took this exhortation seriously found themselves thinking about God, rather than themselves. Self-forgetfulness can be attained only indirectly.

Thus, on one level, there is no doubt that Joseph Fletcher (1966) was right when in the 1960s he claimed Kirk as a source of his defence of 'situation ethics'. The critique of formalism in *The Vision of God* is clearly in the spirit of the defence of liberty of conscience in Kirk's earlier work, as well as of the discussions of 'doubt' and 'perplexity' in *Conscience and its Problems*. In those earlier discussions of morality Kirk had clearly shown appreciation of the fact that 'circumstances alter cases'. Kirk was very suspicious of the stress on moral codes that he saw in the Catholicism and Protestantism of his day. He wanted to stand for gracious and personal moral reasoning against those religiously inadequate and psychologically destructive options.

But there are at least two ways in which Fletcher's theological ethics and Kirk's moral theology are out of synch. One can be seen if we recall Kirk's discussion of custom in *Ignorance, Faith and Conformity*. Far from leading Kirk to advocate radical non-conformity, the rejection of formalism led him to urge patient compliance with custom that had proved itself supportive of attempts at spiritual growth. While it is true that in extreme cases of perplexity he fell back on utilitarian reasoning, this was clearly meant as a rare and undesirable step to take. Thus the whole style and tone of his ethic is different from Fletcher's. Kirk thought that individual Christians should inform themselves about their tradition, pray, reason, and seek advice. Custom and tradition were resources rather than dated moral prejudices, however much it might turn out that the thoughtful Christian had to depart from them.

More fundamentally, Kirk built his understanding of ethics on the importance of character formation and spiritual self-discipline. On that score, formalism was not too hard; it was misguided and too easy. It may well be that Kirk was too hard on the socially necessary impulse to generalize, but if he was, it was because he wanted to defend an ethic that required more than the formal rules of communities can. In his own way Kirk was defending an ethic of virtue, not rules.

This leads to the last component of spiritual discipline that Kirk discusses, the issue of *rigorism*. He was very clear that Christianity required some level of self-renunciation, some form of rigorism, but a large section of *The Vision of God* is devoted to discussion of ways in which the legitimate impulse went astray. Like Troeltsch, Kirk thought that Jesus' ethic was heroic and rigoristic, particularly as regards wealth and money; Paul's ethic was rigoristic about sex. But those starting-points led many Christians to build ideals of life and codifications that got things badly wrong. In general, from the Patristic period to the High Middle Ages, the history of Christian ethics seemed to Kirk to be a series of cycles starting with extensive codification. When those codes proved too rigorous for one reason or another, the result was a lax attitude toward self-discipline, which would then be followed by another rigorist reformation.

Kirk devotes two chapters of *The Vision of God* to the development of monasticism as a rigoristic movement and to the opposition to monastic rigorism in 'humanism'. Kirk has some sympathy with the spiritual quest that drove persons to the desert and then into monastic communities. Seeing the vision of God surely requires renunciation and asceticism. But the early monks too frequently focused their attention on their experience. If self-forgetfulness is our objective, focusing on one's own experience is not the way to get there. And to serve others, as glimpsing the vision of God requires, means that one must remain part of some human community.

Kirk thought that some leaders of monastic movements were right to see that prayer should be the primary Christian activity and to dwell on the contemplation of God in worship. They forgot that to be of value worship should lead to self-forgetfulness and service; they were wrong to insist that the fullest renunciation necessarily required celibacy, poverty, and fasting. What is to be renounced varies more radically from person to person; true renunciation may well not be highly visible.

Kirk is clearly more sympathetic to the 'humanist' alternative to rigorism. He found that in the Basilian and Benedictine reforms of monasticism; he thinks that Benedict's stress on service and de-emphasis on the individual monk's own emotions and experiences was particularly helpful. And he supports the movement from public to private confession on principle, although in fact it led to too much preoccupation with getting the codified penalties for sin correct. Only Abelard's attention to *intention* led to a way to rescue penance from formalism.

Kirk's understanding of the doctrinal bases of humanism is more interesting. He is clear that Christianity can never accept a complete naturalism; but the trick— first seen clearly in Clement—is to combine true Christianity and sound learning. Augustine appears in this context as a hero. On Kirk's terms Augustine opposed rigorism against the Manichees, then turned and opposed naturalism in the

Pelagian controversy. Augustine's great core idea 'that the essence of grace is *love* and the essence of man's salvation that he should become *loving*' could very well stand as the subtitle for Kirk's main claims (1931: 343). He thought that Bernard of Clairvaux captured Augustine's spirit in his attack on negative asceticism and his grasp of the facts that authentic contemplation leads to service and that the great risk of service is spiritual pride.

Fulfilment of the possibilities of Christian humanism, however, had to await the thirteenth century and the work of Thomas Aquinas, 'perhaps the first Christian philosopher to take the corporeal character of human existence calmly' (Kirk 1931: 384). Kirk characterizes Thomas's thought as an other-worldly naturalism or humanism. He had learned from Augustine, Bernard, and the Victorines, but he was clear that monastic or 'religious' life was not the only starting-point for the race to perfection. All religious and moral impulses and practices should be subjected to the test of reason. The goal was not pure intellectualism; the contemplative life was available to all. Indeed the egotism of the intellectual is a serious problem in contemplation.

This led Kirk to defend a version of the double standard for Christians. He found the notion that the standards for the religious and for the ordinary person were intrinsically different to be morally and religiously repugnant, confining most Christians to a second-class citizenship in the City of God. He calls that idea the 'invalid form' of the double standard, but he sees why the institutional church was forced into it: if there is no certain gain for the individual in renouncing the world and entering a convent or monastery, then why make those sacrifices? It's a fine example of the problems associated with *institutionalism*. The important insight that there are many ways to the vision of God was corrupted when it was made into a simplified general ecclesiological policy.

The 'good' form of the double standard acknowledges that individuals are in fact at different stages of spiritual growth, so their appropriate next steps are not all the same; but everyone has the same goal, the same ultimate possibility. We live in a world of pluralism. Everyone tries to grow in participation in the vision of God; monastic life may help some persons at some point in their journey, but there is only one kind of vision, accessible to all people on their journey. Really, for Kirk it's not just a 'double' standard, but a plurality of *de facto* standards for the spiritual life. Worship provides necessary support for all along the way.

Prayer is the centre of worship, but Kirk is quite clear that not all forms of prayer are created equal. He resists petitionary prayer as 'Protestant and pagan', because it amounts to trying to manipulate the deity; nor does he favour meditation with a view to progress in virtue or 'practical self-exhortation to activity'—using worship simply as a crutch to attain pre-chosen ends. That is no prayer at all, and the 'muscular Christian . . . will learn to despise and dispense with reveries of this kind' (Kirk 1931: 441). True prayer is contemplative, and involves an opening of the self to God; it is a kind of listening and learning. Making space for growth.

THE ISSUE OF SEEKING FOR A REWARD

Kirk's strong affirmation of the legitimacy of seeking a reward for oneself set him at odds with both the Protestant movement he knew and many other forms of Protestant ethics. For whatever reason, Kirk worked with a stereotype of Protestantism, and not a very well-informed stereotype at that. He gave little attention to the great Reformers, to Wesley, or really to any non-Catholic figure. He thought that the Protestant movement began with an admirable stress on the promise of God's salvation, but that, as institutionalized, it quickly evolved into a movement that put the stress not on the gracious God but on the Christian's own *experience* of God, and not on moral reasoning but on conformity to a code. It stressed individual experience and rules, rather than the vision of God and moral reasoning. Protestant prayer was, he thought, strictly petitionary; that seemed to him to be just another form of 'auxiliary effort', and quite removed from the contemplative relationship with God that genuine worship nurtures.

On his own terms Kirk was quite justified in rejecting an individualist and rule-constrained piety, and there is much such religiosity in the Protestant and Catholic worlds today. But it is about as relevant to an understanding of the best Protestant theology and worship as the practice of the sale of indulgences is to St Thomas's theological ethics. In fact, however, Kirk's understanding of Christian life and faith was radically different from some emphases in Protestant ethics among theologians who were roughly his contemporaries.

The most striking contrast is with Anders Nygren, whose *Agape and Eros* was discussed in Chapter 25. Nygren drew a stark contrast between the seeking love of *eros* and the giving love of *agapē*. He had great admiration for Augustine's synthesis of these concepts in the doctrine of *caritas*, but Augustine was wrong, or at least misled. The key New Testament notion of love is *agapē*. This is particularly powerful in the thought of St Paul. When Paul wrote that 'nothing can separate us from the love of Christ' (Rom. 8: 35), he meant God's love, but Augustine turns that on its head to mean our loving of God. Luther's rediscovery of the primacy of *agapē* was the linchpin of the Reformation and the rediscovery of genuine Christian ethics.

Among those who learned much from Nygren was Paul Ramsey. In *Basic Christian Ethics*, he suggested that the idea of love for God, emotionally powerful as it might be, was actually a conceptual mistake. *Faith* should characterize the Christian's relationship with God; *love*, properly understood, was a kind of giving or acting to protect others who were in need, a deficient copy of God's archetypal love for us seen in Christ. *Agapē* presupposed faith. Seeking a reward for the self was basically to misunderstand what Christianity is all about. The Christian's own most important needs have been met by the salvation offered by God in Christ. Liberated from concern for self, Christians could turn and devote their lives to meeting the needs of *others*. Whatever the other needs, that *agapē* seeks for him.

True Christian ethics for Ramsey, Barth, and others is an ethics of witness—of testimony to the miracle of salvation.

Kirk could have agreed that someone's relationship with God is the core of any serious Christian ethic; indeed, he held that no ethic in which that relationship is missing could be anything other than an ethic of pride and patronage. But he thought that the Christian moral life must start with recognition of the importance of sustaining our relationship with God. That's what worship is all about. Whatever else it does, the experience of worship reminds someone that she is limited, not God, and appropriately oriented to something beyond herself. Sustaining that identity of humility and enjoyment takes the kind of intentional action to keep one's orientation correct that anyone who responds to an extraordinary opportunity has to engage in. The most certainly reliable form of that intentional action entails making time in the day for contemplation and worship.

Thus Kirk held a distinctly Augustinian, and generally Catholic, understanding of love, in which the legitimacy of the self's quest for fulfilment and the primacy of our self-discipline to that end are acknowledged. Although he did not use these terms, he distinguished self-respect or self-regard from selfishness. The quest for self-respect or genuine self-regard should be associated with seeking fulfilment; that happens in a relationship to something transcendent: God.

Seeking the vision of God is not selfishness, but the way to overcome selfishness. An apparently altruistic theory rests on a false premiss—that any of us can simply assume our salvation and then move to reflection and action. That amounts to a kind of arrogance: forgetting that morally legitimate agency requires spiritual nurture. A more humble approach acknowledges the validity of our concern for self up front. One grows in love; as we come to know and understand God better, our love for others increases. But we have to learn how to be the kind of people who can love; it is not automatic.

SELF-FORGETFULNESS AND
THE VISION OF GOD

Kirk's great psychological insight was that the knot of egotism could only be untied by discovery of something that mattered more than oneself. The claim is reminiscent of Josiah Royce's discussion of loyalty in *The Philosophy of Loyalty*. Royce argued that human beings find their salvation when they learn to live for a cause, when they become fully engaged in the fate of something beyond themselves. He went on to distinguish among loyalties, criticizing some as servile, and praising the highest form as 'loyalty to loyalty', a suggestive but not immediately clear goal. H. R. Niebuhr learned much from Royce, as a reading of *Radical Monotheism and Western Culture* makes clear. But Niebuhr went on crisply to distinguish among polytheistic, henotheistic, and truly monotheistic forms of loyalty.

Comparing Niebuhr's ideas with Kirk's serves to highlight features on both sides. Kirk is explicit that an ethic that is not rooted in some form of the vision of God must go astray, that it can lead only to the philanthropy of patronage—or pride—rather than to an ethic of humility. On the face of it, at least, Niebuhr's understanding of the role of loyalty to God is more irenic. Certainly that was the general force of *Christ and Culture*, one of his most important books. But *Radical Monotheism* doesn't have much positive to say about egoism, polytheism, and henotheism; they are forms of social faith to be rejected.

Niebuhr's analysis of those forms of social faith is a much more nuanced discussion of alternatives to the love of God than a reader will find in Kirk. What is less apparent in Niebuhr's work is discussion of how one comes to discover the God to be loved. With all his limits, Kirk was clearer about this. We should put ourselves in a position where we are likely to focus our attention on God rather than ourselves. Focusing on our own experiences will be counter-productive. How to put oneself in the right position? The short answer, which requires amplification, is 'go to church'! The key, Kirk thought, is the contemplation that worship should stimulate. The idea that worship and ethics can be separated would have struck Kirk as a disastrous mistake. Worship is, or at least should be, the time and place in which selves are properly oriented and enabled to turn and serve conscientiously.

A good Kirkian moralist would write about worship as well as ethics. She or he would devote considerable attention to issues of spiritual discipline—character formation—assisted by worship. Kirk could affirm with Augustine that the Christian should 'love God then do as you will', but his whole point is that coming to love God in a way that will enable a person to be true to God requires a spiritual discipline. Spiritual growth is a necessary, maybe even a sufficient, condition for moral growth. And spiritual growth begins in worship.

WORSHIP AND ETHICS

From Kirk's point of view, moral and ascetic theology are inseparable. Prayer is not only a matter of Christian devotion; it is the spiritual practice field for moral agency and reflection. I have already mentioned Kirk's criticisms of petitionary prayer as 'Protestant and pagan', as well as his dissatisfaction with brooding meditation on how to become a better person. An early twenty-first-century reader might expect these discussions to lead to consideration of liturgy, but they do not. In fact, important as worship is in his overall scheme, he says too little about it. He makes three key affirmations.

First, worship is prior to ethics, because it is through worship that egoism can be transcended. Persons have to be transformed to be moral, and worship is the way in which that process of transformation is initiated.

Second, just what counts as worship is not easy to specify. Ritual can go wrong. Part of this is a matter of human style and intentionality. I have already mentioned his criticisms of various forms of prayer as being overly demanding or moralistic. But more fundamentally, worship is a matter of placing oneself in a position to receive. The Christian waits upon God's action. Truly efficacious worship must start with God; experiences of genuine worship come upon us as accidents, for God is the initiator. Worship simply entails being ready.

Worship depends not upon our own activities, but upon the activities that God brings to bear upon us; to them we are forced to react as worshippers . . . If without self-scrutiny and self-torment a man can remain alive to the goodness in his environment, it will draw out all that is best in him, leading him nearer to the perfect goodness revealed in the Incarnate Lord. (Kirk 1931: 465 f.)

Moreover, as this quotation suggests, worship may well occur outside normal ritual contexts. The requisite attitude of openness is the core of the worship experience. Kirk's understanding of worship was broad. We rightly stress the 'attitude' rather than the 'experience' of worship (Kirk 1931: 464). The vision of God to which it leads is not reserved for the few; mystical experience is the commonest and greatest of human accidents.

Wherever a man's mind has been uplifted, his temptations thwarted, his sorrows comforted, his resolutions strengthened, his aberrations controlled, by purity, innocence, love or beauty—indeed, whenever he has, even for a moment, recognized and responded to the distinction between good and evil, between better or worse,—such a man has had in part the mystical experience. (Kirk 1931: 464)

He does not imply that these experiences are confined to Christians, let alone to experiences of formal worship. God may well be glimpsed in contexts that at first glance seem to be secular. In effect, he is acknowledging the power of natural piety, recognizing that 'the wind blows where it wills' (John 3: 8, RSV).

And thirdly, the word 'attitude' in this discussion is crucial. Worship is associated with an attitude of reverence, of recognizing the reality of God beyond the self. Kirk offered no fully worked-out doctrine of God; it is the beyondness or transcendence of God that is crucial for his moral argument. The moral life starts by looking to God for our fulfilment; we look beyond ourselves. Increasingly, we look in a spirit of reverence and respect to the source of our being. We come to respect ourselves as God's children; we are grateful for our creation and preservation; we love God and the world that God has made. These attitudes are forms of human excellence, or character; they are simultaneously religious and moral. Devotion secures the virtues that are central to the moral life.

Where do we look for a model of devotion and of the Christian life? To the example of the Christ as portrayed in the Gospels and to the Pauline writings. On the one hand, Jesus shows us what it means to devote oneself to God and God's cause. His life, as portrayed by diverse faithful (and broken) disciples, illustrates turning to God and in that turning learning to love each other. There are many ways to love, but all are rooted in the love of God. On the other hand, the portraits of Jesus that have come down to us show us something of the depth of God's love for us.

AN ASSESSMENT

In the USA, the Niebuhrs are the natural people to compare with Kirk; in Germany, Karl Barth and Emil Brunner; in the Catholic world, Jacques Maritain or Bernhard Häring; in Judaism, Martin Buber or Franz Rosenzweig; in the UK, William Temple. For all these writers the experience of World War I was critical; the issue of human identity was central. Kirk served as a chaplain in France in World War I, and eventually became a bishop in the Church of England; he was from the beginning of his professional career a man of, and a leader in, the institutional church. Consistent with this, his work was more oriented to the real life of the Church (or synagogue) than that of any of those contemporaries with the possible exception of Barth or Häring. Compared with Barth, Kirk is an earthling, preoccupied with nitty-gritty individual problems. His *œuvre* is not a great imaginative theological reconstruction, but is meant to be a working out of what being Christian meant in his time and place. His legacy stands in the work of Austin Farrer, Gordon Dunstan, and others.

The other side of this comparison is that Kirk's conception of the task of a Christian moralist was more individualistic than that of most of his great contemporaries. The reader will look in vain to Kirk for a creative discussion of a just society or for commentary on contemporary political issues *per se. Conscience and its Problems* makes clear that Kirk was interested in, and knowledgeable about, social and political issues of the day—indeed, that he was willing to take stands on them. But that was not the purpose of his serious writing. That writing was targeted on clarifying the relationship between a Christian, her God, and her church. His imagined reader was someone who had seen death in the trenches, or its aftermath, and now wanted to lead a Christian life while coping with that experience. His ethic is only indirectly a *social* ethic.

On another level it remains unclear just whom it is an ethic for. On the one hand, the writing and authorities cited, particularly in *The Vision of God*, are very churchy. On the other hand, there is a stress on practical rationality, custom, and the idea that the attitude of worship is in no way confined to Christian liturgical celebrations. As a good Thomist, Kirk supported the *analogia entis* and resisted the idea that faith and reason were radically discontinuous; the UK of his day seemed permeated with cultural forms that were distillations of centuries of faithful Christian observance. Thus substitution of the authority of custom for canonical religious moral teaching made sense.

But is it possible plausibly to maintain this coherence between Christian and secular morality in our time? From Barth to Hauerwas, some of the most creative theologians have thought not. *Nein.* Not after the trenches of the 1910s, the chambers of Auschwitz, or the shallowness of much modern culture. In so far as Kirk had a response to this challenge, it has two parts. On the one hand, he wanted the Church of England freed from subservience to the national state. The two institutions should be distinct. The Church must not be co-opted.

On the other hand, his implicit diagnosis of the problems of his time is different from that of the more radical theologians. It is more psychological (he read William James with great appreciation) and could fit with that of a Frankfurt School writer like Erich Fromm, who argued that the roots of the mid-twentieth century's social pathology lay in religious, particularly German Protestant, insistence on the worthlessness of the self and the value of pure altruism. Totalitarianism enters when self-respect is destroyed. Seeking *one's good* in the vision of God, by contrast, implies the value and worth of the self. A rigorism that devalues all of this world should, therefore, yield to a humanism that celebrates goodness wherever it may be found.

Summing Up

As already suggested, Kirk raised issues pertinent to his own time and relevant to a Western world nearly 100 years after he wrote. The catholicity and down-to-earthness of his approach, the 'Christian humanism' as he would have called it, remain attractive. A learned and disciplined writer, Kirk was anything but a specialist in theoretical issues for their own sake. The real heart of Christianity was the parish, with real Christian people; scholarship should be in their service. No one needed to tell Kirk about diversity, moral recalcitrance, death, and disappointment.

So is reading Kirk now to become acquainted with a sufficient statement of moral theology? This writer suggests some adjustments.

For a writer as concerned with worship as Kirk was, his failure to discuss liturgy is striking. His discussion of worship is quite compatible with a liturgical theology in which the individual contemplates the liturgical drama as the member of an audience watches an opera. The focus of attention is on the elements as *the* sacramental body and blood of Christ. Much work in the liturgical revival—stimulated by the very Anglo-Catholic movement of which Kirk was an intellectual leader—sees liturgy very differently. The worshipper is not an individual member of an audience watching a drama. Rather, the members of the congregation *are* the (social) body of Christ that comes together, breaks itself in the offertory, then receives spiritual renewal through Holy Communion. The focus is not on the personal experience, even contemplation, of the individual, but on the social process, creation and renewal of a special kind of community. Communion, community, and reconciliation are the major events, and a focus on what happens to or with the elements is displaced.

This contemporary liturgical theory has its own problems. It can lead to quasi-deification of the community itself, glossing over the fact that to be the Body of Christ the Church must be faithful to God. Despite use of the Pauline metaphor of the Church as the social body of Christ, anything resembling deification of the church community is very un-Pauline. St Paul asks the factionalized Corinthians 'is Christ divided?' If for him the Church were all there is to the body of Christ, this argument would carry no weight at all, for the Corinthian church surely was divided. Christ's body transcends the church militant; good community is not a sufficient account of the effect of the Eucharist.

Nevertheless, the more recent liturgical theologies do capture something important that Kirk left out of account and that might have strengthened his argument. For they suggest the objectivity of the Eucharistic process without an appeal to magical metaphysics or suspension of disbelief in the minds of the members of the congregation. They have the effect of explaining how the Eucharist breaks down concern for self and replaces it with a sense of membership in community. Egoism is broken without a self-contradictory effort to forget oneself or an introverted focus on one's own experience. That's exactly what Kirk was looking to worship for.

In fact, a more nearly adequate liturgical theology might combine elements of Kirk's view with the more recent theories. The liturgical movements of the latter half of the twentieth century are to a significant extent a form of piety focused on the Holy Spirit, on God's presence with us in the community. As mentioned, this can lead to the community's preoccupation with itself, rather than with God. Kirk's implicit liturgical theology, by contrast, centres attention on the Father, with the Son as our teacher and companion. Keeping that vision as a complement assures that the Father is not displaced and that the Church sees itself as a community of response.

In any case, Kirk was surely right to connect worship with the establishment of Christian attitudes and the formation of Christian character. Participation in the liturgical drama forms the agency of persons; it influences them. Kirk conceded that other experiences might have the same effect. The power of the Spirit is not confined to the Church. But the first step in any genuine, and certainly in any Christian, morality is something like the personal reorientation that Kirk associated with the vision of God. If one is surprised by the vision in some other context, so much the better; but it only makes sense to put oneself in a place where spiritual growth is likely to be nurtured. That means participation in worship. Worship provides the perspective and orientation necessary to Christian agency.

Kirk was a forerunner of much of the late twentieth- and early twenty-first-century moral theory's focus on character and practices, and he saw that Christian *worship* practice was a key component in establishing forms of character that could sustain and reform social practices or customs. Thus, on his account, it makes more sense to speak of a Christian woman or man than of a Christian *rule*. No one finds the vision of God in this life; no one is fully transformed. There are no perfect Christians. But Christianity in the first instance is about selves and their growth; rules are, among other things, means to that end. Thus the relationship between moral rules and the real moral life is always ambiguous. Rules are important, but instrumental, and they have to be flexible. People are playing on different stages throughout their lives, and few are on the same stage at any one time.

Thus Kirk's stress on character as more important than rules has many strengths. It allows him to acknowledge moral complexity in the demands of love, or of any other rule. His embrace of probabilism fits with the intuition that at any one time there may be more than one 'right' answer to a difficult moral issue. Moreover, he recognized that the character of a moralist could not be separated entirely from the quality of his or her intellectual work or advice. Moralists, like all persons, are fallible; moral reflection is not disembodied but comprises a conversation not only with contemporaries but—as the form of Kirk's work clearly shows—with the past.

The most striking thing about Kirk's discussion of rules is the role he gave to custom. The effect is to build flexibility into his perspective and to acknowledge what we all know to be true—that most morality, and some of the best morality, is a matter of habituation. Good customs sustain persons in the face of weakness of will, pride, sensuality, and greed. They can be gently and helpfully educational and corrective.

However, not all customs are good, and Kirk's theory offers little in the way of a general perspective from which general cultural critique might be mounted. The issue can be seen on two levels. Natural law thinkers such as Richard McCormick, SJ, developed a notion of natural law in which a set of general goods for human persons were specified. Rules, cultures, or regimes which made it impossible for human beings to attain these basic goods were then subject to critique. Much the same intellectual move was made by Reinhold Niebuhr and John C. Bennett, who translated the mandates of the Gospel into a set of general social imperatives: to seek justice, preserve order, and secure freedom. If Kirk worked out anything like this schema, it was certainly not central in *The Vision of God*.

Moreover, Kirk has no equivalent to what Michael Walzer (1987) has called 'connected criticism', in which some concepts or commitments central to a culture are reinterpreted and renewed so as to show the extent to which the community has betrayed them. That was the task of the great prophets of Israel: recalling the people to their foundational commitments. Kirk comes closer to this than to the development of a general set of moral standards or ideals, but his use of custom is largely conservative and pastoral rather than interpretive and prophetic. The effect of these two omissions is to leave his ethical perspective more conservative and relativistic than many will find comfortable. The problem is not that Kirk was himself too conservative for his time and place (although this *may* also have been true). The problem is that he did not develop the conceptual resources from which criticism of unjust customs, rules, or institutions might be developed.

Two American Christian ethical theories are stronger on this score, although neither of them shows the appreciation for custom that is so refreshing in Kirk. One is the Niebuhrian perspective previously referred to. For Reinhold Niebuhr himself, the 'love–justice dialectic', with its use of the concept of equality 'love in terms of logic', provided a standard against which rules and customs could be measured. The Niebuhr of *The Children of Light and the Children of Darkness* (1944) did that very pragmatically. John Bennett systematized this idea somewhat, and gave it his own twist. He talked about a set of universally important social goods, and argued that it was important to work out provisional implications of them in any time and place. These were 'middle axioms' or moral imperatives of intermediate generality, rather like the bioethics principle of informed consent. Armed with a concept like this, drawn from his British contemporary and fellow bishop William Temple, Kirk could have both maintained his commitment to custom and found a basis for cultural criticism as needed.

Another option might have presented itself. Kirk was very clear about the importance of loyalty among persons and to the Church. In the United States Paul Ramsey worked out an ethic largely based on loyalty, or what he once called 'covenant fidelity'. Ramsey argued that there were certain forms of relationship—for example, between wives and husbands, physicians and patients, researchers and subjects, soldiers and their enemies—that entailed moral commitments if they were to be truly human and humane relations. Customs that undermined those commitments of fidelity should be challenged, for the moral dimension of those commitments was non-negotiable.

Ramsey's ethic was rigorous, from Kirk's viewpoint too rigorous, and it could seem inflexible. He meant to include the kind of adjustment to uncertainty and fallibility that Kirk stressed, but the controversy-centred form of much of his writing means that discovering the nuances of his view is not always easy. Still, an ethic that combined Kirk's stress on fulfilment in love, Ramsey's fidelity principle, and some Niebuhrian pragmatism would be a formidable heir to the work of those great theological moralists of the twentieth century.

References and Suggested Reading

FLETCHER, J. (1966). *Situation Ethics: The New Morality.* Philadelphia: Westminster Press.

KEMP, E. W. (1959). *The Life and Letters of Kenneth Escott Kirk, Bishop of Oxford 1937–1954.* London: Hodder & Stoughton.

KIRK, K. E. (1920). *Some Principles of Moral Theology and their Application.* London and New York: Longmans, Green and Co.

——(1925). *Ignorance, Faith and Conformity: Studies in Moral Theology.* London and New York: Longmans, Green and Co.

——(1931). *The Vision of God: The Christian Doctrine of the Summum Bonum.* London and New York: Longmans, Green and Co.

——(1999). *Conscience and its Problems: An Introduction to Casuistry.* Louisville, Ky.: Westminster/John Knox Press.

NIEBUHR, R. (1944). *The Children of Light and the Children of Darkness.* New York: Charles Scribner's Sons.

——(1951). *Christ and Culture.* New York: Harper & Brothers.

——(1960). *Radical Monotheism and Western Culture.* Lincoln, Nebr.: University of Nebraska Press.

RAMSEY, P. (1950). *Basic Christian Ethics.* New York: Scribner and Sons.

——(1970). *The Patient as Person.* New Haven: Yale University Press.

ROYCE, J. (1908). *The Philosophy of Loyalty.* New York: Macmillan.

VACEK, E. C. (1994). *Love, Human and Divine: The Heart of Christian Ethics.* Washington: Georgetown University Press.

WALZER, M. (1987). *Interpretation and Social Criticism.* Cambridge, Mass.: Harvard University Press.

CHAPTER 27

H. RICHARD NIEBUHR'S *CHRIST AND CULTURE*

D. M. YEAGER

IN his introduction to the 1960 reissue of Ernst Troeltsch's *The Social Teaching of the Christian Churches*, Niebuhr remarks that Troeltsch valued theology as 'the place where man might have in view his relations both to the eternal and the unconditioned and to the historical and relative in all their intricate interrelations' (Niebuhr 1960: I. 9). It has often been noted (beginning with Niebuhr 1951: p. xii) that *Christ and Culture* extends the work of Troeltsch by enlarging his church/sect/mysticism typology, but the more revealing line of continuity seems to me to lie in their common interest in the situation of the person in relation to the unconditioned and the contingent, eternity and time, God and history.

In Niebuhr's view, Christian ethics finds its meaning, function, and purpose in the field of 'lesser choices' that opens around the agent as the space of responsive encounter. It is a field of freedom (that is, choice), but we occupy it as dependent respondents, not as independent, sovereign selves. Although we act and are accountable for our actions, 'there has always been a choice prior to our own', and the consequences of our acts always depend on the responses of others (Niebuhr 1951: 250). In origin we are doubly dependent. We are flung into existence by a suprahistorical power—variously called Fate or Chance or God—that both establishes and, in the end, brings to nothing every individual mortal life and every civilization. But we are dependent as well on the contingencies of historical location. 'We have not chosen to be social beings, immeasurably dependent on our fellows, nor have we chosen our culture; we have come to consciousness in a society and among established human works' (Niebuhr 1951: 250). Having been 'elected to live' by that transcendent Other and having been equipped to live by some concrete community of others, we then encounter, in a continuing social process, the expectations, deeds, and demands of both God and our innumerable social companions. Our situation is one of freedom, creativity, and hope, but also of anxiety, conflict, and inadequacy, not least because there seems so little obvious harmony between the call to love and serve that absolute Other and the require-ments of making our way in our social world of human achievement, human demands, and human sin. If we are to have any hope of responding well, it seems that we must clarify how these two dimensions are related.

In assessing the success and the value of *Christ and Culture*, commentators understandably focus on the five models of Christian ethics that Niebuhr develops in chapters 2–6. It is, after all, the usefulness of this Weberian typology that has kept the book continuously in print for half a century. Despite widespread criticism, much of which simply misses the mark (see Gustafson 2001; Yeager 2003), the text remains virtually unsurpassed as a teaching tool—a device for introducing the-ology students, the laity, or people who are unfamiliar with Christianity to the predominating 'motifs' or 'positions' that map the variations, fractures, and fissures among Christian patterns of belief (patterns that Niebuhr is careful to say 'cannot be made to coincide with the historic distinctions among the great churches'—that is, the denominations (Niebuhr 1951: 129)). Yet a gaze too fixed on the proffered 'ideal types' can miss the subtle constructive dimension of the text and can even distort our understanding of the typology itself, flattening it out and reducing it to a neutralized tool (or, some would say, an inadequately neutralized tool) for the external understanding of an abstracted 'object': Christian ethics.

FAITH, HISTORY, AND ETHICS

To appreciate the richness of *Christ and Culture*, we have to begin with history. This is a hazardous departure point because, as James Gustafson has forcefully argued in his introduction to the expanded, fiftieth anniversary edition, the book 'is not a history of Christian theological ethics or Christian theology'. As he points out, those who complain about the book on the grounds of 'historical inadequacy' are holding the work to standards that are not applicable to enquiries of this socio-logical genre (Gustafson 2001: pp. xxvi–xxvii).

Yet, as Niebuhr himself remarks, 'History is a notoriously ambiguous term' (1949: 91). In *The Meaning of Revelation* (1941) and in two long-unpublished papers (1949, 1955) written at about the same time that he published *Christ and Culture*, he distinguishes among multiple meanings, including: (1) objective history or 'the course of events in their larger or smaller connections' (1955: 78); (2) 'the recording, remembering and re-enacting of events' (1949: 91) or 'the present activity that makes the human past its object' (1955: 78); and (3) the theory and actuality of social process (1949: 92). This last verges on, but is, I think, more limited than (4) the situation of historical being in time and culture that constitutes, as the human condition, the wide frame of our finitude and contingency—temporal being or timefulness, as contrasted with eternity. The activity of interpreting 'history' may take 'history' in any one of these four senses as its object. In addition to specifying the different objects of interest that are folded under the signifier 'history', Niebuhr also differentiates two diverse intentions that motivate enquiry: 'Every interpretation of history doubtless moves between the polarities of contemplative and practical reason, but there are significant differences here between those who regard [history] ... with worshipping wonder and those who look at it with the concern of doers of deeds' (1949: 93). In the former case, we seek understanding and appreciation; in the latter case, we seek, as accountable agents, to make our responses more honest and discerning, more realistic, and more fruitful—that is, more likely to contribute to what is constructive, good, and God-pleasing, and less likely to harm our companions and to corrupt and destroy that in our social world which is life-giving and life-enhancing.

Christ and Culture is certainly not history in the first sense: it is not a detached, and 'external' study of the 'course of events' involving Christians in the past. We will, however, find much more to appreciate in *Christ and Culture* if we understand the degree to which it is intensely attentive to history in the other three senses, and if we appreciate what Niebuhr demonstrates here about attending to 'history' as doers of deeds. Ten years earlier, in *The Meaning of Revelation*, Niebuhr had written:

It is not enough to say that men live in time and must conceive all things as temporal and historical. Doubtless it is true that all reality has become temporal for us. But our historical relativism affirms the historicity of the subject even more than that of the object; man, it points out, is not only in time but time is in man. Moreover and more significantly, the time that is in man is not abstract but particular and concrete; it is not a general category of time but rather the time of a definite society with distinct language, economic and political relations, religious faith and social organization. (1941: 9–10)

This insight remains central to all of his treatments of ethics, right up through the manuscript on which he was working at the time of his death. The proper background against which *Christ and Culture* should be read is the sociology of knowledge. It is because Niebuhr brings to Christian ethics this social and historicized understanding of human consciousness and the human condition that he sets up 'the enduring problem' as he does.

His reasons for approaching Christian ethics in terms of a Weberian typology of diverse models arise from his deep appreciation of the ethicist's calling as that of one who remembers, reconstructs, and gives an account of 'history' and of the social agent's situation in a social process. In 'Reflections on the Christian Theory of History', an undated essay he left among his unpublished papers, Niebuhr suggests that 'the relation between religious faith, theory of history, and ethics is *triadic*' (n.d.: 84). He believes that the interplay of these mutually modifying factors is as obvious in the work of secular ethicists as in the work of ethicists identified with a religious tradition. 'Faith', then, signifies any deep set of convictions concerning 'the source of life's meaning' and 'the conquering and organizing force in existence' (p. 84). 'Ethics' seems to signify both (a) the human experience of actors and sufferers who self-consciously affect others and are affected by them and (b) accounts of freedom and responsibility that arise out of that experience. 'Theory of history' (referred to as 'eschatology' or 'theology of history' when he focuses on Christianity) signifies an account of the nature, meaning, limits, and possibilities of temporal being. He argues that a properly Christian theory of history denies the meaningfulness of history *per se* because it denies 'the eternity of anything temporal' (p. 86). Yet even as it denies intrinsic meaning to history, it affirms history's 'derivative meaning': 'Creation and resurrection are the affirmation of the meaningfulness of history, as an event which not only refers beyond itself but represents the outgoing love of God' (p. 87). The Christian theory of history does not posit 'two worlds', but one reality, temporal and eternal, in which history is absorbed, transformed, and given meaning as it is drawn up into and transfigured by the kingdom of God in which it is transcended. This twofold interpretation, Niebuhr observes, is always in danger of 'developing into an other-worldliness in which the rejection of this world predominates over acceptance, or into a this-worldliness in which affirmation is unaccompanied by eschatological denial' (p. 87). This twofold theory of history influences Niebuhr's arrangement of the five types in *Christ and Culture* (the types closest to this-worldliness and other-worldliness constitute the outer types of the spectrum), and he differentiates the types partly by reference to contrasting theologies of history (see Table 2 below).

Whether *Christ and Culture* makes a constructive contribution to Christian ethics is a contentious issue. Commentators who think that Niebuhr does incorporate, intentionally or unintentionally, constructive work usually locate it in chapter 6, 'Christ the Transformer of Culture' (the model widely believed to be most congruent with Niebuhr's own theology). Having located it there, they are likely to object either that evaluative judgements do not belong in a typology at all or that some other model actually constitutes the normative standard (usually Christ-against-culture, but occasionally Christ above culture). By contrast, I invite you to consider the possibility that Niebuhr's constructive contribution lies in the project taken as a whole: in his understanding of the fundamental religious and ethical problem, in his reasons for turning to a comparative sociological method, and in the form of moral reflection the book displays.

THE ENDURING PROBLEM

Given Niebuhr's triadic interweaving of faith, history, and ethics, it is not surprising that he identifies the 'enduring problem' at the heart of all forms of Christian ethical theory, discourse, counsel, and behaviour as the problem of the relation of God and history. One dimension of this challenge concerns the struggle of a time-bound, situated, limited creature to discern, or even just trust, what God (revealed in Christ and apprehended in faith) is doing in history. The other dimension is the problem of right response—to the demands both of the God who addresses us and of the neighbour, whom we meet not as an abstract beneficiary but as a concrete claim and duty. These responses can always only be the fallible judgements and half-blind deeds of agents whose consciousness is shaped by social contingencies and who act in, and thus alter, the complex particularities of life in *a* time and *a* place in relation to some actual set of social companions.

This problem arose for the Christian community, Niebuhr suggests, before the church, before the crucifixion, 'in the days of Jesus Christ's humanity' (1951: 2). For support, he turns to the work of a Jewish scholar, Joseph Klausner, who has argued that the radical and destructive message of Jesus was rightly rejected by those whose responsibility it was to preserve the Jewish community and the complex heritage of Jewish civilization. Being material beings, persons depend upon material social arrangements that encompass subsistence, sexuality and nurture, government and law, the arts, work and commerce, education and enquiry, religious practices, memory of the past, and responsible action regarding present and future well-being. A community that does not attend to all these dimensions of life in time perishes; but, rather than proposing to reform deficiencies in Jewish material communal arrangements, Jesus 'ignored' them. Rather than treating religion and ethics as dimensions of life that 'embrace without engulfing' the complex realities of communal life, '[i]n their stead he set up nothing but an ethico-religious system bound up with his conception of the Godhead' (Klausner 1925: 390, quoted in Niebuhr 1951: 3). Or, as Niebuhr summarizes the argument, Jesus 'endangered it [Jewish communal life] by abstracting religion and ethics from the rest of social life, and by looking for the establishment by divine power only of a "kingdom not of this world"' (1951: 3). To show that Klausner's interpretation is neither idiosyncratic nor distinctively Jewish, Niebuhr also notes Edward Gibbon's complaint that

Christians are 'animated by a contempt for present existence and by confidence in immortality' (*Decline and Fall*, quoted 1951: 5), and reminds us that moral thinkers as different as Celsus, Marx, and Nikolai Hartmann have been disturbed by Christian indifference to human effort and achievement.

Thus, according to Niebuhr, the 'enduring problem' is not an error requiring correction but a perplexing challenge received from Christianity's founder. Jesus was 'extreme' with 'the extremism of devotion to the one God, uncompromised by love of any other absolute good' (1951: 16), and he possessed and expressed all virtues in a way that must necessarily seem 'extreme and disproportionate' (p. 19) to time-bound human eyes. Niebuhr understands Jesus to have been radically monotheistic and heroically theocentric, exhibiting absolute trust in and absolute dependence on God. 'He was not dealing with history at all in the first place, but with God, the Lord of time and space. He hoped in the living God.... The object of Jesus' intense expectancy [was] God Himself, the manifestation of divine glory and the revelation of divine righteousness' (p. 21). This accounts for his paradoxically authoritative humility—he was humble only before God; in his relations with persons, he was without inferiority, free of self-abnegation, confident of his power and his actions, and uncompromising.

The pattern here seems familiar: we are confronted with conflicting gods, conflicting loyalties, conflicting faiths—and a situation of decision. We are devoted to the kingdom of this world, and Jesus devotes himself utterly to the kingdom of God. The reader thinks of the rich young ruler and expects Niebuhr's portrayal of 'Christ' to end with an exhortation to give up false gods and devote ourselves to the only true God, to choose between God and civilization, but to reject Klausner's view concerning which constitutes the right choice.

Then, surprisingly, Niebuhr changes the pattern. What we know of Jesus supplies the Christian community not with a choice but a dialectic—'an ambivalent process....a double movement' (p. 28). Loving the Father, Jesus returns from the Father to humanity. This 'doubleness' in Jesus is reflected in a doubleness in the Christian calling. We are 'forever being challenged to abandon all things for the sake of God; and forever being sent back into the world to teach and practice all the things that have been commanded' (p. 29).

Instead of carrying forward Klausner's dichotomizing account of Jesus in his relation to civilization, Niebuhr has introduced a much more complex network of relationships, one which preserves the tension between Jesus' faith and the poly-theistic and henotheistic faiths that govern most human interactions, but which also refuses to force a choice between God and historical, material, social respon-sibilities, and arrangements. Niebuhr, it turns out, does not believe that Jesus 'abstract[ed] religion and ethics from the rest of social life' (Niebuhr's paraphrase of Klausner) in order to 'set up nothing but an ethico-religious system bound up with his conception of the Godhead' (Klausner 1925: 390, quoted Niebuhr 1951: 3). According to Niebuhr, Jesus in his incarnate personhood introduced into history a

Table 1. Love of God and neighbour

Love of God	Love of neighbour
'adoration of the only true good'	'pity for those who are foundering'
gratitude for gifts	generosity and forgiveness
'joy in Holiness'	suffering 'for and in' human viciousness
'consent to Being'; acceptance of what is	summons to repentance; refusal to accept the neighbour as he or she is
'nonpossessive *Eros*'	*agapē*
passion	compassion

perfectly God-centred consciousness: 'the unity of this person lies in the simplicity and completeness of his direction toward God' (p. 16). This altered and intensified ethics, to be sure, but it did not abstract it, for the God who forms this absolute centre is the 'Creator and Governor of all nature and of all history' (p. 24). Loving God rightly, Jesus loved nature and history as well, but loved them as God loves them, not as merely natural and historical creatures do. Niebuhr posits a fundamental asymmetry of loves (pp. 18–19; see Table 1).

There are two sorts of love and virtue here, not one sort directed to two objects or values. Moreover, the two loves 'have no common quality but only a common source' (p. 18). Jesus was able to love nature and history *because* he loved God, and he loved what he found in nature and history with a distinctive kind of love because he loved God rightly. The New Testament gospels present us with a duality, but it is not the duality of the profane and the sacred, or this world and some other: 'It is rather the duality of the Son of Man and Son of God, who loves God as man should love Him, and loves man as only God can love, with powerful pity for those who are foundering' (p. 19). Jesus calls us out of the network of our human loves and responsibilities, calls us to love the absolute God absolutely; however, to do this is to be returned, changed, to the very network of loves and responsibilities that we had thought had been rendered of no account. The Sermon on the Mount and the other hard sayings of Jesus outline the ethics proper to this return.

Another ethicist might have stopped here. Interpretive troubles sufficient to explain both the moral failings of Christians and the perennial variations in Christian teachings arise in plenty from this 'doubleness' alone. Any failure to love God as purely as Jesus loved God will result in wrong loving in our temporal context. The Sermon on the Mount and other teachings lay out a programme of action that few Christian communities have felt able to attempt, and have attempted only with very ambiguous results. Christians are by no means of a common mind with regard to the practical actions that Godly love and compassion require in particular lives and particular situations.

To stop here, however, would be to have only one leg of the triad: the dyad of faith and ethics. That reduction of the triadic relationship leaves ethical reflection vulnerable to (1) the generation of utopian moral expectations that cannot be realized in any temporal practical context and (2) the absolutizing of some temporal interpretation of Jesus as the actual Jesus or some existing temporal arrangement as the will of God for humanity. It is therefore important to see that the ensuing 'Toward the Definition of Culture' is not really a definition of the other end of a stick held at one end by Jesus. It is the filling out of the triad. It brings back into view the particular social context (both the context of Jesus and our own context) without which the teachings and work of Jesus would amount to exactly the abstraction of faith and ethics from social life that Klausner condemns. The discussion of 'culture' actually creates a second problematic overlaid upon, and complicating, the first.

This section owes a great deal to sociologists, and the reference to culture as 'this "reality sui generis"' (p. 32) quotes Emile Durkheim's *The Elementary Forms of Religious Life*. Niebuhr's point is in one sense a simple one: as embodied, temporal creatures, we necessarily belong to, and reason and act within, the conditioning framework of some social 'world' and some material arrangement of food supplies and shelter, of kin networks and other social collectives, of governing institutions, of economic exchanges, of social practices for nurturing the young, caring for the ill, and parting with the dead. He is fully aware of how diversely human societies have organized these things, and I remain perplexed as to how the notion that he treats culture monolithically has gained such credence in the secondary literature. To accuse him of thinking of culture as monolithic is to misread his argument. By speech and action, human beings superimpose an 'artificial, secondary environment' on our biological, ecological reality. There are myriads of secondary environments, as people in different places at different times, co-operating for different purposes, and serving different causes, bring into being, maintain, and reconstruct an evolving, overlapping array of social systems. It is precisely because there is no single, fixed, monolithic, normative, God-ordained 'culture' that there is an 'enduring problem' involving the relationship of God to all this shifty variegated work of human hands and minds and tongues. The social environment of any particular people (which, when it is preserved over time, becomes the 'social heritage' of that particular community) 'comprises language, habits, ideas, beliefs, customs, social organization, inherited artifacts, technical processes, and values' (p. 32). 'Culture' as a signifier does not, in this context, name any substantive entity; it points to 'the total process of human activity' whereby human beings transcend their strictly biological being to generate new and (relatively) durable layers of social reality—as specifiable as constitutions, contracts, power grids, and currencies, and as elusive as webs of conceptual interdependence and patterns of social trust.

Significantly, Niebuhr refuses to define 'culture' in a way that sets it against 'religion' or the churches. Religious faith, practices, and teachings, like religious organizations and institutions, are facets of some identifiable social environment; religion, he says explicitly, is not excluded from, set apart from, or transcendent of, the social matrix of our being and knowing (p. 32). Thus, every interpretive engagement with the teachings of Jesus (including Niebuhr's own) is itself a human achievement reflecting and embodying the values and interests of a complex particular world. Every attempt to love God rightly is the attempt of a historical community. Every effort to love nature and history *as God loves them* is the effort of creatures who are inspired, yet bound. Though we belong to, and encounter, something more than our social world—a reality that moves through, transcends, and judges that social world—we can only ever meet this power here and now.

All this, Niebuhr thinks, was also true of Jesus. That is what it means to say that God became fully human and entered into human history.

Thus, in addition to contending with a Lord who would wrench our love away from creation only to send us back to creation with a different sort of love, we must also contend with the fact that our very knowledge of this calling and this sending is a vulnerable artefact of history. The Christ who points us to a reality deeper than 'the temporality and pluralism of culture' was himself a 'child of a religious culture'. The commission to 'love as I have loved you' sends us back 'to tend his lambs and sheep, who cannot be guarded without cultural work' (p. 39). The anthropocentric social environment that we construct in our material, temporal milieu, which draws us away from theocentric trust and is sometimes openly hostile to such trust, is nonetheless the one and only environment in which we might hear the call to theocentric trust. There is no escape from time and history for the timefull creature whose being is historical being.

THE TYPOLOGY

'Quot homines, tot sententiae.' As many persons as there are, so many knowings will there be. To begin with the historical and particular is to begin with a veritable chaos: 'the manifold richness of historical life...the interfusing, interacting thoughts and deeds of separate men' (1951: 231). 'Types', or models, function in the social sciences as clarifying patterns that can be brought into relation with this overwhelming variety as a means of clustering like with like and generating principles of differentiation that will sort out like and unlike along lines of weighty, signifying tensions, rather than in virtue of the meandering contrasts of accidental or trivial variations. Typologies are thus a means of discerning and understanding social regularities of practice and conviction. The array of conceptually distinctive, self-consistent models may not conform to the self-reported, empirical associations of people into (in this case) churches or denominations, nor do they apply only to people who affiliate with such groups.

This sociological method, which is intrinsically comparative, is an especially apt tool for a socially located and committed ethicist who takes history and the perspectival character of knowledge seriously. It is an appropriate approach to the temporal teachings of a global religion that has persisted for hundreds of years and that has been instantiated in many different historical moments and geopolitical contexts. The 'ideal types', or conceptual models, offer contrasting representations of the relationship that constitutes the chosen axis of concern—they help us see what the plausible interpretive options are and where the points of conflict lie. This method provides a means of acknowledging, without affirming or rejecting, incommensurate beliefs. It allows us to discuss 'Christian ethics' without papering over or otherwise denying the irreducible pluralism of subsystems within the Christian community. A well-developed typology enables participants of each subsystem to see and understand their position relative to other cohesive subsystems. It enables us to differentiate conflicts that arise between competing cohesive systems of interpretation and commitment from conflicts that arise from confusion or self-contradiction. An effective typology facilitates the mutual respect appropriate among persons who seek to love God, act rightly, and teach truly—but who do so as limited creatures with relative points of view. Perhaps most importantly, the method provides an intellectual technique by which an investigator can present and discuss beliefs and practices that conflict with her or his own without subjecting those beliefs and practices to the analyst's own normative standards. The typological method is thus a way of neutralizing the bias and commitment of the scholar conducting the enquiry. (See Gustafson 2001 for a condensed but invaluable analysis of *Christ and Culture* as a Weberian typology, but see also Niebuhr's own briefer reflections in Niebuhr 1942: pp. xxxvii–xxxix.)

The well-known typology developed in chapters 2–6 of *Christ and Culture* proposes five models of the way in which Christian ethicists have dealt with the tension between 'Christ' and 'culture'.

This dominant typology, however, enfolds at least four (and I propose six) subordinate typologies. Among commentators, Douglas Ottati has done a particularly thorough job of bringing out 'the inner logic of each type' with reference to 'four theological relations, points or questions': (1) the relation between reason and revelation, which points to an epistemological question about 'appropriate sources of insight for our vision of God, the world, and ourselves, or for Christian theology and ethics'; (2) the relation of God and world, which points to the Trinitarian question concerning the way in which 'the God who creates and redeems relate[s] to the world as both nature and history'; (3) the relation of sin and goodness, which points to the question as to how 'sin affect[s] human capacities, communities, and institutions'; and (4) the relation of law and grace, which opens on 'the question of moral guidance' (Ottati 2003: 123). Accordingly, each type must be understood as 'a characteristic or patterned resolution of these four theological questions', and '[t]hese resolutions of the four theological relations interact in order to support a coherent Christian stance in the world' (pp. 123, 124). While there are dangers in reducing Niebuhr's multiplex typology to a simple chart, Table 2 serves to disclose

Table 2. Niebuhr's complex typology

	Views of history (quotes are from 1951: 195)	Reason and revelation	Nature and grace (God's relation to creation)	Sin and the good (the effect of the Fall)	Law and Gospel (works and grace)	Church and 'World'
Christ against culture (Tertullian, Tolstoy, monasticism) Ethics as the condemnation of unrighteousness, the call to repentance and right action	'[T]he story of a rising church or Christian culture and a dying pagan civilization'	Separate; in tension. Reason is erroneous and deceptive, leaving revelation as the sole trustworthy source of religious insight and guidance for conduct.	God creates nature, but ungodly action corrupts and obscures God's natural law. Most worldly arrangements are thus unreflective of God's purposes.	The holy community is exempted from sin; sin is associated with the unsaved, who cling to corrupt social forms. This type tends to deny original sin, viewing sin as avoidable fault rather than condition.	Primacy of law. Christ brings a new law, and conduct is an index of faith. Grace is the forgiveness of faults repented and corrected.	Church as alternative community: Jesus/spirit/church vs. nature/creation/world. The church's task is to condemn sin in other social arrangements.
Christ and culture in paradox (Paul, Justin Martyr, Luther, Kierkegaard) Ethics as the restraint and control of sin and corruption	Between the already and the not yet: 'the time of struggle between faith and unbelief', between promise and fulfilment	We stand before man and before God. Reason is given to us for use in our relations with other persons but is useless *coram deo* (before God). Reason is corrupted by idolatry and self-will.	Emphasizes God the governor of creation. Non-religious institutions are a gift of God for governing and limiting the effects of human sinfulness; thus, the temporal realm and God's	Sin is radical, and alienation from God is the defining characteristic of the human condition. This type tends to identify sin and temporality. All works are corrupt, yet we are saved	Primacy of grace and forgiveness. Jesus redeems through the cross. All confidence is placed in grace, and grace is understood purely as the undeserved gift of God. Law restrains evil, but	Church as companion in sin. The church is as infected by sin as any other social/cultural institution.

			redeeming purpose are linked.	and allowed to participate in the goodness of God.	only drives the believer to despair.	
Christ transforming culture (Augustine, Calvin, Edwards, Maurice, Wesley) Ethics as the lifting up and healing of brokenness, the restoration of forgotten possibilities	The story of divine–human interaction, 'of God's mighty deeds and [human] responses'. 'Eternal life is a quality of existence in the here and now'.	Reasoning is corrupted by wrong love, but faith restores reason to trustworthiness by giving it 'a new first principle'; revelation is essential to faith, allowing us to live 'from and toward God's love'.	Emphasizes God the redeemer of creation; centralizes the Incarnation. God is present in history as the power that works for its redemption; the temporal order is good, but it is a corrupted good.	Sin is radical and universal. Conversion of the heart is required, since reason and knowledge otherwise operate within the framework of sinfulness.	Primacy of grace and forgiveness. Jesus redeems through the Incarnation. Grace/Gospel brings about conversion. Law operates not only to restrain evil but also to foster the good.	Church as transforming agent. The church should be a beacon to the world and an example of the possibility of transformation and redemption.
Christ above culture (Aquinas, Anglicanism) Ethics as the fulfilment of the natural law embedded in created nature	Between the already and the not yet: 'a period of preparation under law, reason, gospel, and church for an ultimate communion of the soul with God'	Revelation and reason are in harmony, but revelation goes beyond reason; the Gospel requires more than prudence can discover.	Emphasizes God the creator. Nature is good and rightly ordered; temporal and material arrangements are part of the divine ordering.	Sin is universal, but not radical and ineradicable. Sin can be diminished, and the good can be enhanced, through the support of grace.	Grace is essential to the fullness of the human good. God's law is written into God's creation as God's good will for creation, though God's will requires more than obedience to natural law can assure.	Church as governing power. The Lordship of Christ is equated with the rule of his successors. The church should exercise responsibility for the world.

Table 2. Continued

	Views of history (quotes are from 1951: 195)	Reason and revelation	Nature and grace (God's relation to creation)	Sin and the good (the effect of the Fall)	Law and Gospel (works and grace)	Church and 'World'
Christ of culture (Ritschl, Deism, Fundamentalism, Social Gospel) Ethics as the rational reform and perfection of imperfect temporal arrangements	The story of 'the spirit's encounter with nature.'	Separate but duplicative. Revelation not essential for faith or life; reason and philosophy are adequate and reliable sources; Jesus exemplifies and fulfils society's best insights.	God is present in creation as an immanent, rational, spiritual and moral principle. Spirit must triumph over mere nature.	Reason is exempted from sin. This type tends to deny original sin, locating sin in animal passions (restrainable) and corrupt social systems (reformable). The good has a realm of its own, not in the holy community but in the personal 'spirit'.	Primacy of law. Jesus represents spiritual resources available to all. This type emphasizes self-reliant humanism; reliance on grace is viewed as unstable and irrational.	Church as partner. No tension arises between the church and other constructive social arrangements. The religious task is the conservation of what is good in culture and the improvement of what is not yet good.

the parallel resolutions that constitute the contrasting types. Once the multi-layered character of the typology is laid out, it is easy to see why Niebuhr's models have been so widely used in so many contexts of analysis that people tend to forget that Niebuhr himself was identifying types of Christian *ethics*, in a book that took shape gradually through years of teaching courses in Christian ethics.

To the four categories of analysis that Niebuhr uses explicitly across all five chapters I have added two. First I have laid out the contrasting views of history that Niebuhr correlates with the five types. This set of contrasts is retrospectively specified in chapter 6 (pp. 195–6). Since the 'enduring problem' is, most funda-mentally, the problem of the Christian's simultaneous relation to the absolute and the changing, to God and history, this set of contrasts is particularly important.

I have also included a column tracking the parallel variations in the understand-ing of the relationship of the church and the world, or, as Ottati more precisely frames it, the relationship between 'the community and institution of those who self-consciously acknowledge and are loyal to God-in-Christ' and 'those commu-nities and institutions which apparently do not and are not' (2003: 130). In an earlier article, Ottati, too, had included the church/world polarity among the sets of correlated contrasts that structure the book (Ottati 1988: 320); but in his more recent article, he is more tentative, suggesting only that he believes that Niebuhr's analysis could beneficially be 'extended' to identify the contrasting understandings of the relationship of church and world that each type would entail if it were consistently held. The important thing to notice is that the various conceptions of the relation of the churches (communities and institutions that are dedicated to the nurture and preservation of radical faith) to the 'world' (communities and insti-tutions with other causes and, indeed, other gods) are a subordinate aspect of the typology. While *Christ and Culture* has important things to say about ways in which Christians have construed their individual and institutional relation to temporal and civic arrangements, the book is not in the first instance a direct enquiry into how the Christian churches should relate to secular culture. Church/world relations are not 'the enduring problem'; they are merely one of the several ways in which the enduring problem becomes manifest. Because Christians under-stand the relation of God to history differently, they have therefore developed different understandings of the relation of self-consciously Christian communities to secular or anti-religious communities, as well as to non-Christian religions.

I hope my previous discussion of Niebuhr's way of setting up the problem helps clarify why 'Christ', as Niebuhr uses it here, cannot legitimately be equated with churches or with distinctively Christian values, and why 'culture', as he defines it, cannot legitimately be limited to secular, rationalist, or neo-pagan social institu-tions, practices, or values. To be sure, churches and other Christian movements, communities, and forms of practice are particularly complicated features of culture (because they present in an acute form the paradox involved in trying to apprehend from within a world-view and social process what transcends that viewpoint and process). They are also, from a Christian point of view, particularly important features of culture (because they exist to codify, preserve, and transmit the promise to the rising generations). None the less, they remain cultural phenomena: human achievements wrought by human effort in the idiom of their place and moment. The most that can be said to mark the specialness of 'that community... for whom Jesus Christ—his life, words, deeds, and destiny—is of supreme importance as the key to the understanding of themselves and their world' is that the churches, to the extent that they rise to theocentric faith, are in some peculiar way suspended, 'mov[ing] between the poles of Christ and culture' (1951: 11).

Still, 'church', like 'history', is an 'ambiguous' term. 'Church' can also signify the entire company of those who have been—ever since John began baptizing the repentant in the Jordan—humbly, loyally, and trustingly faithful to the one who redeems his fallen creation. Church in this more capacious sense is not to be identified with any particular 'man or group or historical time' (1951: 256). Yet, even when church is understood in this way, Niebuhr does not consider it to be distinct from or abstracted from culture. It remains the historical company of trusting Christians, all of whom do 'our partial, relative work', deciding and acting in some particular constellation of circumstances within which we have been addressed by God. What distinguishes this entire company, however, is the trust 'that the world of culture—man's achievement—exists within the world of grace—God's Kingdom' (1951: 256).

ETHICS AS INFINITE DIALOGUE

Moral Disagreement

To believe that Christian variation is, in some instances, primordial and irreducible—a function of historicity rather than an index of fault, error, or sin—is to open the way for a more positive understanding of the moral conflicts and ethical disagreements that persist not only among people of good will but within the Christian faith community.

Moral disagreements have many sources. The situations that present themselves as morally problematic are usually remarkably complex and often require more knowledge than decision-makers possess at the time when action must be taken. Moreover, the moral domain comprises quite diverse projects, including, among others, minimizing harm and suffering, responding to immediate human need, preserving moral communities over time, allocating burdens and benefits fairly, encouraging principled action over self-serving action, and establishing the importance of various goods and duties relative to each other. Within and among these projects there is room for considerable conflict. Furthermore, as we are now acutely aware, social location indelibly stamps our sense of what is right and good, with the result that moral judgements frequently vary with the experiences, value hierarchies, and interests of agents and organizations.

Niebuhr's typology provides a powerful analytical tool for differentiating disputes that arise *within* a relatively cohesive set of convictions (and are thus subject to reasoned resolution) from disputes that reflect the long-standing tensions and fissures that mark subsystem boundaries. The latter disagreements arise, not from failures of reason, knowledge, faith, or virtue, but from discordant convictions at levels deeper than the moral judgements themselves. If parties to such disputes are not to remain deaf to one another, the discussion must engage the deeper differences. The typology suggests that conflicting moral judgements of this sort each have a claim to licitness, because each is defensible within a strand of Christian life that arises from foundational documents, teachings, and practices, and has been validated over time. One might conclude that moral conflicts of this sort involve incommensurables and ought to be recognized to be beyond resolution, functioning simply to further define the tensions between cohesive subgroups within the comprehensive community. While that will sometimes be the case, a typological analysis of the variations can also help us see where commonalities may be found, and what goods the various parties to the dispute are concerned to cherish and preserve. Out of such understanding there may arise new and more fruitful ways of framing the issues, a richer sense of the range of effective responses, and a deepened dedication, among all parties, to the indispensable goods that appear to be threatened.

The Relativity of the Relative

Niebuhr places ethics and ethicists in the active tension between, on the one hand, personal encounter with the absolute and, on the other, the manyness, localness, and limitations that condition all historical existence. Influenced though he is by sociological and psychological studies, especially the sociology of knowledge and social psychology, he nevertheless avoids reductive forms of social constructionism. An almost overwhelming sense of the at once terrible and comforting *presence* of God is one of the marks of Niebuhr's theology and his ethics. This is too often overlooked, particularly in academic studies of his work. In a revealing anecdote, James Wharton reports that during a lecture, Niebuhr once fell silent in mid-sentence, withdrawn in thought. After an uncomfortable, mystifying pause, he took up the broken thread of his talk with the remark, 'I think we need to have a moratorium on the use of the word God until we recover the meaning of awe' (Wharton 1999: 30). Niebuhr had no doubt that in the midst of history we meet and are grasped by a towering yet intimate 'Thou'—a sovereign power who will neither let us go nor bend to our will, but also a responsive presence who promises, supports, speaks. We apprehend this action and this word from different perspectives in different circumstances, but it is one power whom we know. And in faith or faithlessness we know this power as the 'infinite absolute'—a stable, irreducible reality who, meeting us, relativizes our proudest achievements, our deepest wisdom, our finest virtues. *Christ and Culture* is, he tells us, his attempt 'to understand... historical relativism in the light of theological and theo-centric relativism'. Drawing attention to Isaiah 10, 1 Corinthians 12, and Augustine's *City of God*, he continues, 'I believe that it is an aberration of faith as well as of reason to absolutize the finite but that all this relative history of finite men and movements is under the governance of the absolute God' (1951: p. xii).

This is why no person, no group, no church, no Christian community, no religious tradition, no historical era can put forward its understanding of transcendent reality as *the* understanding of that presence. Any effort to claim for one's own beliefs the status of final Christian truth would be idolatrous—'an act of usurpation of the Lordship of Christ which at the same time would involve doing violence to the liberty of Christian men and to the unconcluded history of the church in culture. If we should make such an attempt we should need to assume that our particular place in the church and history is so final that we can hear not only the word of God addressed to us but His whole word' (1951: 232).

For this same reason, he views the models as in some sense complementary. By faithful listening to those with whom we disagree, our fallible, finite, partial grasp of that, in turn, faithful reality can grow more penetrating, more comprehensive, and therefore more adequate—if never perfectly so. Thus, Niebuhr invites us to 'infinite dialogue' among ourselves in our relation to this creative, uncreated, and unconditioned Other.

Becoming Critical

The 'social mind' is a pivotal topic that Niebuhr explores in all his books and many of his essays. Reflection on the social mind discloses how much more than an exercise in Weberian social science the typology offered in *Christ and Culture* actually is. In the posthumously published essay 'A Theologian's Approach to History', which was delivered in 1955 and contains a condensed presentation of 'the subject–object situation and its dialectical character' (1955: 78), Niebuhr describes a triad that prefigures those he develops more richly in *The Responsible Self* (1963). He expands the dialectical/dialogical relation of the knower and the known into a more complex triadic relation, because 'knowledge does not happen in the subject–object dialogue unless the subject is also related to another knower, to a companion or companions engaged as he is in dialogue with objects and also engaged in dialogue with him' (1955: 79); thus, not only is all knowledge a feat of interpretation, but it is also 'all social'. We as knowers are thus perpetually 'engaged in a double dialogue—with [our] objects, on the one hand, with our fellow knowers on the other' (p. 79). Just as the subject and the object cannot really be separated, neither can the subject and the social community or the social community and the common object. Whatever it is that I try to understand, 'I come to this object of my inquiry with categories, ideas, patterns of relationships, with certain *a prioris* of experience—these I have derived from my society' (p. 81). This is no less true of human efforts to understand the will and action of God than it is of human efforts to understand the American Civil War or the Lisbon earthquake. Moreover, triadically considered, theological enquiry must be, at least in part, a work of memory. It requires not only dialogue with our contemporaries but sympathetic listening to the rich and varied voices through which, historically, the human experience of God is opened to us.

Much of Western modernity has been defined by a (in Niebuhr's view self-contradictory and futile) rejection of this social and communal dimension of knowledge, as the great theorists of modernity have alternately embraced various forms of scepticism or aspired to establish some indubitable grounds of certain knowledge (the thinking self or 'objective' science). Niebuhr recommends that we embrace and affirm the sociality of all our knowledge. In doing this, we must discipline ourselves

to become critical, to try to understand *a priori* categories and patterns and principles with which I came to the interpretation of my objects, to understand their origin, their development, their degradations in my past, my social past, and to do this by constant reference to my present experience of objects to which my human companions of the past responded in their own way and with their own interpretations, which finally yielded the *a priori* patterns with which I have come to my experience. (pp. 81–2)

Since there is no unmediated asocial access to anything that we find it worthwhile to understand, our only way out of folly, bias, and error—the only way we have of truing our judgements—is through history, understood as 'present re-creation and re-enactment' of the interpretations and struggles of the full company of our companions in enquiry. We are who we are only within some particular constellation of communities, and the depth of our dependency is best acknowledged through the sympathetic indwelling of our equally time-bound companions' efforts to understand that which we, too, struggle to understand.

This 're-enactment of the experiences and ideas of the past' has three benefits. First, by becoming steadily more aware of the social factors that have shaped the views of others, I become more aware of those that shape my own. I thus gain some degree of freedom in relation to those influences. Only by means of such self-knowledge does it become possible for me to modify the social factors that would otherwise determine my responses and to assess the 'value or disvalue of the patterns with which I approach the interpretation of, and with which I guide my responses to, present realities that exercise force on my life' (p. 82). Second, I may recover or discover 'patterns of interpretation' that do a better job than my own received tools in giving 'some order and coherence to my present encounter with my object' (p. 82). Third, by this indwelling and this 'conversation', it becomes possible for me to 'enlarge' the scope of my understanding. This last is particularly important. Though my mind is a social mind (shaped by, responding to, and reconstructing a social world), not everything I do is a consequence solely of social construction. Persons are embodied minds as well as social minds, and we are only beginning to be fully attentive to the interplay of body, mind, and action. Moreover, individuals encounter many realities that are socially interpreted but not socially engendered. We are 'driven', Niebuhr thinks, by a 'thirst for unity' that is neither merely animal curiosity nor social inheritance. We encounter 'the presence of a One in the manyness of subjectivities and objectivities', and 'we find in the recovery of our history, or in our conversation with social and individual wisdom of the past the evidences of the unity from which we came and toward which we aspire in all our aspirations after wisdom' (p. 83). It is possible to love the wholeness of knowledge without being able to possess it, and it is the conflicted and fragmentary apprehension of that whole that makes it possible and necessary for us to be critical in relation to our partialities, even though we know that we can never escape them.

So, yes, Gustafson is quite right to insist that *Christ and Culture* is not what Niebuhr would call 'external' history. Neither the chronological development of Christian thought nor the social history of Christianity is the 'object' examined in this book. The book does, however, engage 'history' in the other senses that Niebuhr has identified, and particularly in the sense he gives to the word in 'A Theologian's Approach to History'. *Christ and Culture* focuses on the multiple ways in which Niebuhr's Christian social companions have, over the centuries, interpreted the will, promise, and demands of 'what they confront in the determination of their destiny, in the why and wherefore of their existence' (pp. 80–1). It is a book that should be read in the same spirit of gentle patience with which it was written, for it is designed, I think, as a spiritual exercise: that we may gain an appreciation of the social rootage and partiality of our own convictions; that we may discover, appreciate, and perhaps recover what is not part of our own favoured strand of Christian heritage; and that we may dimly see, through all the variousness of our broken world and particular visions, some outline of 'the unity from which we came and toward which we aspire'.

REFERENCES AND SUGGESTED READING

BOWKER, J. (1981). 'Religions as Systems', in *Believing in the Church*, Report of the Doctrine Commission of the Church of England, London: SPCK. Repr. in J. Bowker, *Is Anybody Out There? Religions and Belief in God in the Contemporary World* [UK title: *Licensed Insanities*]. Westminster, Md.: Christian Classics, Inc., 1988, 112–43.

Cook, M. L. (1991). *The Open Circle: Confessional Method in Theology.* Minneapolis: Fortress Press.

Gill, R. (1999). 'Churches and Moral Disagreement', in *Churchgoing and Christian Ethics,* Cambridge, and New York: Cambridge University Press, 230–60.

Gilson, E. (1938). *Reason and Revelation in the Middle Ages.* New York: Charles Scribner's Sons.

Gustafson, J. M. (2001). 'Preface: An Appreciative Interpretation', in H. R. Niebuhr, *Christ and Culture,* expanded 50th anniversary edition, New York: HarperSanFranciso, pp. xxi–xxxv.

Jung, C. G. (1971). *Psychological Types,* a revision by R. F. C. Hull of the 1923 translation by H. G. Baynes. Bollingen Series XX. Princeton: Princeton University Press. [Originally published in German in 1921.]

Keiser, R. M. (1996). *The Roots of Relational Ethics: Responsibility in Origin and Maturity in H. Richard Niebuhr.* Atlanta: Scholars Press.

Klausner, J. (1925). *Jesus of Nazareth: His Life, Times, and Teaching,* trans. H. Danby. New York: Macmillan. [Originally published in Hebrew in 1922.]

Mead, G. H. (1934). *Mind, Self, and Society.* Chicago: University of Chicago Press.

Niebuhr, H. R. (1941). *The Meaning of Revelation.* New York: Macmillan. Page numbers are from the 1960 Macmillan paperback edition.

—— (1942). 'Types of Christian Ethics', ed. for publication by D. M. Yeager; posthumously published in Glen H. Stassen, D. M. Yeager, and J. H. Yoder, *Authentic Transformation: A New Vision of Christ and Culture,* Nashville: Abingdon Press, 1996, 15–29. Repr. in H. R. Niebuhr, *Christ and Culture,* New York: HarperSanFranciso, 2001, pp. xxvii–lv. Page citations are from the reprint.

—— (1949). 'Reinhold Niebuhr's Interpretation of History'. Paper prepared for the Theological Discussion Group that met at Union Theological Seminary in New York City. Posthumously published in *Theology, History, and Culture: Major Unpublished Writings,* ed. W. S. Johnson, foreword by R. R. Niebuhr, New Haven and London: Yale University Press, 1996, 91–101.

—— (1951). *Christ and Culture.* New York: HarperSanFranciso. Republished as an expanded 50th anniversary edition, with new front matter, in 2001. Pagination is the same in both editions.

—— (1955). 'A Theologian's Approach to History'. Address to the American History Association, 30 Dec. Posthumously published in *Theology, History, and Culture: Major Unpublished Writings,* ed. W. S. Johnson, foreword by R. R. Niebuhr, New Haven and London: Yale University Press, 1996, 77–83.

—— (1960). 'Introduction', in E. Troeltsch, *The Social Teaching of the Christian Churches,* trans. Olive Wyon, 2 vols., Chicago and London: University of Chicago Press, I. 7–12.

—— (1963). *The Responsible Self: An Essay in Christian Moral Philosophy.* Posthumously published from lectures given in 1960 and 1962, with a preface by R. R. Niebuhr and an introduction by J. M. Gustafson. New York: Harper and Row. Reissued in 1999 by Westminster/John Knox Press, with a new foreword by W. Schweiker.

—— (n.d.). 'Reflections on the Christian Theory of History'. Undated manuscript prepared for the Theological Discussion Group that met at Union Theological Seminary in New York City. Posthumously published in *Theology, History, and Culture: Major Unpublished Writings,* ed. W. S. Johnson, foreword by R. R. Niebuhr, New Haven and London: Yale University Press, 84–90.

OTTATI, D. (1988). 'Christ and Culture', *American Presbyterians*, 66 (Winter), 320–5.

—— (2003). '*Christ and Culture:* Still Worth Reading after All These Years', *Journal of the Society of Christian Ethics*, 23/1, 121–32.

RAMSEY, P. (ed.) (1957). *Faith and Ethics: The Theology of H. Richard Niebuhr*. New York: Harper.

STASSEN, G. H., YEAGER, D. M., and YODER, J. H. (1996). *Authentic Transformation: A New Vision of Christ and Culture*. Nashville: Abingdon Press.

THIEMANN, R. F. (ed.) (1991). *The Legacy of H. Richard Niebuhr*. Minneapolis: Fortress Press.

WERPEHOWSKI, W. (2002). *American Protestant Ethics and the Legacy of H. Richard Niebuhr*. Washington: Georgetown University Press.

WHARTON, J. (1999). Interview with James Wharton, conducted by Terry Muck. *Insights: The Faculty Journal of Austin Seminary*, 115/1 (Fall), 29–30.

YEAGER, D. M. (2003). 'The View from Somewhere: The Meaning of Method in *Christ and Culture*', *Journal of the Society of Christian Ethics*, 23/1, 101–20.

CHAPTER 28

REINHOLD NIEBUHR'S *THE NATURE AND DESTINY OF MAN*

ROBIN W. LOVIN

THE story of Reinhold Niebuhr's *The Nature and Destiny of Man* has a drama that few classics of Christian ethics can match. Niebuhr delivered the work first as the Gifford Lectures at the University of Edinburgh in 1939. This prestigious lectureship, previously held by William James, Alfred North Whitehead, and Karl Barth, gave its own distinction to Niebuhr's words, but the timing made the significance even greater. In the late 1930s, Niebuhr was the most important English-speaking voice in Christian social ethics, and the Gifford invitation placed him at the rostrum as the world moved toward war between the Western democracies and Hitler's Germany. When the lectures began in the spring of 1939, Germany had already annexed Austria and occupied Czechoslovakia. World War II began on 1 September, and the sound of bombs falling on Edinburgh's naval yards could be heard in the background during the lectures in October. Under the circumstances, some were surprised that the public continued to come to hear Niebuhr; but Richard Fox suggests the reason why these lectures were so compelling: '[T]hey probably stuck it out precisely because these were not standard Gifford lectures; they were inspirational if sometimes dense sermons on the Christian view of human destiny. If bombs were going to fall it made sense to make time three afternoons a week for some stirring reflections that went beyond tragedy' (Fox 1996: 191).

Niebuhr's interpretation of human nature and destiny was, however, fitted to more than that moment, however dramatic it may have been. Readiness for Niebuhr's stern realism had been growing for decades, through the disillusionment that followed World War I, the worldwide depression of the 1930s, and the rise of totalitarianism in Spain, Italy, Germany, and the Soviet Union. In September 1939, Britain and the United States faced an uncertain future. The world was far removed from the progressive optimism with which the twentieth century had begun, and Reinhold Niebuhr was one of the few voices who could persuasively relate Christian faith to the grim determination with which the English-speaking world faced the challenge of the new war. People turned out for the Gifford Lectures, and they read the published versions that appeared in 1941 and 1943, because Niebuhr could chart the failures that had led to war and show that there was still important work to be done to salvage the future.

Most important, Niebuhr reminded people that history was not entirely in their own hands. For a generation that had begun the century intending to remake the world by their own faith and energy, the stern message that their failures had been inevitable and that the fulfilment of the human story lies beyond history came as good news. It kept them from despair over their own weakness, and it allowed them to hope for a future they knew they could not make by their own power.

Niebuhr's words would remain good news in a straightforward way for decades to come, as the world divided in new ways between Western democracy and Soviet communism. The moral certainty about Western democracy that some sought to wrest from the struggle with totalitarianism gave way to doubts about colonialist paternalism and racial inequality. People continued to need the realistic warnings that all their achievements were limited and that history has ironic power to reverse even their best intentions. Niebuhr's clear statement of those ideas continued to carry force long after the events that marked the writing and delivery of his Gifford Lectures.

Niebuhr had in some sense been working on *The Nature and Destiny of Man* for at least a decade before he received the Gifford invitation in 1937. He had begun teaching ethics at Union Theological Seminary in New York in 1928, and his reflections on society and theology were already forming during a pastorate in Detroit that began in 1915. Nevertheless, he wrote the lectures with his usual urgency, pressed both by the intensity of his convictions and by the approach of the deadline for their delivery. The first series, on human nature, occupied his time for most of the year before the lectures began on 24 April 1939. The second series, which began on 11 October, was completed in more haste, largely during the long summer vacation which Niebuhr spent with his family in the south of England. Returning to his normal duties at Union in 1940 after the Gifford Lectures had been delivered, Niebuhr revised his notes as he had opportunity, and his usual publisher, Charles Scribner's Sons, brought out the first volume on human nature in 1941 and the second volume on human destiny in 1943. The two series of lectures were always conceived as a whole, with the unifying title, *The Nature and Destiny of Man* and the significant subtitle: *A Christian Interpretation*. Scribner's and its successors kept the work in print for more than fifty years, publishing an edition with a new preface by Niebuhr in 1964. *The Nature and Destiny of Man* is currently available as part of the Library of Theological Ethics, published by Westminster/John Knox Press. (All of the published two-volume editions have the same pagination, so the references to volume and page number (e.g., I. 207) in this essay should serve as a guide to most versions of the work the reader may find available.)

CHRISTIAN REALISM

Niebuhr and his colleagues called their approach to political and economic problems 'Christian realism' (Niebuhr 1992: 43) This realism rejected naïve approaches to political and economic problems that relied solely on Christian love and human good will and ignored the realities of self-interest and power. In so far as it was *Christian* realism, however, it was also an expression of faith that power and self-interest are not the only standards by which events must be judged. Much of the illumination of human nature that audiences experienced in Niebuhr's speaking and writing drew on this juxtaposition of the amorality of social and political life as it is lived and the certainty of moral order known by faith.

Niebuhr had already made a powerful statement about the weakness of moral forces in society and politics in *Moral Man and Immoral Society*, where he suggested that revolutionary movements, with their apocalyptic expectations, might be more effective forces for justice than middle-class Christian idealism (Niebuhr 1932: 277). In the early 1930s, that idea seemed shocking, even irreligious, especially to the Protestant social activists who had already begun to look to Niebuhr for leadership. By 1939, it was not so easy to view history as a steady forward movement or to see religious idealism as a principal force for change. Niebuhr's realistic perspective became more and more persuasive. Through the years of World War II and beyond, into the new era of superpower confrontations and nuclear deterrence, it seemed that power and self-interest would shape the world's future. Reinhold Niebuhr's persistent insistence that we face that grim reality made him America's best-known public intellectual.

At the beginning of the twenty-first century, things have changed remarkably once again, and the world that Reinhold Niebuhr knew seems increasingly distant from our experience. A realism that sought balance between rival superpowers may seem too cautious at a time when only one superpower remains. A realism which understood both the hunger for justice and the inertia of history may seem too conservative for those who have experienced the fall of communism, the end of apartheid, and the emergence of the internet economy. A realism which calls itself Christian may seem insufficiently theological at a time when Christian symbols and sensibilities are rapidly disappearing from a pluralistic culture. Stanley Hauerwas pronounced this verdict on Niebuhr's Christian realism in his own Gifford Lectures in 2001: 'Niebuhr's work now represents the worst of two worlds: most secular people do not find his arguments convincing; yet his theology is not sufficient to provide the means for Christians to sustain their lives' (Hauerwas 2001: 139).

If Hauerwas and other critics are right, Niebuhr is primarily a figure of historical interest, who shows us how Christian thought intersected with historical events during one particularly challenging period of time. The thousands of essays, articles, and speeches that Niebuhr produced indicate the scope of his thought. The admiration for his work expressed by theologians, pastors, and politicians establish his historical importance. The sheer volume of his work and the breadth of his readership easily convince us that what he said made a difference in its time, but they do not immediately tell us whether there are any lessons in it for us.

That is why *The Nature and Destiny of Man* is important for a contemporary reassessment of Christian realism. Here, we can not only ask, 'What did Reinhold Niebuhr think?', but also 'What would it mean to think in this way for our situation today?' That question, too, requires some probing beneath the surface of Niebuhr's text, but *The Nature and Destiny of Man* does a great deal to make clear the complex interweaving of political, moral, and theological ideas that shaped all of Niebuhr's insights. Tracing those underlying themes provides a starting-point for a twenty-first-century Christian realism.

POLITICS

Realism implies in the first place a willingness to investigate the forces that actually shape historical events. It is not enough to know what people ought to do or to describe the world as it would be if they did what they ought. We must pay attention to the forces that actually motivate the conduct of politics and diplomacy; and that, as Niebuhr explained, means understanding how self-interest and the desire for power often lead people to act in ways that contradict what they say they believe (Niebuhr 1953: 119).

Much of Niebuhr's early work was devoted to convincing Christians that the teachings of Jesus do not provide a system of social ethics that we could simply put into practice and thereby end poverty, resolve conflicts, assuage hatreds, and eliminate all the other sad realities that contradict Christian ideals. *Moral Man and Immoral Society* dealt at length with the ways in which Christians confuse the will of God with the interests of their own class and nation. *An Interpretation of Christian Ethics* demonstrated the impossibility of living what Jesus taught (Niebuhr 1979: 22–38). The religion proclaimed by the Hebrew prophets and summed up in the teaching of Jesus demands too much of us to make it real in any particular historical situation. The ideals set out in the teaching of Jesus are always relevant, but they are not relevant as a programme for action. Rather, they provide a standard against which everything that we can accomplish must be measured. Divine judgement, rather than human accomplishment, lies at the centre of the Christian moral life. 'The dominant attitudes of prophetic faith are gratitude and contrition; gratitude for Creation and contrition before Judgment; or, in other words, confidence that life is good in spite of its evil and that it is evil in spite of its good. In such a faith both sentimentality and despair are avoided' (Niebuhr 1979: 64).

Avoiding sentimentality and despair, for Niebuhr, is essential to effective moral activity. Otherwise, we give ourselves over to vague dreams or lapse into the lethargy of those who think there is nothing they can do. We do not escape those dangers, however, simply by a realistic assessment of our own capacities. Gratitude and contrition shape a relationship to God. We are able to act morally, and we are able to sustain that action in the face of failure and tragedy, because we believe that the meaning of life is grounded in a reality that transcends both our momentary successes and our inevitable failures. If the world were not that way, acting on the basis of moral obligation would make no sense, and self-interest and power would have the last word. People who do not believe that the meaning of life lies beyond their own successes and failures eventually lose their sense of moral obligation, and, for them, self-interest and power do have the last word. 'Moral life is possible at all only in a meaningful existence. Obligation can only be felt to some system of coherence and some ordering will' (Niebuhr 1979: 63). This idea of a 'meaningful existence' and its importance for the moral life would remain central to Niebuhr's thought through *The Nature and Destiny of Man* and beyond.

Niebuhr realized, however, that much of our actual living is concerned with self-deceiving assessments of our achievements or with anxious efforts to determine the meaning of events by our own power. Christians are not the only people subject to these unrealistic expectations. Niebuhr also points out the illusions of Marxists, Freudians, and revolutionaries of all sorts. It seems to be characteristic of all human commitments that they lead us to expect the impossible, overstating the completeness and consistency of our goals, underestimating the obstacles to their achievement, and above all, ignoring the ways that our own interests and desires corrupt even the best of them. Pointing out these illusions and self-deceptions in classical and modern systems of thought takes centre stage in the argument of *The Nature and Destiny of Man.*

Cataloguing the mistaken judgements about human nature that inevitably lead to the failure of all forms of rationalism, romanticism, and materialism, including the

National Socialist and Marxist versions, is the primary agenda for the first four chapters of Niebuhr's first volume, but it is also important to identify the partial truths that render these illusions persuasive and attractive. The world is full of people who give their loyalty to impossible ideals of world transformation, and by 1939 it was apparent that not all of them would be as easily disillusioned as middle-class Protestant Christians.

Niebuhr had a keen insight into his Edinburgh audience and those who would read *The Nature and Destiny of Man* after its publication. He knew that they shared the general scepticism of educated modern people, and he knew that they no longer expected much from preaching and moral exhortation. But British and American liberals were confronted by an enemy which had elicited a fearful devotion to nation, blood, and soil, and they were uneasily allied with a Soviet regime which promised a proletarian paradise, once the inevitable revolution was past. Niebuhr's audience was unlikely to develop a similar blind fervour for liberal democracy, but much depended on their confidence that the grand ideas arrayed against them did not have the last word on the human future.

The genius of *The Nature and Destiny of Man* is that it does not make its case by denouncing other systems of ideas and commitments as completely evil. That would reduce it to the level of the wartime propaganda that we now read with historical interest, but also with some degree of embarrassment. In propaganda, enemies are reduced to caricatures that in retrospect show us more about our own ethnocentrism than about the other side of the conflict. Niebuhr did not explain Hitler by reference to traits of German character from which his British and American audiences were happily exempt. Human nature leads us all to claim too much righteousness for ourselves and to accept too little judgement. Nor is Niebuhr concerned simply with a better vision for the post-war world, like the 'war aims' writings with which many British and American intellectuals busied themselves once an allied victory was in sight (Lippman 1944). Rather, at the very beginning of the struggle, while the historical outcome was still unclear, Niebuhr set out to explicate the understandings of human nature on which the contending ideologies had been built. Moral claims made on behalf of the Allied cause had to be grounded in the relative adequacy of the Christian view of human nature, on which Western democracy depended more than it knew (I. 12).

ETHICS

Beginning with human nature set Niebuhr apart from some of the most important developments in Protestant ethics in his generation. He does not begin thinking about the Christian life with the concrete command of God, which is central to

Karl Barth's ethics (Barth 1961: 4); nor does he suggest that the reality of Christ displaces the human search for the good in the way that Dietrich Bonhoeffer begins Christian ethics (Bonhoeffer 1995: 186). Niebuhr's method is apologetic, in the technical sense that the term has in theology. He wants not only to proclaim what Christian ethics is and what it requires, but also to persuade his readers of it in terms that they will understand, beginning with ideas and concepts held in common with those who have alternative views of 'the true meaning of life'.

That is why Niebuhr's Christian ethics begins with human nature. It is an idea deeply rooted in Western thought, at least as far back as Aristotle, that the way human beings ought to live depends on the capacities and limitations that they have by nature. Niebuhr does not make a theological case for this starting-point. The reason for beginning with human nature is that it connects most directly with other ways of thinking about the human good. His apologetic method does not allow him to choose a starting-point for his own theological reasons. He must begin where the rationalists and the idealists, the Stoics and the Romantics, the bourgeoisie and the Marxists, begin.

Niebuhr avoids sweeping claims for his Christian understanding of human nature. He shows appreciation for the insights of other systems of thought, and he acknowledges that many of these systems began historically as plausible corrections to faulty formulations of the Christian idea. He makes his argument by comparison, not by systematic development of a theological idea. What he examines is how the Christian understanding of human nature and each of its rivals make sense of events and enable us to anticipate the future. Chapter by chapter, he builds the argument that 'the Biblical view of the unity of man as body and soul' (I. 13) is relatively more adequate than all its competitors.

What the 'Biblical view' of human nature captures in a variety of ways is the fact that the human being is both 'the image of God' and a finite creature, involved in 'the necessities and contingencies of the natural world' (I. 150). The biblical notion of the person as a unity of body and soul may be too simple for easy application to modern thought, but that unity is superior to the dualisms of the ancient world that treated the physical and the spiritual as independent of, or even hostile to, one another. The Christian interpretation maintains a tension between the freedom of the person, who is finally accountable only to God and not to other persons, and the absolute dependence of that free individual on God's will (I. 57). The balance between freedom and dependence is not easily struck, but this tension depicts human life more accurately than does modern individualism, which makes the individual the final judge of all things and exaggerates the emotional and intellectual freedom that persons have in relation to their social contexts. At the same time, 'prophetic religion...alone does justice to both the natural and the spiritual bases of individuality' (I. 69). Modern materialism and reductive social theories may offer people the momentary satisfaction of knowing exactly, objectively, where they stand in an evolutionary process of historical development, but they miss the dignity and worth that human life maintains, even when the historical movements in which people have found their meaning in life fail.

Niebuhr's Christian interpretation of human nature rests on an insightful comparative argument, applied to historical contexts and many different ways of thinking. The various formulations of the Christian understanding, each shaped by a different context, may sometimes be difficult to connect to one another, but the application of a single Christian principle surely could not sustain the persuasiveness and rhetorical power of *The Nature and Destiny of Man*. What links all of the ways of thinking about the Christian understanding is a human capacity to escape any particular set of limitations imposed by material circumstances or social authorities and yet, at the same time, an incapacity to throw off all limits—the inability to sustain our own lives and the impossibility of knowing our world, or even of knowing ourselves, perfectly. Call it the problem of soul and body, the problem of freedom and determinism, or the problem of the individual and society, the point is that each problem requires a view of human nature that values human self-transcendence, without claiming too much or too little for it. The biblical view that sets the finite human creature in a relationship with the eternal Creator does exactly that. But precisely what this capacity for self-transcendence means cannot be stated once and for all. It can only be clarified again and again in relation to other viewpoints that have not got it quite right:

How difficult it is to do justice to both the uniqueness of man and his affinities with the world of nature below him is proved by the almost unvarying tendency of those philosophies, which describe and emphasize the rational faculties of man or his capacity for self-transcendence to forget his relation to nature and to identify him, prematurely and unqualifiedly, with the divine and the eternal; and of naturalistic philosophies to obscure the uniqueness of man. (I. 4)

There are limits to Niebuhr's imagination as he develops these comparisons. His study of human nature is largely confined to the viewpoints available in Western thought and history, though his historical grasp through that tradition is very broad. Non-Western religions and their views of human nature rarely enter the discussion, and Niebuhr's characterizations of them are brief and flat, as when he dismisses 'religions and philosophies which negate life, and regard a "lifeless" eternity, such as Nirvana, as the only possible end of life' (I. 2). Most consideration of non-Western religions is postponed until the second part, the consideration of alternative views of 'Human Destiny', but even there Eastern religions fail to engage and challenge him in the ways that Western philosophies and social theories do. (See, for example, II. 11–15.) Historians have questioned the details of Niebuhr's account of Western thought, too. Robert Calhoun, historical theologian and Niebuhr's contemporary, dismissed the history in *The Nature and Destiny of Man*, but praised the prophet in its author (Fox 1996: 203). That dualism, too, may be too sharply drawn. Niebuhr's knowledge was vast, and his memory was prodigious, but he selected from what he knew and wove it together for moral purposes, rather than for intellectual refinement. The mind behind *The Nature and Destiny of Man* is the mind of a preacher who has lived long with the text and who is used to applying it to different circumstances; so he sees connections that lie beneath the surface and hears resonances that go beyond what he can spell out logically.

Niebuhr's account of prophetic religion and its relation to Western thought provides him with a clear framework for Christian ethics: 'human life has an ultimate religious warrant for transcending the custom of tribes, rational rules of conduct, and all general and abstract norms of behaviour. Yet Christian morality at its best is not antinomian because it is bound to the will of God as revealed in Christ: "All things are yours but ye are Christ's," said St. Paul' (I. 57–8). Christian ethics calls all codes, systems, and rules into question. Self-transcendence not only escapes material needs and social constraints. It transcends even our ideals of conduct and character. We can question prevailing norms not only with cynicism that seeks to evade their claims, but also from a moral point of view that sees their limitations and demands a higher righteousness of us. Christian ethics subjects all systems of law to the criticism of a 'higher law'. Yet the fact that every law can be questioned does not free us from all law. We are 'bound to the will of God', and this will is known in those forces of nature and history that limit us, even as we partly transcend them. 'No religion or philosophy can change the structure of human existence' (I. 69). Niebuhr is far more ready than most of his Protestant contemporaries to adopt ways of thinking drawn from the natural law tradition (Ramsey 1962: 111–18). Yet he expresses great scepticism about attempts to pin down the requirements of nature with the precision found in Roman Catholic ethics (I. 281). It falls to Christian ethics both to encourage the freedom and creativity with which people transcend the limits of custom and culture and at the same time to warn that there are forces of nature and history that constrain our freedom.

This realism about the 'structure of human existence' sometimes seems to contradict the aspiration for justice that Niebuhr encourages. It can appear profoundly conservative when it is applied to hopeful, new movements of social change. Niebuhr urged caution in the early days of the Civil Rights movement, at least in part because he feared that moving too quickly would provoke massive resistance (Niebuhr 1957: 89). Some critics have seen this as a weakness in Niebuhr's mature Christian realism, as though the radical Christian socialist of the 1930s was prepared at the end of his life to sacrifice justice to the requirements of social stability (Kellerman 1987). The problem, however, is not simply the temperamental conservatism of an older man. As we have seen, Niebuhr suggested at the beginning of his career that change often depends on visionaries whose hope for perfect justice outruns the real possibilities of history and human nature. The Christian realist who encourages the visionary's transcendence of existing injustices may then be in the awkward position of assisting the conservative to apply the brakes of reason to the enthusiastic demand for change. The expectation of perfect justice must be brought under the control of reason, Niebuhr writes at the very end of *Moral Man and Immoral Society*: 'One can only hope that reason will not destroy it before its work is done' (Niebuhr 1932: 277).

But prophetic religion never gives that sort of realism the last word. The capacity for indefinite transcendence over history and nature cannot be reduced to an endless cycle of revolutionary creativity reined in by the necessities of order. In the more complete picture that emerges in *The Nature and Destiny of Man*, freedom is the normative element in human nature. The constraints of human nature and social order may limit our moral aspirations and achievements, but they do not stand in judgement on them. The judgement comes from freedom. Realists will acknowledge the limitations, but also the judgement. 'There is, therefore, no historic structure of justice which can either fulfil the law of love or rest content in its inability to do so' (I. 296).

THEOLOGY

Niebuhr's account of human nature thus provides a framework for Christian ethics; but when we arrive at the end of the first part of *The Nature and Destiny of Man*, we find ourselves in possession of a rather strange apologetics. Niebuhr is not claiming that the Christian understanding of human nature more nearly satisfies our hopes and aspirations. Christianity's promise is, rather, that it more accurately describes our limitations.

That is why Niebuhr's project requires a second part devoted to human destiny. Because the promise of human freedom is incomplete in every historical context, our lives always stand under judgement. The fact that the incompleteness is inevitable does not excuse us from judgement. So meaningful human life is assured only by a destiny that lies beyond every historical context. That destiny includes not only the consummation of individual human searching in what we call 'eternal life', but also, and for Niebuhr especially, the final completion of history in a way that makes of it a meaningful whole (II. 1–6). What we are seeking cannot be achieved in any final way within history.

Niebuhr's genius, as we saw at the outset, was that he turned the inevitable frustration of human aspirations into good news for his generation. For those puzzled and disillusioned by the outcome of their efforts to remake history, it was important to know that it was not their vision, in particular, that was incomplete. The progress of civilization fell short of providing a meaningful history within history because every vision fails in that way. Equally important, perhaps, Niebuhr's generation needed confidence in 1939 that Hitler's vision was not about to succeed where they and their predecessors had failed. But this judgement on every human aspiration is good news, finally, only if a meaningful history is secured by a God who transcends history. Otherwise, we are left with only the small consolation of knowing that we failed because success was impossible. Disillusionment has the last word.

This is the point in Niebuhr's work where the gift of grace meets the needs of nature and where the apologetic purpose of *The Nature and Destiny of Man* is realized. Human beings who see their own limitations clearly are in a position to acknowledge their need for what God alone can provide. But that is a risky apologetics, because it may leave those who hear it lost in their disillusionment, rather than turning them to God.

This is the 'point of contact' between grace and the natural endowments of the soul, which even Luther, despite his doctrine of total depravity, admits and which Karl Barth seeks desperately to deny. As long as there is such a point of contact there is something in man to which appeal can be made; though it must be admitted that men may be driven to despair, rather than repentance, by the events or the appeals which shake the self-confidence of the sinful self. (II. 117)

This transition from human nature to human destiny is the theological centre of Niebuhr's project in *The Nature and Destiny of Man*. While the first part is structured by the comparison between the biblical understanding of human nature and the various classical and modern alternatives to it, the second part is largely devoted to a straightforward exposition of the fulfilment of history promised by Jesus' reinterpretation of Israel's messianic expectations. In the discussion of human destiny, there are reminders of the comparative analysis whereby Niebuhr established his position on human nature. Religions where a Christ is expected are compared with those where a Christ is not expected (II. 6–34). But the question about human destiny does not admit of a comparative answer. The question about human destiny presupposes the Christian answer. 'It is not possible to interpret cultures according to their expectation or want of expectations of *a* Christ without drawing upon the faith that *the* Christ has been revealed' (II. 5).

Historians and theologians applauded the second volume of *The Nature and Destiny of Man* (Fox 1996: 212–15). For historians, it offered a more nuanced view of classical and Renaissance humanism. The harsh polemic of Niebuhr's criticism of Renaissance humanism in the first volume is softened a bit. There is something of a synthesis between the Christian view of history and the Renaissance affirmation of human possibilities (II. 204–12). This change was partly because Niebuhr had in fact learned some things in the preparation of the second volume, and partly because he was less constrained in his account of human destiny by a mode of argument that needed to establish the comparative strength of the Christian view at every point.

For theologians, it demonstrated Niebuhr's sure grasp of a thoroughly orthodox Protestant theology of grace, while offering an alternative to Karl Barth's view that threatened to cut the connection between God's action and human experience altogether. We are situated in a particular place in nature and history, and we learn in experience that we cannot escape its limitations. If we refuse this lesson, we find, paradoxically, that we only become more limited. 'According to the Christian doctrine the sinful self... does not have the power to lift itself out of its narrow interests. It cannot do so because all of its transcendent powers are intimately and organically related to its finiteness. It is tempted by this situation to pretend emancipation; but this pretension is its sin' (II. 113). We are thus powerless to escape the judgement that we experience in our own freedom. That is why those who become fully aware of their human condition are apt to fall into despair. They see all too clearly that there is simply nothing they can do that will resolve the contradictions imposed by their own finitude. They may be more or less successful in achieving some of their immediate goals. They may actually make life better for some of those who share their time in history. But they will not achieve the perfect justice they seek; nor will they escape the judgement that this failure imposes on them. Resolution can come only from beyond the self in a gracious intervention that destroys the attempts at self-justification. 'Yet when the sinful self is broken and the real self is fulfilled from beyond itself, the consequence is a new life rather than destruction. In the Christian doctrine the self is therefore both more impotent and more valuable, more dependent and more indestructible than in the alternate doctrines' (II. 113–14).

A DIVIDED WORLD AND A MEANINGFUL UNIVERSE

Our hope for a meaningful history thus rests not on our own accomplishments, but on a kind of new life that God alone provides. For Niebuhr, the tragedies of contemporary history made that theology of grace compelling. Others, however, were surprised to see this astute political analysis culminate in a theological claim. The philosopher Morton White found Niebuhr's theological convictions incomprehensible, but he quipped that there were 'atheists for Niebuhr' who had learned from his insights into human nature (White 1959: 88).

The secular critics directed their objections not to the details of Niebuhr's theological argument that a transcendent God is the ground of our hope for a meaningful history, but to the prior assumption that a meaningful history is something that human beings need in the first place. A limited, pragmatic, comparative approach to experience not only makes it difficult to establish absolute truths about history. It raises doubts that questions about whether or not history is meaningful make any practical difference. If we are trying to make choices between complex alternatives in what is often a dangerous world, should not our attention be fully devoted to framing those choices accurately and getting the best information we can about the alternatives? A contemporary pragmatist is already well enough aware that the alternatives among which we must choose are relative to one another. What we have to decide is which possibility best serves our present purposes. Does it make any difference whether there is a larger perspective from which the alternatives are all limited and incomplete?

Niebuhr framed the question of human destiny in such a way that the choices it leaves us are repentance or despair. His theological readers appreciated the way in which this brought his analysis of human nature into a closer connection with the doctrine of grace. Niebuhr's secular critics, however, suggested that the urgency of the moment may provide sufficient distraction to render both repentance and despair irrelevant. In a world of rapid change, difficult choices, and over-simplified ideologies, those who do not repent think they have another alternative besides despair. They can refuse such ultimate choices altogether.

Niebuhr's activities in the years after *The Nature and Destiny of Man* have suggested to some that he tacitly agreed with the secular critics. While the structure of *Nature and Destiny* suggested a trajectory from politics to history to theology, Niebuhr became increasingly preoccupied with politics, and he wrote little more on the theological questions that were central to the volume on human destiny. The post-war world soon became as sharply divided as it had been in 1939, and the destructive power available to the United States and the Soviet Union far exceeded anything that those who feared for Western civilization could have anticipated when Niebuhr began his Gifford Lectures a decade earlier. Confronted with this risky new reality, Niebuhr undertook a moral critique of Soviet communism that was, if anything, more aggressive than his attacks on Nazism and fascism in the 1930s. At the same time, he urged a realistic acceptance of the structures of empire that divided the world between the two superpowers, lest leaders eager to vindicate their own righteousness plunge the world into catastrophe (Niebuhr 1959). This was quite enough to do, and it left little time to worry about the meaning of history.

Nevertheless, Niebuhr retained his basic belief in the morally meaningful existence set out in prophetic religion. Not only the alternatives of repentance and despair, but also the possibility of sustained commitment to moral choice and action, depend on a unity that lies beyond what we can achieve in history. Without confidence in the judgement that continually demands a more complete justice, our decisions about justice quickly degenerate into a calculation of self-interest. Without hope for final unity, we lose our motivation to seek the limited achievements that are available to us in history. Langdon Gilkey sees this theology of history as the centre of Niebuhr's work and the critical link between his theology and his ethics.

Unless the meaning of life is in the midst of its passage perfectly clear and fully secure—and [Niebuhr] has surely shown that it is not—then the presence of the power and mercy of God at the Beginning and at the End, to complete what we cannot complete and to purge what we have corrupted, are the sole grounds for any real hope. (Gilkey 2001: 222)

Niebuhr's secular allies wanted to share his moral aims without sharing his theology, and this collaboration became the focus of Niebuhr's prodigious energy during the last part of his career. He was sure that his partners shared his commitment, but he was never confident that they could sustain it unless they caught at least a glimpse of his morally meaningful universe.

So alongside his political work and writings of the late 1940s and 1950s, Niebuhr turned again to the apologetic task. The aim now was not to bring the reader to the stark alternatives of repentance or despair, but to offer a more modest argument that the Christian confidence in a final coherence beyond the partial coherences of history has at least a 'limited rational validation' within history itself (Niebuhr 1949: 152). In short, the method that the first volume of *The Nature and Destiny of Man* applied to the problem of human nature was subsequently to be applied to the question of history and human destiny. To offer a Christian interpretation of the way in which a culture understands history may, as Niebuhr originally suggested, require us to draw upon the faith 'that *the* Christ has been revealed' (II. 5), but having this interpretation widely shared is so vital to Niebuhr's ethical purposes that he had to accept the challenge of making it at least plausible to those who shared those purposes with him. The fanaticism of those who think they have already resolved the incoherence of history and the nihilism of those who think that history has no coherence are both alike so dangerous that no one who seeks justice can afford to leave them unchallenged. That is particularly true because those who seek justice are themselves tempted to nihilism by their own experiences of frustration and failure.

CHRISTIAN REALISM AND NEW REALITIES

The Nature and Destiny of Man is not only Reinhold Niebuhr's most important book. It provides the structure that connects many of his books, essays, sermons, and lectures across his long career. From *An Interpretation of Christian Ethics* at the beginning of his academic career through the pointed essays on race (Niebuhr 1968) and presidential power (Niebuhr 1969) that he wrote near the end of his life, Niebuhr maintained the conviction that divine judgement transcends our partial moral achievements and our inevitable moral failures and that this judgement both sustains the search for justice and restrains our self-righteousness.

In the years after World War II, Niebuhr was increasingly concerned with the problems of stability and order in a world in which the great powers overestimated their ability to control history and revolutionary movements envisioned social transformations that they were not yet equipped to make real. Niebuhr continued to insist that prophetic faith always demands a higher justice than society is currently able to deliver, but his judgements on particular events and movements became more cautious. Subsequent generations of theologians and ethicists, looking back, have tended to view Christian realism through the lens of these later works. They have seen Christian realism as somewhat conservative, despite its prophetic rhetoric, because of its emphasis on the risks and ambiguities of change. Above all, they have found Niebuhr's realism focused on questions regarding control of political and economic power and unable to comprehend the power that is hidden in the resistance of the marginalized.

This criticism is important. Very little in Reinhold Niebuhr's understanding of world politics would have prepared him for the end of apartheid in South Africa, the fall of communism in Eastern Europe, the breakup of the Soviet Union, or the growth of democracy in many parts of Latin America. Niebuhr would no doubt have rejoiced in these changes, but he would not have expected them; and his later writings suggest that he would have worried about developments that seemed to change too much, too fast.

Nevertheless, warnings about the risks of change are not the whole of Niebuhr's legacy, and not the most important part of it. The centre of Niebuhr's realism lies in the more balanced judgement that there is 'no historic structure of justice which can either fulfill the law of love or rest content in its inability to do so' (I. 296). That judgement was derived from the enduring realities of human nature, rather than from transient events, and it is resilient enough both to shake the contentment of the powerful and to provoke the discontent of the weak. The Christian view of human nature and destiny enables us to speak a word of both judgement and hope, and to speak it in whatever situation we find ourselves.

Reinhold Niebuhr was so adept at describing the situation of his generation that his accounts of its problems still engage us, half century and more later. But we are not where they were. Reading *The Nature and Destiny of Man* takes us beyond the details of his generation's problems to the theology that shaped Niebuhr's views. It is that balanced, biblical understanding that we still need, though we may find that its lessons for us are quite different from the ones that Niebuhr's generation had to learn. Judgement today speaks as it did then to the powerful who think too much of what they have already achieved; but it speaks also, and especially, about the power of hope among those for whom hope is the only power they have.

References and Suggested Reading

BARTH, K. (1961). *Church Dogmatics*, III/4. Edinburgh: T. & T. Clark.

BONHOEFFER, D. (1995). *Ethics*. New York: Simon & Schuster.

BROWN, C. C. (2002). *Niebuhr and his Age: Reinhold Niebuhr's Prophetic Role and Legacy*. Philadelphia: Trinity Press International.

DORRIEN, G. (2003). *The Making of American Liberal Theology: Idealism, Realism, and Modernity, 1900–1950*. Louisville, Ky.: Westminster/John Knox Press.

FOX, R. (1996). *Reinhold Niebuhr: A Biography*, rev. edn. Ithaca, NY: Cornell University Press.

GILKEY, L. (2001). *On Niebuhr: A Theological Study*. Chicago: University of Chicago Press.

HAUERWAS, S. (2001). *With the Grain of the Universe: The Church's Witness and Natural Theology*. Grand Rapids, Mich.: Brazos Press.

KELLERMAN, B. (1987). 'Apologist of Power: The Long Shadow of Reinhold Niebuhr's Christian Realism', *Sojourners*, 16 (Mar.), 15–20.

LIPPMANN, W. (1944). *U.S. War Aims*. Boston: Little, Brown and Company.

LOVIN, R. W. (1995). *Reinhold Niebuhr and Christian Realism*. Cambridge: Cambridge University Press.

NIEBUHR, R. (1932). *Moral Man and Immoral Society*. New York: Charles Scribner's Sons.

—— (1949). *Faith and History: A Comparison of Christian and Modern Views of History*. New York: Charles Scribner's Sons.

—— (1953). *Christian Realism and Political Problems*. New York: Charles Scribner's Sons.

—— (1957). 'Civil Rights and Democracy', *Christianity and Crisis*, 17 (8 July), 89.

—— (1959). *The Structure of Nations and Empires: A Study of the Recurring Patterns and Problems of the Political Order in Relation to the Unique Problems of the Nuclear Age*. New York: Charles Scribner's Sons.

—— (1964). *The Nature and Destiny of Man: A Christian Interpretation*. New York: Charles Scribner's Sons.

—— (1968). 'The Negro Minority and its Fate in a Self-Righteous Nation', *Social Action*, 35 (Oct.), 53–64.

—— (1969). 'The King's Chapel and the King's Court', *Christianity and Crisis*, 29 (4 Aug.), 211–13.

—— (1979). *An Interpretation of Christian Ethics*. New York: Seabury Press.

—— (1986). *The Essential Reinhold Niebuhr*. New Haven: Yale University Press.

—— (1992). *Love and Justice: Selections from the Shorter Writings of Reinhold Niebuhr*. Louisville, Ky.: Westminster/John Knox Press.

RAMSEY, P. (1962). *Nine Modern Moralists*. Englewood Cliffs, NJ: Prentice-Hall.

WHITE, M. (1959). *Religion, Politics, and the Higher Learning*. Cambridge, Mass.: Harvard University Press.

CHAPTER 29

JOHN MAHONEY'S
THE MAKING OF
MORAL THEOLOGY

JAMES F. KEENAN, SJ

IN order to appreciate the long-standing significance of John Mahoney's *The Making of Moral Theology: A Study of the Roman Catholic Tradition*, we need to consider the background, the aim, the contents, and the influence of this work. I will proceed through these considerations.

THE BACKGROUND OF MAHONEY'S
THE MAKING OF MORAL THEOLOGY

As Josef Fuchs noted (1993), innovation marked the agenda of most Roman Catholic moral theologians from the 1960s through the 1980s. The innovation was, for the most part, to take moral theology out of the isolating framework in which it had functioned from the end of the sixteenth century until the mid-twentieth century.

During those four centuries, moral theologians stipulated that the task of moral theology was singularly to focus on what belonged to sin and what did not. Thus, their textbooks, commonly referred to as 'moral manuals', were predominantly attempts to outline what actions violated God's, church, and moral law. Moreover, the moral manualists specifically distinguished themselves from those writing about growing in 'perfection' or the ascetical life. In a manner of speaking, for four centuries moral and ascetical theologians split the first principle of the natural law (to do good and to avoid evil) in two: the ascetical manuals instructed on the pursuit of the good; the moral manuals about the avoidance of evil.

We see this distinction clearly in the first Roman Catholic moral manual in English, which appeared in 1908: *A Manual of Moral Theology* by the English Jesuit Thomas Slater (1855–1928). In its preface, Slater acknowledges that other manuals have already appeared in German, Italian, Spanish, and French, and then asserts that moral theology's exclusive preoccupation is sin. By focusing on sin, he affirms that there is no need for moral theology to engage ascetical theology. He writes:

[Moral theology] is the product of centuries of labor bestowed by able and holy men on the practical problems of Christian ethics. Here, however, we must ask the reader to bear in mind that the manuals of moral theology are technical works intended to help the confessor and the parish priest in the discharge of their duties. They are as technical as the text-books of the lawyer and the doctor. They are not intended for edification, nor do they hold up a high ideal of Christian perfection for the imitation of the faithful. They deal with what is of obligation under pain of sin; they are books of moral pathology. They are necessary for the Catholic priest to enable him to administer the sacrament of Penance and to fulfill other duties.

Slater notes the 'very abundant' literature of ascetical theology, but adds that 'moral theology proposes to itself the much humbler but still necessary task of defining what is right and what wrong in all the practical relations of the Christian life.... The first step on the right road of conduct is to avoid evil' (I. 5–6).

From the 1940s through the 1950s several theologians attempted to change the foundations of contemporary moral theology. Among them were three of particular note. First, during and after World War II, a Benedictine monk, Dom Odon Lottin (1880–1965), studied scholastic theology of the twelfth and thirteenth centuries. From 1942 to 1957, he produced eight enormous volumes that treat thematically the Scholastics' positions on the moral epistemology of the agent, intentionality, free will, choice, virtue, etc. Rather than staying within the manualists' demarcated territory of the sinful action, Lottin studied the Scholastics to see how they meticulously sought to understand the nature of moral agency.

As opposed to the manualists, who claimed historical and universal consistency in their teaching about bad moral actions, Lottin found that the Scholastic theologians (pre-dating the neo-Scholastic manualists) were more interested in persons than actions, debate than universal agreement, and historical development than long-standing consistency. Later, Lottin applied these insights to his own contemporary moral theology, and proposed in two works (1947, 1954) the well-ordered and well-intending agent, capable of growth by pursuing the moral virtues (see also Iozzio 1995).

Lottin's investigations of Scholastic theology led him to a more integrated moral theology. By contrast with the manualists, the Scholastics situate moral theology within the broader context of theology itself, engaging the school of perfection rather than ignoring it. For the Scholastics, to define morals as opposed to both systematic or dogmatic theology and ascetical theology, was to bring harm rather than order to the discipline.

Fritz Tillmann's (1874–1953) research paralleled Lottin's. Tillman's own earlier work as a Scripture scholar led him to claim that the goal of Catholic morality is discipleship of Christ: we become disciples by entering into the self-understanding of Christ. Among his works are *The Master Calls: A Handbook of Christian Living*, which celebrates the moral life in terms of the Christian vocation: 'we are made free to share in the magnificent liberty of the children of God' (1960: 23). In order to give this vision flesh, Tillman casts the entire law of Christ into a threefold structure: the love of God, neighbour, and self.

Tillmann's work is a thoroughgoing departure from the neo-Scholasticism of the moral manuals. By turning to the person of Jesus Christ, and by outlining the way of salvation according to the threefold Love Command, Tillmann gives us an integrated moral theology, rooted in the Sacred Scriptures, moving away from sin and toward union with God, neighbour, and self, deeply affected by Christian piety, and founded on love and the person of Jesus Christ. In Roman Catholic moral theology, no other Scripture-based moral handbook for the laity had appeared since the *Enchiridion militis christiani* (1502) of Desiderius Erasmus (1466–1536).

Finally, indebted to Tillmann, Gérard Gilleman proposed in *The Primacy of Charity* a spirituality-based ethics founded on charity, the virtue by which we are in union with God and called to love God, neighbour, and self. Gilleman's work of rediscovering in Thomas Aquinas's writings moral theology's natural and necessary affinity with spirituality provided a deeper and more dynamic understanding of the moral truth that the agent pursues. To reintegrate moral theology with spirituality, Gilleman went from charity, the form of the virtues, to the virtuous life. By re-establishing the primacy of charity, whereby moral subjects discover within themselves their primary identity as children of God, Gilleman developed an anthropology that moved from the depths of the human person to expression in virtuous dispositions and actions. Gilleman's work, essentially a dissertation, is certainly the most important work in fundamental Roman Catholic moral theology in the twentieth century.

After these ground-breaking works, moral theologians rarely looked back at history but, rather, forward to incorporate moral theology into a much more integrated, positive, progressive, personal agenda. Bernhard Häring (1912–88) published a wide-ranging three-volume work (1954, 1961–6) that described moral theology not primarily as an instrument for avoiding sin, but rather as pursuit of the good. The law of Christ is the Love Commandment which we can attain through charity. Häring re-examined the many resources that contemporary Catholics had at their disposal: the Scriptures, grace, the tradition, the natural law, experience, virtues, etc.

Josef Fuchs (1912–2005) promoted moral theology as an enterprise needing to resituate itself within the work of theology which tries to understand God, the human, the world, and the church. Preferring the essay to the book, Fuchs never wrote a comprehensive treatise on this subject, but continually explored the person who seeks through the natural law to realize him or herself rightly in the world (see Graham 2002). Similarly, Louis Janssens (1908–2001) developed a metaphysics of moral truth in the context of personalism.

Though each tried to 'revise' (many refer to these writers and their colleagues and disciples as 'revisionists') the tradition of moral theology, they presented neither a history nor a thematic treatment of the tradition they were trying to reform. Similarly, though they opposed the manualist theology, none made a case against the moral manuals or against the roots of that extended episode of the tradition (see Keenan 2001).

Of course, not everyone was satisfied with innovation and revision. In the English-speaking world, for instance, many Roman Catholics remained inclined to the manualist tradition. The manualist works of Henry Davis and John McHugh and Charles Callan were well regarded. Later theologians like John Ford and Gerald Kelly relinquished their authority to the ever expanding exercise of episcopal and papal magisterial teaching. In turn, bishops and popes followed the manualists' interests in bad actions or sins, though now often named as 'intrinsically evil' actions. Of course, many of the theologians who supported these developments were 'the ghost writers' for these teachers, but still episcopal office, rather than trained competency, became the locus of Roman Catholic moral teaching authority (see Black and Keenan 2001).

In the United States, these attempts were rebuffed by, among others, Charles Curran and Richard McCormick. Unlike their European counterparts, both deliberately aimed to disprove the claims of key elements in the manualist tradition. Curran (1968) invited an impressive array of diverse theologians to consider the claim of moral absolutes, and McCormick, through his *Notes in Moral Theology*, consistently made the case against intrinsic evil. While McCormick mostly attended to bioethical cases, Curran (1980), like his European colleagues, provided a variety of insights that pertained to a revised construction for moral theology. Recently, Curran (1999) has synthesized these insights into a sophisticated, comprehensive moral theology. But not even Curran presented the 'what' of what it was they were trying to replace, or the 'why' as regards why it was so eminently replaceable.

Two very different scholars presented historical investigations of portions of the Roman Catholic moral tradition. John T. Noonan, jun., studied the development of moral teaching, or casuistry, on a variety of very specific topics: abortion, contraception, usury, etc. Louis Vereecke wrote about moral theologians from the fourteenth to the eighteenth century by looking at their cases, particular interests, philosophical influences, etc. Together these writers gave us penetrating studies: Noonan of these particular issues, Vereecke of very specific cases, very particular writers, and very specific philosophical influences. But, like Lottin and Curran, neither ever presented a comprehensive study of the influences that shaped the entire moral tradition; nor did they therefore set about evaluating those influences. Mahoney's *The Making of Moral Theology: A Study of the Roman Catholic Tradition* did just that.

THE AIM OF *THE MAKING* OF *MORAL THEOLOGY*

In 1985 Servais Pinckaers published his study of the sources of moral theology. But that otherwise salutary effort never approached the breadth, depth, and scope of Mahoney's achievement. No one other than Pinckaers ever attempted what Mahoney achieved: an investigation of the central historical themes that comprised moral theology. As Oliver O'Donovan astutely observed, 'we must not miss the importance of his turn to history as a mode of pursuing moral theology. In teaching us that our contemporary disagreements need to be understood in the light of the past that has pursued them, he is directing the community of theological moralists along a path that they badly need to explore' (1988: 350).

In eight chapters, Mahoney first named and examined six major topics that constituted the moral tradition: auricular confession, the legacy of Augustine, the distinction between nature and supernature, magisterial authority, subjectivity, and the language of law. He then turned to a contemporary reading of the convergence of those influences by explicating the writing of *Humanae vitae*, and concluded with a glimpse of his own hope for the future.

Significantly, Mahoney resisted the urge to consider moral theology as expressed solely in the manualist tradition, from the end of the seventeenth to the mid-twentieth century. In this way, he opted to see Catholic morality as Lottin, Tillmann, and Gilleman did, as something richer and more formidable than the moral manuals themselves. Still, some reviewers took him to task for this. James Pollock, who had written on the casuist François Genet, lamented Mahoney's lack of concentration on the manualists: 'no period is more important in the history of moral theology than the late 16th, 17th, and early 18th centuries'. But he then added, 'this is perhaps less a criticism of M. than a reflection on our almost complete ignorance of the primary sources of this central period' (1984: 763). John Gallagher was less forgiving. Because Mahoney did not specifically examine the making of the moral manualists, Gallagher wondered how and what actually pertains to that tradition:

> What strikes me as somewhat amiss in Mahoney's project is that he never clearly defines what he means by moral theology. . . . Mahoney's book is important because it provides us with a general sense of the theological and ecclesiastical forces that over the years framed many of the basic questions as well as most of the possible answers to the moral conun-drums of Christian existence. But this book does not give us a clear sense of what indeed these forces made—what precisely is meant by 'moral theology'. (1989: 280)

A year after making this complaint, Gallagher (1990) answered that moral theology was the manualist tradition.

Mahoney's decision to examine expansively the terrain of moral theology affirms the claims of Lottin and others. Mahoney had, I think, another reason for going beyond manualism. He had a sustained interest in promoting the relevance of the Holy Spirit for moral theology. After his dissertation on the Holy Spirit in the writings of Thomas Aquinas, Mahoney published a collection of essays on the Spirit, fruits of the dissertation as well as the development of other ideas. The essays were published in 1981, the very year Mahoney gave the Martin D'Arcy Lectures, which were the first instance of what would later become *The Making of Moral Theology*. Similarly, in the last pages of *The Making of Moral Theology*, Mahoney turns to the idea of *koinōnia*, or 'the fellowship of the Holy Spirit' (2 Cor. 13: 14) (p. 343). Mahoney recognized that no historical period had done more to eliminate the presence of the Spirit than manualism, a point evident in the text from Slater quoted above. In order to allow for the influence of the Spirit, Mahoney had to acknowledge that moral theology was more than manualism.

Unlike Gallagher, both an expert on the manualists as well as an occasional apologist for them, Mahoney rejected any reductionistic attempts on moral the-ology and clearly allied himself with those who called to expand the shaping of moral theology to be more scriptural (Tillmann), more spiritual (Gilleman), and more theological (Fuchs) (see Patrick 1988; McCormick 1987).

Still, unlike Lottin and Gilleman, as well as Noonan and Vereecke, Mahoney was interested in historical investigation less for the sake of retrieval than for the sake of deconstruction (on the variety of ways that moral theology uses history, see Vereecke 1974; Keenan 2001). Lottin and Gilleman were looking back to history especially to retrieve elements long lost by the manualists. Mahoney, however, wanted effectively to find out what was/is holding us back. For this reason, almost all the reviewers noted that from Mahoney we learned not about the riches of the tradition, but rather the restraining elements.

Endean rightly notes that Mahoney takes 'us back to free us from what can so easily be an unreflective bondage to our past and our traditions' (1988: 683). O'Donovan agrees, and locates Mahoney's book as belonging to the 'genre of theological self-demystification—the most elegant and entertaining example of its kind. He has given his indictment with lucidity and irony.... It is, in fact, a book all about the bad influences which "conspired" to form Moral Theology' (1988: 349). Some reviewers asked whether there might have been a more positive engagement with the shaping of moral theology. David Brown, for instance, comments that 'what one misses from this liberal Catholic is any sympathetic engagement with the past' (1989: 130). But Peter Byrne suggests that Mahoney is offering not the 'harsh exposé of an external sceptic, but the gentle, if persistent, reflection of one who is engaged in examining the basis of his own thinking'. He concludes: 'The resulting effect is to remind us of the limitations and eccentricities of Catholic moral theology that surround its great contribution to the development of the Western moral tradition' (1988: 543).

Mahoney delivered the negative critique, interestingly, without ever presenting the foundations of his own overarching theology. Only in his closing pages does, he propose a vague heuristic guide for the future of moral theology. Thus, he accomplished the critique by examining the tradition on its own terms. Most often his indictment is animated by an appreciation of the totality of factors that need to be adequately considered regarding grace, the supernatural, the natural, sin, moral reasoning, etc. Mahoney is particularly vigilant as regards the proclivity of some keepers of the tradition who try to reduce theological insight to an insufficient or inadequate engagement with reality, the nature of the human, or the tradition itself. For this reason, in the final chapter, in proposing broad guidelines for a more robust tradition, he emphasizes totality, diversity, and mystery. That is, the animated Mahoney turns to the Spirit to liberate the tradition from the constrictive hold that others have placed on it and on the human person.

Finally, this attempt to deconstruct the moral tradition was not unopposed. A year before the publication of *The Making of Moral Theology*, John Mahoney surrendered the *imprimatur* to an earlier work on bioethics (1984). When the book was first published, it received the designation, which meant that the diocesan bishop found a work free from doctrinal or moral error. Others read the *imprimatur*, however, as a diocesan endorsement. To prevent the confusion, Mahoney relinquished the official judgement. At the same time, he resigned as principal of the Jesuit school of theology in London, Heythrop College, and assumed the F. D. Maurice Chair of Moral and Social Theology at King's College, London (see Burns 1987; Hebblethwaite 1986; and 'Moral Theologian's Book loses *imprimatur*'). In that new position, Mahoney turned away from fundamental moral theology and bioethics, resolutely to social and economic ethics. But when he attempted to publish the D'Arcy Lectures, he was met, as William Spohn notes (1988: 90) with 'strenuous efforts made in Rome to censor this study'.

THE CONTENTS OF *THE MAKING*
OF MORAL THEOLOGY

Because of the comprehensive density of Mahoney's treatment of each topic, and because each topic stands as its own lecture, we need to look at the specific chapters in this work.

Clearly, the most important chapter is the first. Brilliantly, Mahoney opens his work: 'To begin a historical study of the making of moral theology with an examination of the influence of auricular confession may appear to some an intriguing, and to others an unattractive prospect; but however one regards it there is no doubt that the development of the practice and of the discipline of moral theology is to be found in the growth and spread of "confession" in the Church' (p. 1).

Mahoney convincingly narrates, from the Patristic era through the penitential and later confessional manuals to the moral manuals, that the moral tradition has been fixated with sin, or what he calls a 'spiritual pathology'. By examining early councils, the penitential tariffs themselves, the imposition of the 'Easter duty' by Innocent III at the Fourth Lateran Council, the Council of Trent, and the subsequent moral textbooks and manuals, Mahoney marshalled the evidence for his indictment of moral theology's obsession with sin. Whereas many moral theologians criticized the manualist era for its emphasis on sin, Mahoney blasts the entire tradition that singularly focused on 'man in his moral vulnerability' (p. 28). He writes:

The pessimistic anthropology from which it started, and which served inevitably to confirm and reinforce itself, particularly when the subject was pursued in growing isolation from the rest of theology and developed as a spiritual arm of the Church's legal system, drove moral theology increasingly to concern itself almost exclusively with the darker and insubordinate side of human existence (p. 28).

He calls this 'miasma of sin' 'not only distasteful but profoundly disquieting' (p. 28).

Mahoney's decision to begin his investigation with a chapter on sin is extraordinarily important. Though he did not make the claim, Mahoney effectively suggests that, aside from the Scholastics, the Catholic moral tradition has never really been interested in the first half of the first principle of the natural law. With singular concern only for avoiding evil, the tradition has not looked at what it means to be a disciple of Christ and to follow in his footsteps. Rather, it has looked solely at the person as spiritually sick and wounded. Thus, moral theology became not an instrument of the Gospel to put into practice the salvific call to discipleship, but rather the ever disarming study that encouraged priests to see nothing but human weakness and moral sickness in themselves and the laity. As if emulating Lot's wife, moral theology became fixated not on the promise of redemption, but on the darkness of human history.

This disabling enterprise, Mahoney argues, contributes to the bleakness of moral theology, which resists any confidence in grace, the Spirit, or Christ. Ironically, because it remained for centuries with such a pathetic self-understanding, it could never appreciate the actual nature of sin. Sin became subdued by the penitential, confessional, and moral manuals; it was compartmentalized into discrete, manageable categories which profiled sin in legal and individualistic terms. Theologians over centuries 'domesticated and trivialized sin', and did 'little to engender and foster a healthy respect for real sin' (p. 32). Beyond a doubt, Mahoney's first salvo was the most penetrating.

The second fell flat. Because his implicit aim was to liberate moral theology from bondage, he chose not to praise Augustine (at all), so as to break the hold of 'the troubled person of Saint Augustine' (p. 38) on moral theology. Whereas many readers were convinced of his arguments in the first chapter, the wholesale denunciation of the Augustinian legacy in the second was not convincing.

Mahoney could have argued, as Antonio Orbe (1987) has, that the tradition would have been better if it had favoured Irenaeus as well as, or more than, Augustine. The former lacks the sense of darkness that often dominates the latter. Similarly, Mahoney could have turned to Augustine's theology of love or his sense of realism to counter the more problematic dimensions of Augustine. But Mahoney chose solely to repudiate Augustine.

Still, Mahoney's target is not Augustine in general, but 'his moral teaching, it is there that the darkness and the sombre pessimism are most in evidence and, it must be said, at their most dogmatic and devastating' (p. 45). He examines Augustine's teachings on grace, specifically in the claim that God does not command the impossible, and on sexual morality.

Mahoney notes that for Augustine, 'grace is almost exclusively isolated in the will of man'. Augustine leaves us with the implicit presupposition that all that is needed in the face of moral dilemma and challenge is 'sufficient effort' (p. 55). Elsewhere Mahoney was more blunt about 'the view of grace which it presupposes, as supercharged willpower regardless of other individual and social resources, or almost miraculously supplying for their absence. It can also too easily sound like maintaining that a sufficiently high upgrade of petrol in a car will make up for a faulty clutch or even for lack of viable roads, for it ignores the Thomist maxim that grace builds on nature and, indeed, human society' (1986: 485). Mahoney's argument against Augustine here is twofold: Augustine reduces moral dilemma to no more than a challenge to the will and, thereby, leaves the Christian with the belief that all challenges are surmountable. Mahoney believes that Augustine's claim lacks a sense of reality: 'with its internally and socially separatist tendencies Augustine's theology of grace is at root unhistorical' (p. 56).

Reductionism again becomes Mahoney's charge when he critiques Augustine's view that 'sexuality was exercised either for children or for lust' (p. 60). Augustine's tendency to exclusive categories leaves us with an either/or approach to evaluating the fundamental complexities of human interrelational experience. Moreover, its unnecessary exclusion of other values or goods shows again a lack of appreciation of the historical. For Mahoney, Augustine grossly limits the range of sexuality, and in many ways frames it according to his own 'introspective make-up', which is nowhere more in evidence than in his view of women: 'He could not for the life of him think of any reason why woman should have been given to man than for the procreation of children, "as the soil is a help to the seed"' (p. 66).

Mahoney's argument is not solely with Augustine, but also with the way the tradition has uncritically embraced his influence. The narrow and at times dualistic world of Augustine becomes the foundation of much contemporary moral teaching, leaving us with a legacy that inhibits a full and adequate ability to provide moral guidance. Indeed, the negative anthropological vision of Augustine accompanies a pathetic obsession with sin and, as Mahoney notes, while quoting *The City of God* (XIX. 27), 'it is no wonder that for Augustine "our righteousness in this life consists in the forgiveness of sins rather than in the perfection of virtues"' (p. 68).

After seeing the deleterious effects of the practice of confession and the tradition's domination by one major Church thinker, Mahoney turns to 'the power of ideas—the control exercised on men's minds by major concepts. Of the ideas which have powerfully shaped moral theology in its long making none have achieved more prominence, or perhaps notoriety, than those of "nature" and of "the supernatural"' (p. 72). So begins the third, and most balanced, of the eight chapters.

Mahoney pursues here the same interest in repudiating exclusive reductionistic distinctions. If the second chapter was a diatribe against Augustine, the third is a guarded, even critical complaint against Aquinas. After noting the richness of Aquinas's notion of law as an order of reason for the common good and of his definition of 'good in terms of those fundamental satisfactions to which every human being is essentially and naturally orientated' (p. 80), Mahoney notes how the natural law emerged in papal teachings toward the end of the nineteenth century. Here he finds that the natural loses out to the supernatural and laments that another theological distinction works not to include, but to exclude. Again blaming Augustine, this time for the cosmic division between the natural and the supernatural, and also the Scholastics for appropriating it, Mahoney argues that 'one consequence of this for moral theology was to lay all the stress on supernatural moral activity as alone sufficient for salvation, to the detriment of merely human, natural, and terrestrial moral behavior. Morality became a two-tiered activity in requiring supernatural motivation and even "infused" moral virtues which alone could count with God' (p. 89).

Mahoney then turns to the parallel distinction between reason and revelation, which becomes problematic for Aquinas because, inasmuch as reason brings order to the natural, revelation merely helps reason to attain better what with difficulty it would eventually grasp. This 'remedial' function for revelation inhibits us from seeing how the natural law could be 'enriched' by revelation, a claim that Mahoney makes but does not develop.

Similarly, Mahoney laments the singular preference of natural law theologians and philosophers to privilege the rational exclusively as the guide of moral judgement. 'Man's nature includes reason but is more than reason. It has other elements of givenness about which man is to act reasonably but which are not identical with reason, such elements as the volitional, emotional, corporeal, and social aspects of his humanity' (p. 111). Again, the critique is made, but not elaborated.

In each instance, Mahoney raises an excluding conceptual distinction that he sees as minimizing the tradition's ability to assess reality precisely, because the distinction dismisses other data as irrelevant. Mahoney's holistic tendency serves then as a critical point of departure for reincorporating what the distinction between the natural and supernatural bifurcated.

Mahoney turns in the fourth chapter to institutional authority, and offers another penetrating glance at how the tradition has demarcated its riches into exclusive categories, and nowhere more than in the teaching and learning church, which identifies the hierarchy with the former, the laity with the latter, and the clergy as the broker between the two. This chapter, his most comprehensive and magisterial, looks at the hierarchy's progressive, evolving claim to an authority to teach that places more weight on the authority than the argument. Mahoney contrasts these assertions of power with other more balanced claims. He notes, for instance, that the validity of a sixteenth-century casuistic argument required both intrinsic and extrinsic probability; that is, it needed to cohere rationally in itself, and it needed to be proffered by someone with recognized authority. Mahoney comments that as we move from the sixteenth to the twentieth century, the Catholic moral teaching tradition looks more to extrinsic probability than to intrinsic probability.

Mahoney studies two significant moments in the evolution of the institutional teaching authority: the Council of Trent and Vatican I. Both treatments manifest the irony inherent in the decisions made at the councils. Regarding Trent's assertion of magisterial authority to teach about faith and morals, Mahoney examines the word *mores* (Latin plural of *mos*), and finds in its use a predominance for 'practices' or 'customs' rather than 'precepts'. That is, Trent was more interested in affirming the hierarchy's competence to determine and promulgate the regulatory norms for right conduct in liturgy, devotions, and other customs important for the ordered life of the Church. Questions of fasting, liturgical vestments, proper penances, clerical life, etc. belonged to the 'mores' that Trent sought to regulate. The more contemporary understanding of authentic teaching on 'mores' as being like precepts—e.g., no direct killing of the innocent—appears occasionally, for instance, in a few statements by Robert Bellarmine, but clearly Trent was asserting its right to determine regulatory practices.

At Vatican I, the papal claim to infallibility was asserted just as Garibaldi broke through the Vatican City walls. In place of his crumbling temporal powers, the pope received from the fathers at Vatican I infallible teaching powers. Mahoney suggests 'that at Vatican I the hidden, perhaps even unconscious, agenda was simply to find a dramatic and perhaps necessary expression of solidarity and loyalty on the part of the Church towards the Holy See and its authority' (p. 167).

As papal teaching authority became more a matter of assertion than of demonstrated argumentation—that is, as extrinsic probability overshadowed the intrinsic—the moral theologians' obligation to teach became eclipsed by papal exercises. As a result, theologians became little more than scribes who explained and validated what the magisterium proposed (see also Black and Keenan 2001). Mahoney concludes this chapter with a compelling proposal for authoritative teaching as respecting subsidiarity, promoting a spirit of service, and subject to both accountability and responsibility for the mode and content of its teaching.

In the fifth chapter, Mahoney raises another distinction: subjective and objective morality. Again, Mahoney's fundamental (and justifiable) complaint is that the distinction does not clarify but rather inhibits our ability to consider adequately the matters at hand. In the first part of this chapter, which really is a propaedeutic for the next one on law, Mahoney critiques the influence of Occam and nominalism as privileging the voluntary over the rational: 'No search is made for the reasons for obligation. It suffices to quote the arguments from authority or of dialectic and to pile up the texts of decrees. The moralist is simply God's lawyer who proclaims, imposes and interprets God's law' (p. 184). (For a fairer reading of Occam see McCord Adams 1987).

He turns then to conscience, where commands are heard (an unfortunate move on Mahoney's part, because conscience in Paul and Aquinas hardly has a voluntaristic context), and eventually moves to the issue of ignorance in conscience and examines another distinction: vincible and invincible ignorance. Cleverly he writes: 'The distinction invoked by Aquinas between ignorance which is vincible, and which is therefore blameworthy since it can be overcome and corrected, and ignorance which is invincible and therefore guiltless, was given impetus, by his authority, to become in the making of moral theology the sanctuary and refuge of non-sinners, and the major escape clause in objective morality' (p. 193).

Mahoney sees that the major escape clause applied to acquitting not only the penitent of moral competence but also the non-Christian of not knowing the 'true faith'. It also served to describe objective morality in such a way as to partition off the subject or the agent completely from objective assessment. The result was that 'objective' moral teaching exercised by papal authority precluded not only the subject but also the subject's world of experience: 'the objective absolute validity of human nature stands or falls by whether or not one conceives nature metaphysically and a priori as being objectively static and absolutely unchangeable, or whether it is conceived of historically and culturally as well as metaphysically' (p. 206).

He concludes the chapter by raising the question of a more integrated view of morality that focuses more on the development of the moral person than on the 'objective' morality of actions. In the most sustained exposition of his own thought yet, Mahoney gives us a glimpse of his appreciation for the emerging field of virtue ethics. This ethics dissolves the distinction between the objective and the subjective by pursuing the objectively right moral course of growth for particular acting subjects.

Finally, in the sixth chapter on law, Mahoney studies another distinction, between voluntarism and rationalism, and discusses Francisco Suarez, who emphasized the will of God over the reasonableness of the law. Mahoney contrasts Suarez with Aquinas on *epicheia*: that is, the right interpretation of law. According to Suarez, it is knowing the mind and will of the lawmaker; to Aquinas it is the right or just application of the law. Mahoney's critique of the law, then, is not the law itself, but rather the preponderance of interest in the wishes of the lawmaker rather than in the rationality of the law and its adequacy in assessing the needs of the common good. In a clear nod to Albert the Great, Mahoney notes, 'the real must not be bent to the rule; it is the rule that must be adapted to the real' (p. 237).

Through these six chapters, Mahoney leads us to the culmination of the making of moral theology in the promulgation of *Humanae vitae* in 1968. There we find the ever expanding magisterial authority, commanding obedience more than understanding, emphasizing a negative Augustinian anthropology that privileges the will, historically remote though metaphysically consistent, conditioned to emphasize the sin to be avoided rather than the good to be pursued, and disposed to eliminate the subjective or the circumstantial from the objective.

James Gustafson called Mahoney's seventh chapter 'the best concise discussion I have read of the impact of the Papal encyclical *Humanae Vitae*' (1990: 75). After twenty years of endless commentaries on the document, the assessment is remarkable. Peter Byrne remarked: 'It is difficult not to see behind Professor Mahoney's treatment of this matter the clear verdict that, in its handling of the ethics of contraception, the Roman Catholic church showed itself to be in a mess as a seat of moral guidance and reflection (partly as a result of those factors in the tradition previously analysed as limiting or mistaken)' (1988: 543).

The chapter deals not only with the events that led to the papal decision, but also with its reception. Mahoney's penetrating exposé ends on a positive note: how the encyclical became a catalyst for the Spirit to prompt individual and collective consciences to ask questions about moral authority, moral truth, and moral living.

In his final chapter, effectively an epilogue, he urges us to reflect on the principle of totality, a concomitant endorsement of diversity, and an appreciation of mystery wherein we humbly acknowledge the need to learn more and define less. Mahoney has helped us to see how limiting, excluding distinctions remove from consideration the matter and the insights of which we are often most in need.

THE INFLUENCE OF *THE MAKING*
OF MORAL THEOLOGY

The work is a *tour de force*. Nothing like it has given Roman Catholics a key to unravelling the endless debates that continue to dominate the field of moral theology. Moreover, it directs us toward a suspicion of eliminating distinctions and reminds us to trust more in the Spirit and less in the call for precipitous decisions.

Moreover, it prompted and sustained research on the magisterium and authority, the natural law, the need to reintegrate the ascetical or spiritual with the moral, the history of moral theology, and the primacy of the conscience. It became the foundational text for revisionists today, and above all it alerted us to the hermeneutics that form the context for teaching and listening, and provided the clergy and the laity with a way of understanding how it is that we are where we are today. In short, it gave us what we were lacking: an understanding and a critique of the moral tradition.

Still, revisiting this text, I am reminded of the work of Thomas Kuhn, who argued that to replace a paradigm, we need not only to demonstrate its inadequacy, but also to propose another operative, functional one. On this further need, I conclude.

First, we need to know not only what of the tradition we should avoid, but, as Lottin, Gilleman, Noonan, and Vereecke showed us, what we can retrieve. What ways of thinking from the Patristic era (from Augustine even), from the medieval era, the later Scholastics, the casuists, or the manualists is worth our investigation?

Second, we need to ask what particular goods we ought to pursue. Mahoney outlines what we need to cast off: our Augustinian mood, our voluntarism, our domesticated notions of sin. But what do we need to pursue? Mahoney hints at a few goods: conscience, responsibility, community, and virtue. But there are other goods entirely absent from *The Making of Moral Theology*: love, Jesus Christ, fidelity to the Scriptures, to name but three.

Third, Mahoney rightly avoided the Gallagher-type suggestion to stay solely within the intellectual history of the manuals and expanded his considerations to the intellectual history of the moral tradition, but he limited his investigation in two very important ways. First, his work bears little resemblance to Curran's *The Catholic Moral Tradition Today* (1999). Unlike Curran, Mahoney has effectively suggested that today's moral theology has been made by popes rather than by theologians. By his indictments, he never acquaints us with how we also got to see the making of the moral theology of Margaret Farley, Enda McDonagh, Kevin Kelly, Lisa Sowle Cahill, Charles Curran, or even John Mahoney himself? Is not there another *Making* that we need to understand? Or did only one *Making* occur?

Similarly, Mahoney has limited the evolution of moral theology by looking solely to the intellectual tradition and the practice of confession, but there were other lessons and texts available (Keenan 2004). The lessons of suffering, conscience, and love were taught from the scriptural and preaching texts about Jesus, discipleship, and the Ten Commandments. These lessons were taught not in the seminary to potential priests, but in classrooms and churches to the whole Church. Similarly we were taught the four cardinal virtues, the lives of the saints, and the corporal and spiritual works of mercy. These were promoted not only in the churches but in lay associations, religious orders, and confraternities, where the moral life was wedded to devotional practices.

Finally, in order to achieve the conviction for his indictment, we can ask whether Mahoney has surrendered too much. At times it seems so. But at other times his indefatigable argument is so compelling that it awakens in us a deeply felt need, sustained by the Spirit, to recognize our bondage, to seek our liberation, and to pursue the light. Inasmuch as that seems to be his purpose, his *Making* animates us then to articulate another *Making*.

REFERENCES AND SUGGESTED READING

BLACK, P. and KEENAN, J. (2001). 'The Evolving Self-Understanding of the Moral Theologian: 1900–2000', *Studia Moralia*, 39, 291–327.

BROWN, D. (1989). 'The Making of Moral Theology', *Scottish Journal of Theology*, 42, 130–1.

BURNS, P. (1987). 'Non *nihil obstat*', *The Tablet*, 31 Oct., 1174–6.

BYRNE, P. (1988). 'The Making of Moral Theology'. *Religious Studies*, 24, 543–4.

CURRAN, C. (ed.) (1968). *Absolutes in Moral Theology?* Washington: Corpus Books.

—— (1980). 'Method in Moral Theology: An Overview from an American Perspective', *Studia Moralia*, 18, 107–28.

—— (1997). *The Origins of Moral Theology in the United States.* Washington: Georgetown University Press.

—— (1999). *The Catholic Moral Tradition Today: A Synthesis.* Washington: Georgetown University Press.

DAVIS, H. (1935). *Moral and Pastoral Theology.* London: Sheed and Ward.

ENDEAN, P. (1988). 'The Making of Moral Theology', *The Month*, 18, 683–5.

FORD, J. and KELLY, G. (1964). *Contemporary Moral Theology.* Westminster, Md.: Newman Press.

FUCHS, J. (1970). *Human Values and Christian Morality.* Dublin: Gill and Macmillan.

—— (1983). *Personal Responsibility and Christian Morality.* Washington: Georgetown University Press.

—— (1984). *Christian Ethics in a Secular Arena.* Washington: Georgetown University Press.

—— (1987). *Christian Morality: The Word Becomes Flesh.* Washington: Georgetown University Press.

—— (1993). 'Innovative Morality', in J. Fuchs (ed.), *Moral Demands and Personal Obligations*, Washington: Georgetown University Press, 114–19.

GALLAGHER, J. (1989). 'The Making of Moral Theology', *Journal of Religion*, 69, 279–80.

—— (1990). *Time Past, Time Future: An Historical Study of Catholic Moral Theology*. New York: Paulist Press.

GILLEMAN, G. (1954). *Le Primat de la charité en théologie morale*. Brussels: Desclée de Brouwer.

—— (1959). *The Primacy of Charity*, trans. W. Ryan and A. Vachon. Westminster, Md.: The Newman Press.

GRAHAM, M. (2002). *Josef Fuchs on Natural Law*. Washington: Georgetown University Press.

GUSTAFSON, J. (1990). 'The Making of Moral Theology', *Ecumenical Review*, 42, 74–6.

HÄRING, B. (1954). *Das Gesetz Christi: Moraltheologie*. Freiburg im Breisgau: Herder.

—— (1961–6). *The Law of Christ: Moral Theology for Priests and Laity*, 2 vols., trans. E. G. Kaiser. Westminster, Md.: Newman Press.

HARRINGTON, D. and KEENAN, J. (2003). *Jesus and Virtue Ethics: Building Bridges between New Testament Studies and Moral Theology*. Chicago: Sheed and Ward.

HEBBLETHWAITE, P. (1986). 'Priest Author Surrenders Church-Stamp', *National Catholic Reporter*, 1 Aug., 21.

IOZZIO, M. J. (1995). *Self-Determination and the Moral Act: A Study of the Contributions of Odon Lottin, O.S.B.* Leuven: Peeters.

JANSSENS, L. (1970). 'Personalist Morals', *Louvain Studies*, 2, 5–16.

—— (1972–3). 'Ontic Evil and Moral Evil', *Louvain Studies*, 4, 115–56.

—— (1976–7). 'Norms and Priorities in a Love Ethics', *Louvain Studies*, 6, 207–38.

—— (1982–3). 'Saint Thomas Aquinas and the Question of Proportionality', *Louvain Studies*, 9, 26–46.

KEENAN, J. (2001). 'Moral Theology and History', *Theological Studies*, 62, 86–104.

—— (2004). *Moral Wisdom: Lessons and Texts from the Catholic Tradition*. Lanham, Md.: Sheed and Ward.

LOTTIN, O. (1942–57). *Psychologie et morale aux XII et XIII siècles*. Louvain: Abbaye du Mont César.

—— (1947). *Principes de morale*. Louvain: Abbaye du Mont César.

—— (1954). *Morale fondamentale*. Tournai: Desclée.

McCORD ADAMS, M. (1987). *William Ockham*. Notre Dame, Ind.: University of Notre Dame Press.

McCORMICK, R. (1981). *Notes in Moral Theology, 1965–1980*. Lanham, Md.: University Press of America.

—— (1985). *Notes in Moral Theology, 1981–1984*. Lanham, Md.: University Press of America.

—— (1987). 'The Spirit, System and Surprise', *The Tablet*, 3 Oct., 1061–2.

MacHUGH, J. and CALLAN, C. (1958). *Moral Theology: A Complete Course based on St. Thomas Aquinas and the Best Modern Authorities*. New York: J. F. Wagner.

MAHONEY, J. (1981). *Seeking the Spirit: Essays in Moral and Pastoral Theology*. London: Sheed and Ward.

—— (1984). *Bioethics and Belief: Religion and Medicine in Dialogue*. London: Sheed and Ward.

—— (1986). 'The Flawed Giant', *The Tablet*, 10 May, 483–5.

—— (1986). 'Moral Theologian's Book Loses *Imprimatur*', *The Tablet*, 26 July, 793–4.

—— (1987). *The Making of Moral Theology: A Study of the Roman Catholic Tradition*. New York: Oxford University Press.

NOONAN, J. T., jun. (1957). *The Scholastic Analysis of Usury*. Cambridge, Mass.: Harvard University Press.

—— (1965). *Contraception: A History of its Treatment by the Catholic Theologians and Canonists*. Cambridge, Mass.: Harvard University Press.

—— (ed.) (1970). *The Morality of Abortion*. Cambridge, Mass.: Harvard University Press.

—— (1995). 'Development in Moral Doctrine', in J. Keenan and T. Shannon (eds.), *The Context of Casuistry*, Washington: Georgetown University Press, 188–204.

O'DONOVAN, O. (1988). 'The Making of Moral Theology', *Journal of Theological Studies*, 39, 348–50.

ORBE, A. (1987). *Introduccion a la teologia de los siglos II y III*. Rome: Gregorian University Press.

PATRICK, A. (1998). 'Imaginative Literature and Renewal in Moral Theology', *New Theology Review*, 11, 43–56.

PINCKAERS, S. (1985). *Les Sources de la morale chrétienne: sa méthode, son contenu, son histoire*. Paris: Editions du Cerf.

—— (1995). *The Sources of Christian Ethics*, trans. Sr M. T. Noble. Washington: Catholic University of America.

POLLOCK, J. (1984). *François Genet: The Man and his Methodology*. Rome: Università Gregoriana Editrice.

—— (1988). 'The Making of Moral Theology', *Theological Studies*, 49, 762–3.

SLATER, T. (1908). *A Manual of Moral Theology*, 2 vols. New York: Benziger Brothers.

SPOHN, W. (1988). 'The Making of Moral Theology', *America*, 159, 90–1.

TILLMANN, F. (1948). *Der Meister ruft: die katholische Sittenlehre gemeinverständlich dargestellt*. Düsseldorf: Patmos-Verlag.

—— (1960). *The Master Calls: A Handbook of Christian Living*, trans. G. Roettger. Baltimore: Helicon Press.

VEREECKE, L. (1974). 'Histoire et morale', *Studia Moralia*, 12, 81–95.

—— (1986). *De Guillaume d'Ockham a Saint Alphonse de Liguori*. Rome: Collegium S. Alfonsi de Urbe.

CHAPTER 30

CATHOLIC SOCIAL TEACHING

STANLEY HAUERWAS
AND JANA BENNETT

LOCATING THE TRADITION

CATHOLIC social teaching is usually identified with the papal encyclicals and a few Vatican II documents, beginning with Leo XIII's great encyclical *Rerum Novarum* (1891) and climaxing in the encyclical of John Paul II *Centesimus Annus* (1991). The 'encyclical tradition' was created by the practice of the popes who referred to past encyclicals in order to set the context for the new encyclical they were promulgating. For example, forty years after *Rerum Novarum* Pius XI celebrated its promulgation by issuing *Quadragesimo Anno* (1931). After *Quadragesimo Anno* it was assumed that modern popes should issue encyclicals about 'social issues', vaguely associated with economic and political developments. These encyclicals would invariably refer to past encyclicals and describe new economic and political developments that needed to be addressed. Often the encyclicals would develop new interpretations of past encyclicals or use different emphases that would open up new lines of analysis.

The list of documents concerning societal issues usually looks like this (Curran 2002: 7):

Rerum Novarum, 'The Condition of Labor' (1891), Pope Leo XIII

Quadragesimo Anno, 'After Forty Years' (1931), Pope Pius XI

Mater et Magistra, 'Christianity and Social Progress' (1961), Pope John XXIII

Pacem in Terris, 'Peace on Earth' (1963), Pope John XXIII

Gaudium et Spes, 'Pastoral Constitution on the Church in the Modern World' (1965), Second Vatican Council

Dignitatis Humanae, 'Declaration on Religious Freedom' (1966), Second Vatican Council

Populorum Progressio, 'On the Development of Peoples' (1967), Pope Paul VI

Octogesima Adveniens, 'A Call to Action on the Eightieth Anniversary of *Rerum novarum*' (1971), Pope Paul VI

Justitia in Mundo, 'Justice in the World' (1971), Roman Synod

Evangelii Nuntiandi, 'Evangelization in the Modern World' (1975), Pope Paul VI

Laborem Exercens, 'On Human Work' (1981), Pope John Paul II

Sollicitudo Rei Socialis, 'On Social Concern' (1987), Pope John Paul II

Centesimus Annus, 'On the Hundredth Anniversary of *Rerum novarum*' (1991), Pope John Paul II

Such lists vary from author to author (cf. Walsh and Davies 2001; Gremillion 1976). By any reckoning, these are a remarkable series of documents that most people consider to constitute the teachings of the Roman Catholic Church on social questions.

Articles about Catholic social teaching usually comment on the individual encyclicals by comparing them with one another. Later encyclicals usually claim to be in agreement with past teachings of the popes, but even the most cursory reading of the encyclicals reveals significant differences about what is thought important, as well as clear disagreements. Leo XIII was anything but a friend of democracy, at least the kind of democracy he identified with developments in France; but Vatican II's *Dignitatis Humanae* suggests that certain forms of democracy are not only compatible with Catholicism but may in fact be the kind of government that Catholic Christians should support. Thus the usual story-line regarding the encyclicals is that they deal with political and economic matters and may be more or less useful depending on the hearers' context.

In the 'Introduction' to their collection of the social encyclicals, David J. O'Brien and Thomas Shannon observe that though *Rerum Novarum* was an attempt to respond to the changing economic conditions and, in particular, the attraction of socialist labour unions for Catholic faithful, the encyclicals of Leo XIII and Pius XI had little effect in America. There were a few American Catholic reformers such as Monsignor John Ryan who used those encyclicals to convince Catholics that they should be for social reform, but:

Leo XIII and Pius XI were too rigid in their theology, too rooted in preindustrial and to some degree antidemocratic ideologies to be directly useful to Americans. With Pope Pius XII's endorsement of democracy and human rights, and especially with publication of Pope John XXIII's *Mater et Magistra* in 1961, that began to change. (O'Brien and Shannon 1992: 1)

We have no reason to deny the differences between the encyclicals, but we think that the story O'Brien and Shannon tell is misleading. Indeed, we believe it is a mistake to restrict Catholic social teaching to lists that include only encyclicals that treat of political and economic matters. This is because this definition of 'social' detracts from the encyclicals' *theological* nature.

Our contention that the encyclicals need to be read theologically may seem odd, given that the encyclicals, particularly the early ones, argue on natural law grounds. While we cannot deal adequately in this article with the questions surrounding the content and status of natural law in the encyclicals, it is important to note that the encyclicals make use, in different ways, of natural law arguments, which can give the impression that the popes assume that the arguments they make in the encyclicals can be defended without appeal to theological convictions. Such an assumption, as we suggest below, is a mistake, because natural law makes sense only against a theological background (Hittinger 2003; Porter 1999).

Leo XIII argues in *Rerum Novarum* that people have a right to private property on the basis of natural law. Leo here critiques how socialists transfer privately owned goods to common ownership because 'they worsen the conditions for all wage-earners' (§4). Though this use of natural law may appear 'conservative', in fact it allows Leo XIII to sound a theme that will continue through the encyclicals of John Paul II: that is, that 'man is older than the state. Before any state came into existence, man had already received from nature the right to make provision for his life and livelihood' (§7). No theme more characterizes the papal encyclicals than that, before all else, persons are to be protected from all schemes that would sacrifice some for the good of others. Thus the popes from Leo XIII to John Paul II argue explicitly that crucial to our ability to enter into the common task of the discovery of the good in common, as well as the protection of human life, is the recognition that we are not our own creators. The recognition of the dignity of each person depends on recognition that God is the beginning and end of existence, and so from beginning to end, theological issues are the burning centre of the popes' understanding of the challenge of modernity for the Church.

The theological agenda of the encyclicals has sometimes been lost, because it has not been recognized that the encyclicals represent the Church's attempt to come to terms with the political and social changes represented by the Enlightenment. For example, Pius IX writes that *Rerum Novarum* is the 'Magna Carta' that should direct Christians' social activity. However, in his extremely important book, Michael Schuck (1991) argues that the encyclicals are not their own best interpreter. Without denying that *Rerum Novarum* represented a different mood in papal encyclicals, Schuck argues that Pius XI was wrong to say in *Quadragesimo Anno* that 'Leo's Encyclical has proved itself the *Magna Carta* upon which all Christian activity in the social field ought to be based, as on a foundation' (Schuck 1991: 39). Leo was wrong, because *Rerum Novarum*, according to Schuck, is best interpreted in the context of the encyclicals written from 1740 to 1877—that is, the encyclicals that were written in response to the French Revolution and the rise of the Enlightenment. Schuck notes that it is tempting to forget these earlier encyclicals, encyclicals such as *Mirari Vos, Singulari Nos*, as well as the infamous *Syllabus of Errors*, because they seem embarrassing from a modern perspective. Yet, when the social encyclicals are read without this background, we can easily miss that, from the perspective of the popes, nothing less than worship, and the morality which depends on right worship, was a stake in their confrontation with the forces unleashed by the French Revolution and the Enlightenment.

A better reading of *Rerum Novarum* makes use of the fact that Leo XIII was not only responding to the rise of socialism and the threat he thought it presented to the Church in Europe, but was also emphasizing, quoting Aquinas, that 'No man is entitled to manage things merely for himself, he must do so in the interest of all, so that he is ready to share them with others in case of necessity. This is why Paul writes to Timothy: "As for the rich of this world, charge them to be liberal and generous"' (§20). Leo XIII saw a social order of different levels, each serving the other in harmony. Of course there are inequalities, but the inequalities that exist do so for the achievement of the common good. Here, as in other encyclicals, 'common good' does not mean the greatest good for the greatest number, nor does it mean the satisfaction of the interests of the majority. Rather, the common good names the good that all people share in common, achieved through their distinctive histories (*Pacem in Terris*, §55). The common good is not whatever people decide they want such a good to be, for the good is discovered, which means that it is not the result of arbitrary willing. The 'state' is therefore subordinate to, and legitimated only if it serves, such a good. In order for a society to be appropriately ordered, therefore, 'the Church, with Jesus Christ for teacher and guide, seeks persistently for more than justice. She warns men that it is by keeping a more perfect rule that class becomes joined to class in the closest neighborliness and friendship. We cannot understand the goods of this mortal life unless we have a clear vision of that other life of immortality' (*Rerum Novarum*, §18).

'Immortality' is not a motif usually associated with 'social teachings', but if the so-called social encyclicals are read abstracted from such theological claims, then their coherence is lost. The primary social challenge according to the encyclicals is quite simply atheism. For example, consider this quote, one that we think informs the perspective of all the encyclicals, from *Quadragesimo Anno*:

The root and font of this defection in economic and social life from the Christian law, and of the consequent apostasy of great numbers of workers from the Catholic faith, are the disordered passions of the soul, the sad result of original sin which has so destroyed the wonderful harmony of many faculties that, easily led astray by his evil desires, he is strongly incited to prefer the passing goods of this world to the lasting goods of Heaven. Hence arises that unquenchable thirst for riches and temporal goods, which has at all times impelled men to break God's laws and trample upon the rights of their neighbors but which, on account of the present system of economic life, is laying far more numerous snares for human frailty. (§132)

Catholic social teachings are misunderstood if they are presented primarily as this or that pope's attitude toward socialism or capitalism. Whatever the popes have to say about socialism or capitalism is framed by their theological analysis of what form social life should take before God.

However, our contention is that we must recognize not only the theological claims inherent in the social encyclical tradition, but also that the social encyclical tradition is not limited to the political and economic sphere, precisely because of those theological claims. The popes never forget that they are first and foremost pastors obligated to remind their flock that God matters not only in so-called 'religious' matters, but also for how all of life, economic, political, *and familial,* is ordered toward life in God. It is no accident, for example, that in nearly every encyclical, the family is addressed, even where the supposed main topic may be working conditions for the poor or political problems with communism and capitalism. We thus deeply disagree with Curran when he makes the seemingly innocuous observation that 'the documents of Catholic social teaching deal primarily with social, economic, and political issues. Some topics—such as the family, the role of women, and the environment—are mentioned in these documents but are developed in greater detail in other papal and hierarchical writings. This book does not deal in depth with these issues precisely because they lie outside the scope of Catholic social teaching' (Curran 2002: 6). By contrast, we argue that Catholic social thought cannot be understood if the Church's stand on sexual ethics is relegated to the sphere of 'moral theology'.

Following a discussion on the 'theopolitics' of the encyclicals, we will therefore conclude this essay with a discussion of some of the encyclicals dealing with family. We think that these encyclicals are not solely (or perhaps even primarily) about the controversial issues of birth control and the nature of the family; rather, they help us see that Catholic social teaching must be interpreted as the ongoing attempt by the Church to respond to the challenge of social orders built on the assumption that we can live as if God does not exist.

THE THEOPOLITICS OF THE ENCYCLICALS

We do not deny that the encyclicals are determinative political and economic documents; but the economic and political judgements of the encyclicals are meant to reflect the presumption that the Church has wisdom about politics and economics available to her because of her theological convictions. This presumption is clearly at work from *Rerum Novarum* to *Centesimus Annus*.

Leo XIII's *Rerum Novarum* was motivated by his concern that Catholic workmen were joining socialist labour movements; yet he addressed his concern for Catholic workers by responding to industrial growth, the rise in poverty for many while a few possess great wealth, and a general decline in 'morality' ($1. 1–1. 2). The recommendations in *Rerum Novarum* are often assumed to favour the rich against the poor, because Leo XIII assumed that it was in the 'nature of things' that society was made up of different classes necessary for the achievement of the common good. 'A community needs to have within it different capacities for action and a variety of services at its disposal; and men are most impelled to supply these by the differences of their condition' ($15). He opposed the socialist presumption that there was a natural 'warfare' between the classes, or that a classless society could be built. He thought that the rich had a paternalistic responsibility to aid the lower classes, but maintained the right of property against any attempt to hold property in common.

Yet Leo XIII's assumption that economic relations were subject to moral judgement meant that he refused to accept the capitalist assumption that economic relations should not be regulated by any considerations apart from the market. In many ways Leo XIII's views, like those of Marx, were so conservative that he represented a radical alternative to capitalist assumptions. Economic relations, from his perspective, had to be subject to politics. He drew on Aquinas to maintain that, while there might be a right to property, this certainly does not mean that there is a corresponding right to use that property in a manner that ignores the need of others ($20). Accordingly, the state has a right to intervene to ensure that 'unpropertied men' are not left to the mercy of those with property ($$33–4). Without denying that the scale of wages can be established by free agreement, Leo XIII none the less maintained that a just wage must be paid. A just wage was determined not by the market, but rather by the needs of 'a temperate and well-behaved worker' who works to sustain his family ($$44–5).

What might be called Leo XIII's theological politics and economics simply did not 'fit' into the secular alternatives of his day. In *Quadragesimo Anno* Pius XI rightly praised Leo XIII's letter, observing that Leo 'sought no help from either Liberalism or Socialism' ($10), and suggesting that he had begun 'a true Catholic social science' that was neither individualistic nor a form of collectivism ($46). Pius XI, even more than Leo XIII, emphasized the social character of ownership and the necessity for the worker to be paid a sufficient wage to support him and his family. Without denying the right of the state to intervene, Pius XI articulated the principle of 'subsidiary function': that is, that the family, for example, should not have its function replaced by the state or other political agencies ($80). This allowed Pius XI to distinguish some forms of socialism acceptable to Catholic social teachings distinct from communism. Yet many criticized these encyclicals for not being sufficiently concrete as to what the Catholic social option might be. The encyclicals seemed to suggest that the popes were committed to some 'third way' between socialism and liberalism, but it was by no means clear what such a third way actually looked like.

John XXIII's encyclical *Mater et Magistra* affirmed the basic principles of the previous encyclicals, but called attention to the disparity in economic wealth of different countries. He was particularly concerned about the fate of agriculture being overwhelmed by industrial development (§125). Accordingly, he emphasized the 'solidarity of the human race', a solidarity anticipated by the Church, which is by divine right universal and capable of embracing all people (§178). Such solidarity depends on recognition of the moral order, which has no existence except from God (§208). Nothing is more pernicious in the modern era than the 'absurd attempt to reconstruct a solid and fruitful temporal order divorced from God, who is, in fact, the only foundation on which it can endure' (§217).

Mater et Magistra heralded John XXIII's very important encyclical *Pacem in Terris*. In this encyclical John XXIII not only introduced a more robust language of 'rights' than had been characteristic of the earlier encyclicals, but, more importantly, he addressed the status and interrelation of states. John XXIII's appeal to rights, like those of the earlier encyclicals, stressed that duties precede rights (§28); but his appeal also makes concessions to liberalism that previous popes had avoided. He argued that 'the universal common good' requires that the needs of refugees be met, that there be a cessation of the arms race, and that the growing economic interdependence between states be just. Though criticized for being 'unrealistic', at the very least John XXIII made questions of international relations and war part of the social encyclical agenda. In doing so, he observed that it was crucial that Christians not allow a separation between their faith and their practices.

Gaudium et Spes, written during the Second Vatican Council, was unique in so far as it began by addressing 'humanity', not bishops or even all Christians. That this pastoral constitution addresses 'humanity' does not mean, however, that the Council represents a 'humanism' divorced from theological commitments. It does so on the assumption that 'in her most benign Lord and master can be found the key, the focal point and the goal of man, as well as of all human history' (§10. 1). To be sure, the document claims that in the depths of his conscience every man detects a law that holds him to obedience (§16), but that law is the source of human dignity found in the call to communion with God (§19). This wide-ranging document addresses every issue from the family to world peace by situating those challenges within the wider problem of faith in God.

In 1967 Paul VI continued John XXIII's attempt to address the international situation in his encyclical *Populorum Progressio*. In this encyclical, Paul VI was particularly critical of wealthy nations for their lack of concern for poorer nations. He called attention to the debt that poorer nations incur with no possibility of relief. As a result, market prices that are freely agreed upon turn out to be the most unfair (§58). In *Redemptor Hominis*, John Paul II continued Paul VI's defence of the poor by maintaining the unity of the human family on the basis of the way in which it has stood the test of centuries—that is, the way indicated by Christ the Lord; as the Council teaches ' "by his incarnation, he, the son of God in a certain way *united himself with each man*." The Church therefore sees its fundamental task in enabling that union to be brought about and renewed continually' (§13).

John Paul II's encyclicals are more Christological and biblical than the earlier 'social encyclicals', but we hope we have made clear that a theological centre has been there from the beginning. With John Paul II, however, there is a theological analysis of social challenges confronting the Church that makes his encyclicals unique. For example, in *Dives in Misericordia* he observes that there is an increasing feeling in the world of being under threat. As he noted in *Redemptor Hominis*, no doubt the feeling of being under threat that many people feel in our day derives from the prospect of a conflict found in the stockpile of nuclear weapons, but he thinks that the threat is to be found not only in the means provided by military technology. The threat also comes from the dangers 'produced by a materialistic society which—in spite of "humanistic" declarations—accepts the primacy of things over persons' (§11). In such a world, any justice to be found will depend on the recovery of the Christian refusal to be satisfied with anything other than the truth.

This same kind of analysis is also characteristic of his encyclical *Laborem Exercens*, issued on the ninetieth anniversary of *Rerum Novarum*. John Paul II clearly tries to end speculation about the Church's 'third way' by focusing on the character of work. This can be seen as a strategy similar to the emphasis on the 'just wage' in the earlier encyclicals, but in *Laborem Exercens* the just wage is given a wider meaning by John Paul II insisting that any society is to be judged by the quality of work that makes possible human flourishing. Accordingly the problem with communism and capitalism is the economization of work which assumes that human labour primarily has an economic purpose (§13. 2). So it is not merely a question of remuneration for work, but whether work is 'marked by the fundamental truth that man, created in the image of God, shares by his work in the activity of the creator and that, within the limits of his own human capabilities, man in a sense continues to develop that activity and perfects it as he advances further and further in the discovery of the resources and values contained in the whole of creation' (§25. 1).

In 1987, John Paul II celebrated the twentieth anniversary of *Populorum Progressio* by issuing *Sollicitudo Rei Socialis*, in which he addressed questions of development between nations. Particularly noteworthy in this encyclical is his use of the word 'solidarity'. He used this word to signal his support for the solidarity movement in Poland that finally led to the 1989 revolution. In this encyclical, which criticizes the arms race as well as the tension between East and West, John Paul II sounds the theme that what is needed is a civilization based on love if we are to meet the challenges of our day. Such a civilization is one in which we must see each person as the image of God, 'called to share in the truth and the good which is God himself. In other words, true development must be based on the love of God and neighbour, and must help to promote the relationships between individuals and society' (§33. 7). Such love is the basis for solidarity, which helps us see the 'other' not just as some kind of instrument, but as on 'on a par with ourselves in the banquet of life to which all are equally invited by God' (§39. 4). Accordingly, John Paul II uses the language favoured by liberation theology to suggest that Christians should have 'a preference for the poor' in how they think about and act in social life.

Perhaps the climax of John Paul II's encyclicals is *Centesimus Annus*, which was issued to celebrate the one hundredth anniversary of *Rerum Novarum*. John Paul begins by noting that *Rerum Novarum* had been preceded by other encyclicals dealing with teachings involving politics. He calls particular attention to *Libertas Praestantissimum* and the claim that the 'bond between human freedom and truth, so that freedom which refused to be bound to the truth would fall into arbitrariness and end up submitting itself to the vilest passions to the point of self-destruction' (§4. 4). That is the context, John Paul II suggests, that is crucial for interpreting *Rerum Novarum*. Moreover, it is the connection between freedom and truth that is the hallmark not only of *Centesimus Annus*, but of all John Paul II's encyclicals.

The spirit of truth can be found in John Paul II's acknowledgement that the socialists got some things right (§12. 2) but failed to see that without God there can be no human dignity. Yet in that respect the socialists were but creatures of the 'rationalism of the Enlightenment, which views human and social reality in a mechanistic way' (§13. 3). John Paul II equally criticizes the same kind of atheism that also characterizes the consumer cultures of the West. He gives a very qualified approval to 'capitalism', if by capitalism is meant an economic system that recognizes the positive role of business and the market under the rule of law; but he remains a vigorous critic of consumer societies, believing that they are but the manifestations of atheistic materialism (§42. 1).

The heart of *Centesimus Annus* is John Paul II's celebration of the year 1989 in which Eastern Europe threw off the shackles of communism. According to the Pope, what is 'worthy of emphasis is the fact that the fall of this kind of "bloc" or empire was accomplished almost everywhere by means of peaceful protest, using only the weapons of truth and justice' (§23. 1). John Paul II is not unaware that many may find his call for a 'civilization of love' to be naïve, but he believes it was love, a truthful love, that triumphed in 1989. That triumph, moreover, testifies to the encyclical tradition's emphasis that at the heart of so-called social problems is the question of faith in God.

We hope this review has sustained our contention that the intelligibility of the social encyclical tradition depends on the theological claims that are necessary to understand the political and economic perspectives taken in the 'social' encyclicals. It should also be apparent that the social encyclicals' understanding of what should and should not be done turns on what preserves and does not preserve the flourishing of families. Therefore we will fail to understand the tradition of the social encyclicals if they are divorced from the Church's teachings about marriage, children, sex, and other such topics. It is to these matters we now turn.

Family and its Theological Significance in the Social Encyclicals

Most of the papal encyclicals, whether or not they deal ostensibly with 'Church and state' as their primary topic, treat the family in relation to the Church and the state. Where this happens, it is not simply a minor referent; rather, its inclusion indicates that 'social' is much broader than Charles Curran and other commentators believe. Although encyclicals such as *Humanae Vitae* are often seen as unrelated to the social encyclicals because they deal with 'sexual ethics' rather than labour, socialism, capitalism, or the just wage, they should be included in the line-up of encyclicals precisely because of the way family is construed as political and seen as constitutive of justice. Moreover, the theological significance of the encyclicals is missed when these documents are not seen as part of the Catholic social tradition. There are numerous encyclicals that we could treat in this section; here we shall discuss *Casti Connubii*, *Humanae Vitae*, and *Evangelium Vitae*.

In *Casti Connubii*, (1930) Pius XI adds a decidedly Thomistic flavour to the Church's understanding of marriage. In his introduction, he places marriage in the context of the new law and the sacramental grace that comes from Christ's redemption. Because he begins with Christ, Pius's concern is the great number of people who are 'forgetful of that divine work of redemption' (§3). Marriage is also a human act (and therefore a moral act), and not solely a divine institution. Pius lays this out by noting the necessity of the will and particularly of 'free consent' in order for a marriage to be valid (§6). Furthermore, paralleling Thomas on moral acts vis-à-vis animals, he says that marriage is 'entirely different both from the union of animals entered into by the blind instinct of nature alone...and also from the haphazard unions of men, which are far removed from all true and honorable unions of the will and enjoy none of the rights of family life' (§7). Marriage may thus be subject to human law in the case of legitimate authority, but such authority can never override the fact that God divinely ordained the institution of marriage.

Having established that entering into marriage connotes a human and moral activity, Pius continues by laying out the blessings obtained in such marriages and then addressing the virtues and vices related to these blessings. The blessings of a marriage are, predictably, the three ends that have been numbered by the Church for centuries: 'offspring, conjugal faith, and the sacrament' (§10). Pius's paragraphs on these blessings assume that the justice of Christ, rather than justice offered by the state, is necessary for rightly understanding the interrelationships of these blessings. For instance, on the blessing of conjugal faith, Pius, following Augustine, suggests that the chastity lived out in the life of a husband and wife

must have, as its primary purpose that man and wife help each other day by day in forming and perfecting themselves in the interior life so that through their partnership in life they may advance ever more and more in virtue, and above all that they may grow in true love toward God and their neighbor. (§23)

The conjugal faith expressed by a couple expresses, in part, the ordering and the justice that God's law requires, and it is not clear that this justice is at all related to the state's justice. Significantly, Pius ends his section on the blessings of marriage by suggesting that

since it is a law of divine Providence in the supernatural order that men do not reap the full fruit of the Sacraments which they receive after acquiring the use of reason unless they cooperate with grace, the grace of matrimony will remain for the most part an unused talent hidden in the field unless the parties exercise these supernatural powers and cultivate and develop the seeds of grace they have received. (§41)

The true justice of marriage and family is a grace that must be recognized and received from God. Following his section on blessings of marriage, Pius discusses the problems and vices relating to the goods of marriage, especially resulting from modernity and the rise in scientific discovery. This section therefore deals directly with the 'social issues' that many contemporary theologians such as Curran see as more strictly belonging to the 'social encyclicals', as opposed to the 'sexual ethics' encyclicals. It is significant that a discussion of such issues comes only after Pius has first rigorously situated the place of marriage with respect to Christ's new law, but the importance of the connection is clear. For example, one key point that Pius makes in this section is the relation of eugenics to the state. Pius is emphatic that 'the family is more sacred than the State'; therefore, the state cannot require certain people to be sterilized, or otherwise forbid their marriages. Here, the state is clearly at odds with the Church and the family; as we will see below, Pius's understanding of family/state relations is quite distinct from that found in *Gaudium et Spes*. In enumerating the corresponding vices (primarily adultery and divorce) for the sacrament of marriage, Pius again emphasizes the origins of marriage in the Church and de-emphasizes the idea that 'matrimony belongs entirely to the profane and purely civil sphere' (§79). He also quotes Leo XIII's encyclical *Arcanum* in this section, in which Leo notes a connection between the destruction of the family and the ruin of the state. Aside from this brief interlude, which is mostly directed against communism rather than the state 'as such', Pius does not whole-heartedly embrace a relationship between the Church and the state, and in fact seems to be writing against his predecessor's encyclicals *Arcanum* and *Rerum Novarum* in terms of their placement of the state in relation to the family.

At the end of the encyclical Pius has a rather stern word for the state, reiterating its responsibility in economic matters and implying that the laws of the state (as seen in his example of the conflict between the civil government of Italy and the Holy See with respect to marriage laws) are made best when copied from canon law. Although Pius gives a nod to the 'supreme authority of the state' in this paragraph, it seems clear nevertheless that he sees the state conceding its supposed authority on these matters to the Church (§126). When we connect this to what he says earlier, that 'the best instruction given by the Church . . . will not alone suffice to bring about once more conformity of marriage to the law of God . . . a steadfast determination of the will [is needed] on the part of husband and wife', it seems that he is positing that the family, when seen in right relationship to Christ and the Church, is its own justice. Here we recall Pius's principle of 'subsidiary function', which we noted above: that the family should not have its function replaced by the state or other political agencies. Elsewhere in *Quadragesimo Anno*, Pius writes: 'Just freedom of action must, of course, be left both to individual citizens and to families, yet only on condition that the common good be preserved and wrong to any individual be abolished' (§25). Pius suggests in this whole section that the state can help the family provide justice (and indeed, through various laws enumerated in §28, it does so), and thus relationships between the family and the state are forged. However, because he insists on the family's great integrity, precisely because it has been created and redeemed by God, the state and the family also experience significant distance from each other.

Indeed, on Pius's terms, we might well wonder if the state is needed at all. In §94, for instance (just following his quotes of Leo and *Arcanum*), Pius reminds his readers of the 'firmly established principle . . . that whatever things have deviated from their right order, cannot be brought back to that original state which is in harmony with their nature except by a return to the divine plan'. All that is necessary is our return to, and reconciliation with, God; the state may possibly but not necessarily be a means toward our end in God. Any justice achieved, any work done for the good of humanity, is work that may only truly be done with an eschatological view toward God and God's creation of us.

Humanae Vitae, the famously controversial document that is seemingly 'about' birth control, may best be seen in line with *Casti Connubii*, because it supports the view of the family taken by Pius XI and therefore of other social issues. Its issuance was shocking to many moral theologians at the time, because conciliar documents written only five years before, such as *Gaudium et Spes*, might be interpreted more favourably with respect to birth control and fertility (e.g., §50. 2). Many in the Church assumed that subsequent Church documents on fertility would follow in the vein of *Gaudium et Spes*, especially since Pope John XXIII had established a commission to study these issues. However, Pope Paul VI wrote decisively against the commission's report, and against such hopes. The storms of protest surrounding *Humanae Vitae* have yet to die down; indeed, in American Catholic circles, this document has probably been more influential than any other Church document, papal or otherwise, for moral theology.

The document begins similarly to *Casti Connubii*. Paul VI notes the institution of marriage in creation, and connects it to the institution of sacramental marriage as conceived by Christ and the Church. Then he moves to consider that marriage is not solely about divine will, but is also about human will in response to God. On this point, Martin Rhonheimer argues that many theologians have made a mistake by focusing on §14, which discusses unlawful methods of birth control (the biologistic section of the encyclical), and skipping over §16, which relates the procreative blessing of marriage to virtues of chastity and justice, or in other words, abstinence. Thus procreation clearly involves human beings' natural functions, but must also be seen in relation to the institution of marriage in the Church, which is associated with the virtues of justice and chastity. Abstinence is therefore not part of a 'method' of birth control, but rather part of the virtue of chastity, and is thus a theological matter for Rhonheimer (2000: 113 ff.).

By showing marriage in relation to virtues and as instituted by God, Paul VI has set the scene for marriage and related issues such as birth control to be inextricably connected to other, supposedly more 'social' issues. On this point David Matzko McCarthy argues:

This second section [of *Humanae Vitae*] discusses Paul VI's critique of modern accounts of economic development, which ironically do not advance but rather diminish human life since they block a full theological understanding of human flourishing. It is not merely coincidental that reductionist proposals for economic progress depend upon contraceptive technology as a means for advancement, for the upward mobility of citizens, and for the development of nations. To this degree, HV's opposition to artificial birth control parallels Paul VI's arguments in documents such as *Populorum Progressio* and *Octogesima Adveniens*. The teaching on contraception is a social teaching, and the social teaching is founded on theological claims about human solidarity and upon the continuity between our natural and supernatural, or eschatological fulfillment. (McCarthy 1999: 700)

Paul VI takes a strong stance against economic systems which support contraception because large families are barriers to economic advancement, but which also assume that productivity and progress happen best when people turn away from so-called domestic affairs and turn toward producing wealth as autonomous individuals.

Like *Casti Connubii*, *Humanae Vitae* is best seen in terms of its description of our last end in God, because both documents argue that when we recognize our God-given nature, we best see how we fulfil our human destiny in God. Conversely, the modern political state and economics reduce human activity to choices, such as how to control births, that are best for 'me' but that do not also lay bare the fact that these choices already subsume us into a world-view in which we must reject some of what makes us human. In fact, the exclusion of the familial encyclicals from social encyclical lists does precisely what our contemporary global economy wants us to do: separate family and marriage from social issues, because family and marriage are matters of choice that should have little to do with the social ills of our time, whereas considerations of poverty and the just wage help society and especially the individual.

John Paul II's encyclical *Evangelium Vitae* (1995) deals precisely with this supposed distinction between the family and the social. As he writes,

> broad sectors of public opinion justify certain crimes against life in the name of the rights of individual freedom, and on this basis they claim not only exemption from punishment but even authorization by the State ... In such a cultural and legislative situation, the serious demographic, social and family problems which weigh upon many of the world's peoples and which require responsible and effective attention from national and international bodies, are left open to false and deceptive solutions, opposed to the truth and the good of persons and nations. (§4)

John Paul II is very clear that the family and what are deemed 'social issues' are intertwined, and that neither should be disposed of as a matter of individual choice.

Evangelium Vitae is the encyclical from which are taken two often used phrases: 'Culture of Death' and 'Culture of Life'. John Paul II here discusses abortion and birth control directly, but throughout he refers to the many other ways in which we, particularly in richer countries, try to assume control over life and death by pretending that these are matters of individual choice. For instance, he references the great injustices of poverty, malnutrition, ecological imbalance, drug use, and the like that are perpetuated in and by our culture even as we, as individuals, seek control over our experience of life and death (§10). 'All this is aggravated', moreover, 'by a cultural climate which fails to perceive any meaning or value in suffering, but rather considers suffering the epitome of evil, to be eliminated at all costs. This is especially the case in the absence of a religious outlook which could help to provide a positive understanding of the mystery of suffering' (§15). Where many might view the Church's stance on birth control and abortion as a blatant lack of concern for the world's over-population, and resultant over-use of global resources, poverty, and malnutrition, the Pope addresses these same problems by turning the blame squarely on those who reject the theological question of what it means to be human. It is not the Church, he says, but rather the Culture of Death, with its love of avoidance of suffering and its preference for inalienable rights and autonomy, that perpetuates the problems which the human global community faces.

CONCLUSIONS

When we view *Casti Connubii*, *Humanae Vitae*, *Evangelium Vitae*, and other supposedly non-social encyclicals as being in the same tradition as the 'social' encyclicals, we see that Catholic social teaching, particularly as found in papal and conciliar encyclicals, reflects some of the best theological argumentation found concerning the Christian life. For instance, In *Rerum Novarum*, often described as a social encyclical concerned with just wages, the family also comes into the discussion. It is seen as a social unit older than the state, which is one important means by which Leo XIII argues against socialism. Socialism is problematic for Leo because it 'dissolves the bonds of family life', and thus causes injustice (*Rerum Novarum*, §26). He also writes that 'no human law can take away the original natural right of a man to marry or in any way impose limits on the principal purpose of marriage ordained by God's authority from the beginning' (§10). Still, for Leo, 'the family is a true society equally with the state and, like the state, it possesses its own source of government, with the authority of the father'. Such views are in tension with the positions taken in *Casti Connubii* and *Humanae Vitae*, which suggest that the family is not a society equal to the state, but one that surpasses the state. While Leo clearly puts forth a similar understanding of natural law, one that makes sense only in connection to our creation in and by God (as opposed to modern understandings of natural law), his view of family does not take into account Christ's new law in the way that *Casti Connubii* and *Humanae Vitae* do. These two later documents restore a theological understanding of Christian marriage and family as grounded in God; in their accounts, therefore, marriage and family are not merely elements whose brokenness demonstrates the destructiveness of socialism or any other governmental structure. Marriage and family enable us to see the character of the God we worship and of our world as one created and endowed by God.

Similarly, *Gaudium et Spes* may be seen as both evaluating previous documents and being theologically critiqued in subsequent documents. This Vatican II document suggests that 'man's social nature makes it evident that the progress of the human person and the advance of society itself hinge on one another. From the beginning, the subject and the goal of all social institutions is and must be the human person' (§25). The human person must be able to attain certain necessary items in order to live a properly human life; among these are 'the right to choose a state of life freely [celibacy or marriage] and to found a family' (§26. 1). Thus *Gaudium et Spes* seems to differ from *Rerum Novarum* just to the extent that in the latter marriage is understood as an elemental and more primitive institution that shows the destructiveness of the state. *Gaudium et Spes*, however, acknowledges that family and state are more complexly related, which means that no account of the good of the human person is adequate in which that good is not first and foremost God. *Humanae Vitae* stands in tension with *Gaudium et Spes* just to the

CATHOLIC SOCIAL TEACHING   535

extent that *Humanae Vitae* reasserts the theology necessary for an understanding of 'the human person'. But this can be shown only if, as we argue, the 'social encyclical list' is made much broader and examined much more deeply for the theological arguments running throughout.

Questions about gender roles, which necessarily arise in discussions of families, also come up in this tradition of argumentation. Feminist scholars, as well as sociologists, often discuss the ways in which women's 'traditional' roles of wife, stay-at-home mother, and child-rearer support a hierarchical and oppressive family structure for women. As Lisa Cahill describes, 'For women, marriage and family are dangerous, at least as traditionally practised' (1996: 198). However, in the past few decades the Church has come to understand that the family is the 'domestic Church' (*Familiaris Consortio*, §21), and that it has a vocation to be a 'community of disciples' concerned with economic and social justice (Cahill 1996: 210). On Cahill's view, this move toward an understanding of family as a community in relationship to the Church represents 'a social and relational appreciation of marriage, now informed by more egalitarian and personalist insights' (1996: 209). Cahill rightly sees this discussion of the family as theological in nature; for her, the family is a '*topos*' in Christian history and theology that has been recovered and reinterpreted in recent years.

The theological points which the encyclical tradition makes about the family and women are not limited to questions of family in relation to Christian discipleship and relationships between men and women. Nor should the encyclicals pertaining to women be read primarily as reactions to feminist theory or as defences of patriarchal understandings of family. Rather, the primary question is how descriptions of 'family' and 'woman' faithfully give theological witness. For instance, in *Casti Connubii*, Pius XI believes that the right ordering of the couple toward God also means 'subjection of wife to husband', which 'may vary according to the different conditions of persons, place, and time.... But the structure of the family and its fundamental law, established and confirmed by God, must always and everywhere be maintained intact' (§28). Paul VI's apostolic letter *Octogesima Adveniens* might be seen as adopting a similar attitude when he speaks against women's 'false equality which would deny the distinctions laid down by the Creator himself and which would be in contradiction with woman's proper role' (§13). Paul VI certainly has in mind the rise of feminist critique in the 1960s and 1970s, but his purpose in the letter is not to deal with this primarily. His is a response to particular historical circumstances, but the history is inscribed within the context of the gospel of Christ. In both Pius's and Paul's letters, the popes make clear the relationship between God's nature as Creator of all and the nature of people and families. The issue for both these popes is that atheism is not only a problem as a 'belief' that is somehow internalized psychologically (which is often the way we think about atheism), but that it is also concretely lived out in familial structures and in daily patterns of life.

In contradistinction to the popes mentioned above, John Paul II suggests a somewhat different reading of the Pauline passages about subjection of women to men, and also a different theological argument. He follows Ephesians 5 in yoking the created dignity of marriage, in which, in their love for one another, man and woman become 'one flesh', to the call for 'mutual subjection out of reverence for Christ (cf. Eph. 5: 21). This is especially true because the husband is called the "head" of the wife *as* Christ is the head of the Church; he is so in order to give "himself up for her" (Eph. 5: 25), and giving himself up for her means giving up even his own life . . . in the relationship between Christ and the Church the subjection is only on the part of the Church, in the relationship between husband and wife the "subjection" is not one-sided but mutual' (*Mulieris Dignitatem*, §24). Admittedly, many contemporary feminists would find as much fault with John Paul II's statements as with claims made in the earlier encyclicals, because the ideas of submission and subjection are present and potentially unhelpful to women who have been subjected to patriarchal authority and have thereby been oppressed. None the less, here the Pope offers a different reading of the relationship between gender and family than his predecessors. *Mulieris Dignitatem* provides some theological responses to feminist concerns by means of Christ's life and work. The question of who 'woman' is, is first put into the context of the history of salvation and the mystery of the Incarnation of a woman bearing God's son (§3). 'Woman' is first a theological matter; contemporary political questions of women's rights are continually read in this light.

In addition to women's roles, we could mention the environment, the nature of the family, the state, and the just wage, which all have theological import and continue to be assessed in the encyclicals and other documents. An artificial delineation of what counts as a social encyclical only detracts from the nature of the encyclicals and causes problems in reading them. What counts as social is also theological; that the popes and the councils have written encyclicals that intertwine all these matters makes this point clear. Our lives are beset on all sides by atheism, and the popes have offered numerous counter-proposals.

References and Suggested Reading

In addition to the collections of encyclicals listed, all encyclicals may be found at the Vatican website or in paper editions from various publishers.

Cahill, L. (1996). *Sex, Gender and Christian Ethics*. Cambridge: Cambridge University Press.

Cavanaugh, W. (2002). *Theopolitical Imagination: Discovering the Liturgy as a Political Act in an Age of Global Consumerism*. Edinburgh: T. & T. Clark.

Curran, C. (2002). *Catholic Social Teaching: 1891–Present: A Historical, Theological and Ethical Analysis*. Washington: Georgetown University Press.

GREMILLION, J. (ed.) (1976). *The Gospel of Peace and Justice: Catholic Social Teaching since Pope John*. Maryknoll, NY: Orbis Books.

HAUERWAS, S. (2000). *A Better Hope: Resources for a Church Confronting Capitalism, Democracy and Postmodernity*. Grand Rapids, Mich.: Brazos Press.

HITTINGER, R. (2002). 'Social Roles and Ruling Virtues in Catholic Social Doctrine', *Annales Theologici*, 16/2, 295–318.

——(2003). *The First Grace: Rediscovering the Natural Law in a Post-Christian World*. Wilmington, Del.: ISI Books.

HOLLENBACH, D. (1999). *Claims in Conflict: Retrieving and Renewing the Catholic Human Rights Tradition*. New York: Paulist Press.

McCARTHY, D. M. (1999). 'Procreation, the Development of Peoples, and the Final Destiny of Humanity', *Communio*, 26 (Winter), 698–721.

O'BRIEN, D. J. and SHANNON, T. (1992). *Catholic Social Thought: The Documentary Heritage*. Maryknoll, NY: Orbis Books.

PORTER, J. (1999). *Natural and Divine Law: Proclaiming the Tradition for Christian Ethics*. Grand Rapids, Mich.: Eerdmans.

RAMSEY, P. (2002). *The Just War: Force and Political Responsibility*, foreword by Stanley Hauerwas. New York: Rowan and Littlefield Publishers.

RHONHEIMER, M. (2000). *Natural Law and Practical Reason: A Thomist View of Moral Autonomy*. New York: Fordham University Press.

SCHUCK, M. (1991). *That They Be One: The Social Teaching of the Papal Encyclicals, 1740–1989*. Washington: Georgetown University Press.

WALSH, M. and DAVIES, B. (eds.) (2001). *Proclaiming Justice and Peace: Papal Documents from Rerum Novarum through Centesimus Annus*, rev. edn. Eugene, Ore.: Wipf and Stock Publishers, 23rd Publications.

Index of Names

INDEX OF SCRIPTURAL REFERENCES